Hands-On Student Workbook
H-WB111A

Vehicle Electrical-Electronics Troubleshooting Training Program
The Starter Kit
Module H-111A

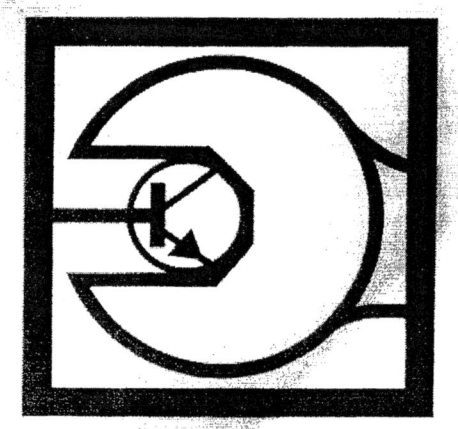

Veejer Enterprises Inc.
Garland, Texas, USA

H-111A Starter Kit
Student Workbook
H-WB111A

Hands-On
Vehicle Electrical-Electronics
Troubleshooting Training Program

Supplement Training To
"The" (60 Lesson Home-Study)
Vehicle Electronics Training Course™

Written and Developed by Vince Fischelli

Published in USA by
VEEJER ENTERPRISES
Garland, Texas

ISBN-10: 1934161225
ISBN-13: 978-1-934161-22-7

Copyright © 2015 Veejer Enterprises.
No part of this workbook or hands-on materials may be reproduced, photocopied
or entered into a computer data base or retrieval system of any kind.
All Rights Reserved.

"The" Hands-On Home-Study
Vehicle Electrical-Electronics
Troubleshooting Training Program

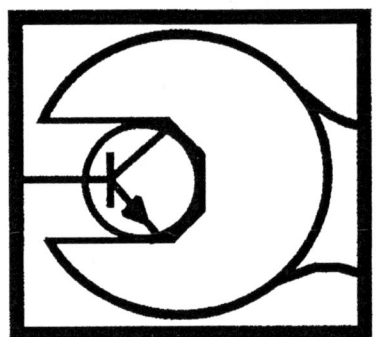

Veejer Enterprises
Garland, Texas
972-276-9642 www.veejer.com

Starter Kit, H-111A ... Table of Contents

- Introduction, comparing H-111 with H-111A
- Getting Started
- Goals and Objectives
- How to begin
- Tips on using this hands-on home-study troubleshooting training program
- Troubleshooting Format
- Resistor Bag-Lamp Circuit
- Recording DMM Troubleshooting Readings
- The H-PS01 Power Supply
- Exploring The Circuit Boards
- Scanning the top of the PCBs
- Operating the circuit boards (S3-S4)
- Introduction to troubleshooting, practice making Vc and Vd circuit measurements
- The six basic problems that occur in any electrical circuit
- 32 practice exercises troubleshooting OPEN CIRCUITS, VOLTAGE DROPS and SHORTS-TO-GROUND in live circuit boards including a section on finding shorts to ground.
- Four short-to-ground problems are grouped together in the back of the workbook with additional instructions on finding shorted loads and shorts-to-ground.
- Tips On Maintaining Troubleshooting Skill
  – Practice – Practice – Practice
- Conducting a troubleshooting contest

"*The*" Hands-On Home-Study
Vehicle Electrical-Electronics
Troubleshooting Training Program

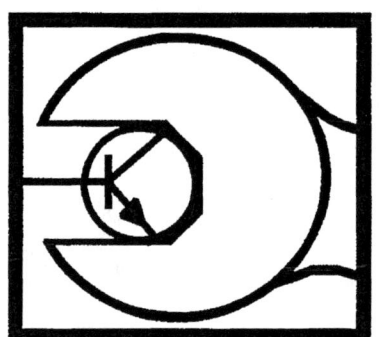

Veejer Enterprises
Garland, Texas
972-276-9642   www.veejer.com

Starter Kit, H-111A
Power Board, H-PCB01A and Lamp Board, H-PCB02A

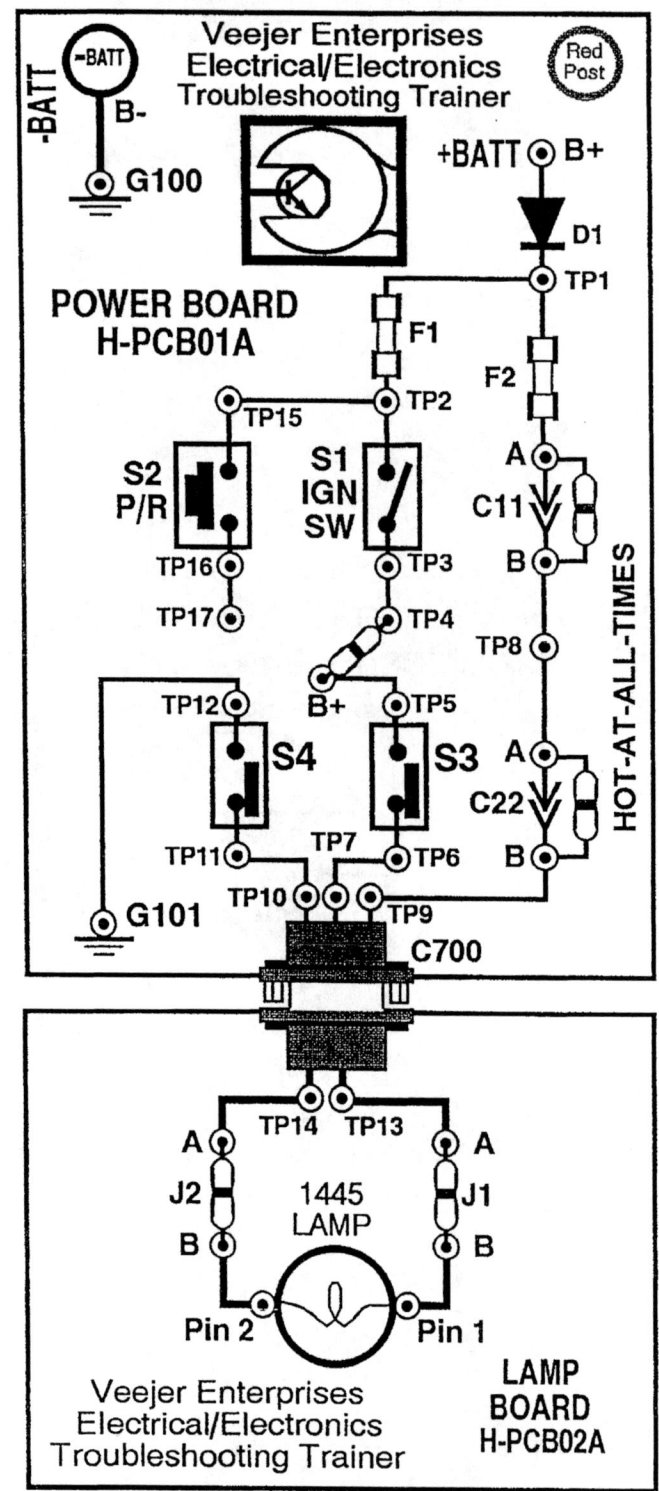

(1) Snap the boards together and squeeze the connector C700 till it snaps together to lock the boards. It is not necessary to use the small screws in the C700 connector to keep the two boards locked together. The locking screws can be removed from the connector.

(2) Notice the electronic circuit components between the Red and Black terminal posts are now mounted on the underside of the Power Board in the revised H-PCB01/02A. These components form the voltage regulator circuit and are not part of the troubleshooting program. Do not allow any metallic object to make contact with the components on the underside (copper) side of the PCB when powered up.

"*The*" Hands-On Home-Study
Vehicle Electrical-Electronics
Troubleshooting Training Program

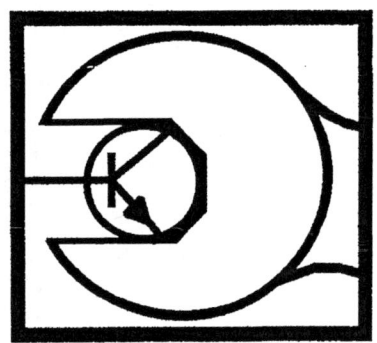

Veejer Enterprises
Garland, Texas
972-276-9642   www.veejer.com

Vehicle Electronics Hands-On Troubleshooting Training Program

VEEJER ENTERPRISES 3701 Lariat Lane, Garland, Texas 75042-5419
Phone: 972-276-9642 Fax: 972-276-8122 Email: contact-us@veejer.com Web Site: www.veejer.com

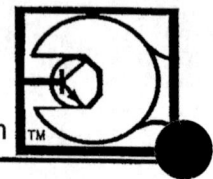

Introduction

The vehicle service industry needs technicians trained in electrical-electronics troubleshooting. We call this highly trained technician a **VEHICLE ELECTRONIC TECHNICIAN**, or **V.E.T.** They are vehicle service technicians who can hands-on troubleshoot vehicle electrical-electronic systems with test equipment using the same methods as electronics technicians have done in the worldwide electronics industry for over 90 years.

It is one thing to discuss how open connections, voltage drops and shorts-to-ground affect circuits and discuss how to troubleshoot those problems on paper. But it's different when live circuits are used to actually experience those problems and effectively troubleshoot with repetitious hands-on practice.

Students perform hands-on troubleshooting at home, in the shop or technical school to develop troubleshooting skill and become hands-on vehicle circuit troubleshooters using this training program.

"The" **Hands-On Program** contains several circuit board training kits. Students begin *"The"* **Hands-On Program** with **The Starter Kit, H-111A**, containing the first two modules we refer to as "PCBs" (printed circuit boards). **The Starter Kit, H-111A**, covers essential troubleshooting technique with the **Lamp Board (H-PCB02A)** connected to the **Power Board (H-PCB01A)**.

Part Number **H-113**, "Troubleshooting DC Motor Circuits" uses a specially designed DC Motor Troubleshooting Trainer circuit board, **H-PCB03**, containing a brushless DC motor. It has 37 DC Motor circuit troubleshooting exercises.

Part Number **H-115**, "Troubleshooting Relay Circuits" using the Relay Circuit Troubleshooting Trainer, **H-PCB05**. The relay is operated and studied as a fuel pump relay circuit to add realism to 75 relay troubleshooting exercises included.

Part Number **H-116**, "Wire Harness Troubleshooting" covers electrical *system troubleshooting* with all the circuit boards connected together to create a **Mini-Electrical-System**, or "M.E.S." for short. The M.E.S. contains over 114 electrical systems problems.

Part Number **H-200**, "CAN Bus Troubleshooting completes the *"The"* **Hands-On Training Program** with 48 CAN Bus troubleshooting circuit problems using the CAN Bus trainer, H-PCB200.

Prerequisite For *"The"* Hands-On Program

There are no specific prerequisites to study The Starter Kit, H-111A, however it is recommended that the first 25 lessons of *"The"* **Vehicle Electronics (60 Lesson) Training Course**™ has been reviewed since much of the circuit explanations in *"The"* **Course** are not repeated in the workbooks contained in this Hands-On Program.

Goals and Objectives

The primary goal of *"The"* **Hands-On Program** is to develop skill in troubleshooting vehicle electrical and electronic systems with hands-on practice. A student of *"The"* **Hands-On Program** who applies what is learned can **begin** to successfully troubleshoot electrical and electronic problems on vehicles after only a few hours of study. Changing parts to troubleshoot electrical problems becomes a thing of the past.

"The" **Hands-On Program** can be studied at home by self-study, or in a study group setting where students share the circuit boards and have their own workbook, or in a classroom led by a teacher. Technicians can take turns sharing the same circuit boards using their own student workbook.

What This Program Offers

"The" **Hands-On Program's** begins by reading this student workbook H-WB111A. The Starter Kit introduces the principles of vehicle electrical and electronic systems troubleshooting techniques with live circuits using real world circuit problems. The Starter Kit, H-111A, contains a DC voltage power supply, **H-PS01**.

> **Please use caution with the H-PS01**
> DO NOT ALLOW THE POWER SUPPLY WIRE TIPS TO EVER "SHORT" TOGETHER WHILE THE POWER SUPPLY IS PLUGGED IN. ALWAYS CONNECT THE RED AND BLACK WIRES TO THE RED AND BLACK POSTS ON THE POWER BOARD BEFORE PLUGGING THE POWER SUPPLY INTO A WALL SOCKET OR POWER STRIP. BEFORE DISCONNECTING THE RED AND BLACK WIRES FROM THE POSTS ALWAYS FIRST UNPLUG THE POWER SUPPLY.

Two printed circuit boards (abbr. PCBs) are included for measuring voltage, resistance and current while troubleshooting circuit problems. The **Power Board H-PCB01A** and **Lamp Board, H-PCB02A.** mimic an actual vehicle circuit. Voltage and resistance readings are in the same range as found in actual vehicle circuits to add realism to the program. Students use their own DMM.

Later on in the program a circuit fault is inserted on the bottom of properly functioning circuit boards to create an electrical problem such as an OPEN, a Voltage drop (abbr. Vd) or a shorted load or short to ground.

Students troubleshoot the live circuit boards from the top of the PCBs, to find the problem using troubleshooting techniques covered in the workbook which would be exactly the same if the circuit were on an actual vehicle.

Vehicle Electronics Hands-On Troubleshooting Training Program

VEEJER ENTERPRISES 3701 Lariat Lane, Garland, Texas 75042-5419
Phone: 972-276-9642 Fax: 972-276-8122 Email: contact-us@veejer.com Web Site: www.veejer.com

> **Notice:**
> The original home-study Student Manual H-SM01/02A and school version S-SM01/02A have been replaced with this new updated version H-WB111A beginning in January 2015.

The PCBs are designed and laid out to represent complete vehicle circuits so live measurements can be taken with a DMM and live readings analyzed. The circuits are not complex in design so that students can focus on developing troubleshooting technique and skill with simple circuits. These troubleshooting techniques can then be employed on more complex circuits without additional training.

A "CONFIDENTIAL" Instructor Guide, H-IG111A (abbr. I/G) is included with complete instructions to insert faults to set up troubleshooting problems and contains all the step-by-step answers to study exercises and troubleshooting problems. If this is being studied in a classroom only the Instructor has the Instructor Guide.

To maximize the benefits of this training program and develop professional troubleshooting skill, technicians should NOT look at the answers to a problem before troubleshooting that problem. Advance knowledge of a fault dilutes the troubleshooting lesson to be learned from that exercise.

If you are working on "*The*" **Hands-On Program** by yourself at home or in the shop, find someone to insert the faults for you for each problem number to achieve best results. While it may be necessary to insert problems for yourself in a self-study setting, it is not an ideal situation. We recommend you show another person how to insert circuit faults for you. In a classroom the Instructor will insert problems.

Students can progress at their own pace and find that after only a couple of hours of study that the troubleshooting principles learned can be immediately applied in the shop on vehicles with electrical or electronic problems even before all of the 32 troubleshooting problems are completed.

How To Begin

Begin "*The*" **Hands-On Program** by reading through the first 39 or so pages in this student workbook Part Number **H-WB111A,** and do the initial exercises in preparation for the 32 problems.

Start troubleshooting problems by inserting a 17 "fault," in the PCBs as explained in the Instructor Guide. Write down your troubleshooting steps and DMM readings in your student workbook until you know exactly what is wrong with each circuit problem. Be careful to write down your answers under the problem number you are troubleshooting at that time. In other words, if you are troubleshooting problem number 4 do not record your answers under problem number 3 in the work book. Compare your answers with the answers in the Instructor Guide for each problem. If in a classroom setting the Instructor will review each problem. **Students should not read the answers to a problem before troubleshooting a circuit problem.**

Troubleshoot one problem at a time and follow them in numerical order for the first go around. Later you may troubleshoot any problem in any order for more practice. Keep track of your troubleshooting progress using the Student Troubleshooting Record on the last page of this student workbook.

Tips Using "*The*" Hands-On Troubleshooting Training Program

(1) STUDENTS SHOULD NOT LOOK AT THE BOTTOM OF THE PCBs PRIOR TO TROUBLESHOOTING A PROBLEM SINCE THE CIRCUIT FAULT MIGHT BE SEEN. DISCOVERING A CIRCUIT FAULT BY OBSERVATION WILL SPOIL THE BENEFIT TO BE GAINED FROM THAT PROBLEM. *DON'T EVEN PEEK!*

(2) A student should have his own Student work book to keep notes, complete reading assignments and record test results obtained in the circuit exercises and troubleshooting problems. Failure to record troubleshooting test results and personal notes will make it impossible to evaluate troubleshooting success later.

(3) Do not insert more than one fault at a time in the PCBs. Follow the instructions for inserting each troubleshooting problem so the fault is correctly inserted. In the classroom the Instructor will insert the problems.

(4) Faults should be removed from the PCBs after finding the problem unless someone is going to troubleshoot the same problem immediately after you. AVOID CONFUSION! Any fault left in a PCB will affect the circuit when a second fault is installed causing false readings and a lot of confusion.

(5) "**Scan the top and bottom**" of the PCBs to verify that no parts are missing on the top of the PCBs before inserting a fault. Scanning the top of the PCBs is covered in this student workbook. Scanning the bottom of the PCBs is covered in the I/G. Do both to properly prepare the PCBs for inserting faults.

The first circuit covered in the Starter Kit, H-111A, is called the **Power Board, H-PCB01A,** to which the second circuit, the **Lamp Board, H-PCB02A,** is connected. A complete but simple lamp circuit is created by connecting (snapping) the two boards together at connector, C700.

A simple circuit of a lamp is used first to introduce

Vehicle Electronics Hands-On Troubleshooting Training Program

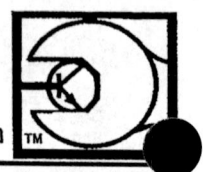

VEEJER ENTERPRISES 3701 Lariat Lane, Garland, Texas 75042-5419
Phone: 972-276-9642   Fax: 972-276-8122   Email: contact-us@veejer.com   Web Site: www.veejer.com

the technician or student to essential troubleshooting skills needed for any circuit. If a technician understands how to troubleshoot a simple lamp circuit he/she can use the same skills to troubleshoot any circuit whether it is an electrical or electronic circuit, simple series circuit, parallel circuit or compound circuit.

All electrical and electronic circuits operate on the same electrical laws. By studying these electrical laws with hands-on exercises and use them in troubleshooting a simple lamp circuit, it is easier to learn more complex troubleshooting procedures.

Resistor Bag–Lamp Circuit H-RB01/02A

The **Resistor Bag–Lamp Circuit** contains an assortment 1/4 watt fixed resistors of different ohmic values for inserting faults into the PCBs. These fixed resistors have four color bands to indicate their resistance value. When told to insert a resistor fault a resistor is randomly selected so it is not necessary to determine resistor values. They can be measured with an ohmmeter if interested in their ohmic value.

A Word About Zero Ohm Resistors

Some components on the top and bottom of the PCBs are not fixed resistors but zero ohm resistors. A **Zero Ohm Resistor**, abbr. 0ΩR is the equivalent of a jumper wire. All zero ohm resistors look like a small "dog-bone" resistor and have a single black band painted in the center of the body.

Inserting some circuit problems for troubleshooting purposes simply require removing a 0ΩR from the bottom of a PCB.

Zero Ohm Resistor

Just pull the 0ΩR straight UP to remove it from the two terminal pins holding it in place when told to do so to create a circuit fault. The leads of the zero ohm resistors are a tight fit in the new mounting pins. It may be difficult to remove a 0ΩR the first time.

USE CAUTION WHEN REMOVING A ZERO OHM RESISTOR THE FIRST TIME TO AVOID BREAKING OFF THE WIRE LEADS OF THE 0ΩR IN THE MOUNTING PINS.
PULL STRAIGHT UP TO REMOVE

It is best to gently pull straight up slowly to remove the 0ΩR the first time. After a 0ΩR is removed and replaced the mounting pins become "broken in" and the 0ΩR can be easily removed and replaced there after.

Some circuit faults call for inserting a fixed resistor in place of a 0ΩR to create a voltage drop. In other troubleshooting scenarios a 0ΩR is inserted to create a shorted load or a short-to-ground. Full instructions are provided in the Confidential Instructor Guide.

There are an assortment of 50Ω, 100Ω and 150Ω resistor values in a small plastic bag labeled Resistor Bag, H-RB01/02. One Resistor Bag is included in each Starter Kit. Each resistor value contained in the Resistor Bag is designed to work with the Lamp Circuit to provide significant circuit faults that can be discovered by DMM voltage readings. The fixed resistors in the Resistor Bag, H-RB01/02 are the only resistor values to be used with the Lamp Circuit.

Follow the instructions given in the Instructor Guide to insert a resistor type fault for a particular problem. **A resistor is randomly selected** from the resistor bag for a voltage drop (Vd) type fault. The resistor is installed on the bottom of the PCBs (as directed in the I/G) to produce a Vd problem at some point in the circuit. It may be helpful to use a long nose pliers for removing the zero ohm resistors and inserting another resistor or 0ΩR. Once the fault is installed begin troubleshooting that problem from the TOP of the PCBs. NEVER TROUBLESHOOT A PROBLEM FROM THE BOTTOM OF THE PCBs.

Recording DMM Troubleshooting Readings

Different resistor values are selected at random to insert a particular problem which affects the actual voltage reading. Readings will vary depending on the resistor value randomly selected for that problem.

Therefore answers in the Instructor Guide do not record actual readings because the reading depends on the value of the fixed resistor used for a problem.

Instead, the I/G answers are word phrases like "Low B+" instead of an actual DMM reading of "10.42V" or 9.35V. The same is true on the ground side of the circuit where a ground side reading is written as "more than 0.1V" or "high B-" instead of an actual DMM reading of "3.25V" or "2.27V." When you check your answers in the I/G they will be recorded as "low B+" rather than an actual reading.

In this way, different resistor values can be used for a wider variety in DMM readings so that you may troubleshoot the same problem more than once and get different readings each time. This also helps increase student familiarity with a wider range of defective circuit DMM readings.

Vehicle Electronics Hands-On Troubleshooting Training Program

VEEJER ENTERPRISES 3701 Lariat Lane, Garland, Texas 75042-5419
Phone: 972-276-9642 Fax: 972-276-8122 Email: contact-us@veejer.com Web Site: www.veejer.com

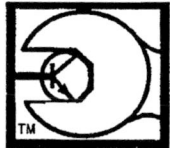

Starter Kit, H-111, Original Version

The Starter Kit, H-111 original version, shown to the right, is the first design of the H-111 PCBs (printed circuit boards). The following explains differences between the original version of H-111 and the new version designated with an "A" as H-111A. Both H-111 and H-111A are identical in operation and either one can be used with any H-111 or H-111A exercise or workbook. Minor changes between the PCBs are discussed below.

Original H-111, Power Board H-PCB01

Notice the voltage regulator circuit components are mounted on the top of the Power Board, H-PCB01, between the Red and Black Posts. **Ignore these components as they are not part of the hands-on troubleshooting training program.** Their function is to provide a regulated 13.8V value of B+ from the unregulated (raw) voltage provided by the Power Supply H-PS01 and are mounted out of the way at the top of the Power Board, H-PCB01.

Positive Post of the Vehicle Battery

The positive post of the vehicle battery IS NOT the Red Post. Instead you are to use the small black Loop Pin marked **+BATT** just below the red post as the positive terminal of the vehicle battery for all measurements and tests.

Test Point TP1

Test Point **TP1** is shown at the top of Fuse F1. The electrical connection point of TP1 is not connected to Fuse F2. In fact Fuse F2 is a direct connection to Diode D1.

Connectors C11 and C22

These are intended to be two connectors in the HOT-AT-ALL-TIMES circuit but they cannot be disconnected on the H-111 Power Board, H-PCB01. They simply simulate where connectors could be inserted in the wiring harness.

Lamp Board H-PCB02

The Lamp Board is essentially the same for all H-111 or H-111A kits. The Lamp Board from either version can be used with either the Power Board H-PCB01 in H-111 or the Power Board H-PCB01A in H-111A.

All these issues are improved with the new version designated H-111A on the next page.

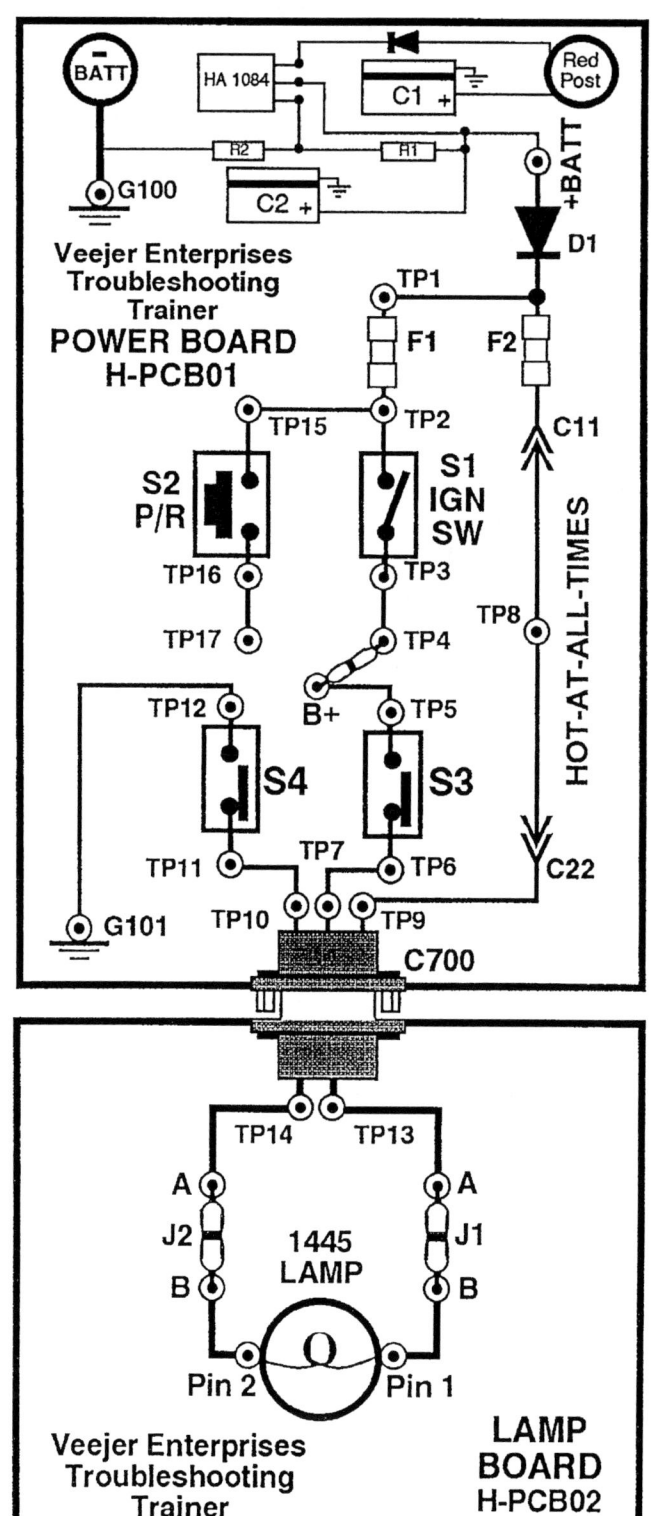

H-111 Original Version

Copyright © 2015 VEEJER ENTERPRISES, Garland, Texas - All Rights Reserved   H-WB111A Page 4

Vehicle Electronics Hands-On Troubleshooting Training Program

VEEJER ENTERPRISES 3701 Lariat Lane, Garland, Texas 75042-5419
Phone: 972-276-9642 Fax: 972-276-8122 Email: contact-us@veejer.com Web Site: www.veejer.com

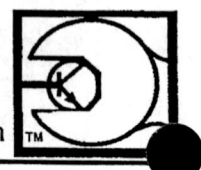

Starter Kit, H-111A Revised Version

The Starter Kit H-111A has minor improvements which do not change operational characteristics of the Starter Kit in any way. **Power Supply H-PS01 and Power Boards from H-111 and H-111A are fully interchangeable with each other as well as Lamp Boards from either H-111 or H-111A.**

H-111A Power Board H-PCB01A

All voltage regulator circuit components are mounted on the bottom (copper) side of the H-PCB01A between the Red and Black posts. This keeps the regulator circuit components out of sight of the student.

Positive Post of the Vehicle Battery

The positive post of the vehicle battery IS NOT the red post. Instead you are to use the small RED Loop Pin marked **+BATT** and **B+** just below the red post as the positive terminal of the vehicle battery for all measurements and tests.

Test Point TP1

Test Point **TP1** is shown moved to the top of Fuse F1 AND Fuse F2. The electrical connection point of TP1 is now connected to both to Fuse F1 and Fuse F2. The B+ voltage to both fuses now comes from **TP1.**

Connectors C11 and C22

C11 and C22 connectors now employ zero ohm resistors in the HOT-AT-ALL-TIMES circuit. REMOVING EITHER ZERO OHM RESISTORS OPENS THAT CONNECTOR. Removing zero ohm resistor C-11 separates C11-A from C11-B When zero ohm resistor C22 is removed the connection between C22-A and C22-B is removed. When the zero ohm resistor is removed consider that one connector is disconnected. For normal operation of the Power Board H-PCB01A with other circuit board connected to C700 it is necessary to insert zero ohm resistors in C11 and C22 to have B+ at TP9.

Lamp Board H-PCB02A

The Lamp Board in H-111A is identical to the Lamp Board in H-111. The only change is noted when the Lamp Board H-PCB02A is disconnected from the Power Board to trace a short-to-ground. Grounding the DMM at TP14 allows the student to "see" the short-to-ground between TP13 and Pin 1. The original Lamp Board H-PCB02 would not allow this.

Mix and Match

It is permissible to mix and match "A" PCBs with original PCBs. The same is true for Power Supply H-PS01 in the H-111 and H-111A. Everything is interchangeable.

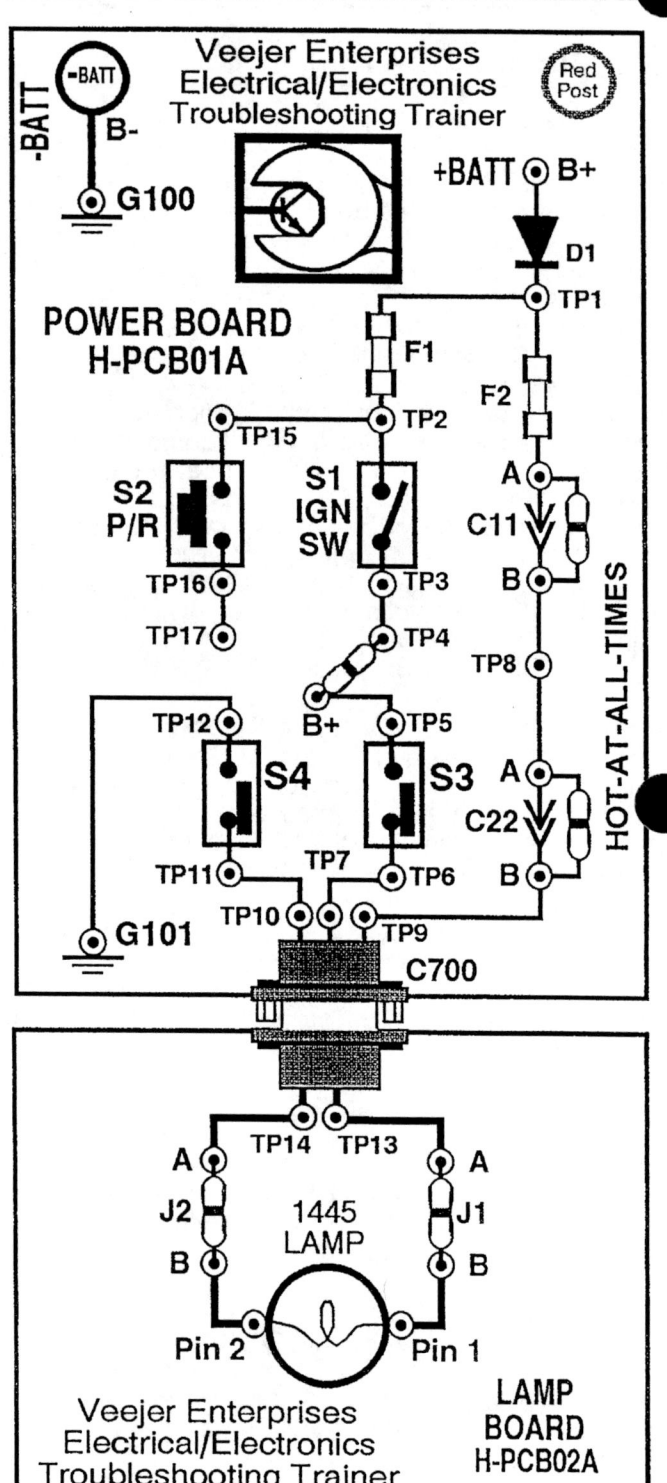

Revised H-111 now referred to as H-111A

Vehicle Electronics Hands-On Troubleshooting Training Program

VEEJER ENTERPRISES 3701 Lariat Lane, Garland, Texas 75042-5419
Phone: 972-276-9642 Fax: 972-276-8122 Email: contact-us@veejer.com Web Site: www.veejer.com

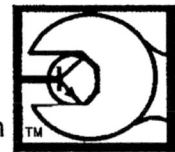

DC Power Supply H-PS01

A small *unregulated* DC power supply, Part Number **H-PS01,** is supplied with "*The*" Hands-On Program's Starter Kit. The H-PS01 plugs into a USA wall socket and has a red and black wire for connection to the Red (+) and Black (-) terminal posts on the Power Board.

> **Please follow these instructions carefully when using the H-PS01 Power Supply.**

DO NOT allow the red and black wires of the H-PS01 to make contact with each other (short together) while the H-PS01 is plugged into a wall socket. This will short circuit and possibly damage the H-PS01 and void the warranty. Tie a knot in either the red lead or black lead from the H-PSO1 to make the leads of different length. This will help prevent the leads from shorting together when disconnected from the two posts.

The H-PS01 power supply has an U.S.A. standard AC plug to fit into a wall socket with 110-120 VAC (Volts Alternating Current). There is no ON/OFF Switch associated with the H-PS01.

- To turn the Power Supply **ON** plug into a 110-120V AC wall outlet.
- To turn the Power Supply **OFF** unplug from the wall outlet.
- Always unplug the H-PS01 power supply from the wall socket when not in use.
- Make it a habit to IMMEDIATELY disconnect the H-PS01 from the wall socket after using.
- Do not leave the H-PS01 plugged in while inserting problems in the PCBs. Disconnect the H-PS01 from the wall socket before inserting faults in the PCBs or when connecting or disconnecting the red and black wires.

ALWAYS observe correct polarity when connecting the red and black wires from the H-PS01 to the terminal posts at the top of the Power Board. The RED WIRE connects to the RED POST. The BLACK WIRE connects to the BLACK POST.

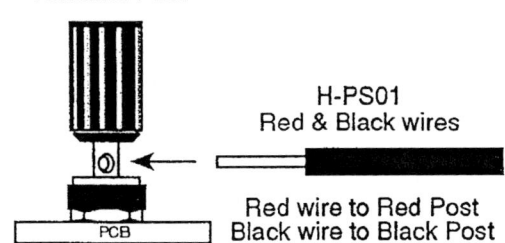

NEVER REVERSE THE CONNECTIONS. Each terminal post has a screw on cap. As the end cap is unscrewed a hole appears in the terminal post shaft as shown below. Insert the red wire into the Red terminal shaft's hole and tighten down the red end cap lightly. Slide the black wire into the Black terminal shaft hole and tighten down the black end cap slightly. **DO NOT over tighten the terminal posts. If they loosen simply tighten the locking nut on the bottom of the post.**

An alternate DC power supply should NOT be used to power the PCBs. The Power Board contains an electronic voltage regulator circuit between the two terminal posts to convert the raw unregulated DC power from the H-PS01 into a regulated DC voltage to simulate the charging voltage of a vehicle's 14 volt system. Using any DC power supply other than the H-PS01 may damage this electronic voltage regulator circuit and void the warranty.

DO NOT use a 12V car battery in place of the H-PS01 power supply. It could damage the electronic voltage regulator circuit.

DO NOT connect a battery charger to a battery being used to power up the PCBs in an attempt to keep the battery charged while troubleshooting.

It's dangerous. *Charging batteries emit gases that are highly explosive if exposed to a spark.* Use only the approved DC power supply H-PS01.

> **CAUTIONS USING THE H-PS01 DC POWER SUPPLY**
>
> (1) ALWAYS UNPLUG THE H-PS01 POWER SUPPLY WHEN NOT IN USE.
>
> (2) ALWAYS UNPLUG THE H-PS01 POWER SUPPLY WHEN INSERTING A CIRCUIT FAULT IN THE PCBs.
>
> (3) DO NOT CONNECT THE H-PS01 RED AND BLACK WIRES TO ANYTHING OTHER THAN THE POWER BOARD RED AND BLACK POSTS.
>
> (4) NEVER ALLOW RED AND BLACK WIRES TO MAKE CONTACT WHILE THE POWER SUPPLY IS PLUGGED IN.

FOLLOW THESE DIRECTIONS AT ALL TIMES. For those countries with 220V electrical systems a power supply is supplied for 220V lines. An extra Power Supply can also be purchased for 220 Euro or UK style electrical sockets.

Vehicle Electronics Hands-On Troubleshooting Training Program

VEEJER ENTERPRISES 3701 Lariat Lane, Garland, Texas 75042-5419
Phone: 972-276-9642   Fax: 972-276-8122   Email: contact-us@veejer.com   Web Site: www.veejer.com

Exploring the POWER BOARD

The first circuit board to review is the **Power Board** which provides the "B+" supply and "B-" the ground circuit to all PCBs plugged into Connector 700 at the bottom of the Power Board. In a vehicle this would be called the *Power Distribution System* of the vehicle. The Power Board and Lamp Board are shown connected in Figure 1.

> **PLEASE STUDY THE POWER BOARD CIRCUIT ANALYSIS CAREFULLY TO AVOID MISTAKES PERFORMING THE EXERCISES.**

The Red Terminal Post

Just below the red terminal post is a **red "loop" test terminal** called the **+BATT** or the **B+** Test Point. This is used as the *FIRST* positive voltage source test point or B+ feed for all circuits in this hands-on training program. **Do not use the red post for any (B+) voltage measurement.** The red post is simply a connection point for the red (+) wire from the H-PS01 Power Supply. The +BATT red loop pin represents the vehicle battery's positive post or the B+ terminal on the back of the generator (alternator).

The Black Terminal Post

The black terminal post at the top left of the Power Board is labeled **-BATT** or **B-** (say B minus). The black terminal post represents the vehicle battery's negative terminal post and is the primary ground point for all testing. **Use the -BATT terminal post for purposes of grounding the DMM for circuit voltage measurements or when tracing shorts-to-ground.**

Trace the Voltage Side of the Power Board

The red loop pin feeds B+ to diode D1, a **Polarity Sensing Diode** located just below the Red Post.

> Polarity sensing diodes are discussed in *"The"* Vehicle Electronics Home Study Training Course in **Lesson 44, Pages 4-5** and **Lesson 49, Pages 1-4**.

Diode, D1, shuts the circuit down (prevents electron current flow) if the H-PS01 power supply red and black leads are connected to the terminal posts in reverse polarity. Reverse polarity means the red wire is accidentally connected to the black post and black wire is accidentally connected to the red post.

Reverse polarity is the same thing as trying to jump start a vehicle with the jumper cables connected in reverse polarity, as covered in **Lesson 17, Page 6; Lesson 49, Pages 1-4.**

Diode D1 protects all circuits from high electron current attempting to flow in the opposite direction due to reverse polarity voltage being connected to the Power Board Red and Black posts.

This can be done on a vehicle during "jump starting" a dead battery and the jumper cables are connected in reverse.

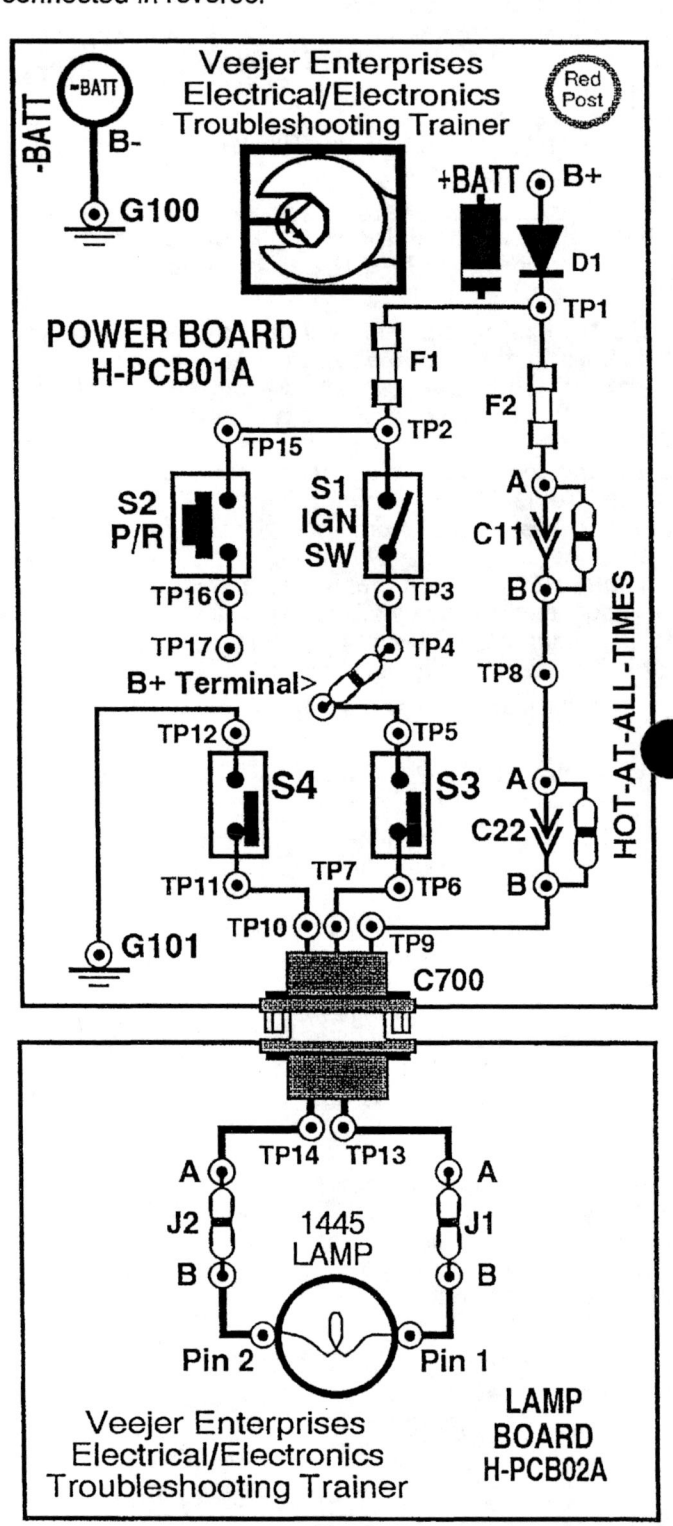

Fig. 1
The H-PCB01A Power Board & Lamp Board H-PCB02A Diode D1 is drawn next to the diode schematic symbol. The painted band on the physical diode corresponds to the line the diode arrow is pointing to.

Vehicle Electronics Hands-On Troubleshooting Training Program

VEEJER ENTERPRISES 3701 Lariat Lane, Garland, Texas 75042-5419
Phone: 972-276-9642   Fax: 972-276-8122   Email: contact-us@veejer.com   Web Site: www.veejer.com

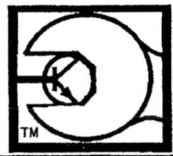

Trace the Voltage Side of the Power Board

TP1 (Test Point #1) is the first B+ test point provided after Diode, D1. The B+ at TP1 splits to supply B+ to two fuses F1 and F2. Fuse, F1 (3A) supplies B+ to TP2, the voltage input terminal to the **IGN**ition **SW**itch, **S1**. TP3 is the output terminal of S1. S1 is a 3 position, surface mount switch. The switch terminals are not accessible for voltage checks from the top of the PCB. Use TP2 to check B+ going into S1 and TP3 to check the B+ coming out of S1 **when S1 is toggled to the UP (top) position.** The Ignition Switch, S1, is only CLOSED when the toggle is pushed UP.

TP3 connects to TP4. A 0ΩR (zero ohm resistor) connects TP4 to what is called the **"B+ Terminal"**. The 0ΩR between the B+ Terminal and TP4 can be moved to connect the B+ Terminal to TP17 so the Push/Release Switch S2 can be used to control a circuit. You will be instructed when to do this in future training programs. For now leave the 0ΩR connected between TP4 and the B+ Terminal.

Switches, S3 and S4 are surface mount slide switches, S3 is on the voltage side and S4 is on the ground side. Each switch has an input test point and an output test point just like S1 and S2 for voltage checks to determine voltage levels at the switch terminals. Back to tracing the voltage side.

The B+ Terminal connects to TP5, the B+ feed or input to switch, S3, the voltage side control switch. TP6 is the output terminal of S3 and connects to TP7 at C700. When the B+ Terminal has B+ and S3 is CLOSED (slide UP), B+ appears at TP7 if the B+ circuit is operating correctly. Any circuit connected to C700 will receive its B+ from TP7. Use TP7 to verify that B+ is available at C700. Do not measure B+ at the exposed pins of C700. That is what TP7 is for. If normal B+ is present at TP7 it can be considered that B+ is available at the proper pin of C700.

Trace the Ground Side of the Power Board

Start at the Black (-BATT) Terminal at the top left of the Power Board. This is the primary ground point for "B-" (say B minus) or the ground side voltage of 0.00 volt written as 0.00V.

The black post connects to G100 which would be the same as the engine ground cable or the accessory (sheet metal) ground cable.

The next ground is G101 at the bottom left of the Power Board. It is understood that G101 connects back to G100 through the engine block or sheet metal.

From G101 the ground circuit connects to TP12, the ground input terminal to S4, the ground side control switch.

When S4 is CLOSED (slide UP) the ground circuit or B- appears at TP11 the output terminal of switch S4. TP11 connects to TP10 to place ground, or B-, at C700 which grounds any PCB plugged into C700 when S4 is CLOSED.

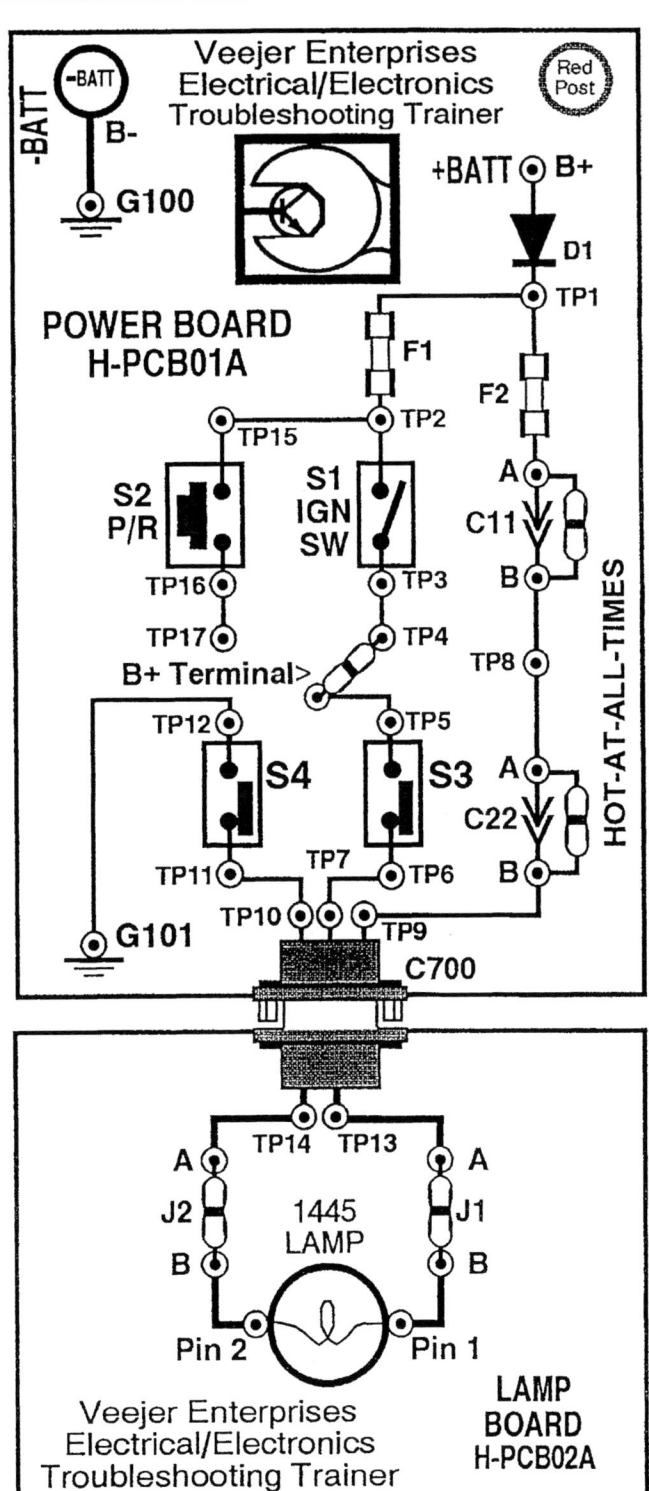

Fig. 1
The H-PCB01A Power Board & Lamp Board H-PCB02A

Vehicle Electronics Hands-On Troubleshooting Training Program

VEEJER ENTERPRISES 3701 Lariat Lane, Garland, Texas 75042-5419
Phone: 972-276-9642   Fax: 972-276-8122   Email: contact-us@veejer.com   Web Site: www.veejer.com

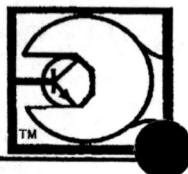

Connector C700

The connector C700 at the bottom on the Power Board contains 12 pins. Do not use the connector pins for troubleshooting test points. A numbered TP is provided for every circuit passing through C700.

Test Point TP7 brings B+ to the connector C700 when S3 is slide UP. On the Lamp Board TP13 is on the opposite side of C700 to provide the B+ to the Lamp Board.

Test Point TP10 brings B- to the connector C700 when S4 is slide UP. On the Lamp Board TP14 is on the opposite side of C700 to provide the B- to the Lamp Board.

Connecting a PCB to C700 completes an operating circuit for study and troubleshooting practice with B+ and B- being available at C700.

Expect a wide range of electrical problems to be inserted into the Power Board and Lamp Board when connected together. Problems occur as OPENs, SHORTS and Voltage drops (Vds) appear at any point in the voltage or ground side of each circuit.

> **Ground DMM During Voltage Measurements**
> **· · · VERY IMPORTANT · · ·**
> **Always connect the DMM's Black Test Lead to the Black (-BATT) Terminal Post at the top of the Power Board when ever it is necessary to ground the DMM black test lead for circuit voltage measurements NO EXCEPTIONS! There is no better ground test point for your DMM's COM (Black) Test Lead.**

When checking circuit voltages, use the black terminal post for grounding the DMM black test lead because the black terminal post is the most negative point electrically (or best ground) on the circuit boards just as it is on a vehicle. This eliminates many potential errors in voltage measurement that will occur by grounding the black test lead at any other ground point in the PCBs.

The same is true on a vehicle. The vehicle battery's negative post (–BATT) is the most negative point (0.00V) and is usually the easiest to access on a vehicle for purposes of grounding the DMM's black test lead. This troubleshooting tip will eliminate errors in voltage measurements especially when checking the voltage on the ground side of vehicle circuits.

Reminders Using The H-PS01 Power Supply

(1) ALWAYS UNPLUG THE H-PS01 POWER SUPPLY WHEN NOT IN USE.

(2) ALWAYS UNPLUG THE H-PS01 POWER SUPPLY WHEN INSERTING A CIRCUIT FAULT IN THE PCBs.

(3) DO NOT ALLOW THE RED AND BLACK WIRES TO MAKE CONTACT WHILE THE POWER SUPPLY IS PLUGGED IN. THIS COULD DESTROY THE POWER SUPPLY.

H-PS01 Power Supply Voltage

The H-PS01 Power Supply is a non-regulated DC power supply which means the voltage output varies widely with the load placed on the power supply.

The H-PS01 works in conjunction with the electronic regulator circuit on the bottom of the Power Board (at the top) to provide the DC voltage to operate a circuit, such as the Lamp circuit, when it is connected to Connector C700 at the bottom of the Power Board..

When the load is zero, the power supply is not supplying current to a circuit and the terminal post voltage is higher.

When the circuit is turned ON, a load is placed on the power supply which lowers the power supply voltage to the normal operating voltage.

Measure H-PS01 Power Supply Voltage

To measure the H-PS01 voltage follow these steps.

(1) Connect the Lamp Board to the Power Board.

(2) Connect the UNPLUGGED H-PS01 red and black leads to the Red and Black terminal posts.

(3) Place the DMM test leads on the red (+) and black (-) **terminal posts** located at the top of the Power Board as shown below in Figure A. Set the DMM to the 20V, 30V or 40V DC range whichever your DMM provides. Do the following.

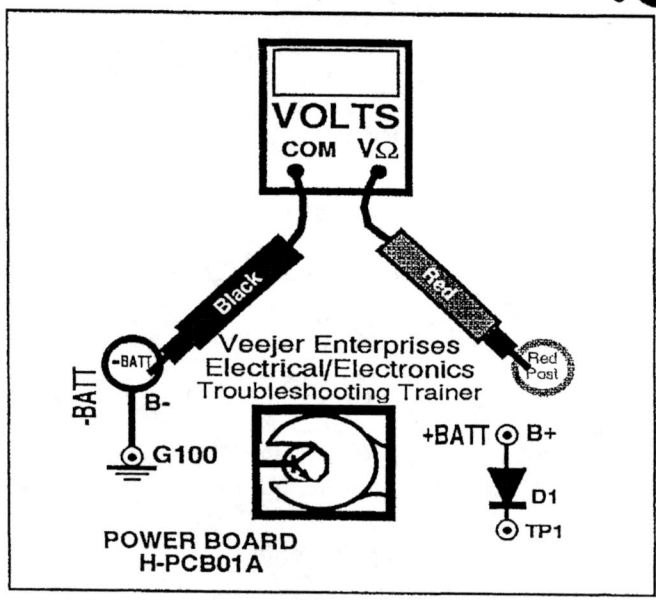

Fig. A

(4) Plug in the H-PS01 to 110-120 VAC wall socket.

(5) On the Power Board turn IGN SW (S1) ON (toggle UP). Slide S3 and S4 UP. The Lamp should be "ON."

(6) Record the voltage at the Power Board Red (+) and Black (-) terminal posts. Write the voltage measured in the DMM display in Figure A. The voltage should be in the range of approximately

16.0-17.50 volts. This is the unregulated (raw) DC voltage produced by the H-PS01.

A regulated power supply is used to maintain a fairly constant output B+ voltage whether the AC power line voltage is a little higher or a little lower between different cities. The actual electronic voltage regulator circuit is mounted on the underside (copper side) of the Power Board between the Red and Black terminal posts to control the output voltage and keep it fairly constant.

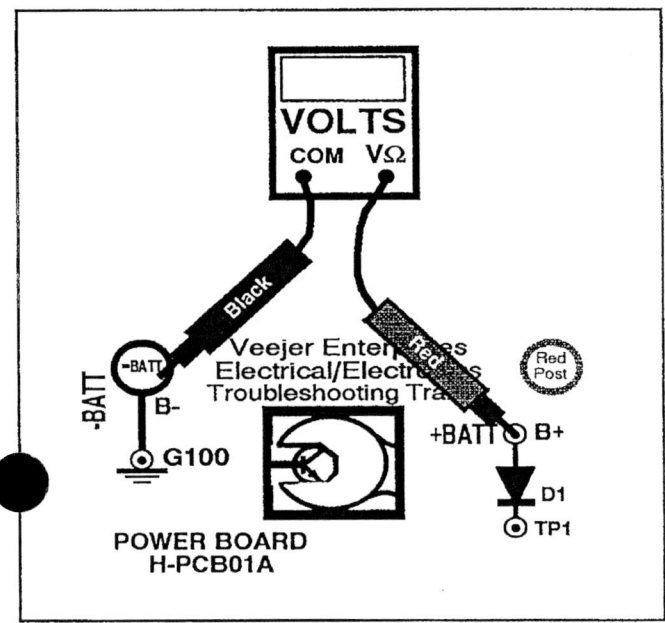

Fig. B

The DMM is shown connected to measure the regulated B+ at the +BATT (B+) (small loop pin) terminal produced by the H-PS01 and the electronic regulator circuit. Follow these steps.

(7) Place DMM test leads as shown in Figure B.

(8) Turn IGN SW, S1, ON (toggle UP), S3 and S4 slide UP. The lamp should be ON.

(9) The voltage measured at the +BATT or B+ Red Loop Pin should be approximately 13.65–13.95V. Write the voltage found in the DMM in Figure B.

The B+ measured at the +BATT or B+ Red Loop Pin changes from no-load (lamp OFF) to loaded condition (lamp ON). The voltage is lower when the lamp is ON as the lamp draws electron current from the power supply (B+). This verifies the proper operation of the voltage regulator circuit.

Hot-At-All-Times Circuit

Figure 2 below shows the **HOT-AT-ALL-TIMES** circuit. This second B+ circuit exists from TP1 through fuse, F2 (3A) which feeds a Hot-at-all-times circuit to TP8 and TP9, the Hot-at-all-times input to C700.

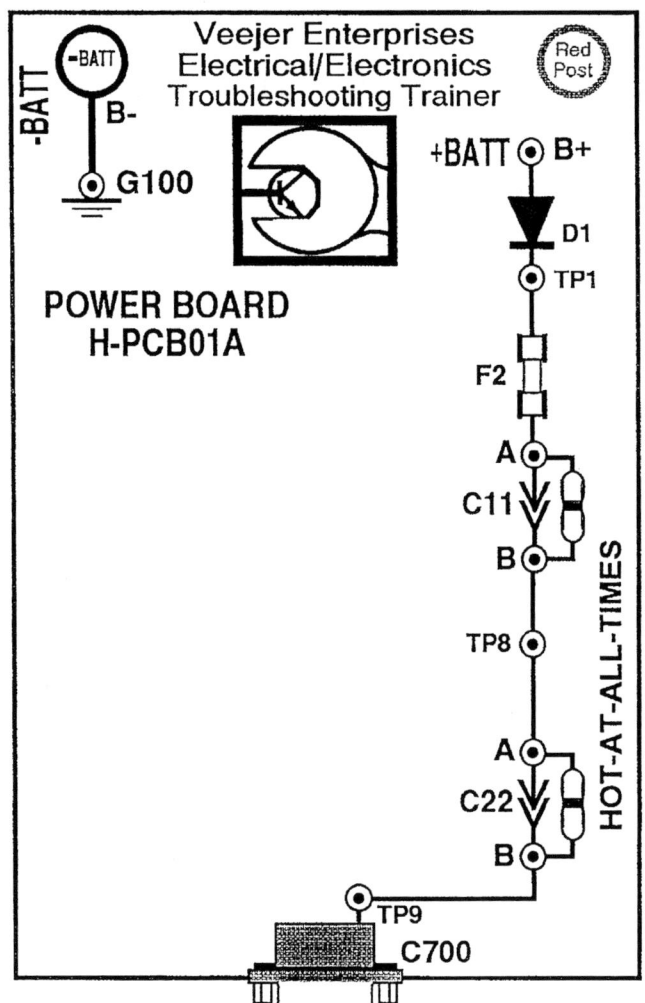

Fig. 2

C11 and C22 **are connectors which have 0ΩRs added to the PCB H-PCB01A (H-111A version).** Each "C" connector now comes with a 0ΩR creating an actual connector. C11 and C22 complete the circuit when a 0ΩR is inserted in C11 and C22. When a 0ΩR is removed, that connector is disconnected or the circuit is OPEN at that point.

TP8 is a test point between the two connectors. The Hot-at-all-times circuit is not used with the Lamp Board but will be used later with the Relay Circuit Troubleshooting Trainer, H-PCB05 (H-115) and The Wire Harness Troubleshooting Trainer, H-PCB06 (H-116).

Vehicle Electronics Hands-On Troubleshooting Training Program

VEEJER ENTERPRISES 3701 Lariat Lane, Garland, Texas 75042-5419
Phone: 972-276-9642   Fax: 972-276-8122   Email: contact-us@veejer.com   Web Site: www.veejer.com

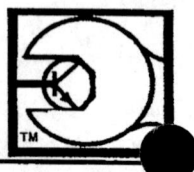

Scanning The Top Of The PCBs

Before using the PCBs for any hands-on exercises or inserting troubleshooting problems, they must be configured (set-up) correctly to operate properly. We call this "**scanning the top of the PCBs.**" This requires a brief visual inspection of the top of the PCBs to verify that everything is in place for proper circuit operation.

(1) Start at the H-PS01. The red/black output leads of the H-PS01 Power Supply are connected to the two terminal posts at the top of the Power Board and make good electrical contact.

(2) The H-PS01 is plugged into a 110-115 VAC wall socket.

(3) Fuses, **F1** (F2 not used with Lamp Board) are good fuses. Do not use more than a **3A fuse.**

(4) There must be a zero ohm resistor between the **B+ Terminal** and **TP4** to use S1 as the **Ignition Switch.**

(5) **S3 & S4** must be CLOSED (slides UP).

(6) There must be zero ohm resistors in **J1** and **J2** on the Lamp Board.

(7) There must be a good #1445 lamp in the lamp socket.

The PCBs are now correctly configured for testing, measuring and troubleshooting problems.

If the lamp does not turn ON when S1 is toggled UP and S3 and S4 are CLOSED (slides UP), it may mean there is a problem on the bottom of the PCBs. "**Scanning the bottom of the PCBs**" for correct set-up conditions is covered in the Instructor Guide H-IG01/02A.

If all set-up conditions on the top and bottom of the PCBs are met and B+ is at the +BATT terminal the lamp will operate when S1, S3 and S4 are CLOSED.

Using Push/Release Switch S2

Future hands-on programs will cover using **S2**, the **Push/Release Switch**. It is not used with the Lamp Board. To use S2 it is necessary to move the 0ΩR to connect between the B+ Terminal and TP17.

Note On Schematic Diagram Symbols

It is customary on schematic diagrams to draw switches (solenoids & relays, etc.) in the OPEN or REST position as is shown in Figure 3 and the other illustrations used in this training program. A technician is expected to *mentally* CLOSE the switch when visualizing circuit operation as in tracing electron current or tracing through a schematic diagram.

Do not misunderstand that the switch is too remain OPEN when operating the circuit. It is understood that to turn a circuit ON the switches must be *physically* CLOSED to complete the circuit.

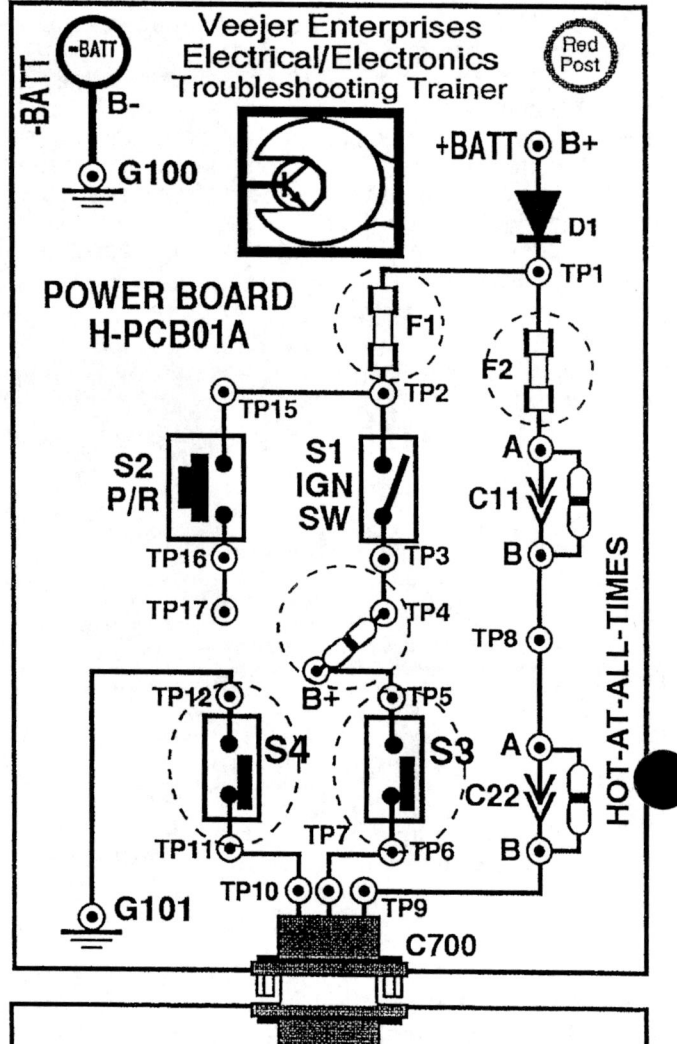

Fig. 3 Scanning the top of H-111A

The Hot-at-all-times Circuit

Future training with the relay board, H-115 and H-116, The Wire Harness Troubleshooting Trainer will use the Hot-at-all-times circuit. Till that time the Hot-at-all-times circuit is not used.

Vehicle Electronics Hands-On Troubleshooting Training Program

VEEJER ENTERPRISES 3701 Lariat Lane, Garland, Texas 75042-5419
Phone: 972-276-9642 Fax: 972-276-8122 Email: contact-us@veejer.com Web Site: www.veejer.com

LOAD SWITCH CONTROL WITH S3 AND S4

All vehicle circuits are controlled by either switching voltage to a load (Switch-to-Voltage control) or switching ground to a load (Switch-to-Ground control) to turn a load ON or OFF.

The "LOAD" in the Lamp Circuit

The "LOAD" in a circuit is the component that the circuit turns ON/OFF. A **series circuit** is a circuit with only **one path** for electron current. There is only one load in a series circuit.

(A **parallel circuit** is a circuit with more than one path for electron current. Each path is called a **branch** of the parallel circuit. A simple parallel circuit is the head lamp circuit of a vehicle where two head lamps are used for night time driving. Each branch or each head lamp is the only load controlled in the branch.)

Switches S3 and S4 on the Power Board are designed to configure a circuit so that either Switch-to-Voltage control (S3) or Switch-to-Ground control (S4) is possible with the Power Board for a wider variety of circuit experiments.

In order to discuss the operation of S3 and S4, the Lamp Board, H-PCB01/02 or H-PCB01/02A must be connected to connector C700 on the Power Board.

Figure 4 at the left is an illustration of the Lamp Board connected to the Power Board to complete the circuit and the location of S3 and S4. Notice the switches are drawn in the OPEN position which is standard schematic convention for switches on schematic diagrams.

The Lamp Board consists of a 1445 lamp as the load. **The load is the component in the circuit that the circuit controls.** TP13 is on the voltage side supplying B+ to Pin 1 of the lamp through 0ΩR (zero ohm resistor) J1. TP14 is on the ground side supplying B- ground to Pin 2 of the lamp through 0ΩR J2.

To provide both power (B+) and ground (B-) to the lamp both switches (S3 and S4) must be CLOSED at the same time. The switch contacts are CLOSED when both S3 and S4 slides are UP as shown below in Figure 5.

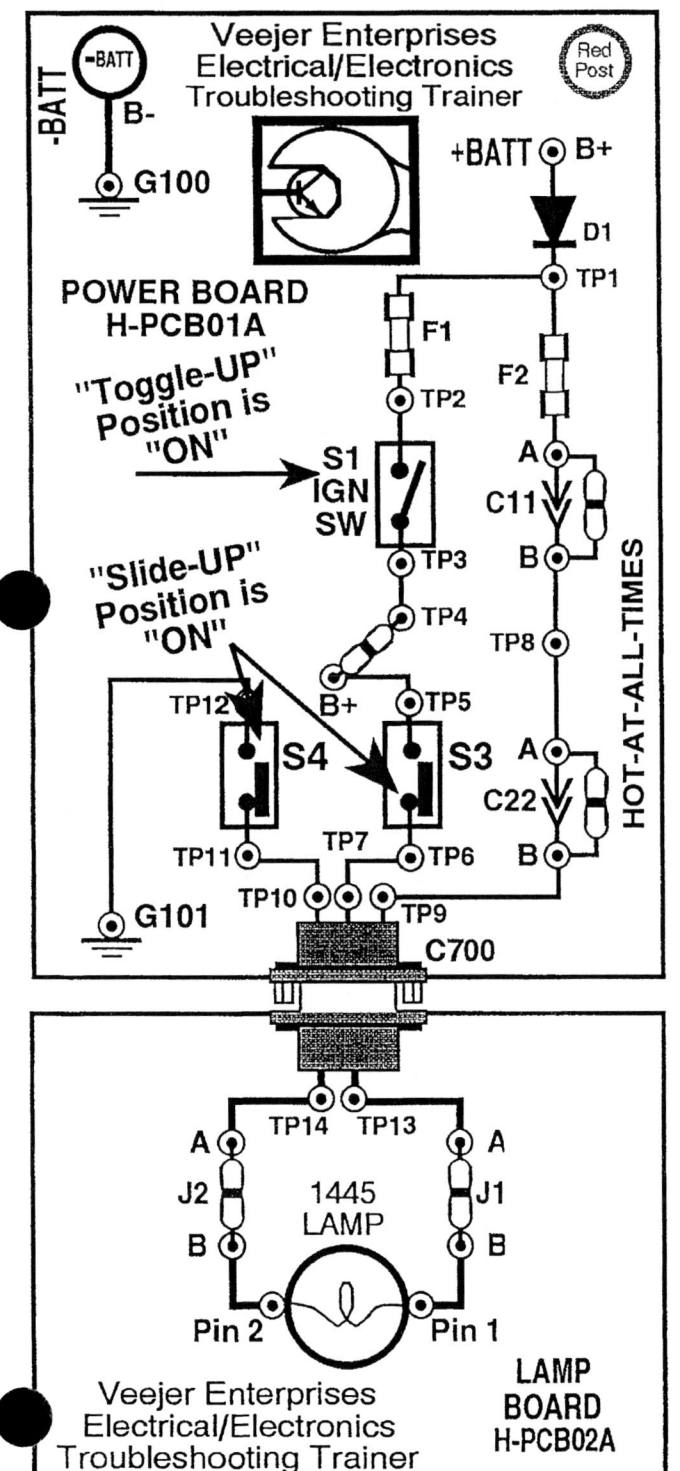

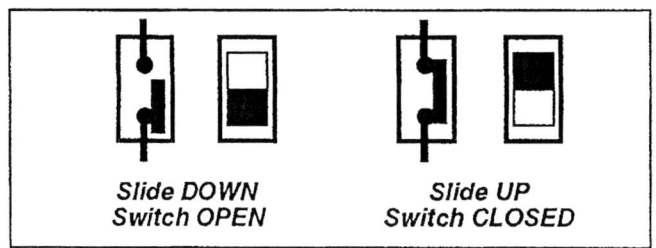

Slide DOWN
Switch OPEN

Slide UP
Switch CLOSED

Fig. 5 S3 & S4 switch configuration

S3 and S4 are mounted on the lower section of the Power Board just above C700 yet play a pivotal role in controlling the lamp (or load) and all other circuits connected to C700 in future training modules to follow.

Fig. 4 Control switches must be "UP" to operate lamp

Vehicle Electronics Hands-On Troubleshooting Training Program

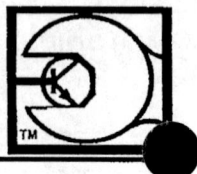

VEEJER ENTERPRISES 3701 Lariat Lane, Garland, Texas 75042-5419
Phone: 972-276-9642 Fax: 972-276-8122 Email: contact-us@veejer.com Web Site: www.veejer.com

Controlling The Lamp With S3 And S4

Figure 6 is a simplified schematic, called a **"straight-line" schematic** of the Lamp Board interconnected to S3 and S4 on the Power Board to illustrate how these two switches can be used to control the load, the lamp in this **PCB**.

A straight line schematic is used in electrical and electronics to re-draw a circuit into a straight line to highlight certain aspects of a circuit so it is easier to understand circuit operation. Some minor circuit details can be eliminated in a straight line schematic for clarity because they might be unnecessary to understanding the circuit's operation or purpose.

In Figure 6 below, the two 0ΩRs in J1 and J2 on the Lamp Board and connector C700 have been deleted from the straight-line schematic to enable us to focus attention on the specific elements of how the circuit is controlled by S3 and S4. The straight line schematic diagram in this example is drawn to point out only how S3 and S4 control the lamp.

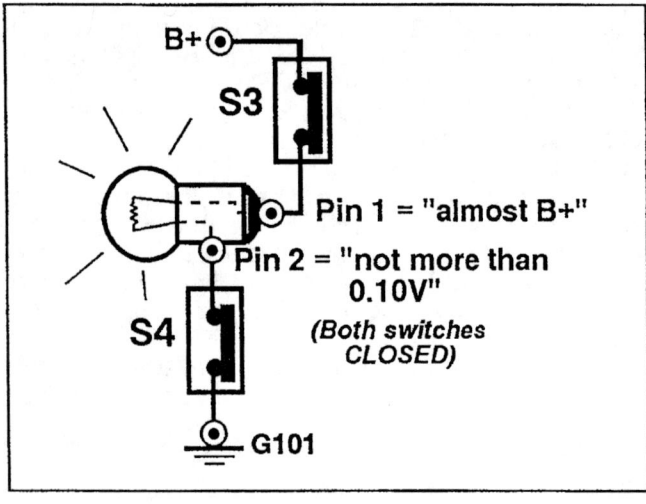

Fig. 6 S3 and S4 controlling the lamp

If both switches, S3 and S4, are CLOSED (slides "UP") at the same time, as shown in Figure 6, the lamp is ON.

Almost B+ is available from the B+ Terminal on the Power Board just above TP5.

Switch S3 places almost B+ (about +13V) on Pin 1 if there is no problem on the voltage side of the circuit. Some B+ is normally dropped on the voltage side of the circuit while the lamp is ON. That is why full B+ is not ever available to Pin 1 of the load. Some voltage drop on the voltage side is considered normal. We will discuss this shortly in detail.

Switch S4 places a ground or B- (or not more than 0.10V) on Pin 2 of the lamp if there is no problem on the ground side of the circuit. A smaller voltage drop on the ground side than the voltage side is considered normal. We will also discuss this shortly in detail.

If the lamp is good and there are no electrical problems in the circuit, OPEN connections or corroded connections causing a Vd, the lamp should operate properly. At this time the lamp should be ON (operating).

Observing Switch-to-Voltage Control

When the control switch is wired into the voltage side of the load it is called a **Switch-to-Voltage** control circuit.

To simulate **Switch-to-Voltage** control, S4 must remain CLOSED to "permanently" complete the ground side of the circuit. Then S3, on the voltage side of the load becomes the control switch which can be **toggled UP/DOWN** to turn the lamp ON/OFF.

Figure 7 below shows the switches set up for Switch-to-Voltage control. S3 is the ON/OFF switch (S4 must remain CLOSED).

To control the lamp ON/OFF, cycle S3 for **Switch-to-Voltage** control of the lamp load. Pin 1 of the lamp is at 0.00V when S3 is OFF/DOWN because B+ voltage has been disconnected from lamp Pin 1.

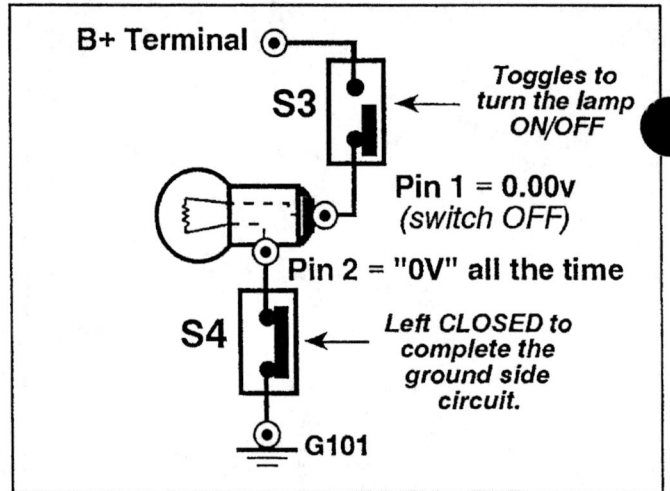

Fig 7 Switch-to-Voltage Control using S3

In Veejer training, Pin 1 is always used to designate the B+ (supply) voltage side pin of the load.

Pin 2 is always used to designate the B- or ground side pin of the load.

Vehicle Electronics Hands-On Troubleshooting Training Program

VEEJER ENTERPRISES 3701 Lariat Lane, Garland, Texas 75042-5419
Phone: 972-276-9642 Fax: 972-276-8122 Email: contact-us@veejer.com Web Site: www.veejer.com

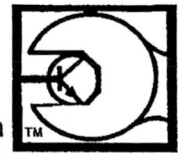

Observing Switch-to-Ground Control

When ground is switched to control a load it is called a **Switch-to-Ground** control circuit. Figure 8 below shows the S3-S4 set up for Switch-to-Ground control of the lamp load. To simulate **Switch-to-Ground** control, S3 must be CLOSED to "permanently" complete the voltage side of the circuit and provide B+ to lamp Pin 1. Then S4 becomes the control switch that is **toggled UP/DOWN** to turn the lamp ON/OFF.

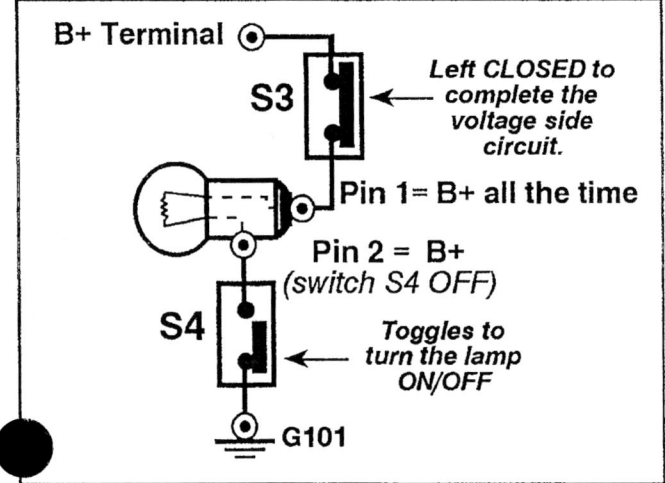

Fig. 8 Switch-to-Ground Control using S4

Pin 2 of the lamp is at B+ when S4 is OFF because ground or B- (0.00V) has been disconnected from the lamp circuit Pin 2.

Remember Pin 2 is always used to designate the B- or ground side pin of the load in Veejer training.

Which Load Side Control Is Best?

It makes no difference to lamp operation which side of the load the control switch is located. Placing the control switch on the voltage side or the ground side does not affect lamp operation at all.

Yet, in some situations a particular circuit may always be connected Switch-to-Voltage or Switch-to-Ground control depending on circumstance decided by the design engineers for purposes of fail-safe.

In other words it may be safer for vehicle operation to control the voltage side versus the ground side of a circuit in a particular situation such as a vehicle accident. But again, this is a decision for the design engineer.

As technicians, in repairing a circuit we should always restore it to its original design of Switch-to-Voltage or Switch-to-Ground control.

Practice Exercise Using S3 and S4

Now for some practice measuring voltages in the lamp circuit using the **load control switches** S3 and S4. Either switch may be used to control the load. Practice measuring the voltages at the lamp terminals, Pin 1 and Pin 2 as follows.

Turn S1 ON. Make sure S3 and S4 are both ON (both slides UP for the CLOSED condition). The lamp is ON and electron current is flowing. (When the lamp is OFF current is not flowing.)

Exercise

Do the following voltage tests with the lamp ON to better understand how S3 and S4 control a load.

(1) Measure the voltage at Lamp Pin 1 and Pin 2 when the lamp is ON (S3 and S4 slide UP) and record voltages below.
MAKE SURE YOUR DMM IS GROUNDED AT THE -BATT BLACK POST AT THE TOP OF THE POWER BOARD. THIS CORRESPONDS TO THE NEGATIVE TERMINAL OF THE VEHICLE BATTERY, -BATT.

Voltage at Pin 1 _____ V
Voltage at Pin 2 _____ V

NOTE: Pin 1 should be about 13 volts (good B+) and Pin 2 should be about 0.0x volts (good B-). The "x" means the digit could be a 0 reading (0.00) or a 9 reading (0.09) with no change in excellent ground circuit performance.

(2) Toggle S3 to turn the lamp OFF. This is **switch-to-voltage** control of the lamp.

Voltage at Pin 1 _____ V
Voltage at Pin 2 _____ V

NOTE: The voltage drops to zero (no B+) on Pin 1 when S3 is OFF (no voltage to the load).

(3) Slide S3 UP and Lamp should be ON.

(4) Toggle S4 to turn the lamp OFF. This is **switch-to-ground** control of the lamp.

Voltage at Pin 1 _____ V
Voltage at Pin 2 _____ V

NOTE: The voltage rises to B+ on Pin 2 when S4 is OFF (no ground or B- to the load).

(5) Slide S3 and S4 UP and Lamp should be ON to complete this exercise.

Vehicle Electronics Hands-On Troubleshooting Training Program

VEEJER ENTERPRISES 3701 Lariat Lane, Garland, Texas 75042-5419
Phone: 972-276-9642 Fax: 972-276-8122 Email: contact-us@veejer.com Web Site: www.veejer.com

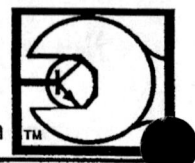

Straight Line Schematics

Figure 9 shows a straight line schematic of the Lamp Board and its interface from the B+ Terminal on the Power Board just above TP5 and includes the ground circuit provided on the Power Board through connector C700.

A **straight line schematic** can be created (re-drawn) to clarify a circuit schematic which may seem difficult to understand the way it is shown in the shop manual.

Notice how confusing the Power Board and Lamp Board schematic is on the ground side of the lamp circuit the way the ground circuit is drawn back in Figure 4 and also appears on the white silk screen on top of the PCBs. A straight line schematic of the circuit can be drawn to clarify the ground circuit of the lamp circuit.

A straight line schematic diagram of both the voltage and ground sides can be drawn placing all components and connections in a straight vertical line between B+ at the top and B- (ground) at the bottom and eliminate confusion in the schematic.

Straight line the lamp circuit schematic starting at the terminals of the load, the lamp. It is on the ground side where the most circuit confusion seems to be and the straight line will help the most. Let's begin at lamp Pin 2 and straight line the ground side of the circuit.

Tracing the Ground Side

The ground side is shown in Figure 9 already drawn in a straight line. Trace through the circuit as described and follow along. **Start at Lamp Pin 2 to trace down the ground side of the lamp circuit.** Ground, B-, is applied to Pin 2 through 0ΩR-J2, TP14 through C700, TP10, TP11, through the CLOSED contacts of S4 (shown drawn OPEN), TP12 to ground connection G101. It should be understood that G101 connects back to G100 and the -BATT negative terminal of the voltage source. On a vehicle this would be -BATT.

Tracing the Voltage Side

Start at Lamp Pin 1 to trace the voltage side of the lamp circuit. B+ is applied to Pin 1 through 0ΩR-J1, TP13, C700, TP7, through the CLOSED contacts of S3, (drawn OPEN as is always done on schematic diagrams), to TP5 which is connected to the B+ Terminal on the Power Board. That's far enough for the voltage side.

Not shown in Figure 9 is a 0ΩR from the B+ Terminal to TP4. TP3 the CLOSED contacts of S1, TP2, Fuse F1, through Diode, D1, to the +BATT or positive terminal of the voltage source (B+).

Complete drawing the voltage side of the lamp circuit for practice beginning at the B+ Terminal and trace back to +BATT, B+. Draw the circuit at the top of Figure 9 as you trace the circuit.

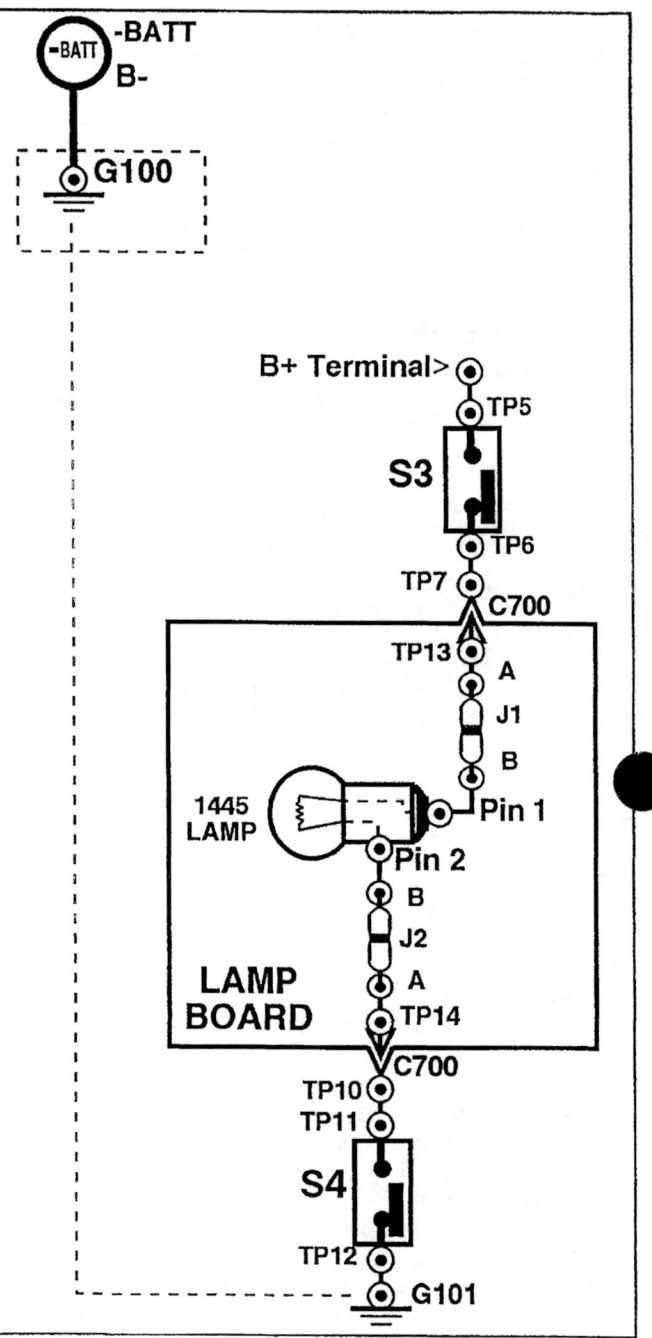

Fig 9 Straight-Line Lamp Board Schematic
Complete the voltage side!

Vehicle Electronics Hands-On Troubleshooting Training Program

VEEJER ENTERPRISES 3701 Lariat Lane, Garland, Texas 75042-5419
Phone: 972-276-9642 Fax: 972-276-8122 Email: contact-us@veejer.com Web Site: www.veejer.com

What Are Voltage Drops?

A **V**oltage **D**rop (a term abbr. as "Vd" in this training program) occurs anytime electron current flows through a resistance. The resistance could simply be the normal resistance of a physical resistor as shown below, or resistance in the length of a wire.

All resistance develops (causes) a Vd as electron current passes through the resistance. Figure 9A below illustrates the symbol for resistance (9A-1) and the polarity of a Vd (9A-3) across a resistance as electrons move from left to right through the resistance.

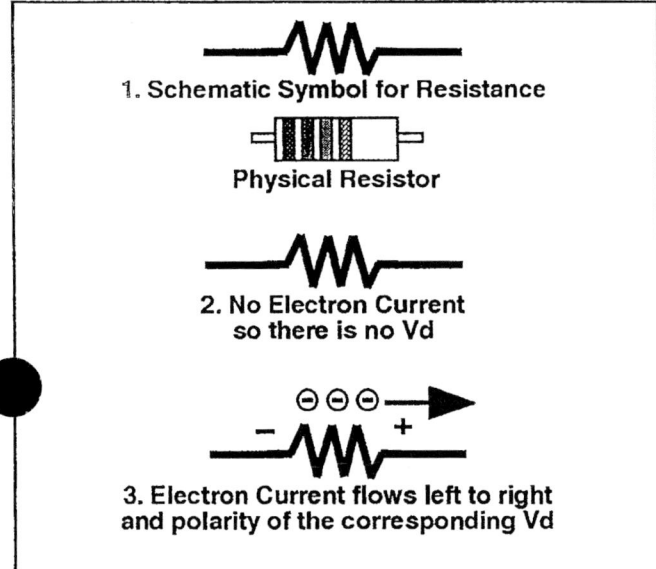

Fig. 9A Polarity of Vd across resistance

Notice above in (9A-2) when there is no electron current through the resistance there is NO Vd. **The Vd appears ONLY when electrons are flowing.** The side the electrons enter the resistance is a negative polarity compared to the opposite side the electrons exit the resistance is a positive polarity.

This is referred to as the **polarity of the voltage drop** across the resistance and can be measured with a DMM. Polarity of a Vd is true regardless of what the resistance actually is. The resistance could be nothing more than a corroded or loose connection. The side electrons enter is negative and the opposite side they exit is positive.

A small amount of Vd in a length of wire is acceptable and proves that the length of wire is able to safely pass the intended level of electron current in amps. The normal Vd of wiring is measured in millivolts per linear foot. **Millivolts is thousandths of volt and abbreviated as "mV."**

All connections have some resistance. A good connection has a very small Vd in the range of millivolts (mV) because it has low resistance if it is a good connection. Should a connection develop resistance from corrosion, the connection Vd will increase to indicate a poor connection.

A circuit load provides the major resistance in a circuit to electron current passing through the circuit. **In fact, the load (works, operates, does it's job) as electrons pass through it. If electron current does not pass through the load will not work, operate nor do it's job.**

The load Vd should be the largest Vd in a circuit approaching almost the level of B+ applied to the circuit. There are three major points to consider when measuring a Vd in a circuit.

(1) **Electron current must be flowing** through the circuit to measure a Vd. If the electron current is turned OFF, as is the case when the circuit is turned OFF, any Vd in the circuit disappears (drops to zero). **Vds across resistance in a circuit do not exist when electron current is NOT flowing.**

(2) **Never disconnect a circuit load** from the circuit to test for Vds. Disconnecting the load is the same thing as turning the circuit OFF. Electron current ceases and Vds disappear.

(3) **Never disconnect a circuit connector** from the circuit to test for voltage or Vds. Disconnecting a connector is the same thing as turning the circuit OFF, electron current ceases and Vds disappear.

Some Vd in wires and connections is considered normal when electron current flows. Too much Vd indicates a circuit problem. The following are **three** basic Vd measurements that can be performed in any circuit on any vehicle to reveal a lot about the electrical conditions in the circuit. How much Vd is an excessive Vd is also addressed.

> *The Vehicle Electronics Training Course*
> **Lessons 15 and 16** explain what voltage drops (Vds) are, how they occur in circuits and how to measure them.

In the next series of **three voltage drop exercises** we will discuss three voltage drop tests that can be performed on any circuit on any vehicle. They are explained using the Power Board and Lamp Board to get familiar with the voltage drop measuring procedure.

These voltage drop tests are fast and easy to perform on any vehicle circuit. They do not require a schematic diagram if the two posts of the battery and the two terminals of the load are accessible. These three voltage drop tests are explained next.

(1) The Vd of the voltage side of the circuit (Vd_{VS}).
(2) The Vd of the ground side of the circuit (Vd_{GS}).
(3) The Vd of the Load of the circuit (Vd_{LOAD}).

Vehicle Electronics Hands-On Troubleshooting Training Program

VEEJER ENTERPRISES 3701 Lariat Lane, Garland, Texas 75042-5419
Phone: 972-276-9642 Fax: 972-276-8122 Email: contact-us@veejer.com Web Site: www.veejer.com

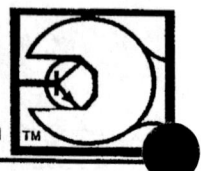

(1) Measure Vd Of The Voltage Side Of Load

The first Vd test to perform on any circuit with the lamp ON (electron current flowing), is the **Vd** (**V**oltage **d**rop) of the **voltage side of the circuit** as shown in Figure 10. The term "**Vd$_{vs}$**" is used for the term "**V**oltage **d**rop of the **V**oltage **S**ide" of a circuit.

The Vehicle Electronics Training Course
Lesson 16, Pages 4-6 discusses checking the Vd of the voltage side of a circuit (**Vd$_{vs}$**).

(1) Turn ON the Ignition Switch, S1.

(2) Make sure S3 and S4 are CLOSED

If the lamp is ON electron current is flowing. If the lamp is OFF electron current is not flowing and a "**Vd$_{vs}$**" measurement cannot be done. **Current must be flowing through the circuit during any Vd test.**

(If the lamp does not turn ON scan the top and bottom of the PCBs to locate any problems that might be present from the last time the PCBs were used.)

With the lamp ON, place the DMM on the 20-30-40 volt range (DMM readout indicates **0.00** before measuring). Connect the DMM test leads to the PCBs as shown in Figure 10 on the next page.

The Red Test Lead connects to +BATT loop pin.
(On a vehicle this would be the positive post of the battery +BATT.)

The Black Lest lead connects to Lamp Pin 1.
(On a vehicle this would correspond to the pin at the load where the B+ appears.)

This places the entire voltage side of the Lamp Circuit between the DMM test leads while the electron current is flowing to obtain the **Vd$_{vs}$** reading.

(3) Record the **Vd$_{vs}$** reading obtained. _____ V

(4) Write the numbers with decimal point in the DMM shown in Figure 10.

A reading of approximately 0.70–0.80 volt is normal for **Vd$_{vs}$** of this circuit if the two circuit boards are functioning correctly and B+ at the +BATT terminal is in the range of 13.8V.

The *lower* Vd$_{vs}$ is in a circuit the better the circuit. A low **Vd$_{vs}$** means less B+ voltage is being dropped (used up) on the voltage side of the load leaving more operating voltage (B+) available to the load. In this case, brighter operation of the lamp represents the load's highest efficiency of operation.

If the **Vd$_{vs}$** reading is higher than that found in a known good lamp circuit (about 1.00V) it means some resistance has developed on the voltage side of the circuit due to possibly a loose 0ΩR on top or the bottom of the PCBs. Gently push all 0ΩRs to see if one 0ΩR seats better in the mounting pins and the **Vd$_{vs}$** drops back to the normal range.

A high **Vd$_{vs}$** also may be due to the fuse holder supporting Fuse F1 is a little loose. Remove the fuse and press the mounting pins together to compress the fuse holder terminals to hold the fuse tighter.

All of these simple fixes may be all the repair that is necessary. Verify that **Vd$_{vs}$** is in the range of 0.75-0.90V.

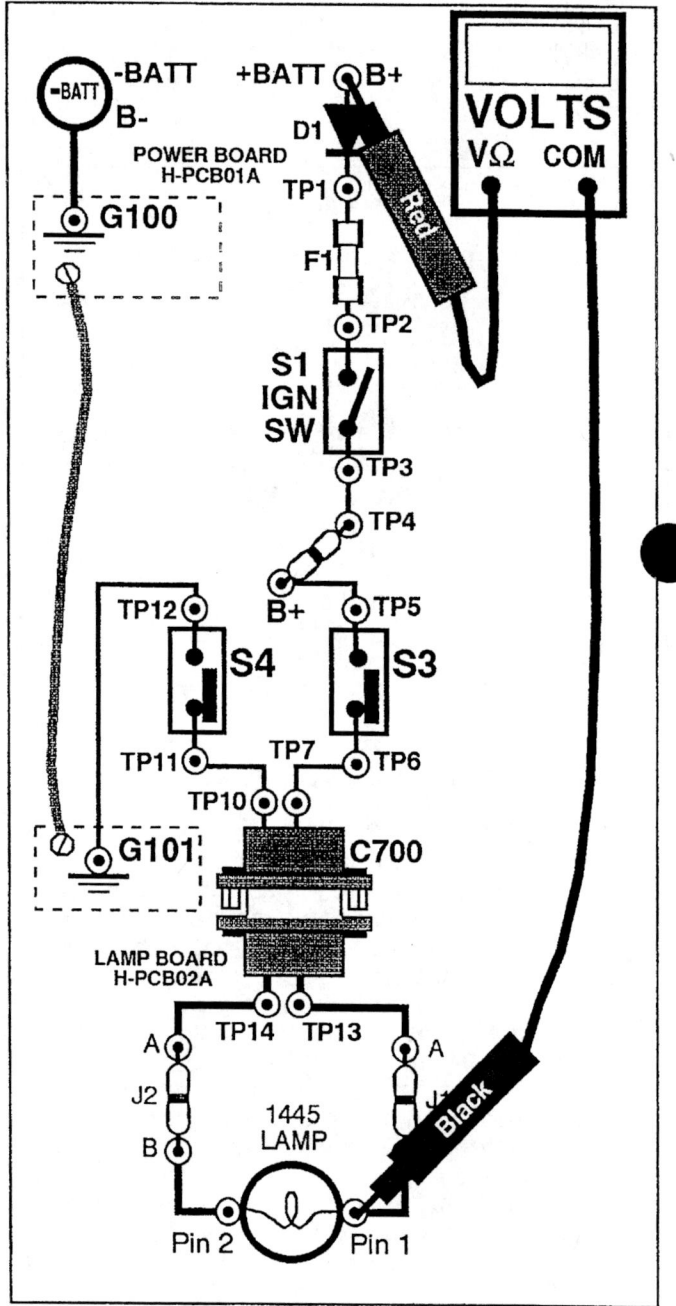

Fig. 10 Checking the Vd of the voltage side, Vd$_{vs}$

Copyright © 2015 VEEJER ENTERPRISES, Garland, Texas - All Rights Reserved

Vehicle Electronics Hands-On Troubleshooting Training Program

VEEJER ENTERPRISES 3701 Lariat Lane, Garland, Texas 75042-5419
Phone: 972-276-9642 Fax: 972-276-8122 Email: contact-us@veejer.com Web Site: www.veejer.com

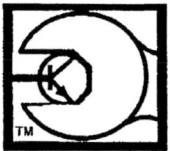

Polarity Sensing Diodes

Diode D1 is a **polarity sensing diode** placed in series with the B+ feed to a circuit. Electron current through the load must pass through the Polarity Diode which only permits electrons to flow one-way (against the arrow). Diodes are used when the load is polarity sensitive and would be damaged if electron current were to attempt to flow in the opposite direction through the load.

The diode is present to protect the circuit from wrong voltage polarity being applied that would force electron current the wrong direction through the circuit, as can happen when jump starting a vehicle with the jumper cables reversed.

If battery voltage is connected backwards, D1 prevents electron current flowing through the circuit in the wrong direction. Diode D1 makes sure of that. Notice electrons only flow AGAINST the arrow in the diode symbol. Lamp current only flows when the Red Post is B+ and the Black Post in B–.

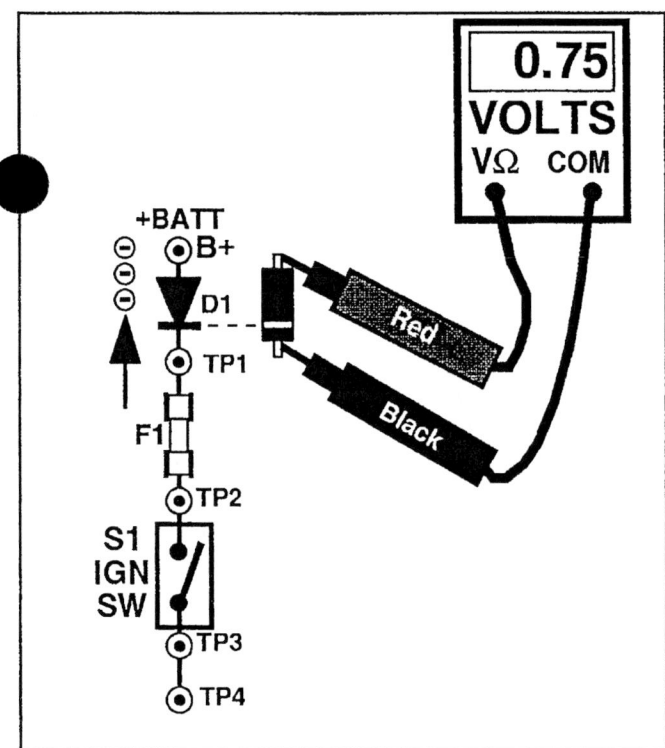

Fig. 10A Measuring Polarity Diode Vd

The reason the Vd_{vs} reading in this Lamp Circuit is high is due to the Vd across the Polarity Diode, D1, of approximately 0.75 volt. This is a normal Vd across a silicon diode. Measure the Vd of the diode as shown in Figure 10A while the Lamp is ON.

The incandescent lamp on the Lamp Board is not polarity sensitive. Electron current can flow in either direction through a lamp. But other circuits, such as solid-state components like transistors and integrated circuits are polarity sensitive. If reverse voltage is applied the solid-state device (transistor or integrated circuit) would be instantly destroyed by electrons flowing the wrong way.

Vd_{vs} In A Vehicle Circuit

In an actual vehicle electrical circuit, a Vd_{vs} reading is considered good if a Vd_{vs} reading is approximately **0.50V** *as a general rule of thumb.* **THE LOWER Vd_{vs} THE BETTER.** The Vd_{vs} reading may be higher on a vehicle depending on the distance between the two points being tested on an individual vehicle circuit. The greater the distance, the longer the wires and the more connectors there may be connecting the two test points which will tend to increase the Vd_{vs} reading.

Practice testing the Vd_{vs} on vehicles will reveal what the Vd_{vs} is on various vehicles and their circuits. A reading of a few tenths of a volt higher Vd_{vs} of (0.8-1.0V) may be normal in some vehicle circuits with a long wire harness and several connectors.

If a polarity sensing diode is connected in series with the wiring of the B+ feed to the load, the Vd_{vs} may be closer to 1.25V to account for the Vd of the Polarity Diode.

Vd_{vs} can be confirmed by checking a known good circuit on a similar vehicle to establish a normal Vd_{vs} reading for that circuit.

Why Vd_{vs} Is Important

This simple Vd test must be performed with the circuit turned ON and the electron current flowing through the load. A Vd_{vs} reading in the general range of what has been learned from checking other similar vehicle circuits eliminates bad wiring and connection problems throughout the voltage side of the circuit. What a time saver this can be.

Intermittent Electrical Problems and Vd_{vs}

Suppose the vehicle has an intermittent electrical problem? An intermittent problem can be caused by a defective connection that sometimes makes good electrical contact so the circuit operates correctly. Then suddenly it makes a poor electrical contact affecting circuit operation. It is clear that intermittent problems can be a difficult task to track down and often consumes a lot of time.

Try measuring the Vd_{vs} of the circuit experiencing the intermittent problem. Many times the Vd_{vs} will be a little higher when there is an intermittent problem in the voltage side of the circuit.

If the Vd_{vs} reading is in the proper range do this. While observing the DMM reading of the Vd_{vs}, move, wiggle and twist all the wires, connectors and connections. When the intermittent area of the circuit is moved, wiggled or twisted, expect to see the DMM reading jump around to indicate where in the circuit is the cause of the intermittent problem. That was easy!

Vehicle Electronics Hands-On Troubleshooting Training Program

VEEJER ENTERPRISES 3701 Lariat Lane, Garland, Texas 75042-5419
Phone: 972-276-9642 Fax: 972-276-8122 Email: contact-us@veejer.com Web Site: www.veejer.com

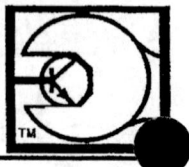

(2) Measure Vd Of The Ground Side Of Load

The second **Vd** measurement to perform on any circuit is the Vd of the ground side of the circuit as shown in Figure 11. The term used for the "**V**oltage **d**rop of the **G**round **S**ide" is **Vd**$_{GS}$.

> The Vehicle Electronics Training Course
> **Lesson 16, Pages 4-6** discusses checking the Vd of the ground side of a circuit, **Vd**$_{GS}$.

DO THIS:
(1) Turn ON S1, the Ignition Switch.
(2) Make sure S3 and S4 are CLOSED

If the lamp is ON, electron current is flowing. If the lamp is OFF, electron current is not flowing and a "**Vd**$_{GS}$" measurement cannot be done. **Current must be flowing through the circuit during any Vd test.**

(If the lamp does not turn ON scan the top and bottom of the PCBs to locate any problems that might be present from the last time the PCBs were used.)

With the lamp ON, place the DMM on the 20-30-40 volt range (DMM readout indicates **0.00** before measuring). Connect the DMM test leads to the PCBs as shown in Figure 11.

The Red Test Lead connects to Lamp Pin 2.
(On a vehicle this would correspond to the pin at the load where the ground side is connected.)

The Black Test Lead connects to the black test post or -BATT.
(On a vehicle this would be the negative post of the battery -BATT.

(1) Record the **Vd**$_{GS}$ reading obtained. _____ V
(2) Write the numbers with the decimal point in the DMM shown in Figure 11.

A reading of about **0.10** volt is normal for **Vd**$_{GS}$ if the ground circuit is in good condition. The *lower* **Vd**$_{GS}$ is in a vehicle circuit the better. Normally, in a vehicle circuit, **Vd**$_{GS}$ is considered a good ground circuit if the **Vd**$_{GS}$ is no more 0.10V.

Do not be surprised if **Vd**$_{GS}$ on the PCBs reads **0.00**V. The resistance in the ground circuit is too small to register a **Vd**$_{GS}$ on the 20-30-40 volt range of a DMM. This is due to two factors. First, the distance of the ground circuit between Pin 2 and the black post is very short in length, about 15 inches of copper trace on the bottom of the PCBs. Secondly, the electron current through the circuit is very small. A 1445 lamp will draw less than 0.150A (150 mA– "milliAmps"). Low electron current and low resistance results in a very low **Vd**$_{GS}$.

Try this.
Set up the DMM to read a low mV (millivolt) reading using the 2-3-4 volt range where the DMM readout indicates **.000** before measuring a voltage.

Measure **Vd**$_{GS}$ again using the DMM's lower range. The reading may now show a low reading, for example, **.003** for 3 mVs. The ground side would be dropping only 3 mV which shows up as **0.00** on the 20-30-40 volt range (too small to be seen on the 20-30-40V range). The reading would have to be **.007-.008** volt to be seen on the 20-30-40 volt range and then it would only indicate as **0.01V**. That's not more than 0.10V.

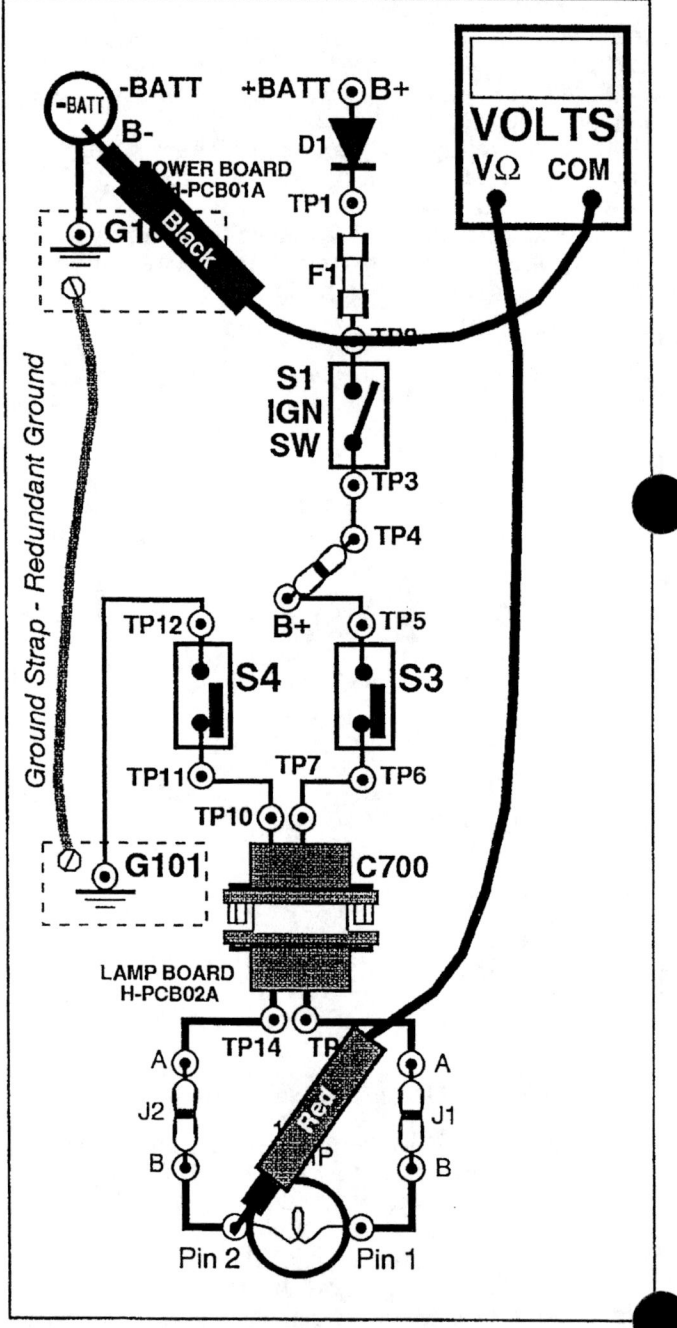

Fig. 11
Measuring Vd of the ground side, Vd$_{GS}$ *showing how ground strap can be tested on the ground circuit.*

Vehicle Electronics Hands-On Troubleshooting Training Program

VEEJER ENTERPRISES 3701 Lariat Lane, Garland, Texas 75042-5419
Phone: 972-276-9642 Fax: 972-276-8122 Email: contact-us@veejer.com Web Site: www.veejer.com

Vd_{GS} On A Vehicle Circuit

If the Vd_{GS} reading is higher than 0.10 volt in a vehicle circuit it may be due to increased resistance on the ground side of the circuit due to corrosion in the ground wiring and connections or possibly a ground strap connection that is not making good electrical contact.

If a Vd_{GS} is slightly higher, say 0.20-0.30V it may not have much impact of the operation of a vehicle circuit as long as normal electron current is flowing through the load and the load is functioning normally. A little experience helps to judge if a Vd_{GS} is too high to impact a circuit. Some vehicles can function well with a Vd_{GS} higher than 0.10V. If a circuit load is functioning as it should, then a 0.30V Vd_{GS} may not be a problem for that circuit. That's good to know.

Ground Straps

A ground strap is installed on a vehicle to connect two sections of sheet metal to provide a better ground path for electron current than relying on sheet metal screws holding the sheet metal together.

Ground straps are used to redirect the ground side electron current through the ground circuit without traveling through engine bearings or the engine water jacket. If a circuit's ground electron current were allowed to pass through engine bearings or the engine water jacket, a problem with bearing failure or water jacket erosion could result. Adding a ground strap between two crucial points on the vehicle ground circuit can be used to redirect the electron current away from engine bearings or the water jacket thus preventing damage from electrolysis.

Ground straps do not always appear on schematic diagrams and they may not always be obvious when looking over the wiring of a vehicle. Sometimes, a ground strap is mounted out of sight.

If a ground strap is missing on a vehicle and it is affecting a circuit's operation, it would be difficult to fix the problem by adding a new ground strap if you didn't know a ground strap is missing in the first place. This is where the Vd_{GS} reading is a great asset.

A higher than normal Vd_{GS} measurement is the only way to determine that a ground strap (redundant ground) may be missing, loose or corroded. A high Vd_{GS} justifies the need to search more closely to find a missing or corroded ground strap especially if no other problem can be found causing the high Vd_{GS}.

Be careful to always ground the DMM black test lead to -BATT on the vehicle so that all of the ground circuit is between the DMM test leads for an accurate and true Vd_{GS} reading. That was easy too!

Vehicle Computer Grounds

There is one point of clarification about ground side Vds and the Vd_{GS} reading specifically. Computers on vehicles today control many critical functions. If a computer controlled system on a vehicle is to function properly the computer ground circuit may have to have a lower Vd_{GS} than 0.10V.

In the early days of computer control, with the 1981 model year, it became apparent that some computer controlled engine management systems would not function properly with poor quality ground circuits. That is, a vehicle would experience a driveability issue with no trouble codes (DTCs) stored in memory. These issues would become known as "no code driveability" problems and strike fear in the hearts of technicians who didn't know what to do without a DTC to give them some clue as to what the driveability problem might be.

Symptoms would include complaints such as, loss of engine power driving up a hill, varying engine idle speed, occasional backfiring, engine miss, not passing a state emissions test and so on.

Through much trial and error it was found that some engine computer systems required the engine computer ground Vd to be approximately 0.05V or 50 mV rather than 0.10V or 100 mV. What a revelation that turned out to be. Checking the engine ground Vd became one of the first things checked when a no code driveability vehicle came in the shop.

How To Check Vehicle Computer Ground Vds

There is a simple way to check any vehicle computer ground. In fact it should be done this way.

(1) GROUND THE DMM TO THE BATTERY NEGATIVE TERMINAL -BATT.

(2) Set DMM to 20-30-40V range which ever your DMM provides. Readout will indicate **0.00** before measuring.

(3) Engine running at idle, warmed up and in CLOSED LOOP.

(4) Touch the DMM red test lead to an easily accessible analog sensor ground, such as the TP (Throttle Position) Sensor.

(5) Confirm the computer system ground Vd_{GS} reading on the DMM is not more than 0.05V.

(6) Rev the engine to 2000 rpm and verify the Vd_{GS} reading does not increase above **0.05V** at higher engine rpm.

Tips checking a computer engine ground

We suggest measuring from an analog sensor since they are often easy to get to. The TP sensor ground wire is a good example of an analog sensor and measured by back probing the TP sensor.

You could also set the DMM to the 2-3-4V range where the DMM reads .000 before measuring. On this range the DMM display should not indicate more than .050 for 50 mV.

the voltage drop of the load is Vd$_{LOAD}$.

> *The Vehicle Electronics Training Course*
> **Lesson 24, Page 1** discusses checking the Vd of the load, **Vd$_{LOAD}$**.

Current must be flowing when measuring **Vd$_{LOAD}$**. If the lamp is ON current is flowing. If the lamp is OFF current is not flowing and this measurement cannot be done. Place the DMM on the 20-30-40 volt range (readout says **0.00**) and connect the test leads as shown in Figure 12.

(1) Record the **Vd$_{LOAD}$** reading obtained. _____ V

(2) Write the numbers with decimal point in the DMM shown in Figure 12.

A reading of close to B+ is normal for Vd$_{LOAD}$ if the circuit is functioning correctly and B+ from the power supply is in the normal range of 13.0 volts.

The *higher* the **Vd$_{LOAD}$** the better and the brighter the lamp (the better the load works). **Vd$_{LOAD}$** can never equal B+ because **Vd$_{VS}$** and **Vd$_{GS}$** are always present and subtract from B+ leaving the value of **Vd$_{LOAD}$**.

The higher **Vd$_{LOAD}$** is in any circuit, the more efficient the circuit and the better the load operates. Lamps are brightest the closer the **Vd$_{LOAD}$** reading is to B+. On a vehicle, **Vd$_{LOAD}$** is good if within 1 volt of B+, or the vehicle charging voltage (with engine running).

> *The Vehicle Electronics Training Course*
> Testing the charging voltage is discussed in **Lesson 22, Pages 5-6.**

On most passenger vehicles, normal charging voltage ranges from a low of 13.50–13.80 volts in hot weather to a high of up to 15.10 volts in cold weather. (This is discussed in **Lesson 21 & 22.**) Therefore **Vd$_{LOAD}$** readings vary as the charging voltage changes with ambient temperature.

In the PCBs, the **Vd$_{LOAD}$** reading is not as close to the B+ supply voltage at the +BATT Terminal as you might expect because of the 0.75 volt drop of polarity diode D1, on the Power Board voltage side. This shows us that any increase in the reading of **Vd$_{VS}$** or **Vd$_{GS}$** begins to decrease the **Vd$_{LOAD}$** reading.

Low **Vd$_{LOAD}$** readings are due to a circuit problem developing (corrosion or loose connections) in the voltage side or the ground side of the circuit. Low B+ or low charging voltage can also cause a low **Vd$_{LOAD}$**.

Whatever the load device is in a circuit happens to be (we use a lamp for our example) and its **Vd$_{LOAD}$** reading begins to decrease, the load will not work as well. Different loads behave weakly when the **Vd$_{LOAD}$** is too low. If the load were a DC motor it would run at a slower rpm with low **Vd$_{LOAD}$**. A relay may not close its contacts. A solenoid may not move its plunger very well.

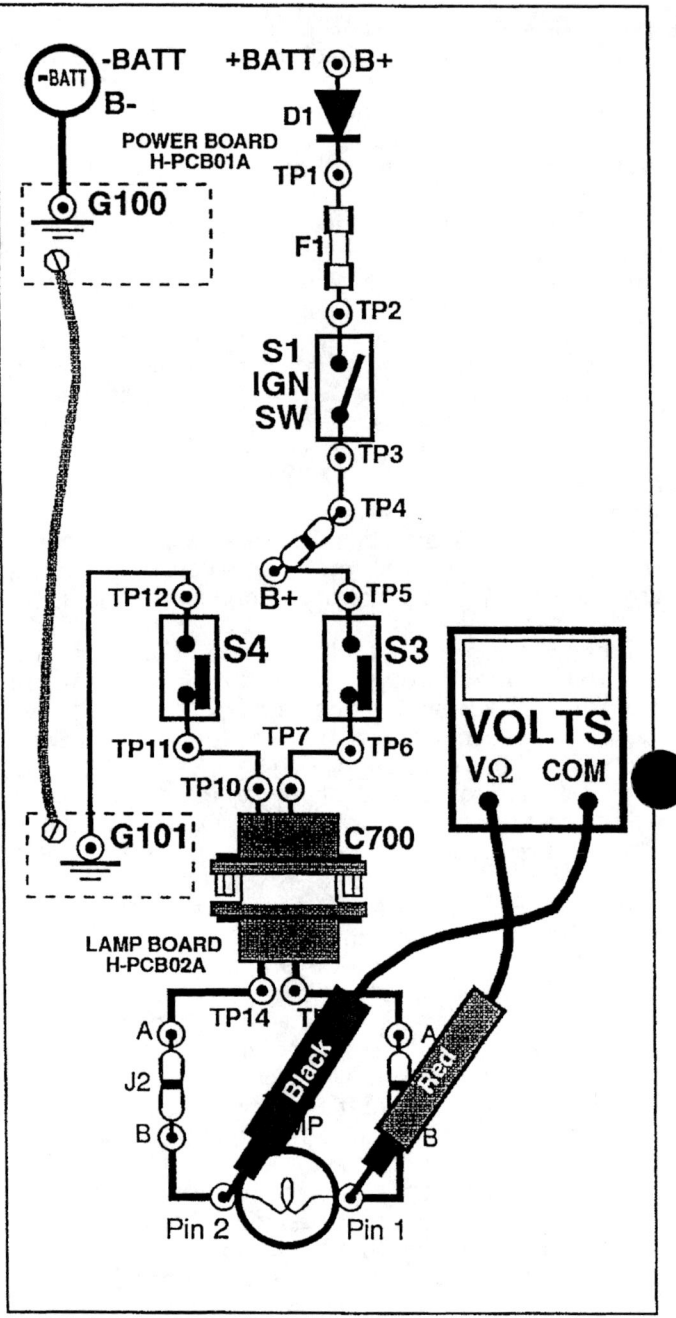

Fig. 12 Measuring Vd of the Load, Vd$_{LOAD}$

Summarizing Vd$_{VS}$ Vd$_{GS}$ and Vd$_{LOAD}$

Measuring **Vd$_{LOAD}$** is NOT the most effective way to test a circuit. Even if **Vd$_{LOAD}$** is one volt less than B+ it doesn't tell if there is a problem on the voltage or ground side of the circuit. It is best to check **Vd$_{VS}$** and **Vd$_{GS}$** separately to clearly define a Vd problem on either side of the load.

Always use this Vd technique when you have circuit with an intermittent problem.

Vehicle Electronics Hands-On Troubleshooting Training Program

VEEJER ENTERPRISES 3701 Lariat Lane, Garland, Texas 75042-5419
Phone: 972-276-9642   Fax: 972-276-8122   Email: contact-us@veejer.com   Web Site: www.veejer.com

"Tracing B+" On The Voltage Side

Should the Vd_{vs} be too high then "Trace B+" which means to check the B+ voltage beginning at the load Pin 1 back to +BATT to find out where the Vd is located on the voltage side.

It is always understood that the DMM's black (COM) test lead is grounded to the -BATT (B-) terminal post on the Power Board. On a vehicle, when tracing B+, the DMM is grounded at (or connected to) the battery negative terminal post.

In Figure 13 the BLACK DMM test lead is shown connected to -BATT (black) terminal post and the placement of the RED DMM test lead for each voltage measurement to be made on the voltage side of the circuit beginning at the load Pin 1.

> *The Vehicle Electronics Training Course*
> **Lesson 11** discusses the voltage side of the circuit. **Lesson 23** discusses Vc measurement.

DO THIS FOR HANDS-ON

- Turn the circuit ON with S1. Lamp should be ON.
- Ground DMM to the -BATT terminal post.
- With the lamp ON, measure the circuit voltage at each point in the circuit shown in Figure 13, first with Lamp Pin 1 and record your readings below.

(1) _____ V (Load Pin 1)
Pins J1-B and J1-A can be used as test points.
(2) _____ V (TP13)
(3) _____ V (TP7)
(4) _____ V (TP6)
(5) _____ V (TP5)
The B+ Terminal can also be used as a test point.
(6) _____ V (TP4)
(7) _____ V (TP3)
(8) _____ V (TP2)
Both fuse ends can be used as test points.
(9) _____ V (TP1)
(10) _____ V (good B+)

Notice the Vc readings **increase slightly** as the measurement point gets closer to B+ or +BATT. Use the two end caps of Fuse F1 for additional test points. Notice a voltage increase of about 0.7 volt from Step 9 to Step 10. The difference between the two DMM readings is the actual Vd of the polarity sensing diode, D1.

Step 10 is also the value of full B+ or the positive terminal of the voltage source, which on the PCBs is the small loop pin at the **+BATT** Terminal. On a vehicle it would be the charging voltage if the engine is running.

This illustrates how a voltage drop problem can be found while "Tracing B+." A bad connection causes a voltage difference from between two points. No voltage difference between two points is excellent. A 0.10 V difference between test points is reasonable. More than that indicates corrosion has begun to develop in the connection and should be corrected.

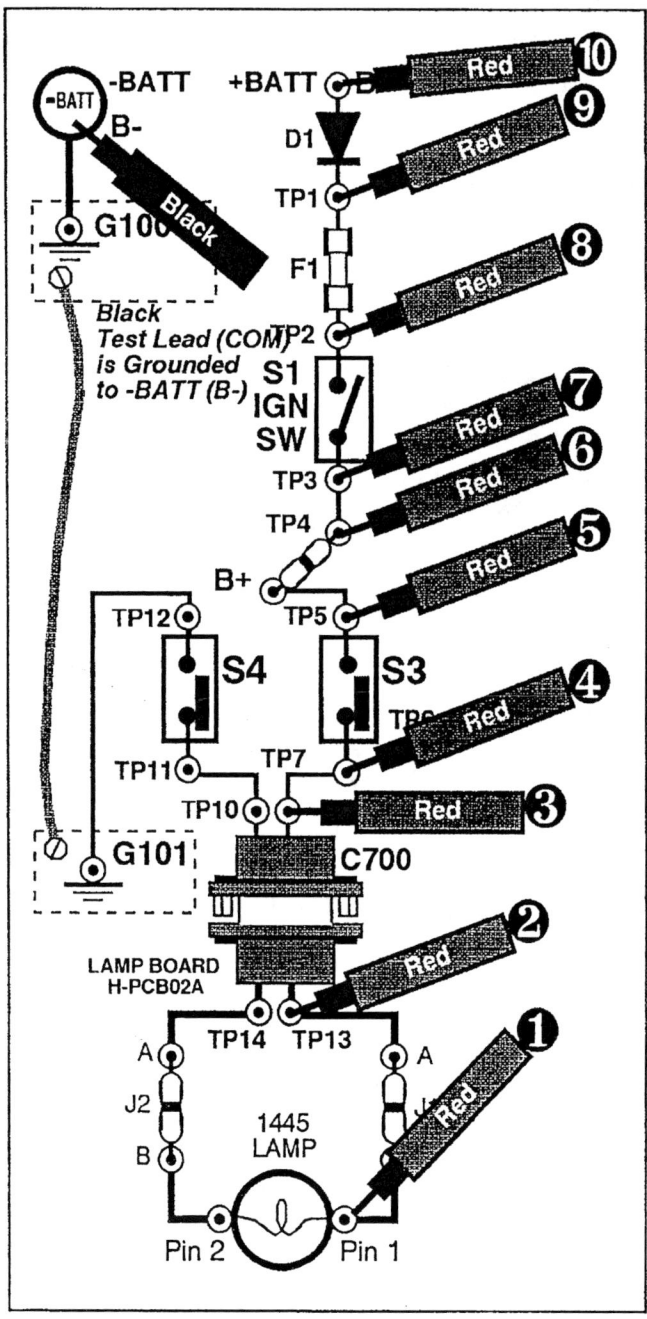

Fig. 13
Tracing B+ circuit voltages (Vc) on the voltage side of the circuit

Remember to always ground the DMM to the negative terminal of the battery when checking a circuit voltage (abbr. Vc) or Tracing B+ in a vehicle circuit.

Vehicle Electronics Hands-On Troubleshooting Training Program

VEEJER ENTERPRISES 3701 Lariat Lane, Garland, Texas 75042-5419
Phone: 972-276-9642 Fax: 972-276-8122 Email: contact-us@veejer.com Web Site: www.veejer.com

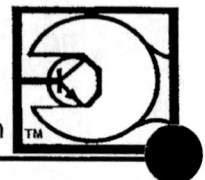

"Tracing B-" On The Ground Side

Again, when measuring a circuit voltage (abbr. "Vc") it *always means* the DMM is understood to be grounded at the battery negative terminal. On a vehicle use the battery's negative terminal post and make a longer DMM ground lead if necessary. On the PCBs use the negative or black terminal post, -BATT.

The BLACK DMM (COM) test lead is shown in Figure 14 connected to -BATT and the placement of the RED DMM (V/Ω) test lead for each Vc measurement to be made on the ground side of the circuit **beginning at load Pin 2**.

> *The Vehicle Electronics Training Course*
> **Lesson 12** discusses the ground side of the circuit.

DO THIS FOR HANDS-ON

- Turn the circuit ON with S1.
- Ground your DMM to the negative terminal post.
- With the lamp ON start to measure the circuit voltage at each point in the circuit beginning at Lamp Pin 2 and record your readings below.

Carefully follow the order of Vc measurements. The DMM test leads are touching the circuit in the correct numerical order to follow in your test steps.

(1) _____ V (Load Pin 2)
Pins J2-B and J2-A can be used as test points.

(2) _____ V (TP14)

(3) _____ V (TP10)

(4) _____ V (TP11)

(5) _____ V (TP12)

(6) _____ V (G101)
The measurement between Steps 6 and 7 checks the quality of the ground strap.

(7) _____ V (G100)

(8) _____ V (-BATT Terminal- Ground)

Notice the Vc readings **decrease slightly** as the measurement point gets closer to the -BATT or negative terminal post of the voltage source.

If the DMM readings are **0.00** (20-30-40V Range) on the ground side (meaning a good ground circuit) change the DMM to the (2-3-4V Range) and the readout says .000. This will allow you to see readings in 1 mV increments, such as .001, .002 etc., which still indicates a good ground circuit but shows the ground side voltage in tiny mV segments.

While "Tracing B-" a bad ground connection causes a reading difference between two ground circuit test points. No voltage difference between two test points indicates a good connection between those two points if the voltage is less than 0.10 volt. More than 0.10 V difference between two ground test points indicates some corrosion has begun to develop in the ground circuit and probably should be corrected by cleaning the connection.

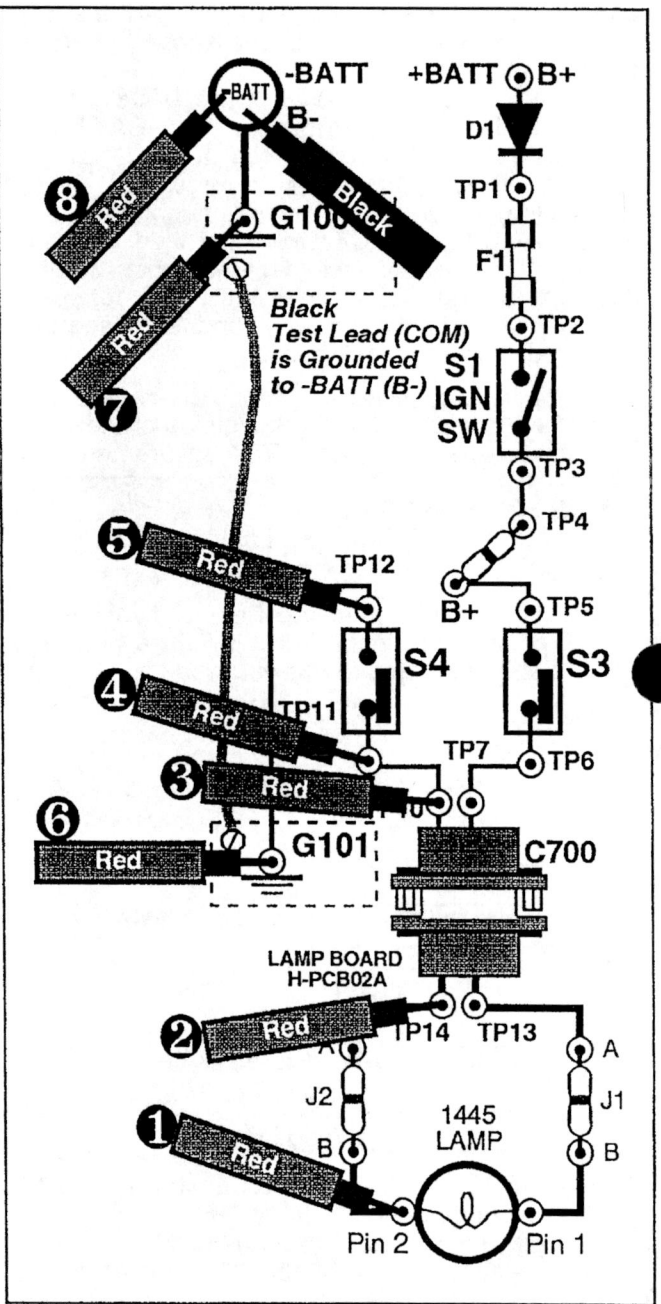

Fig. 14
Tracing B- circuit voltage (Vc) on the ground side of the circuit

Remember to always ground the DMM to the negative terminal of the battery when checking a circuit voltage (abbr. Vc) or Tracing B- in a vehicle circuit.

Vehicle Electronics Hands-On Troubleshooting Training Program

VEEJER ENTERPRISES 3701 Lariat Lane, Garland, Texas 75042-5419
Phone: 972-276-9642 Fax: 972-276-8122 Email: contact-us@veejer.com Web Site: www.veejer.com

Introduction To Troubleshooting

Successful electrical-electronic circuit troubleshooting is based on using proven systematic troubleshooting procedures to reveal a circuit problem in the shortest possible time with almost foolproof accuracy.

Our example is the **"Texas-Two-Step,"** abbreviated as **"TTS"** in this training program. Use the **TTS** from this time forward for foolproof troubleshooting in any vehicle electrical or electronic circuit on any vehicle.

> *The Vehicle Electronics Training Course*
> **Lesson 23** and **Lesson 24** explain the two TTS measurements in detail.

The TTS involves two circuit voltage (or Vc) measurements taken at the load terminals. The DMM black (COM) test lead is grounded to battery negative or **-BATT** as shown at the top of Figure 15. It is *always understood* that the DMM is grounded to the -BATT or at the negative battery post on a vehicle for both TTS readings. The DMM red (V/Ω) test lead is used to measure (1) the B+ at load Pin 1 and (2) the voltage on the ground side at load Pin 2.

STEP 1 of the TTS is abbr. "TTS-1"

Measure the circuit voltage (or Vc) at Load Pin 1. This reading shows how much B+ (charging voltage on a vehicle) gets to the load Pin 1. Expect the reading to be close to B+ (charging voltage on a vehicle) when the voltage side of the load is a good circuit. **The higher the TTS-1 reading the better.** The TTS-1 reading is always the value of B+ minus Vd_{vs}. The higher Vd_{vs} the lower the TTS-1 reading. Any electrical problem on the voltage side of the circuit (OPEN or Vd) will be reflected in a abnormally low TTS-1 reading indicating there is a circuit problem on the voltage side of the load.

STEP 2 of the TTS is abbr. "TTS-2"

Measure the circuit voltage (or Vc) at Load Pin 2. This reading shows how good the ground side circuit is. Expect the reading to be equal to or less than 0.10V for a good ground circuit. **The lower the TTS-2 reading the better.** Any electrical problem on the ground side of the circuit (OPEN or Vd) will be reflected in a abnormally high TTS-2 reading indicating there is a circuit problem on the ground side of the load.

Do This:
(1) Turn ON the circuit.
(2) Verify the DMM is grounded to -BATT.
(3) Perform both TTS measurements with the red DMM (V/Ω) test lead and record the readings to establish normal TTS readings for the Lamp.

TTS-1 _____ volts TTS-2 _____ volts.

These are reasonably normal TTS readings that can be expected if the circuit is good. They can be used to compare against the TTS readings found in a vehicle circuit without an electrical problem.

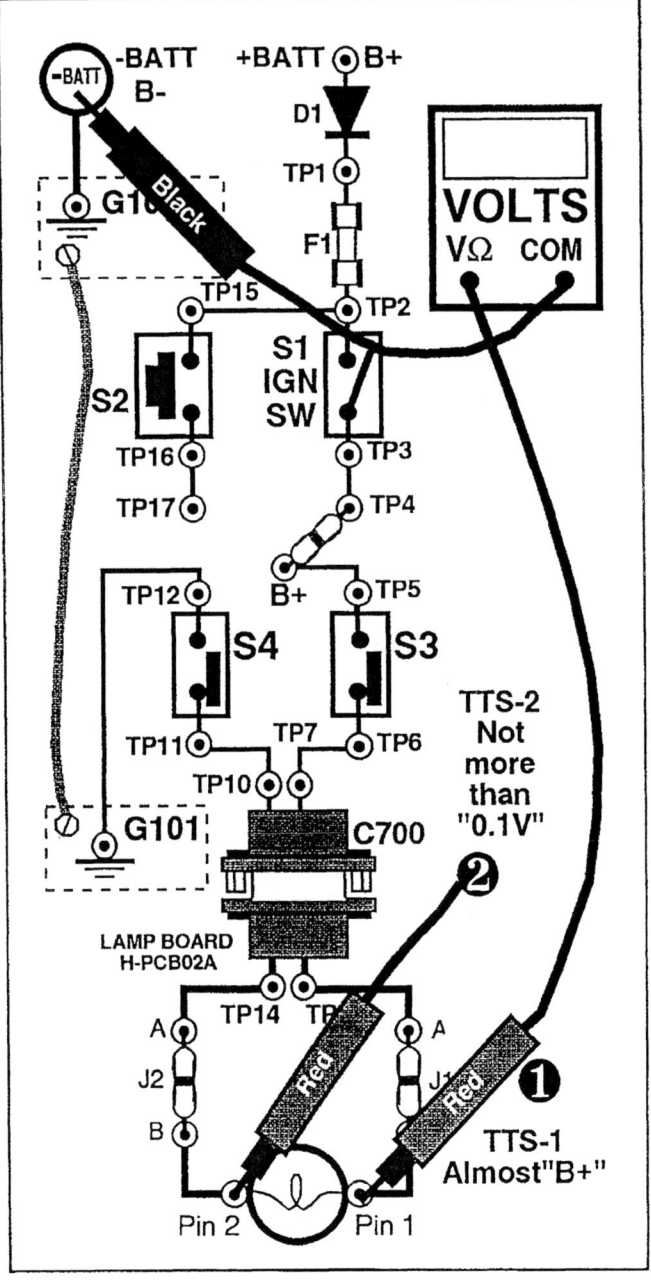

Fig. 15 The Texas-Two-Step (TTS)

ALWAYS PERFORM THE TTS ON KNOWN GOOD VEHICLE CIRCUITS TO ESTABLISH GOOD TTS READINGS FOR FUTURE REFERENCE.

On the next page we begin investigating the six ways a circuit fails. We will learn how to test and measure circuit voltages in a circuit using the TTS to determine what is wrong with a circuit. After these exercises you will begin troubleshooting 32 programmed electrical problems to develop your troubleshooting skill.

Vehicle Electronics Hands-On Troubleshooting Training Program

VEEJER ENTERPRISES 3701 Lariat Lane, Garland, Texas 75042-5419
Phone: 972-276-9642   Fax: 972-276-8122   Email: contact-us@veejer.com   Web Site: www.veejer.com

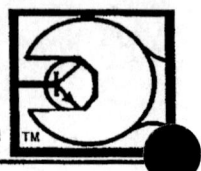

How Electrical Problems Affect A Circuit

The next series of exercises involves inserting a circuit problem, one at a time, **on the top of the PCBs** and analyzing how it affects the load. First there is a comment on how the load performs with each problem from a visual inspection.

Then the TTS is performed and voltage readings recorded to see how the readings are different with each problem. From these exercises you will learn how to troubleshoot and determine what is wrong with a circuit from the test results of the TTS readings.

**Study Circuit Problem Number 1
"OPEN Connection on the Voltage Side"**

Insert An OPEN Connection on the Voltage Side:
Remove (gently pull up) J1 from the top of the Lamp Board to create an open connection in the voltage side of the load. Figure 16 shows jumper J1 removed from the Lamp Board.

The Vehicle Electronics Training Course
Lesson 24, Pages 2-3 analyze basic circuit problem #1.

For Hands-On DO THIS:
• Turn the circuit ON with S1 (S3 & S4 CLOSED).
• Ground DMM negative test lead to -BATT.
• Perform the TTS and record the readings below.

Visual Inspection:
How does an OPEN connection on the voltage side affect the load? _____

(1) TTS-1 reading: _____
    Conclusion: _____

(2) TTS-2 reading: _____
    Conclusion: _____

(3) What is the next troubleshooting step?
    _____

(4) What is concluded when you find B+ at J1 Pin A?
    _____

(5) What did you learn from this problem?
    _____

What You Should Learn From This Problem
An OPEN connection on the voltage side of the load keeps the load from operating. It also means that the 0V reading on Pin 2 (TTS-2) at this time does not indicate a good groundcircuit because there is no electron current through the circuit.

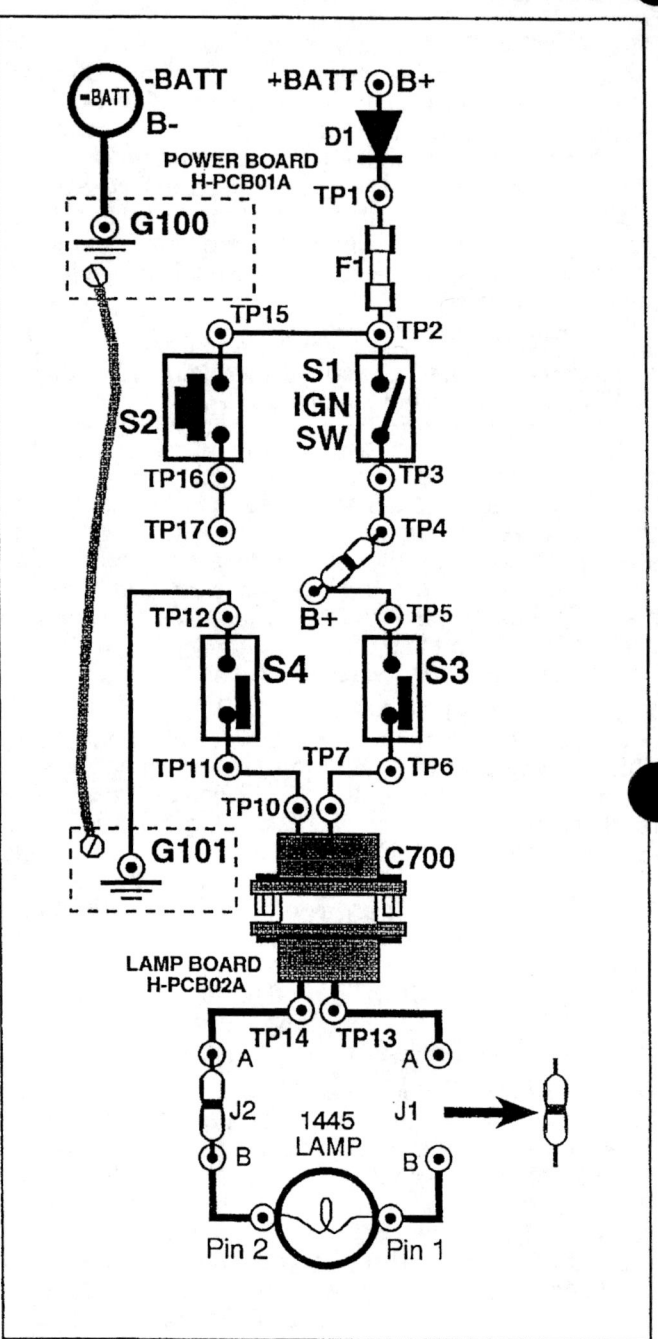

Fig. 16
The 0ΩR in J1 is removed to create an OPEN circuit on the voltage side of the load.

Wrap Up The Problem
Install 0ΩR back into J1 on the Lamp Board when finished. If immediately going on to the next exercise do not replace the 0ΩR. Leave J1 open for the next exercise.

Copyright © 2015 VEEJER ENTERPRISES, Garland, Texas - All Rights Reserved   H-WB111A Page 25

Vehicle Electronics Hands-On Troubleshooting Training Program

Study Circuit Problem Number 2
"A Vd on the Voltage Side"

Insert A Vd on the Voltage Side:
Remove J1 from the top of the Lamp Board if not already removed and insert a 100 ohm resistor in its place. Select a 100 ohm resistor from the Resistor Bag, H-RB01/02 and insert into J1 to create a Vd on the voltage side of the load. **(100Ω color code is Brown-Black-Brown).** Figure 17 shows 0ΩR in J1 removed and a 100Ω resistor inserted in its place.

> *The Vehicle Electronics Training Course*
> **Lesson 24, Pages 3-4** analyze basic circuit problem #2.

TWO NOTES:
(1) The lamp is dim because a Vd is now present on the voltage side of the load due to the 100Ω resistor in J1. Brightness of the lamp varies depending on the amount of resistance creating the Vd. The larger the resistance the greater the Vd and the dimmer the lamp. (2) The 100Ω resistor will get warm during the time this circuit is ON and current is flowing. Let it cool down before removing it.

For Hands-On DO THIS:
- Turn the circuit ON with S1 (S3 & S4 CLOSED).
- Ground DMM negative test lead to -BATT.
- Perform the TTS and record the readings below.

Visual Inspection:
How does a Vd on the voltage side affect the load?
_____

(1) TTS-1 reading: _____
   Conclusion: _____

(2) TTS-2 reading: _____
   Conclusion: _____

(3) What is the next troubleshooting step?
_____

(4) What is concluded when you find B+ at J1 Pin A?
_____

(5) What did you learn from this problem?
_____

What You Should Learn From This Problem
A resistance in the voltage side of the load causes unwanted Vd_{vs} that affects load operation. Above the resistance the Vc (circuit voltage) is almost B+. Below the resistance the Vc is a lower B+ value indicating a voltage drop between J1A and J1B.

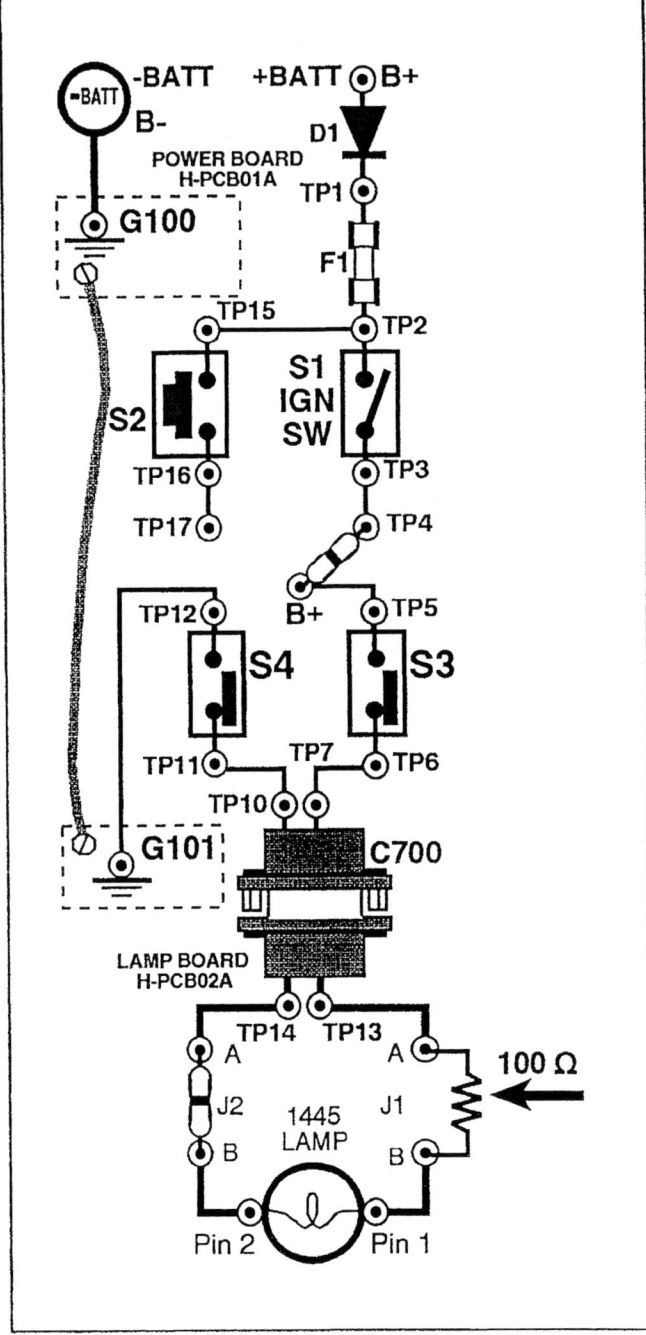

Fig. 17
Vd on the voltage side created when a resistor is inserted into J1

Leave the resistor in the circuit and continue working with Problem #2 on the next page for a very important lesson to learn in troubleshooting.
Next is a circuit principal you must NEVER FORGET.

Vehicle Electronics Hands-On Troubleshooting Training Program

VEEJER ENTERPRISES 3701 Lariat Lane, Garland, Texas 75042-5419
Phone: 972-276-9642 Fax: 972-276-8122 Email: contact-us@veejer.com Web Site: www.veejer.com

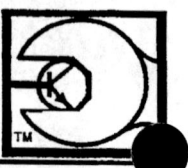

IMPORTANT LESSON FROM STUDY PROBLEM #2

A common mistake made in troubleshooting is to disconnect the load when while performing the TTS or tracing B+ or B- in a circuit.
DO NOT DO THAT. Disconnecting the load stops electron current through the load and hides any Vd problem on the voltage or ground side. To see this for yourself leave the circuit ON with the resistor in J1 and complete this short exercise.

For Hands-On DO THIS:

Figure 18 shows the lamp disconnected. A normal TTS-1 reading will appear even though the problem, a Vd caused by the 100Ω resistor still in the circuit

- Leave the resistor in place of J1
- With the circuit ON and the lamp disconnected do the TTS again.
- TTS-1 reading: _____
- TTS-2 reading: _____

(5) What happened to the TTS-1 reading?
_____

(6) Is the 100Ω resistor still in the circuit? _____

(7) Why is the TTS-1 reading normal with the lamp removed?
_____

(8) What is the lesson to learn from this?
_____

- **NEVER DISCONNECT THE LOAD WHILE MEASURING TTS-1 AND TTS-2.**

- **NEVER DISCONNECT THE LOAD WHILE TRACING B+ or B-.**

- **NEVER STOP CURRENT THROUGH A CIRCUIT when testing a circuit.**
  No electron current = no Vd

What You Should Learn From This Problem

Anything that is done to a circuit that stops electron current from flowing through the circuit, such as creating an OPEN connection on either the voltage or ground side hides any Vd that exists on either the voltage or ground side. In fact, the TTS-1 reading may actually be a little higher than normal because there is no Vd_{vs} when the electron current is not flowing because the load is disconnected.

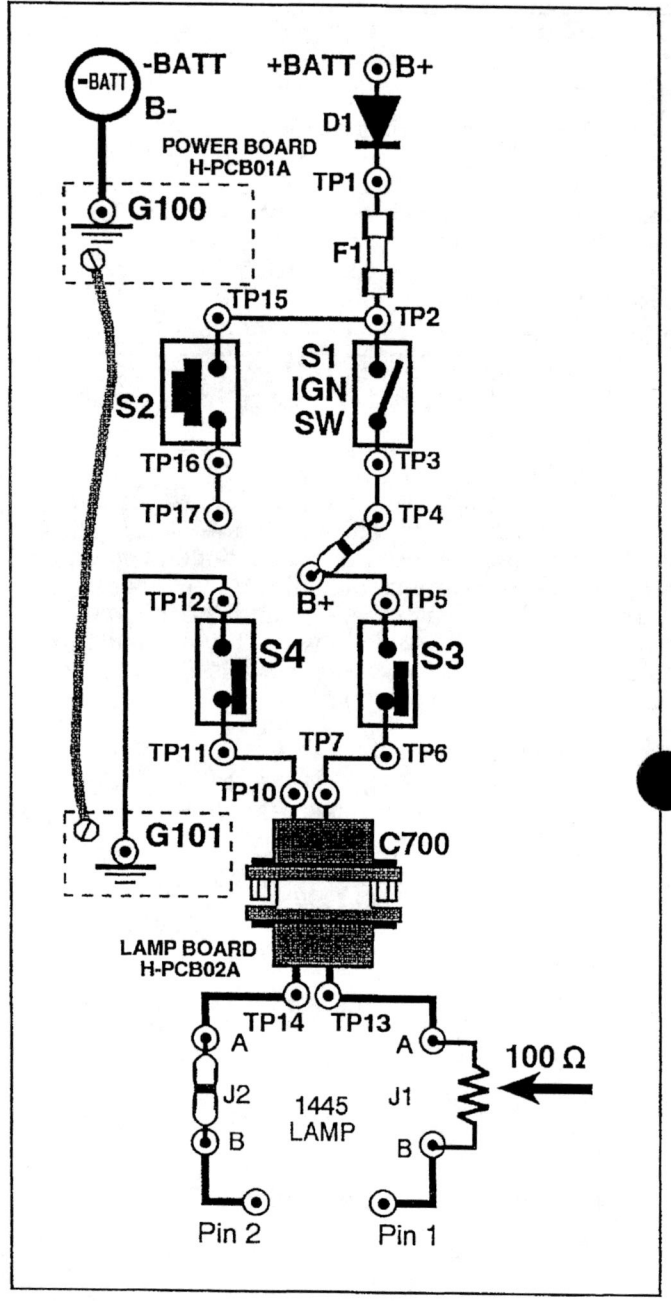

Fig. 18
Removing the load causes TTS-1 to read normal B+ while the resistance problem is still in the circuit.
No electron current = No Vd

Wrap Up The Problem

Remove the 100Ω resistor from J1 and put it back in the resistor bag. The 100Ω resistor will get warm during the time this circuit is ON and current is flowing. Let it cool off a few moments before removing it and use care in removing it. Insert the 0ΩR back into J1 on the Lamp Board to restore the circuit to normal operation.

Copyright © 2015 VEEJER ENTERPRISES, Garland, Texas - All Rights Reserved

Vehicle Electronics Hands-On Troubleshooting Training Program

VEEJER ENTERPRISES 3701 Lariat Lane, Garland, Texas 75042-5419
Phone: 972-276-9642 Fax: 972-276-8122 Email: contact-us@veejer.com Web Site: www.veejer.com

Study Circuit Problem Number 3
"OPEN Connection on the Ground Side"

Insert An OPEN Circuit on the Ground Side:
Remove (gently) J2 from the top of the Lamp Board to create an open connection on the ground side of the load. Figure 19 shows jumper J2 removed from the Lamp Board.

> *The Vehicle Electronics Training Course*
> **Lesson 24, Pages 4-5** analyze basic circuit problem #3.

For Hands-On DO THIS:
- Turn the circuit ON with S1 (S3 & S4 CLOSED).
- Ground DMM negative test lead to -BATT.
- Perform the TTS and record the readings below.

Visual Inspection:
How does an OPEN connection on the ground side affect the load? _____

(1) TTS-1 reading: _____
    Conclusion: _____

(2) TTS-2 reading: _____
    Conclusion: _____

(3) What is the next troubleshooting step?

_____

(4) What is concluded when you find 0V at J2 Pin A?

_____

(5) What did you learn from this problem?

_____

(6) Try this with the lamp in the circuit. Measure the voltage on Pin 2 while watching the DMM, then remove the Lamp.
    What happens to the voltage at Pin 2?

_____

Does the voltage that appears at Pin 2 with the Lamp in the circuit come through the lamp filament? _____

Note: Since the ground circuit is OPEN there is no electron current through the Lamp circuit and there is no electron current through the Lamp. The voltage at Pin 1 appears on Pin 2 as the Lamp filament acts like a wire between Pin 1 and Pin 2. If there is no electron current through the Lamp filament there is no Vd across the Lamp filament. The same voltage appears at both lamp terminals with an OPEN ground circuit.

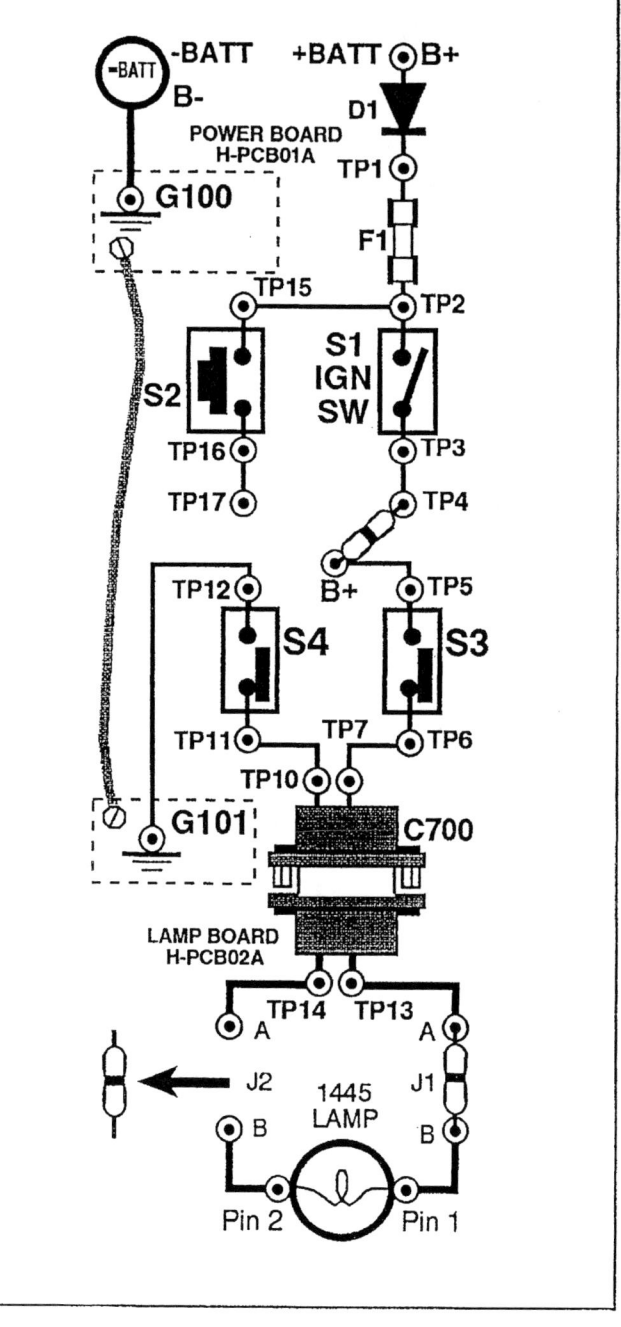

Fig. 19
OPEN circuit on the ground side is created when J2 is removed from the lamp board.

Wrap Up The Problem
Install a 0ΩR back into J2 on the Lamp Board when finished. If immediately going on to the next exercise do not replace the 0ΩR. Leave J2 open for the next exercise.

Vehicle Electronics Hands-On Troubleshooting Training Program

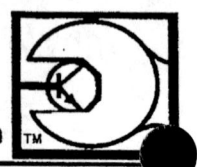

VEEJER ENTERPRISES 3701 Lariat Lane, Garland, Texas 75042-5419
Phone: 972-276-9642 Fax: 972-276-8122 Email: contact-us@veejer.com Web Site: www.veejer.com

Study Circuit Problem Number 4
"Vd on the Ground Side"

Insert A Vd on the Ground Side:
Remove J2 from the top of the Lamp Board. Select a 100 ohm resistor from the Resistor Bag and insert in place of the wire jumper in J2 to create a Vd on the ground side of the load. **(100Ω color code is Brown-Black-Brown.)** Figure 20 shows jumper J2 removed and a 100Ω resistor inserted in its place.

> *The Vehicle Electronics Training Course*
> **Lesson 24, Page 5** analyzes basic circuit problem #4.

For Hands-On DO THIS:
- Turn the circuit ON with S1 (S3 & S4 CLOSED).
- Ground DMM negative test lead to -BATT.
- Perform the TTS and record the readings below.

Visual Inspection:
How does a Vd on the ground side affect the load?
_____

(1) TTS-1 reading: _____
    Conclusion: _____

(2) TTS-2 reading: _____
    Conclusion: _____

(3) What is the next troubleshooting step?
_____

(4) What is concluded when you find 0.1 volt or less at J2 Pin A?
_____

What You Should Learn From This:
A resistance on the ground side of the circuit causes an unwanted Vd on the ground side of the load and is seen in TTS-2. The 100Ω resistor drops some voltage when the electron current is flowing. The voltage at J2-A is 0.10 volt or less, a good reading. On the opposite side of the 100Ω resistor, J2-B, the Vc reading is higher, more than 0.10V, a bad reading.

Keep in mind that a Vc at Pin 2 of the load in the range of 0.20-0.50 volt in some vehicle circuits does not necessarily mean the ground circuit has too much resistance and should be repaired. Some circuits may work well with ground Vc readings above 0.10 volt,. An example is a starter motor ground reading 0.5-0.8 volt and it still cranks the engine.

The Vc at Pin 2 of the load normally will be in the range of 0.10 except for certain high current circuits like starter and blower motor circuits which may be a little higher than 0.10 volt on the ground side.

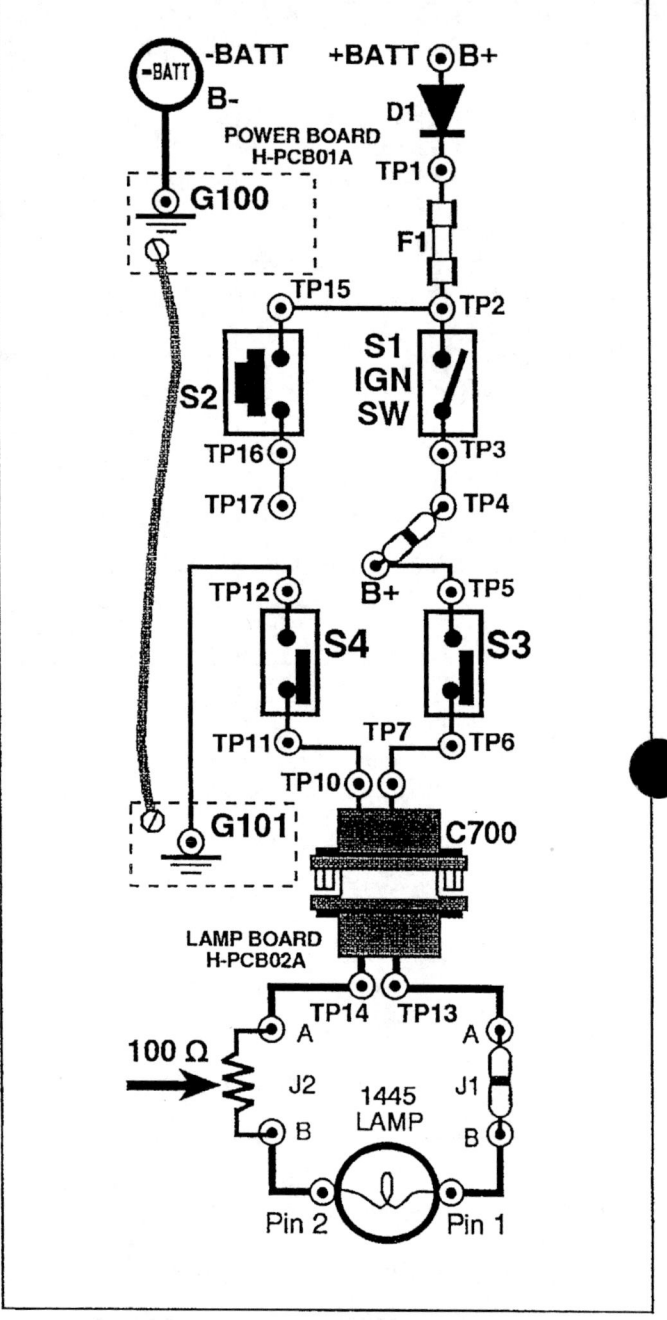

Fig. 20
Vd on the ground side is created when a 100Ω resistor is installed in J2

Leave the fault in the circuit and continue working with Problem #4 on the next page for a very important lesson to learn in troubleshooting.
This is a circuit principal you must NEVER FORGET.

Copyright © 2015 VEEJER ENTERPRISES, Garland, Texas - All Rights Reserved   H-WB111A

Vehicle Electronics Hands-On Troubleshooting Training Program

VEEJER ENTERPRISES 3701 Lariat Lane, Garland, Texas 75042-5419
Phone: 972-276-9642   Fax: 972-276-8122   Email: contact-us@veejer.com   Web Site: www.veejer.com

IMPORTANT LESSON FROM STUDY PROBLEM #4

A common mistake made in troubleshooting is to disconnect the load when performing the TTS or tracing B+ or B- in a circuit.

DO NOT DO THAT. Disconnecting the load stops electron current through the circuit and hides any Vd problem on the ground side. To see this for yourself leave the circuit ON with the 100Ω resistor in J2 and complete this short exercise on this page.

Figure 21 shows the lamp disconnected. A normal TTS-2 reading will appear even though the problem, a Vd caused by the 100Ω resistor on the ground side in J2, is still in the circuit

For Hands-On DO THIS:
- Leave the 100Ω resistor in place of J2
- With the circuit ON, the lamp disconnected, do the TTS again.
- TTS-1 reading: _____
- TTS-2 reading: _____

(5) What happened to the TTS-2 reading?
_____

(6) Is the 100Ω resistor still in the circuit? _____

(7) Why is the reading normal with lamp removed?
_____

(8) What is the lesson to learn from this?
_____

- **NEVER DISCONNECT THE LOAD WHILE MEASURING TTS-1 AND TTS-2.**
- **NEVER DISCONNECT THE LOAD WHILE TRACING B+ or B-.**
- **NEVER STOP CURRENT THROUGH A CIRCUIT when testing a circuit. No current = no Vd**

What You Should Learn From This Problem

Anything that is done to a circuit that stops electron current from flowing through the circuit, such as creating an OPEN connection on either the voltage or ground side hides any Vd that exists on either the voltage or ground side. In fact, the TTS-2 reading will be 0.00V because there is no Vd_{GS} when the electron current is not flowing because the load is disconnected.

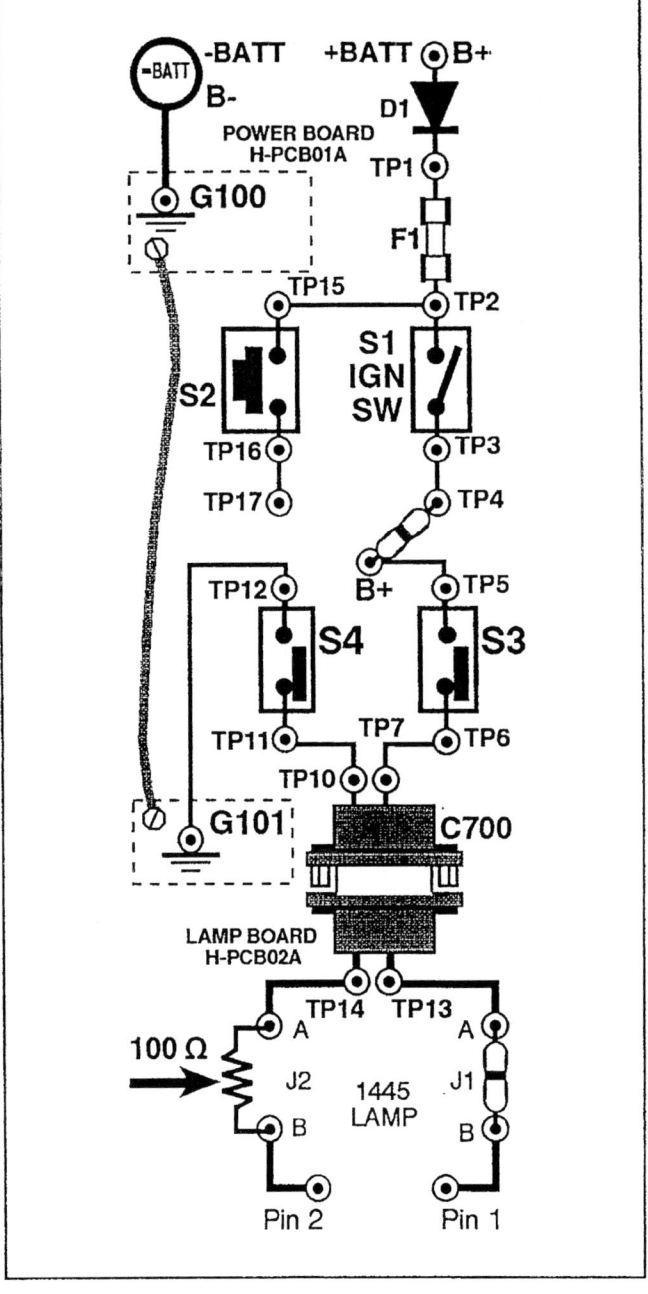

Fig. 21
TTS-2 reads normal when the load is disconnected and the resistor is still in the ground side of the circuit.

Wrap Up The Problem

Remove the 100Ω resistor from J2 and put it back in the resistor bag. The 100Ω resistor will get warm during the time this circuit is ON and current is flowing. Let it cool off a few moments before removing it and use care in removing it. Insert the 0ΩR back into J2 on the Lamp Board to restore the circuit to normal operation.

Vehicle Electronics Hands-On Troubleshooting Training Program

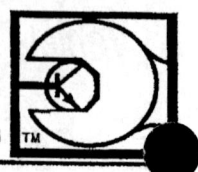

Study Circuit Problem Number 5
"OPEN LOAD"

Insert An OPEN Load condition:
Remove the 1445 lamp from the lamp socket to simulate an OPEN Load. Figure 22 illustrates how an OPEN lamp filament could be the problem in a vehicle circuit. Removing the lamp is the easiest way to simulate an OPEN load for this exercise.

With an OPEN filament there is no path for electron current through the circuit and the load won't operate without electron current passing through it. It would be the same condition if the load were a DC motor or a solenoid. An OPEN load stops all circuit electron current and hides a secondary problem of a possible Vd on the voltage or ground side.

The Vehicle Electronics Training Course
Lesson 24 discusses an OPEN load circuit.

For Hands-On DO THIS:
- Turn the circuit ON with S1 (S3 & S4 CLOSED).
- Ground DMM negative test lead to -BATT.
- Perform the TTS and record the readings below.

Visual Inspection:
How does an OPEN Load affect load operation?
_____

(1) TTS-1 reading: _____
   Conclusion: _____

(2) TTS-2 reading: _____
   Conclusion: _____

(3) What is the next troubleshooting step?
_____

(4) How is load resistance tested?
_____

(5) How is correct load resistance value determined?
   (A.) _____
   (B.) _____

(6) Since the lamp removed from the Lamp Board is good, check its resistance with a **digital ohmmeter** set to the 200 ohm range and record the resistance reading. _____ ohms

(7) What would the ohmmeter indicate if the lamp were really OPEN? _____

(8) If the OPEN load is corrected by installing another good load what problems could still be in the circuit? _____

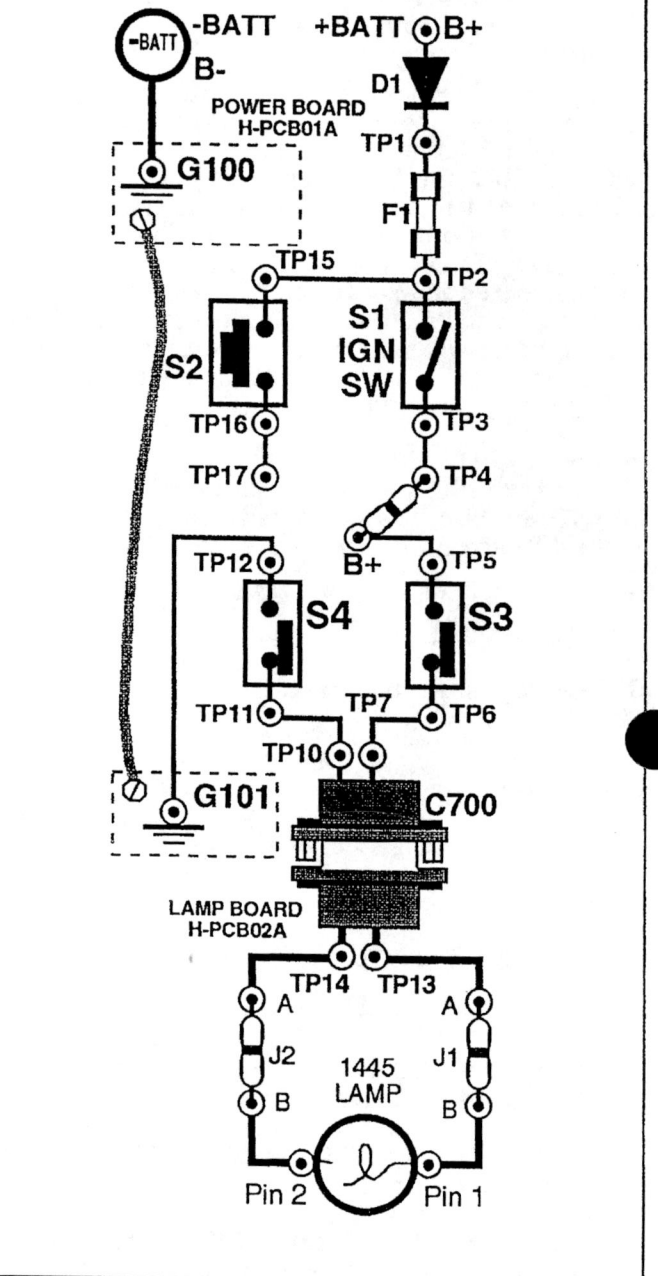

Fig. 22
OPEN load indicated by the lamp filament shown as OPEN.

What You Should Learn From This Problem
Any time an OPEN load is found remember to do the TTS with the new load operating to make sure there is no excessive Vd_{VS} or Vd_{GS}.

Wrap Up The Problem
Put a good lamp back in the lamp socket.

Vehicle Electronics Hands-On Troubleshooting Training Program

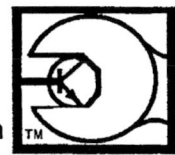

VEEJER ENTERPRISES 3701 Lariat Lane, Garland, Texas 75042-5419
Phone: 972-276-9642 Fax: 972-276-8122 Email: contact-us@veejer.com Web Site: www.veejer.com

Study Circuit Problem Number 6
"SHORTED LOAD"
(Complete Study Problem #5 before attempting Study Problem #6.)

Answer these questions concerning blown fuses.

(1) What blows a fuse?
_____

(2) What are two reasons for current to increase in a circuit above a normal level? Hint: The answer is explained below by Ohm's Law for Current.

$$I = \frac{E}{R}$$

I = electron current in units of **amps**
E = voltage in units of **volts**
R = resistance in units of **ohms**

Ohm's Law explains the relationship between "E" (voltage in volts), "I" (electron current in amps) and "R" (resistance in ohms).
The Ohm's Law formula for "I" (electron current) reveals that the amount of electron current flowing through a circuit depends on the amount of voltage and resistance, and is expressed below. You can also put numbers in the formula and see how I increases or decreases as the E and R values change.

Changes in the amount of voltage:
• If voltage increases, "E" goes up, electron current increases.
(The higher the pressure, the higher the flow.)

• If voltage decreases, "E" goes down, electron current decreases.
(The lower the pressure, the lower the flow.)

Changes in the amount of resistance:
• If resistance increases, "R" goes up, electron current decreases.
(The higher the resistance, the lower the flow.)

• If resistance decreases, "R" goes down, electron current increases.
(The lower the resistance, the higher the flow.)

Now state the two reasons from Ohm's Law that could exist in a circuit for the electron current, "I" to increase.

(3) "E" voltage, would have to _____

(4) "R" resistance, would have to _____

In an electrical or electronic circuit, electron current (in amps) flows *from the negative terminal* of the voltage source, through the circuit load and back *to the positive terminal* of the same voltage source. This is called the **electron theory for current** and is way the scientific community describes electron current flow in a circuit.

The voltage source in a vehicle is the battery if the engine is not running. Battery voltage decreases (battery discharges) as the battery supplies electron current to vehicle circuits. As battery voltage decreases the amount of electron current it can supply decreases.

The generator (alternator) becomes the voltage source when the engine is running which supplies a steady voltage, called "charging voltage." The generator provides a sustained electron current to all electrical circuits as long as the engine runs and recharges the battery at the same time.

The amount of voltage applied to a circuit and the resistance in the load determines how much electron current flows through a circuit which determines the fuse rating. All of this is in complete harmony with Ohm's Law.

Since electron current flows through the load, the amount of electron current flowing through the load is determined by the amount of voltage applied and the amount of resistance in the load.

It could be said that this is the "long way" for electron current to flow around a circuit. It is a fact that load resistance is the primary factor on how much electron current flows through a circuit. Since battery or generator voltage is the same for all circuits but current in vehicle circuits varies considerably between circuits, load resistance determines how much electron current flows through a circuit.

If two circuits are connected to 14V and circuit #1 draws 2 amps and circuit #2 draws 25 amps, it simply means that circuit #2 has a much lower load resistance than circuit #1.

(5) What is a "short" in a circuit?
_____
_____

(6) What two ways can a circuit develop a short?
  (A) _____
  (B) _____

> *(The Vehicle Electronics Training Course)*
> **Lessons that cover troubleshooting shorts:**
> **Lesson 8** Ohmmeter operation
> **Lesson 18** Resistance testing
> **Lesson 24** Study Problem #6
> **Lesson 25** Troubleshooting shorts

Vehicle Electronics Hands-On Troubleshooting Training Program

VEEJER ENTERPRISES 3701 Lariat Lane, Garland, Texas 75042-5419
Phone: 972-276-9642   Fax: 972-276-8122   Email: contact-us@veejer.com   Web Site: www.veejer.com

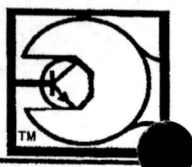

Do This:
Insert a SHORTED Load condition in the PCBs:
Set up these three conditions.

(A.) Unplug the H-PS01 Power Supply from the AC outlet.

(B.) Remove Fuse F1 from the circuit to simulate the fuse is blown.

(C) Remove a 0ΩR (zero ohm resistor) from the Resistor Bag. Install the 0ΩR between the terminals of Lamp Pin 1 and Lamp Pin 2 to create a short circuit around the lamp as shown in Figure 23. Don't cut the leads off the 0ΩR and gently insert into the top of the two pins at Pin 1 and Pin 2.

It is clear that **IF** the PCBs were powered up with the 0ΩR connected across the lamp (load), the electron current would rise high enough to blow the fuse F1. The 0ΩR appears as a no resistance, zero ohm path for electron current. Now electron current can flow unimpeded through the 0ΩR and rise to the highest level the power supply can deliver.

The fuse is placed strategically in the circuit so that the high electron current must pass through the fuse. **The high electron current exceeds the fuse rating so the fuse blows.** This creates an OPEN circuit to stop electron current and prevent an electrical fire.

This also allows the fire department to stay in the fire house and continue their domino game. That's what the fuse if there to do. Keep the fire department in the fire house playing dominos. A circuit with a short path for electron current will burn up and possibly start a vehicle fire.

The 0ΩR across the lamp merely simulates a shorted load (no resistance load) for the electron current to increase. If there is no other significant resistance in the path of electron current, the current will rise high enough to blow the fuse.

Shorted Loads Happen
It could happen that the load of the circuit loses its resistance or, as we say, becomes shorted. One side of a dual filament lamp breaks lose internally and makes contact with the grounded side of the lamp.

A solenoid can develop shorted windings, its resistance decreases and the electron current through the solenoid increases and the fuse blows. The same is true of the coil in a relay.

DC motors can draw too much electron current from running at a slower rpm and blow the fuse which may be a fusible link rather than a small metallic fuse. But it is the same principle. If the load does not supply the correct resistance in a circuit the fuse will blow from the increased electron current.

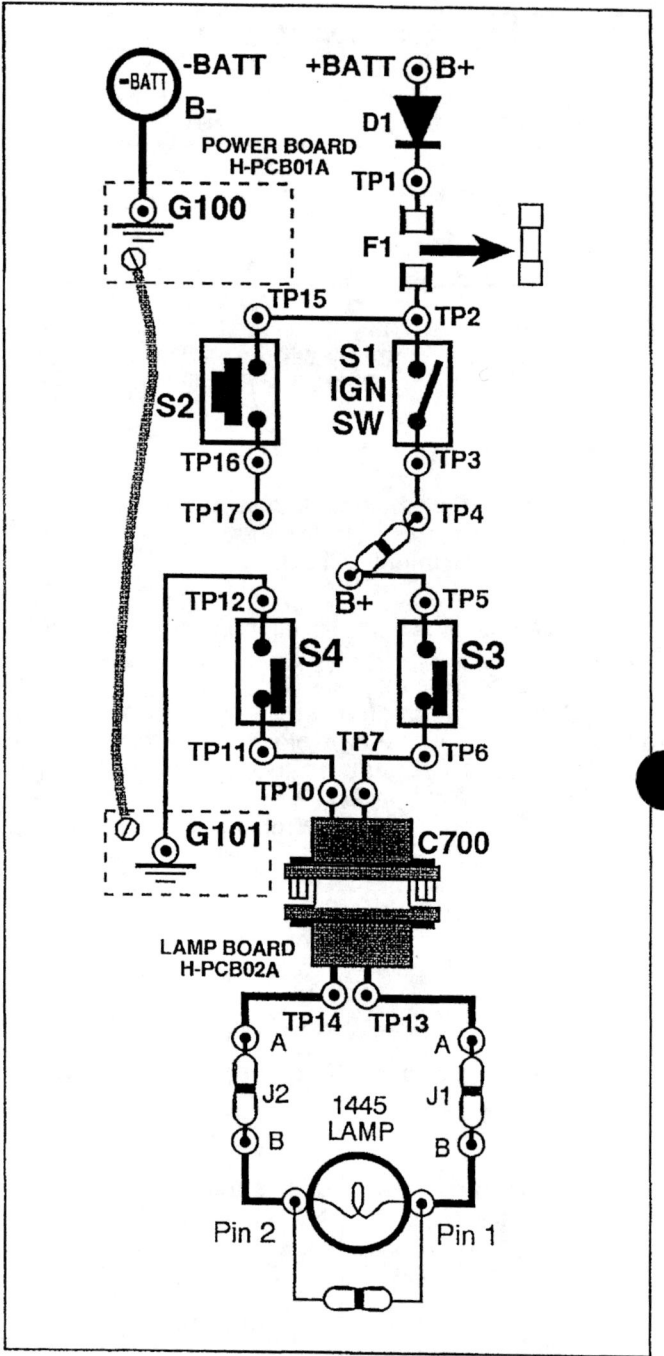

Fig. 23
Shorted Load created with a wire jumper placed between the lamp (load) terminals Pin 1 and Pin 2.

Leave the wire short in Pin 1 and Pin 2 in place to troubleshoot the problem on the next pages where you will learn how to properly troubleshoot a shorted load as well as a voltage side short-to-ground.

Vehicle Electronics Hands-On Troubleshooting Training Program

VEEJER ENTERPRISES 3701 Lariat Lane, Garland, Texas 75042-5419
Phone: 972-276-9642 Fax: 972-276-8122 Email: contact-us@veejer.com Web Site: www.veejer.com

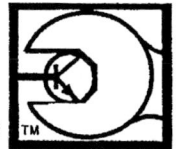

Finding A Shorted Load

In a vehicle situation, when a circuit is dead, technicians will likely check the fuse first to see if it is blown. (If the fuse is good then it is time to check the TTS readings at the load terminals as we have been doing in these previous exercises to find the OPEN in the circuit voltage side or ground side.)

If the fuse is blown, try another fuse. If the fuse disintegrates immediately when the circuit is ON it is because the circuit has a major short-to-ground condition (some would say a "dead short"). If the fuse blows rather slowly (1-2 seconds) it indicates a low resistance condition exists in the circuit. It could be due to low load resistance or a short-to-ground in the circuit which allows current to rise above the fuse rating and the fuse blows. The first logical step is to check load resistance in the circuit as shown in Figure 23A. In this case the load is the lamp.

Ohmmeter tests of the circuit must be used to locate the short because troubleshooting has to be done with the circuit OFF. *Before connecting an ohmmeter to the PCBs always disconnect the H-PS01 Power Supply from the wall socket to remove any voltage in the circuit.*

- **NEVER CONNECT AN OHMMETER TO A LIVE CIRCUIT. AN OHMMETER MAY BE DAMAGED BY CIRCUIT CURRENT FLOWING THROUGH THE OHMMETER.**

(1) Leave the lamp plugged into the lamp socket. Set your DMM to OHMS and the lower 200-300-400 ohm range (which ever your DMM has). If your DMM auto ranges just select Ω (Ohms) and allow it to auto range during the measurement. Record the resistance reading of the lamp (load) between Load Pin 1 and Pin 2 as shown in Figure 23A.
_____ Ω

(2) What does this resistance reading indicate?

_____

(3) Remove the lamp from the lamp socket and check lamp (load) resistance. The lamp should check good, in the range of about 10-15 ohms for a #1445 lamp. The "short" is still in the circuit. Put the lamp back in the lamp socket.

We have determined the load has the correct resistance. It is not shorted since we have a good resistance reading. The low resistance reading between Pin 1 and Pin 2 indicates two possibilities.

(A) lamp socket is shorted
(B) voltage side of the circuit is shorted to ground

If the Lamp (load) was shorted, the ohmmeter would have indicated a lower resistance reading than 10-15 ohms. If a circuit load is tested and found to be shorted, it is replaced to restore normal load resistance to the circuit and stop the fuse from blowing again.

If the load is not shorted but the fuse still blows then the voltage side of the circuit is shorted to ground.

Leave the wire short across the lamp in place to troubleshoot a short to ground on the voltage side. Go to the next page to check for an explanation of finding a voltage side short to ground when the load is NOT shorted and NOT the problem.

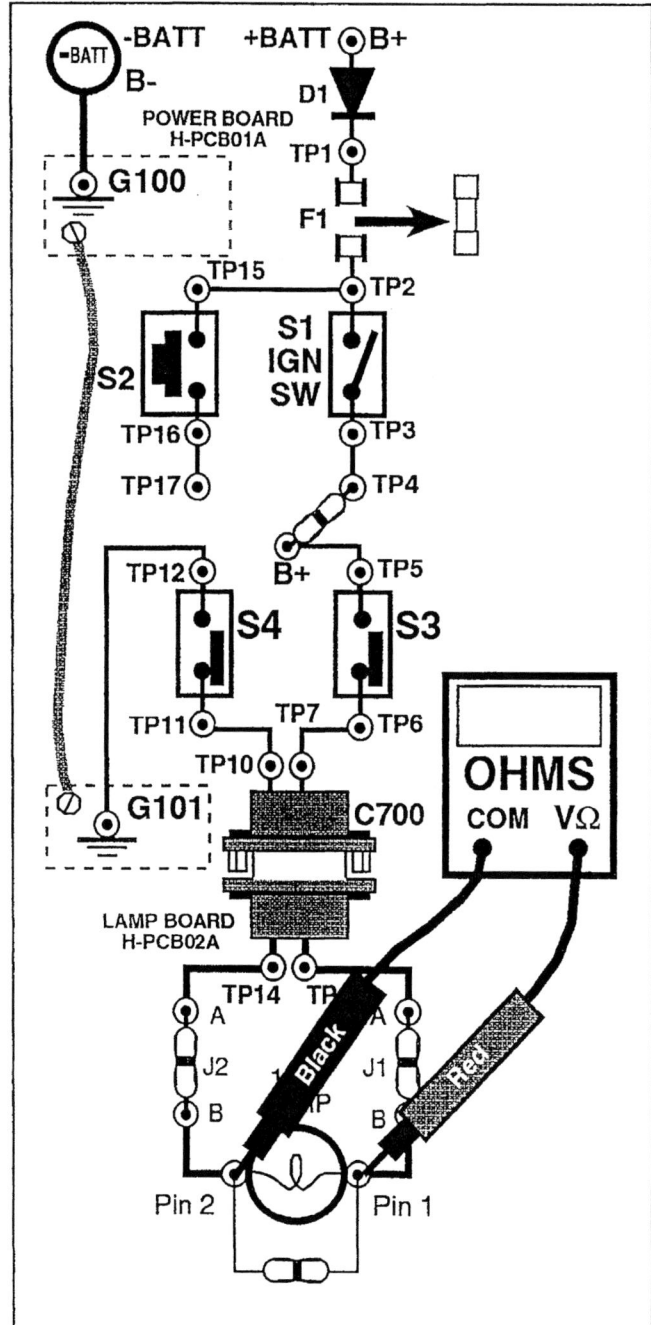

Fig. 23A Ohmmeter detects a shorted load (when the jumper wire is present) as the cause of a blown fuse.

H-WB111A Page 34

Vehicle Electronics Hands-On Troubleshooting Training Program

VEEJER ENTERPRISES 3701 Lariat Lane, Garland, Texas 75042-5419
Phone: 972-276-9642 Fax: 972-276-8122 Email: contact-us@veejer.com Web Site: www.veejer.com

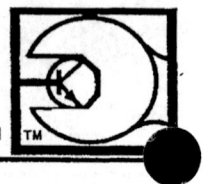

Finding A Voltage Side Short-To-Ground

On the previous page we determined the lamp (the load) is not shorted. The short is the 0ΩR placed across the lamp socket. This creates a short-to-ground on the voltage side of the lamp circuit. It's the same thing as "grounding" the voltage side of the circuit. The fuse blew because the voltage side (insulated) wiring is making electrical contact with ground and there is no resistance in the path of electron current through the short-to-ground.

Electron current increases because there is no resistance (through the 0ΩR) which is a new electron current path. A voltage side short-to-ground could appear anywhere on the voltage side of the circuit.

We can find a short-to-ground in the wiring of the voltage side of a circuit using an ohmmeter to determine where in the voltage side of the circuit the short-to-ground is located.

Do This:
- Make sure the H-PS01 Power Supply is unplugged from the wall socket.
- Remove Fuse F1.
- Turn S1 ON (toggled UP) & CLOSE S3 & S4 (UP)
- Remove the 1445 lamp from the lamp socket.
- Ground DMM negative test lead to -BATT.
- Perform the resistance check shown in Figure 24. Connect the DMM's Red test lead to the **COLD side of the fuse** as shown.

(1) Place DMM's digital ohmmeter on the 200-300-400 ohms range or allow the ohmmeter to auto range if so equipped. *All switches on the voltage side of the circuit (S1, S3,) must be CLOSED and all connectors connected (0ΩRs in B+ Terminal and in J1 and J2. CLOSE S4 because it completes the ground circuit for the DMM ground.*

(2) What does the ohmmeter read when connected to the circuit at the cold side of the fuse as shown in Figure 24? _____ Ω

(NOTE: The ohmmeter is now indicating a very low resistance reading but not necessarily 0.0 ohms. A short-to-ground does not always read exactly 0.0 ohms. It is quite common to read a few tenths of an ohm or even a few ohms due to the resistance in the wiring even when a short-to-ground is present.

A short-to-ground is known to exist anytime the ohmmeter reads a low resistance from the cold side of the fuse and the load is disconnected as we have here in Figure 24.

(3) What does the reading in Step 2 represent? _____

Once the short-to-ground condition on the voltage side of the circuit is corrected, the ohmmeter reading returns to "OL" meaning the short-to-ground is gone.
Remove the 0ΩR from Pin 1 and Pin 2 and note the ohmmeter reading returns to "OL." (Some ohmmeters may say a "1" or "OUCH" instead of "OL.")

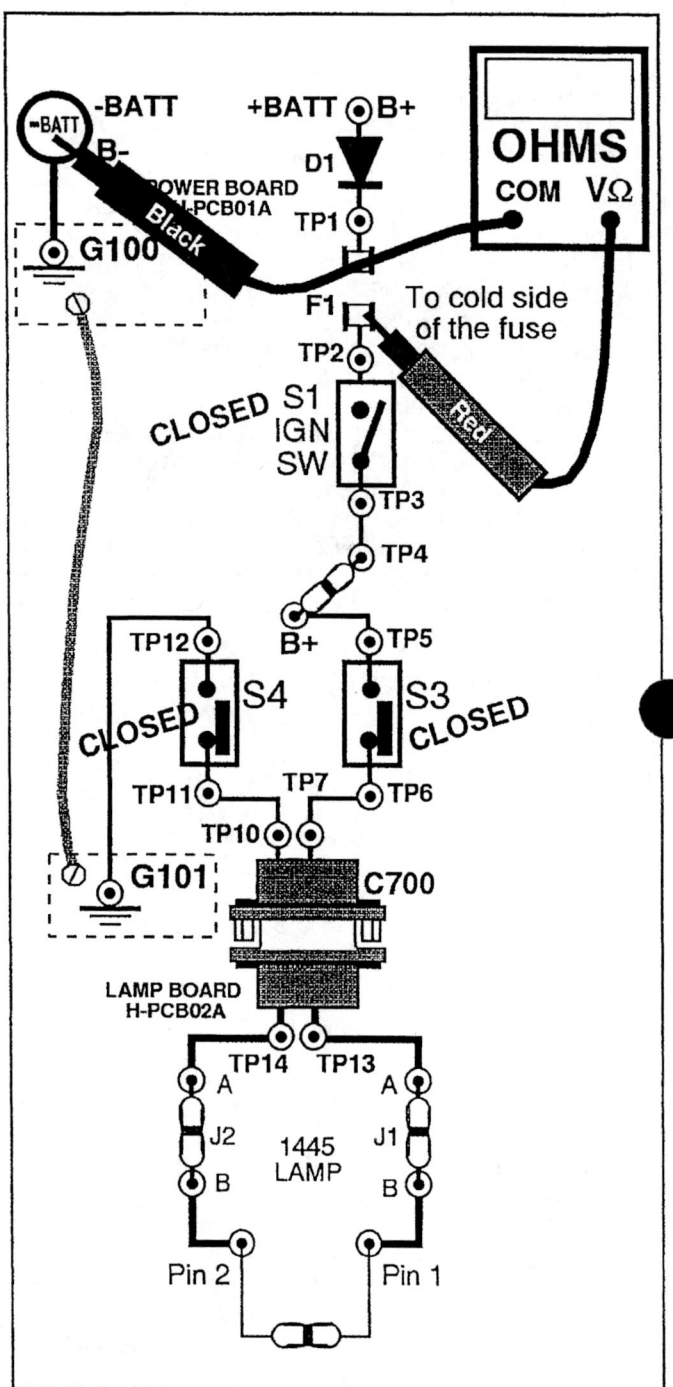

Fig. 24
Ohmmeter detects the voltage side of the circuit is shorted to ground. The 0ΩR grounds the voltage side of the circuit at Pin 1.

Vehicle Electronics Hands-On Troubleshooting Training Program

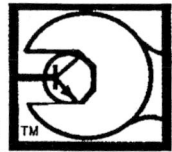

VEEJER ENTERPRISES 3701 Lariat Lane, Garland, Texas 75042-5419
Phone: 972-276-9642 Fax: 972-276-8122 Email: contact-us@veejer.com Web Site: www.veejer.com

At this point we confirm the load (lamp) is not shorted because it is disconnected. The ohmmeter still indicates a low resistance reading because the short-to-ground still exists when measuring between the cold side of the fuse and ground (–BATT or B-). Therefore, the short-to-ground is some where on the voltage side of the load between the cold side of the fuse and Pin 1 of the lamp. Let's find it with the ohmmeter.

When the portion of the circuit with the short-to-ground is disconnected from the circuit the ohmmeter reading changes from a very low reading to a "1" or "OL" reading depending on the ohmmeter used.

A "1" or "OL" reading indicates the ohmmeter no longer "sees" the short-to-ground. This helps to narrow down the point in the circuit where the short-to-ground exists.

Note: Older ohmmeters used a "1" which was either stationary or a blinking "1" to indicate there is an OPEN (no connection) between the ohmmeter probe tips. Newer ohmmeters use "OL" as the new standard. "OL" means "out of limits" or we could say "no path for ohmmeter current exists between the ohmmeter probe tips." In other words, an OPEN exists between the probe tips and no ohmmeter test current flows.

Tracing Down a Voltage Side Short-to-Ground

Several options are possible to narrow down where in the voltage side of the circuit the short-to-ground exists but the following method is suggested as the fastest to speed up the troubleshooting process.

Leave the ohmmeter connected to the cold side of the fuse and the Black test lead connected to the -BATT post. Next disconnect portions of the circuit one section at a time by opening switches or unplugging connectors. When the portion of the circuit with the short-to-ground is disconnected the ohmmeter reading goes from a low reading to "OL".

An "OL" reading means the ohmmeter cannot "see" the short-to-ground any longer. It has been disconnected.

This is the fastest way to troubleshoot a short-to-ground problem in a circuit, especially when tracing a short-to-ground in a vehicle where wiring can cover several feet. When the short-to-ground is isolated (or disconnected) from the cold side of the fuse the ohmmeter reading changes from a low reading to a "1" or "OL" which ever your ohmmeter uses to indicate there is high (maximum) resistance between the test leads, or *"no short - now."* Think of "OL" as *"no short now between the probe tips."*

(4) OPEN S3 (slide DOWN).
    Record ohmmeter reading. _____

(5) What does the reading from Step 4 represent?
_____

(6) What portion of the circuit does not have the short-to-ground? _____

CLOSE S3 again and the low reading reappears on the ohmmeter.

(7) Disconnect the 0ΩR in J1 on the Lamp Board and record the ohmmeter reading. _____ .

(8) What does the reading from Step 7 indicate?
_____

(9) Move the DMM's Red ohmmeter test lead to J1 Pin B on the Lamp Board.
    Record the reading. _____ .

(10) What does the reading from Step 9 indicate?
_____

(11) What is the location of the short-to-ground?
_____

DO THIS WHEN FINISHED:
- **REMOVE 0ΩR between Pin 1 and Pin 2.**
- Install the 0ΩR back into J1 on the Lamp Board.
- Install the 3A fuse in F1.
- Put the lamp back into the lamp socket.
- Turn the circuit ON and the lamp should turn ON.

Remember This Tracing Shorts-To-Ground

> Never touch the Ohmmeter's Red test lead to any point on the ground side of the circuit when tracing a short-to-ground.

The circuit is already "grounded" on the ground side. The ohmmeter will always indicate a very low resistance whether or not the voltage side is shorted-to-ground or not. There is nothing wrong when a zero reading is obtained on the ground side. It's normal.

Yet it might be misunderstood a problem has been found because of the low reading. Many students have been confused by this in the past as well as technicians using this technique in a repair shop.

Always confine the Ohmmeter's Red test lead to the voltage side of the circuit when tracing a shorted load or a short-to-ground.

DMM Ground Lead Tips

(1) The DMM's Black test lead should **always** be connected to -BATT, the negative terminal of the vehicle battery - always - always - for the BEST DMM ground and most accurate measurements.

(2) Make an extended DMM ground lead if needed. Since a DMM's voltmeter section barely uses milliAmps (mA) to sample the voltage in a circuit, an extended ground lead of 30 feet poses no problem for the accuracy of the DMM reading in volts or ohms.

Vehicle Electronics Hands-On Troubleshooting Training Program

VEEJER ENTERPRISES 3701 Lariat Lane, Garland, Texas 75042-5419
Phone: 972-276-9642 Fax: 972-276-8122 Email: contact-us@veejer.com Web Site: www.veejer.com

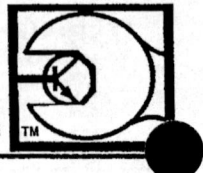

Measuring Circuit Current

At times, measuring electron current helps to determine a circuit problem. Is the current reading normal – too high – too low? This information can help diagnose an electrical circuit problems as we shall see.

Lessons 14, and **Lesson 17** cover current in series and parallel circuits respectively. **Lesson 18** discusses the technique of current measurement. **Lessons 19 & 20** discuss battery current in vehicle circuits. **Lessons 21 & 22** discuss generator (alternator) current in vehicle circuits.

In Figure 25 at the right, a current measurement method is shown that is easily performed on a vehicle circuit because the fuse is easy to access.

(1) Turn the circuit OFF and remove Fuse F1.

(2) Set the DMM to the 10A or 20A range (which ever is on your DMM). Connect as shown in place of the fuse.

(3) Turn the circuit ON.

(4) After the reading is obtained, **turn the circuit OFF before disconnecting the ammeter.**

The reading on the DMM is the current in amps flowing through the circuit. Expect about 0.145A or 145 mA due to the lamp drawing only 145 mA.

Use The Ammeter Properly

This method is satisfactory if the current does not exceed the 10A or 20A range of the DMM. DO NOT allow the DMM to measure the current any longer than necessary to get a reading. If the reading is close to 10 amps, or 20 amps for a DMM rated for that current level, do not leave the DMM connected for more than 10-15 seconds or damage to the DMM could result. Continuos measuring of current close to the maximum rating of the DMM causes the internal measurement resistor to get hot and may melt the solder mounting it to the DMM's internal circuit board. If it is determined that the DMM case is beginning to get warm stop the current measurement.

Interpreting The Ammeter Reading

Normal circuit current is determined by the voltage applied to a circuit and the resistance of the circuit. Basic Ohm's Law is covered in **Lessons 11 & 13.**

Ohm's Law explains that if circuit current is lower than normal, either the applied voltage (B+) is lower than normal or resistance at some point in the circuit has increased. If current is higher than normal either the B+ is higher than normal or circuit resistance has decreased at some point in the circuit.

Therefore, current measurement, while helpful in certain troubleshooting procedures, does not reveal why current is too high or too low, only that it is.

Voltage measurement and the TTS is a more effective method of troubleshooting. With two simple voltage measurements previously explained in the TTS, it can be determined if there is a OPEN or Vd problem on the voltage side or ground side of the load, a problem with the load or the fuse is blown.

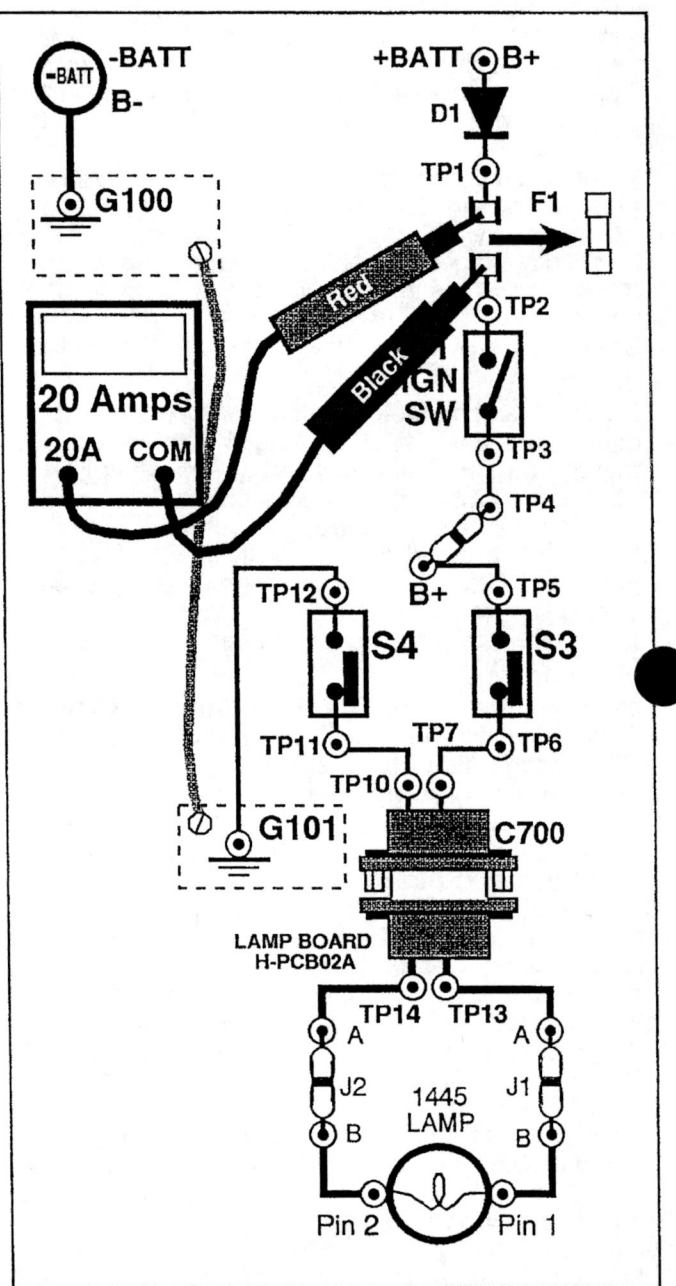

Fig. 25 Measuring circuit current or load current

The TTS should be the first voltage measurements made in any circuit to determine circuit conditions. Current measurement is only used in situations where a current reading can reveal important data about the load's performance, such as a current draw test of a cranking (starter) motor circuit with a current clamp.

Copyright © 2015 VEEJER ENTERPRISES, Garland, Texas - All Rights Reserved   H-WB111A Page 37

Vehicle Electronics Hands-On Troubleshooting Training Program

VEEJER ENTERPRISES 3701 Lariat Lane, Garland, Texas 75042-5419
Phone: 972-276-9642 Fax: 972-276-8122 Email: contact-us@veejer.com Web Site: www.veejer.com

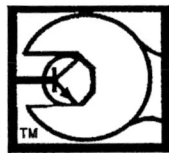

Troubleshooting Problem Format

You are now ready to begin practice exercises to develop your troubleshooting skill. Refer back to the six basic circuit problems for review at any time while troubleshooting these problems if you get stuck or ask your instructor for help if in a classroom.

To the right is an sample of the column format used to record DMM readings for each troubleshooting problem. The box at the top contains the problem number and special instructions. Look up this problem number in the Instructor Guide to find out how to insert the fault in the circuit for that problem if you are working alone. Find someone to help insert problems if you are in home-study.

The schematic diagram number is Figure TS-4A and is provided for reference while troubleshooting.

At **"Performance of the load,"** describe how the load is operating, such as, weak, dead, sluggish, dim, etc. This is followed by **Troubleshooting Step 1.** Decide what is the first DMM measurement (Hint: TTS-1) and describe where you are measuring on the schematic diagram. Record the DMM reading after "Reading" and then check off if the reading is "good" or "bad." Continue taking readings in **Troubleshooting Step 2** (Hint: TTS-2) and describe where you are measuring. Record the DMM reading and check off "good" or "bad."

After the TTS readings you should begin either tracing B+ on the voltage side or tracing B- on the ground side until you know where the problem is in the circuit and what is wrong, either an OPEN or Vd. Take as many steps as necessary to identify the problem in the circuit. Then record specifically what the problem is after **"The Problem Is."**

Finally make any notes you think will be helpful to remember about what you learned from troubleshooting this problem. This will be useful if you go back and review your troubleshooting at a later date. A final reminder is given to remove the fault if no one is to follow you in troubleshooting the same problem.

The column format is used throughout the 32 electrical troubleshooting problems. Consult the Instructor Guide for the answers to the troubleshooting problems.

About Schematic Diagrams:

The straight line schematic diagram, Figure TS-4A is on the right hand column of every odd numbered page for easy reference. This saves time thumbing back and forth through the book looking for a schematic diagram which are available throughout the troubleshooting section in this manner.

Since the white ink on the PCBs (called Silk Screen) is so visible and descriptive about the circuit layout, many students rely on the silk screen to trace the circuit and decide their troubleshooting steps. However, it cannot be stressed enough how important it is to consult the schematic diagrams as a guide in deciding troubleshooting steps instead of using the silk screen on the top of the PCBs.

When working on a vehicle, a silk screen is not available on the vehicle to guide you in troubleshooting. Schematic diagrams are used. Learn to troubleshoot from schematic diagrams now to make it easier to troubleshoot circuits on actual vehicles. Avoid using the silk screen and practice using the schematic diagrams to guide you in tracing the circuit and in selecting troubleshooting points to test the circuit.

Problem 00
Consult Instructor Guide To Insert This Circuit Fault.
Refer to Schematic **Figure TS-4A** for this problem

Begin Troubleshooting After Problem Inserted

Performance of the load: _____

Troubleshooting Step 1: _____
Reading: _____ Good: ____ Bad: ____

Troubleshooting Step 2: _____
Reading: _____ Good: ____ Bad: ____

Troubleshooting Step 3: _____
Reading: _____ Good: ____ Bad: ____

Troubleshooting Step 4: _____
Reading: _____ Good: ____ Bad: ____

Troubleshooting Step 5: _____
Reading: _____ Good: ____ Bad: ____

Troubleshooting Step 6: _____
Reading: _____ Good: ____ Bad: ____

Troubleshooting Step 7: _____
Reading: _____ Good: ____ Bad: ____

Troubleshooting Step 8: _____
Reading: _____ Good: ____ Bad: ____

Troubleshooting Step 9: _____
Reading: _____ Good: ____ Bad: ____

Troubleshooting Step 10: _____
Reading: _____ Good: ____ Bad: ____

Troubleshooting Step 11: _____
Reading: _____ Good: ____ Bad: ____

Troubleshooting Step 12: _____
Reading: _____ Good: ____ Bad: ____

The Problem Is: _____
Notes:

Copyright © 2015 VEEJER ENTERPRISES, Garland, Texas - All Rights Reserved

Vehicle Electronics Hands-On Troubleshooting Training Program

VEEJER ENTERPRISES 3701 Lariat Lane, Garland, Texas 75042-5419
Phone: 972-276-9642   Fax: 972-276-8122   Email: contact-us@veejer.com   Web Site: www.veejer.com

Straight Line Schematic, Figure TS-4A

To the right is a straight-line schematic called Figure TS-4A for reference for troubleshooting 32 lamp circuit problems covered in this section.

A straight line schematic places all components and test points in their proper electrical order, (not necessarily their numerical order) for easier tracing through the voltage side and ground side of a circuit.

Determine a test point to check in the circuit based on the TTS readings which are the first two circuit voltage (Vc) measurements to perform. Find that test point in the straight line schematic to see its relative position in the circuit. If you check a point on the PCBs and do not understand where you are in the circuit or what point to check next, consult the straight line schematic in Figure TS-4A. It works best to follow along with the schematic just as a road map when driving in unfamiliar territory.

Each test point is clearly marked in Figure TS-4A at crucial points in the circuit which makes circuit tracing a lot easier. On an actual vehicle circuit these test points are not always clearly marked as they are in Figure TS-4A but they still exist in the form of wire colors, circuit numbers, labeled connector pins, etc., which should be identified for the test point that they represent. A trained eye can pick out crucial test points in a vehicle circuit schematic but getting to those points on an actual vehicle may be more difficult than it is on the PCBs. No training program can make it easier to get to test points on actual vehicles. That problem will be with us as long as they build vehicles.

At least with this training program, you will become more aware of how to select test points and have an idea of the voltage readings throughout a circuit. With practice you will develop the ability to spot test points in vehicle schematics and know with some certainty what the voltage should be at that point in the circuit. If the reading is too high or too low you will know what to do next if you apply in the vehicle what you learn in this training program.

Another advantage of using the schematic is to follow more of the vehicle style of schematic layout used by many vehicle manufacturers today. They usually start with the B+ source at the top and work down through the circuit to arrive at ground, or -BATT or B- at the bottom of the schematic.

Figure TS-4A appears on the right hand column of every odd number page for ready reference while working through the 32 troubleshooting problems.

Use the I/G (Instructor Guide H-IG01/02A) for instructions on how to insert faults for each problem and for the answers to troubleshooting problems. Do not look at the answers before troubleshooting a problem. If you know in advance what the problem is, it may affect the benefits to be learned in troubleshooting that problem. Find someone to insert problems for you following instructions in the I/G.

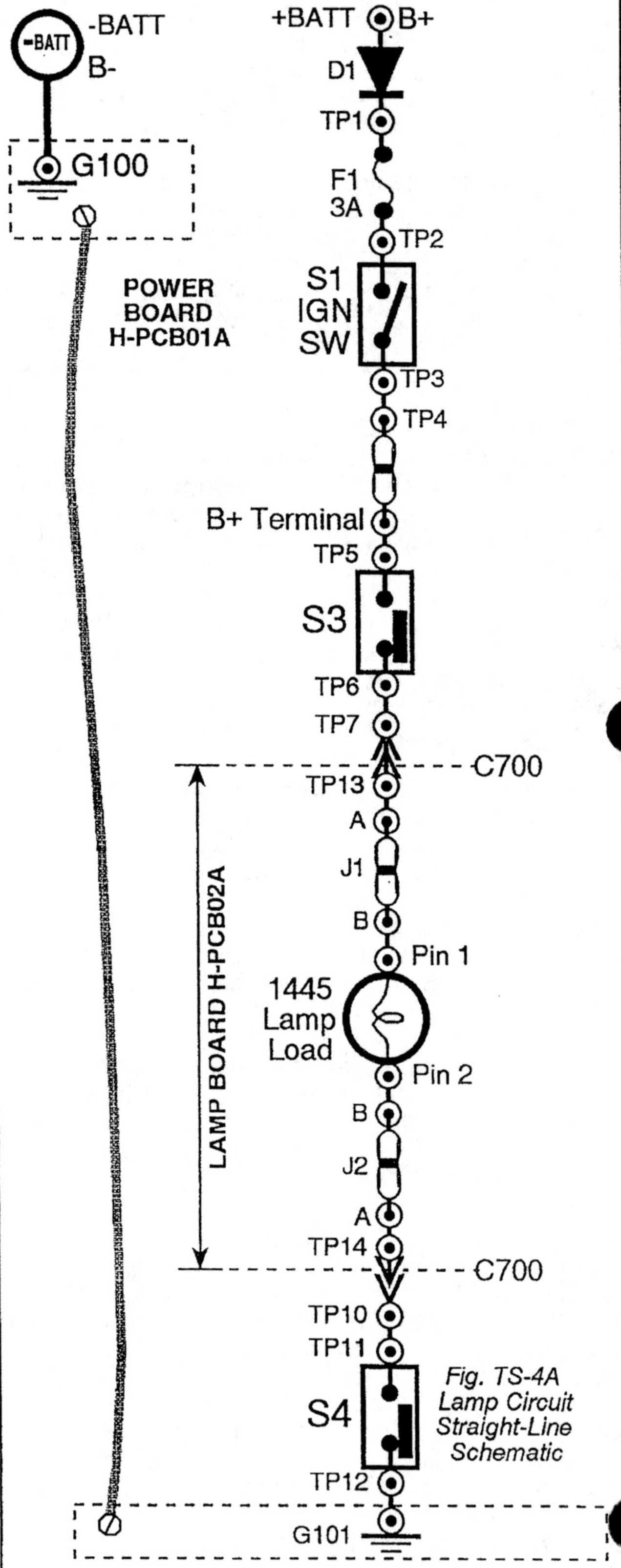

Fig. TS-4A Lamp Circuit Straight-Line Schematic

Copyright © 2015 VEEJER ENTERPRISES, Garland, Texas - All Rights Reserved

Vehicle Electronics Hands-On Troubleshooting Training Program

VEEJER ENTERPRISES 3701 Lariat Lane, Garland, Texas 75042-5419
e: 972-276-9642 Fax: 972-276-8122 Email: contact-us@veejer.com Web Site: www.veejer.com

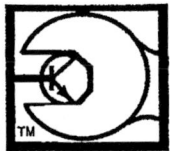

Read this first . . . .
As you begin the 32 troubleshooting exercises of the lamp circuit remember, this is what it's all about, hands-on troubleshooting of electrical and electronics circuits. By learning troubleshooting techniques with a simple circuit such as the lamp circuit, the essential troubleshooting concepts required to troubleshoot more complex circuits come into clear focus with the simple lamp circuit. **Even the most complex vehicle circuits require the same procedures used to troubleshoot the lamp circuit.**

Follow everything that has been have covered in this workbook to prepare you for successful electrical troubleshooting. Don't hesitate to go back and review your notes at any time.

The first 28 problems will be OPEN connections and Vds problem on either the voltage side or the ground side of the circuit. Follow the problems in numerical order except for the 4 short-to-ground problems.

Short-to-Ground Problems
First complete the 28 problems with OPEN connections and Vds. There are 4 short-to-ground problems. Save these four problems for the last 4 problems.

This training program is designed to teach methods to find the problem by troubleshooting with a DMM. The troubleshooting problems encountered in this section are variations of the six basic circuit problems reviewed in the previous pages. Before beginning troubleshooting these problems review the six basic problems and the DMM readings of the TTS that indicate if a problem and which problem is present in the circuit. Then review how to trace back through the circuit to find where in the circuit the problem exists.

Make sure there are no faults in the PCBs before inserting a problem. Scan the top of the PCBs before troubleshooting a problem.

After a fault is inserted begin troubleshooting the problem by recording test readings under the correct Troubleshooting Problem Number in the Student Work Book. The object of troubleshooting each problem is to determine what is wrong in the circuit. Once you know what the problem is you are finished with that problem. You are not required to repair a problem found.

Studying At Home
Ask someone to insert problems for you on the bottom of the PCBs. The I/G (Instructor Guide) has simple instructions so anyone can insert a problem. Before inserting a problem scan the bottom of the PCBs to be sure there is no other problem left from the last problem.
Review the correct answers only AFTER completing a troubleshooting problem. DO NOT look at the answers BEFORE troubleshooting a problem. Correct each problem when it is completed and before inserting the next problem.

Studying in a Tech School
Your Teacher or Instructor will set up procedures for students to troubleshoot circuit problems. Follow instructions given in the classroom.

Final Thoughts
While you are focused on troubleshooting a circuit board don't overlook the fact this is exactly the same way you would troubleshoot a circuit on a vehicle.

Remember to unplug the Power Supply before disconnecting the red and black wires from the red and black posts. Do not leave the power supply lugged in when not in use.

A complete schematic diagram is located in the right hand column of each right hand (odd number) page for easy reference while troubleshooting. The schematic diagram is your "road map" if you loose your direction in troubleshooting

There is a practice troubleshooting problem on the next page which has the answers recorded to guide you through the style of writing down each troubleshooting step, the DMM reading obtained and identifying if the reading is good or bad.

Copyright © 2015 VEEJER ENTERPRISES, Garland, Texas - All Rights Reserved   H-WB111A Page 40

32 Practice Troubleshooting Problems

Vehicle Electronics Hands-On Troubleshooting Training Program

VEEJER ENTERPRISES 3701 Lariat Lane, Garland, Texas 75042-5419
Phone: 972-276-9642 Fax: 972-276-8122 Email: contact-us@veejer.com Web Site: www.veejer.com

Practice Problem

Insert This Practice Problem:
Remove the 0ΩR on top of the Power Board between the B+ Terminal and TP4. Turn the circuit ON and notice the lamp is out. Record your visual inspection of load performance after Performance of the load:.

Begin troubleshooting with the TTS and notice how the blanks are filled in with bold ink. Follow these suggested troubleshooting step answers as a guide for the following 28 problems.

Performance of the load: **Lamp is out (load dead)**

Troubleshooting Step 1: **TTS-1**
Reading: **0V**   Good: ____ Bad: **X**

Troubleshooting Step 2: **ck Vc at J1-B**
Reading: **0V**   Good: ____ Bad: **X**

Troubleshooting Step 3: **ck Vc at J1-A**
Reading: **0V**   Good: ____ Bad: **X**

Troubleshooting Step 4: **ck Vc at TP13**
Reading: **0V**   Good: ____ Bad: **X**

Troubleshooting Step 5: **ck Vc at TP7**
Reading: **0V**   Good: ____ Bad: **X**

Troubleshooting Step 6: **ck Vc at TP6**
Reading: **0V**   Good: ____ Bad: **X**

Troubleshooting Step 7: **ck Vc at TP5**
Reading: **0V**   Good: ____ Bad: **X**

Troubleshooting Step 8: **ck Vc at B+ Terminal**
Reading: **0V**   Good: ____ Bad: **X**

Troubleshooting Step 9: **ck Vc at TP4**
Reading: **B+**   Good: **X** Bad: ____

Troubleshooting Step 10: _____
Reading: _____   Good: ____ Bad: ____

Troubleshooting Step 11: _____
Reading: _____   Good: ____ Bad: ____

Troubleshooting Step 12: _____
Reading: _____   Good: ____ Bad: ____

(Now write down your conclusion of the problem.)
The Problem Is: **There is an OPEN circuit between the B+ Terminal and TP4.**

Notes: **An OPEN on the voltage side of the load blocks B+ from getting to Pin 1 of the load.**

REMINDER: Remove the fault and restore the PCBs to normal operation after the problem is identified if no one else is to troubleshoot this problem.

Comments Troubleshooting Practice

Begin troubleshooting with a visual inspection and note the condition of the load. Load performance is described as "out" or "dead." This means there is a problem that prevents any current from flowing through the load. Either the circuit has an OPEN circuit or an extremely high Vd. **Use your own abbreviations when describing information in the troubleshooting steps. Be consistent with your abbreviations so you don't confuse yourself later when reviewing answers.**

Step 1 is the TTS-1 which measures the Vc at load Pin 1. Writing "TTS-1" is sufficient to describe the first measurement. The reading is 0V and that is bad.

For Step 2 we would normally measure TTS-2 but since TTS-1 is at 0V we know that TTS-2 will also be 0V. Therefore we can skip the TTS-2 measurement this time and immediately begin going back up the circuit looking for B+ (Tracing B+). Step 2 says we are "checking Vc at J1-B." No Vc there is bad. It's a good idea to use any abbreviations you choose to shorten the time writing your answers but use consistent terms. Set up your own system.

Comparing Steps 8 and 9 reveals the Problem. Vc measurements going back up the circuit show B+ is found in Step 9 (at TP4). We conclude that there is an OPEN between The B+ Terminal and TP4. This is described after "The Problem Is" There is no need to perform any more troubleshooting steps once the circuit problem is identified.

Many professional troubleshooters will "split the circuit in half" and take a measurement half way through a circuit rather than take several measurements to get to the half way point in the circuit. Feel free to select test points by jumping ahead and skipping a few test points to save time troubleshooting and writing down each test step and the result you got. If you jump too far ahead and get a good reading then move back down from that test point to find the problem.

Finally make any summary notes to help you remember what you learned troubleshooting each problem. The answers in the Instructor Guide (I/G) will not include any comments for "Notes."

Remove the problem by putting a **zero ohm resistor (0ΩR)** back into the Power Board between the B+ Terminal and TP4 if no one else is to troubleshoot this problem.

Start with Problem #1 on the next page.

Vehicle Electronics Hands-On Troubleshooting Training Program

VEEJER ENTERPRISES 3701 Lariat Lane, Garland, Texas 75042-5419
Phone: 972-276-9642 Fax: 972-276-8122 Email: contact-us@veejer.com Web Site: www.veejer.com

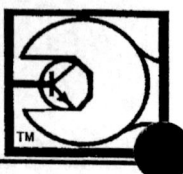

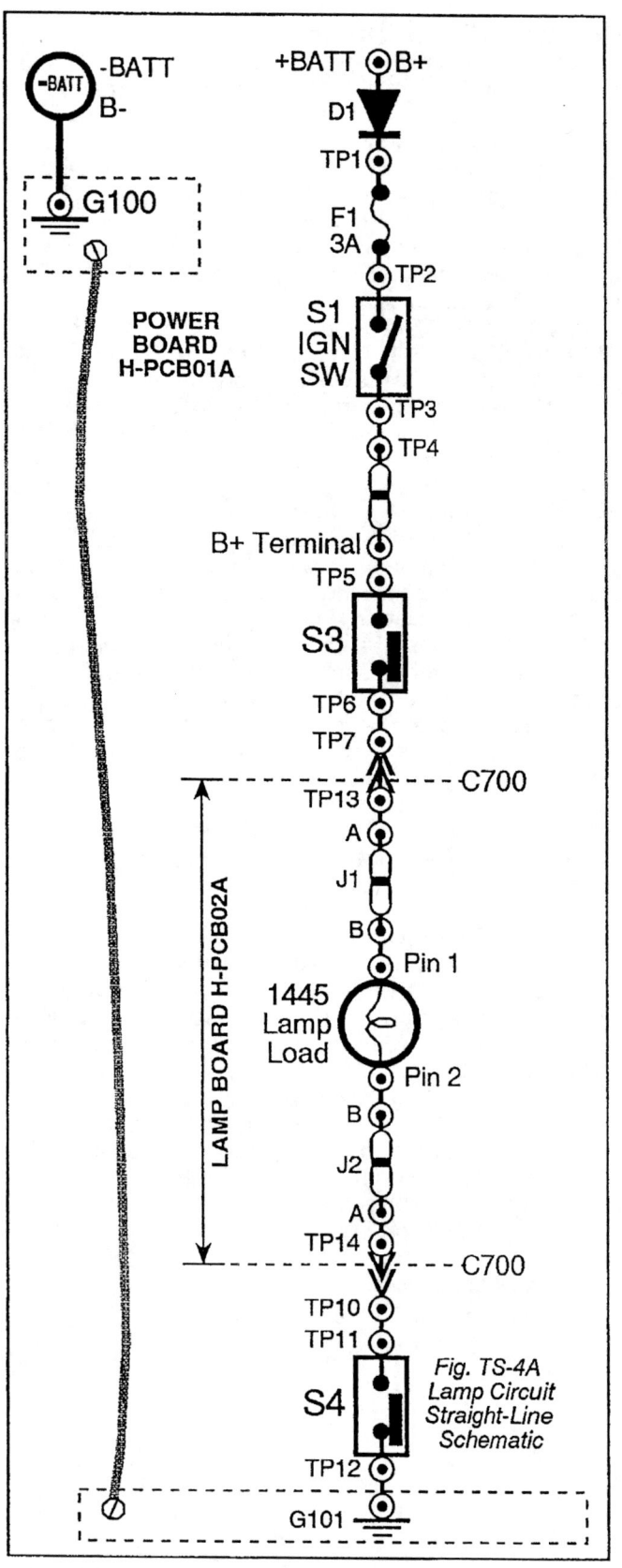

Fig. TS-4A Lamp Circuit Straight-Line Schematic

Problem 01
Consult Instructor Guide To Insert This Circuit Fault.
Refer to Schematic **Figure TS-4A** for this problem

Begin Troubleshooting After Problem Inserted

Performance of the load: _____

Troubleshooting Step 1: __TTS-1__
Reading: _____ Good: ___ Bad: ___

Troubleshooting Step 2: __TTS-2__
Reading: _____ Good: ___ Bad: ___

Troubleshooting Step 3: _____
Reading: _____ Good: ___ Bad: ___

Troubleshooting Step 4: _____
Reading: _____ Good: ___ Bad: ___

Troubleshooting Step 5: _____
Reading: _____ Good: ___ Bad: ___

Troubleshooting Step 6: _____
Reading: _____ Good: ___ Bad: ___

Troubleshooting Step 7: _____
Reading: _____ Good: ___ Bad: ___

Troubleshooting Step 8: _____
Reading: _____ Good: ___ Bad: ___

Troubleshooting Step 9: _____
Reading: _____ Good: ___ Bad: ___

Troubleshooting Step 10: _____
Reading: _____ Good: ___ Bad: ___

Troubleshooting Step 11: _____
Reading: _____ Good: ___ Bad: ___

Troubleshooting Step 12: _____
Reading: _____ Good: ___ Bad: ___

The Problem Is: _____

Notes:

REMINDERS:
Study at home: Remove the fault and restore the PCBs to normal operation after the problem is identified.
Study at Tech School: Follow the Instructor's directions on what to do.

Vehicle Electronics Hands-On Troubleshooting Training Program

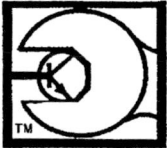

VEEJER ENTERPRISES 3701 Lariat Lane, Garland, Texas 75042-5419
Phone: 972-276-9642   Fax: 972-276-8122   Email: contact-us@veejer.com   Web Site: www.veejer.com

---

Problem 02
Consult Instructor Guide To Insert This Circuit Fault.
Refer to Schematic **Figure TS-4A** for this problem

Begin Troubleshooting After Problem Inserted

Performance of the load: _____

Troubleshooting Step 1: __TTS-1_____
Reading: _____ Good: ___ Bad: ___

Troubleshooting Step 2: __TTS-2_____
Reading: _____ Good: ___ Bad: ___

Troubleshooting Step 3: _____
Reading: _____ Good: ___ Bad: ___

Troubleshooting Step 4: _____
Reading: _____ Good: ___ Bad: ___

Troubleshooting Step 5: _____
Reading: _____ Good: ___ Bad: ___

Troubleshooting Step 6: _____
Reading: _____ Good: ___ Bad: ___

Troubleshooting Step 7: _____
Reading: _____ Good: ___ Bad: ___

Troubleshooting Step 8: _____
Reading: _____ Good: ___ Bad: ___

Troubleshooting Step 9: _____
Reading: _____ Good: ___ Bad: ___

Troubleshooting Step 10: _____
Reading: _____ Good: ___ Bad: ___

Troubleshooting Step 11: _____
Reading: _____ Good: ___ Bad: ___

Troubleshooting Step 12: _____
Reading: _____ Good: ___ Bad: ___

The Problem Is: _____

Notes:

REMINDERS:
Study at home: Remove the fault and restore the PCBs to normal operation after the problem is identified.
Study at Tech School: Follow the Instructor's directions on what to do.

Problem 03
Consult Instructor Guide To Insert This Circuit Fault.
Refer to Schematic **Figure TS-4A** for this problem

Begin Troubleshooting After Problem Inserted

Performance of the load: _____

Troubleshooting Step 1: __TTS-1_____
Reading: _____ Good: ___ Bad: ___

Troubleshooting Step 2: __TTS-2_____
Reading: _____ Good: ___ Bad: ___

Troubleshooting Step 3: _____
Reading: _____ Good: ___ Bad: ___

Troubleshooting Step 4: _____
Reading: _____ Good: ___ Bad: ___

Troubleshooting Step 5: _____
Reading: _____ Good: ___ Bad: ___

Troubleshooting Step 6: _____
Reading: _____ Good: ___ Bad: ___

Troubleshooting Step 7: _____
Reading: _____ Good: ___ Bad: ___

Troubleshooting Step 8: _____
Reading: _____ Good: ___ Bad: ___

Troubleshooting Step 9: _____
Reading: _____ Good: ___ Bad: ___

Troubleshooting Step 10: _____
Reading: _____ Good: ___ Bad: ___

Troubleshooting Step 11: _____
Reading: _____ Good: ___ Bad: ___

Troubleshooting Step 12: _____
Reading: _____ Good: ___ Bad: ___

The Problem Is: _____

Notes:

REMINDERS:
Study at home: Remove the fault and restore the PCBs to normal operation after the problem is identified.
Study at Tech School: Follow the Instructor's directions on what to do.

Vehicle Electronics Hands-On Troubleshooting Training Program

VEEJER ENTERPRISES 3701 Lariat Lane, Garland, Texas 75042-5419
Phone: 972-276-9642   Fax: 972-276-8122   Email: contact-us@veejer.com   Web Site: www.veejer.com

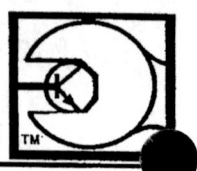

Problem 04
Consult Instructor Guide To Insert This Circuit Fault.
Refer to Schematic **Figure TS-4A** for this problem

Begin Troubleshooting After Problem Inserted

Performance of the load: _____

Troubleshooting Step 1: __**TTS-1**_____
Reading: _____ Good: ____ Bad: ____

Troubleshooting Step 2: __**TTS-2**_____
Reading: _____ Good: ____ Bad: ____

Troubleshooting Step 3: _____
Reading: _____ Good: ____ Bad: ____

Troubleshooting Step 4: _____
Reading: _____ Good: ____ Bad: ____

Troubleshooting Step 5: _____
Reading: _____ Good: ____ Bad: ____

Troubleshooting Step 6: _____
Reading: _____ Good: ____ Bad: ____

Troubleshooting Step 7: _____
Reading: _____ Good: ____ Bad: ____

Troubleshooting Step 8: _____
Reading: _____ Good: ____ Bad: ____

Troubleshooting Step 9: _____
Reading: _____ Good: ____ Bad: ____

Troubleshooting Step 10: _____
Reading: _____ Good: ____ Bad: ____

Troubleshooting Step 11: _____
Reading: _____ Good: ____ Bad: ____

Troubleshooting Step 12: _____
Reading: _____ Good: ____ Bad: ____

The Problem Is: _____

Notes:

REMINDERS:
Study at home: Remove the fault and restore the PCBs to normal operation after the problem is identified.
Study at Tech School: Follow the Instructor's directions on what to do.

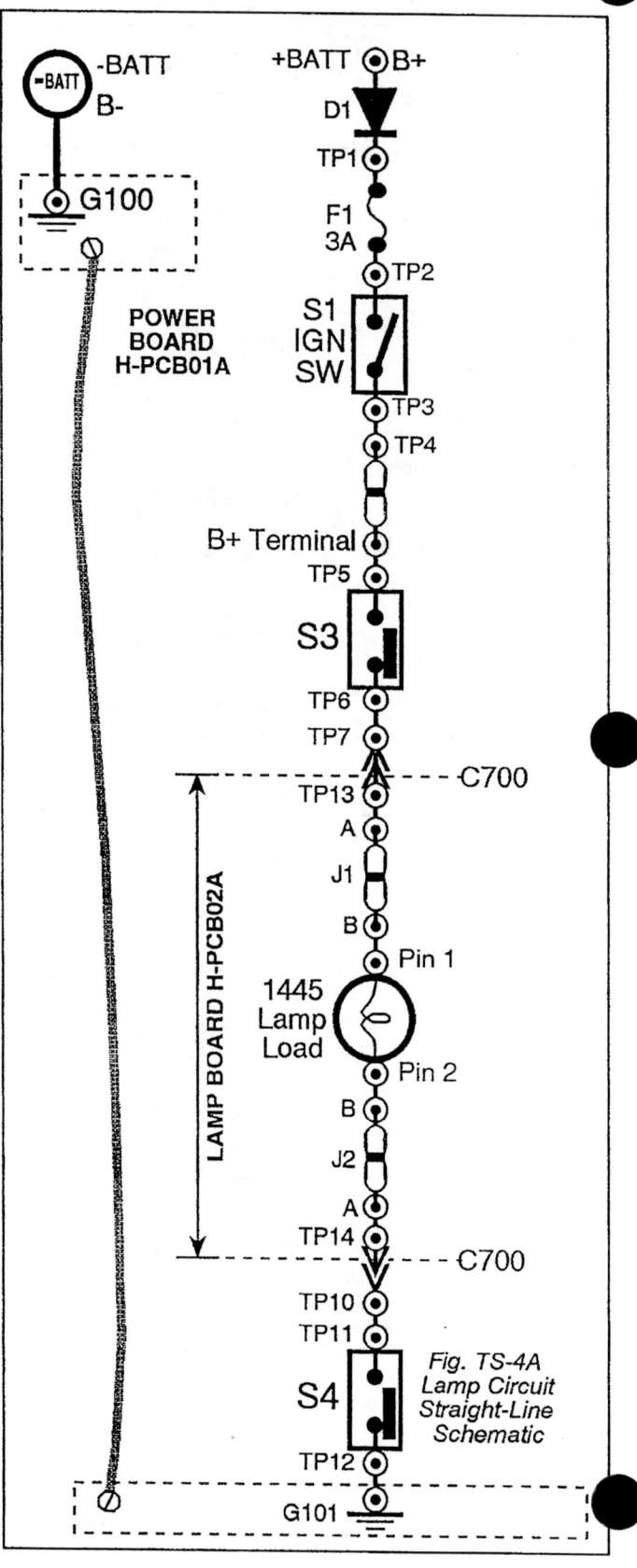

Fig. TS-4A
Lamp Circuit
Straight-Line
Schematic

Copyright © 2015 VEEJER ENTERPRISES, Garland, Texas - All Rights Reserved

Vehicle Electronics Hands-On Troubleshooting Training Program

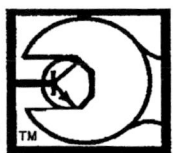

VEEJER ENTERPRISES 3701 Lariat Lane, Garland, Texas 75042-5419
Phone: 972-276-9642 Fax: 972-276-8122 Email: contact-us@veejer.com Web Site: www.veejer.com

Problem 05
Consult Instructor Guide To Insert This Circuit Fault.
Refer to Schematic **Figure TS-4A** for this problem

Begin Troubleshooting After Problem Inserted

Performance of the load: _____

Troubleshooting Step 1: __TTS-1_____
Reading: _____ Good: ____ Bad: ____

Troubleshooting Step 2: __TTS-2_____
Reading: _____ Good: ____ Bad: ____

Troubleshooting Step 3: _____
Reading: _____ Good: ____ Bad: ____

Troubleshooting Step 4: _____
Reading: _____ Good: ____ Bad: ____

Troubleshooting Step 5: _____
Reading: _____ Good: ____ Bad: ____

Troubleshooting Step 6: _____
Reading: _____ Good: ____ Bad: ____

Troubleshooting Step 7: _____
Reading: _____ Good: ____ Bad: ____

Troubleshooting Step 8: _____
Reading: _____ Good: ____ Bad: ____

Troubleshooting Step 9: _____
Reading: _____ Good: ____ Bad: ____

Troubleshooting Step 10: _____
Reading: _____ Good: ____ Bad: ____

Troubleshooting Step 11: _____
Reading: _____ Good: ____ Bad: ____

Troubleshooting Step 12: _____
Reading: _____ Good: ____ Bad: ____

The Problem Is: _____

Notes:

REMINDERS:
Study at home: Remove the fault and restore the PCBs to normal operation after the problem is identified.
Study at Tech School: Follow the Instructor's directions on what to do.

Problem 06
Consult Instructor Guide To Insert This Circuit Fault.
Refer to Schematic **Figure TS-4A** for this problem

Begin Troubleshooting After Problem Inserted

Performance of the load: _____

Troubleshooting Step 1: __TTS-1_____
Reading: _____ Good: ____ Bad: ____

Troubleshooting Step 2: __TTS-2_____
Reading: _____ Good: ____ Bad: ____

Troubleshooting Step 3: _____
Reading: _____ Good: ____ Bad: ____

Troubleshooting Step 4: _____
Reading: _____ Good: ____ Bad: ____

Troubleshooting Step 5: _____
Reading: _____ Good: ____ Bad: ____

Troubleshooting Step 6: _____
Reading: _____ Good: ____ Bad: ____

Troubleshooting Step 7: _____
Reading: _____ Good: ____ Bad: ____

Troubleshooting Step 8: _____
Reading: _____ Good: ____ Bad: ____

Troubleshooting Step 9: _____
Reading: _____ Good: ____ Bad: ____

Troubleshooting Step 10: _____
Reading: _____ Good: ____ Bad: ____

Troubleshooting Step 11: _____
Reading: _____ Good: ____ Bad: ____

Troubleshooting Step 12: _____
Reading: _____ Good: ____ Bad: ____

The Problem Is: _____

Notes:

REMINDERS:
Study at home: Remove the fault and restore the PCBs to normal operation after the problem is identified.
Study at Tech School: Follow the Instructor's directions on what to do.

Vehicle Electronics Hands-On Troubleshooting Training Program

VEEJER ENTERPRISES 3701 Lariat Lane, Garland, Texas 75042-5419
Phone: 972-276-9642   Fax: 972-276-8122   Email: contact-us@veejer.com   Web Site: www.veejer.com

Problem 07
Consult Instructor Guide To Insert This Circuit Fault.
Refer to Schematic **Figure TS-4A** for this problem

Begin Troubleshooting After Problem Inserted

Performance of the load: _____

Troubleshooting Step 1: __TTS-1_____
Reading: _____ Good: ___ Bad: ___

Troubleshooting Step 2: __TTS-2_____
Reading: _____ Good: ___ Bad: ___

Troubleshooting Step 3: _____
Reading: _____ Good: ___ Bad: ___

Troubleshooting Step 4: _____
Reading: _____ Good: ___ Bad: ___

Troubleshooting Step 5: _____
Reading: _____ Good: ___ Bad: ___

Troubleshooting Step 6: _____
Reading: _____ Good: ___ Bad: ___

Troubleshooting Step 7: _____
Reading: _____ Good: ___ Bad: ___

Troubleshooting Step 8: _____
Reading: _____ Good: ___ Bad: ___

Troubleshooting Step 9: _____
Reading: _____ Good: ___ Bad: ___

Troubleshooting Step 10: _____
Reading: _____ Good: ___ Bad: ___

Troubleshooting Step 11: _____
Reading: _____ Good: ___ Bad: ___

Troubleshooting Step 12: _____
Reading: _____ Good: ___ Bad: ___

The Problem Is: _____

Notes:

REMINDERS:
Study at home: Remove the fault and restore the PCBs to normal operation after the problem is identified.
Study at Tech School: Follow the Instructor's directions on what to do.

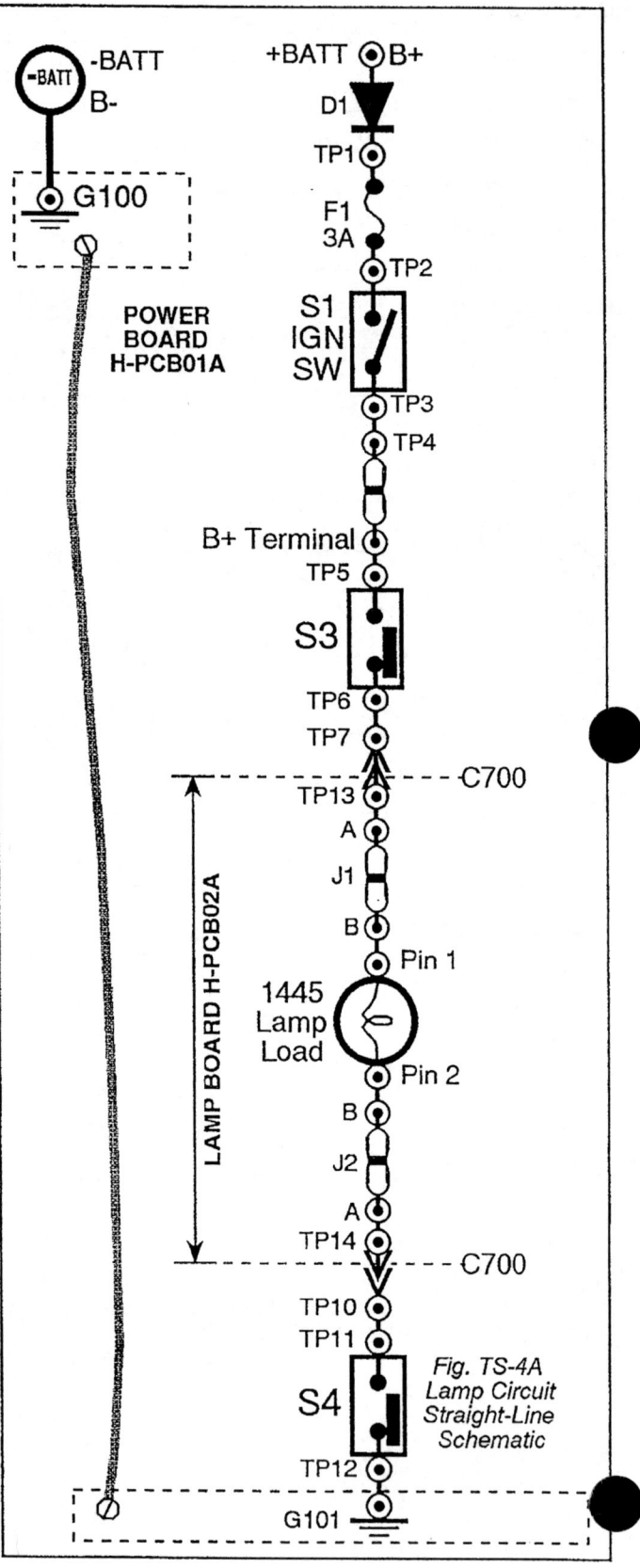

Fig. TS-4A Lamp Circuit Straight-Line Schematic

Copyright © 2015 VEEJER ENTERPRISES, Garland, Texas - All Rights Reserved   H-WB111A Page 47

Vehicle Electronics Hands-On Troubleshooting Training Program

VEEJER ENTERPRISES 3701 Lariat Lane, Garland, Texas 75042-5419
Phone: 972-276-9642 Fax: 972-276-8122 Email: contact-us@veejer.com Web Site: www.veejer.com

Problem 08
Consult Instructor Guide To Insert This Circuit Fault.
Refer to Schematic **Figure TS-4A** for this problem

**Begin Troubleshooting After Problem Inserted
Answers are provided for this problem for
instructional purposes with a new type of
electrical problem.**

Performance of the load: ____ *lamp is dim (weak)* ____

Troubleshooting Step 1: __ **TTS-1** _____
Reading: __ *low B+* _____ Good: ____ Bad: **X**

Troubleshooting Step 2: __ **TTS-2** _____
Reading: __ *0.05 V* _____ Good: **X** Bad: ____

Troubleshooting Step 3: _ *ck Vc at J1-B, J1-A* ____
Reading: __ *low B+* _____ Good: ____ Bad: **X**

Troubleshooting Step 4: __ *ck Vc at TP13* _____
Reading: _ *normal B+* ____ Good: **X** Bad: ____

Troubleshooting Step 5: _____
Reading: _____ Good: ____ Bad: ____

Troubleshooting Step 6: _____
Reading: _____ Good: ____ Bad: ____

Troubleshooting Step 7: _____
Reading: _____ Good: ____ Bad: ____

Troubleshooting Step 8: _____
Reading: _____ Good: ____ Bad: ____

Troubleshooting Step 9: _____
Reading: _____ Good: ____ Bad: ____

Troubleshooting Step 10: _____
Reading: _____ Good: ____ Bad: ____

Troubleshooting Step 11: _____
Reading: _____ Good: ____ Bad: ____

Troubleshooting Step 12: _____
Reading: _____ Good: ____ Bad: ____

The Problem Is: _ *Vd between J1-A and TP13* ____

Notes: A Vd on the voltage side of the load reduces the B+ available to the load Pin 1 which operates, dim, weak, poorly, etc.

REMINDERS:
Study at home: Remove the fault and restore the PCBs to normal operation after the problem is identified.
Study at Tech School: Follow the Instructor's directions on what to do.

Comments Troubleshooting Problem 08

Turn to the Instructor Guide (I/G) to find out what problem is inserted for Problem 08 if you are the one inserting problems. Use the schematic in Figure TS-4A which appears on every odd page number in the right hand column of the page.

Performance of the load is dim or weak. This means there is not an OPEN circuit because some electron current is flowing through the load.

In Step 1 the TTS-1 is measured and a low B+ reading is found. Record the actual DMM reading you find which will be lower than the B+ available at fuse, F1.

NOTE: It is not necessary for the Instructor Guide (I/G) to give you an actual voltage reading since the reading will vary with the ohmic value of the resistor randomly selected from the resistor bag. The larger the resistor value (150 Ω), the larger the Vd, the lower the TTS-1 reading and the dimmer the lamp. The smaller the resistor value (50 Ω) the smaller the Vd, the higher the TTS-1 reading and the less dim the lamp is from its original brightness. It is highly recommended that students write the exact voltage readings found in addition to the comment "low B+" to learn to recognize low B+ readings in circuits.

In Step 2 the TTS-2 is measured since there is some Vc at Pin 1 which will produce some reading on Pin 2 to help evaluate the condition of the ground circuit. A reading of 0.0xV tells us the ground is good, at least with the amount of B+ getting to Lamp Pin 1. If Pin 1 is very low (1-4V) a 0.0xV reading on Pin 2 may not mean the ground is good becasue not much electron current is flowing due to the high Vd on the voltage side. Once the problem on the voltage side is corrected in a vehicle circuit it would be wise to measure TTS-2 again to make sure the ground is good when the circuit problem on the voltage side is corrected. This is explained in Lessons 23 &24.

Since a low TTS-1 reading is the measurement that reveals a Vd problem on the voltage side, go back up the circuit (Trace B+) from Pin 1 looking for a good B+ reading as shown in Steps 3 and 4.

Step 4 is a good B+ reading so there is a Vd between J1 and TP13 which is described after "The Problem Is." A simple comment after "Note" recaps the lesson learned.

Now try Problem 09 on the next page and Check your answers in the I/G for Problem 09.

Vehicle Electronics Hands-On Troubleshooting Training Program

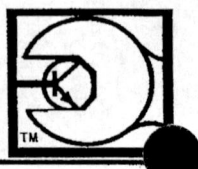

VEEJER ENTERPRISES 3701 Lariat Lane, Garland, Texas 75042-5419
Phone: 972-276-9642   Fax: 972-276-8122   Email: contact-us@veejer.com   Web Site: www.veejer.com

Problem 09
Consult Instructor Guide To Insert This Circuit Fault.
Refer to Schematic **Figure TS-4A** for this problem

Begin Troubleshooting After Problem Inserted

Performance of the load: _____

Troubleshooting Step 1: __TTS-1_____
Reading: _____ Good: ____ Bad: ____

Troubleshooting Step 2: __TTS-2_____
Reading: _____ Good: ____ Bad: ____

Troubleshooting Step 3: _____
Reading: _____ Good: ____ Bad: ____

Troubleshooting Step 4: _____
Reading: _____ Good: ____ Bad: ____

Troubleshooting Step 5: _____
Reading: _____ Good: ____ Bad: ____

Troubleshooting Step 6: _____
Reading: _____ Good: ____ Bad: ____

Troubleshooting Step 7: _____
Reading: _____ Good: ____ Bad: ____

Troubleshooting Step 8: _____
Reading: _____ Good: ____ Bad: ____

Troubleshooting Step 9: _____
Reading: _____ Good: ____ Bad: ____

Troubleshooting Step 10: _____
Reading: _____ Good: ____ Bad: ____

Troubleshooting Step 11: _____
Reading: _____ Good: ____ Bad: ____

Troubleshooting Step 12: _____
Reading: _____ Good: ____ Bad: ____

The Problem Is: _____

Notes:

REMINDERS:
Study at home: Remove the fault and restore the PCBs to normal operation after the problem is identified.
Study at Tech School: Follow the Instructor's directions on what to do.

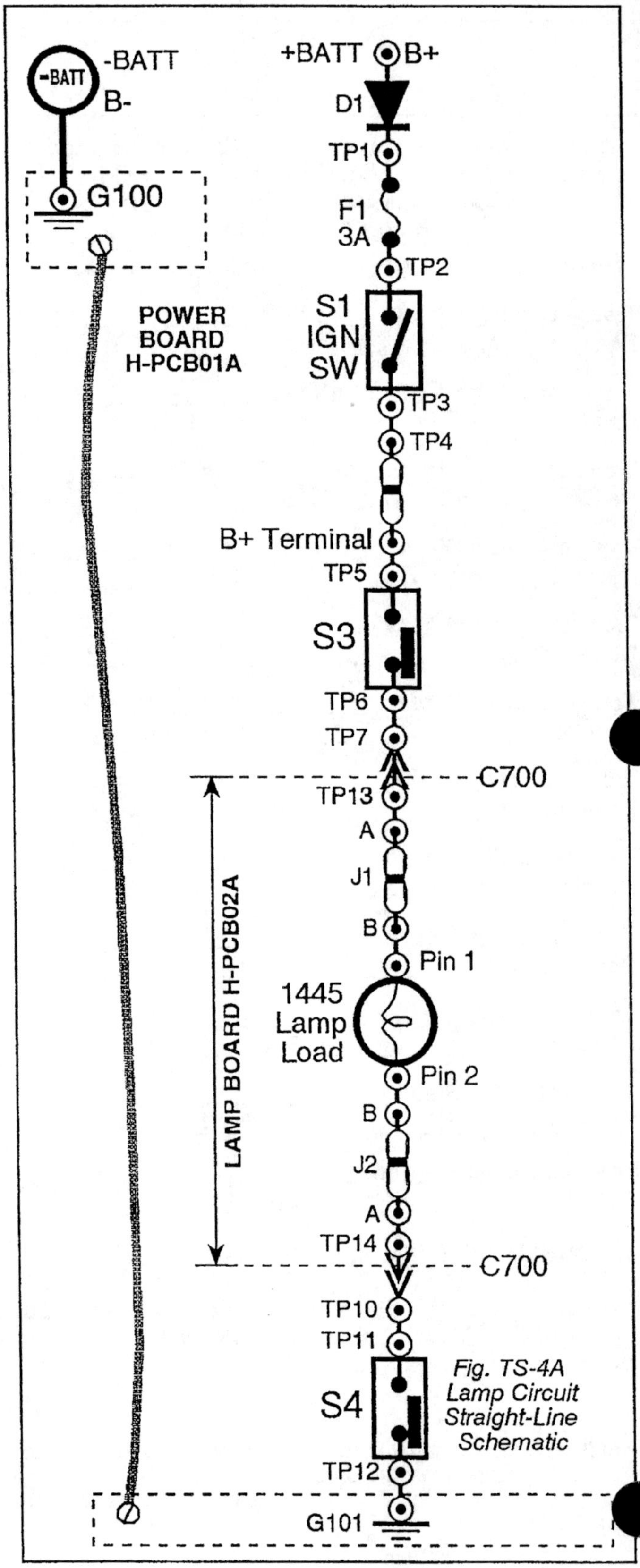

Fig. TS-4A
Lamp Circuit
Straight-Line
Schematic

Copyright © 2015 VEEJER ENTERPRISES, Garland, Texas - All Rights Reserved

Vehicle Electronics Hands-On Troubleshooting Training Program

VEEJER ENTERPRISES 3701 Lariat Lane, Garland, Texas 75042-5419
Phone: 972-276-9642 Fax: 972-276-8122 Email: contact-us@veejer.com Web Site: www.veejer.com

Problem 10
Consult Instructor Guide To Insert This Circuit Fault.
Refer to Schematic **Figure TS-4A** for this problem

Begin Troubleshooting After Problem Inserted

Performance of the load: _____

Troubleshooting Step 1: __TTS-1_____
Reading: _____ Good: ____ Bad: ____

Troubleshooting Step 2: __TTS-2_____
Reading: _____ Good: ____ Bad: ____

Troubleshooting Step 3: _____
Reading: _____ Good: ____ Bad: ____

Troubleshooting Step 4: _____
Reading: _____ Good: ____ Bad: ____

Troubleshooting Step 5: _____
Reading: _____ Good: ____ Bad: ____

Troubleshooting Step 6: _____
Reading: _____ Good: ____ Bad: ____

Troubleshooting Step 7: _____
Reading: _____ Good: ____ Bad: ____

Troubleshooting Step 8: _____
Reading: _____ Good: ____ Bad: ____

Troubleshooting Step 9: _____
Reading: _____ Good: ____ Bad: ____

Troubleshooting Step 10: _____
Reading: _____ Good: ____ Bad: ____

Troubleshooting Step 11: _____
Reading: _____ Good: ____ Bad: ____

Troubleshooting Step 12: _____
Reading: _____ Good: ____ Bad: ____

The Problem Is: _____

Notes:

REMINDERS:
Study at home: Remove the fault and restore the PCBs to normal operation after the problem is identified.
Study at Tech School: Follow the Instructor's directions on what to do.

Problem 11
Consult Instructor Guide To Insert This Circuit Fault.
Refer to Schematic **Figure TS-4A** for this problem

Begin Troubleshooting After Problem Inserted

Performance of the load: _____

Troubleshooting Step 1: __TTS-1_____
Reading: _____ Good: ____ Bad: ____

Troubleshooting Step 2: __TTS-2_____
Reading: _____ Good: ____ Bad: ____

Troubleshooting Step 3: _____
Reading: _____ Good: ____ Bad: ____

Troubleshooting Step 4: _____
Reading: _____ Good: ____ Bad: ____

Troubleshooting Step 5: _____
Reading: _____ Good: ____ Bad: ____

Troubleshooting Step 6: _____
Reading: _____ Good: ____ Bad: ____

Troubleshooting Step 7: _____
Reading: _____ Good: ____ Bad: ____

Troubleshooting Step 8: _____
Reading: _____ Good: ____ Bad: ____

Troubleshooting Step 9: _____
Reading: _____ Good: ____ Bad: ____

Troubleshooting Step 10: _____
Reading: _____ Good: ____ Bad: ____

Troubleshooting Step 11: _____
Reading: _____ Good: ____ Bad: ____

Troubleshooting Step 12: _____
Reading: _____ Good: ____ Bad: ____

The Problem Is: _____

Notes:

REMINDERS:
Study at home: Remove the fault and restore the PCBs to normal operation after the problem is identified.
Study at Tech School: Follow the Instructor's directions on what to do.

Copyright © 2015 VEEJER ENTERPRISES, Garland, Texas - All Rights Reserved

Vehicle Electronics Hands-On Troubleshooting Training Program

VEEJER ENTERPRISES 3701 Lariat Lane, Garland, Texas 75042-5419
Phone: 972-276-9642   Fax: 972-276-8122   Email: contact-us@veejer.com   Web Site: www.veejer.com

---

Problem 12
Consult Instructor Guide To Insert This Circuit Fault.
Refer to Schematic **Figure TS-4A** for this problem

Begin Troubleshooting After Problem Inserted

Performance of the load: _____

Troubleshooting Step 1: __TTS-1_____
Reading: _____ Good: ___ Bad: ___

Troubleshooting Step 2: __TTS-2_____
Reading: _____ Good: ___ Bad: ___

Troubleshooting Step 3: _____
Reading: _____ Good: ___ Bad: ___

Troubleshooting Step 4: _____
Reading: _____ Good: ___ Bad: ___

Troubleshooting Step 5: _____
Reading: _____ Good: ___ Bad: ___

Troubleshooting Step 6: _____
Reading: _____ Good: ___ Bad: ___

Troubleshooting Step 7: _____
Reading: _____ Good: ___ Bad: ___

Troubleshooting Step 8: _____
Reading: _____ Good: ___ Bad: ___

Troubleshooting Step 9: _____
Reading: _____ Good: ___ Bad: ___

Troubleshooting Step 10: _____
Reading: _____ Good: ___ Bad: ___

Troubleshooting Step 11: _____
Reading: _____ Good: ___ Bad: ___

Troubleshooting Step 12: _____
Reading: _____ Good: ___ Bad: ___

The Problem Is: _____

Notes:

REMINDERS:
Study at home: Remove the fault and restore the PCBs to normal operation after the problem is identified.
Study at Tech School: Follow the Instructor's directions on what to do.

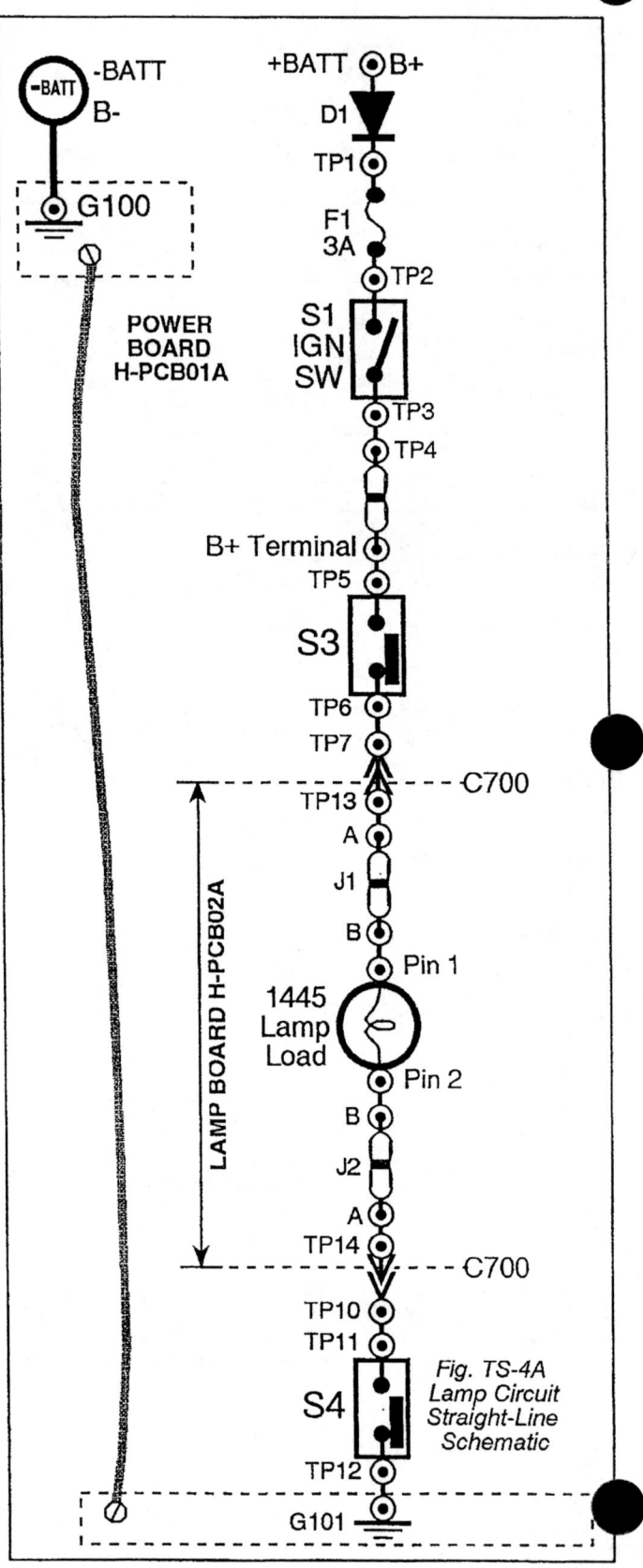

Fig. TS-4A Lamp Circuit Straight-Line Schematic

Copyright © 2015 VEEJER ENTERPRISES, Garland, Texas - All Rights Reserved   H-WB111A Page 51

Vehicle Electronics Hands-On Troubleshooting Training Program

VEEJER ENTERPRISES 3701 Lariat Lane, Garland, Texas 75042-5419
Phone: 972-276-9642 Fax: 972-276-8122 Email: contact-us@veejer.com Web Site: www.veejer.com

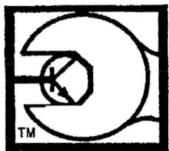

Problem 13
Consult Instructor Guide To Insert This Circuit Fault.
Refer to Schematic **Figure TS-4A** for this problem

Begin Troubleshooting After Problem Inserted

Performance of the load: _____

Troubleshooting Step 1: __TTS-1_____
Reading: _____ Good: ___ Bad: ___

Troubleshooting Step 2: __TTS-2_____
Reading: _____ Good: ___ Bad: ___

Troubleshooting Step 3: _____
Reading: _____ Good: ___ Bad: ___

Troubleshooting Step 4: _____
Reading: _____ Good: ___ Bad: ___

Troubleshooting Step 5: _____
Reading: _____ Good: ___ Bad: ___

Troubleshooting Step 6: _____
Reading: _____ Good: ___ Bad: ___

Troubleshooting Step 7: _____
Reading: _____ Good: ___ Bad: ___

Troubleshooting Step 8: _____
Reading: _____ Good: ___ Bad: ___

Troubleshooting Step 9: _____
Reading: _____ Good: ___ Bad: ___

Troubleshooting Step 10: _____
Reading: _____ Good: ___ Bad: ___

Troubleshooting Step 11: _____
Reading: _____ Good: ___ Bad: ___

Troubleshooting Step 12: _____
Reading: _____ Good: ___ Bad: ___

The Problem Is: _____

Notes:

REMINDERS:
Study at home: Remove the fault and restore the PCBs to normal operation after the problem is identified.
Study at Tech School: Follow the Instructor's directions on what to do.

Problem 14
Consult Instructor Guide To Insert This Circuit Fault.
Refer to Schematic **Figure TS-4A** for this problem

Begin Troubleshooting After Problem Inserted

Performance of the load: _____

Troubleshooting Step 1: __TTS-1_____
Reading: _____ Good: ___ Bad: ___

Troubleshooting Step 2: __TTS-2_____
Reading: _____ Good: ___ Bad: ___

Troubleshooting Step 3: _____
Reading: _____ Good: ___ Bad: ___

Troubleshooting Step 4: _____
Reading: _____ Good: ___ Bad: ___

Troubleshooting Step 5: _____
Reading: _____ Good: ___ Bad: ___

Troubleshooting Step 6: _____
Reading: _____ Good: ___ Bad: ___

Troubleshooting Step 7: _____
Reading: _____ Good: ___ Bad: ___

Troubleshooting Step 8: _____
Reading: _____ Good: ___ Bad: ___

Troubleshooting Step 9: _____
Reading: _____ Good: ___ Bad: ___

Troubleshooting Step 10: _____
Reading: _____ Good: ___ Bad: ___

Troubleshooting Step 11: _____
Reading: _____ Good: ___ Bad: ___

Troubleshooting Step 12: _____
Reading: _____ Good: ___ Bad: ___

The Problem Is: _____

Notes:

REMINDERS:
Study at home: Remove the fault and restore the PCBs to normal operation after the problem is identified.
Study at Tech School: Follow the Instructor's directions on what to do.

Copyright © 2015 VEEJER ENTERPRISES, Garland, Texas - All Rights Reserved

Vehicle Electronics Hands-On Troubleshooting Training Program

VEEJER ENTERPRISES 3701 Lariat Lane, Garland, Texas 75042-5419
Phone: 972-276-9642   Fax: 972-276-8122   Email: contact-us@veejer.com   Web Site: www.veejer.com

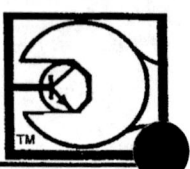

Problem 15
Consult Instructor Guide To Insert This Circuit Fault.
Refer to Schematic **Figure TS-4A** for this problem

Begin Troubleshooting After Problem Inserted

Performance of the load: _____

Troubleshooting Step 1: __TTS-1_____
Reading: _____ Good: ___ Bad: ___

Troubleshooting Step 2: __TTS-2_____
Reading: _____ Good: ___ Bad: ___

Troubleshooting Step 3: _____
Reading: _____ Good: ___ Bad: ___

Troubleshooting Step 4: _____
Reading: _____ Good: ___ Bad: ___

Troubleshooting Step 5: _____
Reading: _____ Good: ___ Bad: ___

Troubleshooting Step 6: _____
Reading: _____ Good: ___ Bad: ___

Troubleshooting Step 7: _____
Reading: _____ Good: ___ Bad: ___

Troubleshooting Step 8: _____
Reading: _____ Good: ___ Bad: ___

Troubleshooting Step 9: _____
Reading: _____ Good: ___ Bad: ___

Troubleshooting Step 10: _____
Reading: _____ Good: ___ Bad: ___

Troubleshooting Step 11: _____
Reading: _____ Good: ___ Bad: ___

Troubleshooting Step 12: _____
Reading: _____ Good: ___ Bad: ___

The Problem Is: _____

Notes:

REMINDERS:
Study at home: Remove the fault and restore the PCBs to normal operation after the problem is identified.
Study at Tech School: Follow the Instructor's directions on what to do.

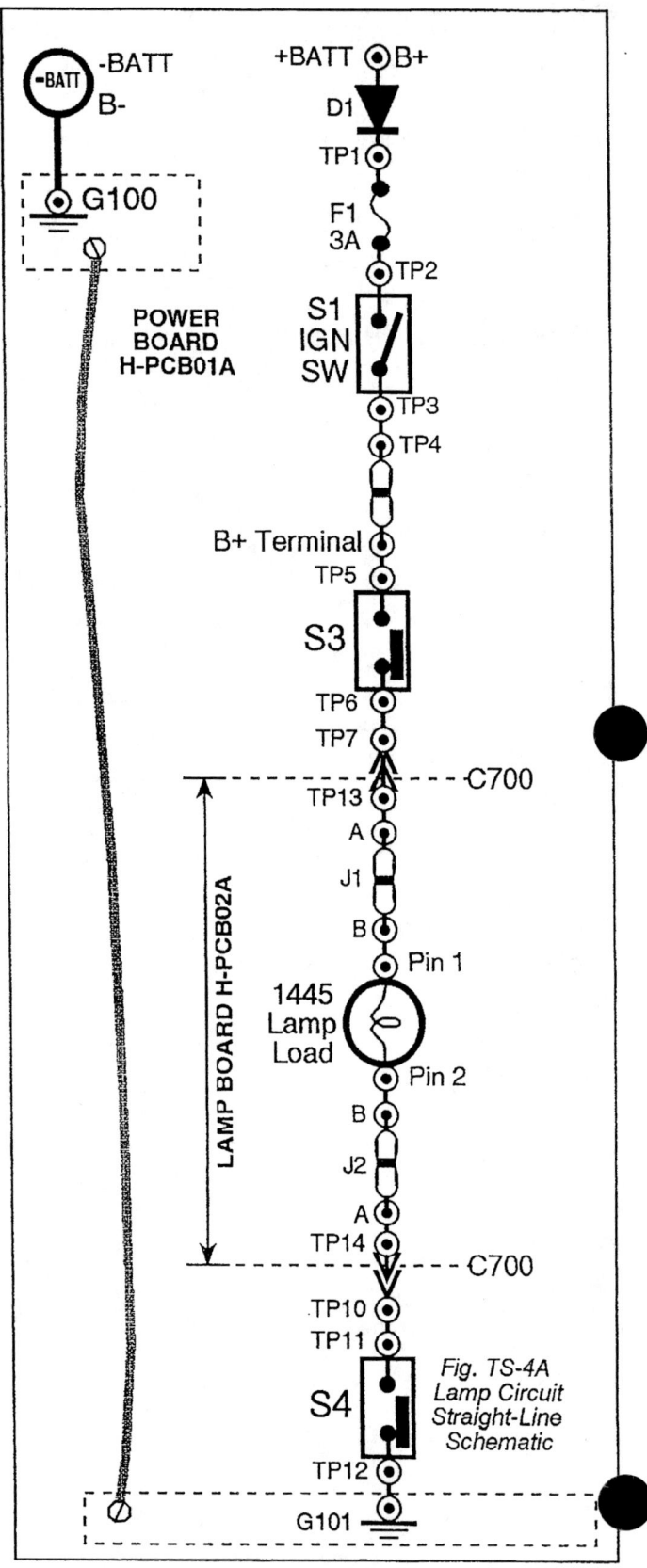

Fig. TS-4A Lamp Circuit Straight-Line Schematic

H-WB111A Page 53

Vehicle Electronics Hands-On Troubleshooting Training Program

VEEJER ENTERPRISES 3701 Lariat Lane, Garland, Texas 75042-5419
Phone: 972-276-9642 Fax: 972-276-8122 Email: contact-us@veejer.com Web Site: www.veejer.com

Problem 16
Consult Instructor Guide To Insert This Circuit Fault.
Refer to Schematic **Figure TS-4A** for this problem

Begin Troubleshooting After Problem Inserted

Performance of the load: _____

Troubleshooting Step 1: __TTS-1_____
Reading: _____ Good: ____ Bad: ____

Troubleshooting Step 2: __TTS-2_____
Reading: _____ Good: ____ Bad: ____

Troubleshooting Step 3: _____
Reading: _____ Good: ____ Bad: ____

Troubleshooting Step 4: _____
Reading: _____ Good: ____ Bad: ____

Troubleshooting Step 5: _____
Reading: _____ Good: ____ Bad: ____

Troubleshooting Step 6: _____
Reading: _____ Good: ____ Bad: ____

Troubleshooting Step 7: _____
Reading: _____ Good: ____ Bad: ____

Troubleshooting Step 8: _____
Reading: _____ Good: ____ Bad: ____

Troubleshooting Step 9: _____
Reading: _____ Good: ____ Bad: ____

Troubleshooting Step 10: _____
Reading: _____ Good: ____ Bad: ____

Troubleshooting Step 11: _____
Reading: _____ Good: ____ Bad: ____

Troubleshooting Step 12: _____
Reading: _____ Good: ____ Bad: ____

The Problem Is: _____

Notes:

REMINDERS:
Study at home: Remove the fault and restore the PCBs to normal operation after the problem is identified.
Study at Tech School: Follow the Instructor's directions on what to do.

Problem 17
Consult Instructor Guide To Insert This Circuit Fault.
Refer to Schematic **Figure TS-4A** for this problem

Begin Troubleshooting After Problem Inserted

Performance of the load: _____

Troubleshooting Step 1: __TTS-1_____
Reading: _____ Good: ____ Bad: ____

Troubleshooting Step 2: __TTS-2_____
Reading: _____ Good: ____ Bad: ____

Troubleshooting Step 3: _____
Reading: _____ Good: ____ Bad: ____

Troubleshooting Step 4: _____
Reading: _____ Good: ____ Bad: ____

Troubleshooting Step 5: _____
Reading: _____ Good: ____ Bad: ____

Troubleshooting Step 6: _____
Reading: _____ Good: ____ Bad: ____

Troubleshooting Step 7: _____
Reading: _____ Good: ____ Bad: ____

Troubleshooting Step 8: _____
Reading: _____ Good: ____ Bad: ____

Troubleshooting Step 9: _____
Reading: _____ Good: ____ Bad: ____

Troubleshooting Step 10: _____
Reading: _____ Good: ____ Bad: ____

Troubleshooting Step 11: _____
Reading: _____ Good: ____ Bad: ____

Troubleshooting Step 12: _____
Reading: _____ Good: ____ Bad: ____

The Problem Is: _____

Notes:

REMINDERS:
Study at home: Remove the fault and restore the PCBs to normal operation after the problem is identified.
Study at Tech School: Follow the Instructor's directions on what to do.

Vehicle Electronics Hands-On Troubleshooting Training Program

VEEJER ENTERPRISES 3701 Lariat Lane, Garland, Texas 75042-5419
Phone: 972-276-9642 Fax: 972-276-8122 Email: contact-us@veejer.com Web Site: www.veejer.com

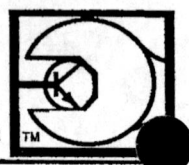

Problem 18
Consult Instructor Guide To Insert This Circuit Fault.
Refer to Schematic **Figure TS-4A** for this problem

Begin Troubleshooting After Problem Inserted

Performance of the load: _____

Troubleshooting Step 1: __TTS-1_____
Reading: _____ Good: ____ Bad: ____

Troubleshooting Step 2: __TTS-2_____
Reading: _____ Good: ____ Bad: ____

Troubleshooting Step 3: _____
Reading: _____ Good: ____ Bad: ____

Troubleshooting Step 4: _____
Reading: _____ Good: ____ Bad: ____

Troubleshooting Step 5: _____
Reading: _____ Good: ____ Bad: ____

Troubleshooting Step 6: _____
Reading: _____ Good: ____ Bad: ____

Troubleshooting Step 7: _____
Reading: _____ Good: ____ Bad: ____

Troubleshooting Step 8: _____
Reading: _____ Good: ____ Bad: ____

Troubleshooting Step 9: _____
Reading: _____ Good: ____ Bad: ____

Troubleshooting Step 10: _____
Reading: _____ Good: ____ Bad: ____

Troubleshooting Step 11: _____
Reading: _____ Good: ____ Bad: ____

Troubleshooting Step 12: _____
Reading: _____ Good: ____ Bad: ____

The Problem Is: _____

Notes:

REMINDERS:
Study at home: Remove the fault and restore the PCBs to normal operation after the problem is identified.
Study at Tech School: Follow the Instructor's directions on what to do.

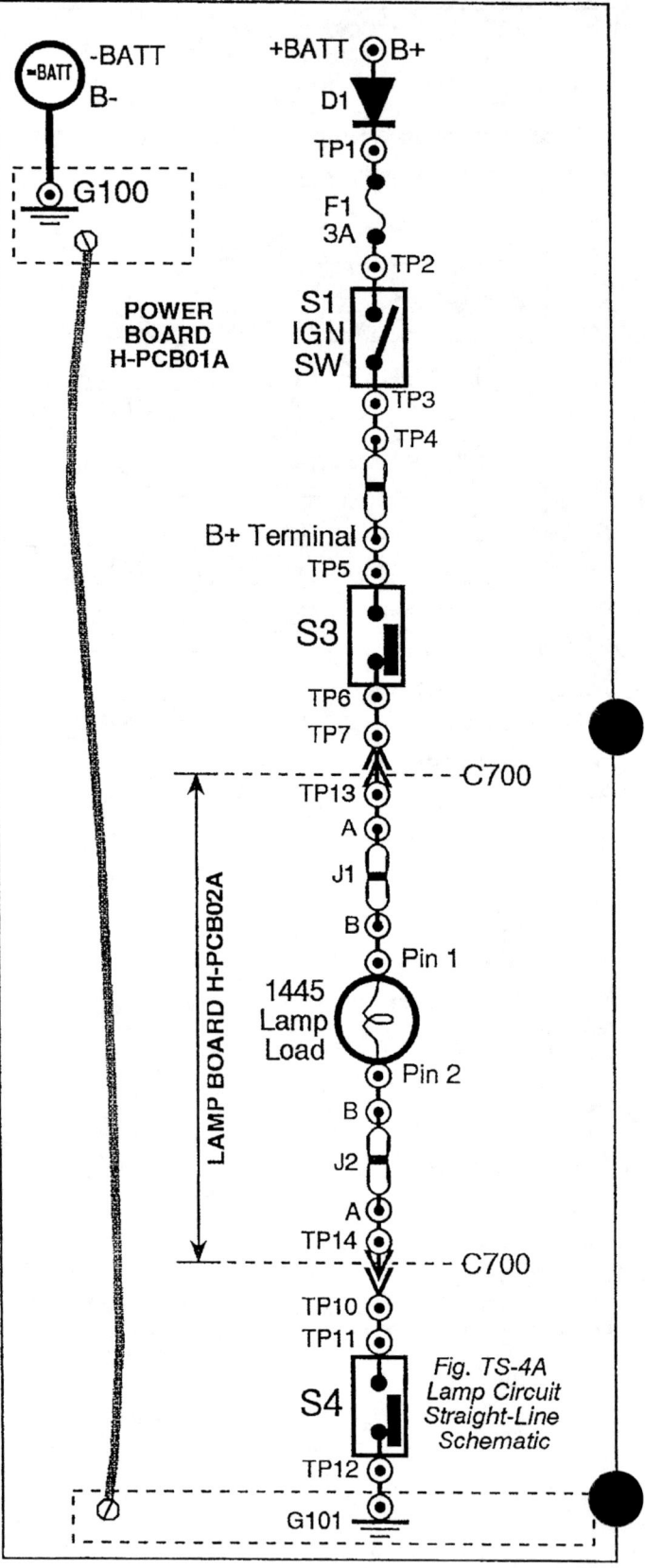

Fig. TS-4A Lamp Circuit Straight-Line Schematic

H-WB111A Page 55

Vehicle Electronics Hands-On Troubleshooting Training Program

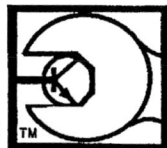

VEEJER ENTERPRISES 3701 Lariat Lane, Garland, Texas 75042-5419
Phone: 972-276-9642 Fax: 972-276-8122 Email: contact-us@veejer.com Web Site: www.veejer.com

Problem 21
Consult Instructor Guide To Insert This Circuit Fault.
Refer to Schematic **Figure TS-4A** for this problem

Begin Troubleshooting After Problem Inserted

Performance of the load: _____

Troubleshooting Step 1: __TTS-1_____
Reading: _____ Good: ____ Bad: ____

Troubleshooting Step 2: __TTS-2_____
Reading: _____ Good: ____ Bad: ____

Troubleshooting Step 3: _____
Reading: _____ Good: ____ Bad: ____

Troubleshooting Step 4: _____
Reading: _____ Good: ____ Bad: ____

Troubleshooting Step 5: _____
Reading: _____ Good: ____ Bad: ____

Troubleshooting Step 6: _____
Reading: _____ Good: ____ Bad: ____

Troubleshooting Step 7: _____
Reading: _____ Good: ____ Bad: ____

Troubleshooting Step 8: _____
Reading: _____ Good: ____ Bad: ____

Troubleshooting Step 9: _____
Reading: _____ Good: ____ Bad: ____

Troubleshooting Step 10: _____
Reading: _____ Good: ____ Bad: ____

Troubleshooting Step 11: _____
Reading: _____ Good: ____ Bad: ____

Troubleshooting Step 12: _____
Reading: _____ Good: ____ Bad: ____

The Problem Is: _____

Notes:

REMINDERS:
Study at home: Remove the fault and restore the PCBs to normal operation after the problem is identified.
Study at Tech School: Follow the Instructor's directions on what to do.

Problem 22
Consult Instructor Guide To Insert This Circuit Fault.
Refer to Schematic **Figure TS-4A** for this problem

Begin Troubleshooting After Problem Inserted

Performance of the load: _____

Troubleshooting Step 1: __TTS-1_____
Reading: _____ Good: ____ Bad: ____

Troubleshooting Step 2: __TTS-2_____
Reading: _____ Good: ____ Bad: ____

Troubleshooting Step 3: _____
Reading: _____ Good: ____ Bad: ____

Troubleshooting Step 4: _____
Reading: _____ Good: ____ Bad: ____

Troubleshooting Step 5: _____
Reading: _____ Good: ____ Bad: ____

Troubleshooting Step 6: _____
Reading: _____ Good: ____ Bad: ____

Troubleshooting Step 7: _____
Reading: _____ Good: ____ Bad: ____

Troubleshooting Step 8: _____
Reading: _____ Good: ____ Bad: ____

Troubleshooting Step 9: _____
Reading: _____ Good: ____ Bad: ____

Troubleshooting Step 10: _____
Reading: _____ Good: ____ Bad: ____

Troubleshooting Step 11: _____
Reading: _____ Good: ____ Bad: ____

Troubleshooting Step 12: _____
Reading: _____ Good: ____ Bad: ____

The Problem Is: _____

Notes:

REMINDERS:
Study at home: Remove the fault and restore the PCBs to normal operation after the problem is identified.
Study at Tech School: Follow the Instructor's directions on what to do.

Vehicle Electronics Hands-On Troubleshooting Training Program

VEEJER ENTERPRISES 3701 Lariat Lane, Garland, Texas 75042-5419
Phone: 972-276-9642 Fax: 972-276-8122 Email: contact-us@veejer.com Web Site: www.veejer.com

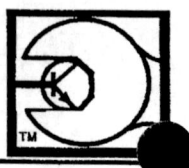

Problem 23
Consult Instructor Guide To Insert This Circuit Fault.
Refer to Schematic **Figure TS-4A** for this problem

Begin Troubleshooting After Problem Inserted

Performance of the load: _____

Troubleshooting Step 1: __TTS-1_____
Reading: _____ Good: ___ Bad: ___

Troubleshooting Step 2: __TTS-2_____
Reading: _____ Good: ___ Bad: ___

Troubleshooting Step 3: _____
Reading: _____ Good: ___ Bad: ___

Troubleshooting Step 4: _____
Reading: _____ Good: ___ Bad: ___

Troubleshooting Step 5: _____
Reading: _____ Good: ___ Bad: ___

Troubleshooting Step 6: _____
Reading: _____ Good: ___ Bad: ___

Troubleshooting Step 7: _____
Reading: _____ Good: ___ Bad: ___

Troubleshooting Step 8: _____
Reading: _____ Good: ___ Bad: ___

Troubleshooting Step 9: _____
Reading: _____ Good: ___ Bad: ___

Troubleshooting Step 10: _____
Reading: _____ Good: ___ Bad: ___

Troubleshooting Step 11: _____
Reading: _____ Good: ___ Bad: ___

Troubleshooting Step 12: _____
Reading: _____ Good: ___ Bad: ___

The Problem Is: _____

Notes:

REMINDERS:
Study at home: Remove the fault and restore the PCBs to normal operation after the problem is identified.
Study at Tech School: Follow the Instructor's directions on what to do.

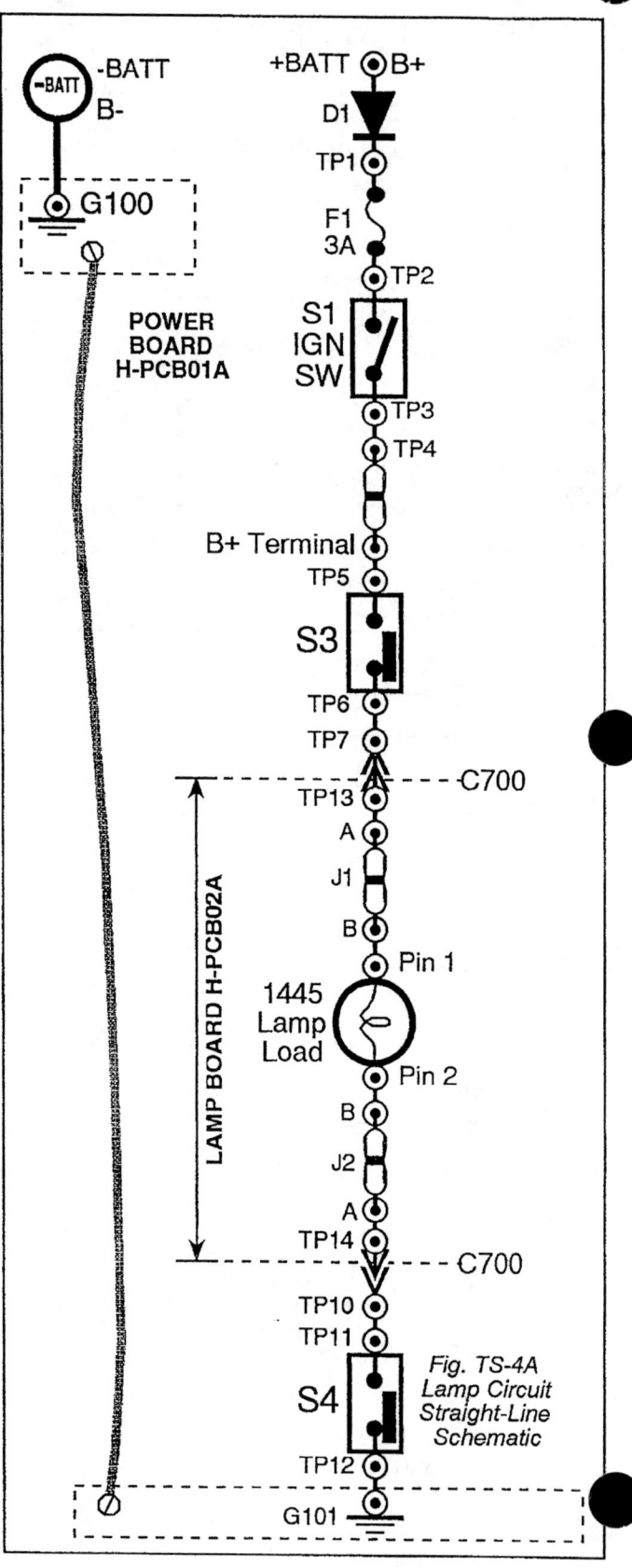

Fig. TS-4A Lamp Circuit Straight-Line Schematic

Copyright © 2015 VEEJER ENTERPRISES, Garland, Texas - All Rights Reserved   H-WB111A Page 57

Vehicle Electronics Hands-On Troubleshooting Training Program

VEEJER ENTERPRISES 3701 Lariat Lane, Garland, Texas 75042-5419
Phone: 972-276-9642 Fax: 972-276-8122 Email: contact-us@veejer.com Web Site: www.veejer.com

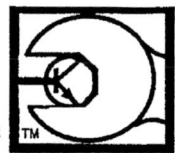

Problem 24
Consult Instructor Guide To Insert This Circuit Fault.
Refer to Schematic **Figure TS-4A** for this problem

Begin Troubleshooting After Problem Inserted

Performance of the load: _____

Troubleshooting Step 1: __TTS-1_____
Reading: _____ Good: ____ Bad: ____

Troubleshooting Step 2: __TTS-2_____
Reading: _____ Good: ____ Bad: ____

Troubleshooting Step 3: _____
Reading: _____ Good: ____ Bad: ____

Troubleshooting Step 4: _____
Reading: _____ Good: ____ Bad: ____

Troubleshooting Step 5: _____
Reading: _____ Good: ____ Bad: ____

Troubleshooting Step 6: _____
Reading: _____ Good: ____ Bad: ____

Troubleshooting Step 7: _____
Reading: _____ Good: ____ Bad: ____

Troubleshooting Step 8: _____
Reading: _____ Good: ____ Bad: ____

Troubleshooting Step 9: _____
Reading: _____ Good: ____ Bad: ____

Troubleshooting Step 10: _____
Reading: _____ Good: ____ Bad: ____

Troubleshooting Step 11: _____
Reading: _____ Good: ____ Bad: ____

Troubleshooting Step 12: _____
Reading: _____ Good: ____ Bad: ____

The Problem Is: _____

Notes:

REMINDERS:
Study at home: Remove the fault and restore the PCBs to normal operation after the problem is identified.
Study at Tech School: Follow the Instructor's directions on what to do.

Problem 26
Consult Instructor Guide To Insert This Circuit Fault.
Refer to Schematic **Figure TS-4A** for this problem

Begin Troubleshooting After Problem Inserted

Performance of the load: _____

Troubleshooting Step 1: __TTS-1_____
Reading: _____ Good: ____ Bad: ____

Troubleshooting Step 2: __TTS-2_____
Reading: _____ Good: ____ Bad: ____

Troubleshooting Step 3: _____
Reading: _____ Good: ____ Bad: ____

Troubleshooting Step 4: _____
Reading: _____ Good: ____ Bad: ____

Troubleshooting Step 5: _____
Reading: _____ Good: ____ Bad: ____

Troubleshooting Step 6: _____
Reading: _____ Good: ____ Bad: ____

Troubleshooting Step 7: _____
Reading: _____ Good: ____ Bad: ____

Troubleshooting Step 8: _____
Reading: _____ Good: ____ Bad: ____

Troubleshooting Step 9: _____
Reading: _____ Good: ____ Bad: ____

Troubleshooting Step 10: _____
Reading: _____ Good: ____ Bad: ____

Troubleshooting Step 11: _____
Reading: _____ Good: ____ Bad: ____

Troubleshooting Step 12: _____
Reading: _____ Good: ____ Bad: ____

The Problem Is: _____

Notes:

REMINDERS:
Study at home: Remove the fault and restore the PCBs to normal operation after the problem is identified.
Study at Tech School: Follow the Instructor's directions on what to do.

Vehicle Electronics Hands-On Troubleshooting Training Program

VEEJER ENTERPRISES 3701 Lariat Lane, Garland, Texas 75042-5419
Phone: 972-276-9642 Fax: 972-276-8122 Email: contact-us@veejer.com Web Site: www.veejer.com

Problem 28
Consult Instructor Guide To Insert This Circuit Fault.
Refer to Schematic **Figure TS-4A** for this problem

Begin Troubleshooting After Problem Inserted

Performance of the load: _____

Troubleshooting Step 1: __TTS-1_____
Reading: _____ Good: ___ Bad: ___

Troubleshooting Step 2: __TTS-2_____
Reading: _____ Good: ___ Bad: ___

Troubleshooting Step 3: _____
Reading: _____ Good: ___ Bad: ___

Troubleshooting Step 4: _____
Reading: _____ Good: ___ Bad: ___

Troubleshooting Step 5: _____
Reading: _____ Good: ___ Bad: ___

Troubleshooting Step 6: _____
Reading: _____ Good: ___ Bad: ___

Troubleshooting Step 7: _____
Reading: _____ Good: ___ Bad: ___

Troubleshooting Step 8: _____
Reading: _____ Good: ___ Bad: ___

Troubleshooting Step 9: _____
Reading: _____ Good: ___ Bad: ___

Troubleshooting Step 10: _____
Reading: _____ Good: ___ Bad: ___

Troubleshooting Step 11: _____
Reading: _____ Good: ___ Bad: ___

Troubleshooting Step 12: _____
Reading: _____ Good: ___ Bad: ___

The Problem Is: _____

Notes:

REMINDERS:
Study at home: Remove the fault and restore the PCBs to normal operation after the problem is identified.
Study at Tech School: Follow the Instructor's directions on what to do.

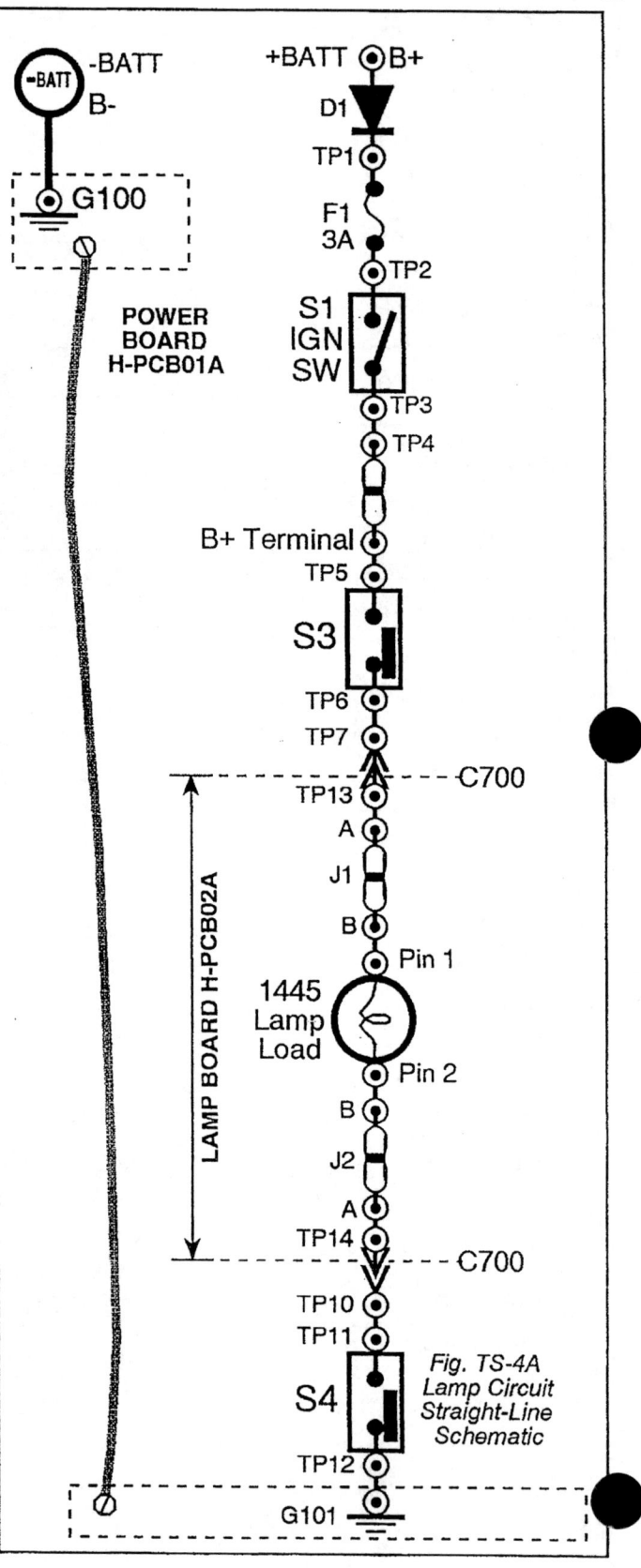

Fig. TS-4A
Lamp Circuit
Straight-Line
Schematic

Copyright © 2015 VEEJER ENTERPRISES, Garland, Texas - All Rights Reserved   H-WB111A Page 59

Vehicle Electronics Hands-On Troubleshooting Training Program

VEEJER ENTERPRISES 3701 Lariat Lane, Garland, Texas 75042-5419
Phone: 972-276-9642 Fax: 972-276-8122 Email: contact-us@veejer.com Web Site: www.veejer.com

---

Problem 29
Consult Instructor Guide To Insert This Circuit Fault.
Refer to Schematic **Figure TS-4A** for this problem

Begin Troubleshooting After Problem Inserted

Performance of the load: _____

Troubleshooting Step 1: __TTS-1_____
Reading: _____ Good: ____ Bad: ____

Troubleshooting Step 2: __TTS-2_____
Reading: _____ Good: ____ Bad: ____

Troubleshooting Step 3: _____
Reading: _____ Good: ____ Bad: ____

Troubleshooting Step 4: _____
Reading: _____ Good: ____ Bad: ____

Troubleshooting Step 5: _____
Reading: _____ Good: ____ Bad: ____

Troubleshooting Step 6: _____
Reading: _____ Good: ____ Bad: ____

Troubleshooting Step 7: _____
Reading: _____ Good: ____ Bad: ____

Troubleshooting Step 8: _____
Reading: _____ Good: ____ Bad: ____

Troubleshooting Step 9: _____
Reading: _____ Good: ____ Bad: ____

Troubleshooting Step 10: _____
Reading: _____ Good: ____ Bad: ____

Troubleshooting Step 11: _____
Reading: _____ Good: ____ Bad: ____

Troubleshooting Step 12: _____
Reading: _____ Good: ____ Bad: ____

The Problem Is: _____

Notes:

REMINDERS:
Study at home: Remove the fault and restore the PCBs to normal operation after the problem is identified.
Study at Tech School: Follow the Instructor's directions on what to do.

Problem 30
Consult Instructor Guide To Insert This Circuit Fault.
Refer to Schematic **Figure TS-4A** for this problem

Begin Troubleshooting After Problem Inserted

Performance of the load: _____

Troubleshooting Step 1: __TTS-1_____
Reading: _____ Good: ____ Bad: ____

Troubleshooting Step 2: __TTS-2_____
Reading: _____ Good: ____ Bad: ____

Troubleshooting Step 3: _____
Reading: _____ Good: ____ Bad: ____

Troubleshooting Step 4: _____
Reading: _____ Good: ____ Bad: ____

Troubleshooting Step 5: _____
Reading: _____ Good: ____ Bad: ____

Troubleshooting Step 6: _____
Reading: _____ Good: ____ Bad: ____

Troubleshooting Step 7: _____
Reading: _____ Good: ____ Bad: ____

Troubleshooting Step 8: _____
Reading: _____ Good: ____ Bad: ____

Troubleshooting Step 9: _____
Reading: _____ Good: ____ Bad: ____

Troubleshooting Step 10: _____
Reading: _____ Good: ____ Bad: ____

Troubleshooting Step 11: _____
Reading: _____ Good: ____ Bad: ____

Troubleshooting Step 12: _____
Reading: _____ Good: ____ Bad: ____

The Problem Is: _____

Notes:

REMINDERS:
Study at home: Remove the fault and restore the PCBs to normal operation after the problem is identified.
Study at Tech School: Follow the Instructor's directions on what to do.

Copyright © 2015 VEEJER ENTERPRISES, Garland, Texas - All Rights Reserved

Vehicle Electronics Hands-On Troubleshooting Training Program

VEEJER ENTERPRISES 3701 Lariat Lane, Garland, Texas 75042-5419
Phone: 972-276-9642   Fax: 972-276-8122   Email: contact-us@veejer.com   Web Site: www.veejer.com

Problem 31
Consult Instructor Guide To Insert This Circuit Fault.
Refer to Schematic **Figure TS-4A** for this problem

Begin Troubleshooting After Problem Inserted

Performance of the load: _____

Troubleshooting Step 1: __TTS-1_____
Reading: _____ Good: ___ Bad: ___

Troubleshooting Step 2: __TTS-2_____
Reading: _____ Good: ___ Bad: ___

Troubleshooting Step 3: _____
Reading: _____ Good: ___ Bad: ___

Troubleshooting Step 4: _____
Reading: _____ Good: ___ Bad: ___

Troubleshooting Step 5: _____
Reading: _____ Good: ___ Bad: ___

Troubleshooting Step 6: _____
Reading: _____ Good: ___ Bad: ___

Troubleshooting Step 7: _____
Reading: _____ Good: ___ Bad: ___

Troubleshooting Step 8: _____
Reading: _____ Good: ___ Bad: ___

Troubleshooting Step 9: _____
Reading: _____ Good: ___ Bad: ___

Troubleshooting Step 10: _____
Reading: _____ Good: ___ Bad: ___

Troubleshooting Step 11: _____
Reading: _____ Good: ___ Bad: ___

Troubleshooting Step 12: _____
Reading: _____ Good: ___ Bad: ___

The Problem Is: _____

Notes:

REMINDERS:
Study at home: Remove the fault and restore the PCBs to normal operation after the problem is identified.
Study at Tech School: Follow the Instructor's directions on what to do.

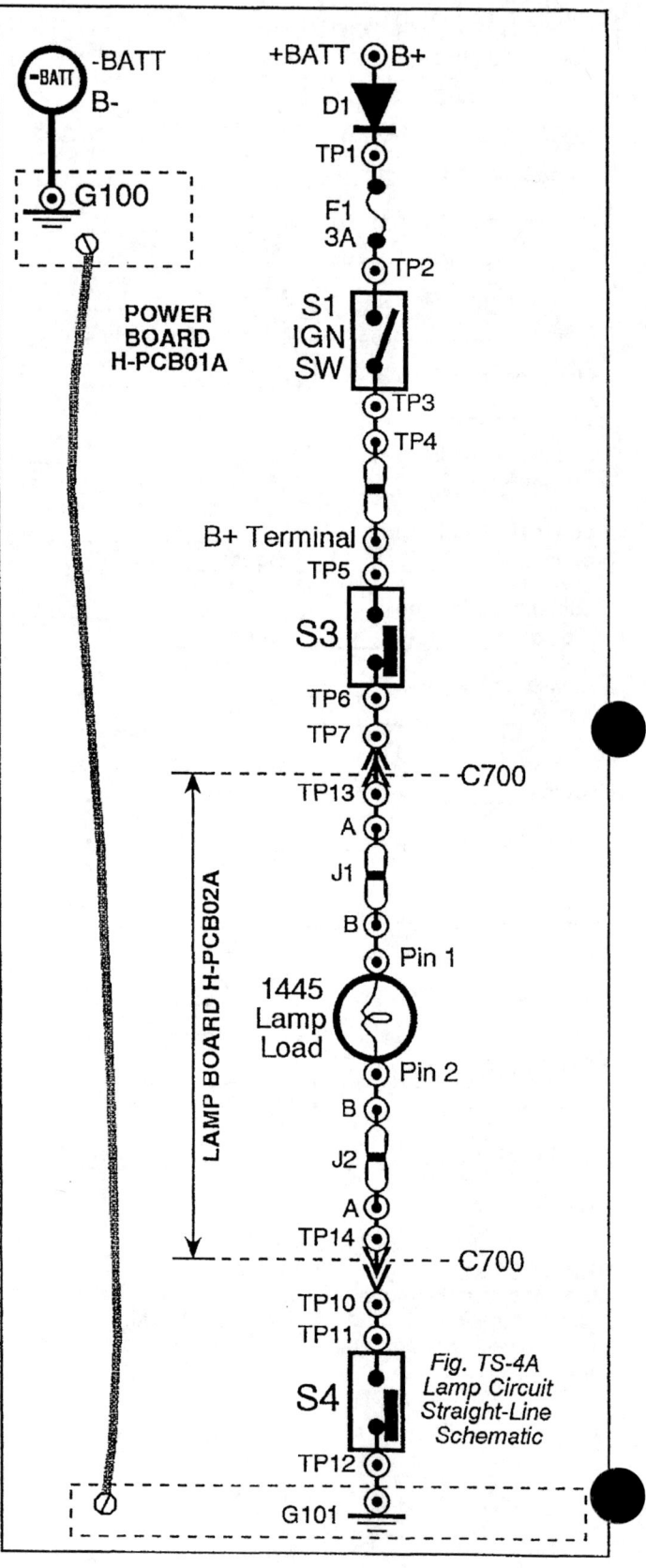

Fig. TS-4A
Lamp Circuit
Straight-Line
Schematic

Copyright © 2015 VEEJER ENTERPRISES, Garland, Texas - All Rights Reserved

Vehicle Electronics Hands-On Troubleshooting Training Program

VEEJER ENTERPRISES 3701 Lariat Lane, Garland, Texas 75042-5419
Phone: 972-276-9642   Fax: 972-276-8122   Email: contact-us@veejer.com   Web Site: www.veejer.com

Problem 32
Consult Instructor Guide To Insert This Circuit Fault.
Refer to Schematic **Figure TS-4A** for this problem

Begin Troubleshooting After Problem Inserted

Performance of the load: _____

Troubleshooting Step 1: __TTS-1_____
Reading: _____ Good: ____ Bad: ____

Troubleshooting Step 2: __TTS-2_____
Reading: _____ Good: ____ Bad: ____

Troubleshooting Step 3: _____
Reading: _____ Good: ____ Bad: ____

Troubleshooting Step 4: _____
Reading: _____ Good: ____ Bad: ____

Troubleshooting Step 5: _____
Reading: _____ Good: ____ Bad: ____

Troubleshooting Step 6: _____
Reading: _____ Good: ____ Bad: ____

Troubleshooting Step 7: _____
Reading: _____ Good: ____ Bad: ____

Troubleshooting Step 8: _____
Reading: _____ Good: ____ Bad: ____

Troubleshooting Step 9: _____
Reading: _____ Good: ____ Bad: ____

Troubleshooting Step 10: _____
Reading: _____ Good: ____ Bad: ____

Troubleshooting Step 11: _____
Reading: _____ Good: ____ Bad: ____

Troubleshooting Step 12: _____
Reading: _____ Good: ____ Bad: ____

The Problem Is: _____

Notes:

REMINDERS:
Study at home: Remove the fault and restore the PCBs to normal operation after the problem is identified.
Study at Tech School: Follow the Instructor's directions on what to do.

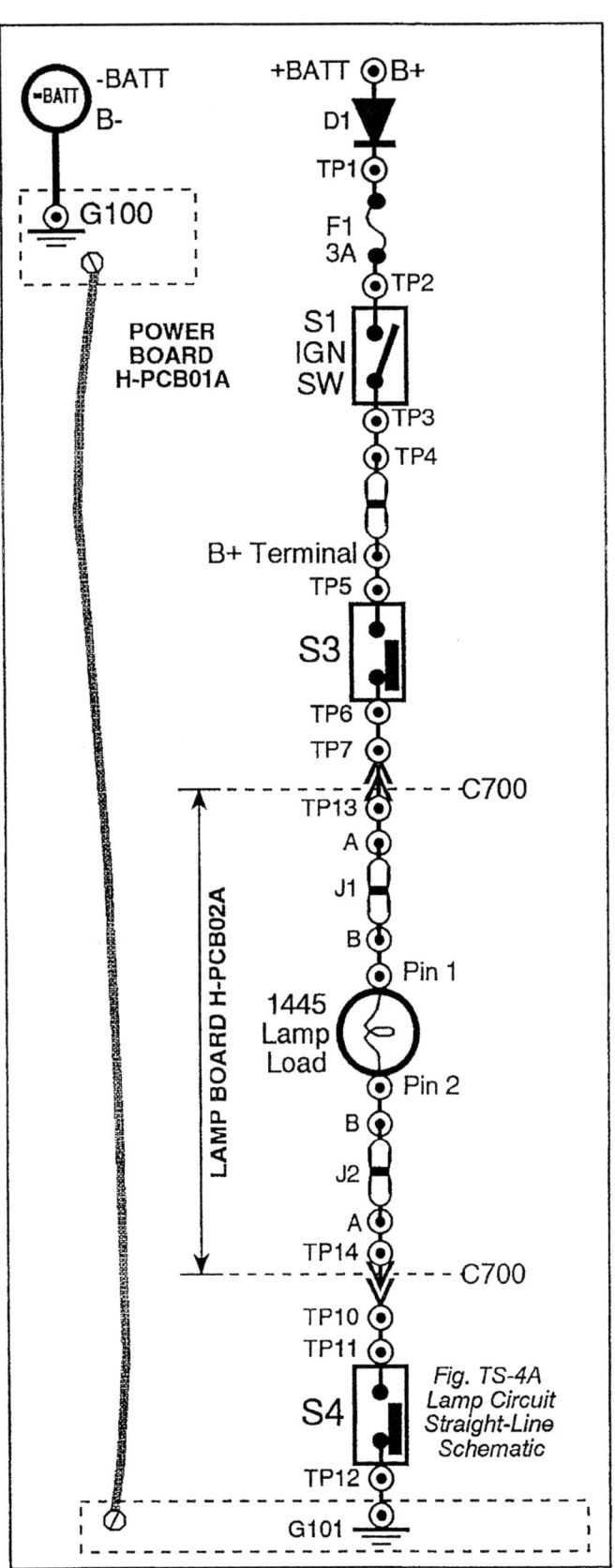

Fig. TS-4A Lamp Circuit Straight-Line Schematic

Copyright © 2015 VEEJER ENTERPRISES, Garland, Texas - All Rights Reserved   H-WB111A Page 62

Troubleshooting Short-to-Ground Problems

You will encounter four problems with either a shorted load or a short-to-ground on the voltage side of the circuit placed at various points in the voltage side of the circuit.

When troubleshooting a short-to-ground on the voltage side you should be able to identify exactly where in the voltage side wiring, between which two points in the circuit, the short-to-ground exists. Once you identify if the load is shorted or exactly where a short-to-ground exists on the voltage side of the circuit you have completed the problem.

Warning: DO NOT LEAVE A GOOD FUSE IN F1 WHILE TROUBLESHOOTING ANY PROBLEM WITH A SHORTED LOAD OR A SHORT TO GROUND ON THE VOLTAGE SIDE.

IF THE FUSE DOESN'T BLOW THE POWER SUPPLY WILL GET HOT AND POSSIBLY BURN UP AS WELL AS DAMAGE THE CIRCUIT BOARDS.

THIS TYPE OF DAMAGE VOIDS THE WARRANTY. EITHER PUT A BLOWN FUSE IN F1 OR REMOVE F1 COMPLETELY IF A BLOWN FUSE IS NOT AVAILABLE TO SUBSTITUTE FOR F1!

IF THE POWER SUPPLY IS BURNED UP OR THE CIRCUIT BOARDS ARE DAMAGED IN THIS WAY THE WARRANTY IS VOIDED.

Vehicle Electronics Hands-On Troubleshooting Training Program

VEEJER ENTERPRISES 3701 Lariat Lane, Garland, Texas 75042-5419
ne: 972-276-9642 Fax: 972-276-8122 Email: contact-us@veejer.com Web Site: www.veejer.com

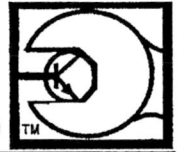

Before Troubleshooting Short-to-Ground Problems 19, 20, 25, & 27 Read This

Four problems have a short to ground. That is, the voltage side of the circuit (the insulated wire side) makes electrical contact with ground causing a short-to-ground that blows Fuse F1. A short-to-ground condition should never happen since it electrically removes the load resistance from the circuit which is the only resistance in the circuit to limit electron current.

If the circuit looses the load's resistance, circuit current increases through the fuse because no resistance is left in the circuit's remaining current path. Current rapidly increases and the fuse blows to shut the circuit OFF. Before you tackle these short-to-ground problems read this section explaining use of an ohmmeter to indicate whether or not a short exists in the load or the voltage side of a circuit.

> These lessons cover ohmmeter operation:
> **Lesson 8** Analog & Digital Ohmmeters
> **Lesson 9** Troubleshooting with Ohmmeters
> **Lesson 25** Troubleshooting Short Circuits

Notice the DMM's digital readout when a digital ohmmeter is placed on the **Ohms (Ω) function** and the test leads probe tips are NOT making contact with each other. Some digital ohmmeters read a "1" or "OUCH" when indicating an OPEN between the test lead probe tips. However, most ohmmeters are now using the *"OL"* indication as the industry standard. Now touch the ohmmeter test leads probe tips together and note the reading changes to less than 0.3 ohms which represents the test leads "see" each other through the resistance 0.3 ohms contained in the test leads.

Figure C shows the voltage (insulated) side of the circuit conductor between TP3 and TP4 is **NOT** shorted-to-ground which is the normal condition.

Fig. C Normally conductor is isolated from chassis

The wire conductor is not shorted to (touching) ground (or the chassis) due to the wire's insulation material preventing (insulating) the wire conductor from making contact with the chassis. The circuit can be tested for a short-to-ground with a digital ohmmeter as shown in Figure D.

> NEVER CONNECT AN OHMMETER TO A LIVE CIRCUIT OR DAMAGE TO THE CIRCUIT & OHMMETER MAY RESULT. ALWAYS REMOVE B+ POWER TO THE CIRCUIT BEFORE CONNECTING AN OHMMETER TO THE CIRCUIT.

The ohmmeter's **black test lead** (COM) connects to ground, the chassis or better yet the negative terminal of the vehicle's battery (-BATT). Our illustrations D and F show the black test lead connected to the chassis to help visually explain the reading of the ohmmeter during this test procedure. **The red test lead touches the conductor while the circuit is powered down.**

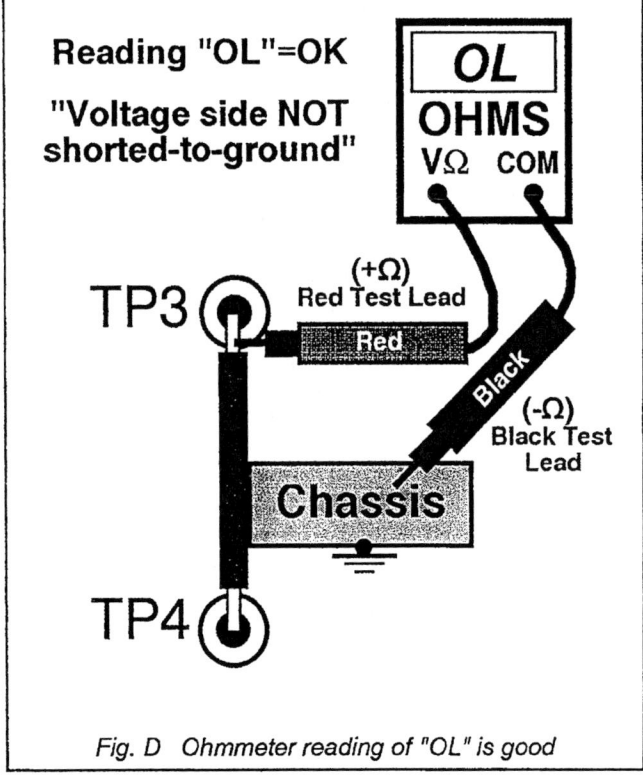

Fig. D Ohmmeter reading of "OL" is good

Since the wire conductor between TP3 and TP4 is NOT shorted to ground the ohmmeter indicates "OL" in Figure D. This represents no electrical contact exists between the two ohmmeter test leads. They don't "see" each other therefore the voltage side conductor wire is NOT shorted-to-ground (touching the chassis).

If the insulation becomes penetrated as is shown in

Vehicle Electronics Hands-On Troubleshooting Training Program

VEEJER ENTERPRISES 3701 Lariat Lane, Garland, Texas 75042-5419
Phone: 972-276-9642 Fax: 972-276-8122 Email: contact-us@veejer.com Web Site: www.veejer.com

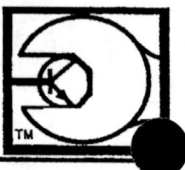

Figure E where the wire rubs against the chassis long enough to penetrate the insulation, the wire conductor makes contact with the chassis causing a "short-to-ground" condition in the circuit. The fuse blows from the high current through the shorted circuit. A new fuse blows as soon as the circuit is turned back ON until the short-to-ground is corrected.

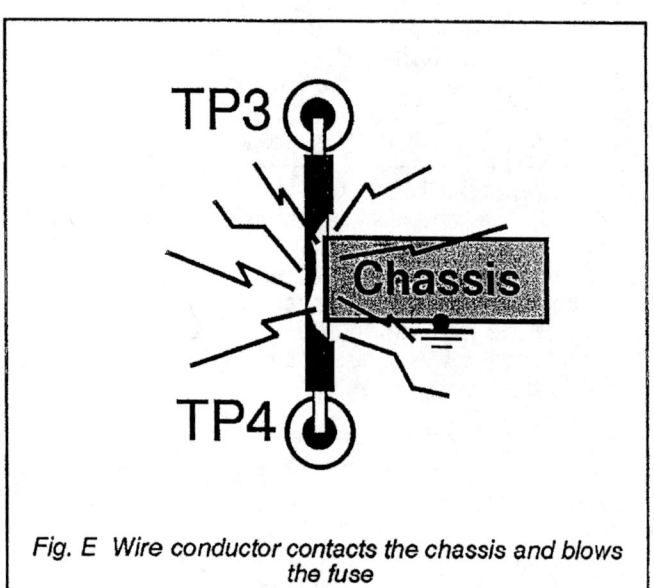

Fig. E Wire conductor contacts the chassis and blows the fuse

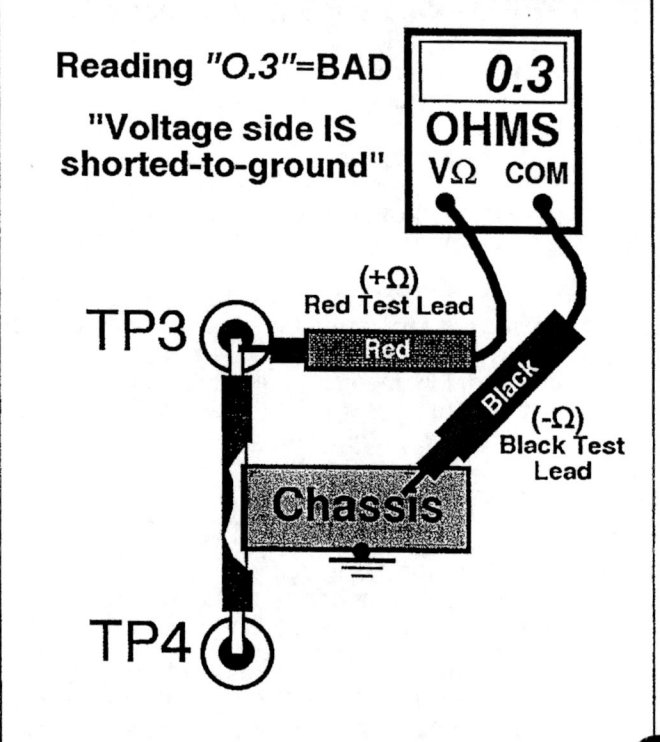

Fig. F Ohmmeter detects a low resistance on the voltage side wiring to detect a short-to-ground has occurred.

In Figure F the ohmmeter is connected to the circuit with the short-to-ground. The black test lead connects to the chassis. The red test lead connects to the wire conductor when the circuit is powered down or turned OFF. Now the ohmmeter's red and black test leads can "see" each other through the short-to-ground location and indicate a low resistance reading.

The ohmmeter indicates a low resistance reading of a few tenths of an ohm due to the few tenths of an ohm resistance detected in the ohmmeter's test leads. (Digital ohmmeters are able to indicate resistance to the tenth of an ohm.)

This method of troubleshooting a short-to-ground with a digital ohmmeter is the fastest way to identify when and where in a circuit a short-to-ground exists. Learn this ohmmeter troubleshooting procedure with the Power and Lamp Boards. Then follow the procedure exactly the same way in a vehicle with a blown fuse to pinpoint where the short-to-ground is in the vehicle. Remember, a short-to-ground could be one of two things.

A. shorted load

B. voltage side short to ground.

Troubleshooting Shorts-to-Ground in The Power Board and Lamp Board

Let the ohmmeter do the work of indicating where the short-to-ground is located in a circuit. Follow these test procedures. Connect the ohmmeter black test lead to -BATT. Connect the ohmmeter red test lead to the cold side (TP2 side) of the fuse. Close all switches in the circuit. That's S1 and S3 on the Power Board. The short-to-ground will appear on the ohmmeter as a low resistance. Now disconnect different parts of the circuit until an *OL* reading is obtained which indicates what was last disconnected contained the short-to-ground. First toggle S1 OFF (Down). If the reading goes to *OL* it indicates the short-to-ground is on the TP3 side of S1. Move the read test lead to TP3 to continue troubleshooting with S1 OFF.

Open S3. If the reading goes to *OL* the short to ground is on the TP6 side of S3. If the reading stays low the short-to-ground is on the TP5 side of S3.

Remove the zero ohm resistor between the B+ terminal and TP4. Touch each terminal, either TP4 or the B+ terminal with the red ohmmeter test lead. The wire that is shorted to ground reads a low resistance while the wire that is not shorted to ground reads *OL*.

If the short-to-ground is on the TP6 side of S3 remove J1 on the Lamp Board. Touch Pins A and B of J1 with the ohmmeter red test lead to see which side of J1 (A or B) is shorted-to-ground.

Vehicle Electronics Hands-On Troubleshooting Training Program

VEEJER ENTERPRISES 3701 Lariat Lane, Garland, Texas 75042-5419
Phone: 972-276-9642 Fax: 972-276-8122 Email: contact-us@veejer.com Web Site: www.veejer.com

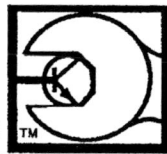

Problem 19
Consult Instructor Guide To Insert This Circuit Fault.
Refer to **Figure 26 on next page** for this problem.
Special Instructions: **Remove Fuse F1**
Scan the top of the PCBs before starting to troubleshoot.

**Begin Troubleshooting After Problem Inserted
Follow with the schematic in Fig. 26
on the next page.**

Performance of the load: __Fuse Blown-Lamp dead__

Note: TTS-1 is 0 volt. Vc is traced back and B+ is found on the hot side of Fuse F1 but not the cold side which means the fuse is blown. A fuse blows because current exceeds fuse current rating.

There are two possibilities that blew the fuse:
(a.) very low load resistance or shorted load
(b.) voltage side of the circuit shorted-to-ground.

Follow these troubleshooting steps:

(1) Disconnect the Power Supply from the wall socket before connecting the DMM's ohmmeter test leads to the circuit boards.

(2) Place the digital ohmmeter on the 200 ohm range or select Ω (Ohms) if your DMM auto ranges. Connect test leads to the PCBs as shown in Figure H-018C on the next page.

(3) CLOSE all switches (S1, S3, S4) to complete the circuit path to ground. The ohmmeter should read about 0 ohms to indicate a short exists in the circuit that blew the fuse. The ohmmeter reading may not be exactly 0.0 ohms due to resistance in the wiring. If the DMM resistance reading is much less than load resistance (remember a #1445 lamp is 10-15 ohms) then the DMM's ohmmeter is indicating the short-to-ground is present or the DMM "sees" the short-to-ground. You have to find it.

(4) Try disconnecting the load (unplug the lamp) first to eliminate a low resistance or shorted load. If the load is shorted the ohmmeter will change to "OL" when the shorted load is removed from the circuit. If the load is not shorted the ohmmeter will continue to indicate 0 ohms which means the short is in the wiring of the voltage side of the circuit.

(5) Slide S3 DOWN to OPEN the switch. If the short-to-ground is above the switch (TP5 side of the switch) the DMM reading stays 0. If the short-to-ground is below S3 (TP6 side of the switch) the DMM readings changes to OL because the DMM's ohmmeter can no longer "see" the short-to-ground on the TP6 side of S3.

(6) You should notice the DMM reading stayed at 0 ohms indicating the short-to-ground is on the TP5 side of S3. We now know the short-to-ground is between the cold side of Fuse F1 and TP5.

(7) Carefully disconnect the 0ΩR between the B+ Terminal and TP4 and notice the DMM reading stays at 0 ohms because the DMM still "sees" the short-to-ground.

(8) Toggle the Ignition Switch S1 DOWN and notice the DMM reading goes to OL. This means the circuit between the cold side of F1 and S1 (TP2) is NOT shorted-to-ground. The short has to be on the cold side of S1 (TP3 side of S1).

(9) Move the DMMs Red ohmmeter test lead to TP3 and notice the reading goes down to 0 ohm again. Therefore the wire from TP3 to TP4 is shorted-to-ground.

Now troubleshoot the same problem:

Start all over. Repeat items #1, 2, and 3 from the previous column and start troubleshooting. Write down each troubleshooting step.

Troubleshooting Step 1: _____
Reading: _____ Good: ____ Bad: ____

Troubleshooting Step 2: _____
Reading: _____ Good: ____ Bad: ____

Troubleshooting Step 3: _____
Reading: _____ Good: ____ Bad: ____

Troubleshooting Step 4: _____
Reading: _____ Good: ____ Bad: ____

Troubleshooting Step 5: _____
Reading: _____ Good: ____ Bad: ____

Troubleshooting Step 6: _____
Reading: _____ Good: ____ Bad: ____

Troubleshooting Step 7: _____
Reading: _____ Good: ____ Bad: ____

Troubleshooting Step 8: _____
Reading: _____ Good: ____ Bad: ____

Troubleshooting Step 9: _____
Reading: _____ Good: ____ Bad: ____

Troubleshooting Step 10: _____
Reading: _____ Good: ____ Bad: ____

Troubleshooting Step 11: _____
Reading: _____ Good: ____ Bad: ____

Troubleshooting Step 12: _____
Reading: _____ Good: ____ Bad: ____

The Problem Is: _____

Notes:

Vehicle Electronics Hands-On Troubleshooting Training Program

VEEJER ENTERPRISES 3701 Lariat Lane, Garland, Texas 75042-5419
Phone: 972-276-9642 Fax: 972-276-8122 Email: contact-us@veejer.com Web Site: www.veejer.com

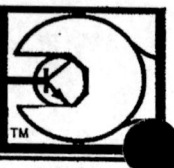

Problem 20
Consult Instructor Guide To Insert This Circuit Fault.
Refer to Schematic in **Figure 26** for this problem
Remove Fuse F1

Begin Troubleshooting After Problem Inserted

Performance of the load: _____

Troubleshooting Step 1: _____
Reading: _____ Good: ___ Bad: ___

Troubleshooting Step 2: _____
Reading: _____ Good: ___ Bad: ___

Troubleshooting Step 3: _____
Reading: _____ Good: ___ Bad: ___

Troubleshooting Step 4: _____
Reading: _____ Good: ___ Bad: ___

Troubleshooting Step 5: _____
Reading: _____ Good: ___ Bad: ___

Troubleshooting Step 6: _____
Reading: _____ Good: ___ Bad: ___

Troubleshooting Step 7: _____
Reading: _____ Good: ___ Bad: ___

Troubleshooting Step 8: _____
Reading: _____ Good: ___ Bad: ___

Troubleshooting Step 9: _____
Reading: _____ Good: ___ Bad: ___

Troubleshooting Step 10: _____
Reading: _____ Good: ___ Bad: ___

Troubleshooting Step 11: _____
Reading: _____ Good: ___ Bad: ___

Troubleshooting Step 12: _____
Reading: _____ Good: ___ Bad: ___

The Problem Is: _____

Notes:

REMINDERS:
Study at home: Remove the fault and restore the PCBs to normal operation after the problem is identified.
Study at Tech School: Follow the Instructor's directions on what to do.

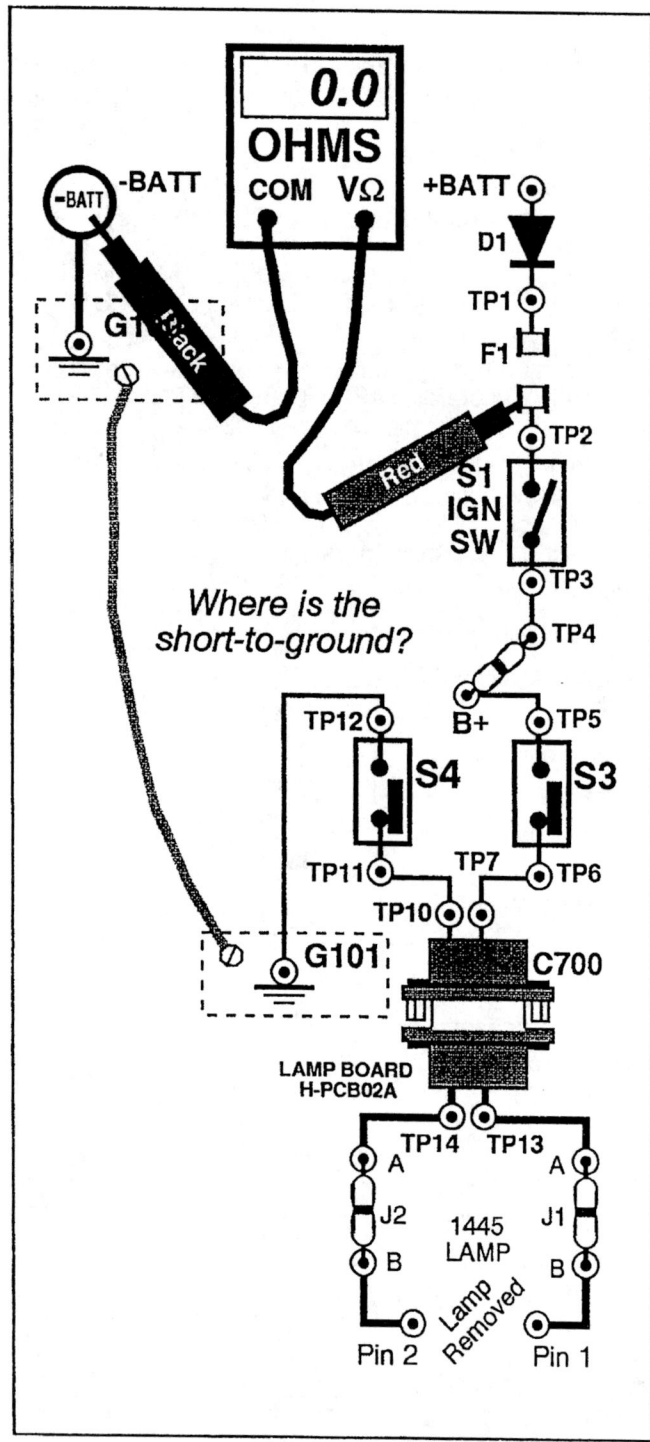

Fig. 26
Checking circuit for a short-to-ground on the voltage side with a DMM' ohmmeter grounded at -BATT

Vehicle Electronics Hands-On Troubleshooting Training Program

VEEJER ENTERPRISES 3701 Lariat Lane, Garland, Texas 75042-5419
Phone: 972-276-9642   Fax: 972-276-8122   Email: contact-us@veejer.com   Web Site: www.veejer.com

Problem 25
Consult Instructor Guide To Insert This Circuit Fault.
Refer to Schematic in **Figure 26** for this problem
Remove Fuse F1

Begin Troubleshooting After Problem Inserted

Performance of the load: _____

Troubleshooting Step 1: _____
Reading: _____ Good: ____ Bad: ____

Troubleshooting Step 2: _____
Reading: _____ Good: ____ Bad: ____

Troubleshooting Step 3: _____
Reading: _____ Good: ____ Bad: ____

Troubleshooting Step 4: _____
Reading: _____ Good: ____ Bad: ____

Troubleshooting Step 5: _____
Reading: _____ Good: ____ Bad: ____

Troubleshooting Step 6: _____
Reading: _____ Good: ____ Bad: ____

Troubleshooting Step 7: _____
Reading: _____ Good: ____ Bad: ____

Troubleshooting Step 8: _____
Reading: _____ Good: ____ Bad: ____

Troubleshooting Step 9: _____
Reading: _____ Good: ____ Bad: ____

Troubleshooting Step 10: _____
Reading: _____ Good: ____ Bad: ____

Troubleshooting Step 11: _____
Reading: _____ Good: ____ Bad: ____

Troubleshooting Step 12: _____
Reading: _____ Good: ____ Bad: ____

The Problem Is: _____

Notes:

REMINDERS:
Study at home: Remove the fault and restore the PCBs to normal operation after the problem is identified.
Study at Tech School: Follow the Instructor's directions on what to do.

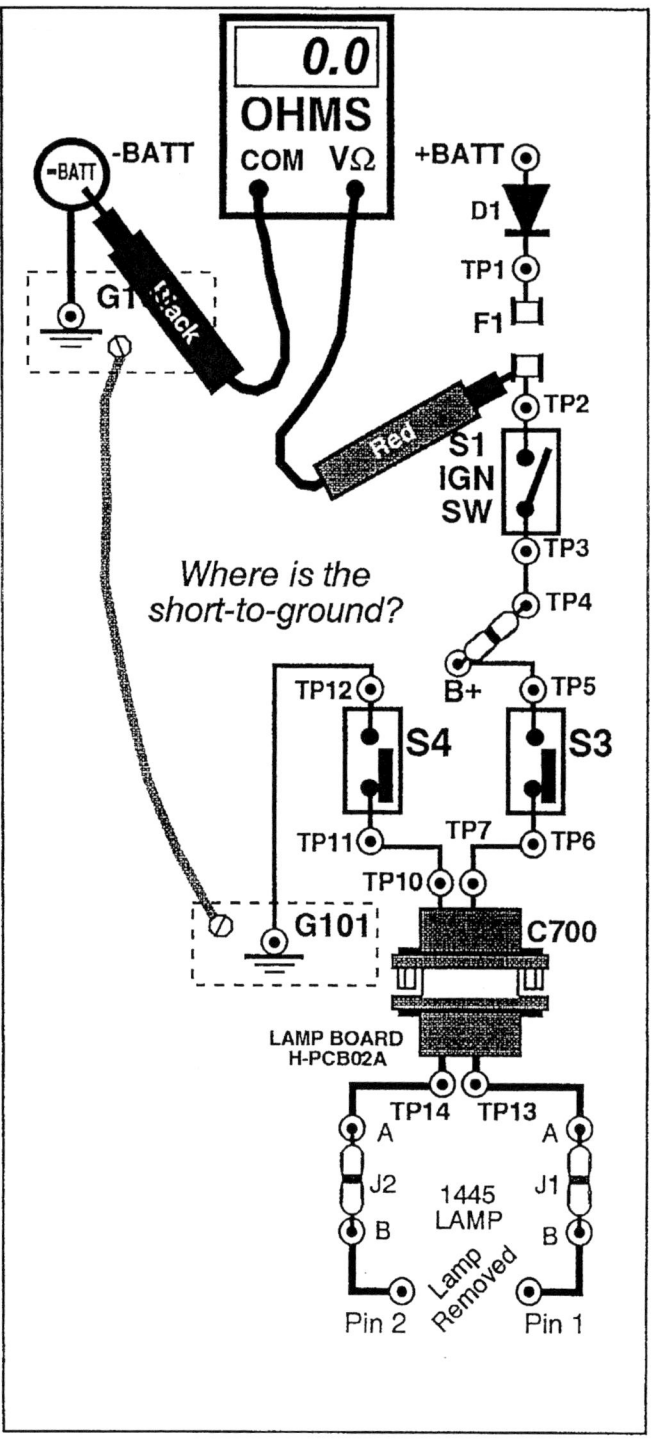

Fig. 26
Checking circuit for a short-to-ground on the voltage side with a DMM' ohmmeter grounded at -BATT

Vehicle Electronics Hands-On Troubleshooting Training Program

VEEJER ENTERPRISES 3701 Lariat Lane, Garland, Texas 75042-5419
Phone: 972-276-9642   Fax: 972-276-8122   Email: contact-us@veejer.com   Web Site: www.veejer.com

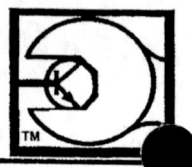

Problem 27
Consult Instructor Guide To Insert This Circuit Fault.
Refer to Schematic in **Figure 26** for this problem
Remove Fuse F1

Begin Troubleshooting After Problem Inserted

Performance of the load: _____

Troubleshooting Step 1: _____
Reading: _____ Good: ___ Bad: ___

Troubleshooting Step 2: _____
Reading: _____ Good: ___ Bad: ___

Troubleshooting Step 3: _____
Reading: _____ Good: ___ Bad: ___

Troubleshooting Step 4: _____
Reading: _____ Good: ___ Bad: ___

Troubleshooting Step 5: _____
Reading: _____ Good: ___ Bad: ___

Troubleshooting Step 6: _____
Reading: _____ Good: ___ Bad: ___

Troubleshooting Step 7: _____
Reading: _____ Good: ___ Bad: ___

Troubleshooting Step 8: _____
Reading: _____ Good: ___ Bad: ___

Troubleshooting Step 9: _____
Reading: _____ Good: ___ Bad: ___

Troubleshooting Step 10: _____
Reading: _____ Good: ___ Bad: ___

Troubleshooting Step 11: _____
Reading: _____ Good: ___ Bad: ___

Troubleshooting Step 12: _____
Reading: _____ Good: ___ Bad: ___

The Problem Is: _____

Notes:

REMINDERS:
Study at home: Remove the fault and restore the PCBs to normal operation after the problem is identified.
Study at Tech School: Follow the Instructor's directions on what to do.

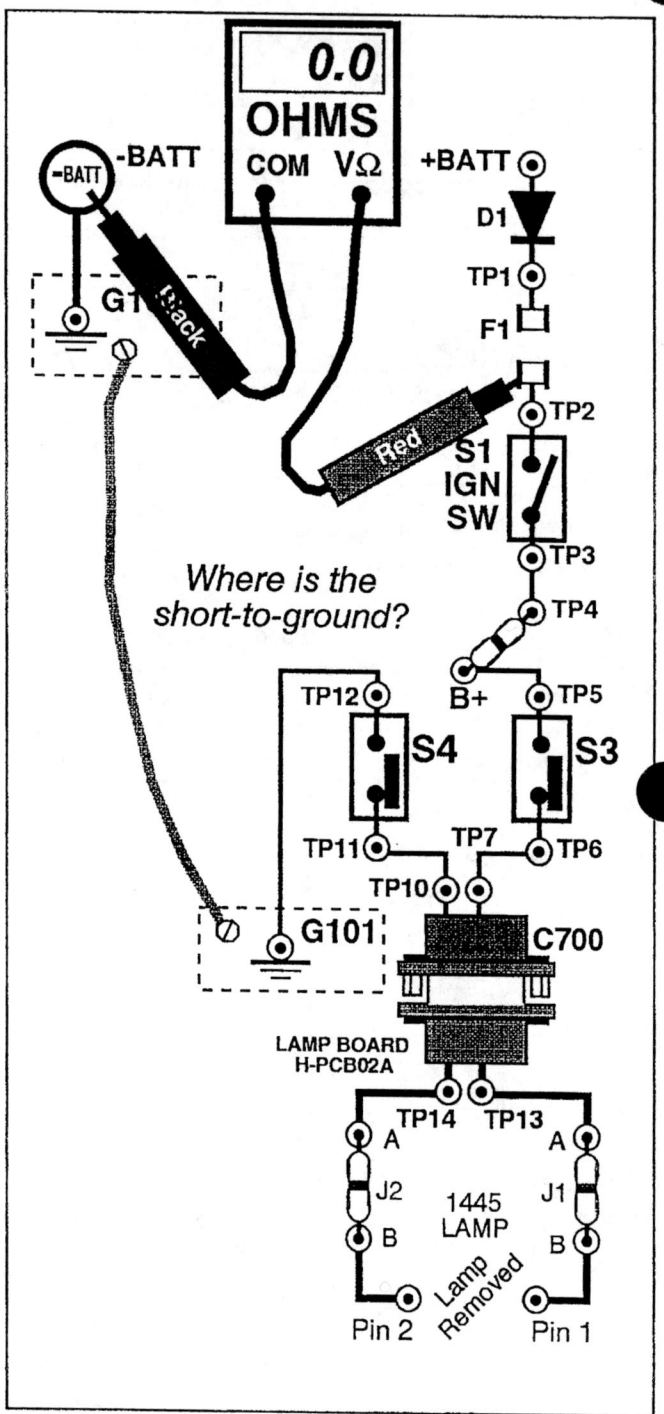

Fig. 26
Checking circuit for a short-to-ground on the voltage side with a DMM' ohmmeter grounded at -BATT

H-WB111A   Page 69

Vehicle Electronics Hands-On Troubleshooting Training Program

VEEJER ENTERPRISES 3701 Lariat Lane, Garland, Texas 75042-5419
Phone: 972-276-9642   Fax: 972-276-8122   Email: contact-us@veejer.com   Web Site: www.veejer.com

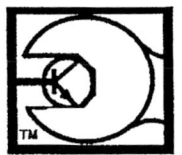

Tips On Maintaining Troubleshooting Skill
Practice – Practice – Practice – Practice

Once all the troubleshooting problems have been completed for the first time you can still use the PCBs to keep your troubleshooting skills sharp and ready to go if you continue practicing by repeating the troubleshooting exercises at random. Remember the old "**use it or lose it**" adage? It's true.

Here are three ways to use the PCBs over and over to keep your troubleshooting skills sharp.

Do not use U10, U11, U12 or U-NO3 located in the Hot-at-all-times B+ feed to TP9 locations for inserting problems with the Lamp Board Circuit since they are not used in the Lamp Circuit.

(1) Insert OPENs:
Randomly remove a **zero ohm resistor** from the bottom of the PCBs to insert an OPEN connection in the circuit. Do not use U10, U11, U12. Troubleshoot from the top of the PCBs in the normal manner. After you find the OPEN circuit problem reinstall a **zero ohm resistor**.

(2) Insert Voltage Drops (Vds):
Randomly select a resistor from the Resistor Bag-Lamp Circuit. Then remove a randomly selected **zero ohm resistor** from the bottom of the PCBs and insert the resistor in its place to create a Vd at some point in the circuit. Do not use U10, U11, U12 or any U-NOx location. Begin troubleshooting in the normal manner from the top of the PCBs. After you find the Vd problem remove the resistor and reinstall a **zero ohm resistor** back into that U-jumper location.

> **Do not insert a resistor into a U-NOx jumper location. This will damage the PCBs and void the warranty.**

(3) Insert SHORTS and SHORTS-TO-GROUND
IMPORTANT: Inserting a zero ohm resistor into a U-NO jumper location of the bottom of a PCB produces a short to ground on the voltage side of the circuit. **YOU MUST CHANGE FUSE F1 TO A BLOWN FUSE OR REMOVE IT FROM THE POWER BOARD** to simulate a blown fuse. Failure to do so will damage the H-PS01 Power Supply and both PCBs.

Practice troubleshooting shorts to ground and shorted loads by inserting a **zero ohm resistor** into a U-NO-jumper location. **Do not use U-NO3**. After the short or short-to-ground problem is found remove the wire jumper from the U-NO jumper location and replaced fuse F1 with a good 2A fuse.

> **The warranty of "The" Hands-On Program does not cover a burned up H-PS01 Power Supply or PCB damage from failure to use a burned fuse or removing a fuse when a zero ohm resistor is placed in a U-NOx location.**

Practice With A Troubleshooting Contest

Insert a random problem in the PCBs and then time each tech until he finds the problem. Total the time each tech spends troubleshooting the same problems. Mix up the problems between OPEN, SHORTS and Vds. Keep score. The one with the least amount of time spent is the Top Troubleshooter.

The next circuit board in "**The**" **Hands-On Troubleshooting Training Program** is the DC motor Board, H-113 with over 45 troubleshooting problems concerning DC motor circuits.

This is followed by, H-115, Troubleshooting Relay Circuits with 75 troubleshooting problems in relay circuits.

This is followed by troubleshooting wire harness problems with H-116, Wire Harness Troubleshooting which has more than 100 electrical problems.

Stay sharp – keep practicing your troubleshooting!

> "**The**" Vehicle Electronics *Hands-On Home-Study*
> **Troubleshooting Training Program**
> **Written by Vince Fischelli**
> Published by VEEJER ENTERPRISES, Garland, Texas
> Copyright © 2000, 2004, 2006, 2009, 2015
> Veejer Enterprises. No part of these manual or training material may be reproduced, photocopied, copied into a computer data base or copied by any means. All rights reserved.
> Phone: 972-276-9642   Fax: 972-276-8122
> Email: sales@veejer.com   Web Site: www.veejer.com

Vehicle Electronics Hands-On Troubleshooting Training Program

VEEJER ENTERPRISES 3701 Lariat Lane, Garland, Texas 75042-5419
Phone: 972-276-9642 Fax: 972-276-8122 Email: contact-us@veejer.com Web Site: www.veejer.com

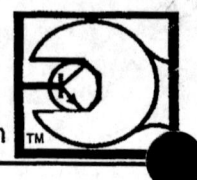

Student Troubleshooting Record

Keep track of your troubleshooting progress below.

OPENs and Voltage Drop (Vd) Problems

Problem #	Date Comp.	Grade/Result/Do Again	Notes on this problem:
01			
02			
03			
04			
05			
06			
07			
08			
09			
10			
11			
12			
13			
14			
15			
16			
17			
18			
21			
22			
23			
24			
26			
28			
29			
30			
31			
32			

Short-to-Ground Problems:

19			
20			
25			
27			

Copyright © 2015 VEEJER ENTERPRISES, Garland, Texas - All Rights Reserved

Hands-On Student Workbook
H-WB113

Troubleshooting DC Motor Circuits Module H-113

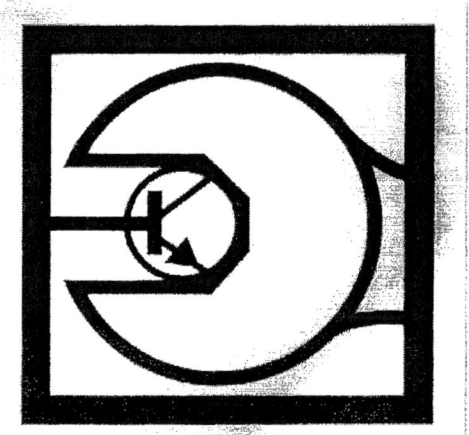

Veejer Enterprises Inc.
Garland, Texas, USA

Hands-On Student Workbook H-WB113

Troubleshooting DC Motor Circuits
Module H-113

Supplement to
"*The*" (60 Lesson Home-Study) Vehicle Electronics Training Course™

Written by Vince Fischelli

Published in USA by
VEEJER ENTERPRISES INC.
Garland, Texas, USA

Copyright © 2015 Veejer Enterprises Inc.
No part of these Lessons or Course Materials may be reproduced, photocopied, entered into a computer data base or retrieval system of any kind.
All Rights Reserved.

"*The*" **Hands-On Vehicle Electronics
Troubleshooting Training Program**

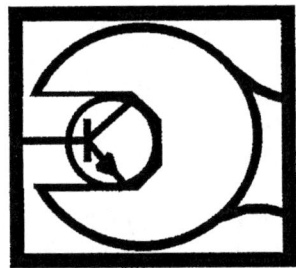

Veejer Enterprises
Garland, Texas
972-276-9642   www.veejer.com

Contents

- Introduction to Module H-113, Troubleshooting DC Motor Circuits
- Brushless DC Motors and the DC Motor Board, H-PCB03
- Controlling DC Motor Operation
- Testing Brushless DC Motors & Circuits
- Testing Brushless DC Motors with an Analog Ohmmeter
- Testing Brushless DC Motors with a Digital Ohmmeter
- Testing Brushless DC Motors with the Diode Test Function
- Checking Polarity Diodes
- Scanning the Top of the PCBs
- The Ground Side of the Circuit
- DC Motor and CEMF - Seeing CEMF in Action
- Measuring Vd_{VS}, Vd_{GS} and Vd_{LOAD}
- Measuring Circuit Voltages on the Voltage Side and the Ground Side
- Systematic Troubleshooting, The Texas-Two-Step
- The Six Basic Circuit Problems
- Shorts to Voltage Explained
- Checking Starter Draw
- Checking DC Blower Motor Current
- Straight Line Schematic Diagram 3TS-5
- Troubleshooting Record
- Standard Troubleshooting Problems 33 through 69
- Advanced Troubleshooting Problems 70A, 71A, 72A, 73A

"*The*" Hands-On Vehicle Electronics Troubleshooting Training Program

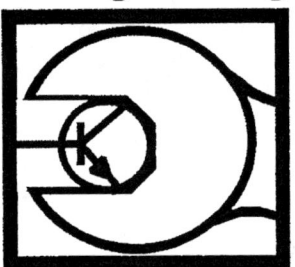

Veejer Enterprises
Garland, Texas
972-276-9642 www.veejer.com

Vehicle Electronics Hands-On Home-Study Troubleshooting Training

VEEJER ENTERPRISES 3701 Lariat Lane, Garland, Texas 75042-5419
Phone: 972-276-9642 Fax: 972-276-8122 Email: info@veejer.com Web Site: www.veejer.com

Hands-On Troubleshooting Training DC Motor Circuit Troubleshooting Module H-113

Hands-on auto and truck electrical and electronics troubleshooting workshops by Vince Fischelli since 1985 have been very successful in teaching service technicians how to troubleshoot auto and truck electrical and electronic circuits. The success of these hands-on workshops and the unique troubleshooting training that made them so effective led to the development of a written training program called *"THE"* VEHICLE ELECTRONICS (60 Lesson Home-Study) TRAINING COURSE,™ simply referred to as *"The"* Course.

"The" Course achieved its training objectives but was limited by the absence of hands-on application of the various troubleshooting techniques presented. Students often asked for hands-on supplements to *"The"* Course.

Lessons **34, 35, 36** and **37** of *"The"* Course cover DC motor circuits but do not provide the opportunity for students to apply hands-on what they learn about troubleshooting DC motor circuits.

This led to the development of a supplemental training program emphasizing hands-on training that became know as the *"The"* **Hands-On (Home-Study) Training Program**, Part Number H-111A featuring **The Starter Kit**.

"The" **Hands-On Program,** is designed to supply the hands-on training needed to master live circuit troubleshooting by offering students the opportunity to practice hands-on troubleshooting at home or in the shop. Techs develop troubleshooting skill and confidence to become hands-on vehicle electronic system troubleshooters combining *"The"* Course and *"The"* Hands-On Program.

Once *"The"* **Hands-On Program** is purchased it allows students to refresh their troubleshooting skills from time to time by going back to the circuit boards to practice and review live troubleshooting.

Students must begin *"The"* **Hands-On Program** with **The Starter Kit** containing the first two circuit boards which covers essential troubleshooting technique using the *Lamp Circuit Board* connected to the *Power Board.* These provide power and ground distribution circuits similar to a typical vehicle circuit schematic format (B+ at the top of the schematic and B- at the bottom.) This initial circuit board set-up is used to introduce hands-on principles of specific auto and truck electrical and electronic system troubleshooting techniques with live circuits and the capability to insert realistic circuit problems into the circuit.

After the Starter Kit program is completed, a foundation in essential troubleshooting is developed and the student is ready for this **Module H-113** covering troubleshooting DC motors and the unique situations peculiar to DC motor circuits.

Part number H-113, uses a specially designed Motor circuit board, **H-PCB03**, which is connected to the Power Board (H-PCB01) and provides a platform for troubleshooting brushless DC Motor circuit problems.

The DC Motor used is a 60mm x 25mm brushless DC Motor. The home-study Student Manual is Part Number **H-SM03**. The Instructor Guide, (I/G03) is Part Number **H-IG03**. Also included are 5 advanced problems that should be attempted only after completing problems 33-69. Module H113 is followed by additional modules.

Module H-115, Relay Circuit Troubleshooting
Relay circuit troubleshooting uses a specially designed relay circuit board, H-PCB05 which is connected to the Power Board to operate the relay circuit and provide a platform for troubleshooting relay circuit problems.

Module H-116, Wire Harness Troubleshooting
H-PCB06, the Wire Harness circuit board, connects the Power Board, the Lamp Board, the DC Motor Board and the Relay Board into a complete mini-electrical system called, the "M.E.S." or Mini-Electrical System.

Module H-200, CAN Bus Troubleshooting
H-PCB200, VAN Bus circuit board connects to Power Board from H-111A, There are 20 problems with the CAN Bus network wiring and 24 problems simulating Node voltage feeds and ground circuits failures.

Prerequisite For Program H-113
It is understood that before starting, H-113, Module 03, DC Motor Troubleshooting, the student has mastered the Starter Kit, H-111A with the Power Board, H-PCB01 and the Lamp Board, H-PCB02 along with the 32 troubleshooting problems presented in the Starter Kit. NO EXCEPTIONS. Some essential material presented in the Starter Kit, H-111A, is not repeated in Program H-113.

Goals and Objectives
H-113 focuses on troubleshooting brushless DC motor circuits and wire wound DC motors such as the starter motor and the blower motor. There are unique problems and troubleshooting procedures, such as measuring electron current in DC motor circuits that was not such an issue in the Lamp Circuit.

How To Begin
Begin this program by reading this Student Text, H-SM03, pages 1 - 39. It will guide you through the DC Motor hands-on circuit troubleshooting program of Module H-113. Answers to review questions available in the Instructor Guide H-I/G03.

Vehicle Electronics Hands-On Home-Study Troubleshooting Training

VEEJER ENTERPRISES 3701 Lariat Lane, Garland, Texas 75042-5419
Phone: 972-276-9642   Fax: 972-276-8122   Email: info@veejer.com   Web Site: www.veejer.com

Tips Using The H-113 " *The*" Hands-On Troubleshooting Training Program

(1) NEVER LOOK AT THE BOTTOM OF THE PCBs (Printed Circuit Boards) PRIOR TO TROUBLE-SHOOTING A PROBLEM SINCE THE CIRCUIT FAULT INSERTED FOR THAT PROBLEM MIGHT BE OBVIOUS. DISCOVERING A CIRCUIT FAULT BY OBSERVATION SPOILS THE BENEFIT TO BE GAINED FROM THAT PROBLEM. *DON'T EVEN PEAK!*

(2) Each student should have their personal Student Workbook, H-WB113 to keep notes and record test results obtained in the circuit troubleshooting exercises. Failure to record troubleshooting test results will make it impossible to evaluate troubleshooting performance.

(3) Do not insert more than one fault at a time in the PCBs until the final 5 advanced problems. Follow the instructions for each particular troubleshooting problem to be sure the fault is correctly inserted if you are the one inserting faults.

(4) Remove the fault from the PCBs after finding the problem unless someone is going to troubleshoot the same problem immediately after you. Any fault left in a PCB will affect the circuit when a second fault is later inserted causing false readings and confusion.

(5) "Scan the top and bottom" of the PCBs to verify that no fault exists before inserting a fault. Scanning the top of the PCBs is covered in this text and scanning the bottom of the PCBs is covered in the I/G03 Instructor Guide to aid in preparing PCBs and inserting faults.

Resistor Bag (H-RB03) – DC Motor Circuit

The **Resistor Bag, DC Motor Circuit, Part Number H-RB03** contains several 1/2 watt resistors of different ohmic values for inserting voltage drop faults in the DC Motor circuit troubleshooting problems. Fixed carbon resistors have 4 color bands to indicate the resistance of the resistor.

For practice with the resistor color code, you may review **Lesson 4, Page 4 and Lesson 5** of *"The"* **Vehicle Electronics Training Course** to interpret the resistor color code of the various fixed resistors in H-RB03. Another option is to check the resistance of the resistors with a digital ohmmeter.

"The" **Vehicle Electronics Training Course** is now available on line. Go to **http://training.veejer.com** to view lesson content. A link allows students to subscribe to read and print lessons for additional study.

References to lesson numbers is given that relate to the exercises in this workbook for additional reading.

Zero Ohm Resistors

Some circuit faults require removing a wire jumper from the bottom of a PCB to insert a problem. These wire jumpers look like a small resistor and are called **"zero ohm resistors."** They have a single black color band in the center. They are equivalent to a wire jumper.

Zero Ohm Resistor (0ΩR)

REMOVING A 0ΩR FOR THE FIRST TIME MAY BE TIGHT. PULL STRAIGHT UP AND OUT. DO NOT TRY TO WIGGLE IT OUT. After one or two times the mounting pins become broken in and removal is much easier. Some circuit problems call for inserting a fixed carbon resistor in place of a zero ohm resistor to create a voltage drop problem. In other troubleshooting problems a 0ΩR (zero ohm resistor) is inserted to create a shorted load or a short to ground. Instructions are provided in the Instructor Guide. The **Resistor Bag, DC Motor Circuit, Part Number H-RB03** is shown below.

RESISTOR BAG - DC MOTOR BOARD & CIRCUIT Part # H-RB03

5 ea. Zero-Ohm Resistors
1 Foot Solid Hook-Up Wire

Fixed Resistors
2 - 50 Ω 0.5 W
2 - 100 Ω 0.5 W
2 - 150 Ω 0.5 W
2 - 270 Ω 0.5 W

Veejer Enterprises
Garland, Texas
Ph. 972-276-9642
www.veejer.com

The resistor values used are **50 Ω, 100 Ω, 150 Ω and 270 Ω**. All are 0.5 watt (1/2 watt) resistors. Each resistor value contained in the Resistor Bag is designed to work with the DC Motor Circuit to provide significant circuit voltage drops that can be seen with DMM voltage readings. The resistors in the **H-RB03** are the resistor values to be used with the DC Motor Circuit when troubleshooting these problems.

Follow the instructions given in the Instructor Guide to insert a resistor type fault for a particular problem number.

A resistor is often randomly selected from the resistor bag to be installed on the bottom of the PCBs (as directed in the I/G) in place of a 0ΩR to produce a voltage drop (Vd) problem. Some problems require a specific resistor values be used.

It may be helpful to use a long nose pliers for removing the zero ohm resistors and inserting fixed resistors. Once the fault is installed begin troubleshooting the problem.

Brushless DC Motor – DC Motor Board

The DC Motor used in the DC Motor circuit board is a small, 60mm x 25mm **brushless** type DC motor often used in electronic equipment to keep circuit boards air cooled in electronic equipment.

This type of DC Motor technology is gaining wide acceptance in automotive and truck technology as larger versions of brushless DC Motors are used in cars and trucks to cool engines instead of the old wire wound brush style DC fan motors.

A drawing of the DC Motor used in "*The*" Hands-On Program, DC Motor Circuit Board, H-113, is shown below. The center circle supports the fan blades which rotate to move air.

A brushless DC motor contains **solid-state control circuitry** to both operate and control motor rpm. Each application of a brushless DC motor can be designed for unique operating characteristics to meet operational requirements through the use of specifically designed solid-state micro-circuitry packaged inside the motor housing.

The DC Motor Circuit Board

The DC Motor Circuit Board is shown to the right. The DC motor's Red wire goes to Pin 1 and the Blue wire goes to Pin 2. DO NOT cross these wires as the motor will not operate. A zero ohm resistor should be installed in J3 and J4.

To add more realism to the troubleshooting problems with the DC Motor Board we will refer to the DC Motor as an **Engine Cooling Fan Motor**.

If a brushless DC Motor does not rotate the blades when it is turned ON, a tech should carefully give the blades a spin using a screw driver or pencil to see if the blades continue to rotate after a little help to get rotation started before assuming the DC Motor is defective.

A serious voltage drop in a brushless DC Motor circuit may prevent enough voltage to self-start the blades rotating and a little push may be needed to get blade rotation started. If the blades continue to rotate slowly it could likely be a circuit voltage drop problem keeping the blades from rotating at normal rpm rather than a DC Motor failure. If the blades stop by themselves after a little push it means the brushless DC Motor may be defective or there is a major circuit problem. Of course, to determine if the problem is in the circuit or inside the brushless DC Motor's control circuitry requires troubleshooting.

More on this later in this module.

Be sure to spin the blades anytime the blades don't start rotating on their own. Do this with the brushless DC Motor used on the H-PCB03 as well as on brushless DC Motors on vehicles. **DO NOT USE YOUR FINGERS.**

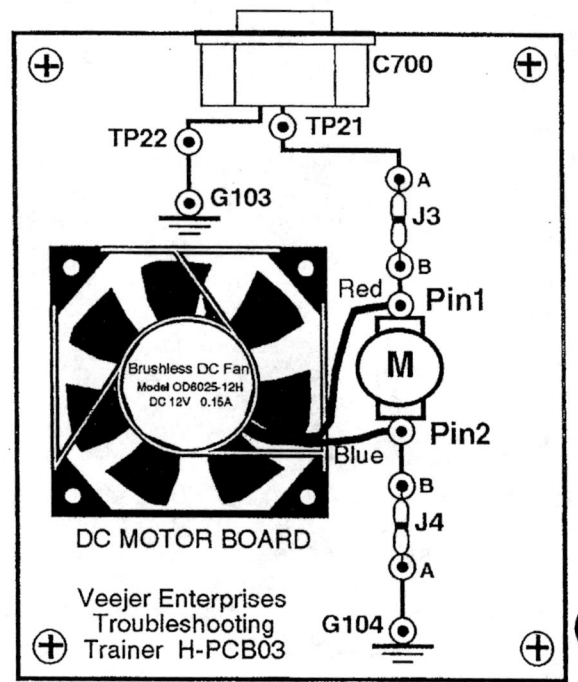

With the DC Motor operating, notice the strength of the air being moved by the DC motor to establish operation of a known good circuit. Evaluating air flow is the method to determine if the DC Motor (cooling fan) circuit is operating correctly.

One method is to simply place your hand over the motor into the air stream and "feel" the air moving. Another method, *purely optional,* is to make a "paper vane" using a small piece of light weight paper as a flap held in place over the DC motor with one piece of tape at the top as shown below. It may be necessary to work at this trying different weights of paper, paper size and tape to get the best effect of a rising vane proportional to air flow.

As the DC Motor operates, the air flow will push the paper vane upwards depending on the amount of air flow produced. This will make air flow some what easier to determine.

Vehicle Electronics Hands-On Home-Study Troubleshooting Training

VEEJER ENTERPRISES 3701 Lariat Lane, Garland, Texas 75042-5419
Phone: 972-276-9642   Fax: 972-276-8122   Email: info@veejer.com   Web Site: www.veejer.com

DC Motor Board Set-Up

Connect the DC Motor Troubleshooting Trainer, H-PCB03 to the Power Board, H-PCB01. When the DC Motor Board is securely connected to the Power Board a snap is heard as the two C700 connectors mate. Toggle S1 UP and slide S3 and S4 UP. The DC Motor should operate and blow air up from board.

Controlling DC Motor Operation

This exercise and the one on the next page demonstrates how to determine if a DC motor (or any electrical load for that matter) is switch-to-voltage or switch-to-ground controlled when the method of load control is clearly shown on the schematic diagram,

There are two ways to control a DC motor. Either switch B+ to a permanently grounded DC motor (Switch-to-Voltage Control) or switch ground to a DC motor permanently connected to B+ (Switch-to Ground Control).

Lesson 23 discusses basic load control concepts.
Lesson 36 discusses controlling DC motors.

Switch-to-Voltage Control

Figure 3H-041, to the right, illustrates the method of *switch-to-voltage control*. S3 is used as the ON/OFF switch to control the DC Motor's voltage side. S4 on the ground side of the DC motor is not shown in this schematic since it is CLOSED to "permanently" complete the ground side circuit.

Do This:

(1) Turn S1 ON (toggle UP), S4 (Slide UP), S3 (Slide DOWN), The DC Motor does not operate because S3 is not CLOSED.

(2) When S3 is CLOSED (slide UP) the DC motor is ON or operating.
   Voltage at Pin 1 is _____ volts
   Voltage at Pin 2 is _____ volts

(3) When S3 is OPEN (slide DOWN) the DC Motor is OFF.
   Voltage at Pin 1 is _____ volts
   Voltage at Pin 2 is _____ volts

(4) Leave S3 OFF (slide DOWN). Since there is no voltage on the motor terminals when the control switch, S3, is OFF, it is safe to connect an ohmmeter to the terminals to see which side of the DC motor is permanently grounded.

(5) Select the OHMS function on a DMM and ground the DMM's BLACK Test Lead to -BATT Terminal Post.

(6) Touch RED Test Lead to Pin 1.
   What is the reading? _____ ohms

(7) Touch RED test Lead to Pin 2.
   What is the reading? _____ ohms

(8) According to the two ohmmeter readings, which terminal on the DC Motor is permanently grounded? _____ .

You see a very low resistance at Pin 2 (Motor's Blue Wire). This confirms the circuit is a switch-to-voltage control circuit since the Pin 2 side of the DC motor is permanently grounded. B+ voltage on Pin is required to operate the DC Motor.

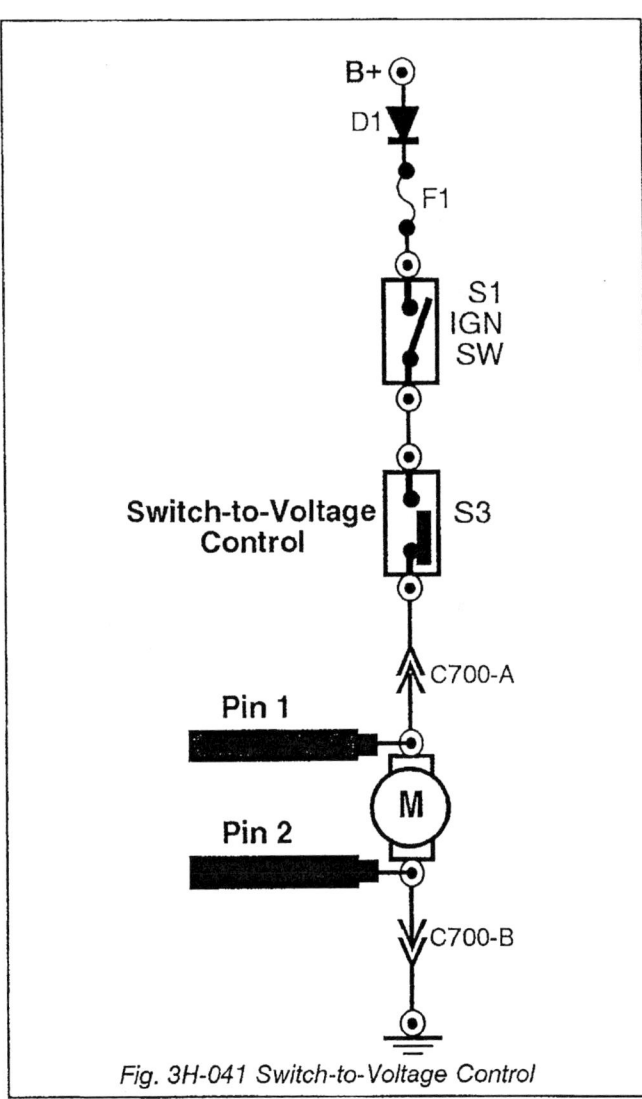

Fig. 3H-041 Switch-to-Voltage Control

If a mechanical switch (like S3), is used to apply voltage to the load and the load doesn't operate the switch could have OPEN contacts or it may not be connected to B+, possibly because the fuse is blown, a broken wire or a connector is not making good contact.

Switch-to-Ground Control

Figure 3H-042, to the right, illustrates the method of *switch-to-ground control*. S4 is used as the ON/OFF switch to control the DC Motor's ground side. S3 on the voltage side of the DC motor is not shown in this schematic since it is CLOSED to "permanently" complete the voltage side circuit.

Do This:

(1) Turn S1 ON (toggle UP), S3 (slide UP), S4 (slide DOWN).

(2) When S4 is CLOSED (slide UP) the DC Motor is ON or operating.

    Voltage at Pin 1 is _____ volts

    Voltage at Pin 2 is _____ volts

(3) When S4 is OPEN (slide DOWN) the DC motor is OFF.

    Voltage at Pin 1 is _____ volts

    Voltage at Pin 2 is _____ volts

(4) Leave S4 OFF (slide DOWN). Since there is B+ on both DC motor terminals the ohmmeter should not be connected to the DC Motor terminals. With the DC motor not operating there is B+ on both DC motor terminals. It can be concluded the DC motor is missing a ground therefore it must be considered a switch-to-ground control circuit.

If a mechanical switch (like S4), is used to ground the load and the load doesn't operate the switch could have OPEN contacts or it may not be grounded. There could also be a broken wire or a connector that is disconnected.

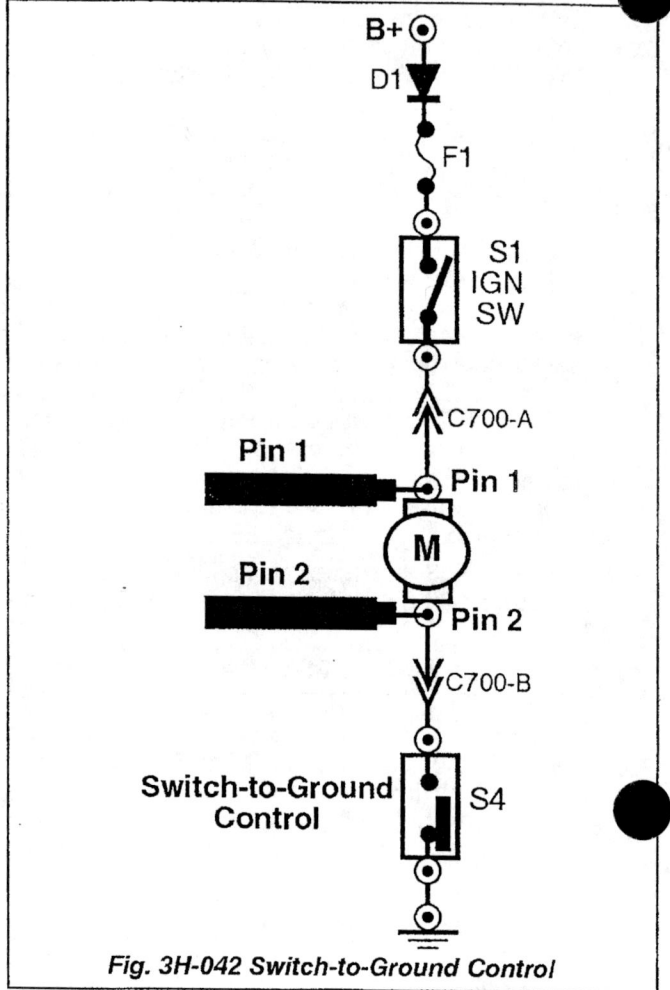

Fig. 3H-042 Switch-to-Ground Control

Summarizing Load Control Analysis

Anytime a DC Motor, or any load device such as a solenoid, relay coil or lamp is not operating when the circuit is turned ON, it means the load is missing B+ on the voltage side or ground (B-) on the ground side. Measure the voltage or resistance on both load terminal wires as necessary to troubleshoot the problem.

Both Terminals Have B+

The problem is on the ground side. Disconnect both wires and measure the voltage on both wires to see which wire has the B+. The other wire is the ground side of the load. Trace that wire to find the problem on the ground side of the circuit.

Both Terminals Have 0V

The problem is on the voltage side. Disconnect both wires and measure the resistance to ground at each wire. The wire with a low resistance reading is the ground side. The other wire is the voltage wire. Trace that wire to find the problem on the voltage side of the circuit.

Vehicle Electronics Hands-On Home-Study Troubleshooting Training

VEEJER ENTERPRISES 3701 Lariat Lane, Garland, Texas 75042-5419
Phone: 972-276-9642 Fax: 972-276-8122 Email: info@veejer.com Web Site: www.veejer.com

Computer Control of DC Motor Operation

Figure 3H-042A below shows a computer (PCM) providing a ground through driver transistor "Q1" to turn ON the DC Motor. The solid-state transistor, labeled Q1 is used in place of a mechanical switch. We understand this is called switch-to-ground "computer" control since the transistor in the PCM and it is on the ground side of the load.

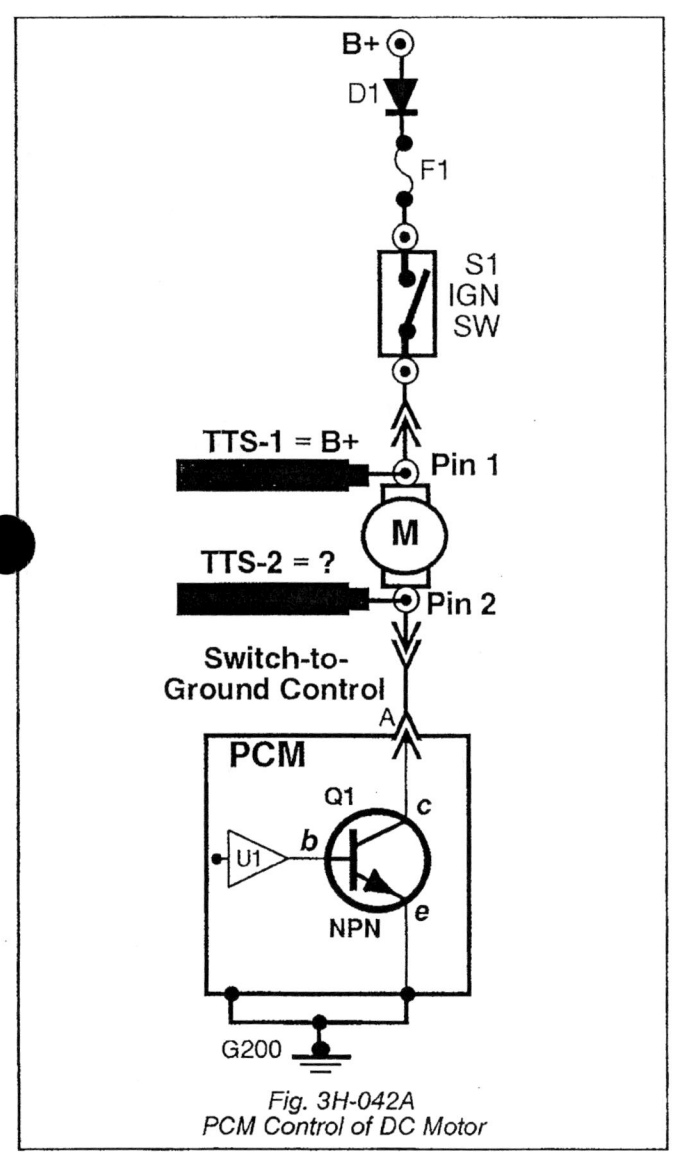

Fig. 3H-042A
PCM Control of DC Motor

A transistor has three leads or wires to connect it to the circuit. This is true of all NPN (and PNP) transistors.

On the schematic diagram in Figure 3H-042A the **Emitter** lead is designated with a lower case "e." The **Base** is designated with a lower case "b." The **Collector** is designated with a lower case "c." Schematic diagrams do not usually show these letters but the transistor leads are understood in the schematic symbol of a transistor.

The TTS-1 reading at DC Motor Pin 1 is B+ as long as S1 is closed. The TTS-2 reading is determined by the ON/OFF state of Q1, a NPN driver transistor. The Base lead is the control lead of the transistor and the voltage applied to the base controls the transistor.

When Transistor Q1 is "OFF"

The transistor, Q1 is OFF when base voltage is 0V. There is no electron current through Q1 so the DC Motor is not operating. It is not possible to measure the base voltage on the transistor inside the computer. The fact of B+ being measured at TTS-2 indicates the transistor is not sending electron current through the DC Motor. You could say the DC Motor is not being grounded (Problem #3 – OPEN Ground).

Other possibilities are as follows. There could be no voltage on the Base or the transistor driver. The driver transistor could be defective. It should also be considered that the PCM does not have B+ (voltage) and B- (ground) on the correct pins at the PCM connector for proper operation.

When Transistor Q1 is "ON"

Since the Base is the transistor control lead, placing a small positive voltage (1.0V-2.5V) on the Base of a NPN transistor causes the transistor to turn "ON." It would be the same thing as CLOSING a mechanical switch to operate the DC Motor.

Transistor Q1 allows electrons to flow up from ground into the Emitter, pass through the Base into the Collector and exit the Collector wire.

This electron current is the same electron current that operates the DC Motor. As electrons exit the DC Motor they travel up to B+ to complete the electron current path. Don't overlook the fact that the ground side of the circuit must be good for electrons to flow through the ground circuit to enter Ground 200 and supply the emitter with electrons.

When the PCM decides it is time to operate the DC Motor the PCM circuit "U1" puts the required voltage on the Base of Q1 causing Q1 conduct (pass) electron current through the DC Motor.

During DC Motor ON-time the TTS-2 reading is in the range 0.8V due to the voltage drop across driver transistor Q1. The actual voltage at TTS-2 or Pin A of the PCM must be measured on a known good PCM controlled circuit since the voltage will vary depending on what type of solid-state driver is used to control the DC Motor.

When the PCM decides to turn OFF the DC Motor, U1 removes the Base voltage which drops to 0V so Q1 turns "OFF." The TTS-2 reading becomes B+ again because the DC Motor looses the ground provided through the driver transistor.

What we have covered in the last two exercises about determining load control still applies whether the control switch is a mechanical switch or a solid-state driver transistor.

Copyright © 2015 VEEJER ENTERPRISES, Garland, Texas - All Rights Reserved   Text H-WB113 Page 6

Vehicle Electronics Hands-On Home-Study Troubleshooting Training

VEEJER ENTERPRISES 3701 Lariat Lane, Garland, Texas 75042-5419
Phone: 972-276-9642   Fax: 972-276-8122   Email: info@veejer.com   Web Site: www.veejer.com

If a driver transistor in an on-board control unit doesn't ground the load, it could be caused by a defective computer driver transistor circuit. The driver transistor could have failed OPEN and the DC Motor never turns ON. The driver transistor could have failed SHORTED and the DC Motor runs all the time when the Ignition Switch is ON.

Testing Driver Transistor with an Ohmmeter

The driver transistor in the PCM or other on-board computer controlling a load, presents a problem for the technician to determine if the driver transistor is good or bad. An ohmmeter can be somewhat helpful to check the resistance of the driver transistor as shown in Figure 3H-042B to the right.

A driver transistor will have a resistance value that will help determine if it is good or bad – as long as – a good resistance value is known for comparison. This is determined by checking a similar good circuit on another vehicle with an ohmmeter.

There are many differences between ohmmeters and that will be discussed on the next pages. For this exercise let's consider running this driver transistor test with a standard digital ohmmeter.

> Our DC Motor circuit uses S4 to ground the DC Motor and does not employ a transistor driver. This test cannot be performed with the circuit boards and result in a reading that would be found in a vehicle. This test should be done on a vehicle. We are using the H-113 circuit boards to practice the test set up.

First of all the load must be disconnected to stop B+ from getting to Pin 2 through the DC Motor. This can be accomplished by removing the circuit fuse or disconnecting the DC Motor's red wire to Pin 1. Pin 2 now measures 0V. It is therefore safe to connect the ohmmeter to Pin 2 without disconnecting the load.

Figure 3H-042B shows a digital ohmmeter connected to Pin 2 to check for a grounded Pin 2 circuit. The digital ohmmeter "sees" the driver transistor (in the OFF state) as a very high resistance. How high a resistance depends on the driver used by the manufacturer. The only way to tell what a good reading is would be to "CHAKGO" (check a known good one). Expect to see several million ohms.

If the driver is OPEN the reading will be substantially higher than a good reading. If the driver is shorted the ohmmeter will indicate a low resistance reading of only a few ohms and that explains why the DC Motor is operating all the time.

This type of troubleshooting takes a lot of practice checking known good circuits to get familiar with normal ohmmeter readings which will vary slightly from one circuit to another and with different ohmmeters being used. The final good reading should only be decided after you have checked several known good circuits to establish the range of normal resistance values to indicate a good transistor driver circuit. The normal good reading is determined by what driver transistor is used and practice.

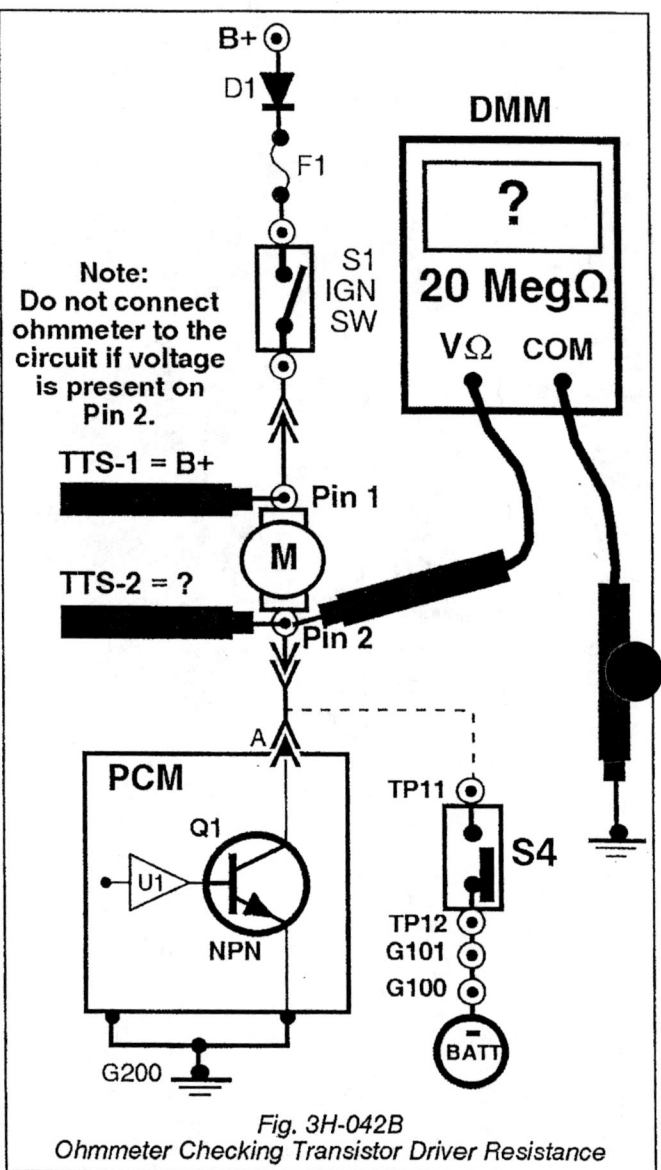

Fig. 3H-042B
Ohmmeter Checking Transistor Driver Resistance

Before any computer/control unit is replaced, determine that all sensor, voltage and ground inputs to the on-board computer are correct. If one input is not correct it may prevent a computer or control unit from grounding a specific load. *A computer or control unit requires all inputs to be correct before it can do its job grounding a specific load.*

Try This:

With the digital ohmmeter connected as shown the DC Motor Module the reading will be "OL" with OPEN and a zero ohm reading with S4 CLOSED.

Vehicle Electronics Hands-On Home-Study Troubleshooting Training

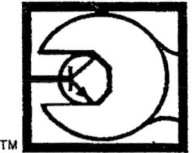

VEEJER ENTERPRISES 3701 Lariat Lane, Garland, Texas 75042-5419
Phone: 972-276-9642   Fax: 972-276-8122   Email: info@veejer.com   Web Site: www.veejer.com

Testing Brushless DC Motors & Circuits

Circuit voltage checks (Vc), voltage drop measurements (Vd), and electron current readings provide sufficient information in solving most brushless DC motor circuit problems and that is what is thoroughly covered in *"The"* Hands-On Program, **Module H-113**.

DC motor problems are easily duplicated in the DC Motor circuit board and will add realism to the troubleshooting problems by **referring to the DC Motor as an engine cooling fan.** DC Motor performance is evaluated in terms of how much air the DC Motor is moving. Normal air flow means the cooling fan is OK and the engine runs at the proper operating temperature. Weak or no air flow means the cooling fan circuit has a problem and the engine overheats.

Due to the internal construction of a brushless DC motor it is not possible to check motor winding condition as is the case with an old style DC fan motor with a wire wound motor winding. Wire wound DC motors have a winding resistance that can be checked with either a digital or analog ohmmeter (digital is better than analog for this) to determine if the winding has the proper resistance, or is OPEN or SHORTED.

Brushless DC motors, on the other hand, have internal solid-state components (diodes, transistors and integrated circuits) that make useful DC motor resistance testing with an ohmmeter more difficult and less conclusive about the condition of the brushless DC Motor. These solid-state components are included in brushless DC Motors because it allows the brushless DC Motor to become "smart." That is, a brushless DC Motor can be programmed to do certain things.

Here's an example comparing an old style wire wound cooling fan with a brushless cooling fan. A standard wire wound cooling fan can burn up from drawing high current if the fan blades are blocked, as might happen in a front end accident where the grill is pushed in. The wiring harness may burn up from the high motor current resulting in an electrical fire.

A brushless DC Motor, because of internal electronic circuitry, can be designed to automatically shut down and stop drawing current when the fan blades are blocked from rotating When the fan blade blockage is removed and the blades can move normally, the brushless cooling fan resumes normal operation and there is no damage to the brushless DC motor or wiring harness. Expect to see more applications in vehicle electronics using brushless DC Motors instead of the old style wire wound DC Motors that draw high electron current when the fan blades are not turning properly.

To undertake testing of the internal solid-state circuitry of a brushless DC motor, a *thorough understanding of ohmmeters and their testing characteristics is required.*

This information is covered in *"The"* Course:
Lesson 8: "Analog and Digital Ohmmeters"
Lesson 9: "Troubleshooting with Ohmmeters"
Lesson 44: "Troubleshooting Diodes"

These lessons explain in detail how analog and digital ohmmeters indicate good and bad diodes as a prelude to testing circuits containing solid-state components like brushless DC motors and making sense of the ohmmeter readings.

It is not practical to take these few lessons out of *"The"* **Course** without the benefit of the other lessons that precede and follow them and include them at this point in *"The"* Hands-On Program. Too much background information would be lost that these lessons depend on for clarity of information about ohmmeters.

Yet we need to be able to test a brushless DC Motor with an ohmmeter to help our analysis and troubleshooting procedures of brushless motors.

Ohmmeter troubleshooting will have great importance in future troubleshooting training modules covering relay circuits so a little about ohmmeters here will come in handy for this module and for what's ahead.

We approach troubleshooting with ohmmeters with a limited understanding of ohmmeter operation and simply test the brushless DC Motor with three different meters:

(1) **analog ohmmeter**

(2) **digital ohmmeter**

(3) **Diode Test**

These three meter functions can be used to test the electronic control circuit of a brushless DC Motor.

At the same time we will introduce some ohmmeter basics without lengthy explanations as to "why." This will serve to introduce you to basic analog and digital ohmmeter operation, some of the quirks of the different types of ohmmeters and provide some practice in ohmmeter testing. This will serve greater purpose later in *"The"* Hands-On Program as well as the troubleshooting that can be accomplished on vehicle electronic systems.

This understanding of ohmmeters can be used to test a number of solid-state devices that are beginning to show up in vehicles today. This used to be taught in electronics schools as recently as the 1980's. Now these electronics schools are closing down since the electronics manufacturers can build circuit boards cheaper than it cost to train an electronics technician to repair them. Unfortunately, these troubleshooting techniques with ohmmeters is being forgotten when it could still be helpful.

Vehicle Electronics Hands-On Home-Study Troubleshooting Training

VEEJER ENTERPRISES 3701 Lariat Lane, Garland, Texas 75042-5419
Phone: 972-276-9642   Fax: 972-276-8122   Email: info@veejer.com   Web Site: www.veejer.com

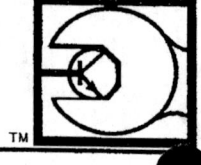

Testing Brushless DC Motor Resistance with an Analog Ohmmeter

Analog ohmmeters have an internal ohmmeter test battery to provide a small voltage to test solid-state devices like diodes and transistors.

Older analog ohmmeters have a 1.5V test voltage using a single AA or "C" cell battery to generate the ohmmeter test voltage of 1.5V. Some newer analog ohmmeters have a 3.0V test voltage using two AA batteries in series to obtain the 3.0V test voltage, Consider these ohmmeters as *high performance* analog ohmmeters. The higher test voltage of 3.0V is necessary to test some of the new solid-state components being used in current vehicle electronics technology because the older style 1.5V ohmmeter test voltage cannot enable (or turn ON) solid-state junctions in many of the newer solid-state devices.

Two Ohmmeter Characteristics

Get to know your ohmmeter's characteristics. You must know two parameters of an ohmmeter before using it to test a solid-state device (diode or transistor):
(1) the amplitude (how much) test voltage
(2) the polarity of an ohmmeter's test voltage

Once you know this you are ready to interpret the ohmmeter readings. Failing to know these characteristics about your ohmmeter results in a lot of mistakes and misunderstanding of ohmmeter tests.

Check Ohmmeter Test Voltage Amplitude

Measure the ohmmeter test voltage at the ohmmeter probe tips using a separate digital voltmeter (DMM) set to read DC VOLTS.

Place your ohmmeter on the OHMS Function and select the different ohmmeter ranges (Rx1, Rx10, Rx1k, etc.,). The voltage reading on the DMM indicates the ohmmeter test voltage in your analog ohmmeter for each ohmmeter range.

Check Ohmmeter Test Voltage Polarity

Next determine the polarity of the ohmmeter test voltage as you test it for voltage. Most analog ohmmeters are often **reverse polarity** from what you would ASSUME.

Red Ohmmeter Test Lead

You would expect the Red ohmmeter test lead to be the positive side of the ohmmeter test voltage but most likely it is the negative side of the test voltage. We designate the negative side of the ohmmeter test voltage by the term **-Ohmmeter** or (-Ω) for short.

Black Ohmmeter Test Lead

You would expect the Black ohmmeter test lead to be the negative side of the ohmmeter test voltage but it is most likely the positive side. We designate the positive side of the ohmmeter test voltage as **+Ohmmeter** or (+Ω) for short..

This is typical of analog ohmmeter test voltage polarity since their development in the 1920's. However, in the last 40 years some analog ohmmeters have been built with normal polarity, that is, the Red test lead is +Ohmmeter (+Ω) and the Black test lead is -Ohmmeter (–Ω).

That is why it is so important that you check your ohmmeter before you start using it. You only have to check your ohmmeter once with a voltmeter because it never changes polarity.

It is necessary to use a 3.0V analog ohmmeter for these tests because of the extensive circuitry in brushless DC Motors. A 1.5V ohmmeter could be used in a pinch but the reading is much higher.

DO THIS TWO STEP TEST WITH AN ANALOG ("swing needle") OHMMETER:

(1) Disconnect the DC Motor wires (red) from Pin 1 and (blue) from Pin 2 on the DC Motor Board.
(2) Zero the analog ohmmeter on the **Rx1k** range. (Rx1k = 1,000 ohm range)

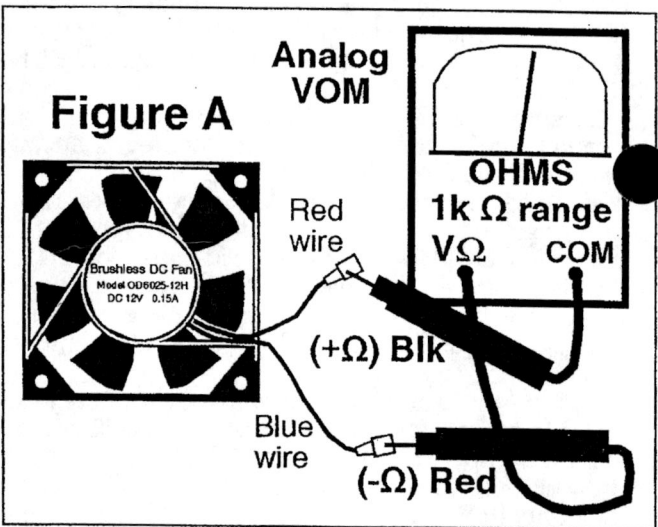

Figure A

(3) Connect +Ohmmeter Test Lead, +Ω, (positive test lead, usually the Black) to the DC Motor's Red wire as shown in Figure A.
(4) Connect the -Ohmmeter Test Lead, -Ω, (minus or negative Ohmmeter Test Lead, usually the Red test lead) to the DC Motor's Blue wire as in Fig. A.
(5) The reading is approximately 13k-15k ohms. You reading may vary depending on your analog ohmmeter.
(6) Reverse the ohmmeter leads as shown in Figure A1 and the reading is infinity because this polarity of the ohmmeter test voltage cannot enable the solid-state junctions in the circuitry.

Copyright © 2015 VEEJER ENTERPRISES, Garland, Texas - All Rights Reserved   Text H-WB113   Page 9

Vehicle Electronics Hands-On Home-Study Troubleshooting Training

VEEJER ENTERPRISES 3701 Lariat Lane, Garland, Texas 75042-5419
Phone: 972-276-9642   Fax: 972-276-8122   Email: info@veejer.com   Web Site: www.veejer.com

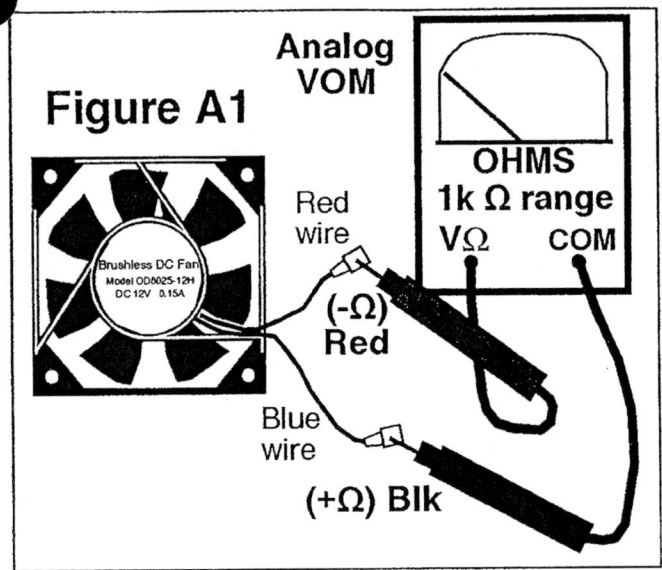

Figure A1

The reading you obtain may vary from those given because analog ohmmeter batteries can be a little weaker or stronger than the ohmmeter the author used for this test and do not indicate a good or bad brushless DC Motor.

The difference in readings when the test leads are reversed indicates the presence of internal solid-state components in the DC motor which "turn-ON" when the DC Motor's red wire is (+Ohmmeter) and the Blue wire is (-Ohmmeter). That is the normal voltage polarity needed to operate (enable) the DC Motor circuit. When the ohmmeter test leads are reversed, the Red DC Motor wire gets the (-Ohmmeter) and the Blue motor wire gets the (+Ohmmeter) which "turns-OFF" the internal circuitry of the motor causing the reading of infinity (the VOM's pointer stays at the left end of the scale).

If this test is performed with a 1.5V analog ohmmeter the reading is infinity because the 1.5V test voltage cannot enable the solid-state junctions in the semiconductors inside the brushless DC motor. That means, 1.5V cannot "turn-ON" the solid-state components inside the brushless DC Motor. It does NOT mean the brushless DC Motor is OPEN and helps to explain why newer analog ohmmeters have a 3.0V test voltage instead of the old 1.5V versions.

Testing Brushless DC Motor Resistance with a Digital Ohmmeter (DMM).

Digital ohmmeters have what we call normal ohmmeter test voltage polarity which means the DMM's Red test lead is +Ohmmeter and the Black test lead is -Ohmmeter. This is true of every digital ohmmeter we have tested since they have been available.

However, digital ohmmeters have a much lower ohmmeter test voltage, usually around 0.05 volt while the test leads are measuring a resistance. This is just another quirk of ohmmeters that must be understood. **A digital ohmmeter is not designed to measure solid-state circuitry or "enable" (turn ON) their junctions** due to their low ohmmeter test voltage during a test. DON'T USE A DIGITAL OHMMETER TO TEST SOLID-STATE COMPONENTS.

When a brushless DC Motor resistance is measured with a digital ohmmeter, expect to see a very high resistance reading. Some digital ohmmeters may indicate an OPEN circuit, a "1", or an "OL" or an "Ouch" reading depending on the DMM you use. However, some digital ohmmeters may read a very high reading of 10-15-20 Megohms because they are very sensitive and capable of indicating very high resistance values. These are not valid readings to determine condition of the solid-state circuitry in a brushless DC Motor except to conclude the circuitry is not SHORTED.

Some DMMs have "Auto ranging" capabilities which means selecting the "Ω" function and the DMM automatically selects the proper ohmmeter range based on the value of resistance being measured at that time. This is highly desirable because it eliminates technician errors in selecting the correct ohmmeter range. If you have a "manually selectable" DMM you must select the correct range by setting the Main Function knob to the correct ohmmeter range. Follow the directions below to apply this with hands-on practice.

DO THIS WITH A DIGITAL OHMMETER:

(1) Disconnect the DC Motor wires from Pin 1 and Pin 2 on the DC Motor Board.

(2) Select **OHMS** on your DMM (Digital Multimeter) and be prepared to see a very high resistance reading.

If you have an **Auto ranging DMM** select the "Ω" Function and let the DMM Autorange to automatically select the correct ohmmeter range during these next two measurements.

If you have a **manually selectable DMM** turn the function knob to the **highest ohmmeter range** available. This would be 20 MegΩ, 30 MegΩ or 40 MegΩ depending on the ohmmeter brand and model.

(3) Connect +Ohmmeter Test Lead (Red test lead) to the DC Motor's Red wire as shown in Fig. B.
(4) Connect the -Ohmmeter (minus or negative Ohmmeter) Test Lead (Black test lead) to the DC Motor's Blue wire as show in Figure B.

(4) Connect the -Ohmmeter (minus or negative Ohmmeter) Test Lead (Black test lead) to the DC Motor's Blue wire as show in Figure B.

Vehicle Electronics Hands-On Home-Study Troubleshooting Training

VEEJER ENTERPRISES 3701 Lariat Lane, Garland, Texas 75042-5419
Phone: 972-276-9642 Fax: 972-276-8122 Email: info@veejer.com Web Site: www.veejer.com

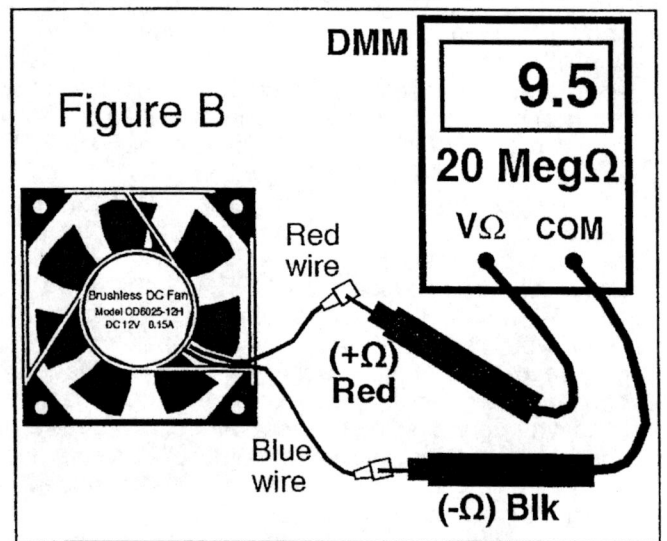

Figure B

DIODE TEST Checks Brushless DC Motor Control Circuit

Since a digital ohmmeter's test voltage is too low to turn-ON solid-state junctions in diodes and transistors (force them to pass a small ohmmeter test current), the DIODE TEST feature is added to DMMs. A higher test voltage most often in the range of about 3.0 volts allows the DMM to test diodes.

You can confirm this higher test voltage by measuring the voltage at the Diode Test lead probe tips with another DMM. Notice polarity of the Diode Test leads appear normal. That is, red is positive and black is negative.

The **Red** test lead is (plus) **+Diode Test** and indicated as "**+DT**" in our illustrations.

The **Black** test lead is (negative.) **–Diode Test** and indicated as "**-DT**" in our illustrations.

Understanding Diode Test Readings

The readout of the DIODE TEST Function indicates the voltage drop across the component placed between the probe tips while the DMM is in the DIODE TEST mode and testing a solid-state component.

DIODE TEST reading of 1.500 is 1.5 volts.

DIODE TEST reading of 1.000 is 1.0 volt.

DIODE TEST reading of .750 is 0.75 volt (750 mV)

DIODE TEST reading of .050 is 0.05 volt (50 mV)

DIODE TEST reading of .006 is 0.006 volt (6 mV)

A normal reading of a good silicon diode is in the range of 0.50 – 0.70. This means 0.50V – 0.70V is dropped across the diode. If the diode is not conducting (passing) enough test current, the reading will be **higher** than 0.70. If the diode is conducting too much test current, the reading will be **lower** than 0.50.

TO ESTABLISH NORMAL READINGS FOR A DIODE ALWAYS TEST MORE THAN ONE DIODE OF THE SAME TYPE TO CONFIRM NORMAL READINGS FOR THAT TYPE DIODE. AT TIMES A PARTICULAR (special purpose) DIODE MAY READ LESS OR MORE THAN THE VALUES GIVEN HERE.

DO THIS WITH DIODE TEST FEATURE OF DMM:

(1) Disconnect the DC Motor wires from Pin 1 and Pin 2 on the DC Motor Board.

(2) Select **DIODE TEST** on your DMM.

(3) Connect Red test lead (+DT) to the DC Motor's Red wire as shown in Figure C.

(4) Connect the Black test lead (-DT) to the DC Motor's Blue wire as show in Figure C. This turn-ON the DC Motor control circuit.

---

(5) The reading is approximately 9-10 MegΩ for this brushless DC Motor. Your reading may vary depending on the brand and model of DMM. Some DMM ohmmeters may not show a reading because of low 9V ohmmeter battery.

(6) Reverse the ohmmeter leads and the reading is a "1", or "OL" or "Ouch" depending on brand of DMM which indicates the meter cannot detect any resistance between its probe tips.

Although a resistance reading is obtained in Step 5, it has little significance to the operating condition of the internal solid-state circuitry of a brushless DC Motor because the low DMM ohmmeter test voltage cannot enable (turn-ON) the solid-state components inside the brushless DC Motor control circuitry. The DMM ohmmeter simply looks at the solid-state circuitry as if it were a **large value fixed resistor.** .

If the solid-state DC Motor circuitry fails by becoming a complete SHORT the DMM would indicate a few ohms to identify the SHORTED problem. If the solid-state circuitry fails by becoming OPEN the reading might indicate "OL", or "1" or "Ouch" depending on the DMM brand to identify the problem. But be careful. Some DMMs may indicate "OL" anyway because of their own inability to read very high resistance values. The solution is to **CHECK-A-KNOWN-GOOD-ONE** or "CAKGO" as we say in "*The*" Course.

From all this we observe the very limited value of a digital ohmmeter when checking solid-state components unless they are SHORTED or OPEN.

We can conclude that a digital ohmmeter, with it's low ohmmeter test voltage under load is insufficient to test solid-state components. A digital ohmmeter cannot properly check a diode (Lesson 44), a transistor or an integrated circuit (abbr. IC). That is why DMMs incorporate a DIODE TEST Feature.

Copyright © 2015 VEEJER ENTERPRISES, Garland, Texas - All Rights Reserved   Text H-WB113

Vehicle Electronics Hands-On Home-Study Troubleshooting Training

VEEJER ENTERPRISES 3701 Lariat Lane, Garland, Texas 75042-5419
Phone: 972-276-9642 Fax: 972-276-8122 Email: info@veejer.com Web Site: www.veejer.com

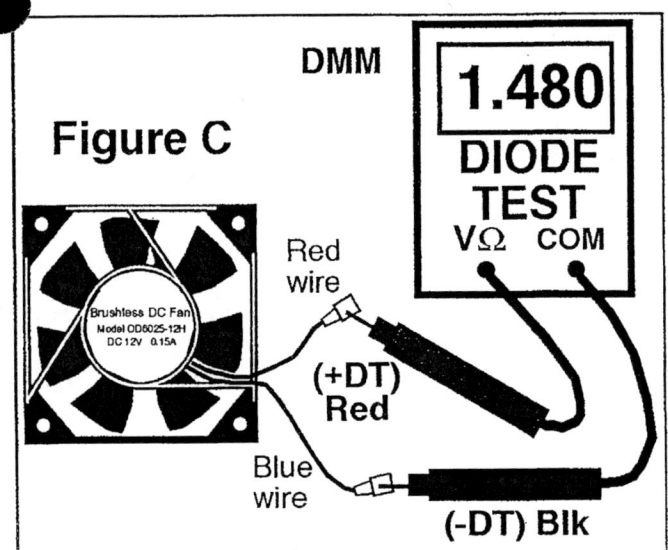

Figure C

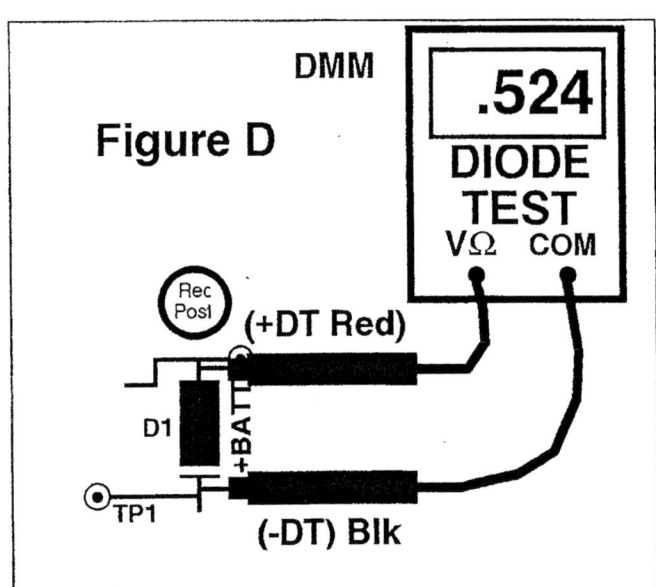

Figure D

CHECK POLARITY DIODE - POWER BOARD

Diode D1 on the Power Board (near the red post) is a (silicon) **polarity sensing diode** to protect the circuit if the two wires from the H-PS01 Power Supply are connected in reverse polarity to the two binding posts.

A diode only allows electron current to flow in one direction. The diode prevents circuit current in the wrong direction as when reverse polarity is applied to the Power Board. The diode can be checked for good condition using the Diode Test of your DMM.

DO THIS TO CHECK THE POLARITY DIODE

(1) UNPLUG Power Supply.
(2) Disconnect wires from the H-PS01 connected to the two binding posts.
(3) Select the DIODE TEST feature on your DMM.
(4) Place test leads as shown in Figure D.

(4) The reading for this brushless DC Motor is in the range of 1.300 - 1.700 because DC Motor control circuit is passing a test current. Readings vary depending on brand of DMM used. (Note: The author used three different DMM ohmmeter brands and got three slightly different readings all within the range of 1.300 - 1.700. The reading means the Diode Test voltage drop of the DC Motor control circuit is within the proper range due to correct amount of Diode Test current passing through. It also means the control circuit is not OPEN.

(5) Reverse Diode Test leads and the reading should be a "1", or "OL" or "Ouch" depending on brand of DMM. This indicates the meter cannot detect a circuit between its probe tips as it should do. This also means the control circuit is not SHORTED.

The DIODE Test reading for this known good brushless DC Motor is obtained by this test and falls within the range given above depending on the make and model of your DMM. The Diode Test reading is the voltage drop of the solid-state circuitry in the brushless DC motor's control circuitry. The combined solid-state circuitry of diodes and transistors is what determines the actual Diode Test reading.

A normal reading indicates a good possibility the DC control circuit is OK and the motor should operate provided the external circuit is OK. However, both an analog and a digital ohmmeter's Diode Test Feature could have normal readings yet the brushless DC Motor might still fail to operate.

This requires additional voltage and current measurements to determine the good/bad condition of any brushless DC Motor in a circuit or if the circuit around the DC Motor has a problem preventing proper DC Motor operation. These issues will be addressed in the troubleshooting exercises to come.

(4) Reading in the range of 0.500-0.700 is the voltage drop across the diode's internal junction. Diode Test "enables" diode to pass DMM test current and reading is the voltage drop across a **good** silicon diode while conducting test current.

(5) Reverse the test leads and the reading should be a normal "OL" indicating the diode is not shorted.

To summarize the differences in ohmmeters, an analog ohmmeter and a Diode Test feature of a DMM are effective in checking diodes and individual solid-state components. A digital ohmmeter is not designed to do this because of lower ohmmeter test voltage so the Diode Test was incorporated in modern DMMs for this purpose.

Yet, none of the three ohmmeters can conclusively prove the control circuit is good. They only tell you there is a good chance the circuit is good. Testing voltage and current measurements are required.

Vehicle Electronics Hands-On Home-Study Troubleshooting Training

VEEJER ENTERPRISES 3701 Lariat Lane, Garland, Texas 75042-5419
Phone: 972-276-9642 Fax: 972-276-8122 Email: info@veejer.com Web Site: www.veejer.com

Review Questions About Ohmmeters

(1) What two characteristics must you know about an ohmmeter before using it to properly interpret readings?
   A. if it auto ranges or is manually selectable
   B. the size of the readout
   C. test voltage amplitude and polarity
   D. voltage and current limits

(2) An analog ohmmeter can test a solid-state component better than a digital because
   A. a digital is less accurate at low resistance.
   B. a digital uses normal test voltage polarity.
   B. an analog has more test voltage.
   C. most analogs are reversed polarity.

(3) A digital ohmmeter indicates 'OL" when
   A. the load is OPEN.
   B. the load is a high resistance.
   C. the load is a low resistance.
   D. the 9V battery is weak.

(4.) What does the Diode Test of a DMM measure across a solid-state component that is enabled?
   A. a voltage drop in millivolts
   B. the internal resistance in ohms
   C. the current in milliAmps
   D. none of the above

(5) To test the polarity sensing diode on the Power Board with an ohmmeter
   A. only a digital ohmmeter is suitable.
   B. the Diode Test feature cannot be used.
   C. the circuit must be powered up.
   D. an analog ohmmeter is suitable.

Recording DMM Troubleshooting Readings

Since more than one value fixed carbon resistor is included in the resistor bag, different resistor values are selected at random for inserting a specific problem and that changes the voltage readings. This is intended because it adds variety to the readings obtained in troubleshooting each problem. Using different resistor values causes DMM readings to vary depending on the resistor value randomly selected for each problem. If you troubleshoot the same problem again for additional practice and select a different resistor value the readings will be different adding some variety when troubleshooting the same problem a second or third time.

Recording B+ (Voltage) Side Problems

Rather than attempt to put actual DMM readings for answers to each troubleshooting step, readings in the I/G (Instructor Guide) are recorded with word phrases. "Low B+" is used instead of an actual DMM reading of "10.42V" or 5.35V when checking a circuit voltage on the voltage side of the circuit. The actual voltage reading is not given in the Instructor Guide since it depends on what size resistor was used to insert the problem. By saying "low B+" in the I/G you can use the actual voltage value you got in the measurement and still know it is the same thing as "low B+."

Recording B- (Ground) Side Problems

The same is true on the ground side of the circuit which can be referred to as the **B-** side (just as the voltage side is referred to as the B+ side).

A ground side voltage reading is recorded as "more than 0.100V" for a bad ground side voltage reading instead of an actual DMM reading of "3.25V" or "2.27V." The I/G will define answers for ground side problems as **"high B-"** meaning more than 0.10 volt or a bad ground side voltage reading.

This method allows different resistor values to be used for a wide variety in DMM readings so that students may troubleshoot the same problem more than once and get different readings each time a different resistor value is used. It also helps increase student familiarity with a wide range of defective DMM readings without the need to document a separate troubleshooting answer sheet in the I/G for each conceivable combination of resistors values.

Additional troubleshooting practice can enhance your troubleshooting skills. Practice often.

Note On Schematic Diagram Symbols

It is customary on schematic diagrams to draw switches (solenoids and relays, etc.) in the OPEN or REST position as is shown in all the schematics in this training program. A technician is expected to *mentally* CLOSE the switch when visualizing circuit operation, tracing or studying the schematic diagram.

Do not misunderstand that the switch is too remain OPEN when operating the circuit. It is understood that to turn a circuit ON the switches must be *physically* CLOSED to complete the circuit.

Using Push/Release Switch S2

S2 on the Power Board is not used with the DC Motor circuit and is deleted from most schematics used in this manual. Future hands-on exercises and troubleshooting problems will cover the solenoid and relay circuits which will require using **S2**, the Push/Release Switch as the primary ON/OFF control instead of S1.

Vehicle Electronics Hands-On Home-Study Troubleshooting Training

VEEJER ENTERPRISES 3701 Lariat Lane, Garland, Texas 75042-5419
Phone: 972-276-9642 Fax: 972-276-8122 Email: info@veejer.com Web Site: www.veejer.com

Scanning The Top Of The PCBs

Connect the DC Motor board to the Power Board by the C700 Connector. Make a tight fit by inserting the board connector till they "snap" into a locked position.

Before using the PCBs for any hands-on experiments, or inserting troubleshooting problems, the PCBs must be configured (set-up) correctly to operate properly. We call this **"scanning the top of the PCBs."** This requires a brief visual inspection of the top of the PCBs to verify that everything is in place for proper circuit operation. The schematic is shown to the right in Figure 3H-PCB03.

(1) Start at the H-PS01. The red/black leads of the H-PS01 Power Supply are connected to the two binding posts at the top of the Power Board and good electrical contact is made (Red to Red and Black to Black).

(2) The H-PS01 is plugged into a 110-115 VAC wall socket.

(3) Fuses, **F1** and **F2** are good 2A fuses. Do not use more than a **2A** fuse.

(4) There is a wire jumper or zero ohm resistor between the **B+** terminal and **TP4** to use S1 as the **IGN**ition **SW**itch.

(5) On the DC Motor Board there are wire jumpers or zero ohm resistors in **J3** and **J4**.

(6) The two wires from the DC motor are connected correctly to Pin 1 and Pin 2. The RED wire goes to Pin 1 and the BLUE or BLACK wire goes to Pin 2. **When the DC motor is operating air should be moving UP from the circuit board.**

The PCBs are now correctly configured from the top of the PCBs for testing, measuring and troubleshooting problems. When S1, S3 and S4 are CLOSED, voltage and ground should be applied to the DC Motor Board.

If the DC Motor does not operate, it may mean there is a problem on the bottom of the PCBs that was left in the PCBs from a previous problem or a zero ohm resistor has fallen out of the circuit board's copper side. To determine if a problem exists on the bottom of the PCBs scan the bottom of the PCBs as covered in the Instructor Guide, H-I/G03 which should only be reviewed by an instructor or an individual student using this training program for home-study.

If all set-up conditions on the top and bottom of the PCBs are met and B+ is at the +BATT terminal the DC Motor should operate when S1 (toggled UP), S3 and S4 are CLOSED (slides UP). If the DC Motor does not operate it's time to troubleshoot isn't it?

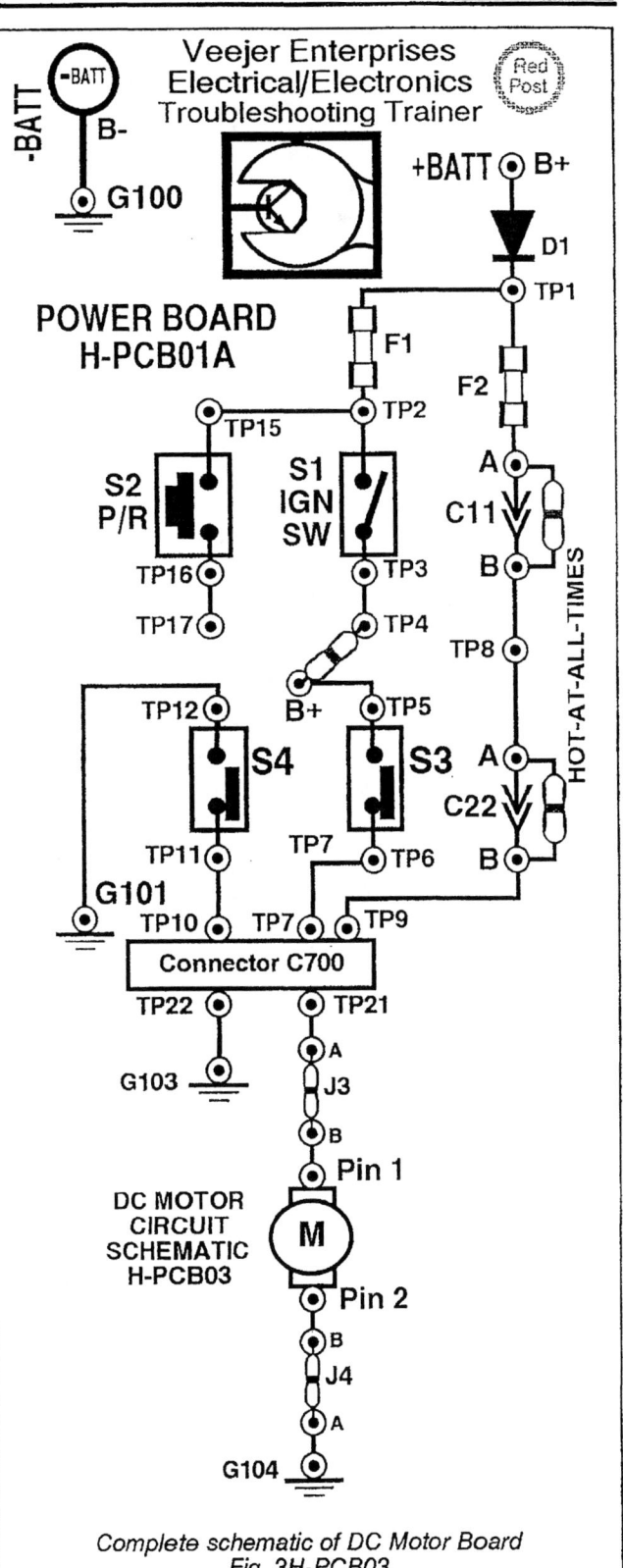

Complete schematic of DC Motor Board
Fig. 3H-PCB03

Vehicle Electronics Hands-On Home-Study Troubleshooting Training

VEEJER ENTERPRISES 3701 Lariat Lane, Garland, Texas 75042-5419
Phone: 972-276-9642   Fax: 972-276-8122   Email: info@veejer.com   Web Site: www.veejer.com

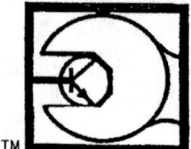

The Ground Side of The Circuit

When a circuit load is grounded it simply means the ground side of the load eventually connects to the B-terminal of the power source, usually through the sheet metal (G103-G101) or engine block which has already been "grounded" by a battery cable from the battery's negative terminal (G100). This reality is represented in our schematics by the circled -BATT terminal post (Black) connected to G100. representing the negative side of the voltage source.

The ground side of the circuit in the DC Motor Board is identical to the Lamp Board in the Starter Kit with an additional ground, G103 added on the DC Motor Board. The DC Motor Board schematic is drawn a little different than was shown with the Lamp Board to accommodate the new ground connection.

Comparing the two schematic versions of the DC Motor board shown in Figure 3H-021 may help to understand the ground side of the circuit with the new added ground connection, G103. A dotted line separates the two schematics into A. and B. sections.

Schematic Figure 21A:
The A. side of the schematic shows the ground circuit like it appears in the circuit board drawings and schematics although a little horizontally compressed to fit on the page. Pin 2 of the DC motor grounds to G104 through the zero ohm resistor in J4. G104 is grounded by G103 which connects to TP22 through C700 to TP10. TP10 connects to TP11 which connects to TP12 through the CLOSED contacts of S4. TP12 is grounded by G101. G101 is grounded by G100 which connects the ground circuit to the negative terminal of the voltage source, -BATT.

Schematic Figure 21B:
The B. side of the schematic is a straight-line schematic showing the same ground circuit. In the straight line schematic drawing, the sequence of ground connections is clearly evident showing how Pin 2 of the DC Motor connects to the -BATT binding post (Black) to complete the ground circuit.

Let there be no misunderstanding about grounding the DMM during circuit voltage (Vc) measurements. **ALWAYS GROUND THE DMM'S BLACK TEST LEAD TO THE BATTERY'S NEGATIVE TERMINAL FOR Vc MEASUREMENTS.** It is the most negative point on the vehicle that is easy to access on most vehicles. The only other point on a vehicle that is more negative is the Generator (Alternator) housing (ground) when the engine is running and the generator is producing charging voltage.

Since the generator may be difficult to access on many vehicles the battery negative terminal is a good substitute. Make a 10-15 foot ground lead to ground your DMM on vehicles. When troubleshooting "The" Hands-On Program simply ground the DMM BLACK Test Lead to the Black binding post at the top of the Power Board.

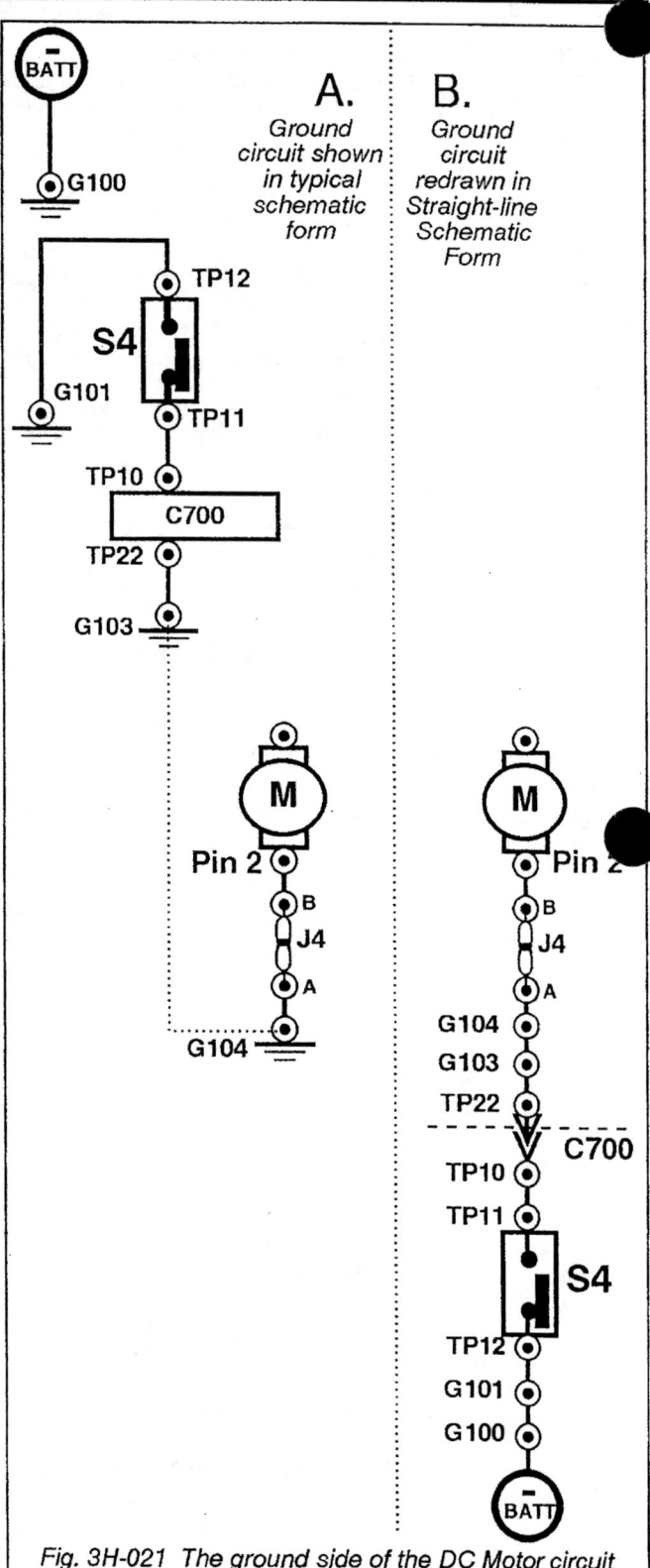

A. Ground circuit shown in typical schematic form

B. Ground circuit redrawn in Straight-line Schematic Form

Fig. 3H-021 The ground side of the DC Motor circuit

Vehicle Electronics Hands-On Home-Study Troubleshooting Training

VEEJER ENTERPRISES 3701 Lariat Lane, Garland, Texas 75042-5419
Phone: 972-276-9642 Fax: 972-276-8122 Email: info@veejer.com Web Site: www.veejer.com

DC Motor and CEMF

The resistance of a component has a major impact on the amount of current that can pass through a circuit. The higher a component's resistance the *lower* the current through the circuit containing the component. If a component's resistance decreases in a circuit the circuit's current *increases*. That's basic Ohm's Law in action.

DC motors in circuits act the same as any other circuit component with resistance but DC motors present an added twist. DC Motors *change their resistance* with their rpm which changes the current passing through the DC motor winding. A DC motor is said to have the property of *dynamic (changing) resistance* because DC motors vary current passing through them as DC motor rpm changes. A DC motor's dynamic resistance is called **counter electromotive force,** abbreviated **cemf**. Cemf is a force that opposes electromotive force **(emf),** the force that pulls/pushes electrons through a circuit. The two forces work against each other as current flows through a DC motor. Cemf is discussed in **Lesson 34** of *"The"* Course.

Cemf is a *counter force* present in a DC motor that *opposes* the current flowing through a motor just as the resistance of a resistor opposes current flowing through the resistor. The only difference is a DC Motor changes its resistance with rpm. The cemf that a DC motor develops in a circuit determines the amount of current flowing through the DC motor. Low DC motor rpm *decreases cemf* (resistance) so DC motor *current rises*, sometimes rather drastically causing damage to the motor winding and wiring.

The effect of cemf can be used to troubleshoot DC motor circuits. DC motor cemf affecting motor current is good because we can use current measurement to determine if a DC motor is running at the correct rpm.

If the DC motor is drawing the correct current (determined by specifications or checking a known good similar DC motor circuit for current draw) we know it is turning at the correct rpm as long as the current draw is in the normal range found on other similar circuits.

DC motor cemf dramatically affects motor electron current. Suppose a DC motor is mechanically prevented from running at normal rpm. Cemf (resistance) is low so there is a significant rise in motor electron current which can damage circuit wiring by melting the wire insulation and heating the insulation in adjacent conductors in a wiring harness. This can create shorts-to-ground and shorts-to-voltage. High motor current can also damage the DC motor's winding.

There are two reasons for a DC motor to turn at lower than normal rpm. If the mechanical assembly turned by the DC motor cannot allow proper rpm due to worn motor bearings then motor current rises. If the DC motor has worn or defective bearings the motor shaft cannot rotate at the proper rpm and motor current rises.

Two examples:

(1) In the case of a **starter motor** used to crank an engine, "starter draw" is excessively high when the starter motor is cranking a very cold engine or the starter motor has worn bearings causing the armature to drag on the field coils. In both cases low starter cranking rpm causes a high starter draw that is much higher than normal and an indication that something is slowing starter rpm.

(2) In the case of a **blower fan motor,** current rises quickly if blower motor air passages are restricted or worn motor bearings cause low blower rpm. Wires to the blower motor may get so hot they melt the insulation exposing the conductor which makes contact with other wires in the same harness. Once the current stops the insulation cools and fuses the wires together creating shorts-to-voltage and or shorts-to-ground. Figure 3H-023 shows a simple technique of checking DC blower motor current to determine if current is in a normal range.

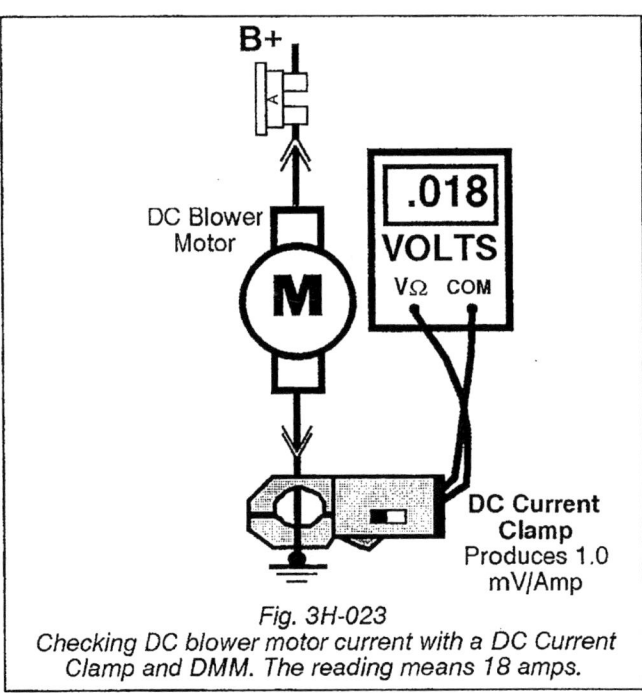

Fig. 3H-023
Checking DC blower motor current with a DC Current Clamp and DMM. The reading means 18 amps.

The DMM indicates the blower motor is pulling 18 amps. If the current is in the range of 25-30 amps it could be concluded the blower motor is running at a lower rpm.

Lesson 34, Page 3 of the 60 lesson course discusses using a DC Current Clamp. **Lesson 35** discusses troubleshooting blower motor problems.

Anytime wiring to a DC motor circuit shows signs of over heating, such as melted insulation that has cooled into an abnormal shape, motor current should be checked as shown above to identify DC motor circuit problems especially in high current circuits.

Vehicle Electronics Hands-On Home-Study Troubleshooting Training

VEEJER ENTERPRISES 3701 Lariat Lane, Garland, Texas 75042-5419
Phone: 972-276-9642 Fax: 972-276-8122 Email: info@veejer.com Web Site: www.veejer.com

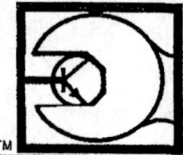

Seeing CEMF In Action

It is possible to see current rise as motor rpm decreases. Simply drag down DC motor rpm while measuring the current.

Do This.

(1) Connect the DC Motor Board to the Power Board.

(2) Turn ON the DC Motor by toggling S1 UP and slide S3 and S4 UP.

(3) The DC Motor should operate and move air.

(4) Turn S1 OFF.

(5) Remove Fuse F1.

(6) Set-up the DMM as shown in Fig. 3H-022. Set DMM to the 10 AMP range and connect to the two fuse terminals. Connect the Red DMM Test Lead to the top fuse terminal (hot side) and the Black DMM Test Lead to the bottom fuse terminal (cold side).

(7) Turn S1 ON and the DC Motor should operate again.

(8) Notice the current reading of about 0.14 to 0.18 amps, or 140 mA or 180 mA. Your reading may vary slightly and this is normal.

(9) Carefully, now, place your finger UNDER the circuit board and gently push up on the large flat base plate of the DC Motor's armature (as shown below) at the center point of the rotating blades. Press gently to slow down the DC Motor by applying some mechanical drag on the rotor blades. DO NOT MAKE CONTACT WITH THE ROTOR BLADES THEMSELVES. As the fan slows down note a slight rise in motor current on the DMM to about 0.24 - 0.25 amps.

Underside of DC motor

The rise is DC Motor current is due to the rpm slowing down and cemf decreasing which allows the increase in DC Motor electron current. Basic Ohm's Law states: As resistance (motor cemf) decreases, current increases. The rise in current is slight with this DC Motor because it is a brushless DC motor and carries only a small current of approximately 0.18 amps or 180 mA in normal operation. The rise in current would be much more noticeable if the DC Motor being tested was a starter motor **(Lesson 34)** or a blower motor **(Lesson 35)** and it was operating at a lower rpm due to a mechanical problem dragging of a DC motor. Disconnect the ammeter from the fuse holder terminals and install the fuse F1 to proceed.

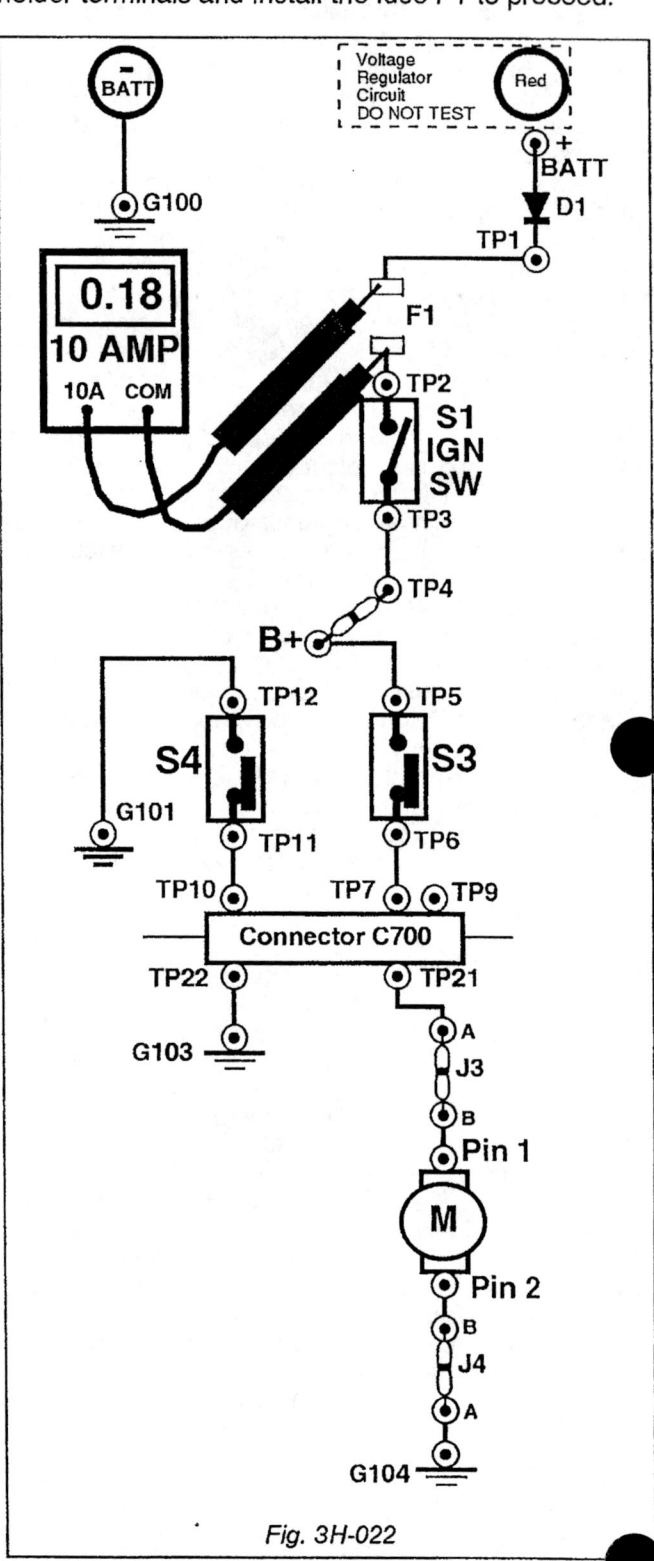

Fig. 3H-022

Copyright © 2015 VEEJER ENTERPRISES, Garland, Texas - All Rights Reserved

Vehicle Electronics Hands-On Home-Study Troubleshooting Training

VEEJER ENTERPRISES 3701 Lariat Lane, Garland, Texas 75042-5419
Phone: 972-276-9642 Fax: 972-276-8122 Email: info@veejer.com Web Site: www.veejer.com

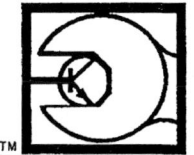

There are **three** basic voltage drop measurements that can be made on any circuit including DC motor circuits on any vehicle to reveal a lot about the electrical conditions in the circuit.

1. Measure Vd Of The Voltage Side Of Load

With the DC Motor ON (current flowing through motor, moving proper amount of air) the first voltage check to perform is the Vd of the voltage side, **Vd$_{vs}$**, of the circuit as shown in Figure 3H-024.

Lessons 15 and 16 explain what Vds are, how they occur in circuits and how to measure them. **Lesson 16, Pages 4-6** discusses checking Vd$_{vs}$. **Lesson 35** discusses measuring DC motor circuit Vds. Current must be flowing when measuring **Vd$_{vs}$**.

Do This:
(1) Turn S1 ON.
(2) Verify S3 and S4 are CLOSED (slide UP) and if the DC Motor is moving proper amount of air. If the DC Motor is OFF current is not flowing and a **Vd$_{vs}$** measurement cannot be done.

Scan the top and bottom of the PCBs to locate any problems that might be present from the last time the PCBs were used. Current must be flowing when measuring any voltage drop including **Vd$_{vs}$**. Place the DMM on the 20-30-40 volt range (readout indicates **0.00** before measuring) and connect the DMM test leads to the PCBs as shown in Figure 3H-024.

(3) Record the **Vd$_{vs}$** reading obtained. _____ V

(4) Write the numbers with decimal point in the DMM shown in Figure 3H-024.

A reading of about 0.70–0.80 volt is normal for **Vd$_{vs}$** if the circuit is functioning correctly. The *lower* **Vd$_{vs}$** is in a circuit the better. The more air the DC Motor moves the higher the efficiency of operation.

Vd$_{vs}$ In A Vehicle Circuit

In any vehicle electrical circuit, a **Vd$_{vs}$** reading is considered normal if the reading is approximately **0.50V** or less. A reading of a few tenths of a volt higher (0.6-0.8V) may be normal in some circuits when a solid-state component is present such as diode, D1, which provides the function of **polarity protection** of the circuit from reverse operating voltage (B+)

Polarity Protection Diode, D1

Should the operating voltage be connected to the circuit in reverse, that is, the red power lead (B+) to the black post and the black power lead (B-) to the red post, the diode prevents current from flowing through the circuit.

Diodes may be placed in the voltage feed of any circuit (as D1 is on the Power Board) to protect the circuit from reverse polarity such as when attempting to jump start a vehicle with the jumper cables connected in reverse polarity to the dead battery.

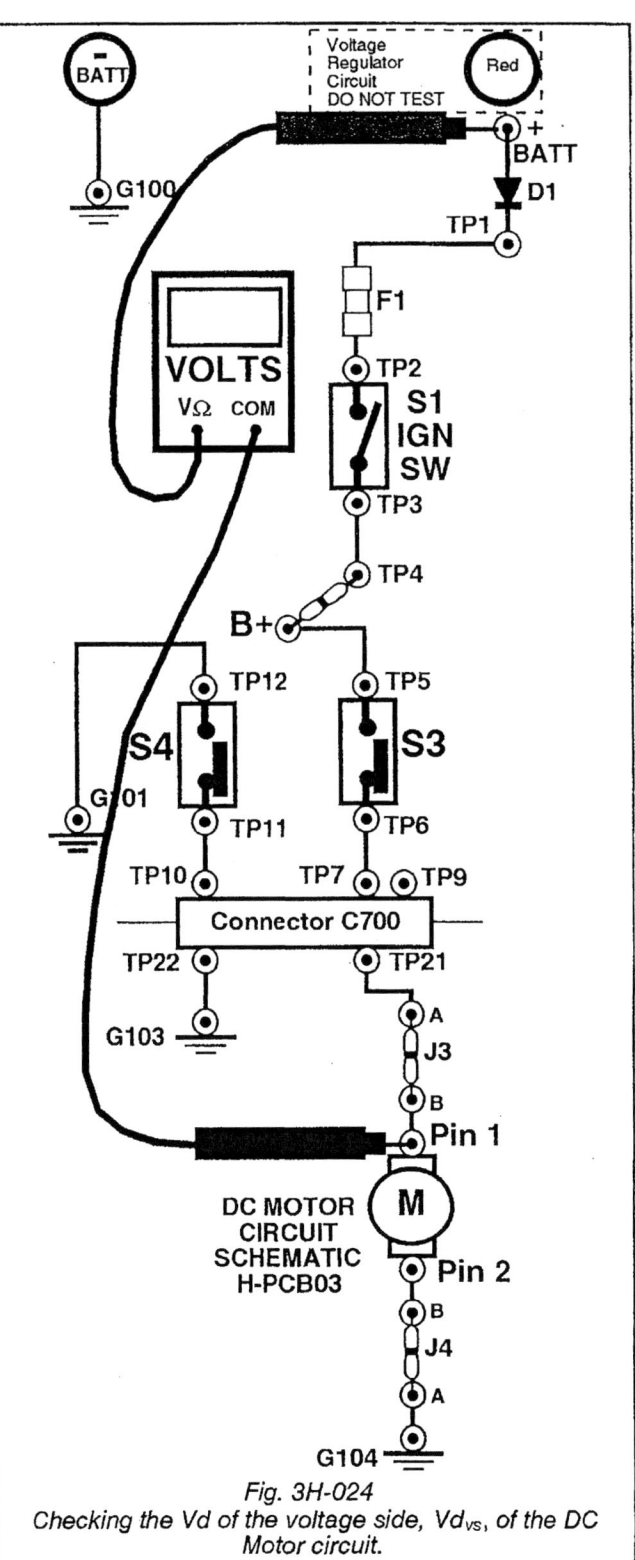

Fig. 3H-024
Checking the Vd of the voltage side, Vd$_{vs}$, of the DC Motor circuit.

2. Measure Vd Of The Ground Side Of Load

A second Vd check to perform is the Vd of the ground side of the circuit, or **Vd$_{GS}$** as shown in Figure 3H-025.

Lesson 16, Pages 4-6 discusses checking the Vd of the ground side of a circuit and **Lesson 35** discusses **Vd$_{GS}$** in DC motor circuits. Current must be flowing when measuring **Vd$_{GS}$**.

Do This:
(1) Turn S1 ON.
(2) Make sure S3 and S4 are CLOSED (slides UP).
(3) Place the DMM on the 20-30-40 volt range (readout says **0.00**) and connect the test leads as shown in Figure 3H-025.

(4) Record the **Vd$_{GS}$** reading obtained. _____ V

(5) Write the numbers with decimal point in the DMM shown in Figure H-007A

A reading of about **0.10** volt is normal for **Vd$_{GS}$** if the ground circuit is in good condition. The *lower* **Vd$_{GS}$** is in a vehicle circuit the better. Normally, on a vehicle, **Vd$_{GS}$** of most vehicle electrical circuits is considered to be a good ground circuit if the **Vd$_{GS}$** is no more 0.10V. The reason that **Vd$_{GS}$** is so low in the PCBs is due to the short distance of the ground circuit. Do not be surprised if **Vd$_{GS}$** on the PCBs reads **0.00V**. It shows the ground circuit is such a short distance between the -BATT terminal post and Lamp Pin 2 that the resistance is too small to register a **Vd$_{GS}$** on the 20-30-40 volt range of a DMM.

If the **Vd$_{GS}$** reading is higher than 0.10 volt in a vehicle circuit it means there is increased resistance on the ground side due to corrosion in the wiring and connections or possibly a ground jumper connection is not making good contact.

Vd$_{GS}$ On A Vehicle Circuit

The ground side of a circuit on a vehicle may have ground jumpers connecting two pieces of metal to complete the ground circuit of some electrical circuits. These ground jumpers are called **redundant grounds** and are usually not shown on vehicle schematic diagrams so it is difficult to know when they are present and if they are defective causing a ground side problem. If one of these redundant ground jumper connections is loose or corroded it may cause **Vd$_{GS}$** to be higher than normal so you will know a problem on the ground side exists.

Since the ground jumpers do not appear on schematic diagrams and they may not always be obvious when looking over the wiring of a vehicle, a **Vd$_{GS}$** measurement is the only way to determine that a ground side wire jumper is loose or corroded.

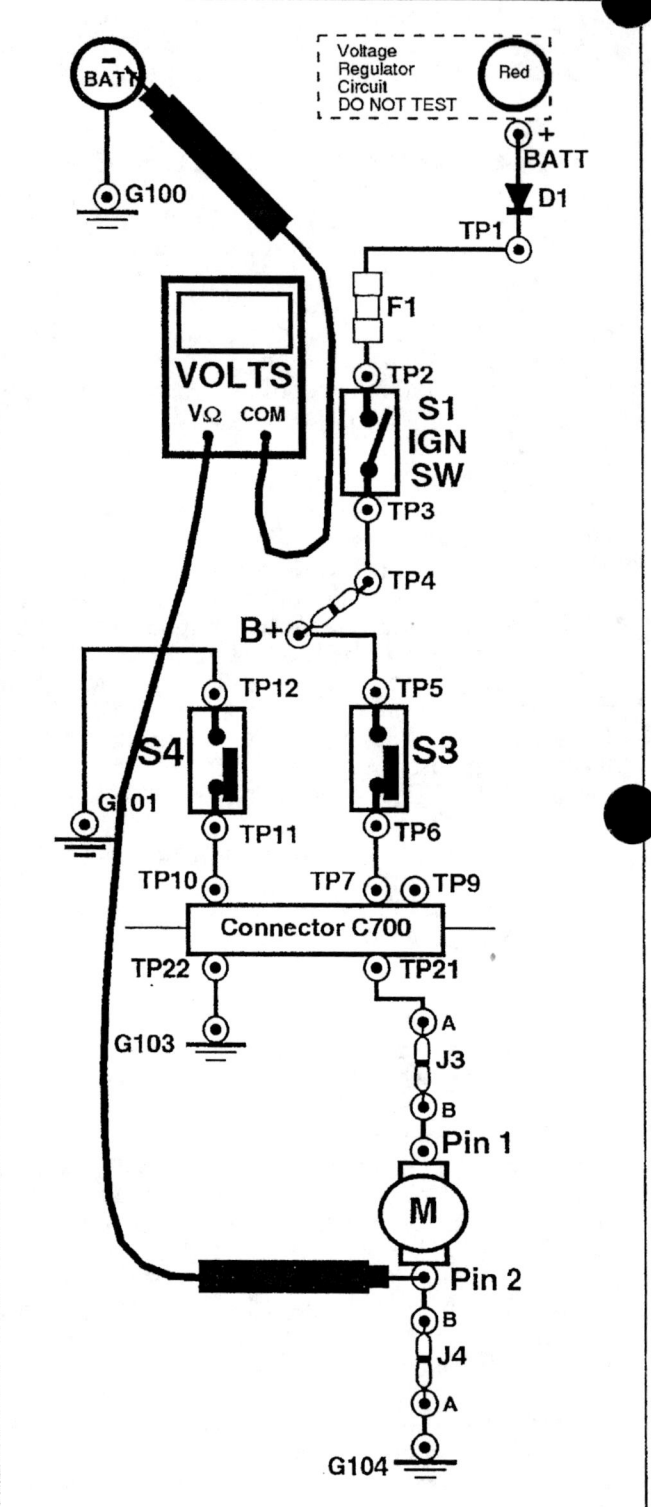

Fig. 3H-025 Measuring Vd of the ground side, Vd$_{GS}$ of the DC Motor circuit.

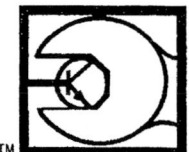

Vehicle Electronics Hands-On Home-Study Troubleshooting Training

VEEJER ENTERPRISES 3701 Lariat Lane, Garland, Texas 75042-5419
Phone: 972-276-9642   Fax: 972-276-8122   Email: info@veejer.com   Web Site: www.veejer.com

3. Measure Vd Of The Load

A third Vd check to perform is the Vd of the load as shown in Figure 3H-026 The term used for the voltage drop of the load is **Vd$_{LOAD}$**.

Lesson 24, Page 1 discusses checking **Vd$_{LOAD}$**, and **Lesson 35** discusses **Vd$_{LOAD}$** in DC Motor Circuits.

Current must be flowing when measuring **Vd$_{LOAD}$**. The current is flowing if the DC Motor is running and moving air. Place the DMM on the 20-30-40 volt range (readout says **0.00**) and connect the test leads as shown in Figure 3H-026

(1) Record the **Vd$_{LOAD}$** reading obtained. _____ V

(2) Write the numbers with decimal point in the DMM shown in Figure 3H-026.

A reading of close to B+ should be expected for **Vd$_{LOAD}$**. The *higher* **Vd$_{LOAD}$** the better and the brighter the lamp. **Vd$_{LOAD}$** can never equal B+ because **Vd$_{VS}$** and **Vd$_{GS}$** are always present and subtract from **Vd$_{LOAD}$**. This is discussed in **Lesson 24**.

The higher **Vd$_{LOAD}$** is in a circuit, the more efficient the circuit and the better the load operates. Lamps are brightest as their **Vd$_{LOAD}$** gets closer to B+. DC Motors operate at the highest rpm, relays close contacts better, solenoids move their plunger more efficiently when they have the highest **Vd$_{LOAD}$**. On a vehicle, **Vd$_{LOAD}$** is good if within 1 volt of B+, the vehicle charging voltage.

> Testing the charging voltage is discussed in **Lesson 22, Pages 5-6.**

On most passenger vehicles, normal charging voltage ranges from a low of 13.50–13.80 volts in hot weather to a high of 15.10 volts in cold weather. (This is discussed in **Lesson 21 & 22**.) Therefore **Vd$_{LOAD}$** varies as the charging voltage changes with ambient temperature.

In the PCBs, the **Vd$_{LOAD}$** reading is not as close to the B+ supply voltage at the +BATT Terminal because of the 0.75 volt drop of diode, D1, on the voltage side.

This shows us that any increase of **Vd$_{VS}$** or **Vd$_{GS}$** decreases **Vd$_{LOAD}$**. A low **Vd$_{LOAD}$** reading is due to a circuit problem developing corrosion or loose connections in the voltage side or the ground side of the circuit. Low B+ or charging voltage can also lower **Vd$_{LOAD}$**.

Whatever the load device in a circuit happens to be (we use a DC Motor for our example here) and its **Vd$_{LOAD}$** reading begins to decrease, it will not work as well (rpm is lower). A solenoid may not move its plunger very well. A relay may not close its contacts. Loads work best in any circuit the higher the **Vd$_{LOAD}$** reading.

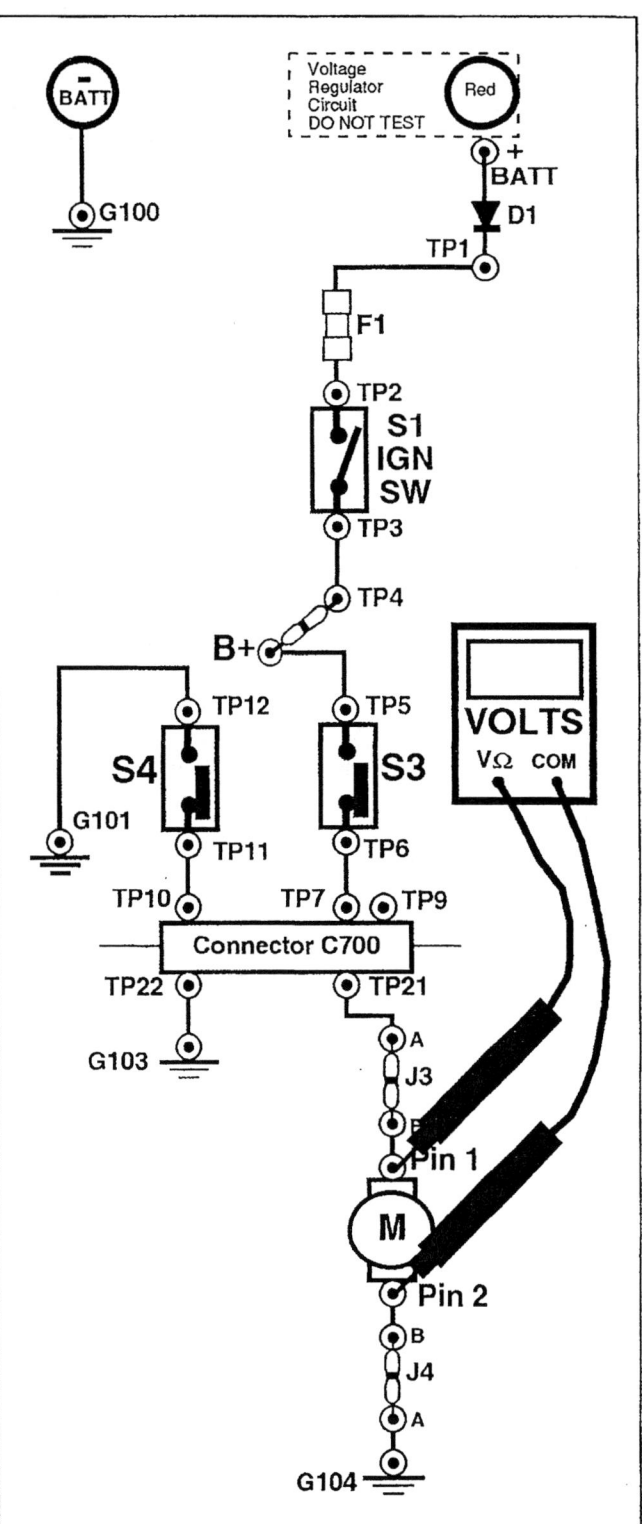

Fig. 3H-026 Measuring Vd of the Load, Vd$_{LOAD}$, of the DC Motor circuit.

Vehicle Electronics Hands-On Home-Study Troubleshooting Training

VEEJER ENTERPRISES 3701 Lariat Lane, Garland, Texas 75042-5419
Phone: 972-276-9642 Fax: 972-276-8122 Email: info@veejer.com Web Site: www.veejer.com

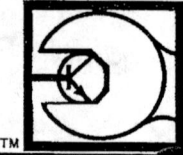

Measure Circuit Voltages (Vc) Voltage Side
Trace voltage side Vc or B+:

When measuring a circuit Voltage (abbr. "Vc") it **always means the DMM is understood to be grounded at the -BATT terminal post.** On a vehicle, a Vc measurement means the DMM is grounded at the battery negative terminal post.

In Figure 3H-027 the BLACK DMM test lead is understood to be connected to the negative -BATT terminal post and is not shown to save space in the illustration.

Figure 3H-027 shows the placement of the RED DMM test lead for each Vc measurement to be made on the voltage side of the circuit and the sequence of the measurements. **Lesson 11** discusses the voltage side of the circuit. **Lesson 23** discusses Vc measurement. **Lesson 35** covers Vc measurements in DC motor circuits.

DO THIS:

- Scan the top and bottom of the PCBs to make sure the PCBs have no faults.
- Place S3 and S4 in the UP position (CLOSED).
- Turn the circuit ON with S1. DC Motor should be moving the proper amount of air.
- Ground DMM to the -BATT Black terminal post.
- Measure the Vc at each point in the voltage side of the circuit as shown in Figure 3H-027 beginning at load Pin 1 and record your readings below. Note what each Vc measurement reveals about the circuit.

(1) _____ V (Load Pin 1)
(2) _____ V (TP21–good B+ to board)
(3) _____ V (TP7–good B+ to C700)
(4) _____ V (TP6–good B+ from S3)
(5) _____ V (TP5–good B+ to S3)
(6) _____ V (TP4–good 0Ω resistor)
(7) _____ V (TP3–good B+ from S1)
(8) _____ V (TP2–good fuse F1)
(9) _____ V (TP1–good B+ from D1)
(10) _____ V (good B+ supply)

Notice how the Vc readings **increase slightly** as the measurement point gets closer to the positive terminal of the voltage source, the **+BATT Terminal**. At TP10 the Vc is equal to the B+ of the power source for the PCBs.

Notice the voltage increase from Step 9 to Step 10. The difference between the two readings is the Vd of the polarity sensing diode, D1.

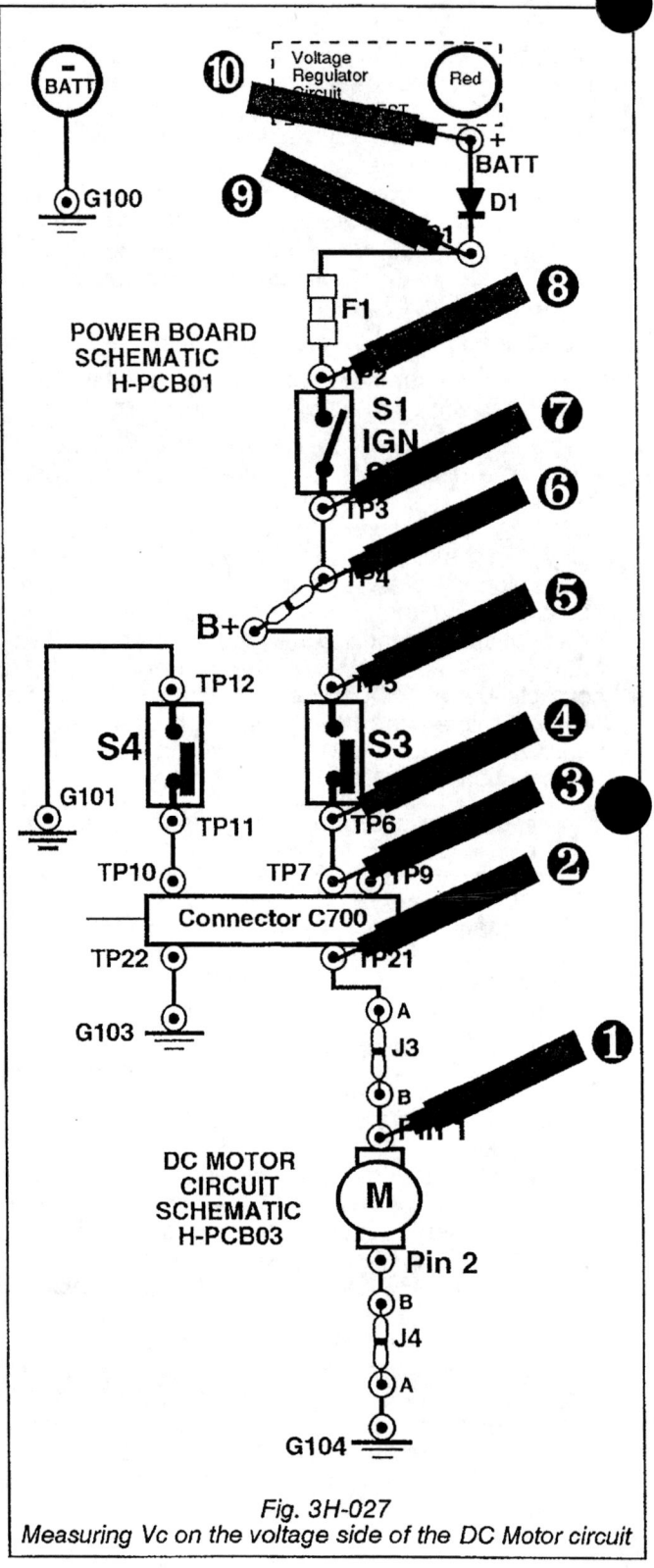

Fig. 3H-027
Measuring Vc on the voltage side of the DC Motor circuit

Copyright © 2015 VEEJER ENTERPRISES, Garland, Texas - All Rights Reserved   Text H-WB113 Page 21

Vehicle Electronics Hands-On Home-Study Troubleshooting Training

VEEJER ENTERPRISES 3701 Lariat Lane, Garland, Texas 75042-5419
Phone: 972-276-9642   Fax: 972-276-8122   Email: info@veejer.com   Web Site: www.veejer.com

Measure Circuit Voltages (Vc) Ground Side
Trace ground side Vc or B-:

When measuring Vc (circuit voltage) it *always means* the DMM is understood to be grounded at the battery negative terminal. On the vehicle use the battery's negative terminal. On the PCBs use the negative or black terminal post, -BATT.

Figure 3H-028 shows the placement of the RED DMM test lead for each Vc measurement to be made on the ground side of the circuit. **Lesson 12** discusses the ground side of the circuit. **Lesson 35** discusses Vc measurements.

DO THIS:

- Scan the top and bottom looking for faults left in the PCBs.
- Turn the circuit ON with S1 so the DC Motor is moving air (S3 and S4 slide UP).
- Ground DMM to the negative terminal post.
- With the DC Motor operating normally measure the Vc at each ground side point in the circuit beginning at Lamp Pin 2 and record your readings below.

Carefully follow the order of Vc measurements. The DMM test leads are touching the circuit in the correct numerical order however numbers next to the DMM test leads *only appear* out of order.

(1) _____ V (Load Pin 2)
(2) _____ V (G104 – good ground)
(3) _____ V (G103   "   ")
(4) _____ V (TP22   "   ")
(5) _____ V (TP10   "   ")
(6) _____ V (TP11   "   ")
(7) _____ V (TP12   "   ")
(8) _____ V (G101   "   ")
(9) _____ V G100   "   ")
(10) _____ V (-BATT Terminal Ground)

Notice the Vc readings **decrease slightly** as the measurement point gets closer to the -BATT or negative terminal of the voltage source.

If the DMM readings are **0.00** (20-30-40V Range) on the ground side (meaning a really good ground circuit) change the DMM to the (2-3-4V Range) where the readout says **.000** before measuring. This will allow you to see readings in 1 mV increments, .001=1 mV, .002=2 mV, .012-12 mV, etc., to better observe the subtle Vc changes on the ground side of the circuit.

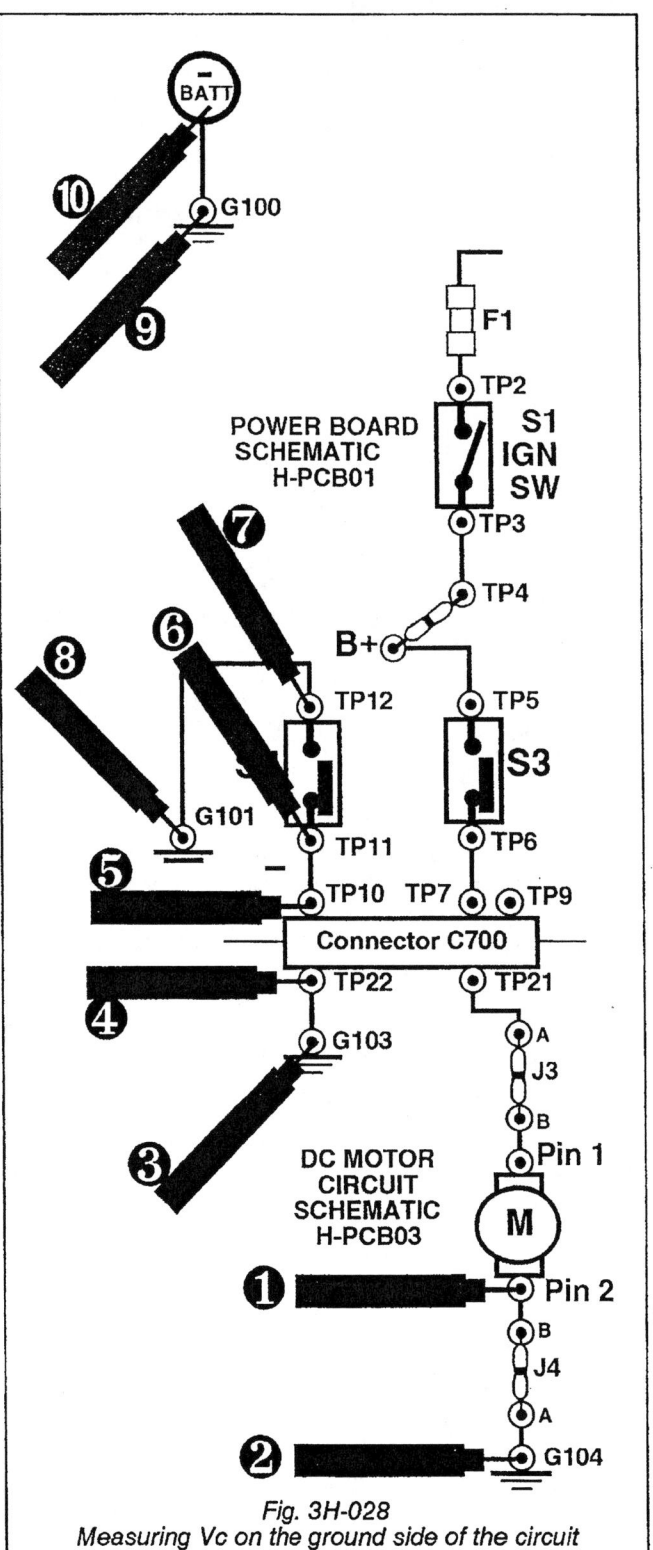

Fig. 3H-028
Measuring Vc on the ground side of the circuit

Vehicle Electronics Hands-On Home-Study Troubleshooting Training

VEEJER ENTERPRISES 3701 Lariat Lane, Garland, Texas 75042-5419
Phone: 972-276-9642 Fax: 972-276-8122 Email: info@veejer.com Web Site: www.veejer.com

Systematic Troubleshooting

Successful automotive and truck electronic system troubleshooting is based on systematic troubleshooting procedures developed and proven to reveal a circuit problem in the shortest possible time with almost foolproof accuracy. We covered the "Texas-Two-Step," abbr. as "TTS" in Module 01/02, the Power Board/Lamp Circuit. The **TTS** is adequate to test DC motor circuits as well. **Lesson 23** and **Lesson 24** explain TTS measurement in detail. **Lesson 36** covers the TTS as it applies to DC motor circuits.

The TTS involves two Vc measurements at the load terminals. The DMM black test lead is grounded to battery negative which we call **-BATT** as shown at the top of Figure 3H-029 illustrating the two Vc measurements at the load's terminals of the DC Motor circuit. It is *always understood* that the DMM is grounded to the Power Board (-BATT) for the TTS.

STEP 1 of the TTS is abbr. "TTS-1":
Measure the Vc at Load Pin 1. This reading shows how much B+ gets to the load pin 1. **Expect the reading to be close to B+** when the voltage side of the load is a good circuit. **The higher the TTS-1 reading the better.** The TTS-1 reading is always the value of B+ minus Vd_{vs}. The higher Vd_{vs} the lower the TTS-1 reading. Any electrical problem on the voltage side of the circuit (OPEN or Vd) will be reflected in a **lower than normal** TTS-1 reading.

STEP 2 of the TTS is abbr. "TTS-2":
Measure the Vc at Load Pin 2. This reading shows how good the ground is for the load. **Expect the reading to be about 0.10V for a good ground circuit. The lower the TTS-2 reading the better.** Any electrical problem on the ground side of the circuit (OPEN or Vd) will be reflected in a **higher than normal** TTS-2 reading.

Do This: Turn ON the circuit. Verify that the DMM is grounded to -BATT. Now perform both TTS measurements with the red DMM test lead and record the readings to establish normal TTS readings for the DC Motor circuit.

TTS-1 _____ volts TTS-2 _____ volts.

These are normal TTS readings that should be expected in the DC Motor circuit. Compare actual TTS readings in a circuit with these "known-good" values to identify a circuit problem with the DC Motor circuit.

On the next page we begin investigating the six ways a circuit fails. We will learn how to test and measure Vc in the circuit using the TTS to determine what is wrong in a circuit. After that we begin troubleshooting all the programmed troubleshooting problems to improve your troubleshooting skill.

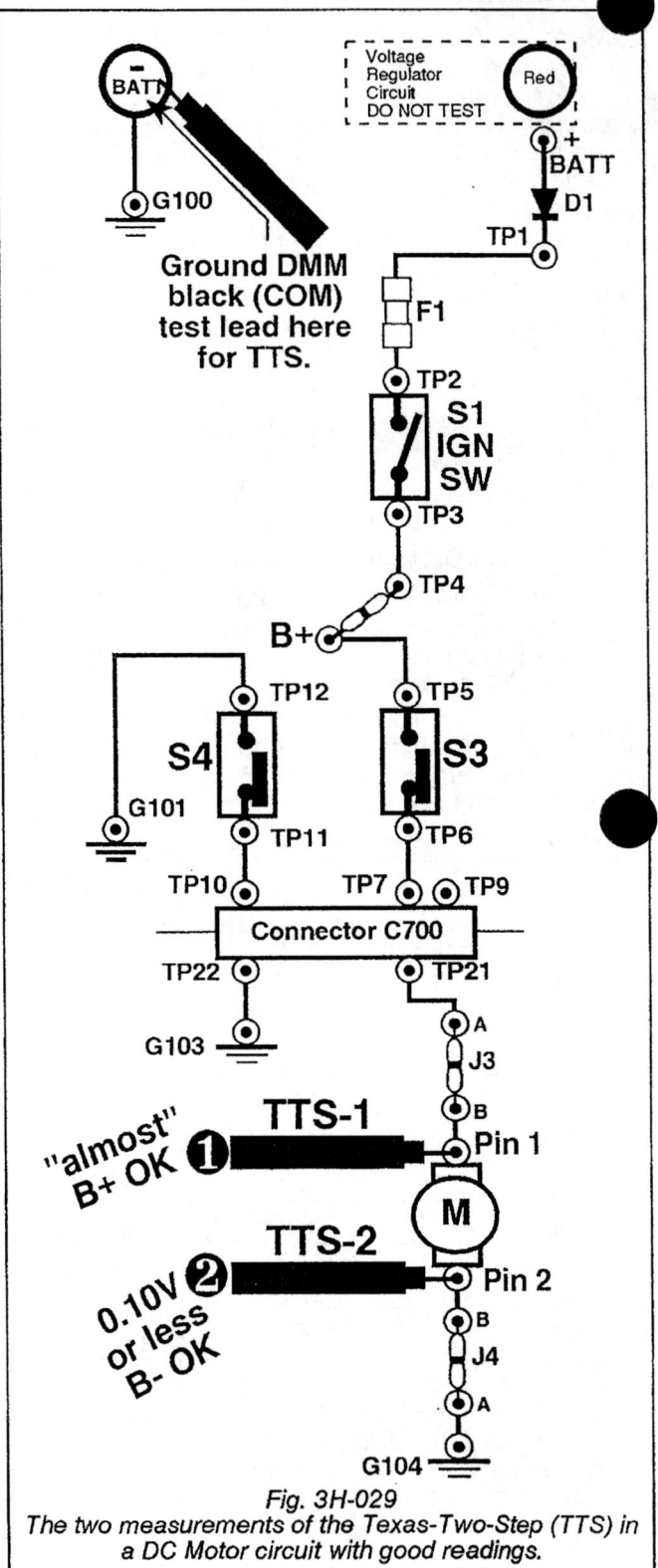

Fig. 3H-029
The two measurements of the Texas-Two-Step (TTS) in a DC Motor circuit with good readings.

Vehicle Electronics Hands-On Home-Study Troubleshooting Training

VEEJER ENTERPRISES 3701 Lariat Lane, Garland, Texas 75042-5419
Phone: 972-276-9642 Fax: 972-276-8122 Email: info@veejer.com Web Site: www.veejer.com

Basic Circuit Problem Number 1
"OPEN Circuit on the Voltage Side"

Insert An OPEN Circuit on the Voltage Side:
Remove the 0ΩR (zero ohm resistor) from J3 on the top of the DC Motor Board to create an open circuit on the voltage side of the DC Motor circuit. Figure 3H-030 shows the 0ΩR in J3 removed from the DC Motor Board.

Lesson 24, Pages 2-3 analyze basic circuit problem #1.
Lesson 36, Page 3 analyses problem #1 in DC Motors.

How does an OPEN circuit on the voltage side affect DC Motor operation? _____

Do This:
◦ Turn the circuit ON with S1 (S3 & S4 slide UP)
◦ Ground DMM negative test lead to -BATT.
◦ Perform the TTS with the 0ΩR removed from J3. Record the readings below and in Figure 3H-030.

(1) TTS-1 reading: _____
Conclusion: _____

(2) TTS-2 reading: _____
Conclusion: _____

(3) What is the next troubleshooting step?
_____
_____

(4) What is concluded when you find B+ at J3 Pin A?
_____
_____

(5) What You Should Learn From This.

An OPEN on the voltage side of the load causes zero volt at the voltage side of the load.

_____

Leave the 0ΩR out of J3 for the next exercise on the next page.

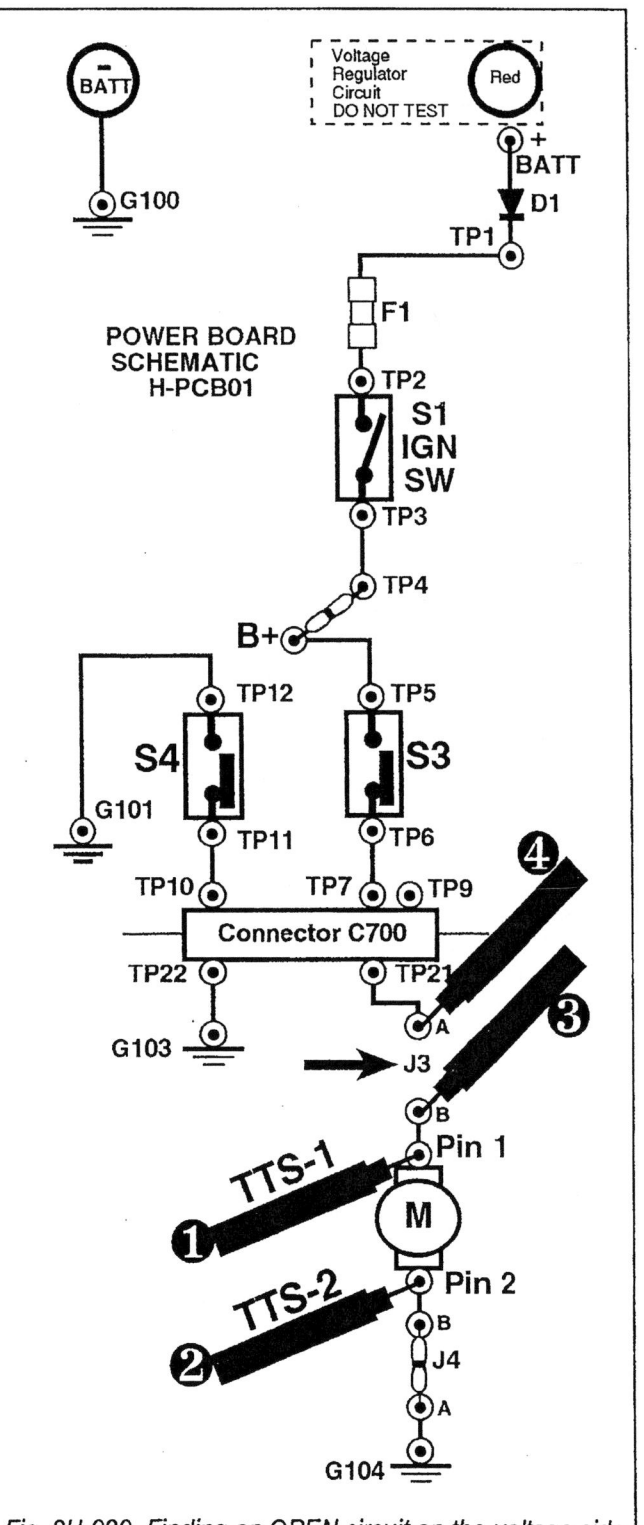

Fig. 3H-030 Finding an OPEN circuit on the voltage side

Copyright © 2015 VEEJER ENTERPRISES, Garland, Texas - All Rights Reserved

Vehicle Electronics Hands-On Home-Study Troubleshooting Training

VEEJER ENTERPRISES 3701 Lariat Lane, Garland, Texas 75042-5419
Phone: 972-276-9642   Fax: 972-276-8122   Email: info@veejer.com   Web Site: www.veejer.com

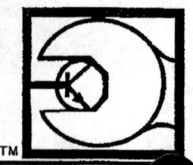

Study Circuit Problem Number 2
"A Vd on the voltage side"

Insert A Vd on the Voltage Side:
Remove J3 from the top of the DC Motor Board and insert a 150 ohm resistor in its place. Select a 150 ohm resistor from the Resistor Bag, H-RB03, and insert it in place of the 0ΩR in J3 to create a Vd on the voltage side of the DC Motor. **(150Ω color code is Brown-Green-Brown.)** Figure 3H-031 shows jumper J3 removed and a 150Ω resistor inserted in its place.

Lesson 24, Pages 3-4 discusses basic circuit problem #2. **Lesson 36, Page 3** discusses problem #2 in DC motor circuits.

How does a Vd on the voltage side affect DC Motor operation? _____

TWO NOTES:
(1) The DC Motor runs at a lower rpm and moves less air because a large Vd is present on the voltage side of the load due to the 150Ω resistor in J3. Later when troubleshooting the programmed troubleshooting problems, the rpm of the DC Motor and the amount of air it moves will vary depending on the size of the fixed resistor used to create a Vd. Since different resistor values are selected DC Motor rpm will vary in each circuit problem. This adds some interesting variety to the troubleshooting problems.

(2) The 150Ω resistor will get warm during the time this circuit is ON and current is flowing. Use care in removing the resistor.

Do This:
- Turn the circuit ON with S1 (S3 & S4 slide UP).
- Ground DMM negative test lead to -BATT.
- Perform the TTS and record the readings below.

(1) TTS-1 reading: _____ V
Conclusion: _____

(2) TTS-2 reading: _____ V
Conclusion: _____

(3) What is the next troubleshooting step?
_____

(4) What is concluded when you find B+ at J3 Pin A?
_____

What You Should Learn From This:
A resistance at the wrong place in the voltage side of a circuit causes an undesirable Vd. Above the resistance the Vc (circuit voltage) is almost B+ and below the resistance the Vc is low B+. Leave the fault in the circuit and continue working with Problem #2

on the next page for a very important lesson to le[arn] in troubleshooting. **It's a principal you must NEVER FORGET.**

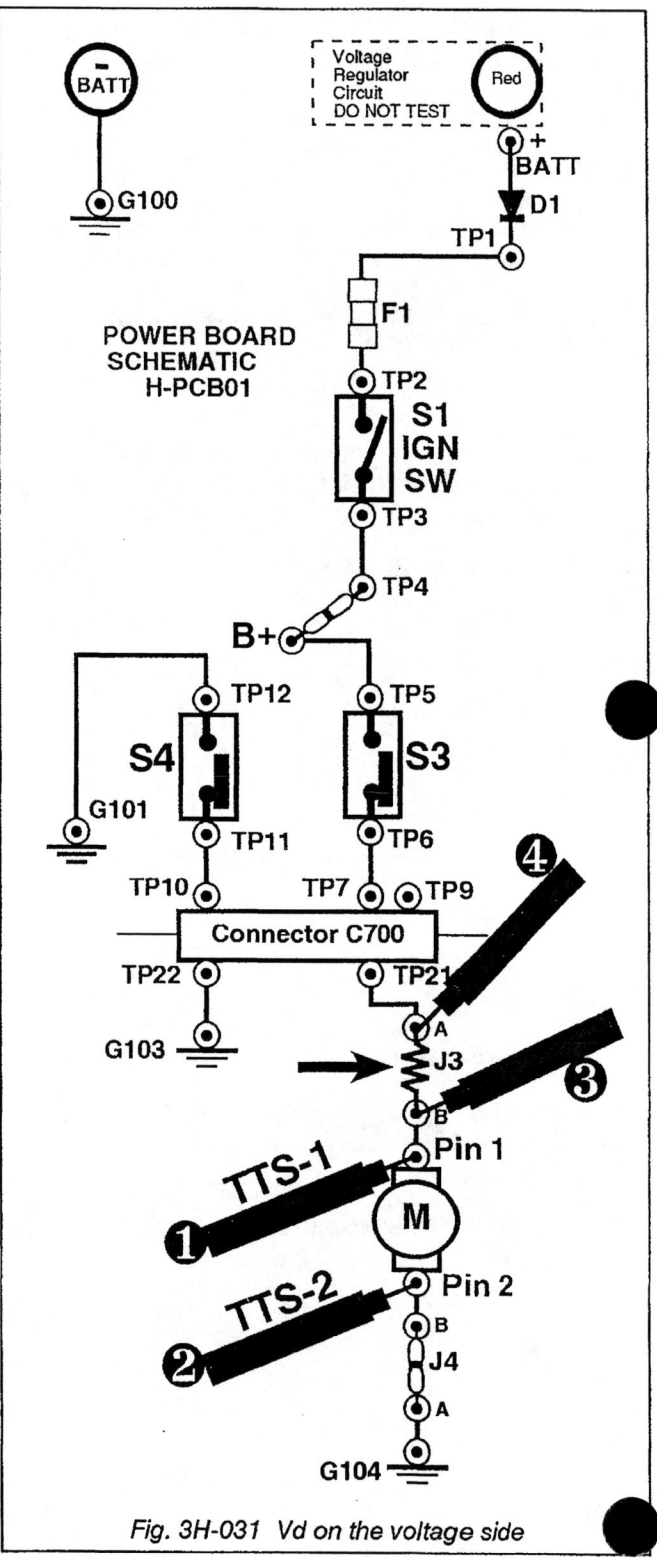

Fig. 3H-031 Vd on the voltage side

Copyright © 2015 VEEJER ENTERPRISES, Garland, Texas - All Rights Reserved

Vehicle Electronics Hands-On Home-Study Troubleshooting Training

VEEJER ENTERPRISES 3701 Lariat Lane, Garland, Texas 75042-5419
Phone: 972-276-9642 Fax: 972-276-8122 Email: info@veejer.com Web Site: www.veejer.com

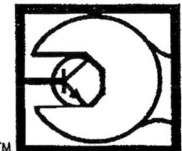

IMPORTANT LESSON FROM STUDY PROBLEM #2

A common mistake made in troubleshooting is to disconnect the load when measuring Vc in a circuit. Disconnecting the load stops circuit current and hides any Vd problem at any point in the circuit.

To see this on the PCBs DISCONNECT THE DC MOTOR'S RED WIRE FROM THE TERMINALS AT PIN 1. Leave the fixed resistor installed in J3.

Figure 3H-032 shows the load disconnected and a normal TTS-1 reading even though the problem, a resistance on the voltage side in J3 is still in the circuit

For Hands-On DO THIS:
- Leave the resistor in place of J3
- With the circuit ON and the DC Motor Red wire disconnected, do the TTS again.
- TTS-1 reading: _____ V
- TTS-2 reading: _____ V

(5) What happened to the TTS-1 reading?

_____

(6) Is the 150Ω resistor still in the circuit? _____

(7) Why is the reading normal with the DC Motor's wire disconnected from the pin?

_____

_____

(8) What is the lesson to learn from this?

The voltage drop disappears when the load is disconnected because electron current stops. If electron current is not flowing, a voltage drop across the resistance (bad connection) cannot be created.

Remove the problem:
- Remove the 150Ω resistor from J3 and put it back in the resistor bag, H-RB03.
- Insert a 0ΩR back into J3.
- Reconnect the DC Motor's wire to Pin 1.

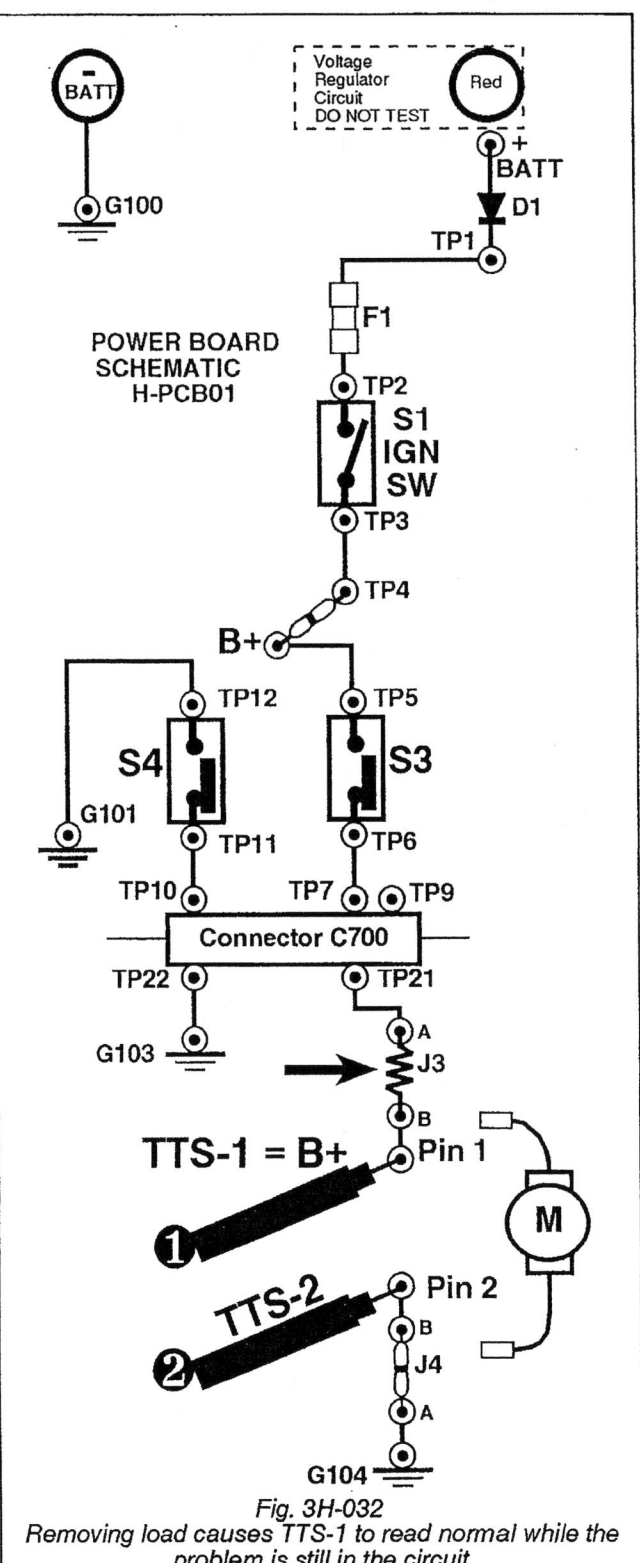

Fig. 3H-032
Removing load causes TTS-1 to read normal while the problem is still in the circuit

Copyright © 2015 VEEJER ENTERPRISES, Garland, Texas - All Rights Reserved

Vehicle Electronics Hands-On Home-Study Troubleshooting Training

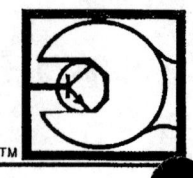

VEEJER ENTERPRISES 3701 Lariat Lane, Garland, Texas 75042-5419
Phone: 972-276-9642   Fax: 972-276-8122   Email: info@veejer.com   Web Site: www.veejer.com

Study Circuit Problem Number 3
"OPEN on the ground side"

Insert An OPEN Circuit on the Ground Side:
Remove J4 from the top of the DC Motor Board to create an open circuit on the ground side of the load. Figure 3H-033 shows jumper J4 removed from the DC Motor Board.

Lesson 24, Pages 4-5 discusses basic circuit problem #3. **Lesson 36, Page 5** discusses basic problem #3 in DC Motor Circuits.

How does an OPEN circuit on the ground side affect DC Motor operation? _____

Do This:
- Turn the circuit ON with S1 (S3 & S4 CLOSED).
- Ground DMM negative test lead to -BATT.
- Perform the TTS and record the readings below.

(1) TTS-1 reading: _____ V
Conclusion: _____

(2) TTS-2 reading: _____ V
Conclusion: _____

Note: Notice the reading on the ground side is not full B+ as found in the Lamp Module. The reason the voltage is lower than full B+ when the ground circuit is OPEN is due to the presence of solid-state control circuitry inside the brushless DC Motor. The control circuitry acts like a big resistor in series with the DMM's Red Test lead at Pin 2 which is grounded through the DMM by the Black Test Lead. This creates a voltage divider circuit (**Lesson 54**) between the control circuitry and the DMM. Since the DMM's internal resistance is much higher than the DC Motor's control circuitry, the DMM drops most of the voltage while the control circuitry drops a little so the reading for TTS-2 is close to, but not quite equal to B+.

(3) What is the next troubleshooting step?

_____

_____

(4) What is concluded when you find 0V at J4 Pin A?

_____

_____

What You Should Learn From This:
Above an OPEN on the ground side the Vc is either *close to* B+ or *equal to* B+ *depending on the load's resistance.* The higher the load resistance the less chance of reading full B+ on the ground side of the load when the ground circuit is OPEN because the DMM completes a circuit to ground. Below the OPEN on the ground side the Vc is still 0.00 volt. Leave OPEN for the next exercise.

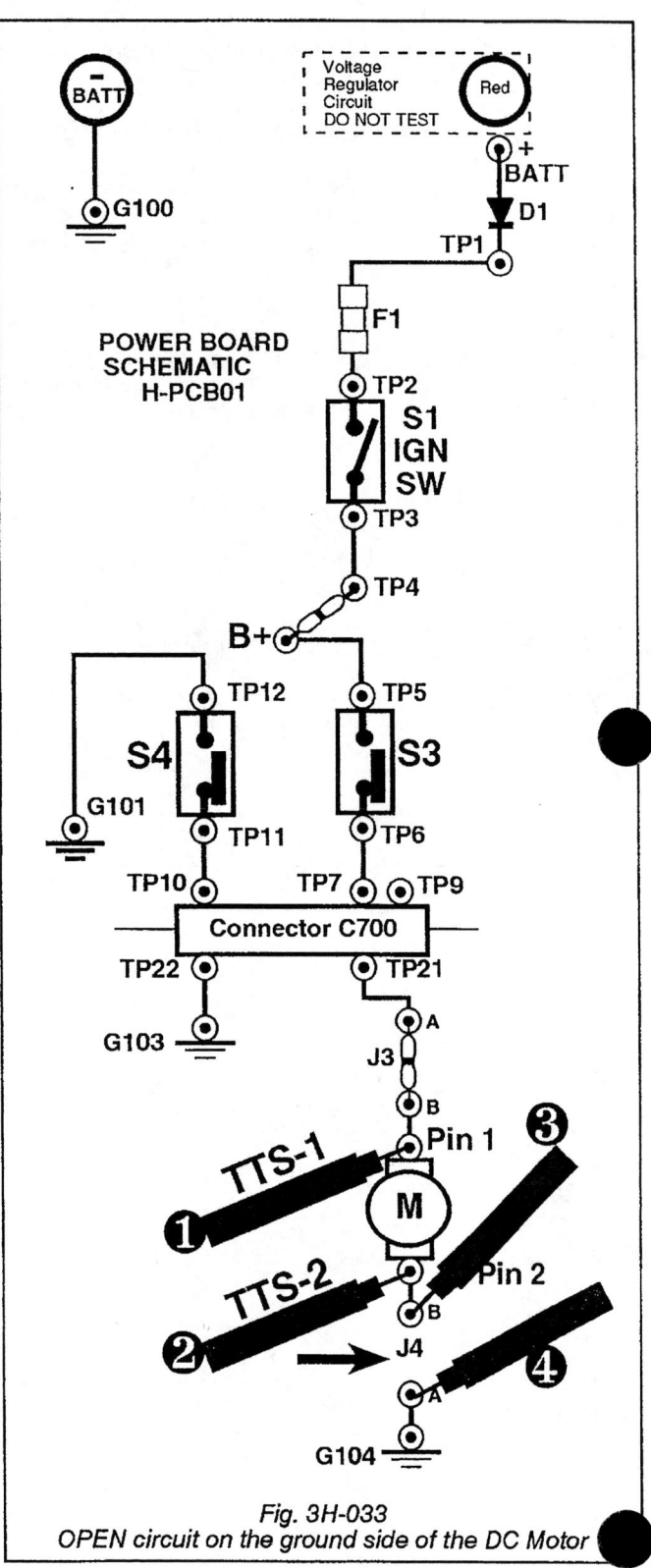

Fig. 3H-033
OPEN circuit on the ground side of the DC Motor

Copyright © 2015 VEEJER ENTERPRISES, Garland, Texas - All Rights Reserved   Text H-WB113   Page 27

Vehicle Electronics Hands-On Home-Study Troubleshooting Training

VEEJER ENTERPRISES 3701 Lariat Lane, Garland, Texas 75042-5419
Phone: 972-276-9642 Fax: 972-276-8122 Email: info@veejer.com Web Site: www.veejer.com

Study Circuit Problem Number 4
"Vd on the ground side"

Insert A Vd on the Ground Side:
Remove J4 from the top of the DC Motor Board and insert a 150 ohm resistor in its place. Select a 150 ohm resistor from the Resistor Bag, H-RB03 to create a Vd on the ground side of the load. **(150Ω color code is Brown-Green-Brown.)** Figure 3H-034 shows jumper J4 removed and a 150Ω resistor inserted in its place.

Lesson 24, Page 5 discusses basic circuit problem #4. **Lesson 36, Page 5** discusses basic problem #4 as it applies to DC Motor circuits.

How does a Vd on the ground side affect DC Motor operation? _____

Do This:
- Turn the circuit ON with S1 (S3 & S4 CLOSED).
- Ground DMM negative test lead to -BATT.
- Perform the TTS and record the readings below.

(1) TTS-1 reading: _____ V

Conclusion: _____

(2) TTS-2 reading: _____ V

Conclusion: _____

(3) What is the next troubleshooting step?
_____
_____

(4) What is concluded when you find 0V at J4 Pin A?
_____
_____

What You Should Learn From This:
A resistance at the wrong place in the circuit causes an undesirable Vd even on the ground side. Above the resistance (Test Lead #3) the Vc is more than 0.10 volt below the resistance (Test Lead #4) the Vc is less than 0.10 volt.

Keep in mind that a Vc at Pin 2 of the load in the range of 0.20-0.50 volt does not necessarily mean the ground circuit has too much resistance and should be serviced. Some DC Motor circuits work well with ground Vc readings above 0.10 volt, such as a starter motor ground. But for smaller electrical circuits expect the TTS-2 reading to be less than 0.1 volt.

Leave the resistor in J4 and continue working with Problem #4 on the next page for a very important lesson to learn in troubleshooting. **It's a principal you must NEVER FORGET.**

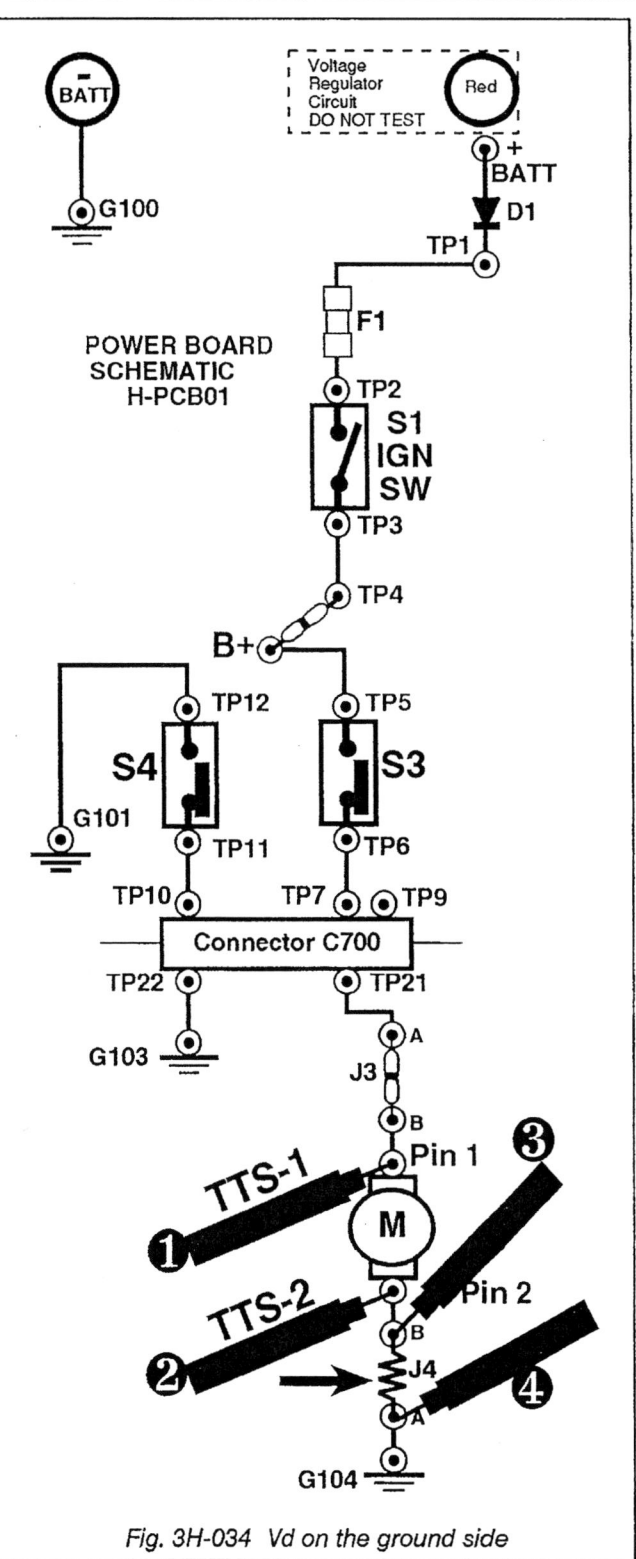

Fig. 3H-034 Vd on the ground side

Copyright © 2015 VEEJER ENTERPRISES, Garland, Texas - All Rights Reserved

Vehicle Electronics Hands-On Home-Study Troubleshooting Training

VEEJER ENTERPRISES 3701 Lariat Lane, Garland, Texas 75042-5419
Phone: 972-276-9642   Fax: 972-276-8122   Email: info@veejer.com   Web Site: www.veejer.com

IMPORTANT LESSON FROM STUDY PROBLEM #4

A *common mistake made in troubleshooting* is to disconnect the load when measuring the TTS. In this example, disconnecting the DC Motor stops circuit electron current and hides the Vd problem on the ground side of the circuit.

To see this on the PCBs DISCONNECT THE DC MOTOR'S RED WIRE FROM Pin 1. Figure 3H-035 shows the DC Motor disconnected and a normal TTS-2 reading even with the problem, resistance on the ground side, (bad connection) still in the circuit

To illustrate DO THIS:
- Leave the resistor in place of J4
- With the circuit ON, and the DC Motor's Red wire disconnected, do the TTS again.
  ◦ TTS-1 reading: _____ V
  ◦ TTS-2 reading: _____ V

(5) What happened to the TTS-2 reading?

_____

(6) Is the 150Ω resistor still in the circuit? _____

(7) Why is the TTS-2 reading at Pin 2 normal with the DC Motor disconnected?

_____
_____

(8) What is the lesson to learn from this?

_____
_____

Remove the fault:
- Remove the 150Ω resistor and put it back in the resistor bag, H-RB03.
- Insert a 0ΩR back into J4.
- Reconnect the DC Motor's Red wire to Pin 1.

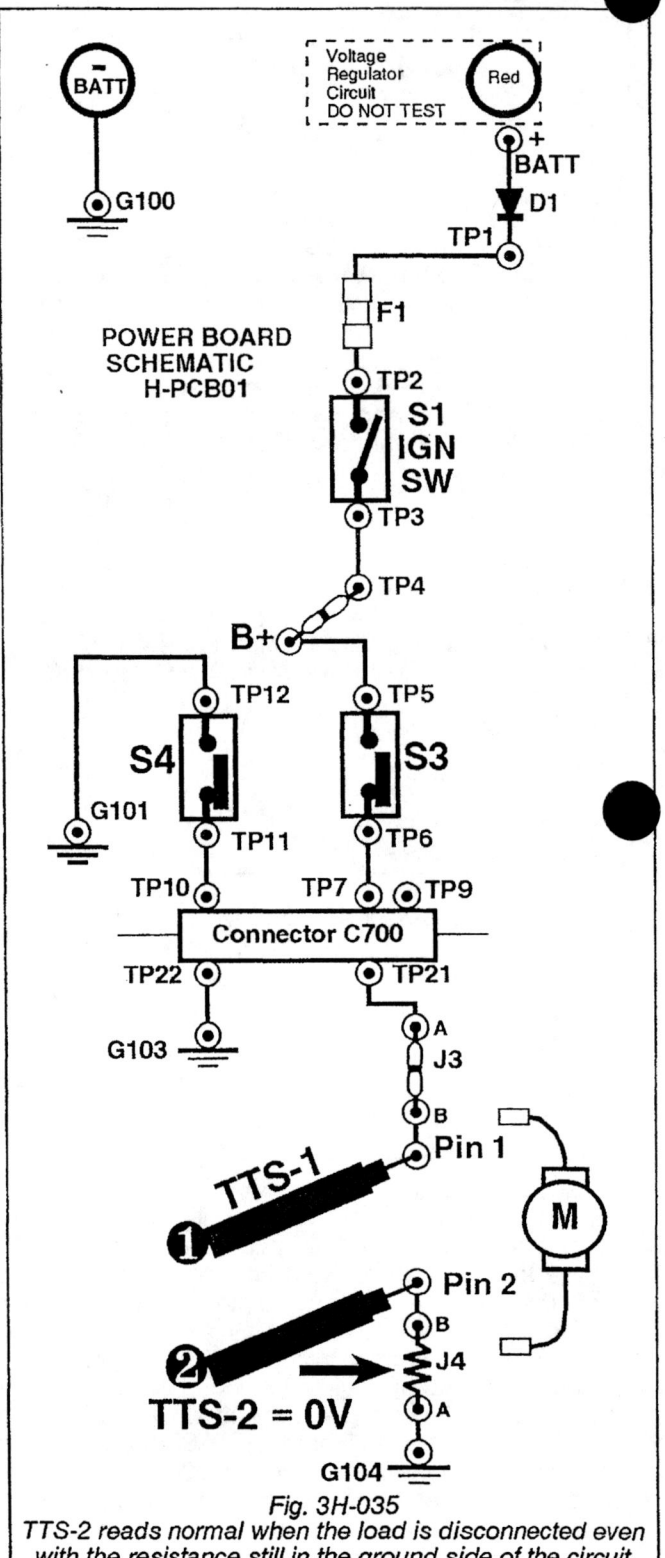

Fig. 3H-035
TTS-2 reads normal when the load is disconnected even with the resistance still in the ground side of the circuit.

Vehicle Electronics Hands-On Home-Study Troubleshooting Training

VEEJER ENTERPRISES 3701 Lariat Lane, Garland, Texas 75042-5419
Phone: 972-276-9642 Fax: 972-276-8122 Email: info@veejer.com Web Site: www.veejer.com

Study Circuit Problem Number 5
"OPEN LOAD"

Insert An OPEN Load condition:
Disconnect at least one of the wires of the DC Motor from Pin 1 and Pin 2 as illustrated in Figure 3H-036. Disconnecting either DC Motor wire simulates an OPEN DC Motor in the circuit. This is the only way to simulate an OPEN DC Motor in H-PCB03 and has to suffice for this simulation.

Lesson 24 discusses an OPEN load circuit.
Lesson 37, Page 1 discusses an OPEN DC Motor in a circuit.

How does an OPEN Load affect DC Motor operation?
_____

Do This:
• Turn the circuit ON with S1 (S3 & S4 CLOSED).
• Ground DMM negative test lead to -BATT.
• Perform the TTS and record the readings below.

(1) TTS-1 reading: _____ V
Conclusion: _____

(2) TTS-2 reading: _____ V
Conclusion: _____

(3) What is normally the next troubleshooting step?
_____

Note: The TTS readings indicate B+ and B- are present at the DC Motor terminals but the motor doesn't operate. Manually spin the rotor blades to see if the motor starts to run with a little push to help it get started. It will not run by itself so the DC Motor is defective.

(4) How is a brushless DC Motor tested by itself?
_____

(5) How is a DC Motor checked that has a old style motor winding with brushes tested directly with an ohmmeter, such as a blower motor, a fan, or a window or seat motor?
_____

(6) What would an ohmmeter indicate if a wire wound DC motor winding with brushes were actually OPEN?
_____

Remove the fault by connecting the leads of the DC Motor back to Pin 1 and Pin 2 terminals.

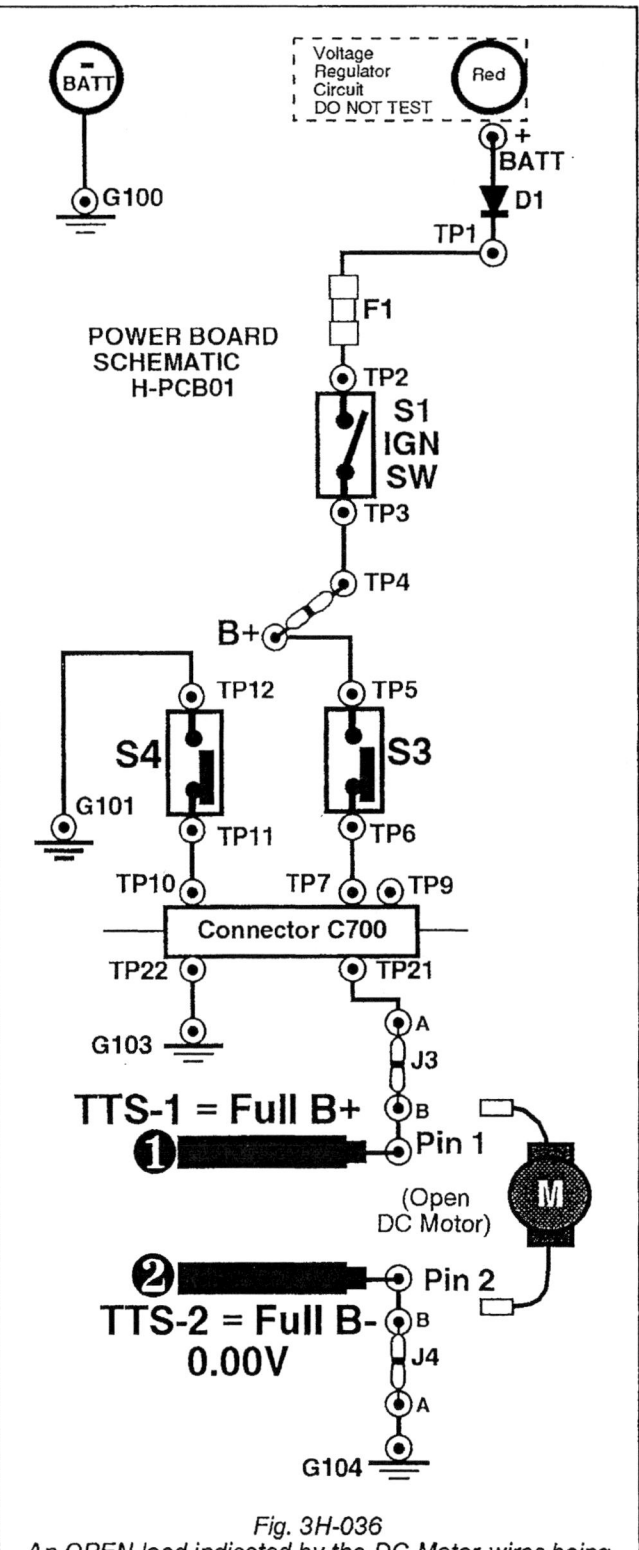

Fig. 3H-036
An OPEN load indicated by the DC Motor wires being disconnected from Pin 1 and Pin 2.

Vehicle Electronics Hands-On Home-Study Troubleshooting Training

VEEJER ENTERPRISES 3701 Lariat Lane, Garland, Texas 75042-5419
Phone: 972-276-9642 Fax: 972-276-8122 Email: info@veejer.com Web Site: www.veejer.com

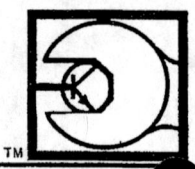

Study Circuit Problem Number 6
"SHORTED LOAD"

Insert a SHORTED Load condition in PCBs:
Insert these two conditions in the PCBs.

(A.) **IMPORTANT: Remove F1 from the circuit to simulate the fuse is blown.**

(B.) Insert a wire jumper with small alligator clips to the terminals of DC Motor Pin 1 and Pin 2 to create a short circuit around the load as shown in Figure 3H-037. This simulates a shorted DC Motor that blew the fuse.

Lessons that cover material pertaining to troubleshooting shorts for review:
Lesson 8 discusses ohmmeter operation.
Lesson 18 discusses resistance testing.
Lesson 24 discusses Study Problem #6.
Lesson 25 discusses troubleshooting shorts.
Lesson 37 discusses shorts in DC Motor circuits.

(1) What is it that blows a fuse?
_____

(2) What are two reasons for current to increase in a circuit above a normal level?

(A) _____

(B) _____

(3) What is a "short" in a circuit?
_____
_____

(4) What two ways can a circuit develop a short?

(A.) _____

(B.) _____

Leave the wire short across the DC Motor terminals in place to troubleshoot the problem on the next page where we explain how to properly troubleshoot a shorted load.

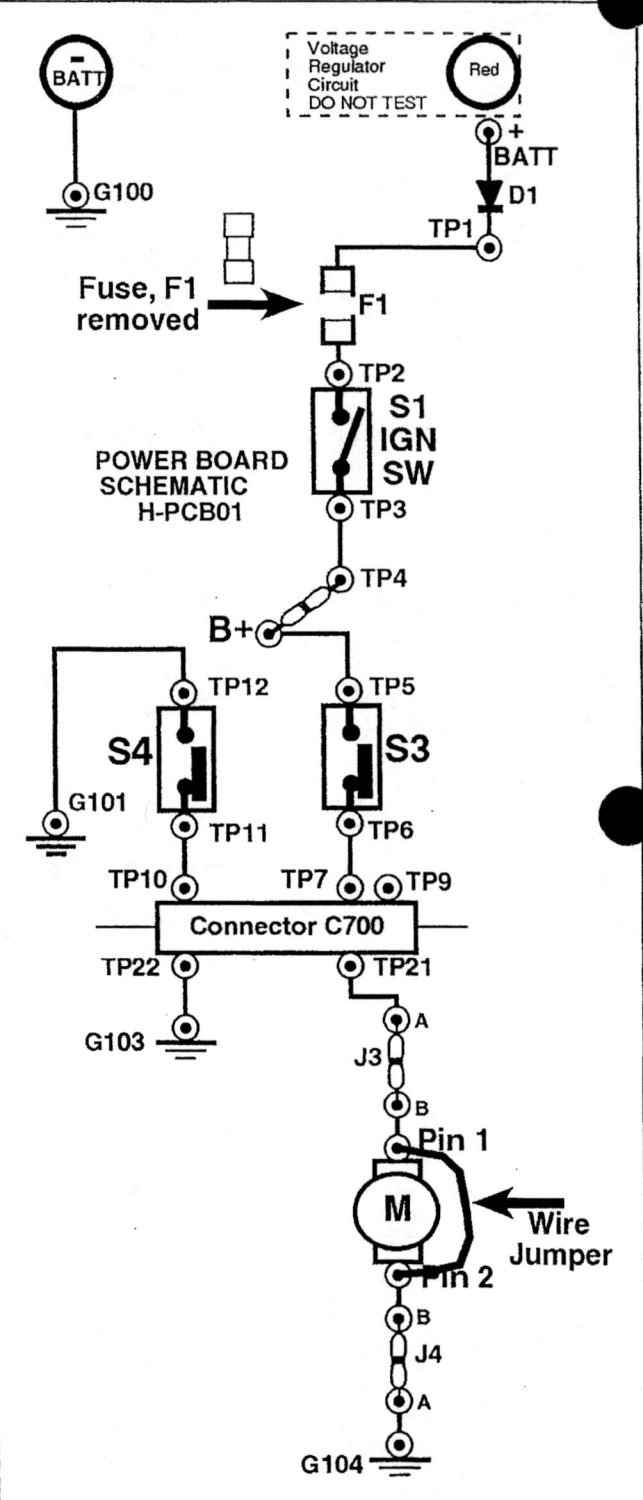

Fig. 3H-037 Shorted Load created with a wire jumper placed between the load Pin 1 and 2 terminals.

Copyright © 2015 VEEJER ENTERPRISES, Garland, Texas - All Rights Reserved   Text H-WB113 Page 31

Vehicle Electronics Hands-On Home-Study Troubleshooting Training

VEEJER ENTERPRISES 3701 Lariat Lane, Garland, Texas 75042-5419
Phone: 972-276-9642   Fax: 972-276-8122   Email: info@veejer.com   Web Site: www.veejer.com

Finding A Shorted Load

Do This:
- CLOSE S1 (toggle UP), Slide S3 & S4 UP.
- Ground DMM negative test lead to -BATT.
- Perform the TTS and record the readings below.

(5) TTS-1 reading: _____

Conclusion: _____

(Note 1: Measure several Vc readings back up the voltage side of the circuit in Figure 3H-038 looking for B+. There is no B+ on the cold side of the fuse but B+ is present at the hot side of the fuse. This indicates the fuse is blown.

Note 2: When discovering a blown fuse it means high current blew the fuse, If current is too high it means low resistance in the circuit has developed. Ohmmeter tests are the quickest and best way to find the cause because troubleshooting must be done with the circuit OFF. *Before connecting an ohmmeter to the PCBs always disconnect the H-PS01 Power Supply from the wall socket and wait 1 minute to remove any voltage that could exist at any point in the circuit.* **NEVER CONNECT AN OHMMETER (Analog or Digital) TO A LIVE CIRCUIT BECAUSE IT WILL DAMAGE THE OHMMETER.**

(6) What two circuit failure possibilities could exist in a circuit with a blown fuse?

  (A) _____

  (B) _____

(7) What is the next troubleshooting step after finding the fuse is blown? Refer back to **Lesson 25, Pages 1-3** for detailed circuit explanations if necessary. **Lesson 37** has details about shorts in DC motor circuits. _____

(8) With the short across the DC Motor terminals, set a DMM to the 200-300-400 ohm range. Record the resistance reading obtained between Load Pin 1 and Pin 2 as shown in Figure 3H-038.
   _____ Ω

(9) What does this resistance reading indicate about DC Motor load resistance? _____

Note: Some wire wound blower motors and cooling fans at rest will read very low resistance because their windings normally have only a few tenths of an ohm. Check known good DC blower motors at rest on actual vehicles to verify normal resistance readings of wire wound DC Motors with brushes.

We are able to determine the load, the DC Motor is shorted (ohmmeter says 0 ohms) and should be replaced if this were an actual DC Blower or Cooling Fan motor on a vehicle.

Remove wire short across DC Motor terminals.
    Go to the next page.

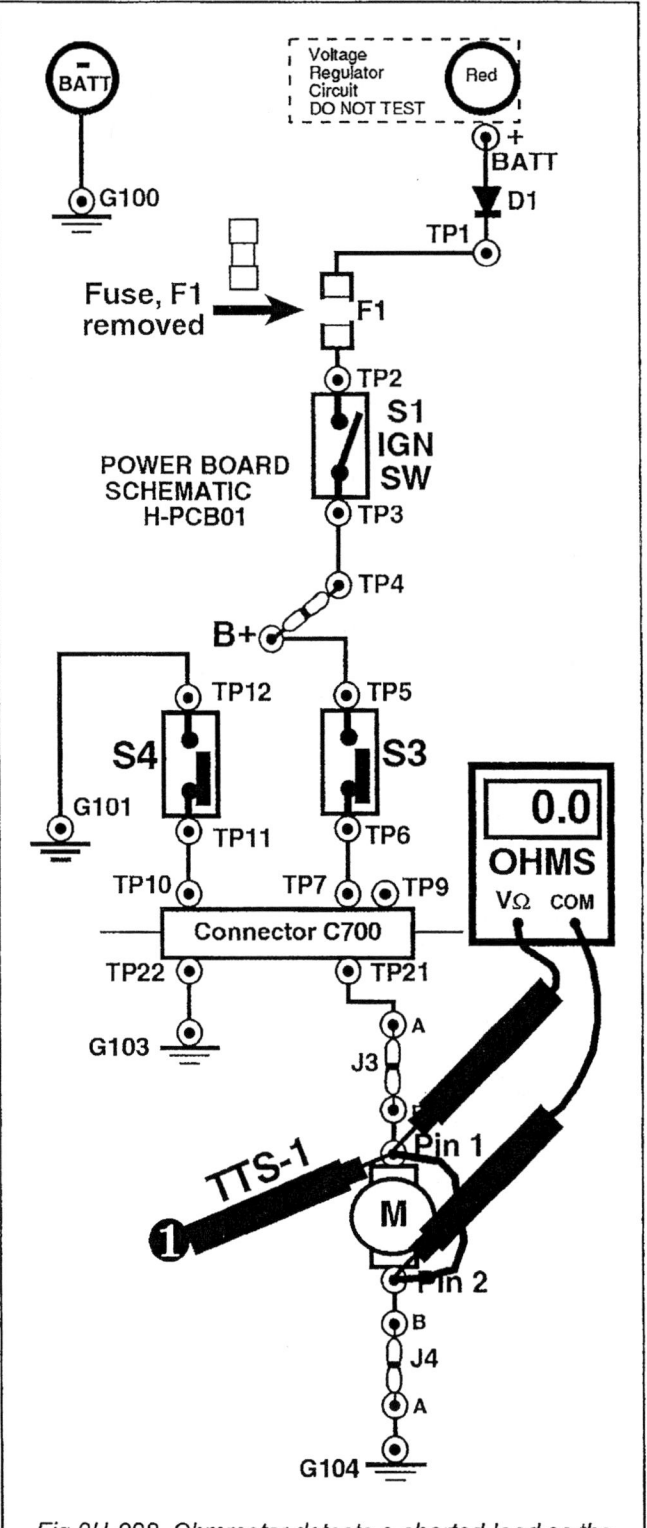

Fig 3H-038 Ohmmeter detects a shorted load as the cause of a blown fuse.

Vehicle Electronics Hands-On Home-Study Troubleshooting Training

VEEJER ENTERPRISES 3701 Lariat Lane, Garland, Texas 75042-5419
Phone: 972-276-9642 Fax: 972-276-8122 Email: info@veejer.com Web Site: www.veejer.com

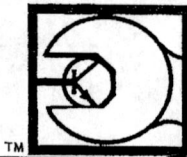

Finding A Voltage Side Short To Ground

It is also possible for the voltage side to be shorted to ground instead of the load being shorted. Continue to learn how to find shorts to ground in the voltage side.

Do This First:
- Unplug the H-PS01 Power Supply from wall socket.
- Disconnect the DC Motor's RED wire from Pin 1 to disconnect the motor from the circuit once it is determined the DC Motor is NOT SHORTED.
- Connect a wire jumper from Pin 1 to G103 to short the voltage side of the DC Motor circuit to ground.
- Turn S1 ON (toggle UP) to complete the circuit.
- CLOSE S3 & S4 (slide UP) to complete the circuit.
- Continue with (10) below.

This test procedure is explained in detail in **Lesson 25, Pages 3-4** and **Lesson 37, Pages 2-3**.

(10) Place a digital ohmmeter on the 200 ohm range. Connect the ohmmeter test leads to the PCBs as shown in Figure 3H-039. Since the PCBs have no power applied there is no voltage in the circuit and the ohmmeter will not be damaged.

(11) What does the ohmmeter read? _____ Ω

(12) What does the reading in Step 11 represent?
_____

(13) OPEN S1 (toggle down) and move Red Test Lead to TP3. Record reading. ___ Ω

(14) What does the reading in Step 13 mean?
_____

(15) Leave Red Test Lead on TP3 and OPEN S3 (slide down). Record reading _____ Ω

(16) What does the reading in Step 15 mean?
_____

(17) Leave S3 OPEN and move Red Test Lead to TP6. Record reading. _____ Ω

(18) What does the reading in Step 17 mean?
_____

(19) Disconnect J3 from the DC Motor Board. Record ohmmeter reading from TP6. _____

(20) What does the reading in Step 19 mean?
_____
_____

Conclusion: _____

Restore PCBs:
__ Remove the wire jumper from Pin 1 to G103.
__ Re-install 0ΩR in J3.
__ Connect red wire of DC Motor to Pin 1.
__ Put a good fuse in F1.

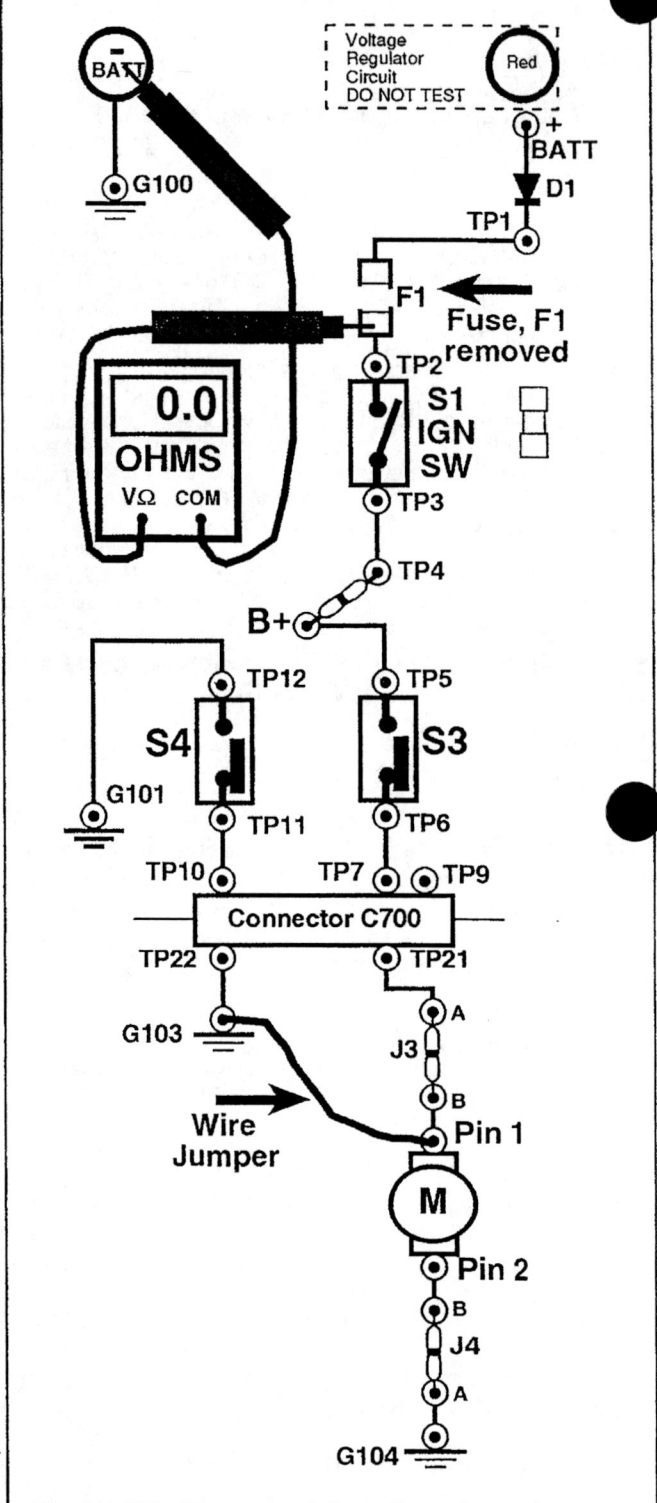

Fig. 3H-039 Ohmmeter detects the voltage side of the circuit is shorted to ground.

Vehicle Electronics Hands-On Home-Study Troubleshooting Training

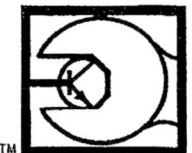

VEEJER ENTERPRISES 3701 Lariat Lane, Garland, Texas 75042-5419
Phone: 972-276-9642 Fax: 972-276-8122 Email: info@veejer.com Web Site: www.veejer.com

Short to Voltage Problems

We have discussed shorts to ground where either the load is shorted or the voltage side of the circuit is shorted to ground because a voltage side wire conductor has the insulation penetrated and the bare conductor contacts the chassis (ground). A problem can also develop on the voltage side where the wire insulation is penetrated and the bare conductor connected to DC Motor Pin 1 contacts another wire conductor carrying B+. This is known as a "short to voltage." This problem was not discussed with the Lamp Board but is covered here because it can be a very likely failure in DC Motor Circuits.

A DC motor forced to run at a lower rpm draws higher current. If the current gets excessive, it could easily melt the insulation surrounding the voltage side wiring. If the DC Motor wire gets hot enough to melt the insulation it may also melt the insulation of wires next to it in the harness. If enough heat is generated the insulation of the various wires in the harness will melt to the point that the different conductors make unfortunate electrical contact. When the DC motor is switched OFF, the insulation cools down and becomes solid again allowing the various conductor wires to remain in electrical contact creating a "short to voltage." The blower fan continues to run when the control switch S3 is turned OFF.

There are two possibilities.

(1) If an adjacent wire to the DC motor voltage side wire conductor is a ground wire and the insulation melts to the point that they both make contact, the DC motor wire becomes shorted to ground quickly blowing the DC motor fuse. This has already been discussed as Basic Circuit Problem Number 6.

(2) Another possibility is that the adjacent wire is carrying B+. When the DC motor voltage side wire comes in contact with the B+ wire there is no indication of a problem because the DC motor is in operation with B+ from its own fuse. The problem only becomes apparent when the DC motor is shut OFF but keeps running because it is getting B+ from the adjacent wire. This is called a "short to voltage" and is often a problem around wiring controlling DC motors such as seat and window DC motors but especially high current DC blower and starter motor circuits.

Do This To Simulate The Problem:
- H-PS01 connected and good fuses in F1 and F2
- Operate DC Motor – Toggle S1 UP, S3 & S4 Slide UP to verify proper operation.
- Create short to voltage by connecting TP7 and TP9 with jumper wire as shown in Figure 3H-040. Nothing appears wrong as motor continues to run.
- Toggle S3 down to shut OFF DC motor and notice the DC motor keeps running. B+ is getting to Pin 1 of the DC Motor through the short to voltage at TP7-TP9.
- Remove F2 to identify the path of the extra B+ and the DC motor shuts OFF. This confirms the DC motor

is getting B+ from F2 and the associated voltage feed wire which must be shorted to the normal voltage feed wire to the DC Motor, Pin 1. **In a vehicle harness look for insulation that shows signs of melting. That is the place where a short to voltage is most likely to occur.** Remove wire SHORT.

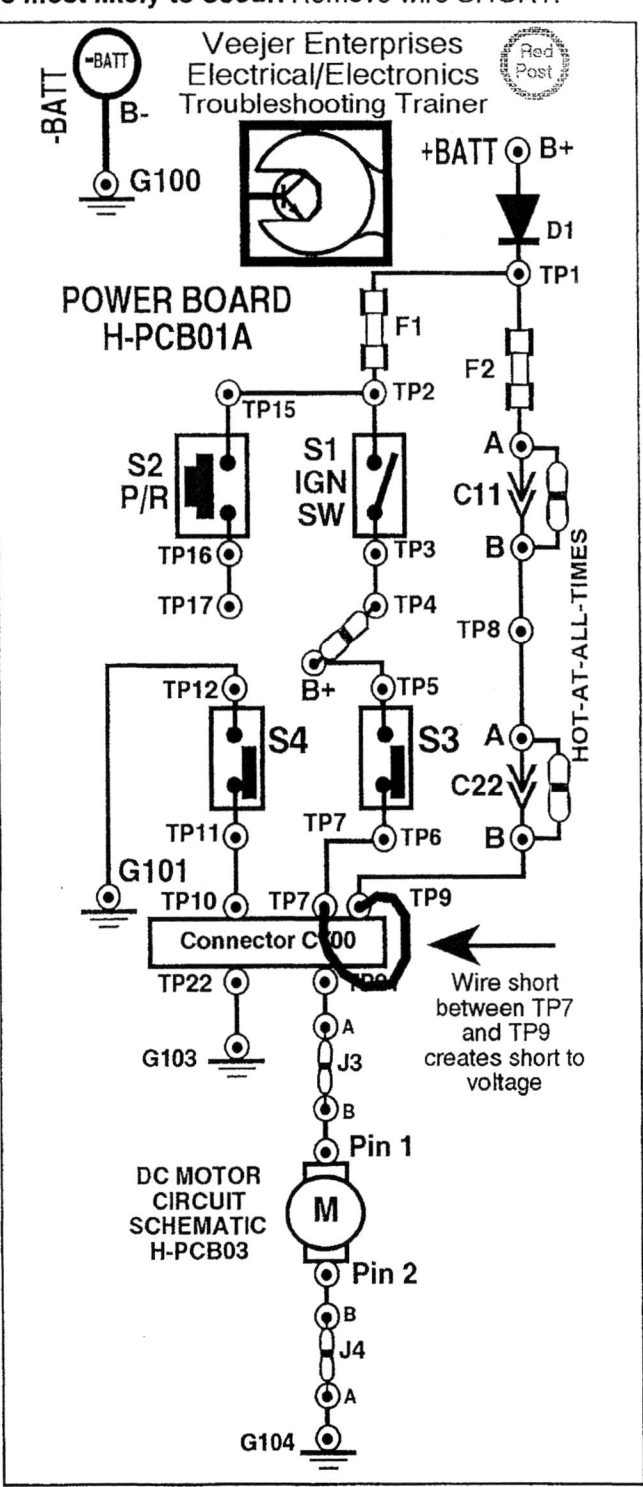

Copyright © 2015 VEEJER ENTERPRISES, Garland, Texas - All Rights Reserved   Text H-WB113 Page 34

Vehicle Electronics Hands-On Home-Study Troubleshooting Training

VEEJER ENTERPRISES 3701 Lariat Lane, Garland, Texas 75042-5419
Phone: 972-276-9642   Fax: 972-276-8122   Email: info@veejer.com   Web Site: www.veejer.com

These next two exercises are designed to offer practice checking high current **brush type DC motors** used on a cars and trucks that have been the mainstay of vehicle electrical motors since the beginning of the automotive industry..

Checking Starter Motor Draw

An engine starter motor is a heavy duty DC Motor often pulling over 100 amps to crank an engine. To measure high current over 10 amps requires a DC Current Clamp. If a DC Current Clamp is not available these tests on a car cannot be done.

> A DC Current Clamp is available on our web site at **www.veejer.com**. Click on the Button **"Electronic Test Equipment"** in the red border at the left side of the screen to see a picture of a DC Current Clamp. It will work with all DMMs that have standard meter jacks and can be ordered from the web site.

Lesson 34 of "*The*" **Course** covers principles of measuring current in starter motor circuits using a DC Current Clamp connected to a DMM.

Measure starter draw on a car:
- Connect DC Current Clamp to DMM just as would be done connecting test leads to measure DC Volts.
- Set DMM to read low DC Volts using the 2-3-or-4 volt range whichever is available on your DMM. DMM readout should indicate **.000** when on the 2-3-or-4 volt range.
- Turn ON and zero adjust Current Clamp so the readout is steady at **.000**.
- Open DC Current Clamp jaws and surround the heavy duty battery cable that grounds the battery to the engine block, as shown in Figure 3H-043. Then close the jaws.
- Crank the engine and allow engine to roll-over several times to get a consistent starter draw reading. It may be necessary to put car in clear flood mode or remove the ignition fuse so car won't start running while checking starter draw.

Interpreting DMM Readings

Figure 3H-043 shows the DMM indicating **.145** with the Current Clamp. The reading means 145 amps.

A DMM reading of . . . . .
.095 means **95 amps**;
.175 means **175 amps**;
.220 means **220 amps**;
.310 means **310 amps**, etc.

A shop manual may give approximate starter motor draw in amps for a given engine size for each make and model. Smaller engines like 4 cylinders have a *lower* cranking current while 8 cylinder engines have a *higher* cranking current. It takes more power to crank a bigger engine.

Engine temperature also affects cranking current. Colder engines have a higher cranking current than warmer engines because a cold engine's cold oil lowers cranking rpm. Practice checking starter motor draw on good engines will aid in determining correct starter draw for various engines.

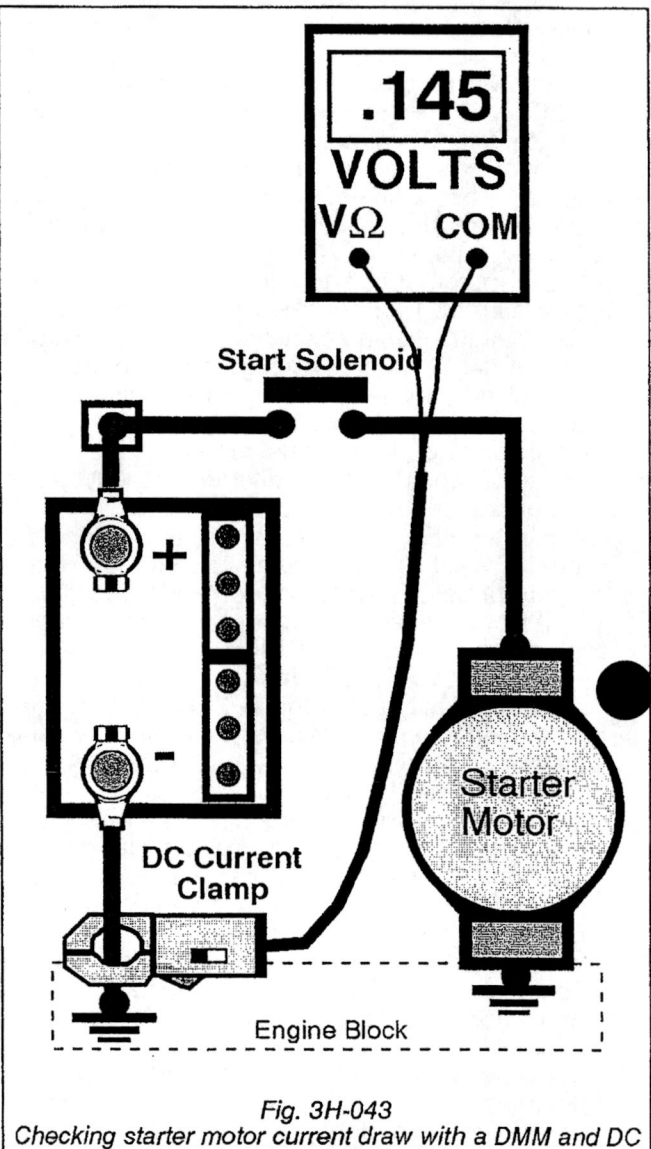

Fig. 3H-043
Checking starter motor current draw with a DMM and DC Current Clamp.

If **starter draw is higher than the normal** range usually found it indicates the starter is turning at lower than normal rpm. Listen for the sound of lower cranking rpm to confirm. It is most likely due to defective armature bearings in the starter or the starter is improperly spaced to the ring gear.

If the **starter draw is lower than normal** it means the starter has some of the following problems: worn armature brushes; bad connection in wiring, weak battery, etc. Finding these types of problems requires troubleshooting simulated to what you will have the opportunity to practice in this module, H-113.

Copyright © 2015 VEEJER ENTERPRISES, Garland, Texas - All Rights Reserved

Vehicle Electronics Hands-On Home-Study Troubleshooting Training

VEEJER ENTERPRISES 3701 Lariat Lane, Garland, Texas 75042-5419
Phone: 972-276-9642   Fax: 972-276-8122   Email: info@veejer.com   Web Site: www.veejer.com

Checking DC Blower Motor Current

DC Blower Motors are another **brush type** motor that must move enough air to cool down or warm up the passenger compartment. After many hours of operation a brush type DC motor begins to run at a lower rpm and moves less air due to wear and tear on the motor bushings supporting the motor's armature. The change in air flow decreases gradually so it is not initially noticed by the driver. Measuring DC Blower Motor current will tell the tale about the blower motor's condition.

A sample DC Blower Motor Circuit is shown in Figure 3H-044. This circuit schematic is taken from **Lesson 35** of "**The**" **Course**. The blower motor receives B+ at Pin 1 from the Blower Switch Assembly. Pin 2 of the blower motor is grounded to the sheet metal to complete the negative side of the circuit. The speed of the blower motor and the resultant air moved is determined by the switch position of the Blower Switch Assembly.

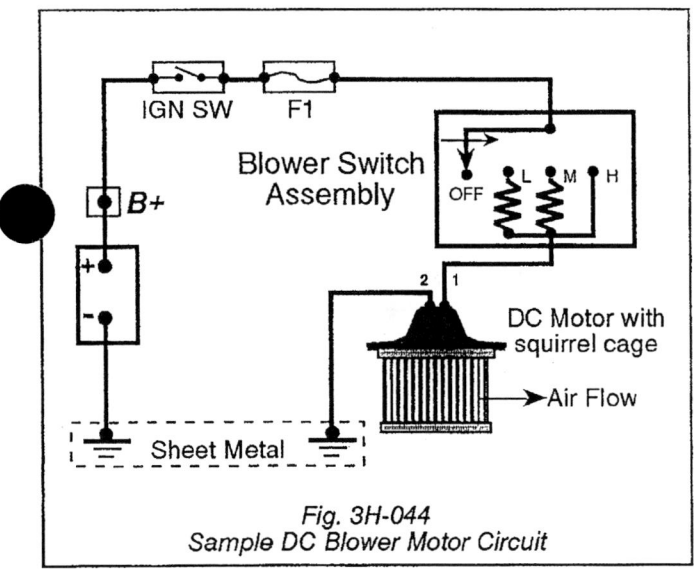

Fig. 3H-044
Sample DC Blower Motor Circuit

When the switch is in the "L" (LOW) position less B+ gets to the blower motor due to the internal resistor voltage drop causing the motor to operate at a lower rpm. Moving the switch to "H" (HIGH) applies full B+ to Pin 1 which allows the blower motor to operate at maximum rpm moving maximum air.

The current draw for a blower motor may be available in service literature. If not, you can always "check-a-known-good-one" or "CAKGO." Always put the blower fan into the high speed mode and simply set up the DMM and current clamp as explained on the previous page for starter draw tests.

Place only one of the wires to the blower fan (not both wires) inside the jaws of the current clamp to measure the highest current flowing through the blower motor, as shown in Figure 3H-045. The DMM in Figure 3H-045 indicates **.020** which is interpreted as 20 amps.

If the blower fan has worn bearings, expect the current to increase several amps indicating the blower fan is drawing excessive current due to lower than normal rpm. As the current increases as the blower motor bearings bind up, the wiring will begin to get hot to the point the insulation melts shorting wires together in the wiring harness creating shorts to ground or shorts to voltage. Measuring blower fan current will detect defective blower motors before they reach the point they damage the wiring harness.

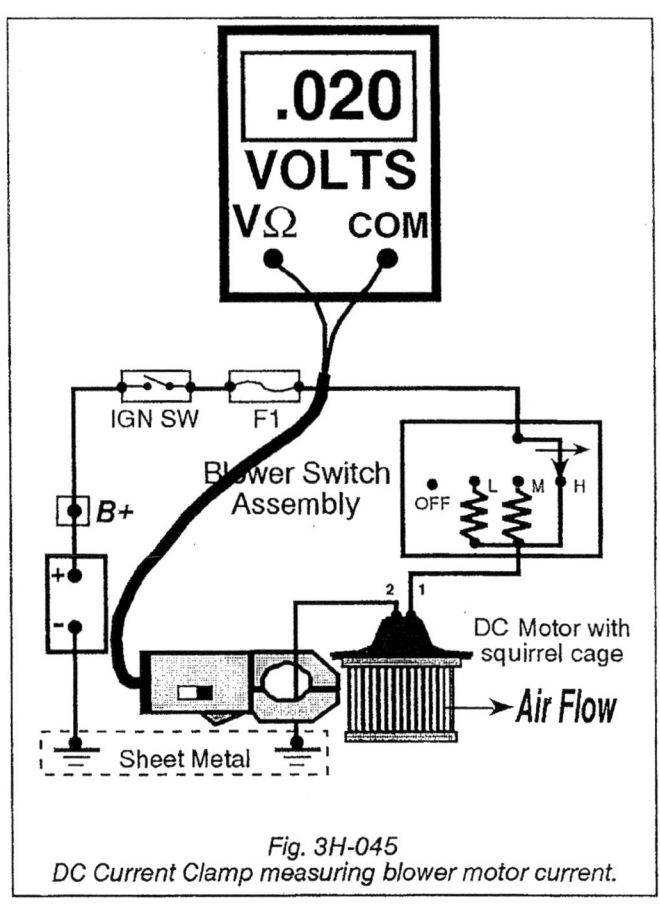

Fig. 3H-045
DC Current Clamp measuring blower motor current.

A little practice checking various blower fans on high speed will give you an idea of various current draws for different makes and models. The same techniques can be used for fuel pump circuits.

Checking starter draw and blower fan current have been included in this manual because a technician should be able to test any type DC motor on a vehicle whether it is a brush type or brushless DC Motor.

The brushless DC Motor used on the DC Motor Troubleshooting Trainer has different technology than brush type DC Motors, yet brushless DC motors are becoming more common in today's high tech vehicles for many low power applications. We will now begin troubleshooting exercises using the brushless DC Motor on the DC Motor Troubleshooting Trainer.

DC Motor With Computer Control

DC Motors draw higher electron current in normal operation compared to the electron current through a lamp, solenoid or relay coil circuit. If the DC Motor begins to develop armature rotation problems, such as worn armature bearings that prevent the DC Motor from reaching normal rpm (dragging), the DC Motor doesn't develop sufficient counter-electromotive force. As a result, the DC motor draws even higher electron current than normal causing the wiring to get hot and possibly melt the wire's insulation.

> TIP: Any time you encounter vehicle wiring with insolation that appears to have been deformed by excessive heat, look to see if a DC Motor is the load in the circuit. It could indicate the DC Motor is drawing excessive electron current and will have to be replaced.

In previous automotive years, 1930's through 1970's before solid-state technology (computers) became so common, a DC Motor drawing higher than normal electron current through a mechanical control switch would cause switch contact damage and melted wire insulation. Many times the DC Motor would be left in service drawing higher than normal current once the mechanical switch or melted wiring was repaired.

This cannot be done with an on-board computer control unit using a solid-state driver (switch) to control a DC Motor. It is necessary to test for correct DC Motor electron current draw. The reason for this test is that the DC Motor's electron current is supplied by a (solid-state) transistor or a special MOSFET component (solid-state relay) inside the control unit.

Recent advances in solid-state component technology has made it possible to mount these high current handling solid-state driver (switch) circuits inside an on-board computer or control unit. Excessive DC Motor current through the solid-state driver circuit will destroy it and the control unit must be replaced.

As the DC Motor bearings begin to cause the armature to turn at a lower rpm the electron current through the DC Motor begins to increase putting a greater burden on the solid-state driver circuit inside the computer. If this high current condition lasts long enough it will cause a solid-state driver circuit failure.

When the vehicle is in the shop for repairs the technician determines the on-board control unit has failed and replaces it without testing for excessive electron current through the DC Motor. The new on-board control unit becomes a victim of the high DC Motor electron current draw just like the original computer.

In Figure 3H-046, we show the correct procedure to test a DC Motor when it is controlled by an on-board control unit. The on-board control unit is disconnected from the circuit. A heavy duty wire jumper grounds the DC Motor allowing full electron current through the DC Motor. The DC Motor is able to run at full rpm. A Current Clamp is shown measuring the DC Motor current through the jumper wire.

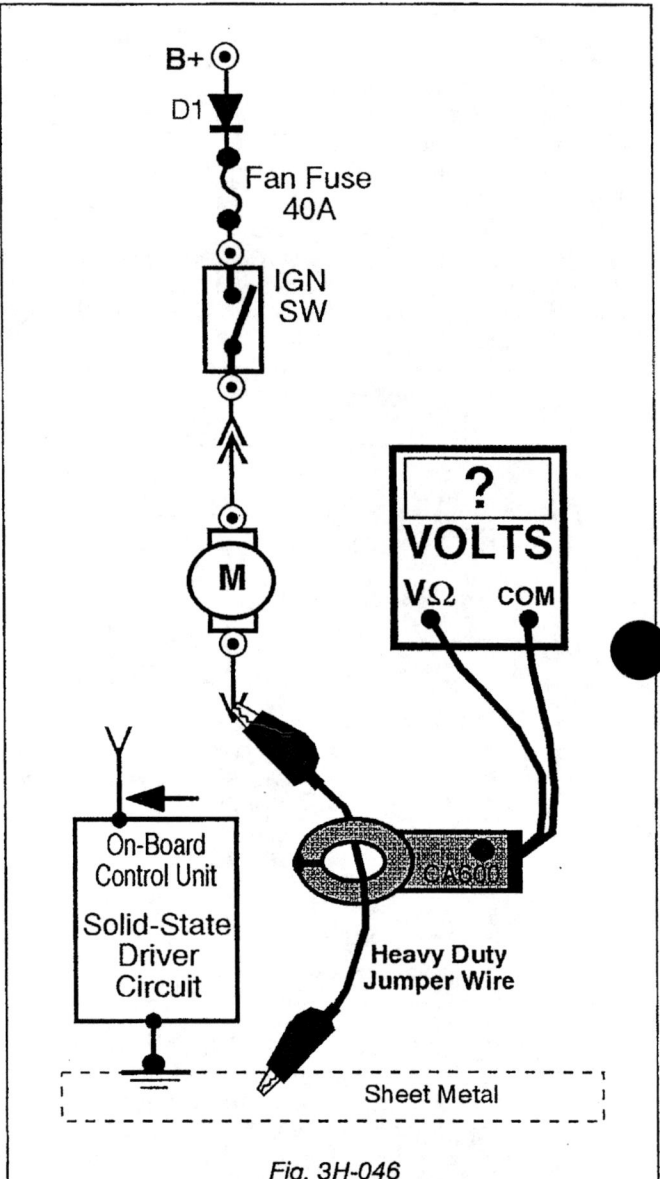

Fig. 3H-046
Testing DC Motor draw when controlled by an on-board computer (control unit)

Once the normal DC Motor's high electron current reading is determined from first checking a known good circuit, it can be compared to the reading obtained on the vehicle that has experienced an on-board computer failure. A higher than normal current draw would indicate the DC Motor is defective and should be replaced before the new on-board computer is installed.

Vehicle Electronics Hands-On Home-Study Troubleshooting Training

VEEJER ENTERPRISES 3701 Lariat Lane, Garland, Texas 75042-5419
Phone: 972-276-9642 Fax: 972-276-8122 Email: info@veejer.com Web Site: www.veejer.com

Straight Line Schematic 3TS-5

To the right is a straight line reference schematic, Figure 3TS-5, for troubleshooting DC Motor circuit problems covered in Program H-113.

A straight line schematic places all components and test points in their proper electrical order, (not necessarily their numerical order) for easier tracing through the voltage side and the ground side of the circuit. If the electronic voltage regulator circuit is present between the red post and the -BATT Black Terminal (H-PCB01) disregard the V/R Circuit.

First step is to take the TTS readings which are the first two voltage measurements to perform. Find each test point in the straight line schematic like a map to determine its electrical position in the circuit. If you check a point on the PCBs and do not understand where you are in the circuit or what point to check next, consult the straight line schematic in Figure 3TS-5.

Each test point is clearly marked in Figure 3TS-5 at crucial points in the circuit which makes circuit tracing a lot easier. On an actual vehicle circuit these test points are not always clearly marked as they are in Figure 3TS-5 but they still exist in the form of wire colors, circuit numbers, connector pins, etc., which must be identified for the test point that they represent. A trained eye can pick out crucial test points in a vehicle circuit schematic but getting to those points on an actual vehicle is much more difficult than it is on the PCBs. No training program can make it easier to get to test points on actual vehicles. That problem will be with us as long as they build vehicles.

At least with "*The*" **Hands-On Program** you will become more aware of how to select test points and have an idea of the voltage readings throughout a circuit. With practice you will develop the ability to spot test points in vehicle schematics and know with some certainty what the voltage should be at that point in the vehicle. If the reading is too high or too low you will know what to do next if you apply what you learn in "*The*" **Hands-On Program.**

Another advantage of using the schematic is to follow more of the vehicle style of schematic layout used by many vehicle manufacturers today. They usually start with the B+ source at the top and work down through the circuit to arrive at ground, B-, at the bottom of the schematic.

Figure 3TS-5 appears on the right hand column of every odd number page for the remainder of the student manual for ready reference while working through the troubleshooting problems.

Use the I/G for instructions on how to insert faults for each problem and for the answers. Do not look at the answers before troubleshooting a problem. It will affect the benefits to be learned in troubleshooting that problem.

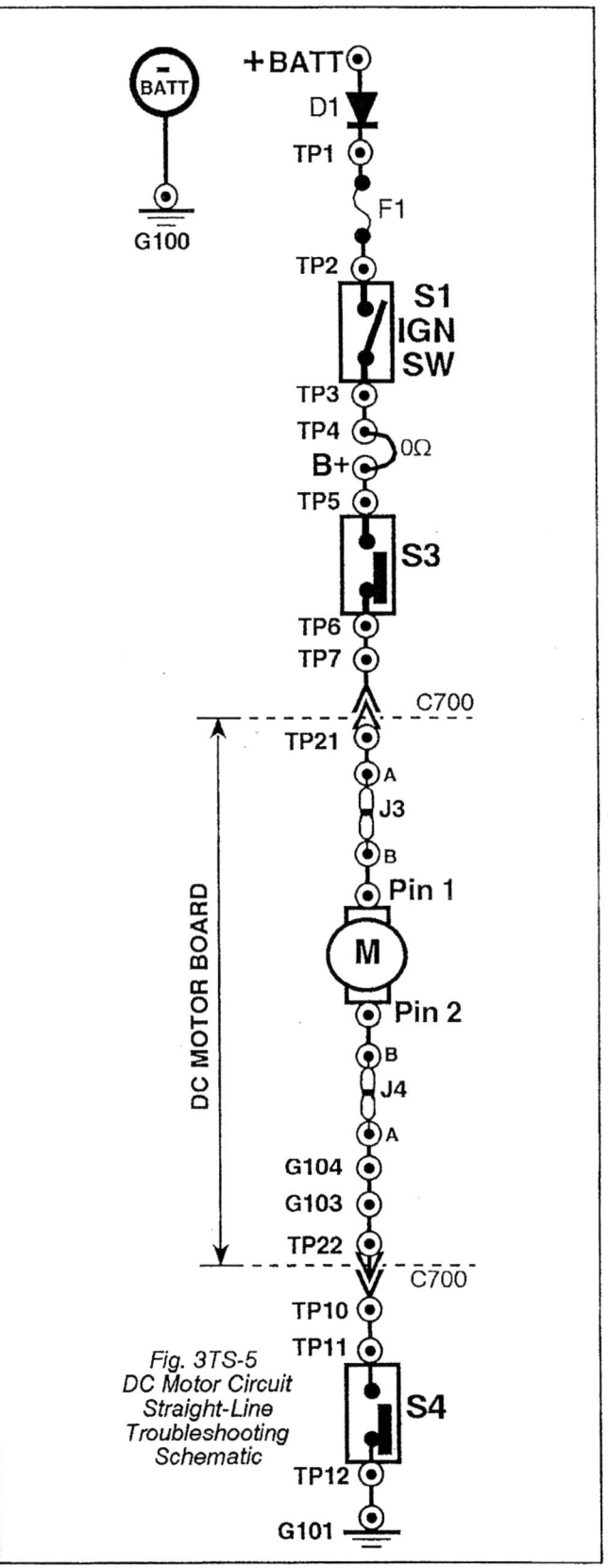

Fig. 3TS-5
DC Motor Circuit
Straight-Line
Troubleshooting
Schematic

Vehicle Electronics Hands-On Home-Study Troubleshooting Training

VEEJER ENTERPRISES 3701 Lariat Lane, Garland, Texas 75042-5419
Phone: 972-276-9642   Fax: 972-276-8122   Email: info@veejer.com   Web Site: www.veejer.com

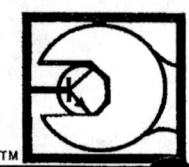

33-69 Practice Troubleshooting Problems

Read This First

TROUBLESHOOT PROBLEMS IN NUMERICAL ORDER. The troubleshooting problems encountered in this section are variations of the six basic circuit problems plus short-to-voltage problems.

You must have already completed the 32 troubleshooting problems in the Starter Kit using the Power Board and the Lamp Board. Procedures for inserting problems and troubleshooting are the same for the DC Motor Circuit. Make sure there are no faults in the PCBs before inserting a problem by scanning the top and bottom of the PCBs. VERIFY THAT BOTH F1 AND F2 ARE GOOD 3A FUSES.

Have someone else install each fault if possible so student does not have any idea what type of problem is inserted. The Instructor Guide has instructions for inserting the fault in each problem. Troubleshoot one problem at a time.

After a fault is inserted, begin troubleshooting the problem and recording test readings under the correct Troubleshooting Problem Number in the Student Manual. **If the DC Motor is not operating try spinning the blades to help get the DC Motor started. It may or may not keep running at low rpm. This is necessary to clearly understand each circuit problem when the DC Motor blades do not start rotating.**

A complete schematic diagram is located in the right hand column of each right hand (odd number) page for easy reference while troubleshooting.

Check the I/G (Instructor Guide) for the correct answers only AFTER completing a troubleshooting problem. DO NOT look at the answers BEFORE troubleshooting a problem.

To add realism to the troubleshooting problems the DC Motor is described as an **engine cooling fan.** *If the fan doesn't operate the engine quickly overheats. If the fan turns slowly the engine still overheats but it takes longer. The slower the fan turns the faster the engine overheats. A symptom is given in the box at the top of each problem which refers to the DC Motor as a "fan" or "cooling fan."* READ EACH INSTRUCTION BOX FIRST!

Five **"advanced troubleshooting" problems** have been added at the end for additional training. **For maximum benefit of advanced problems have someone else install these problems for you.**

Vehicle Electronics Hands-On Home-Study Troubleshooting Training

VEEJER ENTERPRISES 3701 Lariat Lane, Garland, Texas 75042-5419
Phone: 972-276-9642   Fax: 972-276-8122   Email: info@veejer.com   Web Site: www.veejer.com

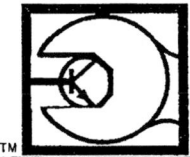

Problem 33
Consult Instructor Guide To Insert Circuit Fault 33
Refer to Schematic **Figure** 3TS-5 for this problem
Engine overheats after running a few minutes.

Performance of the load: _____

Troubleshooting Step 1: _____TTS-1_____
Reading: _____ Good: ____ Bad: ____

Troubleshooting Step 2: _____TTS-2_____
Reading: _____ Good: ____ Bad: ____

Troubleshooting Step 3: _____
Reading: _____ Good: ____ Bad: ____

Troubleshooting Step 4: _____
Reading: _____ Good: ____ Bad: ____

Troubleshooting Step 5: _____
Reading: _____ Good: ____ Bad: ____

Troubleshooting Step 6: _____
Reading: _____ Good: ____ Bad: ____

Troubleshooting Step 7: _____
Reading: _____ Good: ____ Bad: ____

Troubleshooting Step 8: _____
Reading: _____ Good: ____ Bad: ____

Troubleshooting Step 9: _____
Reading: _____ Good: ____ Bad: ____

Troubleshooting Step 10: _____
Reading: _____ Good: ____ Bad: ____

Troubleshooting Step 11: _____
Reading: _____ Good: ____ Bad: ____

Troubleshooting Step 12: _____
Reading: _____ Good: ____ Bad: ____

The Problem Is: _____

REMINDER: Remove the fault and restore the PCBs to normal operation after the problem is identified.

Problem 34
Consult Instructor Guide To Insert Circuit Fault 34
Refer to Schematic **Figure** 3TS-5 for this problem
Engine overheats in a few minutes.

Performance of the load: _____

Troubleshooting Step 1: _____TTS-1_____
Reading: _____ Good: ____ Bad: ____

Troubleshooting Step 2: _____TTS-2_____
Reading: _____ Good: ____ Bad: ____

Troubleshooting Step 3: _____
Reading: _____ Good: ____ Bad: ____

Troubleshooting Step 4: _____
Reading: _____ Good: ____ Bad: ____

Troubleshooting Step 5: _____
Reading: _____ Good: ____ Bad: ____

Troubleshooting Step 6: _____
Reading: _____ Good: ____ Bad: ____

Troubleshooting Step 7: _____
Reading: _____ Good: ____ Bad: ____

Troubleshooting Step 8: _____
Reading: _____ Good: ____ Bad: ____

Troubleshooting Step 9: _____
Reading: _____ Good: ____ Bad: ____

Troubleshooting Step 10: _____
Reading: _____ Good: ____ Bad: ____

Troubleshooting Step 11: _____
Reading: _____ Good: ____ Bad: ____

Troubleshooting Step 12: _____
Reading: _____ Good: ____ Bad: ____

The Problem Is: _____

REMINDER: Remove the fault and restore the PCBs to normal operation after the problem is identified.

Copyright © 2015 VEEJER ENTERPRISES, Garland, Texas - All Rights Reserved

Vehicle Electronics Hands-On Home-Study Troubleshooting Training

VEEJER ENTERPRISES 3701 Lariat Lane, Garland, Texas 75042-5419
Phone: 972-276-9642   Fax: 972-276-8122   Email: info@veejer.com   Web Site: www.veejer.com

Problem 35
Consult Instructor Guide To Insert Circuit Fault 35
Refer to Schematic **Figure 3TS-5** for this problem
Engine overheats after a few minutes.

Performance of the load: _____

Troubleshooting Step 1: ____TTS-1____
Reading: _____ Good: ___ Bad: ___

Troubleshooting Step 2: ____TTS-2____
Reading: _____ Good: ___ Bad: ___

Troubleshooting Step 3: _____
Reading: _____ Good: ___ Bad: ___

Troubleshooting Step 4: _____
Reading: _____ Good: ___ Bad: ___

Troubleshooting Step 5: _____
Reading: _____ Good: ___ Bad: ___

Troubleshooting Step 6: _____
Reading: _____ Good: ___ Bad: ___

Troubleshooting Step 7: _____
Reading: _____ Good: ___ Bad: ___

Troubleshooting Step 8: _____
Reading: _____ Good: ___ Bad: ___

Troubleshooting Step 9: _____
Reading: _____ Good: ___ Bad: ___

Troubleshooting Step 10: _____
Reading: _____ Good: ___ Bad: ___

Troubleshooting Step 11: _____
Reading: _____ Good: ___ Bad: ___

Troubleshooting Step 12: _____
Reading: _____ Good: ___ Bad: ___

The Problem Is: _____

REMINDER: Remove the fault and restore the PCBs to normal operation after the problem is identified.

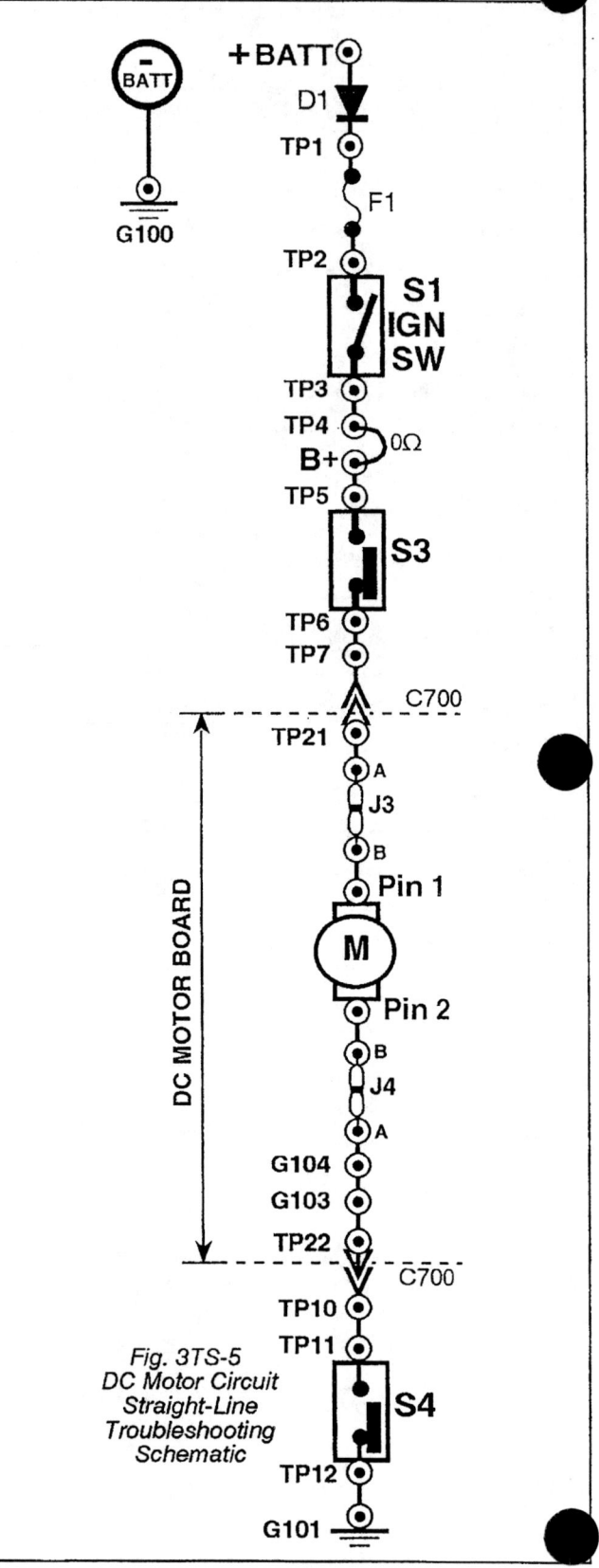

Fig. 3TS-5 DC Motor Circuit Straight-Line Troubleshooting Schematic

Copyright © 2015 VEEJER ENTERPRISES, Garland, Texas - All Rights Reserved   Text H-WB113

Vehicle Electronics Hands-On Home-Study Troubleshooting Training

VEEJER ENTERPRISES 3701 Lariat Lane, Garland, Texas 75042-5419
Phone: 972-276-9642   Fax: 972-276-8122   Email: info@veejer.com   Web Site: www.veejer.com

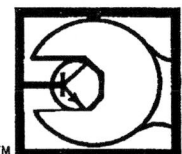

Problem 36
Consult Instructor Guide To Insert Circuit Fault 36
Refer to Schematic **Figure 3TS-5** for this problem
Engine overheats after a few minutes.

Performance of the load: _____

Troubleshooting Step 1: _____TTS-1_____
Reading: _____ Good: ____ Bad: ____

Troubleshooting Step 2: _____TTS-2_____
Reading: _____ Good: ____ Bad: ____

Troubleshooting Step 3: _____
Reading: _____ Good: ____ Bad: ____

Troubleshooting Step 4: _____
Reading: _____ Good: ____ Bad: ____

Troubleshooting Step 5: _____
Reading: _____ Good: ____ Bad: ____

Troubleshooting Step 6: _____
Reading: _____ Good: ____ Bad: ____

Troubleshooting Step 7: _____
Reading: _____ Good: ____ Bad: ____

Troubleshooting Step 8: _____
Reading: _____ Good: ____ Bad: ____

Troubleshooting Step 9: _____
Reading: _____ Good: ____ Bad: ____

Troubleshooting Step 10: _____
Reading: _____ Good: ____ Bad: ____

Troubleshooting Step 11: _____
Reading: _____ Good: ____ Bad: ____

Troubleshooting Step 12: _____
Reading: _____ Good: ____ Bad: ____

The Problem Is: _____

REMINDER: Remove the fault and restore the PCBs to normal operation after the problem is identified.

Problem 37
Consult Instructor Guide To Insert Circuit Fault 37
Refer to Schematic **Figure 3TS-5** for this problem
Engine overheats very quickly.

Performance of the load: _____

Troubleshooting Step 1: _____TTS-1_____
Reading: _____ Good: ____ Bad: ____

Troubleshooting Step 2: _____TTS-2_____
Reading: _____ Good: ____ Bad: ____

Troubleshooting Step 3: _____
Reading: _____ Good: ____ Bad: ____

Troubleshooting Step 4: _____
Reading: _____ Good: ____ Bad: ____

Troubleshooting Step 5: _____
Reading: _____ Good: ____ Bad: ____

Troubleshooting Step 6: _____
Reading: _____ Good: ____ Bad: ____

Troubleshooting Step 7: _____
Reading: _____ Good: ____ Bad: ____

Troubleshooting Step 8: _____
Reading: _____ Good: ____ Bad: ____

Troubleshooting Step 9: _____
Reading: _____ Good: ____ Bad: ____

Troubleshooting Step 10: _____
Reading: _____ Good: ____ Bad: ____

Troubleshooting Step 11: _____
Reading: _____ Good: ____ Bad: ____

Troubleshooting Step 12: _____
Reading: _____ Good: ____ Bad: ____

The Problem Is: _____

REMINDER: Remove the fault and restore the PCBs to normal operation after the problem is identified.

Copyright © 2015 VEEJER ENTERPRISES, Garland, Texas - All Rights Reserved

Vehicle Electronics Hands-On Home-Study Troubleshooting Training

VEEJER ENTERPRISES 3701 Lariat Lane, Garland, Texas 75042-5419
Phone: 972-276-9642 Fax: 972-276-8122 Email: info@veejer.com Web Site: www.veejer.com

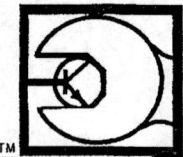

Problem 38
Consult Instructor Guide To Insert Circuit Fault 38
Refer to Schematic **Figure 3TS-5** for this problem

Customer complains the battery won't stay charged. The last shop that had his car sold him a new battery but it still goes dead. The charging system checks OK. **NOTE:** *CLOSE S4 to complete the ground circuit and leave it CLOSED during this problem. Use S3 as the On/Off Switch to control the DC Motor acting as the cooling fan. The problem: After the ignition key (S1) is turned off the cooling fan can be heard running. The car does not have a cooling fan circuit that runs a few minutes after the engine is turned off.*

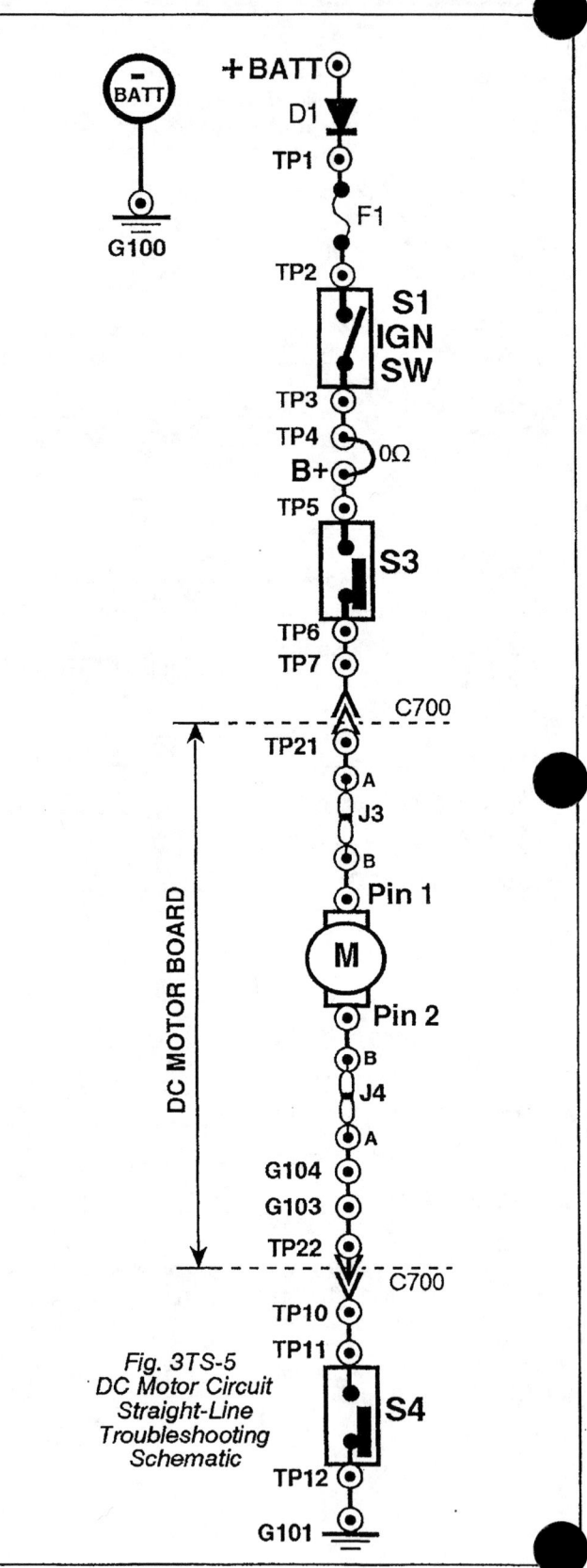

*Fig. 3TS-5
DC Motor Circuit
Straight-Line
Troubleshooting
Schematic*

Performance of the load: _____

Troubleshooting Step 1: _____TTS-1_____
Reading: _____ Good: ___ Bad: ___

Troubleshooting Step 2: _____TTS-2_____
Reading: _____ Good: ___ Bad: ___

Troubleshooting Step 3: _____
Reading: _____ Good: ___ Bad: ___

Troubleshooting Step 4: _____
Reading: _____ Good: ___ Bad: ___

Troubleshooting Step 5: _____
Reading: _____ Good: ___ Bad: ___

Troubleshooting Step 6: _____
Reading: _____ Good: ___ Bad: ___

Troubleshooting Step 7: _____
Reading: _____ Good: ___ Bad: ___

Troubleshooting Step 8: _____
Reading: _____ Good: ___ Bad: ___

Troubleshooting Step 9: _____
Reading: _____ Good: ___ Bad: ___

Troubleshooting Step 10: _____
Reading: _____ Good: ___ Bad: ___

Troubleshooting Step 11: _____
Reading: _____ Good: ___ Bad: ___

Troubleshooting Step 12: _____
Reading: _____ Good: ___ Bad: ___

The Problem Is: _____

REMINDER: Remove the fault and restore the PCBs to normal operation after the problem is identified.

Vehicle Electronics Hands-On Home-Study Troubleshooting Training

VEEJER ENTERPRISES 3701 Lariat Lane, Garland, Texas 75042-5419
Phone: 972-276-9642   Fax: 972-276-8122   Email: info@veejer.com   Web Site: www.veejer.com

---

Problem 39
Consult Instructor Guide To Insert Circuit Fault 39
Refer to Schematic **Figure 3TS-5** for this problem
Engine runs hot.

Performance of the load: _____

Troubleshooting Step 1: ____**TTS-1**_____
Reading: _____ Good: ___ Bad: ___

Troubleshooting Step 2: ____**TTS-2**_____
Reading: _____ Good: ___ Bad: ___

Troubleshooting Step 3: _____
Reading: _____ Good: ___ Bad: ___

Troubleshooting Step 4: _____
Reading: _____ Good: ___ Bad: ___

Troubleshooting Step 5: _____
Reading: _____ Good: ___ Bad: ___

Troubleshooting Step 6: _____
Reading: _____ Good: ___ Bad: ___

Troubleshooting Step 7: _____
Reading: _____ Good: ___ Bad: ___

Troubleshooting Step 8: _____
Reading: _____ Good: ___ Bad: ___

Troubleshooting Step 9: _____
Reading: _____ Good: ___ Bad: ___

Troubleshooting Step 10: _____
Reading: _____ Good: ___ Bad: ___

Troubleshooting Step 11: _____
Reading: _____ Good: ___ Bad: ___

Troubleshooting Step 12: _____
Reading: _____ Good: ___ Bad: ___

The Problem Is: _____

REMINDER: Remove the fault and restore the PCBs to normal operation after the problem is identified.

Problem 40
Consult Instructor Guide To Insert Circuit Fault 40
Refer to Schematic **Figure 3TS-5** for this problem
Engine runs hot.

Performance of the load: _____

Troubleshooting Step 1: ____**TTS-1**_____
Reading: _____ Good: ___ Bad: ___

Troubleshooting Step 2: ____**TTS-2**_____
Reading: _____ Good: ___ Bad: ___

Troubleshooting Step 3: _____
Reading: _____ Good: ___ Bad: ___

Troubleshooting Step 4: _____
Reading: _____ Good: ___ Bad: ___

Troubleshooting Step 5: _____
Reading: _____ Good: ___ Bad: ___

Troubleshooting Step 6: _____
Reading: _____ Good: ___ Bad: ___

Troubleshooting Step 7: _____
Reading: _____ Good: ___ Bad: ___

Troubleshooting Step 8: _____
Reading: _____ Good: ___ Bad: ___

Troubleshooting Step 9: _____
Reading: _____ Good: ___ Bad: ___

Troubleshooting Step 10: _____
Reading: _____ Good: ___ Bad: ___

Troubleshooting Step 11: _____
Reading: _____ Good: ___ Bad: ___

Troubleshooting Step 12: _____
Reading: _____ Good: ___ Bad: ___

The Problem Is: _____

REMINDER: Remove the fault and restore the PCBs to normal operation after the problem is identified.

Vehicle Electronics Hands-On Home-Study Troubleshooting Training

VEEJER ENTERPRISES 3701 Lariat Lane, Garland, Texas 75042-5419
Phone: 972-276-9642   Fax: 972-276-8122   Email: info@veejer.com   Web Site: www.veejer.com

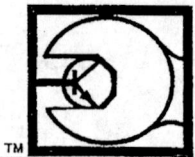

Problem 41
Consult Instructor Guide To Insert Circuit Fault 41
Refer to Schematic **Figure 3TS-5** for this problem
Engine tends to run a little hot. Changed the cooling fan but the problem persists.

Performance of the load: _____

Troubleshooting Step 1: ____TTS-1_____
Reading: _____ Good: ___ Bad: ___

Troubleshooting Step 2: ____TTS-2_____
Reading: _____ Good: ___ Bad: ___

Troubleshooting Step 3: _____
Reading: _____ Good: ___ Bad: ___

Troubleshooting Step 4: _____
Reading: _____ Good: ___ Bad: ___

Troubleshooting Step 5: _____
Reading: _____ Good: ___ Bad: ___

Troubleshooting Step 6: _____
Reading: _____ Good: ___ Bad: ___

Troubleshooting Step 7: _____
Reading: _____ Good: ___ Bad: ___

Troubleshooting Step 8: _____
Reading: _____ Good: ___ Bad: ___

Troubleshooting Step 9: _____
Reading: _____ Good: ___ Bad: ___

Troubleshooting Step 10: _____
Reading: _____ Good: ___ Bad: ___

Troubleshooting Step 11: _____
Reading: _____ Good: ___ Bad: ___

Troubleshooting Step 12: _____
Reading: _____ Good: ___ Bad: ___

The Problem Is: _____

REMINDER: Remove the fault and restore the PCBs to normal operation after the problem is identified.

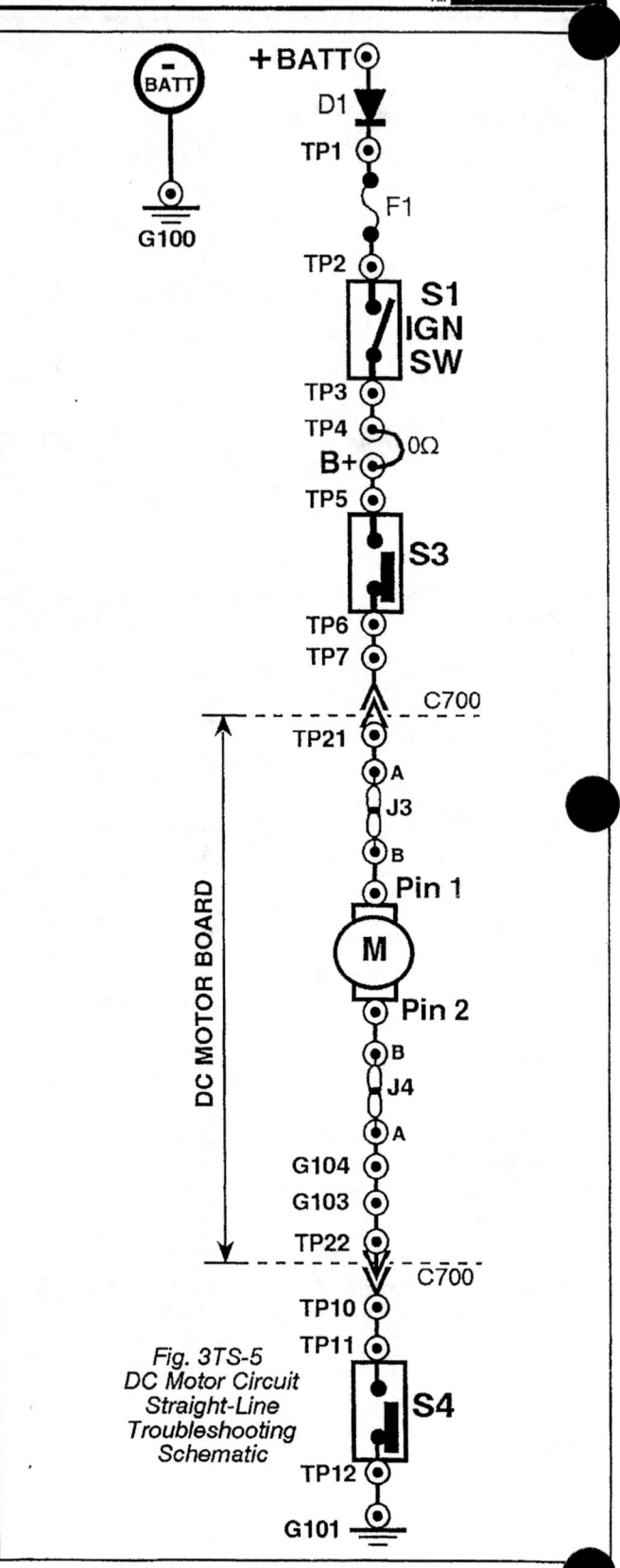

Fig. 3TS-5
DC Motor Circuit
Straight-Line
Troubleshooting
Schematic

Text H-WB113 Page 45

Vehicle Electronics Hands-On Home-Study Troubleshooting Training

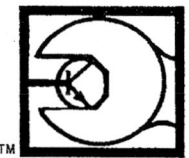

VEEJER ENTERPRISES 3701 Lariat Lane, Garland, Texas 75042-5419
Phone: 972-276-9642   Fax: 972-276-8122   Email: info@veejer.com   Web Site: www.veejer.com

---

Problem 42
Consult Instructor Guide To Insert Circuit Fault 42
Refer to Schematic **Figure 3TS-5** for this problem
Cooling Fan runs slow and engine gets hot.

Performance of the load: _____

Troubleshooting Step 1: _____TTS-1_____
Reading: _____ Good: ____ Bad: ____

Troubleshooting Step 2: _____TTS-2_____
Reading: _____ Good: ____ Bad: ____

Troubleshooting Step 3: _____
Reading: _____ Good: ____ Bad: ____

Troubleshooting Step 4: _____
Reading: _____ Good: ____ Bad: ____

Troubleshooting Step 5: _____
Reading: _____ Good: ____ Bad: ____

Troubleshooting Step 6: _____
Reading: _____ Good: ____ Bad: ____

Troubleshooting Step 7: _____
Reading: _____ Good: ____ Bad: ____

Troubleshooting Step 8: _____
Reading: _____ Good: ____ Bad: ____

Troubleshooting Step 9: _____
Reading: _____ Good: ____ Bad: ____

Troubleshooting Step 10: _____
Reading: _____ Good: ____ Bad: ____

Troubleshooting Step 11: _____
Reading: _____ Good: ____ Bad: ____

Troubleshooting Step 12: _____
Reading: _____ Good: ____ Bad: ____

The Problem Is: _____

REMINDER: Remove the fault and restore the PCBs to normal operation after the problem is identified.

Problem 43
Consult Instructor Guide To Insert Circuit Fault 43
Refer to Schematic **Figure 3TS-5** for this problem
Car overheats very fast.

Performance of the load: _____

Troubleshooting Step 1: _____TTS-1_____
Reading: _____ Good: ____ Bad: ____

Troubleshooting Step 2: _____TTS-2_____
Reading: _____ Good: ____ Bad: ____

Troubleshooting Step 3: _____
Reading: _____ Good: ____ Bad: ____

Troubleshooting Step 4: _____
Reading: _____ Good: ____ Bad: ____

Troubleshooting Step 5: _____
Reading: _____ Good: ____ Bad: ____

Troubleshooting Step 6: _____
Reading: _____ Good: ____ Bad: ____

Troubleshooting Step 7: _____
Reading: _____ Good: ____ Bad: ____

Troubleshooting Step 8: _____
Reading: _____ Good: ____ Bad: ____

Troubleshooting Step 9: _____
Reading: _____ Good: ____ Bad: ____

Troubleshooting Step 10: _____
Reading: _____ Good: ____ Bad: ____

Troubleshooting Step 11: _____
Reading: _____ Good: ____ Bad: ____

Troubleshooting Step 12: _____
Reading: _____ Good: ____ Bad: ____

The Problem Is: _____

REMINDER: Remove the fault and restore the PCBs to normal operation after the problem is identified.

Vehicle Electronics Hands-On Home-Study Troubleshooting Training

VEEJER ENTERPRISES 3701 Lariat Lane, Garland, Texas 75042-5419
Phone: 972-276-9642   Fax: 972-276-8122   Email: info@veejer.com   Web Site: www.veejer.com

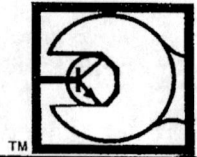

Problem 44
Consult Instructor Guide To Insert Circuit Fault 44
Refer to Schematic **Figure 3TS-5** for this problem
Cooling Fan inop. Car gets hot very quickly. "A new cooling fan still won't work after all that work for nothing installing a new cooling fan. Now the Boss is upset with me . . . again! I've got to learn how to troubleshoot with a DMM before he demotes me to just pumping gas and washing windshields."

Performance of the load: _____

Troubleshooting Step 1: _____TTS-1_____
Reading: _____ Good: ___ Bad: ___

Troubleshooting Step 2: _____TTS-2_____
Reading: _____ Good: ___ Bad: ___

Troubleshooting Step 3: _____
Reading: _____ Good: ___ Bad: ___

Troubleshooting Step 4: _____
Reading: _____ Good: ___ Bad: ___

Troubleshooting Step 5: _____
Reading: _____ Good: ___ Bad: ___

Troubleshooting Step 6: _____
Reading: _____ Good: ___ Bad: ___

Troubleshooting Step 7: _____
Reading: _____ Good: ___ Bad: ___

Troubleshooting Step 8: _____
Reading: _____ Good: ___ Bad: ___

Troubleshooting Step 9: _____
Reading: _____ Good: ___ Bad: ___

Troubleshooting Step 10: _____
Reading: _____ Good: ___ Bad: ___

Troubleshooting Step 11: _____
Reading: _____ Good: ___ Bad: ___

Troubleshooting Step 12: _____
Reading: _____ Good: ___ Bad: ___

The Problem Is: _____

REMINDER: Remove the fault and restore the PCBs to normal operation after the problem is identified.

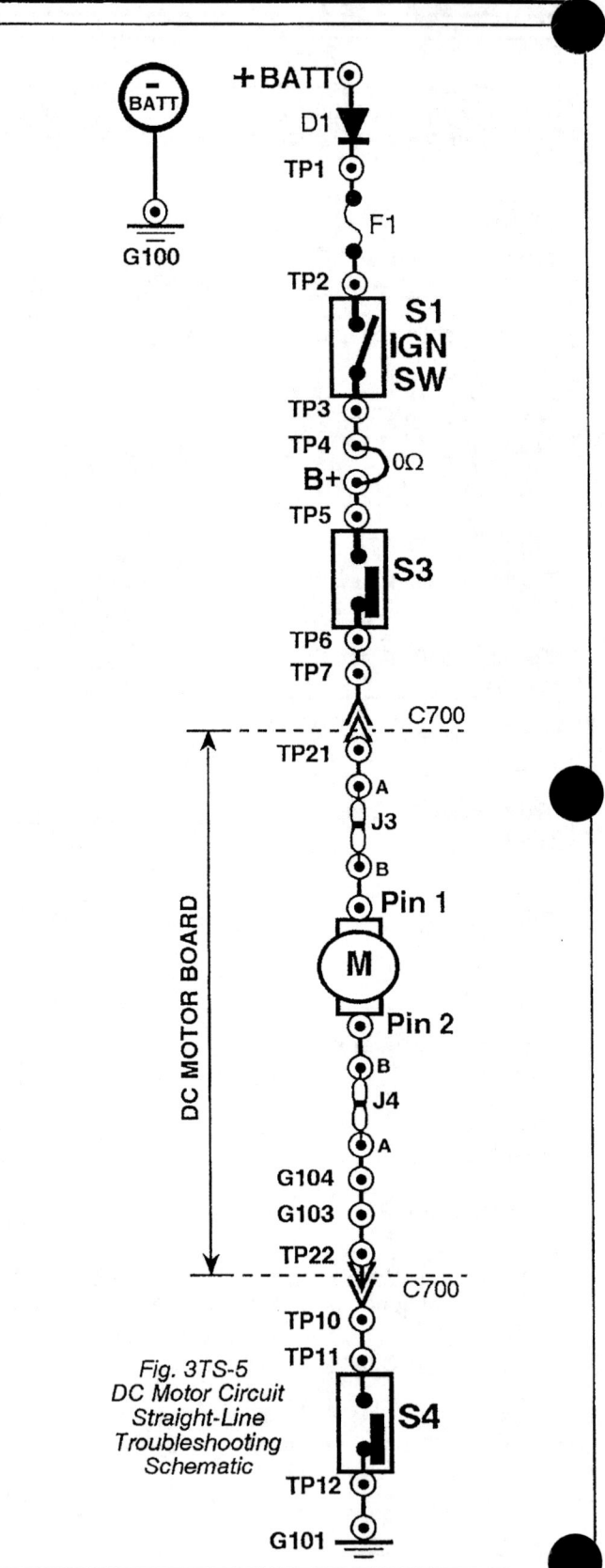

*Fig. 3TS-5
DC Motor Circuit
Straight-Line
Troubleshooting
Schematic*

Copyright © 2015 VEEJER ENTERPRISES, Garland, Texas - All Rights Reserved

Vehicle Electronics Hands-On Home-Study Troubleshooting Training

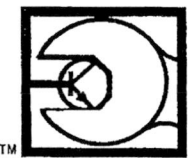

VEEJER ENTERPRISES 3701 Lariat Lane, Garland, Texas 75042-5419
Phone: 972-276-9642   Fax: 972-276-8122   Email: info@veejer.com   Web Site: www.veejer.com

Problem 45
Consult Instructor Guide To Insert Circuit Fault 45
Refer to Schematic **Figure 3TS-5** for this problem
Engine tends to overheat.

Performance of the load: _____

Troubleshooting Step 1: _____TTS-1_____
Reading: _____ Good: ____ Bad: ____

Troubleshooting Step 2: _____TTS-2_____
Reading: _____ Good: ____ Bad: ____

Troubleshooting Step 3: _____
Reading: _____ Good: ____ Bad: ____

Troubleshooting Step 4: _____
Reading: _____ Good: ____ Bad: ____

Troubleshooting Step 5: _____
Reading: _____ Good: ____ Bad: ____

Troubleshooting Step 6: _____
Reading: _____ Good: ____ Bad: ____

Troubleshooting Step 7: _____
Reading: _____ Good: ____ Bad: ____

Troubleshooting Step 8: _____
Reading: _____ Good: ____ Bad: ____

Troubleshooting Step 9: _____
Reading: _____ Good: ____ Bad: ____

Troubleshooting Step 10: _____
Reading: _____ Good: ____ Bad: ____

Troubleshooting Step 11: _____
Reading: _____ Good: ____ Bad: ____

Troubleshooting Step 12: _____
Reading: _____ Good: ____ Bad: ____

The Problem Is: _____

REMINDER: Remove the fault and restore the PCBs to normal operation after the problem is identified.

Problem 46
Consult Instructor Guide To Insert Circuit Fault 46
Refer to Schematic **Figure 3TS-5** for this problem
Engine tends to overheat.

Performance of the load: _____

Troubleshooting Step 1: _____TTS-1_____
Reading: _____ Good: ____ Bad: ____

Troubleshooting Step 2: _____TTS-2_____
Reading: _____ Good: ____ Bad: ____

Troubleshooting Step 3: _____
Reading: _____ Good: ____ Bad: ____

Troubleshooting Step 4: _____
Reading: _____ Good: ____ Bad: ____

Troubleshooting Step 5: _____
Reading: _____ Good: ____ Bad: ____

Troubleshooting Step 6: _____
Reading: _____ Good: ____ Bad: ____

Troubleshooting Step 7: _____
Reading: _____ Good: ____ Bad: ____

Troubleshooting Step 8: _____
Reading: _____ Good: ____ Bad: ____

Troubleshooting Step 9: _____
Reading: _____ Good: ____ Bad: ____

Troubleshooting Step 10: _____
Reading: _____ Good: ____ Bad: ____

Troubleshooting Step 11: _____
Reading: _____ Good: ____ Bad: ____

Troubleshooting Step 12: _____
Reading: _____ Good: ____ Bad: ____

The Problem Is: _____

REMINDER: Remove the fault and restore the PCBs to normal operation after the problem is identified.

Vehicle Electronics Hands-On Home-Study Troubleshooting Training

VEEJER ENTERPRISES 3701 Lariat Lane, Garland, Texas 75042-5419
Phone: 972-276-9642 Fax: 972-276-8122 Email: info@veejer.com Web Site: www.veejer.com

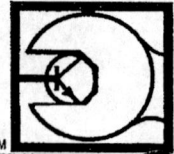

Problem 47

Consult Instructor Guide To Insert Circuit Fault 47
Refer to Schematic **Figure 3TS-5** for this problem

Cooling fan won't work. Engine overheats really fast and the Boss won't let me try a new cooling fan again. He said "Get out your DMM and tell him what's wrong with the circuit before you change any parts." Got any ideas?

Performance of the load: _____

Troubleshooting Step 1: _____TTS-1_____
Reading: _____ Good: ___ Bad: ___

Troubleshooting Step 2: _____TTS-2_____
Reading: _____ Good: ___ Bad: ___

Troubleshooting Step 3: _____
Reading: _____ Good: ___ Bad: ___

Troubleshooting Step 4: _____
Reading: _____ Good: ___ Bad: ___

Troubleshooting Step 5: _____
Reading: _____ Good: ___ Bad: ___

Troubleshooting Step 6: _____
Reading: _____ Good: ___ Bad: ___

Troubleshooting Step 7: _____
Reading: _____ Good: ___ Bad: ___

Troubleshooting Step 8: _____
Reading: _____ Good: ___ Bad: ___

Troubleshooting Step 9: _____
Reading: _____ Good: ___ Bad: ___

Troubleshooting Step 10: _____
Reading: _____ Good: ___ Bad: ___

Troubleshooting Step 11: _____
Reading: _____ Good: ___ Bad: ___

Troubleshooting Step 12: _____
Reading: _____ Good: ___ Bad: ___

The Problem Is: _____

REMINDER: Remove the fault and restore the PCBs to normal operation after the problem is identified.

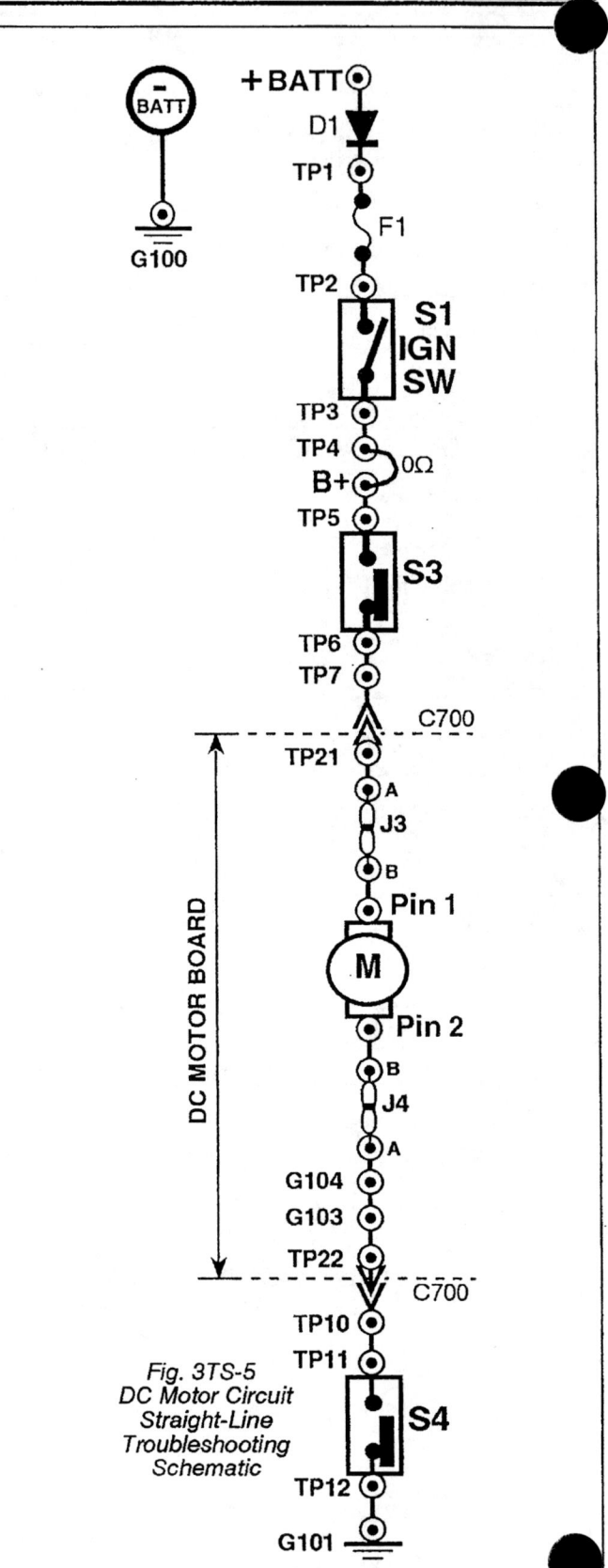

Fig. 3TS-5
DC Motor Circuit
Straight-Line
Troubleshooting
Schematic

Copyright © 2015 VEEJER ENTERPRISES, Garland, Texas - All Rights Reserved   Text H-WB113 Page 49

Vehicle Electronics Hands-On Home-Study Troubleshooting Training

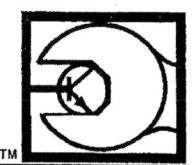

VEEJER ENTERPRISES 3701 Lariat Lane, Garland, Texas 75042-5419
Phone: 972-276-9642   Fax: 972-276-8122   Email: info@veejer.com   Web Site: www.veejer.com

Problem 48
Consult Instructor Guide To Insert Circuit Fault 48
Refer to Schematic **Figure 3TS-5** for this problem

"Now what? I just found a short to ground in Problem 47 and repaired the wire short-to-ground. Now the cooling fan won't spin fast enough to keep the engine from overheating. It never fails. Just when I think I've got it all figured out I get a car with two problems in the same circuit. Hey, Louie, can I borrow your DMM again? Awww . . . come on man, I'll buy my own DMM the next time the tool truck comes around, I promise."

Performance of the load: _____

Troubleshooting Step 1: _____**TTS-1**_____
Reading: _____ Good: ____ Bad: ____

Troubleshooting Step 2: _____**TTS-2**_____
Reading: _____ Good: ____ Bad: ____

Troubleshooting Step 3: _____
Reading: _____ Good: ____ Bad: ____

Troubleshooting Step 4: _____
Reading: _____ Good: ____ Bad: ____

Troubleshooting Step 5: _____
Reading: _____ Good: ____ Bad: ____

Troubleshooting Step 6: _____
Reading: _____ Good: ____ Bad: ____

Troubleshooting Step 7: _____
Reading: _____ Good: ____ Bad: ____

Troubleshooting Step 8: _____
Reading: _____ Good: ____ Bad: ____

Troubleshooting Step 9: _____
Reading: _____ Good: ____ Bad: ____

Troubleshooting Step 10: _____
Reading: _____ Good: ____ Bad: ____

Troubleshooting Step 11: _____
Reading: _____ Good: ____ Bad: ____

Troubleshooting Step 12: _____
Reading: _____ Good: ____ Bad: ____

The Problem Is: _____

REMINDER: Remove the fault and restore the PCBs to normal operation after the problem is identified.

Problem 49
Consult Instructor Guide To Insert Circuit Fault 49
Refer to Schematic **Figure 3TS-5** for this problem

One of your techs had the dash partially removed on this car to fix a bad connection at a fuse terminal in the Fuse Box, After the customer drove away he came back in a few minutes complaining his car is getting extremely hot. You confirm this is true as steam pours out from under the hood. The other tech who worked on this car took off for the rest of the day so you have to fix it for the customer because he is bigger than you and is very angry. He also happens to be a lawyer and is threatening a lawsuit.

Performance of the load: _____

Troubleshooting Step 1: _____**TTS-1**_____
Reading: _____ Good: ____ Bad: ____

Troubleshooting Step 2: _____**TTS-2**_____
Reading: _____ Good: ____ Bad: ____

Troubleshooting Step 3: _____
Reading: _____ Good: ____ Bad: ____

Troubleshooting Step 4: _____
Reading: _____ Good: ____ Bad: ____

Troubleshooting Step 5: _____
Reading: _____ Good: ____ Bad: ____

Troubleshooting Step 6: _____
Reading: _____ Good: ____ Bad: ____

Troubleshooting Step 7: _____
Reading: _____ Good: ____ Bad: ____

Troubleshooting Step 8: _____
Reading: _____ Good: ____ Bad: ____

Troubleshooting Step 9: _____
Reading: _____ Good: ____ Bad: ____

Troubleshooting Step 10: _____
Reading: _____ Good: ____ Bad: ____

Troubleshooting Step 11: _____
Reading: _____ Good: ____ Bad: ____

Troubleshooting Step 12: _____
Reading: _____ Good: ____ Bad: ____

The Problem Is: _____

REMINDER: Remove the fault and restore the PCBs to normal operation after the problem is identified.

Vehicle Electronics Hands-On Home-Study Troubleshooting Training

VEEJER ENTERPRISES 3701 Lariat Lane, Garland, Texas 75042-5419
Phone: 972-276-9642   Fax: 972-276-8122   Email: info@veejer.com   Web Site: www.veejer.com

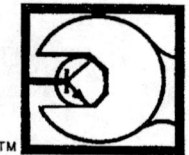

Problem 50
Consult Instructor Guide To Insert Circuit Fault 50
Refer to Schematic **Figure 3TS-5** for this problem

Car has been subjected to a lot of road salt corrosion. Bottom of fenders are eaten away and the hub caps are missing. Customer complains of a lot of electrical things that don't always work right and sometimes he has cranking problems but now he came in because his car is overheating and barely runs. His wife is afraid to drive with him as long as smoke is coming out from under the hood.

Performance of the load: _____

Troubleshooting Step 1: _____TTS-1_____
Reading: _____ Good: ____ Bad: ____

Troubleshooting Step 2: _____TTS-2_____
Reading: _____ Good: ____ Bad: ____

Troubleshooting Step 3: _____
Reading: _____ Good: ____ Bad: ____

Troubleshooting Step 4: _____
Reading: _____ Good: ____ Bad: ____

Troubleshooting Step 5: _____
Reading: _____ Good: ____ Bad: ____

Troubleshooting Step 6: _____
Reading: _____ Good: ____ Bad: ____

Troubleshooting Step 7: _____
Reading: _____ Good: ____ Bad: ____

Troubleshooting Step 8: _____
Reading: _____ Good: ____ Bad: ____

Troubleshooting Step 9: _____
Reading: _____ Good: ____ Bad: ____

Troubleshooting Step 10: _____
Reading: _____ Good: ____ Bad: ____

Troubleshooting Step 11: _____
Reading: _____ Good: ____ Bad: ____

Troubleshooting Step 12: _____
Reading: _____ Good: ____ Bad: ____

The Problem Is: _____

REMINDER: Remove the fault and restore the PCBs to normal operation after the problem is identified.

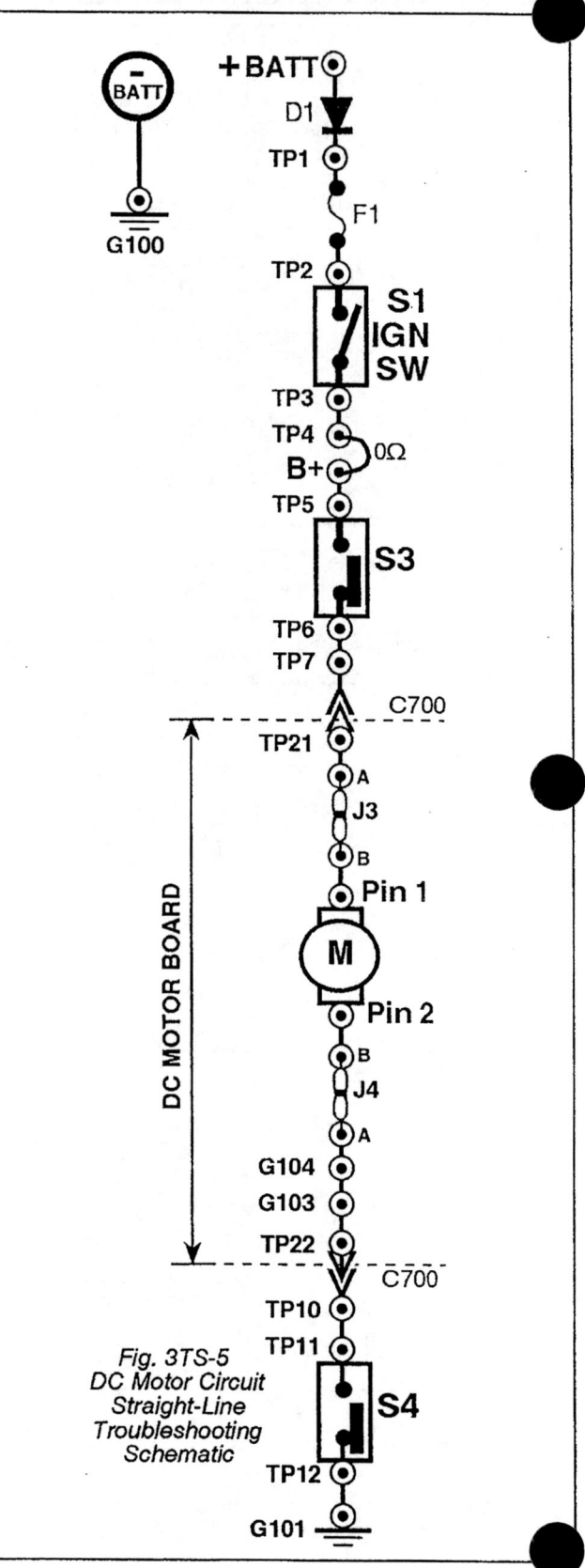

Fig. 3TS-5 DC Motor Circuit Straight-Line Troubleshooting Schematic

Copyright © 2015 VEEJER ENTERPRISES, Garland, Texas - All Rights Reserved   Text H-WB113

Vehicle Electronics Hands-On Home-Study Troubleshooting Training

VEEJER ENTERPRISES 3701 Lariat Lane, Garland, Texas 75042-5419
Phone: 972-276-9642 Fax: 972-276-8122 Email: info@veejer.com Web Site: www.veejer.com

Problem 51
Consult Instructor Guide To Insert Circuit Fault 51
Refer to Schematic **Figure 3TS-5** for this problem
Engine overheats quickly.

Performance of the load: _____

Troubleshooting Step 1: _____TTS-1_____
Reading: _____ Good: ____ Bad: ____

Troubleshooting Step 2: _____TTS-2_____
Reading: _____ Good: ____ Bad: ____

Troubleshooting Step 3: _____
Reading: _____ Good: ____ Bad: ____

Troubleshooting Step 4: _____
Reading: _____ Good: ____ Bad: ____

Troubleshooting Step 5: _____
Reading: _____ Good: ____ Bad: ____

Troubleshooting Step 6: _____
Reading: _____ Good: ____ Bad: ____

Troubleshooting Step 7: _____
Reading: _____ Good: ____ Bad: ____

Troubleshooting Step 8: _____
Reading: _____ Good: ____ Bad: ____

Troubleshooting Step 9: _____
Reading: _____ Good: ____ Bad: ____

Troubleshooting Step 10: _____
Reading: _____ Good: ____ Bad: ____

Troubleshooting Step 11: _____
Reading: _____ Good: ____ Bad: ____

Troubleshooting Step 12: _____
Reading: _____ Good: ____ Bad: ____

The Problem Is: _____

REMINDER: Remove the fault and restore the PCBs to normal operation after the problem is identified.

Problem 52
Consult Instructor Guide To Insert Circuit Fault 52
Refer to Schematic **Figure 3TS-5** for this problem
Engine overheats quickly.

Performance of the load: _____

Troubleshooting Step 1: _____TTS-1_____
Reading: _____ Good: ____ Bad: ____

Troubleshooting Step 2: _____TTS-2_____
Reading: _____ Good: ____ Bad: ____

Troubleshooting Step 3: _____
Reading: _____ Good: ____ Bad: ____

Troubleshooting Step 4: _____
Reading: _____ Good: ____ Bad: ____

Troubleshooting Step 5: _____
Reading: _____ Good: ____ Bad: ____

Troubleshooting Step 6: _____
Reading: _____ Good: ____ Bad: ____

Troubleshooting Step 7: _____
Reading: _____ Good: ____ Bad: ____

Troubleshooting Step 8: _____
Reading: _____ Good: ____ Bad: ____

Troubleshooting Step 9: _____
Reading: _____ Good: ____ Bad: ____

Troubleshooting Step 10: _____
Reading: _____ Good: ____ Bad: ____

Troubleshooting Step 11: _____
Reading: _____ Good: ____ Bad: ____

Troubleshooting Step 12: _____
Reading: _____ Good: ____ Bad: ____

The Problem Is: _____

REMINDER: Remove the fault and restore the PCBs to normal operation after the problem is identified.

Copyright © 2015 VEEJER ENTERPRISES, Garland, Texas - All Rights Reserved

Vehicle Electronics Hands-On Home-Study Troubleshooting Training

VEEJER ENTERPRISES 3701 Lariat Lane, Garland, Texas 75042-5419
Phone: 972-276-9642 Fax: 972-276-8122 Email: info@veejer.com Web Site: www.veejer.com

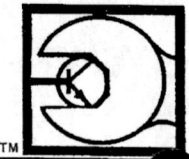

Problem 53
Consult Instructor Guide To Insert Circuit Fault 53
Refer to Schematic **Figure 3TS-5** for this problem
Engine runs hot.

Performance of the load: _____

Troubleshooting Step 1: _____TTS-1_____
Reading: _____ Good: ___ Bad: ___

Troubleshooting Step 2: _____TTS-2_____
Reading: _____ Good: ___ Bad: ___

Troubleshooting Step 3: _____
Reading: _____ Good: ___ Bad: ___

Troubleshooting Step 4: _____
Reading: _____ Good: ___ Bad: ___

Troubleshooting Step 5: _____
Reading: _____ Good: ___ Bad: ___

Troubleshooting Step 6: _____
Reading: _____ Good: ___ Bad: ___

Troubleshooting Step 7: _____
Reading: _____ Good: ___ Bad: ___

Troubleshooting Step 8: _____
Reading: _____ Good: ___ Bad: ___

Troubleshooting Step 9: _____
Reading: _____ Good: ___ Bad: ___

Troubleshooting Step 10: _____
Reading: _____ Good: ___ Bad: ___

Troubleshooting Step 11: _____
Reading: _____ Good: ___ Bad: ___

Troubleshooting Step 12: _____
Reading: _____ Good: ___ Bad: ___

The Problem Is: _____

REMINDER: Remove the fault and restore the PCBs to normal operation after the problem is identified.

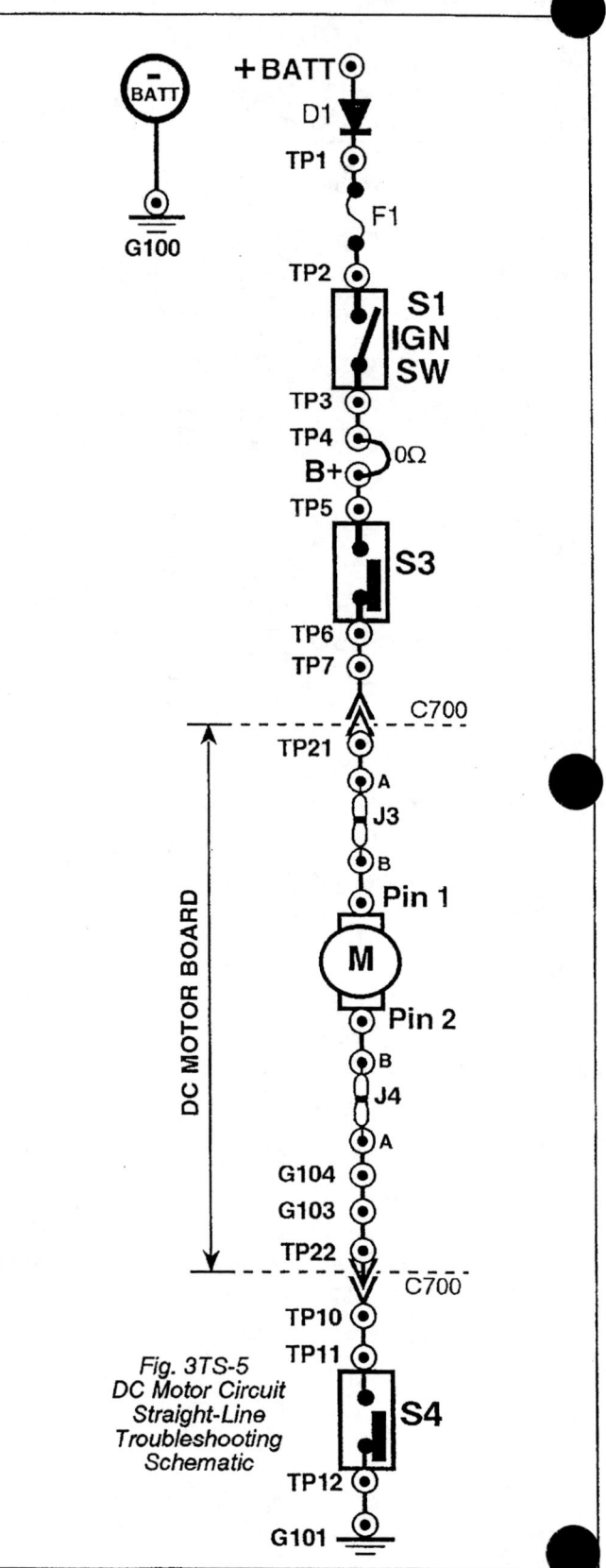

Fig. 3TS-5 DC Motor Circuit Straight-Line Troubleshooting Schematic

Copyright © 2015 VEEJER ENTERPRISES, Garland, Texas - All Rights Reserved

Vehicle Electronics Hands-On Home-Study Troubleshooting Training

VEEJER ENTERPRISES 3701 Lariat Lane, Garland, Texas 75042-5419
Phone: 972-276-9642   Fax: 972-276-8122   Email: info@veejer.com   Web Site: www.veejer.com

Problem 54
Consult Instructor Guide To Insert Circuit Fault 54
Refer to Schematic **Figure 3TS-5** for this problem
Engine runs hot.

Performance of the load: _____

Troubleshooting Step 1: _____TTS-1_____
Reading: _____ Good: ____ Bad: ____

Troubleshooting Step 2: _____TTS-2_____
Reading: _____ Good: ____ Bad: ____

Troubleshooting Step 3: _____
Reading: _____ Good: ____ Bad: ____

Troubleshooting Step 4: _____
Reading: _____ Good: ____ Bad: ____

Troubleshooting Step 5: _____
Reading: _____ Good: ____ Bad: ____

Troubleshooting Step 6: _____
Reading: _____ Good: ____ Bad: ____

Troubleshooting Step 7: _____
Reading: _____ Good: ____ Bad: ____

Troubleshooting Step 8: _____
Reading: _____ Good: ____ Bad: ____

Troubleshooting Step 9: _____
Reading: _____ Good: ____ Bad: ____

Troubleshooting Step 10: _____
Reading: _____ Good: ____ Bad: ____

Troubleshooting Step 11: _____
Reading: _____ Good: ____ Bad: ____

Troubleshooting Step 12: _____
Reading: _____ Good: ____ Bad: ____

The Problem Is: _____

REMINDER: Remove the fault and restore the PCBs to normal operation after the problem is identified.

Problem 55
Consult Instructor Guide To Insert Circuit Fault 55
Refer to Schematic **Figure 3TS-5** for this problem
Engine runs hot.

Performance of the load: _____

Troubleshooting Step 1: _____TTS-1_____
Reading: _____ Good: ____ Bad: ____

Troubleshooting Step 2: _____TTS-2_____
Reading: _____ Good: ____ Bad: ____

Troubleshooting Step 3: _____
Reading: _____ Good: ____ Bad: ____

Troubleshooting Step 4: _____
Reading: _____ Good: ____ Bad: ____

Troubleshooting Step 5: _____
Reading: _____ Good: ____ Bad: ____

Troubleshooting Step 6: _____
Reading: _____ Good: ____ Bad: ____

Troubleshooting Step 7: _____
Reading: _____ Good: ____ Bad: ____

Troubleshooting Step 8: _____
Reading: _____ Good: ____ Bad: ____

Troubleshooting Step 9: _____
Reading: _____ Good: ____ Bad: ____

Troubleshooting Step 10: _____
Reading: _____ Good: ____ Bad: ____

Troubleshooting Step 11: _____
Reading: _____ Good: ____ Bad: ____

Troubleshooting Step 12: _____
Reading: _____ Good: ____ Bad: ____

The Problem Is: _____

REMINDER: Remove the fault and restore the PCBs to normal operation after the problem is identified.

Copyright © 2015 VEEJER ENTERPRISES, Garland, Texas - All Rights Reserved   Text H-WB113

Vehicle Electronics Hands-On Home-Study Troubleshooting Training

VEEJER ENTERPRISES 3701 Lariat Lane, Garland, Texas 75042-5419
Phone: 972-276-9642   Fax: 972-276-8122   Email: info@veejer.com   Web Site: www.veejer.com

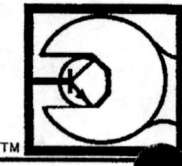

Problem 56
Consult Instructor Guide To Insert Circuit Fault 56
Refer to Schematic **Figure 3TS-5** for this problem
Engine runs hot.

Performance of the load: _____

Troubleshooting Step 1: ____TTS-1____
Reading: _____ Good: ___ Bad: ___

Troubleshooting Step 2: ____TTS-2____
Reading: _____ Good: ___ Bad: ___

Troubleshooting Step 3: _____
Reading: _____ Good: ___ Bad: ___

Troubleshooting Step 4: _____
Reading: _____ Good: ___ Bad: ___

Troubleshooting Step 5: _____
Reading: _____ Good: ___ Bad: ___

Troubleshooting Step 6: _____
Reading: _____ Good: ___ Bad: ___

Troubleshooting Step 7: _____
Reading: _____ Good: ___ Bad: ___

Troubleshooting Step 8: _____
Reading: _____ Good: ___ Bad: ___

Troubleshooting Step 9: _____
Reading: _____ Good: ___ Bad: ___

Troubleshooting Step 10: _____
Reading: _____ Good: ___ Bad: ___

Troubleshooting Step 11: _____
Reading: _____ Good: ___ Bad: ___

Troubleshooting Step 12: _____
Reading: _____ Good: ___ Bad: ___

The Problem Is: _____

REMINDER: Remove the fault and restore the PCBs to normal operation after the problem is identified.

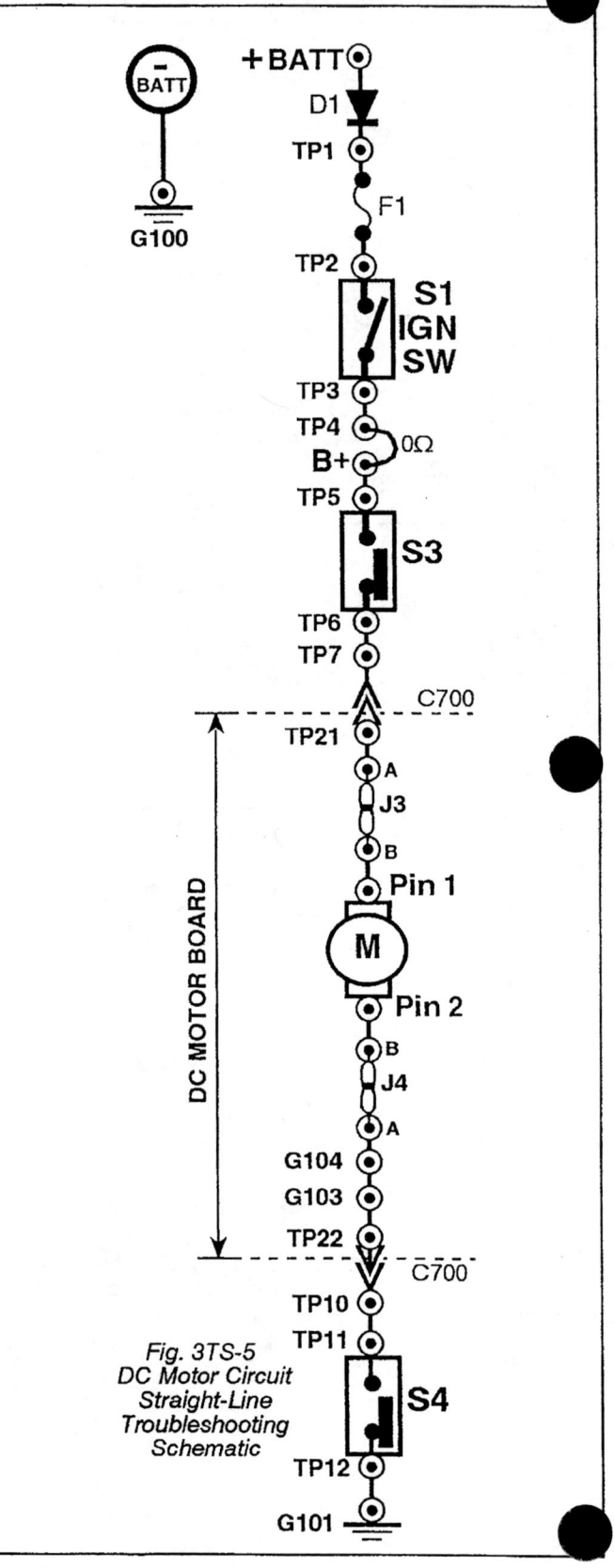

Fig. 3TS-5 DC Motor Circuit Straight-Line Troubleshooting Schematic

Copyright © 2015 VEEJER ENTERPRISES, Garland, Texas - All Rights Reserved   Text H-WB113 Page 55

Vehicle Electronics Hands-On Home-Study Troubleshooting Training

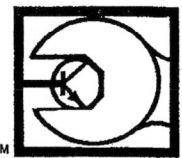

VEEJER ENTERPRISES 3701 Lariat Lane, Garland, Texas 75042-5419
Phone: 972-276-9642   Fax: 972-276-8122   Email: info@veejer.com   Web Site: www.veejer.com

---

Problem 57
Consult Instructor Guide To Insert Circuit Fault 57
Refer to Schematic **Figure 3TS-5** for this problem
Engine runs hot.

Performance of the load: _____

Troubleshooting Step 1: _____TTS-1_____
Reading: _____ Good: ____ Bad: ____

Troubleshooting Step 2: _____TTS-2_____
Reading: _____ Good: ____ Bad: ____

Troubleshooting Step 3: _____
Reading: _____ Good: ____ Bad: ____

Troubleshooting Step 4: _____
Reading: _____ Good: ____ Bad: ____

Troubleshooting Step 5: _____
Reading: _____ Good: ____ Bad: ____

Troubleshooting Step 6: _____
Reading: _____ Good: ____ Bad: ____

Troubleshooting Step 7: _____
Reading: _____ Good: ____ Bad: ____

Troubleshooting Step 8: _____
Reading: _____ Good: ____ Bad: ____

Troubleshooting Step 9: _____
Reading: _____ Good: ____ Bad: ____

Troubleshooting Step 10: _____
Reading: _____ Good: ____ Bad: ____

Troubleshooting Step 11: _____
Reading: _____ Good: ____ Bad: ____

Troubleshooting Step 12: _____
Reading: _____ Good: ____ Bad: ____

The Problem Is: _____

REMINDER: Remove the fault and restore the PCBs to normal operation after the problem is identified.

Problem 58
Consult Instructor Guide To Insert Circuit Fault 58
Refer to Schematic **Figure 3TS-5** for this problem
Engine overheats

Performance of the load: _____

Troubleshooting Step 1: _____TTS-1_____
Reading: _____ Good: ____ Bad: ____

Troubleshooting Step 2: _____TTS-2_____
Reading: _____ Good: ____ Bad: ____

Troubleshooting Step 3: _____
Reading: _____ Good: ____ Bad: ____

Troubleshooting Step 4: _____
Reading: _____ Good: ____ Bad: ____

Troubleshooting Step 5: _____
Reading: _____ Good: ____ Bad: ____

Troubleshooting Step 6: _____
Reading: _____ Good: ____ Bad: ____

Troubleshooting Step 7: _____
Reading: _____ Good: ____ Bad: ____

Troubleshooting Step 8: _____
Reading: _____ Good: ____ Bad: ____

Troubleshooting Step 9: _____
Reading: _____ Good: ____ Bad: ____

Troubleshooting Step 10: _____
Reading: _____ Good: ____ Bad: ____

Troubleshooting Step 11: _____
Reading: _____ Good: ____ Bad: ____

Troubleshooting Step 12: _____
Reading: _____ Good: ____ Bad: ____

The Problem Is: _____

REMINDER: Remove the fault and restore the PCBs to normal operation after the problem is identified.

Copyright © 2015 VEEJER ENTERPRISES, Garland, Texas - All Rights Reserved   Text H-WB113

Vehicle Electronics Hands-On Home-Study Troubleshooting Training

VEEJER ENTERPRISES 3701 Lariat Lane, Garland, Texas 75042-5419
Phone: 972-276-9642 Fax: 972-276-8122 Email: info@veejer.com Web Site: www.veejer.com

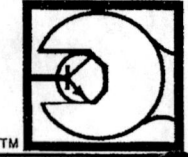

Problem 59
Consult Instructor Guide To Insert Circuit Fault 59
Refer to Schematic **Figure** 3TS-5 for this problem
Engine overheats fast.

Performance of the load: _____

Troubleshooting Step 1: _____TTS-1_____
Reading: _____ Good: ____ Bad: ____

Troubleshooting Step 2: _____TTS-2_____
Reading: _____ Good: ____ Bad: ____

Troubleshooting Step 3: _____
Reading: _____ Good: ____ Bad: ____

Troubleshooting Step 4: _____
Reading: _____ Good: ____ Bad: ____

Troubleshooting Step 5: _____
Reading: _____ Good: ____ Bad: ____

Troubleshooting Step 6: _____
Reading: _____ Good: ____ Bad: ____

Troubleshooting Step 7: _____
Reading: _____ Good: ____ Bad: ____

Troubleshooting Step 8: _____
Reading: _____ Good: ____ Bad: ____

Troubleshooting Step 9: _____
Reading: _____ Good: ____ Bad: ____

Troubleshooting Step 10: _____
Reading: _____ Good: ____ Bad: ____

Troubleshooting Step 11: _____
Reading: _____ Good: ____ Bad: ____

Troubleshooting Step 12: _____
Reading: _____ Good: ____ Bad: ____

The Problem Is: _____

REMINDER: Remove the fault and restore the PCBs to normal operation after the problem is identified.

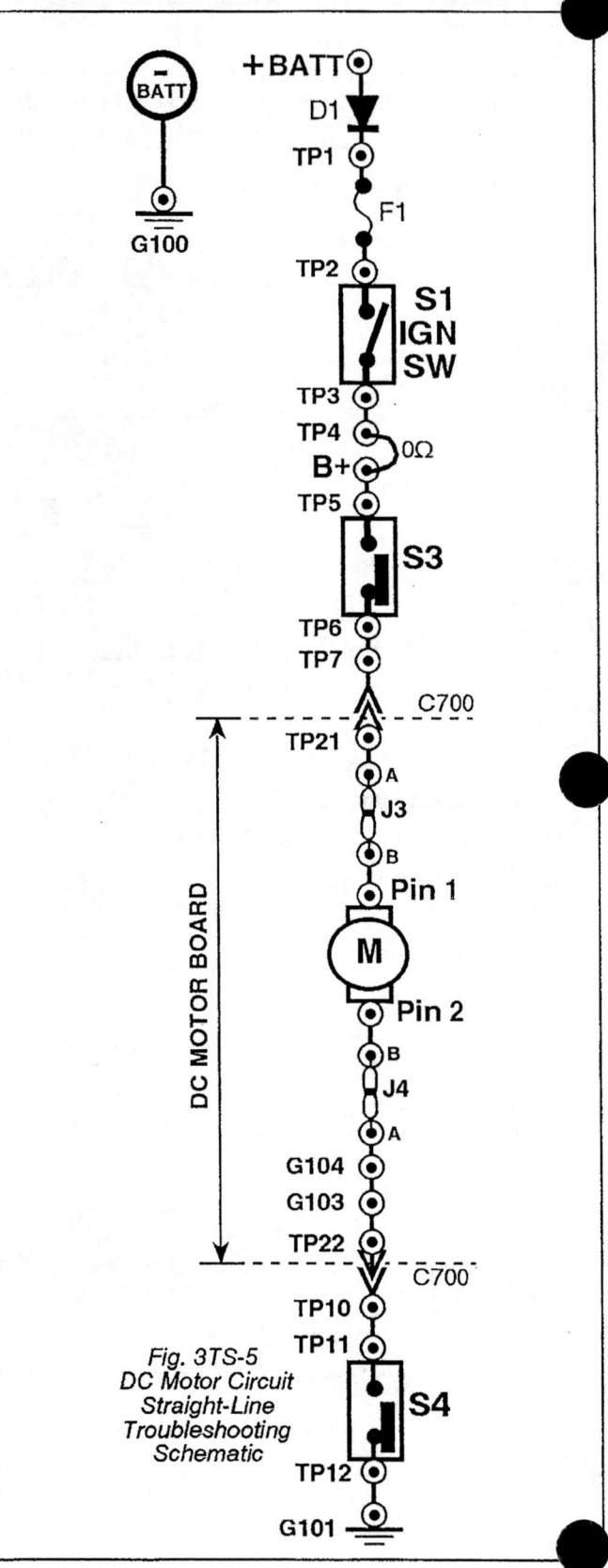

Fig. 3TS-5 DC Motor Circuit Straight-Line Troubleshooting Schematic

Copyright © 2015 VEEJER ENTERPRISES, Garland, Texas - All Rights Reserved   Text H-WB113 Page 57

Vehicle Electronics Hands-On Home-Study Troubleshooting Training

VEEJER ENTERPRISES 3701 Lariat Lane, Garland, Texas 75042-5419
Phone: 972-276-9642   Fax: 972-276-8122   Email: info@veejer.com   Web Site: www.veejer.com

Problem 60
Consult Instructor Guide To Insert Circuit Fault 60
Refer to Schematic **Figure** 3TS-5 for this problem
Engine runs hot.

Performance of the load: _____

Troubleshooting Step 1: _____TTS-1_____
Reading: _____ Good: _____ Bad: _____

Troubleshooting Step 2: _____TTS-2_____
Reading: _____ Good: _____ Bad: _____

Troubleshooting Step 3: _____
Reading: _____ Good: _____ Bad: _____

Troubleshooting Step 4: _____
Reading: _____ Good: _____ Bad: _____

Troubleshooting Step 5: _____
Reading: _____ Good: _____ Bad: _____

Troubleshooting Step 6: _____
Reading: _____ Good: _____ Bad: _____

Troubleshooting Step 7: _____
Reading: _____ Good: _____ Bad: _____

Troubleshooting Step 8: _____
Reading: _____ Good: _____ Bad: _____

Troubleshooting Step 9: _____
Reading: _____ Good: _____ Bad: _____

Troubleshooting Step 10: _____
Reading: _____ Good: _____ Bad: _____

Troubleshooting Step 11: _____
Reading: _____ Good: _____ Bad: _____

Troubleshooting Step 12: _____
Reading: _____ Good: _____ Bad: _____

The Problem Is: _____

REMINDER: Remove the fault and restore the PCBs to normal operation after the problem is identified.

Problem 61
Consult Instructor Guide To Insert Circuit Fault 61
Refer to Schematic **Figure** 3TS-5 for this problem
Engine runs hot.

Performance of the load: _____

Troubleshooting Step 1: _____TTS-1_____
Reading: _____ Good: _____ Bad: _____

Troubleshooting Step 2: _____TTS-2_____
Reading: _____ Good: _____ Bad: _____

Troubleshooting Step 3: _____
Reading: _____ Good: _____ Bad: _____

Troubleshooting Step 4: _____
Reading: _____ Good: _____ Bad: _____

Troubleshooting Step 5: _____
Reading: _____ Good: _____ Bad: _____

Troubleshooting Step 6: _____
Reading: _____ Good: _____ Bad: _____

Troubleshooting Step 7: _____
Reading: _____ Good: _____ Bad: _____

Troubleshooting Step 8: _____
Reading: _____ Good: _____ Bad: _____

Troubleshooting Step 9: _____
Reading: _____ Good: _____ Bad: _____

Troubleshooting Step 10: _____
Reading: _____ Good: _____ Bad: _____

Troubleshooting Step 11: _____
Reading: _____ Good: _____ Bad: _____

Troubleshooting Step 12: _____
Reading: _____ Good: _____ Bad: _____

The Problem Is: _____

REMINDER: Remove the fault and restore the PCBs to normal operation after the problem is identified.

Vehicle Electronics Hands-On Home-Study Troubleshooting Training

VEEJER ENTERPRISES 3701 Lariat Lane, Garland, Texas 75042-5419
Phone: 972-276-9642   Fax: 972-276-8122   Email: info@veejer.com   Web Site: www.veejer.com

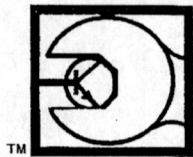

Problem 62
Consult Instructor Guide To Insert Circuit Fault 62
Refer to Schematic **Figure** 3TS-5 for this problem
Engine tends to run hot.

Performance of the load: _____

Troubleshooting Step 1: ____TTS-1_____
Reading: _____ Good: ___ Bad: ___

Troubleshooting Step 2: ____TTS-2_____
Reading: _____ Good: ___ Bad: ___

Troubleshooting Step 3: _____
Reading: _____ Good: ___ Bad: ___

Troubleshooting Step 4: _____
Reading: _____ Good: ___ Bad: ___

Troubleshooting Step 5: _____
Reading: _____ Good: ___ Bad: ___

Troubleshooting Step 6: _____
Reading: _____ Good: ___ Bad: ___

Troubleshooting Step 7: _____
Reading: _____ Good: ___ Bad: ___

Troubleshooting Step 8: _____
Reading: _____ Good: ___ Bad: ___

Troubleshooting Step 9: _____
Reading: _____ Good: ___ Bad: ___

Troubleshooting Step 10: _____
Reading: _____ Good: ___ Bad: ___

Troubleshooting Step 11: _____
Reading: _____ Good: ___ Bad: ___

Troubleshooting Step 12: _____
Reading: _____ Good: ___ Bad: ___

The Problem Is: _____

REMINDER: Remove the fault and restore the PCBs to normal operation after the problem is identified.

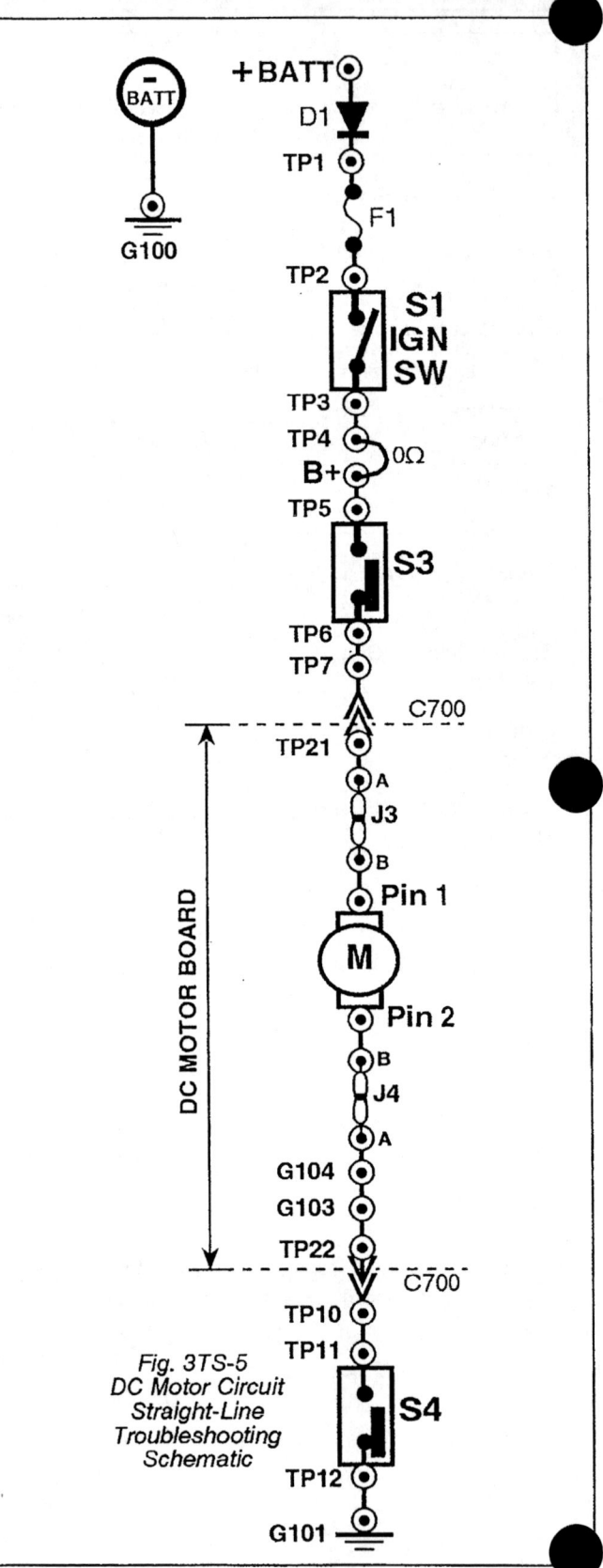

*Fig. 3TS-5
DC Motor Circuit
Straight-Line
Troubleshooting
Schematic*

Copyright © 2015 VEEJER ENTERPRISES, Garland, Texas - All Rights Reserved   Text H-WB113 Page 59

Vehicle Electronics Hands-On Home-Study Troubleshooting Training

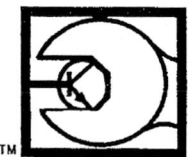

VEEJER ENTERPRISES 3701 Lariat Lane, Garland, Texas 75042-5419
Phone: 972-276-9642   Fax: 972-276-8122   Email: info@veejer.com   Web Site: www.veejer.com

---

Problem 63
Consult Instructor Guide To Insert Circuit Fault 63
Refer to Schematic **Figure 3TS-5** for this problem
Engine overheats after a few minutes.

Performance of the load: _____

Troubleshooting Step 1: _____**TTS-1**_____
Reading: _____ Good: ____ Bad: ____

Troubleshooting Step 2: _____**TTS-2**_____
Reading: _____ Good: ____ Bad: ____

Troubleshooting Step 3: _____
Reading: _____ Good: ____ Bad: ____

Troubleshooting Step 4: _____
Reading: _____ Good: ____ Bad: ____

Troubleshooting Step 5: _____
Reading: _____ Good: ____ Bad: ____

Troubleshooting Step 6: _____
Reading: _____ Good: ____ Bad: ____

Troubleshooting Step 7: _____
Reading: _____ Good: ____ Bad: ____

Troubleshooting Step 8: _____
Reading: _____ Good: ____ Bad: ____

Troubleshooting Step 9: _____
Reading: _____ Good: ____ Bad: ____

Troubleshooting Step 10: _____
Reading: _____ Good: ____ Bad: ____

Troubleshooting Step 11: _____
Reading: _____ Good: ____ Bad: ____

Troubleshooting Step 12: _____
Reading: _____ Good: ____ Bad: ____

The Problem Is: _____

REMINDER: Remove the fault and restore the PCBs to normal operation after the problem is identified.

Problem 64
Consult Instructor Guide To Insert Circuit Fault 64
Refer to Schematic **Figure 3TS-5** for this problem
Engine overheats quickly.

Performance of the load: _____

Troubleshooting Step 1: _____**TTS-1**_____
Reading: _____ Good: ____ Bad: ____

Troubleshooting Step 2: _____**TTS-2**_____
Reading: _____ Good: ____ Bad: ____

Troubleshooting Step 3: _____
Reading: _____ Good: ____ Bad: ____

Troubleshooting Step 4: _____
Reading: _____ Good: ____ Bad: ____

Troubleshooting Step 5: _____
Reading: _____ Good: ____ Bad: ____

Troubleshooting Step 6: _____
Reading: _____ Good: ____ Bad: ____

Troubleshooting Step 7: _____
Reading: _____ Good: ____ Bad: ____

Troubleshooting Step 8: _____
Reading: _____ Good: ____ Bad: ____

Troubleshooting Step 9: _____
Reading: _____ Good: ____ Bad: ____

Troubleshooting Step 10: _____
Reading: _____ Good: ____ Bad: ____

Troubleshooting Step 11: _____
Reading: _____ Good: ____ Bad: ____

Troubleshooting Step 12: _____
Reading: _____ Good: ____ Bad: ____

The Problem Is: _____

REMINDER: Remove the fault and restore the PCBs to normal operation after the problem is identified.

Vehicle Electronics Hands-On Home-Study Troubleshooting Training

VEEJER ENTERPRISES 3701 Lariat Lane, Garland, Texas 75042-5419
Phone: 972-276-9642 Fax: 972-276-8122 Email: info@veejer.com Web Site: www.veejer.com

Problem 65
Consult Instructor Guide To Insert Circuit Fault 65
Refer to Schematic **Figure 3TS-5** for this problem
Engine runs hot.

Performance of the load: _____

Troubleshooting Step 1: ____TTS-1____
Reading: _____ Good: ___ Bad: ___

Troubleshooting Step 2: ____TTS-2____
Reading: _____ Good: ___ Bad: ___

Troubleshooting Step 3: _____
Reading: _____ Good: ___ Bad: ___

Troubleshooting Step 4: _____
Reading: _____ Good: ___ Bad: ___

Troubleshooting Step 5: _____
Reading: _____ Good: ___ Bad: ___

Troubleshooting Step 6: _____
Reading: _____ Good: ___ Bad: ___

Troubleshooting Step 7: _____
Reading: _____ Good: ___ Bad: ___

Troubleshooting Step 8: _____
Reading: _____ Good: ___ Bad: ___

Troubleshooting Step 9: _____
Reading: _____ Good: ___ Bad: ___

Troubleshooting Step 10: _____
Reading: _____ Good: ___ Bad: ___

Troubleshooting Step 11: _____
Reading: _____ Good: ___ Bad: ___

Troubleshooting Step 12: _____
Reading: _____ Good: ___ Bad: ___

The Problem Is: _____

REMINDER: Remove the fault and restore the PCBs to normal operation after the problem is identified.

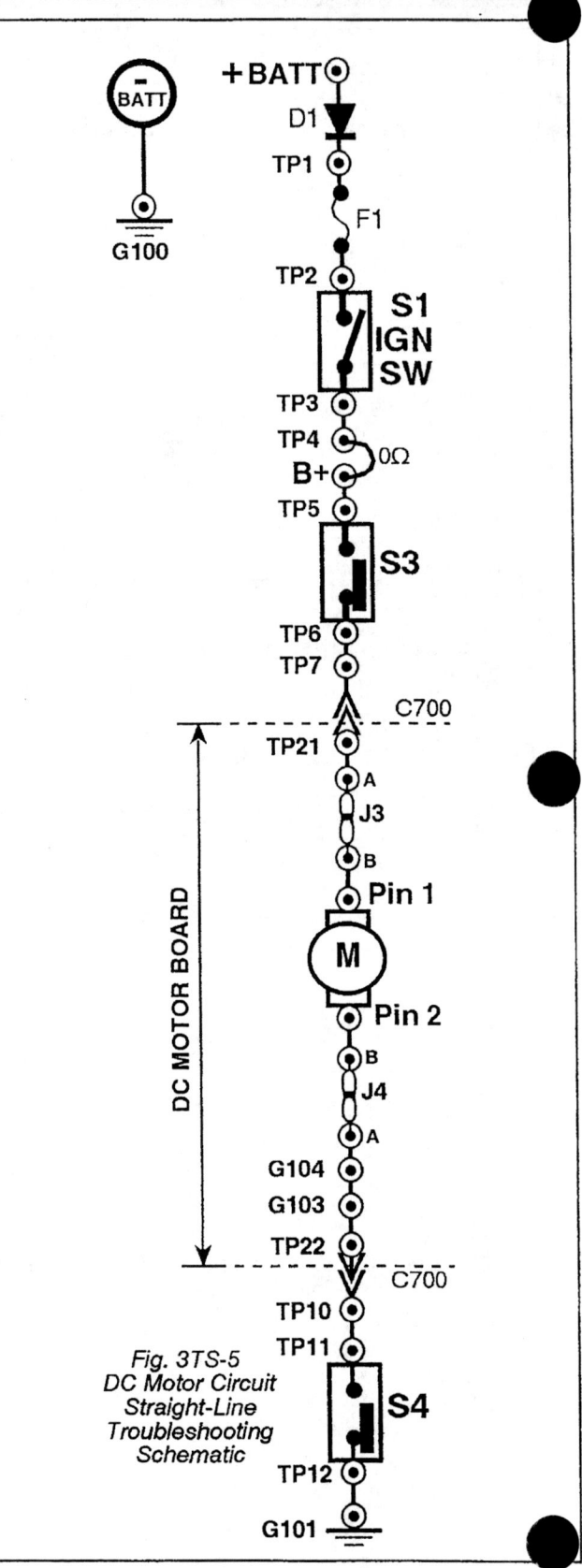

Fig. 3TS-5 DC Motor Circuit Straight-Line Troubleshooting Schematic

Vehicle Electronics Hands-On Home-Study Troubleshooting Training

VEEJER ENTERPRISES 3701 Lariat Lane, Garland, Texas 75042-5419
Phone: 972-276-9642 Fax: 972-276-8122 Email: info@veejer.com Web Site: www.veejer.com

Problem 66
Consult Instructor Guide To Insert Circuit Fault 66
Refer to Schematic **Figure 3TS-5** for this problem
Engine tends to overheat.

Performance of the load: _____

Troubleshooting Step 1: _____TTS-1_____
Reading: _____ Good: ____ Bad: ____

Troubleshooting Step 2: _____TTS-2_____
Reading: _____ Good: ____ Bad: ____

Troubleshooting Step 3: _____
Reading: _____ Good: ____ Bad: ____

Troubleshooting Step 4: _____
Reading: _____ Good: ____ Bad: ____

Troubleshooting Step 5: _____
Reading: _____ Good: ____ Bad: ____

Troubleshooting Step 6: _____
Reading: _____ Good: ____ Bad: ____

Troubleshooting Step 7: _____
Reading: _____ Good: ____ Bad: ____

Troubleshooting Step 8: _____
Reading: _____ Good: ____ Bad: ____

Troubleshooting Step 9: _____
Reading: _____ Good: ____ Bad: ____

Troubleshooting Step 10: _____
Reading: _____ Good: ____ Bad: ____

Troubleshooting Step 11: _____
Reading: _____ Good: ____ Bad: ____

Troubleshooting Step 12: _____
Reading: _____ Good: ____ Bad: ____

The Problem Is: _____

REMINDER: Remove the fault and restore the PCBs to normal operation after the problem is identified.

Problem 67
Consult Instructor Guide To Insert Circuit Fault 67
Refer to Schematic **Figure 3TS-5** for this problem
Engine tends to overheat.

Performance of the load: _____

Troubleshooting Step 1: _____TTS-1_____
Reading: _____ Good: ____ Bad: ____

Troubleshooting Step 2: _____TTS-2_____
Reading: _____ Good: ____ Bad: ____

Troubleshooting Step 3: _____
Reading: _____ Good: ____ Bad: ____

Troubleshooting Step 4: _____
Reading: _____ Good: ____ Bad: ____

Troubleshooting Step 5: _____
Reading: _____ Good: ____ Bad: ____

Troubleshooting Step 6: _____
Reading: _____ Good: ____ Bad: ____

Troubleshooting Step 7: _____
Reading: _____ Good: ____ Bad: ____

Troubleshooting Step 8: _____
Reading: _____ Good: ____ Bad: ____

Troubleshooting Step 9: _____
Reading: _____ Good: ____ Bad: ____

Troubleshooting Step 10: _____
Reading: _____ Good: ____ Bad: ____

Troubleshooting Step 11: _____
Reading: _____ Good: ____ Bad: ____

Troubleshooting Step 12: _____
Reading: _____ Good: ____ Bad: ____

The Problem Is: _____

REMINDER: Remove the fault and restore the PCBs to normal operation after the problem is identified.

Copyright © 2015 VEEJER ENTERPRISES, Garland, Texas - All Rights Reserved

Vehicle Electronics Hands-On Home-Study Troubleshooting Training

VEEJER ENTERPRISES 3701 Lariat Lane, Garland, Texas 75042-5419
Phone: 972-276-9642   Fax: 972-276-8122   Email: info@veejer.com   Web Site: www.veejer.com

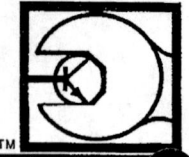

Problem 68
Consult Instructor Guide To Insert Circuit Fault 68
Refer to Schematic **Figure 3TS-5** for this problem
Engine overheats very quickly.

Performance of the load: _____

Troubleshooting Step 1: ____TTS-1____
Reading: _____ Good: ___ Bad: ___

Troubleshooting Step 2: ____TTS-2____
Reading: _____ Good: ___ Bad: ___

Troubleshooting Step 3: _____
Reading: _____ Good: ___ Bad: ___

Troubleshooting Step 4: _____
Reading: _____ Good: ___ Bad: ___

Troubleshooting Step 5: _____
Reading: _____ Good: ___ Bad: ___

Troubleshooting Step 6: _____
Reading: _____ Good: ___ Bad: ___

Troubleshooting Step 7: _____
Reading: _____ Good: ___ Bad: ___

Troubleshooting Step 8: _____
Reading: _____ Good: ___ Bad: ___

Troubleshooting Step 9: _____
Reading: _____ Good: ___ Bad: ___

Troubleshooting Step 10: _____
Reading: _____ Good: ___ Bad: ___

Troubleshooting Step 11: _____
Reading: _____ Good: ___ Bad: ___

Troubleshooting Step 12: _____
Reading: _____ Good: ___ Bad: ___

The Problem Is: _____

REMINDER: Remove the fault and restore the PCBs to normal operation after the problem is identified.

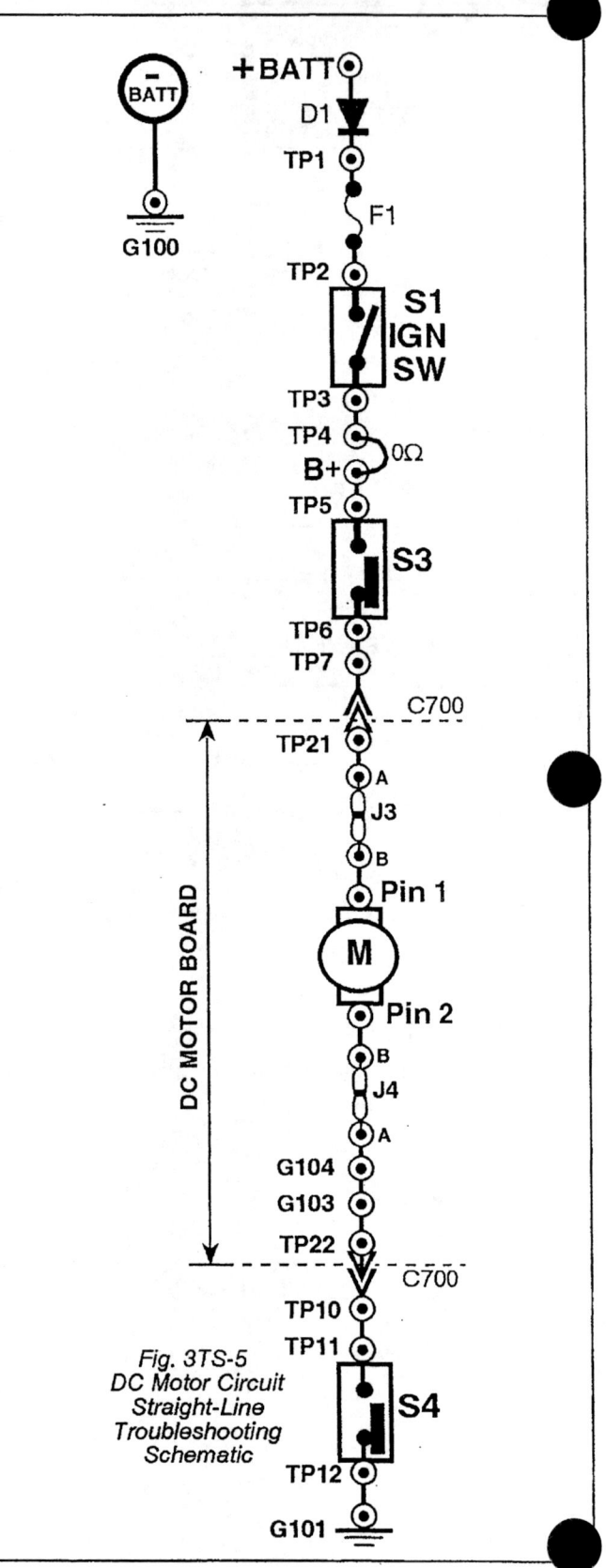

*Fig. 3TS-5
DC Motor Circuit
Straight-Line
Troubleshooting
Schematic*

Vehicle Electronics Hands-On Home-Study Troubleshooting Training

VEEJER ENTERPRISES 3701 Lariat Lane, Garland, Texas 75042-5419
Phone: 972-276-9642   Fax: 972-276-8122   Email: info@veejer.com   Web Site: www.veejer.com

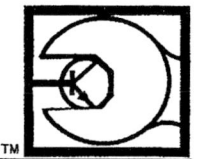

Problem 69
Consult Instructor Guide To Insert Circuit Fault 69
Refer to Schematic **Figure 3TS-5** for this problem
At times this car will not crank. When it does crank it runs very poorly and also gets hot very fast. The car is barely running at this time and is extremely hot.

Performance of the load: _____

Troubleshooting Step 1: ____TTS-1_____
Reading: _____ Good: ____ Bad: ____

Troubleshooting Step 2: ____TTS-2_____
Reading: _____ Good: ____ Bad: ____

Troubleshooting Step 3: _____
Reading: _____ Good: ____ Bad: ____

Troubleshooting Step 4: _____
Reading: _____ Good: ____ Bad: ____

Troubleshooting Step 5: _____
Reading: _____ Good: ____ Bad: ____

Troubleshooting Step 6: _____
Reading: _____ Good: ____ Bad: ____

Troubleshooting Step 7: _____
Reading: _____ Good: ____ Bad: ____

Troubleshooting Step 8: _____
Reading: _____ Good: ____ Bad: ____

Troubleshooting Step 9: _____
Reading: _____ Good: ____ Bad: ____

Troubleshooting Step 10: _____
Reading: _____ Good: ____ Bad: ____

Troubleshooting Step 11: _____
Reading: _____ Good: ____ Bad: ____

Troubleshooting Step 12: _____
Reading: _____ Good: ____ Bad: ____

The Problem Is: _____

REMINDER: Remove the fault and restore the PCBs to normal operation after the problem is identified.

ADVANCED TROUBLESHOOTING PROBLEMS

Advanced problems are provided for those who would like more of a troubleshooting challenge. DO NOT ATTEMPT ADVANCED PROBLEMS UNTIL THE REGULAR PROBLEMS UP TO PROBLEM 69 HAVE BEEN COMPLETED.

Each advanced problem is unique and all instructions for that problem should be followed precisely. **Advanced problems may contain more than one problem at the same time.**

The problem numbers continue in numerical order but have a suffix "A" to signify it is an advanced problem, such as "70-A."

Verify that both fuses on the Power Board, F1 and F2 are good 2A fuses for all advanced problems. Follow all instructions carefully to proceed through advanced problems because each advanced problem is unique.

Copyright © 2015 VEEJER ENTERPRISES, Garland, Texas - All Rights Reserved   Text H-WB113 Page 64

Vehicle Electronics Hands-On Home-Study Troubleshooting Training

VEEJER ENTERPRISES 3701 Lariat Lane, Garland, Texas 75042-5419
Phone: 972-276-9642 Fax: 972-276-8122 Email: info@veejer.com Web Site: www.veejer.com

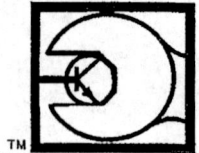

Problem 70A

Consult Instructor Guide To Insert Circuit Fault 70A
Refer to Schematic **Figure 3TS-5** for this problem

Special Instructions for Problem 70A:
(1) **CLOSE S4** to "permanently" complete the ground side for this problem.
(2) Use S1 to turn the "car" ON/OFF.
(3) Use S3 as the Cooling Fan ON/OFF Switch.

Two Problems: Engine overheats and the battery runs down. The customer has already had a new battery installed and a new cooling fan installed at two different shops but still has the same two problems.

Performance of the load: _____

Which problem should you tackle first? _____

Why? _____

Troubleshooting Step 1: ____**TTS-1**_____
Reading: _____ Good: ___ Bad: ___

Troubleshooting Step 2: ____**TTS-2**_____
Reading: _____ Good: ___ Bad: ___

Troubleshooting Step 3: _____
Reading: _____ Good: ___ Bad: ___

Troubleshooting Step 4: _____
Reading: _____ Good: ___ Bad: ___

Troubleshooting Step 5: _____
Reading: _____ Good: ___ Bad: ___

Troubleshooting Step 6: _____
Reading: _____ Good: ___ Bad: ___

Troubleshooting Step 7: _____
Reading: _____ Good: ___ Bad: ___

Troubleshooting Step 8: _____
Reading: _____ Good: ___ Bad: ___

Troubleshooting Step 9: _____
Reading: _____ Good: ___ Bad: ___

Troubleshooting Step 10: _____
Reading: _____ Good: ___ Bad: ___

The Problems are:
(1) _____
(2) _____
(3) Is the short to voltage on the Power Board or on the DC Motor Board? _____

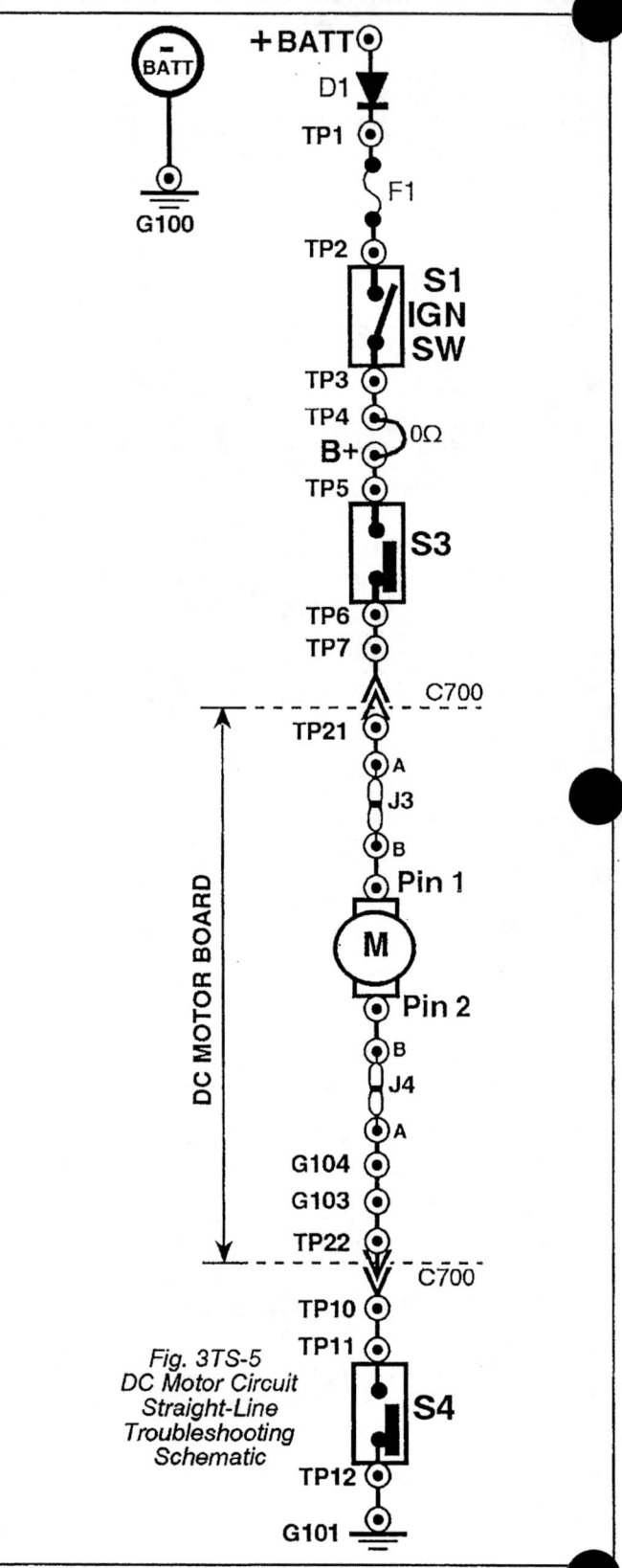

Fig. 3TS-5
DC Motor Circuit
Straight-Line
Troubleshooting
Schematic

Copyright © 2015 VEEJER ENTERPRISES, Garland, Texas - All Rights Reserved   Text H-WB113   Page 65

Vehicle Electronics Hands-On Home-Study Troubleshooting Training

VEEJER ENTERPRISES 3701 Lariat Lane, Garland, Texas 75042-5419
Phone: 972-276-9642   Fax: 972-276-8122   Email: info@veejer.com   Web Site: www.veejer.com

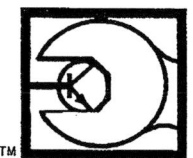

Problem 71A
Consult Instructor Guide To Insert Circuit Fault 71A
Refer to Schematic **Figure 3TS-5** for this problem

Special Instructions for Problem 71A:
(1) CLOSE S4 to "permanently" complete the ground side for this problem.
(2) Use S1 to turn the "car" ON/OFF.
(3) Use S3 as the Cooling Fan ON/OFF Switch.

Problems: Customer complains of multiple electrical problems that have plagued this car for the past year. Now the problem is the engine overheats. Another shop has flushed the radiator, then replaced the radiator but engine still overheats.

Performance of the load: _____

Troubleshooting Step 1: ____**TTS-1**_____
Reading: _____ Good: ___ Bad: ___

Troubleshooting Step 2: ____**TTS-2**_____
Reading: _____ Good: ___ Bad: ___

Troubleshooting Step 3: _____
Reading: _____ Good: ___ Bad: ___

Troubleshooting Step 4: _____
Reading: _____ Good: ___ Bad: ___

Troubleshooting Step 5: _____
Reading: _____ Good: ___ Bad: ___

Troubleshooting Step 6: _____
Reading: _____ Good: ___ Bad: ___

Troubleshooting Step 7: _____
Reading: _____ Good: ___ Bad: ___

Troubleshooting Step 8: _____
Reading: _____ Good: ___ Bad: ___

Troubleshooting Step 9: _____
Reading: _____ Good: ___ Bad: ___

Troubleshooting Step 10: _____
Reading: _____ Good: ___ Bad: ___

Troubleshooting Step 11: _____
Reading: _____ Good: ___ Bad: ___

Troubleshooting Step 12: _____
Reading: _____ Good: ___ Bad: ___

The Problem Is: _____

REMINDER: Remove the fault and restore the PCBs to normal operation after the problem is identified.

Fig. 3TS-5 DC Motor Circuit Straight-Line Troubleshooting Schematic

Copyright © 2015 VEEJER ENTERPRISES, Garland, Texas - All Rights Reserved   Text H-WB113 Page 66

Vehicle Electronics Hands-On Home-Study Troubleshooting Training

VEEJER ENTERPRISES 3701 Lariat Lane, Garland, Texas 75042-5419
Phone: 972-276-9642 Fax: 972-276-8122 Email: info@veejer.com Web Site: www.veejer.com

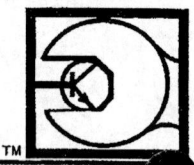

Problem 72A
Consult Instructor Guide To Insert Circuit Fault 72A
Refer to Schematic **Figure 3TS-5** for this problem

Special Instructions for Problem 72A:
(1) CLOSE S4 to "permanently" complete the ground side for this problem.
(2) Use S1 to turn the "car" ON/OFF.
(3) Use S3 as the Cooling Fan ON/OFF Switch.
Problem: Engine overheats on hot days. The first shop flushed the radiator. Another shop fixed a "bad ground connection" in the cooling fan harness. The engine still overheats. It's your turn.

Performance of the load: _____

Troubleshooting Step 1: ____TTS-1____
Reading: _____ Good: ___ Bad: ___

Troubleshooting Step 2: ____TTS-2____
Reading: _____ Good: ___ Bad: ___

Troubleshooting Step 3: _____
Reading: _____ Good: ___ Bad: ___

Troubleshooting Step 4: _____
Reading: _____ Good: ___ Bad: ___

Troubleshooting Step 5: _____
Reading: _____ Good: ___ Bad: ___

Troubleshooting Step 6: _____
Reading: _____ Good: ___ Bad: ___

Troubleshooting Step 7: _____
Reading: _____ Good: ___ Bad: ___

Troubleshooting Step 8: _____
Reading: _____ Good: ___ Bad: ___

Troubleshooting Step 9: _____
Reading: _____ Good: ___ Bad: ___

Troubleshooting Step 10: _____
Reading: _____ Good: ___ Bad: ___

Troubleshooting Step 11: _____
Reading: _____ Good: ___ Bad: ___

Troubleshooting Step 12: _____
Reading: _____ Good: ___ Bad: ___

The Problem Is: _____

REMINDER: Remove the fault and restore the PCBs to normal operation after the problem is identified.

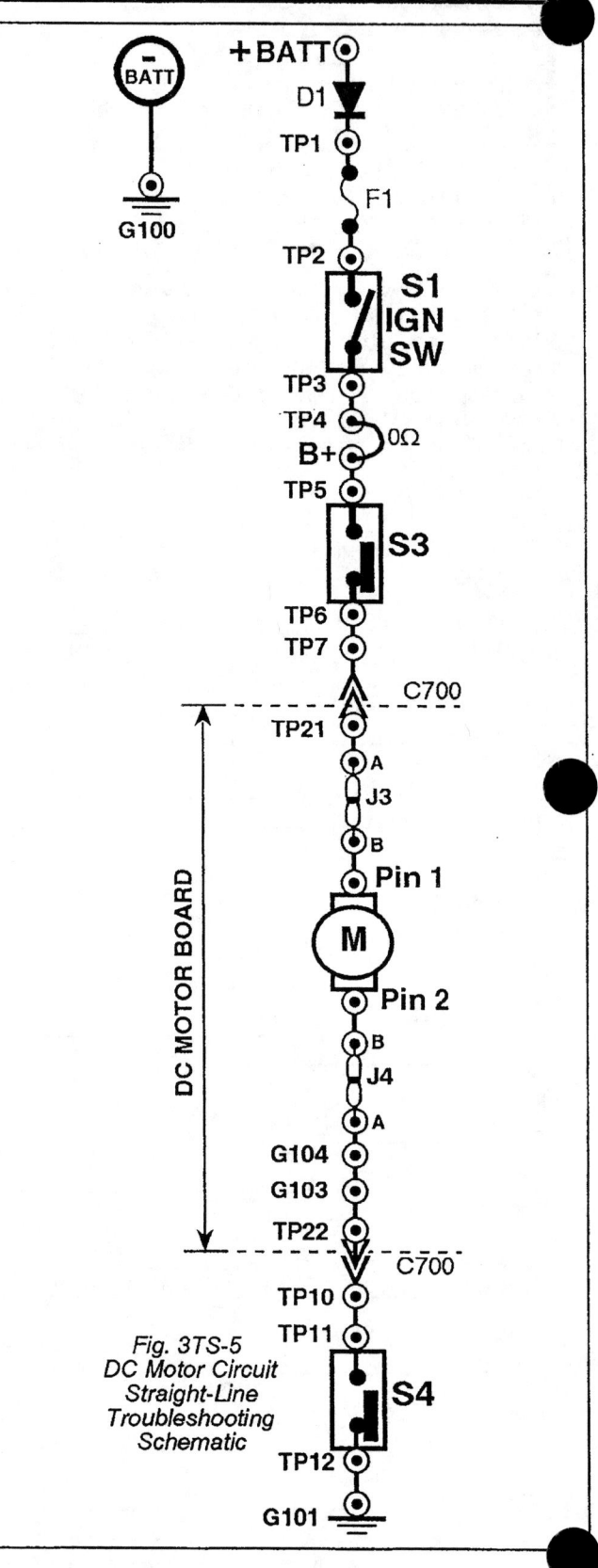

Fig. 3TS-5
DC Motor Circuit
Straight-Line
Troubleshooting
Schematic

Copyright © 2015 VEEJER ENTERPRISES, Garland, Texas - All Rights Reserved   Text H-WB113 Page 67

Vehicle Electronics Hands-On Home-Study Troubleshooting Training

VEEJER ENTERPRISES 3701 Lariat Lane, Garland, Texas 75042-5419
Phone: 972-276-9642   Fax: 972-276-8122   Email: info@veejer.com   Web Site: www.veejer.com

Problem 73A
Consult Instructor Guide To Insert Circuit Fault 73A
Refer to Schematic **Figure** 3TS-5 for this problem
Engine runs hot.

Performance of the load: _____

Troubleshooting Step 1: _____TTS-1_____
Reading: _____ Good: ___ Bad: ___

Troubleshooting Step 2: _____TTS-2_____
Reading: _____ Good: ___ Bad: ___

Troubleshooting Step 3: _____
Reading: _____ Good: ___ Bad: ___

Troubleshooting Step 4: _____
Reading: _____ Good: ___ Bad: ___

Troubleshooting Step 5: _____
Reading: _____ Good: ___ Bad: ___

Troubleshooting Step 6: _____
Reading: _____ Good: ___ Bad: ___

Troubleshooting Step 7: _____
Reading: _____ Good: ___ Bad: ___

Troubleshooting Step 8: _____
Reading: _____ Good: ___ Bad: ___

Troubleshooting Step 9: _____
Reading: _____ Good: ___ Bad: ___

Troubleshooting Step 10: _____
Reading: _____ Good: ___ Bad: ___

Troubleshooting Step 11: _____
Reading: _____ Good: ___ Bad: ___

Troubleshooting Step 12: _____
Reading: _____ Good: ___ Bad: ___

The Problem Is: _____

REMINDER: Remove the fault and restore the PCBs to normal operation after the problem is identified.

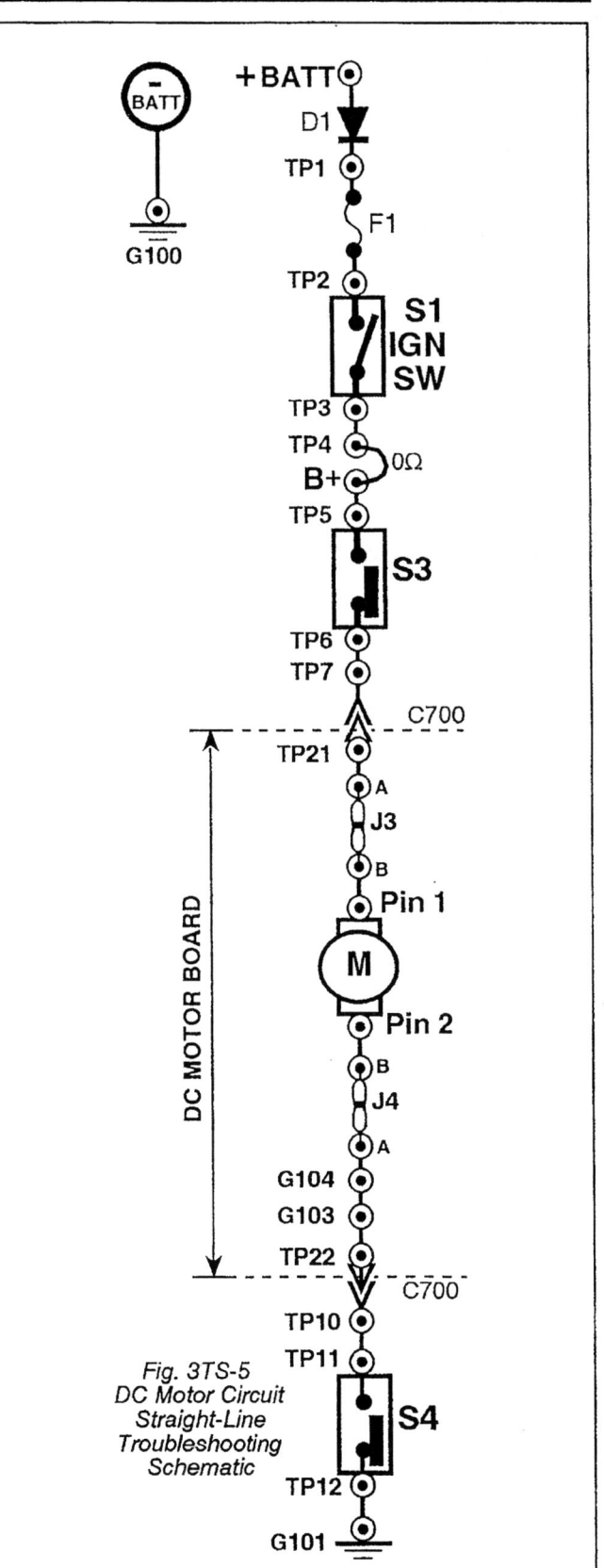

Fig. 3TS-5
DC Motor Circuit
Straight-Line
Troubleshooting
Schematic

Copyright © 2015 VEEJER ENTERPRISES, Garland, Texas - All Rights Reserved   Text H-WB113 Page 68

Vehicle Electronics Hands-On Home-Study Troubleshooting Training

VEEJER ENTERPRISES 3701 Lariat Lane, Garland, Texas 75042-5419
Phone: 972-276-9642 Fax: 972-276-8122 Email: info@veejer.com Web Site: www.veejer.com

Problem 74A
Consult Instructor Guide To Insert Circuit Fault 74A
Refer to Schematic **Figure 3TS-5** for this problem
Engine runs hot.

Performance of the load: _____

Troubleshooting Step 1: _____TTS-1_____
Reading: _____ Good: ___ Bad: ___

Troubleshooting Step 2: _____TTS-2_____
Reading: _____ Good: ___ Bad: ___

Troubleshooting Step 3: _____
Reading: _____ Good: ___ Bad: ___

Troubleshooting Step 4: _____
Reading: _____ Good: ___ Bad: ___

Troubleshooting Step 5: _____
Reading: _____ Good: ___ Bad: ___

Troubleshooting Step 6: _____
Reading: _____ Good: ___ Bad: ___

Troubleshooting Step 7: _____
Reading: _____ Good: ___ Bad: ___

Troubleshooting Step 8: _____
Reading: _____ Good: ___ Bad: ___

Troubleshooting Step 9: _____
Reading: _____ Good: ___ Bad: ___

Troubleshooting Step 10: _____
Reading: _____ Good: ___ Bad: ___

Troubleshooting Step 11: _____
Reading: _____ Good: ___ Bad: ___

Troubleshooting Step 12: _____
Reading: _____ Good: ___ Bad: ___

The Problem Is: _____

REMINDER: Remove the fault and restore the PCBs to normal operation after the problem is identified.

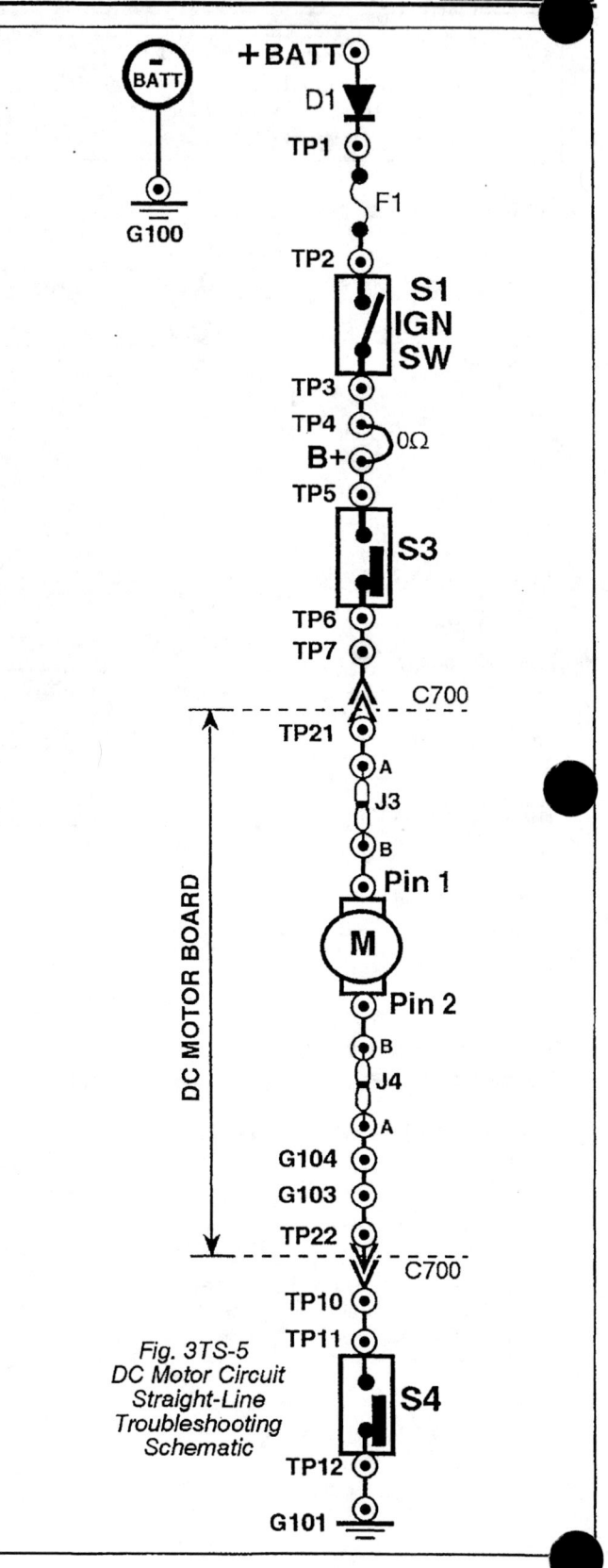

Fig. 3TS-5 DC Motor Circuit Straight-Line Troubleshooting Schematic

Copyright © 2015 VEEJER ENTERPRISES, Garland, Texas - All Rights Reserved

Vehicle Electronics Hands-On Home-Study Troubleshooting Training

VEEJER ENTERPRISES 3701 Lariat Lane, Garland, Texas 75042-5419
Phone: 972-276-9642   Fax: 972-276-8122   Email: info@veejer.com   Web Site: www.veejer.com

Tips On Maintaining Troubleshooting Skill
Practice – Practice – Practice – Practice

Once all the troubleshooting problems have been completed continue to use the PCBs to keep your troubleshooting skills sharp and ready to go. Continue practicing by repeating the troubleshooting exercises at random.

Remember the old "**use it or lose it**" statement? It's true. Here are three ways to use the PCBs over and over to keep your troubleshooting skills sharp.

Do not use U10, U11, U12, U19 or U-NO3 located in the Hot-at-all-times B+ feed to TP9 locations for inserting problems with the DC Motor Circuit. These are not used in the DC Motor Circuit.

(1) Insert OPENS:
Randomly remove a **zero ohm resistor** from the bottom of the PCBs to insert an OPEN connection in the circuit. Troubleshoot from the top of the PCBs in the normal manner. After you find the OPEN circuit problem reinstall a **zero ohm resistor.**

(2) Insert Vds:
Randomly select a resistor from the Resistor Bag-Lamp Circuit. Then remove a randomly selected **zero ohm resistor** from the bottom of the PCBs and insert the resistor in its place to create a Vd at some point in the circuit. Begin troubleshooting in the normal manner from the top of the PCBs. After you find the Vd problem remove the resistor and reinstall a **zero ohm resistor** back into that U-jumper location.

> Do not insert a resistor into a U-NO jumper location. This may damage the PCBs and void the warranty.

(3) Insert SHORTS and SHORTS-TO-GROUND
IMPORTANT: When inserting a zero ohm resistor into a U-NO jumper location of the bottom of a PCB ALWAYS change fuse F1 to a blown fuse or remove it from the circuit to simulate a blown fuse to prevent damage to the H-PS01 Power Supply and PCBs.

Practice troubleshooting shorts to ground and shorted loads by inserting a **zero ohm resistor** into a U-NO-jumper location. Do not use U-NO3. After the short or short-to-ground problem is found remove the wire jumper from the U-NO jumper location and replaced fuse F1 with a good 2A fuse.

(4) Practice the five advanced problems 70A, 71A, 72A, 73A and 74A over and over as long as somebody else inserts the problems for you.

> The warranty of "*The*" Hands-On Program does not cover a burned up H-PS01 Power Supply or PCB damage from failure to use a burned fuse or removing a fuse when a zero ohm resistor is placed in a U-NOx location.

Conduct A Troubleshooting Contest

Insert a random problem in the PCBs and then time each student until he finds the problem. Total the time each student or tech spends troubleshooting the same problems. Mix up the problems between OPEN, SHORTS and Vds. Keep score. The one with the least amount of time spent is the Top Troubleshooter.

Stay sharp – keep practicing troubleshooting!

The next circuit board to be offered in "*The*" **Hands-On Program** is the Solenoid Board which is to be connected to the Power Board. Following that will be a Relay Circuit. If interest continues more circuit boards will be developed.

Vehicle Electronics Hands-On Home-Study Troubleshooting Training

VEEJER ENTERPRISES 3701 Lariat Lane, Garland, Texas 75042-5419
Phone: 972-276-9642 Fax: 972-276-8122 Email: info@veejer.com Web Site: www.veejer.com

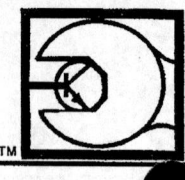

Troubleshooting Record
Keep track of your troubleshooting progress below.
Check off each completed problem.

Problem #	Date Comp.	Grade/Result/Do Again
33		
34		
35		
36		
37		
38		
39		
40		
41		
42		
43		
44		
45		
46		
47		
48		
49		
50		
51		
52		
53		
54		
55		
56		
57		
58		
59		
60		
61		
62		
63		
64		
65		
66		

Problem #	Date Comp.	Grade/Result/Do Again
67		
68		
69		

ADVANCED PROBLEMS

Problem #	Date Comp.	Grade/Result/Do Again
70A		
71A		
72A		
73A		
74A		

"The" Vehicle Electronics *Hands-On Home-Study*
Troubleshooting Training Program
Written by Vince Fischelli
Published by VEEJER ENTERPRISES, Garland, Texas
Copyright © 2012 Veejer Enterprises. No part of these manual or training material may be reproduced, photocopied, entered into a computer data base or copied by any means. All rights reserved.

Phone: **972-276-9642** Fax: **972-276-8122**
Email: **sales@veejer.com** Web Site: **www.veejer.com**

Hands-On Student Workbook
H-WB115

Troubleshooting Relay Circuits Module H-115

Veejer Enterprises Inc.
Garland, Texas, USA

Hands-On Student Workbook H-WB115

Troubleshooting Relay Circuits Module H-115

Supplement to
"The" (60 Lesson Home-Study) **Vehicle Electronics Training Course**™

Written by Vince Fischelli

Published in USA by
VEEJER ENTERPRISES INC.
Garland, Texas, USA

Copyright © 2015 Veejer Enterprises Inc
No part of these Lessons or Course Materials may be reproduced, photocopied, entered into a computer data base or retrieval system of any kind.
All Rights Reserved.

"*The*" Hands-On Vehicle Electronics
Troubleshooting Training Program

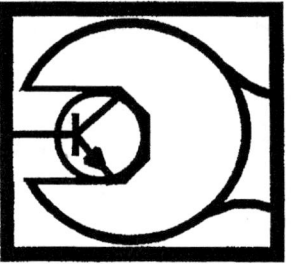

Veejer Enterprises
Garland, Texas
972-276-9642   www.veejer.com

H-115 Contents

- Introduction to Module H-115, Troubleshooting Relay Circuits
- The Relay Troubleshooting Trainer
- How we will study relays
- About solenoid circuits
- What is a relay?
- Relay schematic symbol
- Relay coil
- Relay operation – S.P.S.T. (Single-Pole-Single-Throw)
- D.P.S.T. (Double-Pole-Single-Throw)
- Relay schematic in relay board
- Spike suppression diode operation
- Spike voltage suppression options
- Comparing spike diode vs. resistor
- Getting Started
- Relay Board simulates a fuel pump circuit
- Tips using this hands-on home-study troubleshooting training program
- Resistor Bag - relay circuit - RB05
- Resistor color code guide
- Scanning the Power Board-Relay Board
- Divide and conquer relay circuits
- Significance of a relay's "CLICK"
- Load switch control with S3 and S4
- Relay circuit straight line schematic
- Reading schematic diagrams
- Grounding the DMM
- Review of ohmmeters
- Testing relay coil resistance
- Testing spike suppression diodes
- Measure Vd_{VS} of voltage side of relay primary circuit
- Measure Vd_{VS} of voltage side of relay secondary circuit
- Measure Vd_{GS} of ground side of relay primary circuit
- Measure Vd_{GS} of ground side of relay secondary circuit
- Measure Vd_{LOAD} of relay primary circuit
- Measure Vd_{LOAD} of relay secondary circuit
- Tracing B+ in relay primary circuit
- Tracing B+ in relay secondary circuit
- Tracing B- in relay primary circuit
- Tracing B- in relay secondary circuit
- Testing relay contacts
- Introduction - troubleshooting relays

- Relay primary circuit –open circuit voltage side– problem number "1P"
- Relay secondary circuit –open circuit voltage side– problem number "1S"
- Relay primary circuit Vd_{vs} problem number "2P"
- Important lesson when a Vd_{vs} problem exists on primary voltage side
- Relay secondary circuit problem number "2S"
- Important lesson when a Vd_{vs} problem exists on secondary voltage side
- Relay primary circuit –open circuit ground side– problem number "3P"
- Relay secondary circuit –open circuit ground side– problem number "3S"
- Relay primary circuit Vd_{GS} problem number "4P"
- Important lesson when a Vd_{GS} problem exists on primary ground side
- Relay secondary circuit Vd_{GS} problem number "4S"
- Important lesson when a Vd_{GS} problem exists on secondary ground side
- Relay primary circuit –open load– problem number "5P"
- Relay secondary circuit –open load– problem number "5S"
- Relay primary circuit –shorted load– problem number "6P"
- Relay secondary circuit –shorted load– problem number "6S"
- Relay primary circuit –short-to-ground voltage side– problem number "6P"
- Relay secondary circuit –short-to-ground voltage side– problem number "6S"
- Relay circuit –short-to-voltage– problem number 7
- Current in relay primary circuit
- Current in relay secondary circuit
- Computer control of relays
- How relays damage computers
- Relay circuit troubleshooting exercises
- Troubleshooting problem format
- 75 Practice Troubleshooting Problems

Vehicle Electronics Hands-On Troubleshooting Training Program

VEEJER ENTERPRISES 3701 Lariat Lane, Garland, Texas 75042-5419
Phone: 972-276-9642 Fax: 972-276-8122 Email: sales@veejer.com Web Site: www.veejer.com

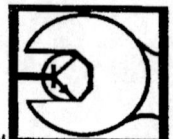

Introduction

It is important that the student beginning this relay circuit troubleshooting module, H-115, has completed the two previous modules in *"The"* **Hands-On Troubleshooting Training Program**, The Starter Kit, **H-111A**, and Troubleshooting DC Motor Circuits, **H-113**. Both these modules provide instruction and information required as a prerequisite for troubleshooting relay circuits. Skipping either of the previous two modules will make this module more difficult.

This hands-on relay troubleshooting training program goes through relay troubleshooting procedures with detailed instructions. However, *explanations* about electrical and electronics theory and how it relates to relay circuits studied in this module are contained in *"The"* **Vehicle Electronics (60-Lesson) Training Course.™** If there are more questions about a particular point on relays refer back to *"The"* **60 Lesson Course.™** This student text lists specific lesson numbers where appropriate for consulting *"The"* **Course™** for more in-depth information. Visit **training.veejer.com** to read the lessons on-line.

Sufficient technical material about relays needed to understand and successfully troubleshoot relay circuits is included in the first 62 pages of this manual. It provides a brief introduction to the theory and terminology of relays necessary to understand and troubleshoot relay circuits. This should be studied thoroughly along with the embedded exercises in the text before beginning the hands-on problem troubleshooting. Simply follow the pages in numerical order.

The Relay Troubleshooting Trainer

The Relay Troubleshooting Trainer Board, part number, H-PCB05, is shown at the right in Figure 5H-050. The silk screen, the white ink on top of the relay circuit board, outlines the relay circuit schematic while the physical relay and the diode D5 are placed off to the left side. On some circuit boards the diode D5 is on the copper side of the board.

Convenient relay test points are provided for measurement purposes on the silk screen. It is not intended that students access relay pins where the relay is soldered into the PCB. Use all test points on the silk screen on top of the PCB to access any relay pin or circuit test point. The same applies to the diode. Do not test the diode using the leads on the physical diode. Test the diode using pins "DA" and DB" which are two terminal test points of the spike suppression diode drawn into the silk screen.

The relay used on the Relay Circuit Troubleshooting Trainer is a typical relay used in vehicle electrical and electronic circuits.

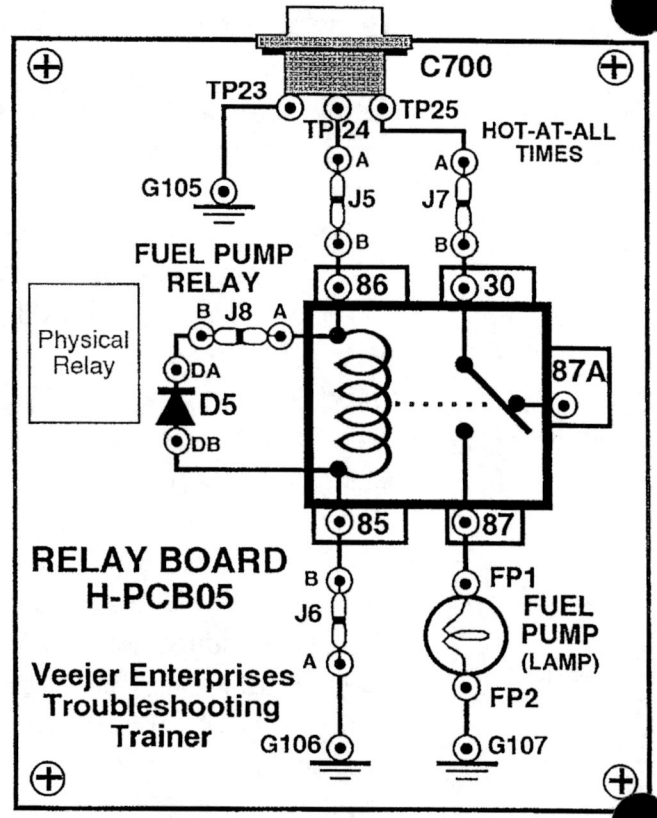

Fig. 5H-050 The Relay Troubleshooting Trainer Board, Part Number, H-PCB05

"0ΩR" (zero ohm resistors) are placed in J5, J6, J7 and J8. These are equivalent to a wire jumper. There are extra 0ΩRs in the Resistor Bag, RB05, if needed. The lamp is a 1445 lamp and is controlled by the relay contacts. The pins around the relay schematic on the Relay Circuit Board are numbered according to a standard relay numbering system used in relay circuits. **A vehicle manufacturer may use a different relay pin numbering system than used in this relay but the function of the relay is the same.**

How We Will Study Relays

In this relay module, H-115, many practice exercises are imbedded in the text of explanations so address these as you read through the text and follow the instructions given.

Module H-115 continues advanced ohmmeter training which began in the last module, H-113. Students will be using a digital ohmmeter, an analog ohmmeter and the Diode Test feature of a DMM to test spike suppression diodes. It would be good to go back and review ohmmeters in module H-113 if a refresher is needed working with ohmmeters.

We emphasize the use of an **analog ohmmeter**, found in old style VOMs, as a necessary tool troubleshoot spike suppression diodes connec across solenoids and relay coils. You will learn that

Vehicle Electronics Hands-On Troubleshooting Training Program

VEEJER ENTERPRISES 3701 Lariat Lane, Garland, Texas 75042-5419
Phone: 972-276-9642 Fax: 972-276-8122 Email: sales@veejer.com Web Site: www.veejer.com

the Diode Test of a DMM cannot test this diode while it is connected to the relay coil and why this is so.

About Solenoid Circuits

Before we get into our discussion on relay circuits a few words on solenoid circuits are appropriate. When *"The"* Hands-On Program was first envisioned in 1997, the fourth module (H-114) was to be devoted to solenoid circuits. It was later determined that this module would not be necessary since the troubleshooting techniques of solenoid circuits is so similar to relay circuits that producing a solenoid program just before a relay program would be unnecessarily redundant. Therefore, at this time, the Solenoid Circuit has been deleted from *"The"* Hands-On Program.

A solenoid is simply a coil of wire that becomes an electromagnet when an electron current passes through it. A relay coil acts the same way electrically. A solenoid plunger or shaft placed inside the solenoid coil or an armature (the moving part) next to the coil is held in a desired position by spring tension. An electromagnetic field around the solenoid coil that occurs when current is flowing through the coil moves the plunger, shaft or armature (overpowering spring tension) which causes the solenoid's mechanical part to move and accomplish a physical task.

For example, the mechanical part of a solenoid that moves could cause the closing of an a/c clutch to turn an a/c compressor, the closing of the heavy duty contacts of a starter solenoid to operate a starter motor, the energizing of a transmission solenoid to shift a transmission and the moving of the pintle in a fuel injector are just some of the jobs a solenoid accomplishes.

The training to electrically troubleshoot a relay coil circuit is identical to the process for troubleshooting solenoid circuits.

Figure A shows a solenoid circuit and a relay circuit connected to the same voltage (B+) source. The only difference between the two circuits is that the relay has relay contacts as part of its electrical circuit. The solenoid circuit does not have electrical contacts. Yet electrically, a solenoid coil circuit schematic appears identical to the coil in the relay circuit in Figure A.

Switch S1 controls B+ to the solenoid circuit and switch S2 controls B+ to the relay circuit. CLOSE S1 and the solenoid is energized. CLOSE S2 and the relay is energized. The solenoid and the relay coil have a spike suppression diode and independent grounds. Troubleshooting a solenoid circuit is no different than troubleshooting the coil of a relay circuit. Therefore, *"The"* Hands-On Program for relays focuses primarily on how electrically operated relays are used, wired and troubleshot in vehicle applications. The same troubleshooting principles (TTS-1 & TTS-2) that apply to relay circuits also applies to solenoid circuits.

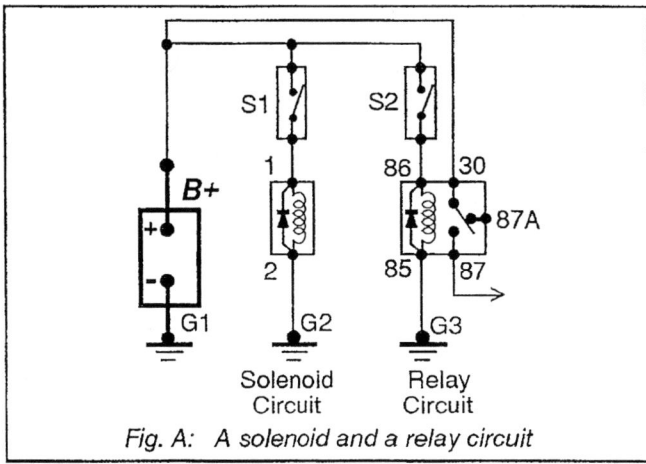

Fig. A: A solenoid and a relay circuit

The following lessons from *"The"* **60 Lesson Course** are available for more in-depth study of inductor (or coil) electrical properties, principles of operation and troubleshooting of coil and solenoid circuits.

Lesson 28 Inductors & Inductance, Part 1
Lesson 29 Inductors, Part 2
Lesson 30 Inductors, Part 3

Lesson 31 "Capacitors & Coils Working Together" in *"The"* Course™ discusses how capacitors and coils work together.

Two lessons in *"The"* Course™ discuss coil circuits.
Lesson 32 Coil Circuits, Part 1
Lesson 33 Coil Circuits, Part 2

Four lessons in *"The"* Course™ discuss relay circuits.
Lesson 38 Relay Circuits, Part 1
Lesson 39 Relay Circuits, Part 2
Lesson 40 Relay Circuits, Part 3
Lesson 41 Relay Circuits, Part 4

Consult these lessons for in-depth discussion and circuit analysis of inductors, coil circuits and relay circuits. However, this training manual provides a portion of some of the same information to enable the student to effectively troubleshoot relay circuits using only the Troubleshooting Trainer, H-PCB05, and Manual, H-SM05.

"The" 60 Lesson Course" is now available on-line at **training.veejer.com** to supplement your studies.

Vehicle Electronics Hands-On Troubleshooting Training Program

VEEJER ENTERPRISES 3701 Lariat Lane, Garland, Texas 75042-5419
Phone: 972-276-9642 Fax: 972-276-8122 Email: sales@veejer.com Web Site: www.veejer.com

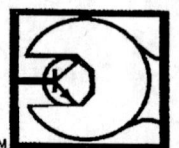

What Is A Relay?

A **relay is an electrical switch** that can be operated either mechanically or electrically. The type of relay most often used in vehicles is an electrically operated relay where a control current flows through a coil creating an electromagnet that is surrounded by invisible **lines of flux.** The relay's switch consists of a soft iron armature (the moving part) which is connected to a movable relay contact. The armature is placed close to the coil so that the lines of flux surrounding the coil attract the armature. The relay's armature contact moves (magnetically attracted) when the relay is energized (turned ON) to either CLOSE or OPEN the relay contacts depending on the configuration of the relay and how the relay is wired into the circuit.

Relay Schematic Symbol

A typical vehicle relay schematic symbol with only two relay contacts is shown in Figure 5H-051 using standard pin numbering common in the vehicle industry.

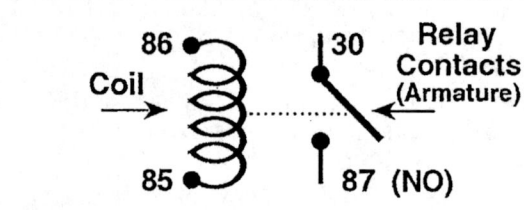

Fig. 5H-051 Basic relay schematic with S.P.S.T. AT REST - contacts Normally OPEN (NO)

A relay consists of a coil and a set of relay contacts that OPEN (separate) or CLOSE (make physical contact). The relay contacts can be connected into a circuit in various configurations depending on the number of contacts.

Relay Coil

Pins 86 and Pin 85 connect to the relay coil. An electrical current can flow in either direction through a coil and CLOSE the contacts. Therefore, a relay coil can be connected to a voltage source in either polarity direction. That is Pin 86 can connect to B+ and Pin 85 to B-, or Pin 86 can connect to B- and Pin 85 to B+ and still close the relay contacts. **However, when a spike suppression diode is connected across a relay coil, Pin 86 must always be the B+ pin and Pin 85 must always be the B- pin.** If the relay coil is connected the opposite way, the spike diode will be forward biased by B+ at Pin 85 and blow the relay circuit fuse or burn up a computer controlling the relay. This will be discussed later in *"The"* Hands-On Program.

Relay Operation – S.P.S.T. (Single-Pole Single-Throw)

The relay in Figure 5H-051 is called a "Single-Pole Single-Throw" relay or "S.P.S.T." for short describe the configuration of a relay with two contacts. In a "S.P.S.T." relay Pins 30 and 87 experience movement of **the armature (Pin 30)** to make contact with Pin 87.

The armature is the movable contact and is sometimes called the **"swinging contact."** The dotted line illustrates the relay contact to be moved by the coil but it does not always appear in the schematic symbol. However, it should be understood to be present. Pin 87 can be designated as the **N**ormally **O**PEN ("NO") contact.

Relay AT REST

When a relay is AT REST the contacts are OPEN as shown in Figure 5H-051. There is no physical contact between Pins 30 and 87 with the relay AT REST.

Relay Voltage Control Levels

Relays require a higher voltage to CLOSE their contacts than they require to keep the contacts CLOSED. The relay used on the Relay Board, H-PCB05, has a relay coil rated at 12VDC. The contacts actually CLOSE in the voltage range of 7.0-7.5 volts. The contacts do not open until B+ drops to a low of 2.8-3.2 volts. Even with low B+ a relay can CLOSE its contacts or keep them CLOSED.

Relay is Energized or Turned "ON"

When a DC current flows through the relay coil as illustrated in Figure 5H-052, the swinging contact moves to make physical contact with Pin 87 completing a connection between Pins 30 and 87. The relay is turned "ON" and the contacts CLOSE.

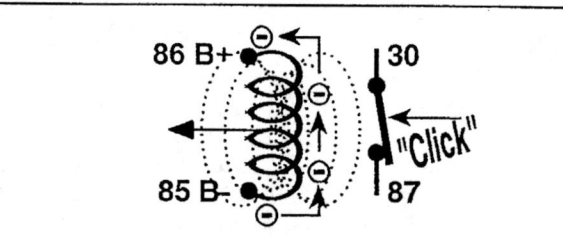

Fig. 5H-052 Basic relay schematic showing S.P.S.T. Relay ENERGIZED - contacts 30-87 CLOSED

When B+ is connected to Pin 86 and B- is connected to Pin 85, electron current flows through the relay coil entering Pin 85 and exiting Pin 86, as shown in Figure 5H-052. The electron current produces an electromagnetic field (lines of flux) around the coil which magnetically attracts the swinging contact Pin 30 to make physical contact with Pin 87. Physical contact exists between the pins like closing a switch.

Relay De-energized or Turned "OFF"

When current through the coil ceases, (either B+ or B- is removed), the electromagnetic field collapses removing the magnetic attraction. The swinging contact moves away from Pin 87 and back to its position due to its spring tension. The relay is now

Vehicle Electronics Hands-On Troubleshooting Training Program

VEEJER ENTERPRISES 3701 Lariat Lane, Garland, Texas 75042-5419
Phone: 972-276-9642 Fax: 972-276-8122 Email: sales@veejer.com Web Site: www.veejer.com

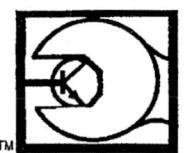

de-energized and returns to the REST condition. The relay contacts are OPEN.

A relay sequence of the energizing and de-energizing sequence is shown in Figure 5H-052A.

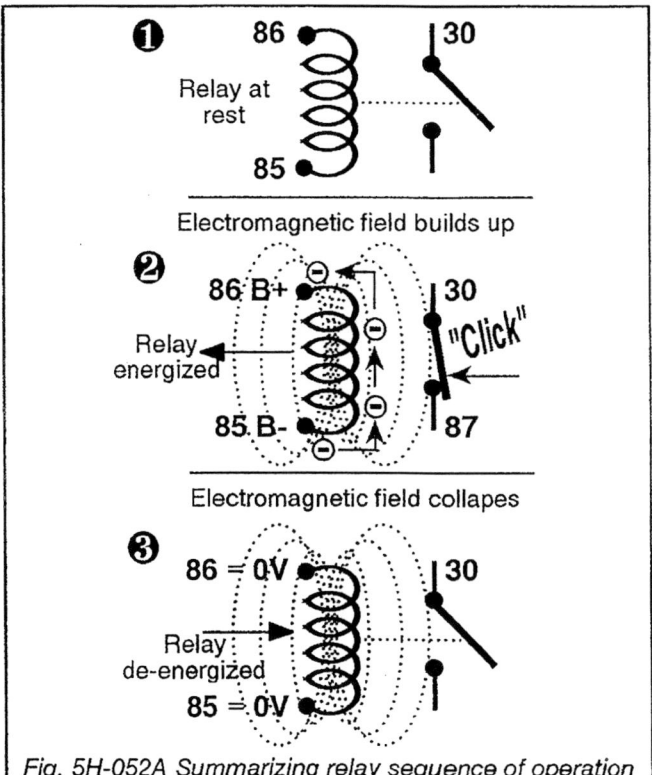

Fig. 5H-052A Summarizing relay sequence of operation

(1) Relay is at rest, contacts are OPEN.

(2) Voltage applied to relay winding terminals produces a current through the coil which creates an electromagnetic field that attracts the swinging contact. The armature connected to Pin 30 moves and makes contact with Pin 87 producing an audible *"Click."*

(3) When voltage is removed from the coil, current stops, the electromagnetic fields collapses and the swinging contact returns to its rest position.

As long as a sufficient current flows through the relay coil the electromagnetic field is sustained, the relay remains energized and the contacts remain CLOSED.

It takes a minimum threshold voltage often less than full B+ to drive sufficient excitation current through a relay coil and initially CLOSE the contacts. Once the relay contacts are CLOSED, the B+ can decrease and the excitation current reduced yet the contacts remain CLOSED.

The minimum threshold voltage necessary to energize a relay is called the **"kick-in voltage."** The decrease in voltage that allows the relay to de-energize is called the **"drop-out voltage."** These relay specs are included in the specifications sheet of a particular relay. Each relay part number has a slightly different **"kick-in voltage"** and excitation current to CLOSE the contacts and keep them CLOSED. As soon as the voltage drops below the **"drop-out voltage,"** coil current decreases, the strength of the electromagnetic field decreases and the relay contacts OPEN.

We need to remember that once a relay is energized and the contacts are CLOSED, the voltage can drop below the initial voltage needed to energize the relay and the relay contacts will remain CLOSED until the lower "drop-out" voltage is reached.

S.P.D.T. (Single Pole Double Throw)

The relay in Figure 5H-053 is a "Single-Pole Double-Throw" relay or "S.P.D.T." for short to describe the configuration of a relay with two contacts and a single movable armature. In a "S.P.D.T." relay Pin 30 "swings" between Pin 87 and a new pin labeled 87A.

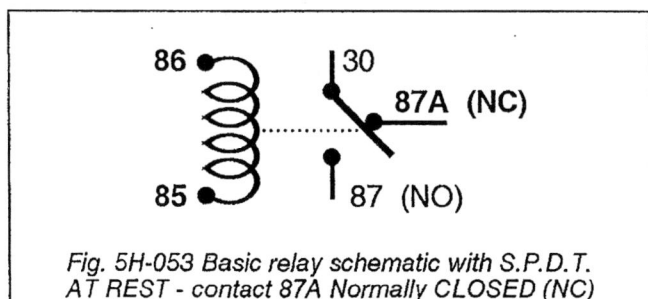

Fig. 5H-053 Basic relay schematic with S.P.D.T. AT REST - contact 87A Normally CLOSED (NC)

Pin 87 is still called "NO" contact while Pin 87A is added to the relay and labeled the **N**ormally **C**losed contact or **"NC"** contact.

When the relay is AT REST, Pin 30 and 87A are CLOSED or make physical contact. When a DC current flows through the S.P.D.T. relay coil the swinging contact moves towards the coil swinging away from Pin 87A to make physical contact with Pin 87 and a "CLICK" is heard. A connection between Pins 30 and 87 is shown in Figure 5H-054.

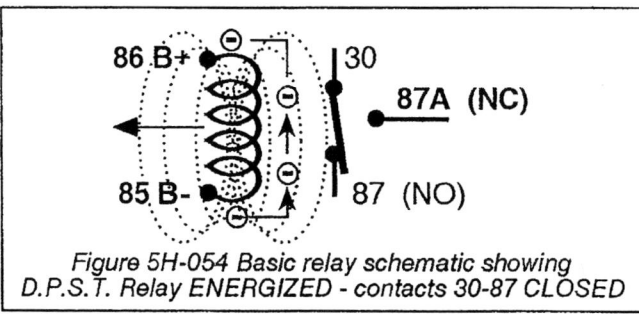

Figure 5H-054 Basic relay schematic showing D.P.S.T. Relay ENERGIZED - contacts 30-87 CLOSED

When current through the coil ceases, the swinging contact moves away from Pin 87 to "make" (re-establish) contact with Pin 87A. The relay is now back to the AT REST condition.

The position of Pin 30's movable armature can be determined by the presence of voltage on Pins 87A or 87. If Pin 87A has B+ then Pin 30 is connected to Pin 87A and the relay is AT REST. If Pin 87 has B+

Vehicle Electronics Hands-On Troubleshooting Training Program

VEEJER ENTERPRISES 3701 Lariat Lane, Garland, Texas 75042-5419
Phone: 972-276-9642 Fax: 972-276-8122 Email: sales@veejer.com Web Site: www.veejer.com

then Pin 30 is connected to pin 87 and the relay is energized. It is possible for the movable armature to be in contact Pin 87 while the relay is de-energized but then the relay has SHORTED (stuck CLOSED) relay contacts and is defective.

A Little Electronics Theory About Spike Voltage Suppression

Refer to Fig. 5H-54A below. When Switch S5 is CLOSED, an electron current flows through the coil. This creates an electromagnetic field that builds up and stores electrical energy in the field as illustrated by the dotted lines and the arrows pointing outward. The electromagnetic field is maintained as long as electron current passes through the solenoid winding or relay coil.

The polarity of the voltage drop across the coil is maintained as long as electron current flows through the coil with the a polarity (+) positive at the top and a (–) negative at the bottom of the coil

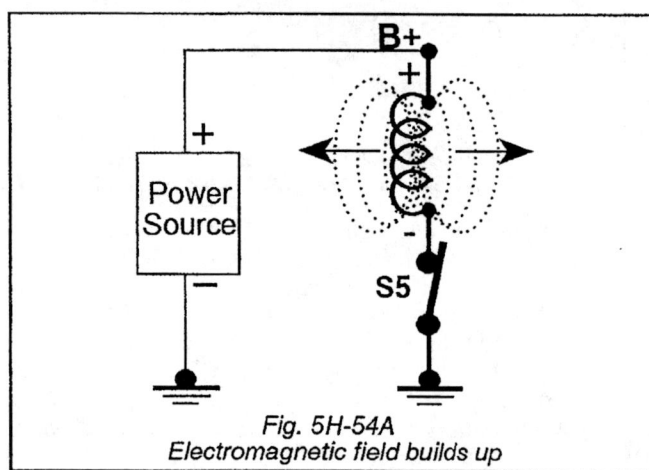
Fig. 5H-54A
Electromagnetic field builds up

The electromagnetic field represents considerable amount of electrical energy that builds up. The problem occurs when the switch OPENS and the electron current stops flowing through the coil or relay coil.

IMMEDIATELY the field collapses creating a **reverse voltage drop across the coil.** The reverse polarity (–) negative at the top and (+) positive at the bottom drives an electron current back the long way around the circuit to supply electrons to the now (+) positive point at the bottom of the coil. *Keep in mind electrons always seek the most positive point in a circuit.*

Next in Figure 5H-54B switch S5 is opened which stops electron current through the coil.

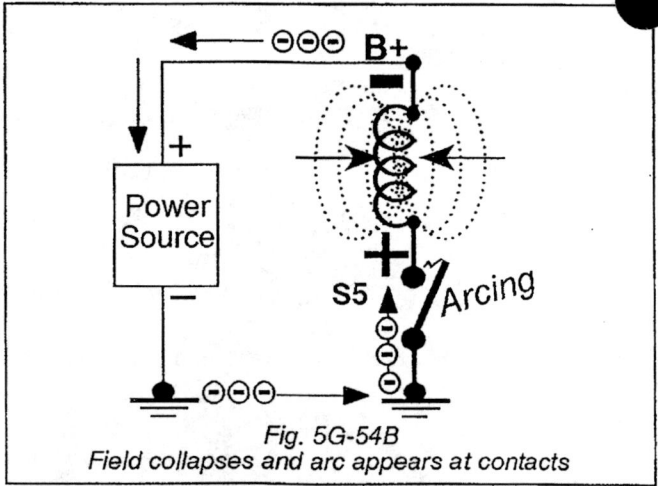
Fig. 5G-54B
Field collapses and arc appears at contacts

The rush of electrons produced by the collapsing electromagnetic field is called an **"energy dump."** The energy dump, lasts for less than a mSec (millisecond) and causes an arc of electrons across the just opened switch contacts. Over time the switch contacts may become corroded from the arcing.

It is a simple matter to control the energy dump so as not to damage switch contacts or a solid-state transistor driver. That is the job of the diode.

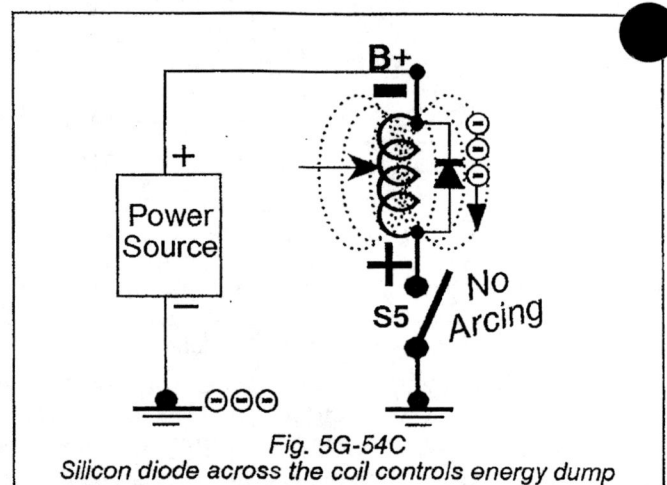
Fig. 5G-54C
Silicon diode across the coil controls energy dump

A silicon diode is placed across the coil, as shown above in Figure 5H-54C. The energy dump drives electrons through the diode to supply electrons to the bottom of the coil. No arcing occurs at the switch contacts since the energy dump flows through the diode as electrons fill the high positive spot at the bottom of the coil. The diode saves the day.

What happens when the field collapses if the switch is a control unit such as the PCM containing a solid-state switch called a **driver transistor,** as shown next in Figure 5H-54D?

Copyright © 2015 VEEJER ENTERPRISES, Garland, Texas - All Rights Reserved Student Workbook H-WB115 Page 5

Vehicle Electronics Hands-On Troubleshooting Training Program

VEEJER ENTERPRISES 3701 Lariat Lane, Garland, Texas 75042-5419
Phone: 972-276-9642 Fax: 972-276-8122 Email: sales@veejer.com Web Site: www.veejer.com

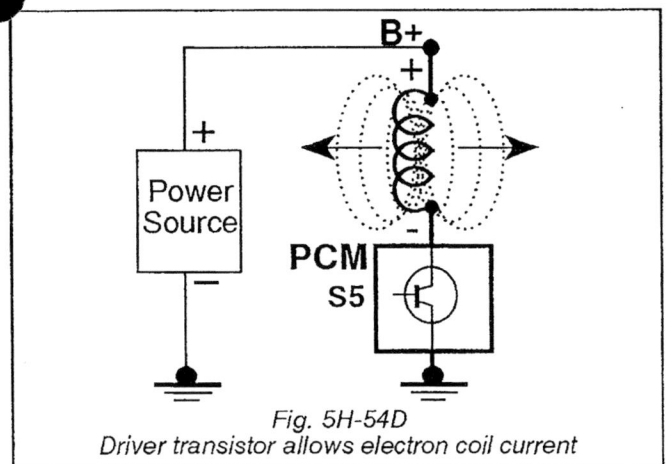

Fig. 5H-54D
Driver transistor allows electron coil current

The driver transistor is turned ON and supplies the electron current to operate the coil. This creates an electromagnetic field just as the mechanical switch did when it allowed electron current to pass through the coil.

When the time comes for the PCM to turn OFF (power down) the coil, the transistor driver stops allowing electron current to pass through the coil, as show in Figure 5H-54E. The field collapses as indicated by the arrows pointing inward.

If the electromagnetic field around an energized relay coil is allowed to randomly dissipate back into the circuit when the relay turns OFF, the energy dump (surge current) from the collapsing electromagnetic field drives an electron current the "long way" around the circuit to supply electrons to the bottom of the coil. This surge electron current could easily destroy a solid-state driver transistor inside a vehicle computer as it passes through the "turned OFF" transistor driver in Fig. 5H-54E.

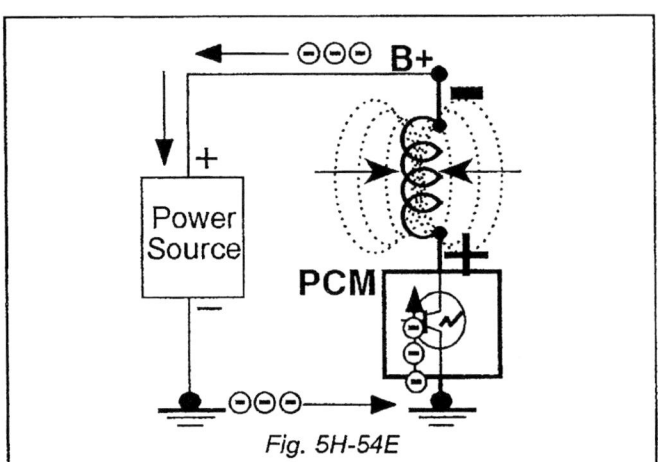

Fig. 5H-54E

When the time comes for the PCM to turn OFF (power down) the coil, the transistor driver stops allowing electron current to pass through the coil, as show in Figure 5H-54E. The field collapses as indicated by the arrows pointing inward. IMMEDIATELY the field creates a **reverse voltage drop across the coil just as it did with the switch.**

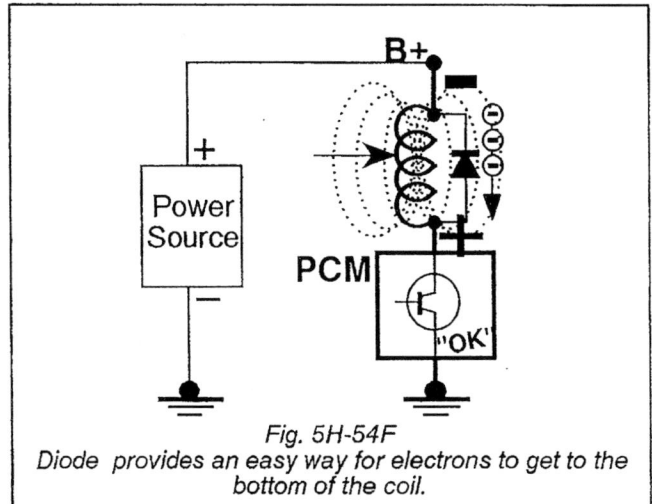

Fig. 5H-54F
Diode provides an easy way for electrons to get to the bottom of the coil.

The energy dump drives electrons through the diode rather than the long way around the circuit to supply electrons to the bottom of the coil. The driver transistor is protected from the surge electron current the energy dump never passes through the driver transistor. The spike diode saves the day.

Relay Schematic on Relay Board

Figure 5H-055 shows the relay schematic used on the relay PCB trainer, H-PCB05.

Relays shown on schematic diagrams are always drawn in the rest position. That is, Pin 30 contacts Pin 87A.

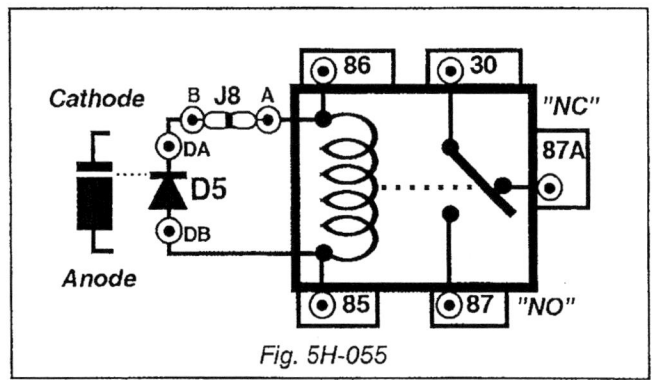

Fig. 5H-055

Diode, D5, is connected in parallel with the coil to protect the circuit when the field collapses. The diode terminals are identified as **DA,** for the cathode side and **DB** for the anode side of the diode.

Normally a spike suppressor diode is mounted inside the relay housing and is not visible outside the relay housing.

We have mounted the spike suppression diode external to the relay so that we can explore relay coil

Vehicle Electronics Hands-On Troubleshooting Training Program

VEEJER ENTERPRISES 3701 Lariat Lane, Garland, Texas 75042-5419
Phone: 972-276-9642 Fax: 972-276-8122 Email: sales@veejer.com Web Site: www.veejer.com

testing possibilities with or without a spike suppression diode present to examine how different types of ohmmeters can be used.

Removing the zero ohm resistor in J8 disconnects the spike suppression diode from the relay coil for various diode/coil testing exercises later on.

The relay coil connects between Pins 86 and 85. Pin 30 is the swinging contact. Pin 87A is the "NC" normally CLOSED contact. Pin 87 is the "NO" normally OPEN contact. The diode is connected through 0ΩR J8 to Pins 86 and 85 for spike voltage suppression. The painted band of the diode always connects to Pin 86.

A spike suppression diode is mandatory when a solid-state driver transistor provides the coil electron current. This true for both solenoids and relay coils.

If coil current is provided by a mechanical switch, as in Relay Circuit Board H-PCB05, (S3 or S4) on the Power Board, a spike diode is not needed since there is no driver transistor involved. However, the electromagnetic field still collapses and this causes an arc across the switch contacts (S3 or S4) that over time will degrade the switch contacts.

We are using the spike suppression diode for instructional purposes in troubleshooting training since many relays in vehicle electronic systems have them and technicians need to know about them and how to test them.

> **All it takes is one defective spike suppression diode in a vehicle circuit (solenoid or relay) to destroy a vehicle computer's solid-state driver transistor.**

In a relay circuit, the diode's cathode (side of diode with the painted band) is connected to Pin 86 and the anode (side of diode without the painted band) is connected to Pin 85 as shown in Figure 5H-056.

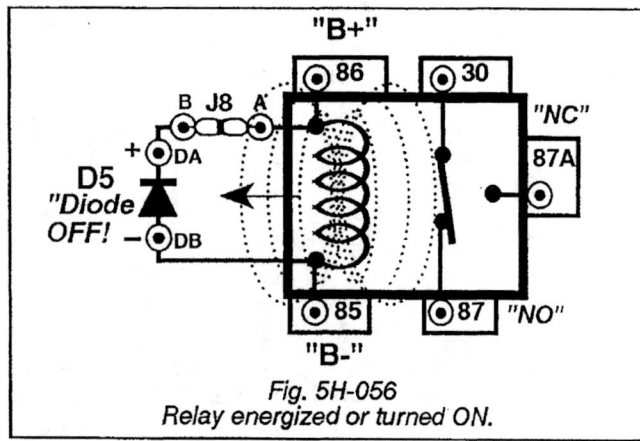

Fig. 5H-056
Relay energized or turned ON.

The diode is OFF while the field is developed and maintained by continuous electron current through the coil. Pin 86 is (+) positive and Pin 85 is (–) negative.

Figure 5H-057 illustrates the change in polarity at Pins 86 and 85 **while the electromagnetic field collapsing** and the resultant electron current from the energy dump flows through the spike suppression diode.

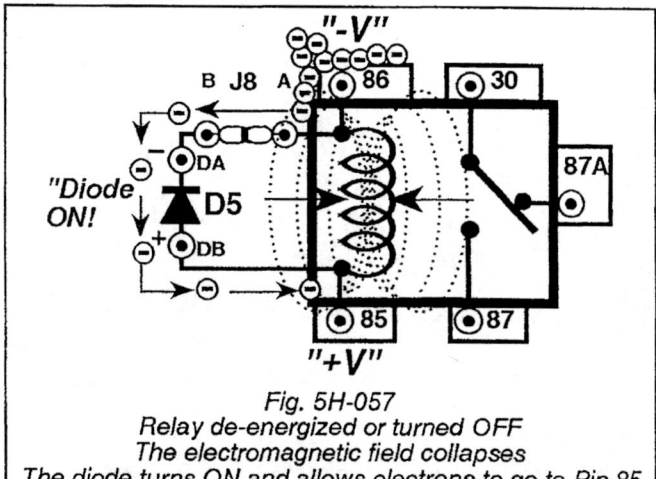

Fig. 5H-057
Relay de-energized or turned OFF
The electromagnetic field collapses
The diode turns ON and allows electrons to go to Pin 85

As the electromagnetic field (lines of flux) collapse, the voltage polarity reverses at the coil's terminals (86-85) but only **while the electromagnetic field is collapsing** as illustrated in Figure 5H-057.

The momentary voltage polarity reversal turns ON the diode. Now that the diode is biased ON the diode allows excess electrons accumulating at Pin 86 from the collapsing electromagnetic field to pass through the diode (electrons flow against a diode's arrow) and go to Pin 85 which is momentarily a positive polarity indicating it needs electrons.

Electrons flow from the negative polarity voltage (Pin 86), through the diode and to the positive polarity voltage (Pin 85) to neutralize the charge difference between Pins 86 and 85 until all the energy in the electromagnetic field is fully dissipated.

All the energy stored in the electromagnetic field is fully dissipated through the diode. No more excess electrons accumulate at Pin 86 and the relay again assumes an AT REST condition (Pin 30 connects to Pin 87A.).

The spike suppression diode "appears" to absorb the energy dump caused by the collapsing electromagnetic field around the coil. What it actually does is let electrons produced by the collapsing electromagnetic field at Pin 86 find a quick and short path to get to the opposite side of the coil (Pin 85) where the electrons are needed to bring balance to the circuit. Once the same number of electrons exist on both Pins 86 and 85 there is no charge difference between the pins. The energy dump is then fully dissipated.

Vehicle Electronics Hands-On Troubleshooting Training Program

VEEJER ENTERPRISES 3701 Lariat Lane, Garland, Texas 75042-5419
Phone: 972-276-9642 Fax: 972-276-8122 Email: sales@veejer.com Web Site: www.veejer.com

Spike Voltage Suppression Options

There are two options for spike voltage suppression in relays and solenoids circuits. Both spike suppression options are shown in Figure 5H-058A and 58B. Either a diode or a resistor can get the spike suppression job done, but each option has advantages and disadvantages.

A spike suppression resistor or diode may also be used in a vehicle circuit where a mechanical switch is used to turn a circuit OFF when it is possible the energy dump electron current could affect some solid-state memory chips in neighboring on-board computers.

Diode Spike Suppression (Fig. 58A):

The spike suppression diode in Figure 58A is shown inside the relay housing as expected. The painted band on the diode must always be connected to Pin 86 because the diode makes the relay coil circuit **polarity sensitive.** Pin 86 must always be wire to B+ and Pin 85 must always be wired to B- (ground side)

Diode Spike Suppression Advantage:

(1) A diode provides a rapid reaction time to turn ON as the electromagnetic field collapses. The diode limits the voltage spike to less than one volt using an inexpensive silicon diode.

(2) The spike diode draws no electron current while the relay is energized.

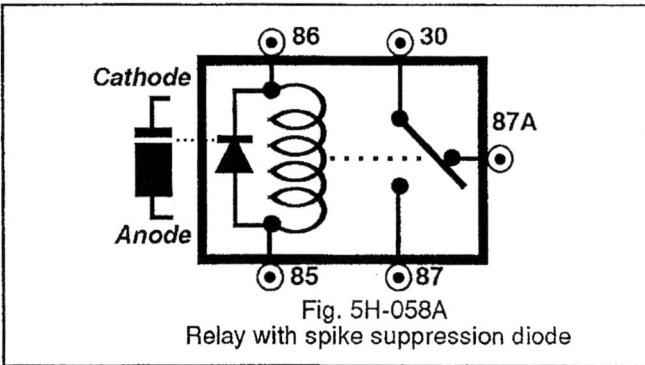

Fig. 5H-058A
Relay with spike suppression diode

Diode Spike Suppression Disadvantage:

(1) The diode is polarity sensitive. Diode electron current only flows against the arrow in the diode symbol. If reverse polarity is applied to the relay coil (Pin 85 wired to B+ and Pin 86 wired to B-) the diode turns ON and draws maximum current from the transistor driver providing the coil current. This will instantly burn up the transistor driver before a problem is recognized. The relay doesn't energize because the computer's transistor driver is damaged.

Resistor Spike Suppression (Fig. 58B)

Figure 58B shows a resistor to serve the same function of spike voltage suppression.

Resistor Spike Suppression Advantage:

A resistor is NOT polarity sensitive. Electron current can flow in either direction through a resistor therefore a relay coil with a spike resistor can be connected either way in a circuit. Pin 86 is B+ and Pin 85 is B- or Pin 86 is B- or Pin 85 is B+. This eliminates the possibility of wiring a relay coil in reverse polarity and damaging a computer. Resistor suppression indicates the relay coil can be wired in in either direction.

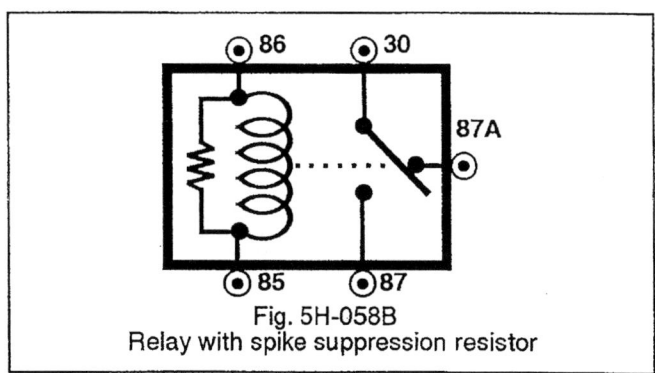

Fig. 5H-058B
Relay with spike suppression resistor

Resistor Spike Suppression Disadvantage:

The resistor draws some current when the relay is energized placing an additional current load on the transistor driver which must supply current to the relay coil and the spike suppression resistor at the same time. This is not a problem if the driver transistor is designed to handle the additional electron current load of the resistor.

Three Things to Observe With Relays

(1) Notice how Pin 86 is wired. If Pin 86 goes to B+ a replacement relay with a diode is safe to use.

BUT, if Pin 86 is wired to B- (ground side) **DO NOT** use a replacement relay with a diode. You must use a relay with a spike suppression resistor.

If a replacement relay has a diode and is plugged into a relay socket with Pin 86 connected to B- (ground side), the transistor driver in the control unit will be destroyed.

(2) Always check relay coil resistance with a digital ohmmeter to determine coil resistance. Select a replacement relay that is within 15% resistance of the original relay coil.

(3) Never use a replacement relay with no spike suppression if there are any electronics on-board the vehicle.

Vehicle Electronics Hands-On Troubleshooting Training Program

VEEJER ENTERPRISES 3701 Lariat Lane, Garland, Texas 75042-5419
Phone: 972-276-9642   Fax: 972-276-8122   Email: sales@veejer.com   Web Site: www.veejer.com

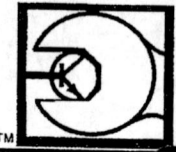

Getting Started

Connect the Relay Board H-PCB05 to the Power board and follow this review of how the two Troubleshooting Trainers work together. The Relay Troubleshooting Trainer, H-PCB05 is shown to the right connected to the Power Board in Figure 5H-059.

1. Plug in the Relay Board, H-PCB05 to connector C700 on the Power Board.
2. Connect the H-PS01 Power Supply to the Power Board's red and black terminal posts.
3. Plug in the H-PS01 power supply.
4. Turn ON S1, IGN SW, (toggle UP).
5. Turn ON S3 and S4 (slide UP).

The relay should be energized (CLICKS) and the lamp should be ON. When the relay de-energizes (any one switch OPEN) the lamp turns OFF.

If S1, IGN SW is turned OFF (toggled DOWN) the relay is shut down. The relay de-energizes and the lamp is out.

If S3 only is turned OFF (slide DOWN) the lamp is out because B+ has been removed from the relay winding. **Sliding S3 ON/OFF simulates controlling the relay by switch-to-voltage control. Try it.**

If S4 is turned OFF (slide DOWN) the lamp is out because B- (ground) has been removed from the relay coil. **Sliding S4 ON/OFF simulates controlling the relay by switch-to-ground control. Try it.**

Relay Board Simulates Fuel Pump Circuit

The Relay Board is designed to teach technicians how to troubleshoot any relay circuit. The Lamp on the Relay Board is the circuit's load the relay is controlling. The relay is referred to as the **FUEL PUMP RELAY** and the lamp is referred to as the actual **"FUEL PUMP"** itself. This adds realism to the troubleshooting exercises so technicians relate relay problems they encounter in the Troubleshooting Trainers to real world situations. Three possible conditions exist in relating the brightness of the lamp to a vehicle's fuel pump operation.

(1) When the **lamp is ON bright** the fuel pump is operating at full capacity and normal fuel pressure is present in the fuel rail.

(2) When the **lamp is ON but dim** the fuel pump is operating at less than full capacity resulting in less than normal fuel pressure in the fuel rail.

(3) When the **lamp is OFF** the fuel pump is NOT operating and there is NO fuel pressure in the fuel rail.

For our initial discussion of the relay circuit we will refer to the relay and lamp as "a relay" and "a lamp." But when we get to the troubleshooting exercises we will call the relay a Fuel Pump Relay and the lamp the actual Fuel Pump.

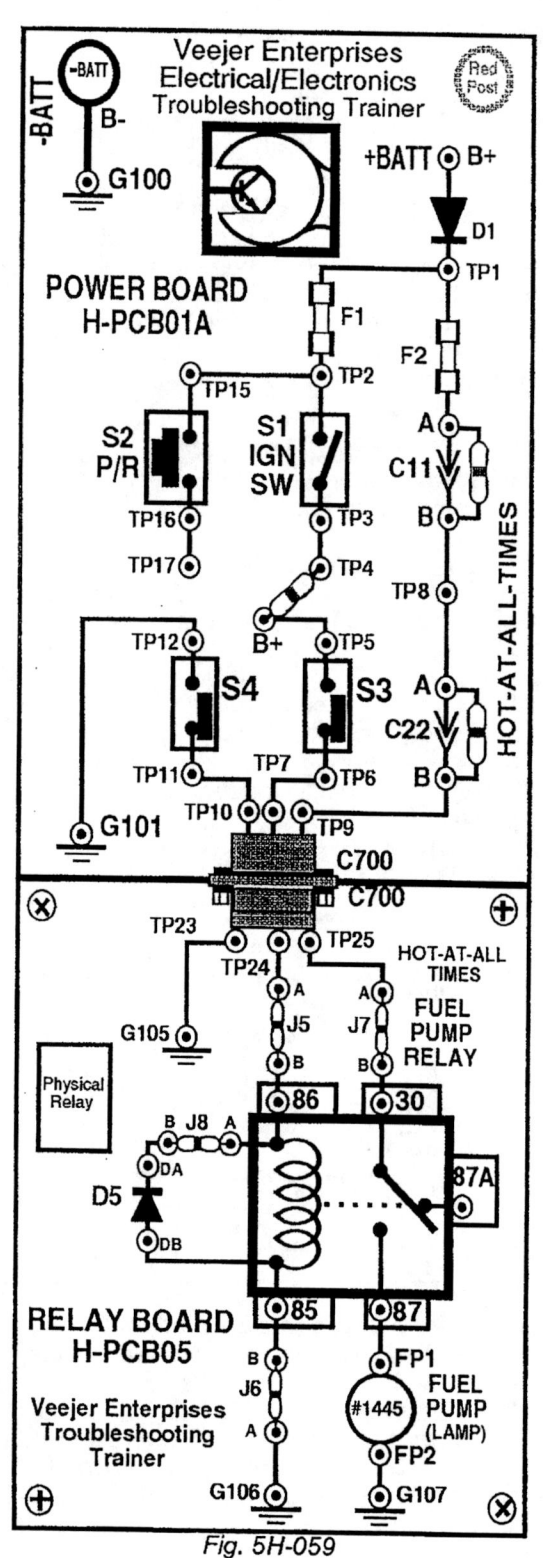

Fig. 5H-059

Vehicle Electronics Hands-On Troubleshooting Training Program

VEEJER ENTERPRISES 3701 Lariat Lane, Garland, Texas 75042-5419
Phone: 972-276-9642 Fax: 972-276-8122 Email: sales@veejer.com Web Site: www.veejer.com

Tips Using This Hands-On Troubleshooting Training Program

• STUDENTS SHOULD NEVER LOOK AT THE BOTTOM OF THE PCBs PRIOR TO TROUBLESHOOTING A PROBLEM SINCE THE CIRCUIT FAULT MIGHT BE OBVIOUS. DISCOVERING THE CIRCUIT FAULT BY OBSERVATION WILL SPOIL THE BENEFIT TO BE GAINED FROM TROUBLESHOOTING THAT PROBLEM. **DON'T EVEN PEEK!**

• Each student should have his own Student Manual to keep notes and record test results obtained in the circuit exercises and troubleshooting problems. Failure to record personal notes and troubleshooting test results will make it impossible to evaluate troubleshooting progress and impede the learning experience.

• Follow the instructions for each particular troubleshooting problem to be sure the fault is correctly inserted.

• Remove the fault from the PCBs after finding the problem unless someone is going to troubleshoot the same problem immediately after you. Any fault left in a PCB will affect the circuit when a second fault is installed causing false readings and a lot of confusion. AVOID CONFUSION!

• "Scan the top and bottom" of the PCBs to verify that no fault exists before inserting a fault. Scanning the top is covered in this text and scanning the bottom is covered in the Instructor Guide, IG05.

Resistor Bag – Relay Circuit – RB05

The **Resistor Bag RB05** contains several resistors of different ohmic values for inserting faults in the relay circuit. Each resistor ohmic value contained in the Resistor Bag is designed to work with the relay circuit to provide actual relay circuit failures that can be seen with DMM readings. These are the only resistor values to be used with the relay circuit for inserting problems.

Follow the instructions given in the Instructor Guide and it will tell you what ohmic value and what U-jumper location to insert a resistor type fault.

> A major difference when inserting faults in the relay circuit is that selected circuit problems require a specific resistor value be used for that problem. Follow instructions for inserting each problem to ensure the problem appears as intended to get the most benefit from each relay circuit problem.

If a prescribed resistor value in ohms is not used for specific problems the benefit of that circuit problem will not appear as intended. The benefit of troubleshooting a specific relay circuit failure will be lost. Simply follow the instructions in the Instructor Guide when inserting each problem.

For practice with the resistor color code, **review Lessons 4, 5 and 6 of "The" Vehicle Electronics Training Course**™ to study details about the resistor color code of the various resistors in the Resistor Bag RB05. The resistor bag label is shown below with a list of the resistor quantity and resistance values in ohms. All resistors are 1/4 watt.

RESISTOR BAG H-RB05 RELAY CIRCUIT, H-115

Fixed Resistors
2 - 50 Ω 1/4 W
2 - 100 Ω 1/4 W
2 - 150 Ω 1/4 W
2 - 220 Ω 1/4 W
2 - 330 Ω 1/4 W
2 - 560 Ω 1/4 W
2 - 910 Ω 1/4 W

5 ea. Zero-Ohm Resistors

Veejer Enterprises
Garland, Texas
Ph. 972-276-9642
www.veejer.com

Guide to Resistor Color Code

Resistors use color coded bands painted on the resistor body to identify the resistance in ohms of a particular resistor. Lesson 6 covers the resistor color code system. Since you must use a specific resistor ohmic value for inserting problems in the circuit boards for some of the troubleshooting exercises, we have listed the color code description below for all resistors used with the Relay Circuit Troubleshooting Trainer, H-PCB05. The colors of the first three color bands denote the ohmic value of the resistor. The fourth band denotes the ±% tolerance of the resistor which we can ignore in the "The" Hands-On Program exercises since the resistors are pre-selected.

50 Ω green-brown-black *abbr..* **grn-bro-blk**
(the color code is provided abbreviated in bold type)

100 Ω brown-black-brown *abbr..* **bro-blk-bro**

150 Ω brown-green-brown *abbr..* **bro-grn-bro**

220 Ω red-red-brown *abbr..* **red-red-bro**

330 Ω orange-orange-brown *abbr..* **org-org-bro**

560 Ω green-blue-brown *abbr..* **grn-blu-bro**

910 Ω white-brown-brown *abbr..* **wht-bro-bro**

When a specific ohmic value resistor is required to set up a circuit problem in "The" Hands-On Program, the color code is preceded by "cc:" in the text for "color code." Then the abbreviated three color bands is given. For example when a 100Ω resistor is required it will be listed as **100Ω–cc:bro-blk-bro**. Select a resistor with color code of brown-black-brown. The 4th band is the tolerance value (5%, 10%, etc., and can be ignored. If there is any doubt in the resistance value simply check a resistor with a digital ohmmeter.

Vehicle Electronics Hands-On Troubleshooting Training Program

VEEJER ENTERPRISES 3701 Lariat Lane, Garland, Texas 75042-5419
Phone: 972-276-9642 Fax: 972-276-8122 Email: sales@veejer.com Web Site: www.veejer.com

Scanning the POWER BOARD-RELAY BOARD

Before beginning an exercise or troubleshooting a problem, **scan the top of the circuit boards** FIRST to verify everything on top of the boards is correct. Items which need to be checked are circled in Figure 5H-060. Starting at the top are two terminal posts.

Black Terminal Post, -BATT:

The negative (black) terminal post **(B-)** connects to the black lead from the power supply H-PS01. The black terminal post represents the battery negative terminal (-BATT) **for purposes of grounding the DMM for Vc voltage measurements.**

Red Terminal Post:

The positive (red) post is used only as a connection point for the red (+) wire from the Power Supply. Use the **+BATT** terminal just below the red post as the positive terminal of the voltage source, or **B+**. It simulates the positive battery post or the B+ terminal at the back of the generator/alternator of a vehicle.

The +BATT terminal feeds B+ to diode D1, a polarity sensing diode which was discussed in **Lesson 44, Pages 4-5 and Lesson 49, Pages 1-4.** D1 shuts the circuit down (prevents circuit current) if the power supply leads are connected to the red/black posts in reverse polarity. It would be the same thing as jump starting a vehicle with the jumper cables connected in reverse polarity. **Lesson 17, Page 6; Lesson 49, Pages 1-4** discuss the concept of reverse polarity.

The two fuses, F1 and F2, must be good 2A fuses for the relay circuit to function properly. Fuse, F1, supplies B+ to TP2, the input to the ignition switch, S1. Fuse, F2, supplies B+ to the relay contacts to provide B+ voltage to operate the load connected to the relay contacts. Fuse, F2, feeds the Hot-at-all-times circuit to TP9 at C700. C11 and C22 are connectors in this leg of the circuit. Both are drawn into the Hot-at-all-times circuit and are simulated physical connectors. TP8 is a test point between the two connectors to test connector operation and detect connector problems for additional troubleshooting practice.

A zero ohm resistor (0ΩR) or wire jumper must connect TP4 to the "B+ Terminal." Switches, S3 and S4 must be CLOSED (slides UP). Depending which switch is CLOSED and which switch is OPEN, the relay circuit can be controlled by switching ground to the load (closing S3 and operating S4 as the ON/OFF switch), or, switching voltage to the load (closing S4 and operating S3 as the ON/OFF switch).

The Relay Board should have a zero ohm resistor in J5, J6, J7 and J8. A 1445 lamp should be in the lamp socket simulating the Fuel Pump. Once all these conditions are met the PCBs are ready to use.

The relay should be energized and the lamp ON bright when the PCBs are ready to go.

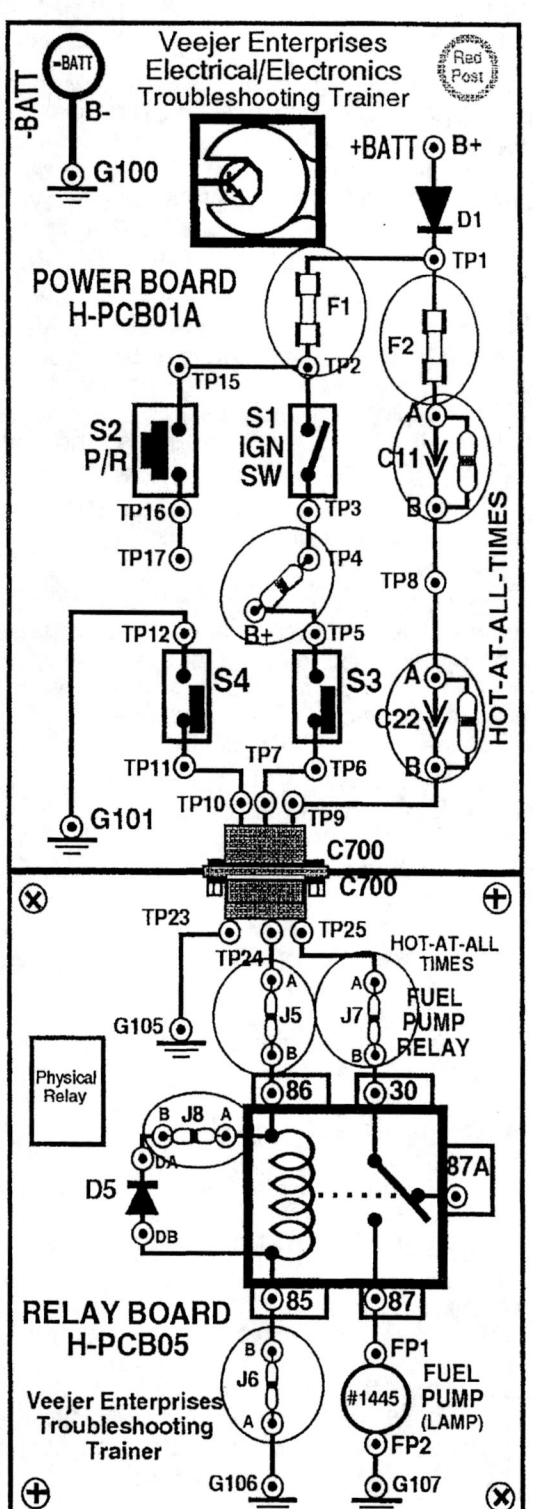

Fig. 5H-060

Copyright © 2015 VEEJER ENTERPRISES, Garland, Texas - All Rights Reserved Student Workbook H-WB115 Page 11

Vehicle Electronics Hands-On Troubleshooting Training Program

VEEJER ENTERPRISES 3701 Lariat Lane, Garland, Texas 75042-5419
Phone: 972-276-9642   Fax: 972-276-8122   Email: sales@veejer.com   Web Site: www.veejer.com

Divide and Conquer Relay Circuits

Troubleshooting a relay problem is not difficult if the relay circuit is divided into two individual circuits as shown in Fig. 5H-061. The relay primary circuit (coil circuit) is referred to as the **Relay's Primary Circuit** and the relay contacts side of the circuit is referred to as the **Relay's Secondary Circuit**.

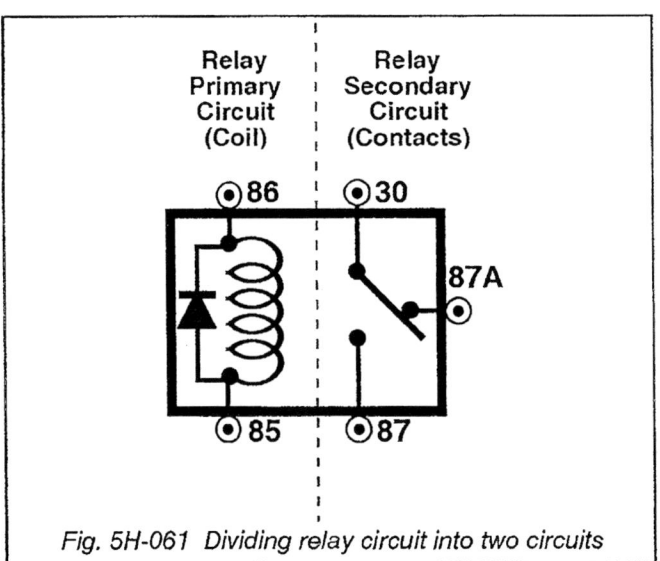

Fig. 5H-061 Dividing relay circuit into two circuits

Use the *"CLICK"* vs. *"NO CLICK""* concept in troubleshooting relay circuits as shown next. From the perspective of dividing a relay circuit into two individual circuits we can quickly begin to analyze a relay circuit problem. The relay will either *"CLICK"* or it will NOT *"CLICK"* when energized. The *"CLICK"* reveals a lot about a relay circuit

Significance of a Relay's *"CLICK"*

An audible *"CLICK"* is heard as a relay is energized and the contacts make initial physical contact, as shown in Figure 5H-061A. The audible *"CLICK"* is confirmation the relay coil side of the circuit is functioning. As long as current through the coil is maintained, the electromagnetic field is sustained to keep the contacts CLOSED. Some relays even make another lower level audible *"CLICK"* when the contacts OPEN (relay de-energizes).

A *"CLICK"* is useful in troubleshooting relay circuits because a *"CLICK"* indicates the relay coil circuit is energized and the swinging contact has moved. It does NOT mean the contacts make sufficient contact to be a good electrical switch. The contacts may CLOSE but fail to provide good electrical contact between the relay contacts. The *"CLICK"* may be loud enough to hear by holding an ear close to the relay when it is energized.

Listen for the *"CLICK"*:

Use slide switch, S3, to control the relay ON/OFF because it makes less noise than the ignition switch, S1, when it is toggled. Listen for the relay's *"CLICK"* when S3 is CLOSED. Try it several times.

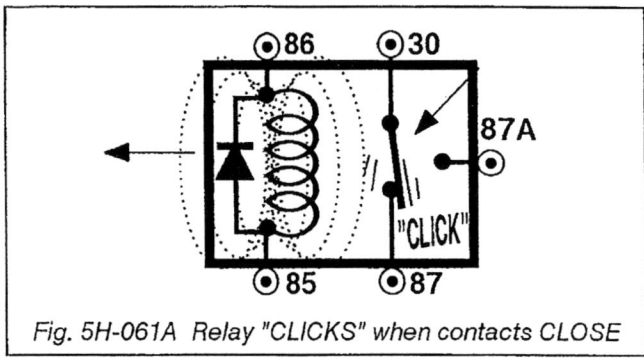

Fig. 5H-061A Relay "CLICKS" when contacts CLOSE

If background (shop) noise is too high the relay's *"CLICK"* may not be audible above the noise. It may be necessary to use the other methods listed below to determine if a relay *"CLICKS"* when turned ON.

(1) Place a finger on the relay and see if you "feel" a vibration from the *"CLICK"* as a relay energizes and the contacts move. Be careful to not mistake a vibration from some other source and think the relay is clicking when it is not.

(2) Touch the top of the relay with a long screw driver and put your ear on the screw driver's handle to listen for the *"CLICK"*.

(3) Use a stethoscope to listen for the relay *"CLICK"*.

If a Relay *"CLICKS"*:

The primary (coil) side must be working to produce the *"CLICK"*. This means the coil has B+ and B- applied. Current is flowing through the coil and the armature contact is being attracted to CLOSE the contacts. Therefore, do not waste time checking voltages around the primary relay (coil) circuit if the relay *"CLICKS"*. Voltages will all check good because the relay coil circuit is working properly. **Start by troubleshooting the secondary side of the relay circuit and performing the TTS (Texas Two Step) on the load's terminals (lamp) on the relay contact side to identify the problem.**

If the relay DOES NOT *"CLICK"*

Start troubleshooting the primary (coil) side of the relay circuit by performing the **TTS on the relay coil if the relay does not *"CLICK"*.** Do not waste time by checking voltages around the secondary side of the relay circuit. Voltages may check good and/or bad where you measure because the relay coil circuit is NOT working and the contacts are not CLOSED.

We will study testing the relay circuit in *"The"* Hands-On Program and explore all the possibilities including listening for the *"CLICK"*.

Vehicle Electronics Hands-On Troubleshooting Training Program

VEEJER ENTERPRISES 3701 Lariat Lane, Garland, Texas 75042-5419
Phone: 972-276-9642 Fax: 972-276-8122 Email: sales@veejer.com Web Site: www.veejer.com

Load Switch Control with S3 and S4

The Relay Board connected to the Power Board allows control of the relay by either (switch-to-voltage) S3 or (switch-to-ground) S4 as shown in Figure 5H-062. The concepts of load switching the voltage or ground side is covered in **Lesson 23**.

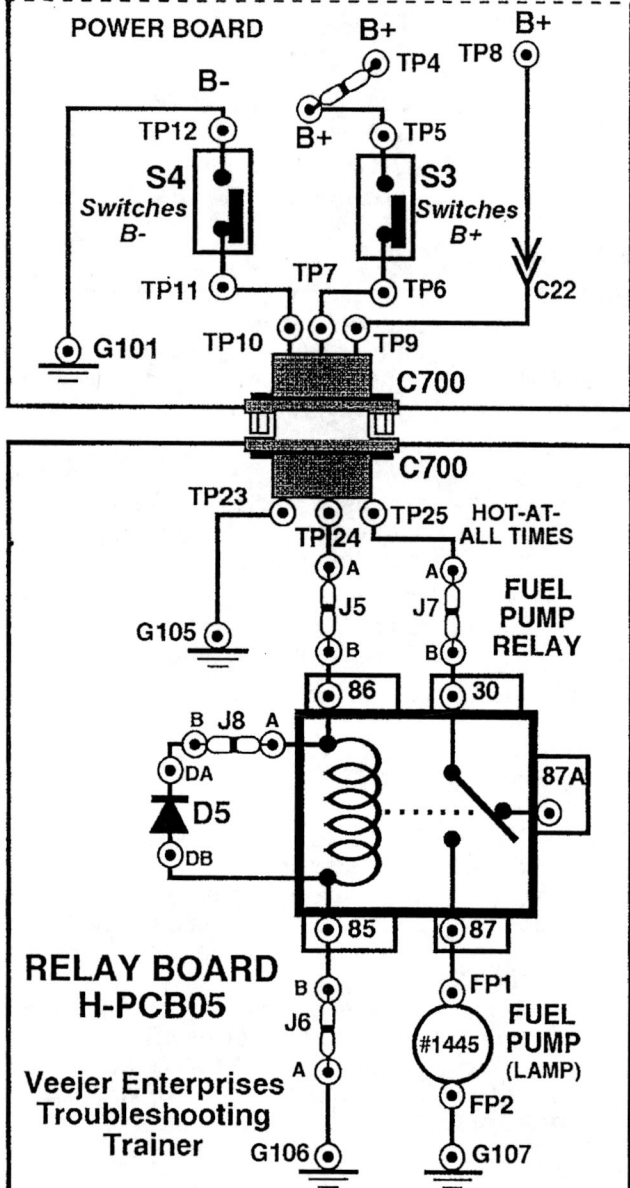

Fig. 5H-062

The relay secondary circuit (relay contacts) may be connected in the voltage side of the load, as we have in the relay board, or the relay contacts may be connected to the load for ground side switching. It is possible to control the relay primary side (coil circuit) with one method of switching and use the opposite method of controlling the load connected to the relay contacts. It makes no difference to the relay.

Figure 5H-062A is an abbreviated schematic diagram of the relay circuit showing crucial circuit test points to review using S3 and S4 to control the relay.

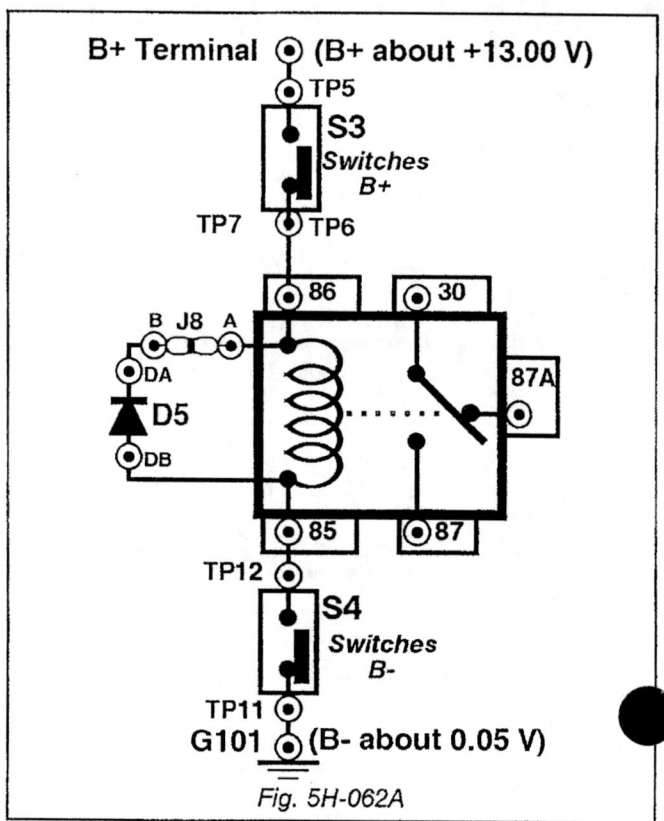

Fig. 5H-062A

Review Exercise of Relay Control
Do This:
- Connect the Relay Board to the Power Board.
- Connect the H-PS01 Power Supply to the Power Board and plug into a wall socket.
- Toggle S1 UP
- Slide S3 UP
- Slide S4 UP
- Verify the relay is energized and the lamp is ON

Turn relay OFF by sliding S3 DOWN.
(1) Measure the TTS at the relay coil.
   TTS-1 at Pin 86 _____ volts.
   TTS-2 at Pin 85 _____ volts.

Slide S3 UP to turn relay ON.

Turn relay OFF by sliding S4 DOWN.
(3) Measure the TTS at the relay coil.
   TTS-1 at Pin 86 _____ volts.
   TTS-2 at Pin 85 _____ volts.

When a load is turned OFF the TTS readings reveal how a load is controlled. If the TTS readings are both 0V the circuit is switch-to-voltage controlled. If the TTS readings are both B+ the circuit is switch-to-ground controlled.

Vehicle Electronics Hands-On Troubleshooting Training Program

VEEJER ENTERPRISES 3701 Lariat Lane, Garland, Texas 75042-5419
Phone: 972-276-9642 Fax: 972-276-8122 Email: sales@veejer.com Web Site: www.veejer.com

Relay Circuit Straight Line Schematic

Figure 5H-063 is a "straight line schematic" of the Relay Board with B+ at the +BATT Terminal at the top down to B-, at the -BATT Terminal. A straight line schematic puts the entire circuit into a format that improves circuit comprehension when tracing the circuit to learn what components make up the circuit, their position in the circuit and their electrical relationship to each other.

Reading Schematic Diagrams

Here are some simple techniques to employ when reading a schematic diagram.

(1) Trace the relay's primary circuit beginning with the voltage side of the load, the coil at Pin 86 and trace back to +BATT. Trace the ground side of the circuit starting at the relay coil's Pin 85 and trace back to -BATT.

(2) Trace the relay's secondary circuit beginning with the voltage side of the circuit and the ground side of the circuit starting at the load terminals controlled by the relay contacts, the lamp. Start at Pins FP1 and FP2.

If this were a circuit on an actual vehicle you were not already familiar with, you would have determined many of the major features of the circuit using this simple circuit tracing technique. You would have discovered what switches, fuses and connectors comprise the relay's primary circuit as well as the source of B+ and B- to energize the relay. On the secondary side of the circuit the same crucial elements of the circuit are also now known by tracing the circuit as well as what components the relay contacts are controlling.

This tracing technique may seem very simple at this point because you are already somewhat familiar with the relay circuit. But, once you try this schematic tracing technique on a schematic diagram you haven't seen before you will realize how helpful this technique can be.

Grounding the DMM

Consistently in *The" Hands-On Troubleshooting Training Program*, we have stressed over and over the need to always ground the DMM at the most negative point on the vehicle, the negative battery terminal. The straight line schematic in Figure 5H-063 helps to show why grounding a DMM's black test lead at the negative battery post is the best DMM ground point. When there is an OPEN connection or a Vd (voltage drop) on either side of the circuit, correct grounding of the DMM ensures the DMM indicates a reading to reflect the circuit problem because the problem is always between the test lead probe tips.

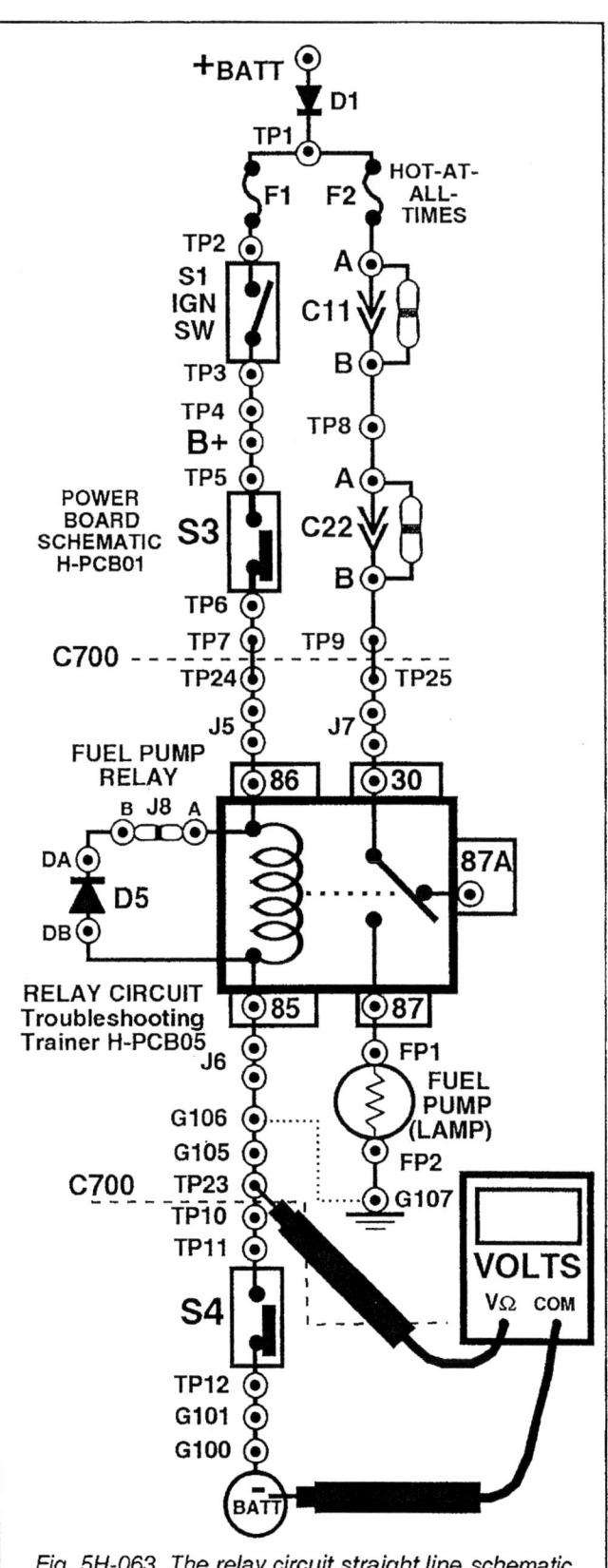

Fig. 5H-063 The relay circuit straight line schematic

Copyright © 2015 VEEJER ENTERPRISES, Garland, Texas - All Rights Reserved

Vehicle Electronics Hands-On Troubleshooting Training Program

VEEJER ENTERPRISES 3701 Lariat Lane, Garland, Texas 75042-5419
Phone: 972-276-9642 Fax: 972-276-8122 Email: sales@veejer.com Web Site: www.veejer.com

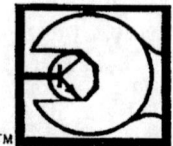

Review of Ohmmeters

An ohmmeter is essential for checking relay coil resistance. Before we discuss testing relay coil resistance here is a brief overview of the two types of ohmmeters, analog and digital. An ohmmeter uses an internal voltage source (usually a small battery) to generate an ohmmeter test voltage and current to sense the resistance of a device placed between it's probe tips. An ohmmeter measures the level of ohmmeter test current passing through the test resistance and indicates a reading in ohms.

> Additional information about ohmmeters is available in *"The"* Course.™
>
> **Lesson 8** Analog & Digital Ohmmeters
> **Lesson 9** Troubleshooting with Ohmmeters
> **Lesson 10** Working with Resistance in Vehicle Circuits

There are two things that must be known to make correct resistance checks using an ohmmeter:

(1) **Polarity** of ohmmeter test voltage, and
(2) **Amplitude** of ohmmeter test voltage.

Use a DMM to test the voltage at the analog ohmmeter's probe tips with the analog ohmmeter on the Rx1 range to determine polarity and amplitude.

Analog Ohmmeter Overview

An analog ohmmeter is found in a VOM (Volt-Ohm-Milliamp) analog meter using a meter movement with a pointer. An analog ohmmeter indicates resistance as a pointer moves across an ohmmeter scale printed on the meter face. The resistance value is determined by noting where the pointer stops on the scale. This requires careful observation of the pointer location on the scale to determine the correct measured resistance value.

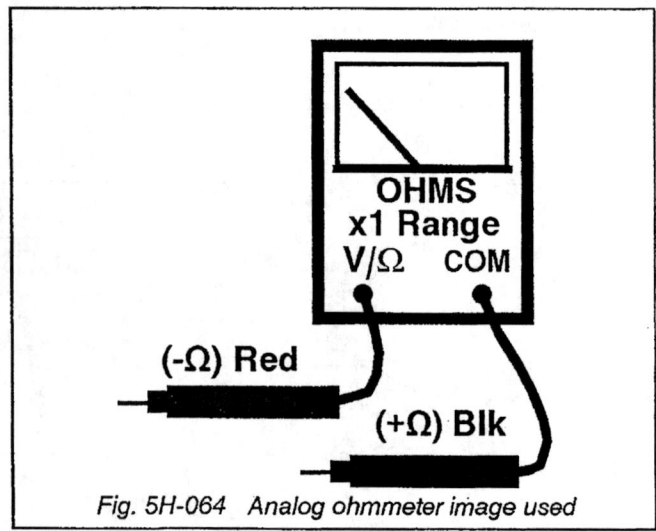

Fig. 5H-064 Analog ohmmeter image used

Figure 5H-064 shows the image for an analog ohmmeter we use in *"The"* **Hands-On Program.**

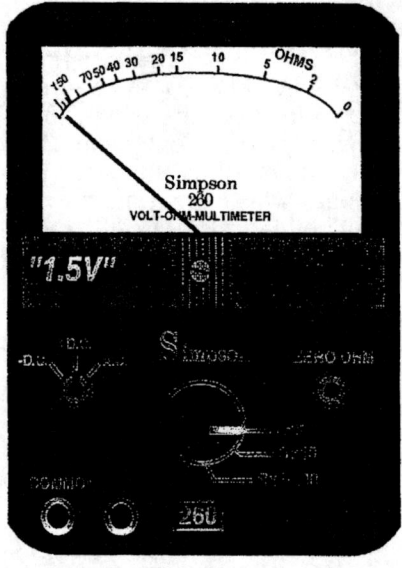

Old style Simpson 260 VOM shown above with Ohms Rx1 Range selected. Notice pointer rests at the left side of the scale when not measuring resistance as is common with most VOMs.
(1) Test lead **probe tip polarity of this VOM can be selected** so that the Red test lead can be either +Ohmmeter or -Ohmmeter.
(2) Ohmmeter test voltage amplitude is normally **1.5V** for older style VOM ohmmeters.

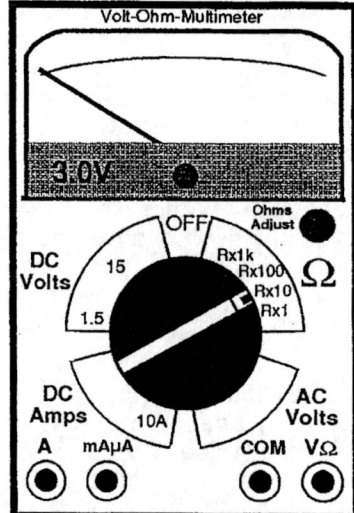

A later version VOM is shown above with the Rx10 Ohmmeter Range selected.
(1) Test lead **probe tip polarity is fixed** so that the Black test lead is always +Ohmmeter.
(2) Ohmmeter test voltage amplitude is most often **3.0V** for testing some newer solid-state components.

Vehicle Electronics Hands-On Troubleshooting Training Program

VEEJER ENTERPRISES 3701 Lariat Lane, Garland, Texas 75042-5419
Phone: 972-276-9642   Fax: 972-276-8122   Email: sales@veejer.com   Web Site: www.veejer.com

Analog Test Voltage Polarity:

The test voltage polarity of most analog ohmmeters is the reverse of the test lead colors. The RED test lead (in the V/Ω jack) is the **negative side (–)** of the test voltage and is designated as (–Ω) or –Ohmmeter in this text. The BLACK test lead (in the COM jack) is the **positive side (+)** of the test voltage and is designated as (+Ω) or +Ohmmeter in this text.

Analog Test Voltage Amplitude:

Older 1.5V analog ohmmeters use a single AAA, AA or C-cell battery so the ohmmeter test voltage is always 1.5V. You can tell when the ohmmeter test battery is getting weak. As the battery voltage begins to decrease it becomes impossible to "Zero" the ohmmeter.

How to "Zero" an analog ohmmeter:

(1) Select the ohmmeter range to be used such as Rx1, Rx10, etc.

(2) Short the test lead probe tips together and watch the pointer move across the scale and verify that it reaches the zero ohm mark at the far right of the Ohms scale.

(3) If the pointer does not reach the Zero Ohm mark on the scale rotate the **Ohms Adjust** knob to move the pointer to zero ohms at the far right on the scale.

If the pointer reaches the zero ohm mark the ohmmeter is now said to be "zero-ed." The internal ohmmeter test battery is good. Ohmmeter readings will now be as accurate as possible with an analog ohmmeter.

If the Ohms Adjust knob will not move the pointer far enough to reach the zero ohm mark you know the internal ohmmeter test battery is weak and should be replaced.

Recent developments in analog ohmmeters has increased the test voltage to 3.0V (2xAA or 2x C-cell) to meet the testing requirements of the newest solid-state devices. An ohmmeter with a 1.5V ohmmeter test voltage is not sufficient voltage to "turn-ON" many new solid-state devices when testing them. They will require more than 1.5V. This resulted in some newer analog ohmmeters having a 3.0V ohmmeter test voltage.

Be aware a test voltage of 3.0V may be harmful to some solid-state components. So be careful with a 3.0V ohmmeter. Never probe the wiring in a vehicle with a 3.0V ohmmeter as the test current generated could harm solid-state components in on-board computers.

Digital Ohmmeter Overview

A digital ohmmeter reads resistance to the tenth of an ohm (0.1Ω) and displays the measured resistance value on a digital readout. This makes a digital ohmmeter much more accurate than an analog ohmmeter. They also have a very low ohmmeter test voltage so they are safer to use in the wiring harness.

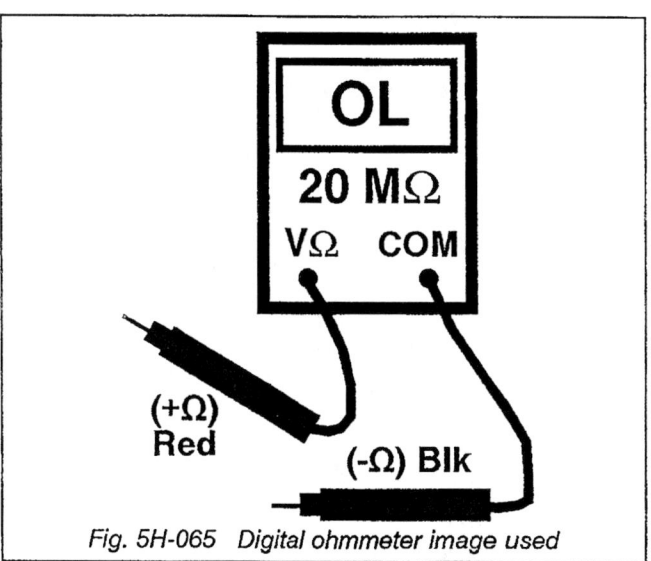

Fig. 5H-065   Digital ohmmeter image used

Digital Ohmmeter Test Voltage Polarity:

Digital ohmmeter test voltage polarity is normal. That is digital ohmmeter polarity always follows the test lead color code. The RED test lead (in the V/Ω jack) is always (+Ω) or +Ohmmeter. The BLACK test lead (in the COM jack) is always (–Ω) or –Ohmmeter.

Digital Ohmmeter Test Voltage Amplitude:

Digital ohmmeter test voltage amplitude has a low test voltage of only 0.05V – 0.10V while measuring a resistance. This makes a digital ohmmeter very safe for testing circuits with sensitive solid-state circuits because they can't "turn-ON" solid-state components.

If the ohmmeter test voltage is measured at the probe tips with a voltmeter – when the ohmmeter is not measuring resistance – the voltage may be as high as 3.0 volts. This is not a problem since the test voltage drops to 0.05V –01.0V during the resistance test.

In the next exercises we see how to choose the right ohmmeter for a specific resistance test and why.

Vehicle Electronics Hands-On Troubleshooting Training Program

VEEJER ENTERPRISES 3701 Lariat Lane, Garland, Texas 75042-5419
Phone: 972-276-9642 Fax: 972-276-8122 Email: sales@veejer.com Web Site: www.veejer.com

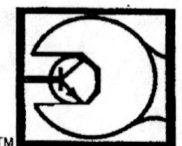

Testing Relay Coil Resistance

The next series of exercises review procedures for testing relay coil resistance with an analog ohmmeter, a digital ohmmeter and using the Diode Test of a DMM. These are some very important exercises to understand using ohmmeters and the Diode Test.

This type of relay coil ohmmeter test is extremely important when the relay is controlled by a computer. A driver transistor inside the computer is used to provide the relay coil current necessary to energize the relay. If the relay coil resistance decreases or if the coil becomes SHORTED, coil current increases and the computer driver transistor in the on-board computer will fail.

If the faulty relay is left in the vehicle and a new on-board computer is installed you can expect the new computer to fail just like the original computer.

A simple ohmmeter test of a relay coil will reveal if the relay coil has the correct resistance to protect the computer's driver transistor. However, you should know the polarity and test voltage of the ohmmeter you are using. Different ohmmeters will result in different readings and confusion about what is right or wrong.

Coil Resistance & Analog Ohmmeters

An analog ohmmeter's Red test lead is **-ohmmeter** (minus polarity) and the Black test lead is **+ohmmeter** (positive polarity).

As stated earlier, the polarity of most analog ohmmeters have a test voltage polarity that is the opposite of the test lead colors. It's one of the oddities of analog ohmmeters a technician must be aware of to correctly test solid-state components like diodes especially when the diode is connected across a solenoid or coil.

> Lesson 44 of "*The*" Course™ covers diode testing with analog ohmmeters.

Figure 5H-066 is checking relay coil resistance with an analog ohmmeter using the Rx1 range. Use the Relay Circuit Troubleshooting Trainer, H-PCB05, and follow these two steps using an analog ohmmeter.

Always make two resistance measurements when using an ohmmeter by reversing the ohmmeter test leads for the second step and compare the readings.

Step 1 (of 2 steps): Test Coil Resistance

Connect analog ohmmeter test leads to the relay terminals as shown in Figure 5H-066. The Red test lead **-ohmmeter** connects to Pin 86. The Black test lead **+ohmmeter** connects to Pin 85.

Notice how the ohmmeter pointer moves across the Rx1 ohmmeter scale and comes to a stop indicating a low resistance reading. The actual reading obtained varies with the type of analog ohmmeter used and this requires some explanation.

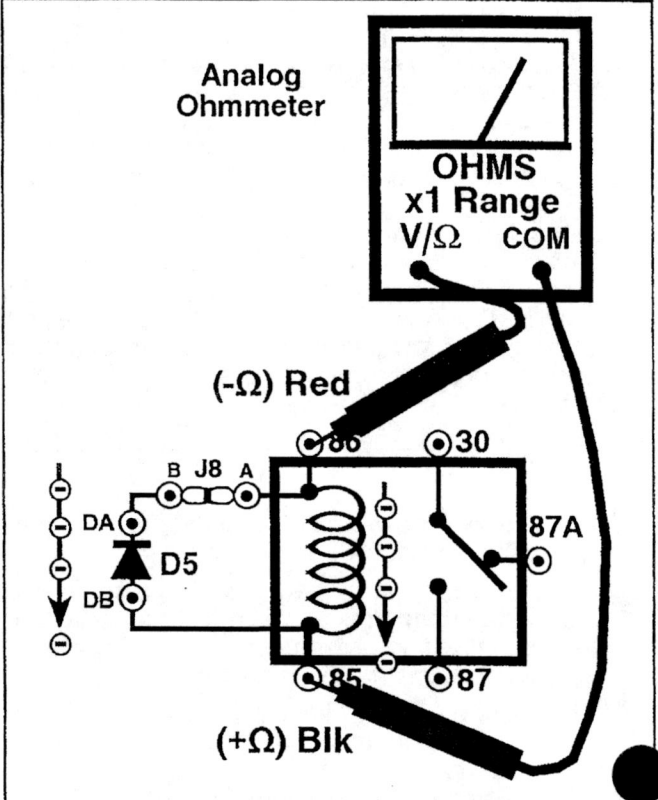

Fig. 5H-066 Testing coil resistance with analog ohmmeter – Step 1 of 2 steps

Another oddity about analog ohmmeters is now evident in the reading obtained in Figure 5H-066. As mentioned on the previous page, analog ohmmeters may use one AAA battery, one AA battery or a C-cell battery to produce ohmmeter test voltage. All these are 1.5V so the ohmmeter test voltage is always 1.5V with the Red test lead being **-ohmmeter** and Black test lead being **+ohmmeter** *for most brands* of analog ohmmeters.

The reading obtained in the first resistance measurement shown in Figure 5H-066 depends on the type of battery in the ohmmeter. The reading to expect according to battery energy capacity of your analog ohmmeter follows.

AAA battery the reading is about 16-22 ohms
AA battery the reading is about 11-14 ohms
C-cell battery the reading is about 9-11 ohms

The reading varies depending on accuracy of the ohmmeter, state of charge of the ohmmeter test battery and proper calibration (zeroing the ohms range) of the analog ohmmeter before using.

The reason the battery type changes the resistance reading obtained is due to the **ohmmeter battery's energy capacity.** The higher the energy capacity cells) the higher the test voltage during the resista

Vehicle Electronics Hands-On Troubleshooting Training Program

test and the more current that can be provided through the component being tested – coil and diode in this case. The higher the test current the lower the good resistance reading.

An AAA battery has the least energy capacity while the C-cell has the highest energy of the three battery types. The lowest resistance reading obtained in the measurement shown in Figure 5H-066 using an analog ohmmeter with a single C-cell battery for ohmmeter test voltage is in the range of 10-12 ohms.

The reading obtained with the test leads connected as shown in Figure 5H-066 is due to ohmmeter test current flowing through the relay coil AND the spike suppression diode at the same time. Electrons always flow against the arrow in the diode symbol and Pin 86 is connected to the -Ω Black test lead.

The diode is **forward biased** by the polarity of the ohmmeter test voltage and provides a path for ohmmeter test current which lowers the ohmmeter reading to the point that it cannot be determined if the relay coil is OPEN or has the correct resistance. The reading obtained is the same reading if the diode were tested separate from the relay coil.

In effect this first ohmmeter test step – turning ON the diode – proves the following conditions which are all very important to verify about the relay coil circuit.

(1) diode is in place
(2) it is not connected backwards
(3) the diode is ON (conducting current–good)

A reading of close to zero ohms or an actual zero ohm reading would indicate that either the relay coil is shorted OR the diode is shorted. The diode and the relay coil would have to be separated and their resistance tested independently to determine if the diode or the relay coil is the shorted component. Don't waste time doing that. You already know the relay has to be replaced because the coil circuit resistance is too low. Now let's reverse the analog ohmmeter test leads for the second reading.

Step 2 - Reverse Test Leads:

For the second ohmmeter test step simply reverse the ohmmeter test leads at the relay coil terminals as shown in Figure 5H-066A. The Black test lead **+ohmmeter** connects to Pin 86 and the Red test lead **-ohmmeter** connects to Pin 85. Ohmmeter test current only flows through the relay coil in Step 2 since the polarity of the analog ohmmeter test voltage is **reverse bias** to the diode and no current flows through the diode this time. The only ohmmeter test current is through the relay coil so the resistance reading is the coil resistance without being influenced by the diode which is OFF.

The ohmmeter reading is about 400 ohms. The actual reading is difficult to determine on the Rx1 range at the left side of the ohmmeter scale because the pointer barely moves to indicate 400 ohms if the ohmmeter range selected is Rx1. The extreme left hand side of the ohmmeter scale indicates high resistance in a very small area of the scale making the left side of the ohmmeter scale a very inaccurate portion of the ohms scale.

A slight movement of the pointer on the left side of the scale could be a difference of a few thousand ohms of resistance. However, the slight movement of the pointer in Step 2 indicates an ohmmeter test current is flowing through the relay coil yet the exact resistance of the relay coil cannot be accurately determined when the pointer barley moves on the left side of the scale.

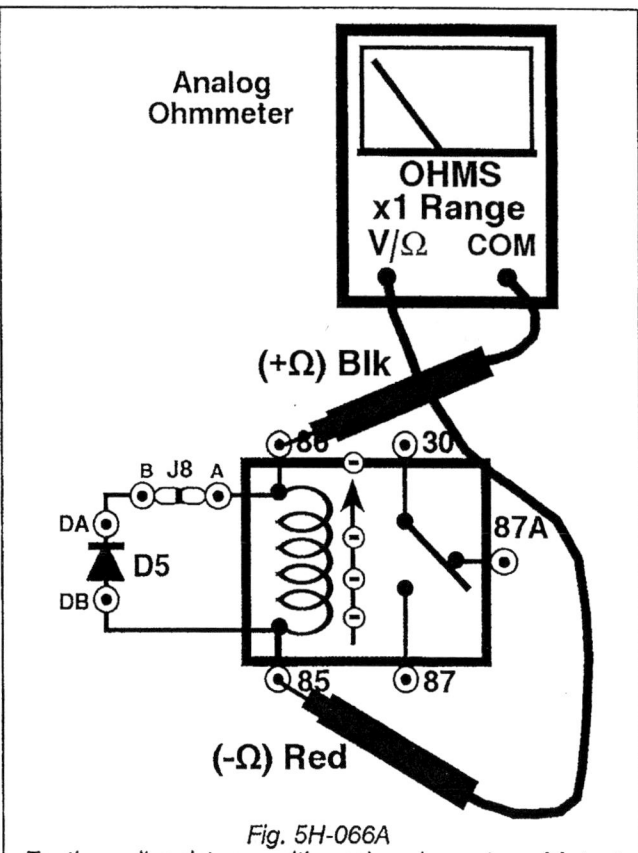

Fig. 5H-066A
*Testing coil resistance with analog ohmmeter **with test leads reversed** – Step 2 of two steps.*

We can conclude that using an analog ohmmeter on **the Rx1 range is an effective tester for the condition if the spike suppression diode remains connected to the relay coil,** more so than to determine the resistance of the relay coil.

It would also be practical to switch the analog ohmmeter to the Rx10 range to see a more accurate reading of the relay coil's resistance in Step 2. The Rx10 range would also have a lower impact on the reading obtained in Step 1 when the diode is forward biased.

Technicians who have extensive experience in testing diodes and transistors usually prefer the Rx1 range and are careful to zero the ohmmeter before using because more accurate readings of most solid-state components are obtained on the Rx1 range. If the resistance of the relay coil is to be determined a digital ohmmeter is more accurate.

High Performance Ohmmeters

We have to consider what we call **"high performance ohmmeters"** to give them a name. This type of ohmmeter is a standard analog VOM that uses an ohmmeter test voltage of 3.0V, instead of the more common 1.5V, by using two AA or two C-cell batteries **in series** so the voltage of the two batteries adds together (1.5 V + 1.5V = 3.0V).

The only way to tell if an analog ohmmeter is a "high performance" ohmmeter is to measure the voltage at the probe tips when the ohmmeter is on the Rx1 or Rx10 range. A reading of 3V tells you it is a high performance ohmmeter and you now know to be very careful with these high performance ohmmeters should you ever encounter one.

Recent developments in solid-state components (advanced diode and transistor devices) make it necessary to use a 3.0V ohmmeter test voltage in order to turn ON (forward bias) these newer solid-state devices. The older conventional 1.5V ohmmeter does not have enough voltage to turn ON these new devices.

When we test the relay coil as shown in Figure 5H-066 using a 3.0V (high performance) ohmmeter the first reading is low on the Rx1 scale in the range of 6-7 ohms. A low resistance reading indicates the higher ohmmeter test voltage turns ON the diode to a higher level of conduction than a 1.5V ohmmeter. If using a 1.5V analog ohmmeter the first reading will be a few ohms higher indicating the diode is turned ON but at a lower level using 1.5V.

These subtle differences in ohmmeter readings is a very effective method to determine the spike suppression diode is good and able to turn ON to provide spike voltage suppression.

Coil Resistance with Digital Ohmmeter

A digital ohmmeter in a DMM (Digital Multimeter) is the most precise ohmmeter available.

The **polarity of the digital ohmmeter test voltage** is always positive at the Red test lead (+Ω) or +Ohmmeter. The negative or the Black test lead is always (-Ω) or –Ohmmeter.

The **amplitude of the digital ohmmeter test voltage** is very low when testing a resistance placed between the test leads. If the digital ohmmeter test voltage is measured at the probe tips with another DMM, while the probe tips are not connected to a device for testing, the open circuit voltage at the probe tips can be as high as 3.0V for most DMMs set to the Ohms function. This does not mean the test voltage is 3.0V during a resistance test.

If the DMM's ohmmeter probe tip voltage is measured during a resistance test, expect to see about 0.05V – 0.10V at the probe tips. The voltage is dropped inside the digital ohmmeter during a resistance test to protect sensitive electronic circuits containing ICs (integrated circuits) which can be destroyed with an ohmmeter test voltage exceeding as little as 0.5V.

A relay coil resistance test with a DMM (digital) ohmmeter is shown below in Figure 5H-067. Be sure to set your DMM to the 2k Ohmmeter Range since we now have determines the coil resistance is over 200 ohms. If the relay coil is tested on the 200Ω Range the ohmmeter will say "OL" which would seem to indicate the coil is OPEN when in reality the DMM is on the wrong range.

If you have an autoranging DMM select the Ohms function and let the DMM automatically select the correct range to get a resistance reading.

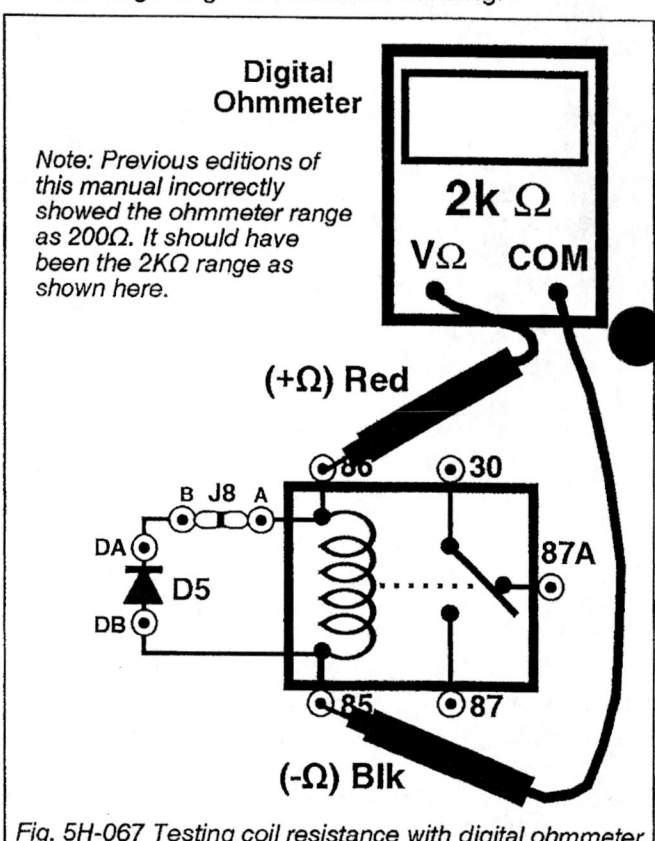

Fig. 5H-067 Testing coil resistance with digital ohmmeter

Step 1 (of 2 steps): Test Relay Coil Resistance
(1) Verify a 0ΩR (zero ohm resistor) is in J8.
(2) Place the test leads of a digital ohmmeter as shown in Figure 5H-067.
(3) Write down the reading indicated by the DMM in Figure 5H-067.

The reading should be about 400 ohms, the approximate resistance of the relay coil. **The ohmmeter should be on the 2k-3k-4k ohmmeter range depending on which brand DMM is used.**

Vehicle Electronics Hands-On Troubleshooting Training Program
VEEJER ENTERPRISES 3701 Lariat Lane, Garland, Texas 75042-5419
Phone: 972-276-9642   Fax: 972-276-8122   Email: sales@veejer.com   Web Site: www.veejer.com

Step 2: Reverse Test Leads
Reverse the test leads as shown in Figure 5H-067A and write down the resistance reading in the window of the DMM in Figure 5H-067A.

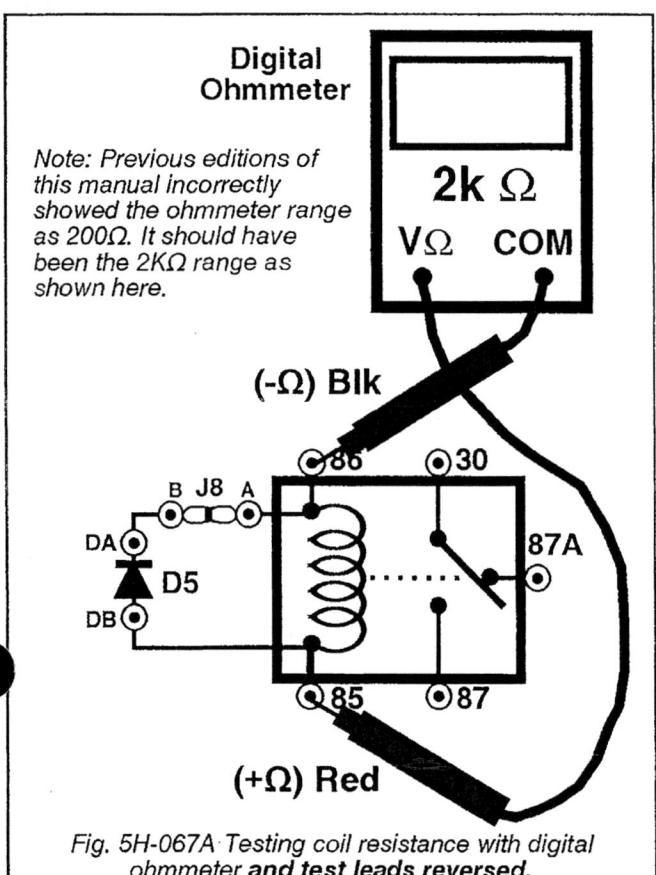

Fig. 5H-067A Testing coil resistance with digital ohmmeter and test leads reversed.

Notice the reading in Step 2 is the same as obtained in Step 1. A digital ohmmeter measures relay coil resistance either way it is connected across the relay coil whether a spike suppression diode is present or not.

A DMM's digital ohmmeter cannot "see" the spike suppression diode in Step 2 because its test voltage is less than the required 0.7V level needed to forward bias the diode to turn it ON.

> **We can conclude that a digital ohmmeter cannot be used to test a spike suppression diode across a solenoid or relay coil**

THIS IS A BIG DEAL!
This is a major digital ohmmeter issue to understand because it represents benefits as well as limitations of different ohmmeters testing diodes. As we have just seen an analog ohmmeter CAN check a spike suppression diode connected across a relay coil but a digital ohmmeter CANNOT.

Yet, a digital ohmmeter is more accurate in indicating coil resistance than an analog ohmmeter. Both type ohmmeters are necessary for complete testing of solenoid and relay circuits when a spike suppression diode is connected in parallel with the solenoid or relay coil and the diode cannot (should not) be disconnected.

Testing a Spike Suppression Diode with a DMM's "Diode Test"
THIS IS A BIG DEAL!
The Diode Test feature of a DMM is designed to test a solid-state diode by measuring the Vd (voltage drop) created across the diode during the Diode Test. DMM electron current produces a Vd in millivolts (mV) across the diode which is the reading displayed in the DMM readout.

Black epoxy coated silicon diodes (used for polarity circuit protection or spike voltage suppression) normally read in the range of a high of 0.600 (600 mV) to a low of 0.400 (400 mV).

Germanium diodes, glass coated diodes, (used in digital circuits) normally read in the range 0.300 (300 mV) to a low of 0.200 (mV) but they are not used for spike voltage suppression.

If a diode reads higher it indicates the diode is going bad because it cannot pass a normal amount of electron current.

If a diode reads lower it indicates the diode is going bad because it passes more than a normal amount of electron current.

If testing a diode for the first time and the Diode Test reading is higher or lower than expected it could be that the diode is a special purpose diode and it is normal to read higher or lower. ALWAYS CHECK A KNOWN GOOD SIMILAR DIODE TO BE SURE OF THE CORRECT READING.

The Diode Test feature of a DMM is needed because a DMM's digital ohmmeter, as we have just seen, is **unable** to test a solid-state diode when disconnected from the circuit or the diode is connected across a solenoid or relay coil for spike suppression.

A DMM ohmmeter won't test a diode if the diode is disconnected at both ends from the circuit. This is due to a DMM ohmmeter having very low ohmmeter test voltage in the range of 0.05V – 0.10V during the diode resistance test. This is NOT sufficient test voltage to forward bias and turn ON a diode.

The DMM's Diode Test on the other hand, is designed to provide enough test voltage to forward bias a diode **as long as the diode is disconnected at one end from the circuit.**

BUT – The Diode Test feature of a DMM cannot test a diode connected across a solenoid or coil. The coil resistance affects the Diode Test reading.

Copyright © 2015 VEEJER ENTERPRISES, Garland, Texas - All Rights Reserved   Student Workbook H-WB115

Vehicle Electronics Hands-On Troubleshooting Training Program

VEEJER ENTERPRISES 3701 Lariat Lane, Garland, Texas 75042-5419
Phone: 972-276-9642 Fax: 972-276-8122 Email: sales@veejer.com Web Site: www.veejer.com

Follow the DMM set up below in Figure 5H-068 to see the shortcomings of the Diode Test while testing a diode connected across a relay coil.
- Select the Diode Test function.
- Connect DMM test leads to the relay coil with diode D5 connected to the relay coil (zero ohm resistor in J8).

The Red test lead is designated as +DT Red (Diode Test positive side) and the Black test lead is designated as -DT Black (Diode Test negative side).
- Connect +DT to Pin 86 and -DT to Pin 85.

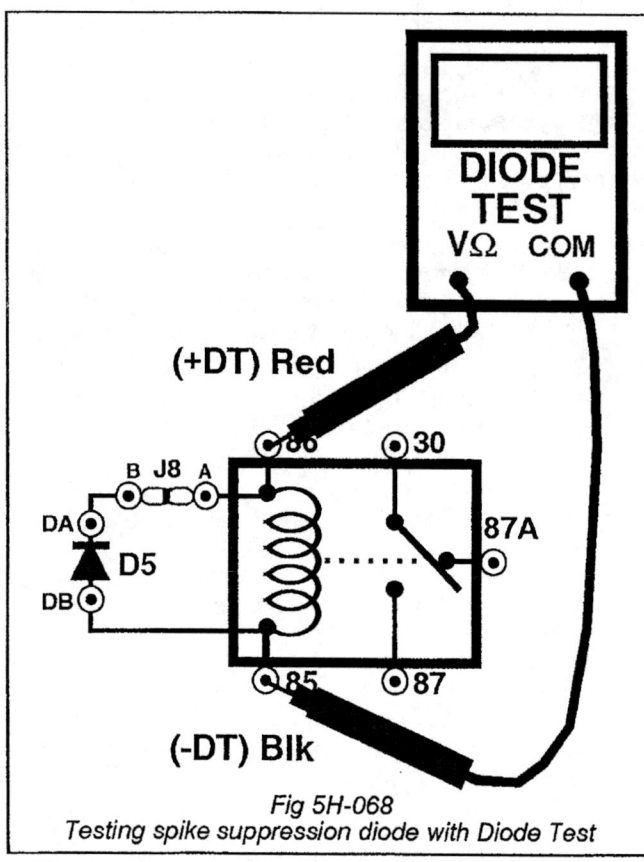

Fig 5H-068
Testing spike suppression diode with Diode Test

The reading obtained depends on the make and model DMM used since all Diode Test features vary slightly in test voltage between make and model DMM. The following readings in volts were obtained with different three DMM Diode Tests.

Fluke 87 reading is 0.322
Fluke 27 reading is .411
Knight 225B reading is .361

The Diode Test feature indicates a voltage drop in volts developed across the relay coil.

The Diode Test reading is not in ohms as with analog or digital ohmmeters. A Diode Test reading of 0.322 is actually a voltage drop reading of 0.322 volts

Notice that 1 mV of Diode Test voltage is approximately equal to 1 ohm of resistance. The relay coil is determined to be about 400 ohms with a digital ohmmeter. The Diode Test obtained with various DMMs varied between .323 and .411 depending on the DMM. That's approximately 1.0 mV for each ohm of coil resistance.

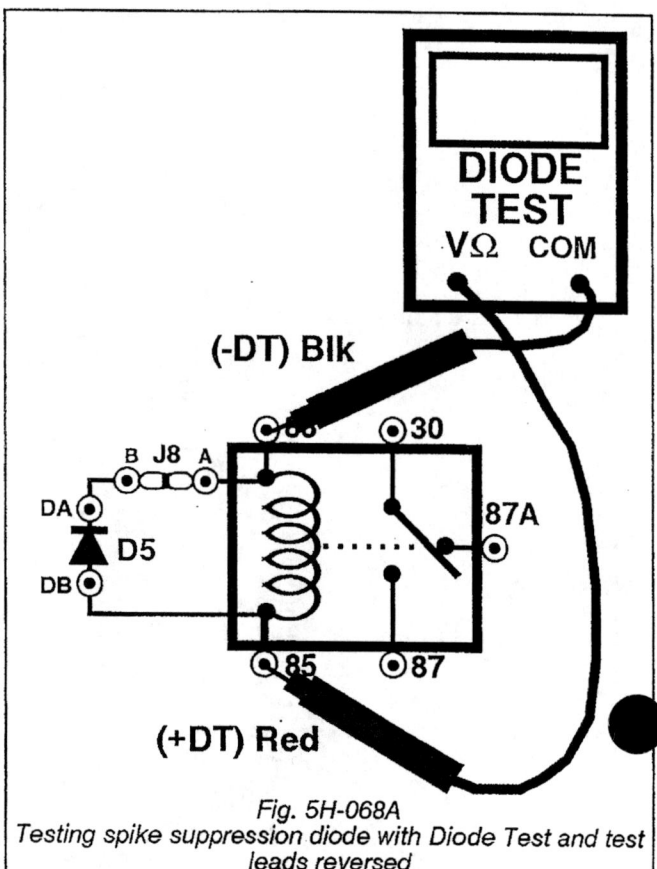

Fig. 5H-068A
Testing spike suppression diode with Diode Test and test leads reversed

Continue on. Just a little bit more to understand the Diode Test benefits and limitations. Notice what happens when the Diode Test's test leads are reversed across the relay as in Figure 5H-068A. **The Diode Test reading is the same in both steps.**

This indicates the Diode Test feature is unable to "see" the diode connected across the coil because the test voltage placed at the probe tips when connected across the relay coil is too low to forward bias the diode. The reading obtained is a Vd (voltage drop) reading developed across the relay coil. The diode is electrically not being tested even though the DMM is set to "Diode Test." **The truth is the Diode Test can only test a diode when the diode is disconnected at least at one end from the relay coil.**

Leave the DMM on Diode Test and the test leads connected across the relay coil and continue exploring the limitations of the Diode Test.

Remove the 0ΩR (zero ohm resistor) from J8 as shown in Figure 5H-068B. Notice the Diode Test reading does not change. This proves the Diode Test feature cannot test a diode when the diode connected or disconnected across a solenoid or relay coil.

Copyright © 2015 VEEJER ENTERPRISES, Garland, Texas - All Rights Reserved Student Workbook H-WB115

Vehicle Electronics Hands-On Troubleshooting Training Program

VEEJER ENTERPRISES 3701 Lariat Lane, Garland, Texas 75042-5419
Phone: 972-276-9642   Fax: 972-276-8122   Email: sales@veejer.com   Web Site: www.veejer.com

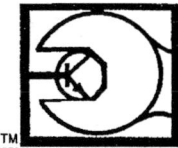

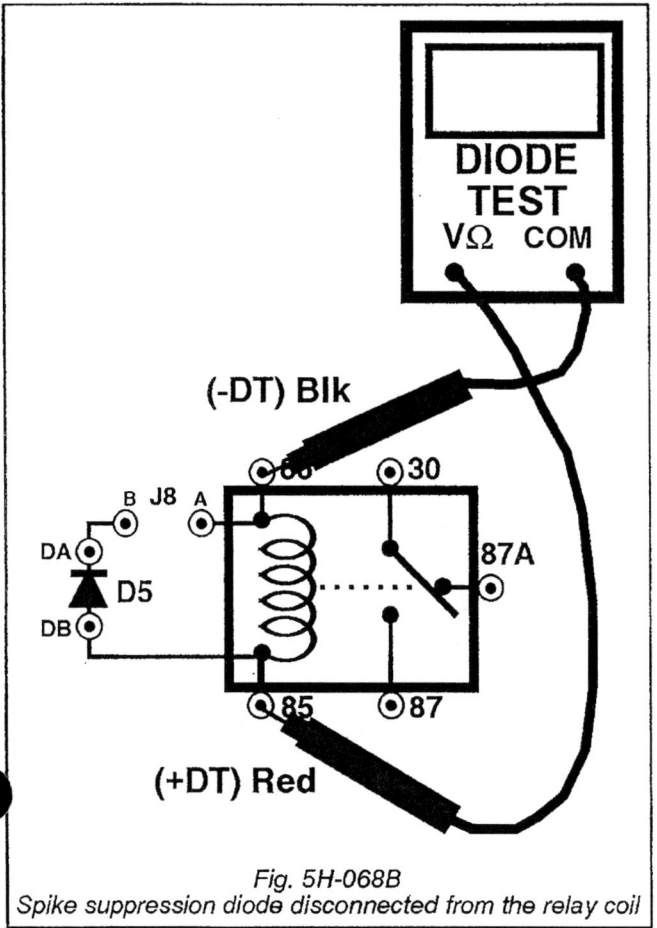

Fig. 5H-068B
Spike suppression diode disconnected from the relay coil

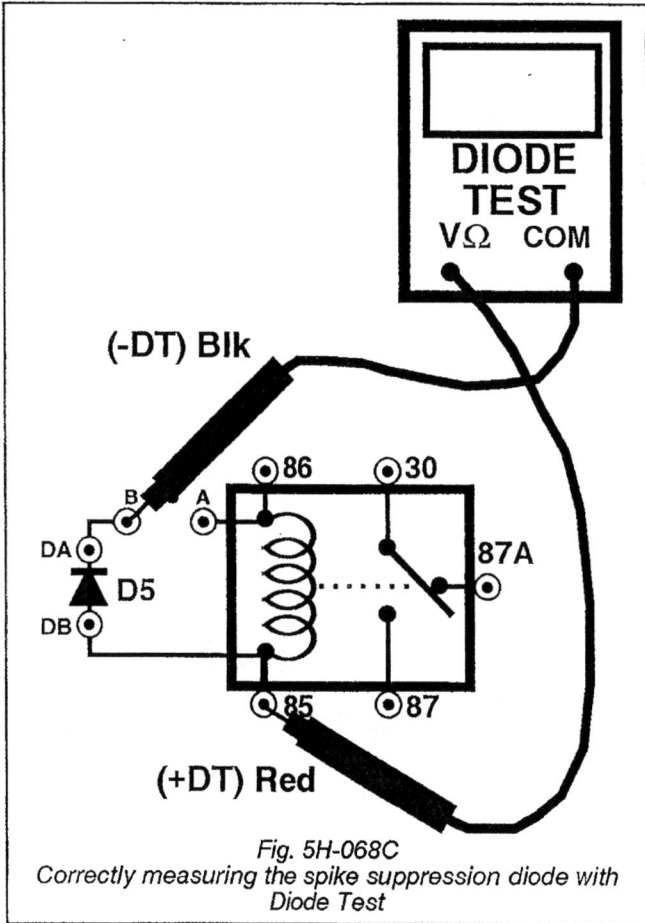

Fig. 5H-068C
Correctly measuring the spike suppression diode with Diode Test

Following what is shown in Figure 5H-068C, leave the 0ΩR out of J8 and move the **-DT Black** test lead from Pin 86 to Pin B of J8 or Test Pin "DA". Leave the **+DT Red** test lead at Pin 85.

The change to the -DT test lead is shown in Figure 5H-068C.

> **NOTE: When checking diode D5 always use the two test points marked "DA" and "DB" as the two terminals of the diode.** On some relay boards diode D5 is mounted on the top side in full view. On newer relay boards the diode has been mounted on the bottom side out of view.

DO NOT test the diode by placing test lead probe tips directly on the physical diode itself. When circuit problems are inserted to simulate a bad diode, test points DA and DB must be used to see the problem. Diode failures are simulated between test points DA and DB.

With the 0ΩR in J8 removed the DMM's Diode Test is able to "see" the diode apart from the relay coil and indicate an official "diode test" reading of 0.540-0.575 for a good diode depending on DMM Diode Test make and model.

Learning DMM & Analog Ohmmeter Readings

Before using a DMM for the first time, check a good diode disconnected from a circuit to determine the Diode Test reading for a good diode. As mentioned earlier, DMMs have slightly different readings for a good diode. The only way to know what the indication is for a good diode with your DMM is to check a good diode.

The same thing is true about using an analog ohmmeter. Check a known good diode disconnected from a circuit to learn the analog ohmmeter readings for a good diode. Try both the Rx1 and Rx10 ranges to get familiar with the readings.

> Lesson 44 in "*The*" Course™ discusses troubleshooting diodes with an analog ohmmeter and a DMM's Diode Test.

Next is a review of Vd (voltage drop) measurement techniques as applied to a relay circuit.

Vehicle Electronics Hands-On Troubleshooting Training Program

VEEJER ENTERPRISES 3701 Lariat Lane, Garland, Texas 75042-5419
Phone: 972-276-9642 Fax: 972-276-8122 Email: sales@veejer.com Web Site: www.veejer.com

Measure Vd_{vs} of Voltage Side of Relay Primary Circuit

If the lamp does not turn ON, scan the top and bottom of the PCBs to make sure there is no circuit fault present. Scanning the bottom of the circuit boards is explained in the Instructor Guide.

Turn ON S1 (toggle UP). Make sure S3 and S4 are ON (slides UP). Current must be flowing when measuring Vd_{vs}. (The term Vd_{vs} is used for an abbreviation of the term "voltage drop of the voltage side" of a circuit.)

> **Lesson 16** discusses checking the Vd of the voltage side of a circuit, Vd_{vs}.
> **Lesson 40** discusses Vd_{vs} measurements in relay circuits.

If the relay "CLICKS" current is flowing in the relay primary circuit. If the relay does NOT "CLICK" current is not flowing and Vd_{vs} cannot be measured.

Place the DMM on the 20-30-40 volt range (readout says **0.00** when not measuring a voltage) and connect the test leads as shown in Figure 5H-069.

With the relay energized (lamp ON), perform the Vd_{vs} as shown. Carefully follow the placement of the test leads.

(1) Record the actual reading obtained. _____ V

(2) Write down the numbers with decimal point in the DMM in Figure 5H-069

A reading of about 0.80–0.89 volt is normal for Vd_{vs} if the circuit is functioning correctly and B+ from the power supply is in the normal range of 13.8 volts.

Vd_{vs} On A Vehicle Relay Circuit

In any vehicle relay circuit, the Vd_{vs} of the primary relay circuit is good if the Vd_{vs} reading is approximately **0.50V**. In an actual vehicle circuit the *lower* the Vd_{vs} reading is the better the relay primary circuit is. A reading of a few tenths of a volt higher may be normal in certain circuits and that should be confirmed by checking known good similar circuits on similar vehicles.

If the Vd_{vs} reading is higher than 0.50V when 0.50V or less is known to be a good reading it means there is excessive resistance developing on the voltage side due to corrosion in the wiring and connections or a connector that is not making good contact. Check wiring and connections while watching the Vd_{vs} reading. When the wire or connector with a problem is moved the reading will fluctuate indicating where the problem is located.

Don't overlook a possibly defective ignition switch. Tap on the vehicle's ignition switch while watching the Vd_{vs} reading. The Vd_{vs} reading will fluctuate while **gently tapping** on a defective ignition switch.

The reason that Vd_{vs} is higher than 0.50V in the relay circuit is due to the Vd of D1 which is about 0.7V by itself. Check it to see the Vd across the diode. Place both DMM test leads across the diode terminals. Expect a reading of 0.72-7.9 depending on the diode.

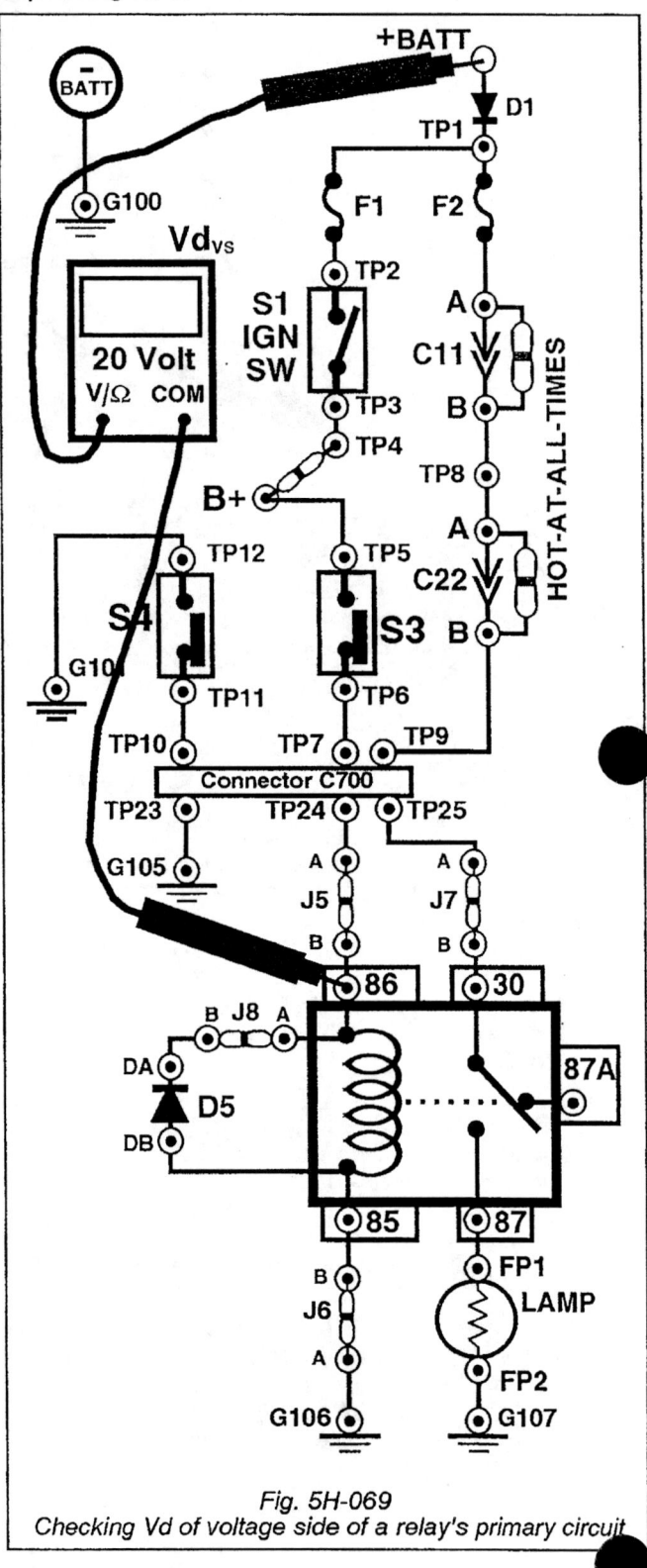

Fig. 5H-069
Checking Vd of voltage side of a relay's primary circuit

Copyright © 2015 VEEJER ENTERPRISES, Garland, Texas - All Rights Reserved   **Student Workbook H-WB115**

Vehicle Electronics Hands-On Troubleshooting Training Program

VEEJER ENTERPRISES 3701 Lariat Lane, Garland, Texas 75042-5419
Phone: 972-276-9642   Fax: 972-276-8122   Email: sales@veejer.com   Web Site: www.veejer.com

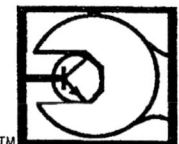

Measure Vd_{vs} of Voltage Side of Relay Secondary Circuit

Turn ON S1 (toggled UP). Make sure S3 and S4 are ON (slides UP). Current must be flowing when measuring Vd_{vs}. If the relay "CLICKS" and the lamp turns ON, current is flowing in the secondary circuit. If the relay does NOT "CLICK" and the lamp is OFF, current is not flowing and Vd_{vs} in the relay secondary circuit cannot be measured.

Place the DMM on the 20-30-40 volt range (readout says **0.00** when not measuring a voltage) and connect the test leads as shown in Figure 5H-070.

Move the DMM Black test lead from Pin 86 on the relay coil to Pin 1 on the Lamp, the load on the relay secondary side of the circuit.

(1) Record the actual reading obtained. _____ V

(2) Write down the numbers with decimal point in the DMM in Figure 5H-070.

A reading of about 0.70–0.89 volt is normal for Vd_{vs} on the relay secondary side.

Vd_{vs} Primary Circuit vs. Vd_{vs} Secondary Circuit

It may be the Vd_{vs} reading on the relay secondary circuit is slightly higher than the Vd_{vs} reading on the relay primary circuit. This is due to a slightly higher current flowing in the relay secondary circuit than in the relay primary circuit on the relay circuit board H-PCB05 and the different components involved in each side of the relay circuit.

The relay primary circuit has resistance from the contacts of the Ignition Switch S1 and slide switch, S3. The relay coil has a resistance of 400 ohms. All this resistance affects the current and the Vd_{vs} of the relay primary circuit.

(3) Measure the current in the relay primary circuit. Remove Fuse F1 and connect a digital ammeter between the fuse terminals.
_____ Amps; converted to mA _____ .

The relay secondary side has a different load, the lamp, which is a lower resistance than coil resistance.

(4) Measure the current in the relay secondary circuit. Remove Fuse F2 and connect a digital ammeter between the fuse terminals.
_____ Amps; converted to mA _____ .

The relay secondary circuit is always a higher current than the relay primary current in actual automotive circuits because relay contacts carry more load current than the relay coil requires.

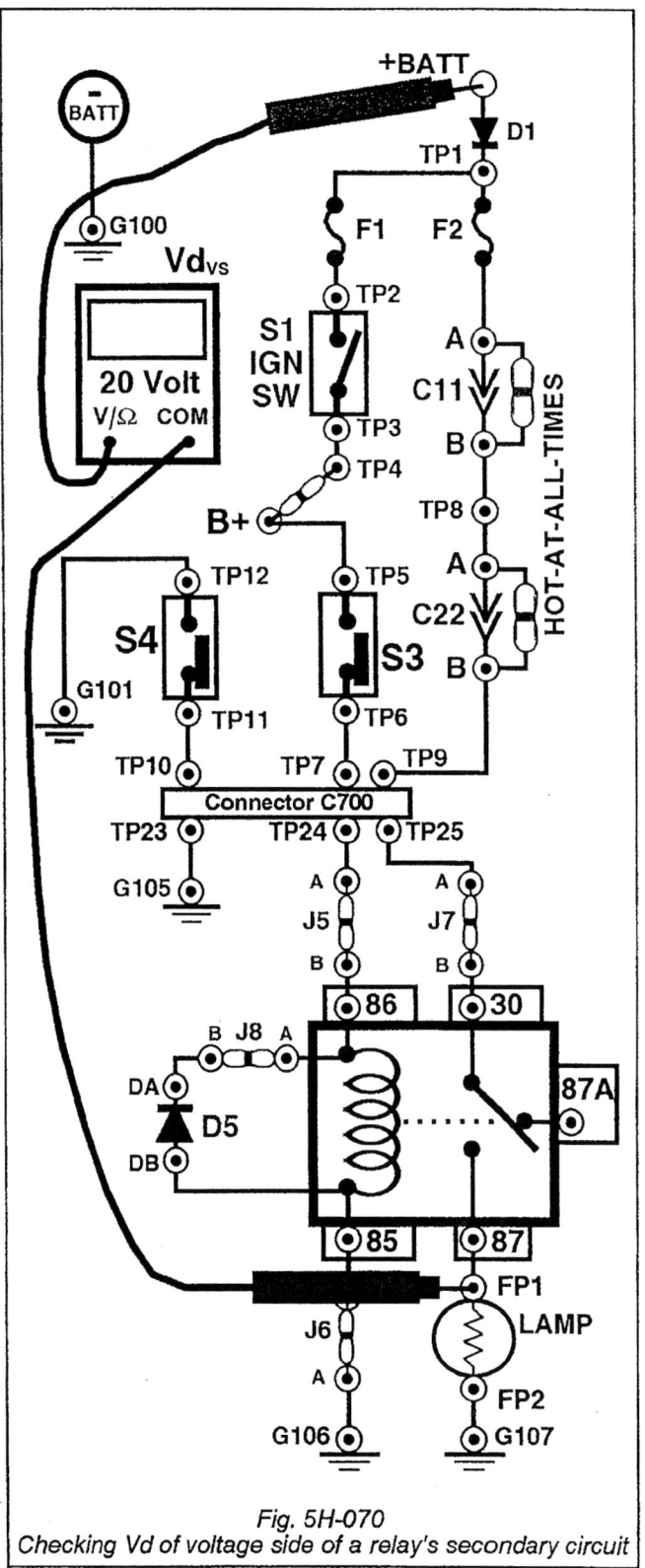

Fig. 5H-070
Checking Vd of voltage side of a relay's secondary circuit

Copyright © 2015 VEEJER ENTERPRISES, Garland, Texas - All Rights Reserved   Student Workbook H-WB115   Page 24

Vehicle Electronics Hands-On Troubleshooting Training Program

VEEJER ENTERPRISES 3701 Lariat Lane, Garland, Texas 75042-5419
Phone: 972-276-9642 Fax: 972-276-8122 Email: sales@veejer.com Web Site: www.veejer.com

Measure Vd_{GS} of Ground Side of Relay Primary Circuit

The Vd of the ground side of the relay's primary circuit is shown in Figure 5H-071. The term used in *"The" Course* for the voltage drop of the ground side is Vd_{GS}. Notice **redundant ground connections** are added to the schematic between G106/G107 & G105. Ground G105 connects to G101 through C700 and S4. Another redundant ground connects G101 and G100. Schematic diagrams often do not show these redundant grounds so it may not be know if they are present in the circuit to cause Vd_{GS} problems on the ground side. All redundant grounds are verified good if Vd_{GS} is 0.10V or less.

> **Lesson 16** discusses checking the Vd of the ground side of a circuit, Vd_{GS}.
> **Lesson 40** discusses Vd_{GS} in relay circuits.

Current must be flowing when measuring Vd_{GS}. If the lamp is ON current is flowing. If the lamp is OFF current is not flowing and this measurement cannot be done. Scan the top of the PCBs if the relay is not energized. Turn ON S1. Make sure S3 and S4 are ON (slides both UP). Check the fuses and the lamp. Make sure the wire jumper from the B+ terminal is connected to TP4 and making good contact. Verify a 0ΩR is in J5, J6 & J7 on the Relay Board.

Place the DMM on the 20-30-40 volt range and connect the test leads as shown in Figure 5H-071.

(1) Record the actual reading obtained. _____ V

(2) Write down the numbers with decimal point in the DMM shown in Figure 5H-071.

A reading of about **0.10** volt is normal for Vd_{GS} if the relay ground circuit is in good condition. The *lower* Vd_{GS} is in a relay primary circuit the better. Normally, on a vehicle, Vd_{GS} of most relay circuits connected directly to ground are considered good if the Vd_{GS} is no more 0.10V. The reason that Vd_{GS} is lower than 0.10V in the PCBs is due to the short distance of the ground circuit.

Try this.
Set the DMM to read mV (millivolts). On the mV range the DMM readout indicates **.000** when not measuring a voltage. Measure Vd_{GS} again using the mV range. The reading may show, as an example, .050 for 50 mVs.

High Vd_{GS}

If the Vd_{GS} reading is higher than 0.1V in a relay circuit with a direct connection to ground it may not prevent the relay from energizing until the voltage reaches several volts. But more than 0.1V means there is resistance developing on the ground side due to corrosion in the wiring and connections or possibly a ground jumper connection is not making good contact. The Vd_{GS} will increase over time if not repaired and eventually the relay will cease to energize.

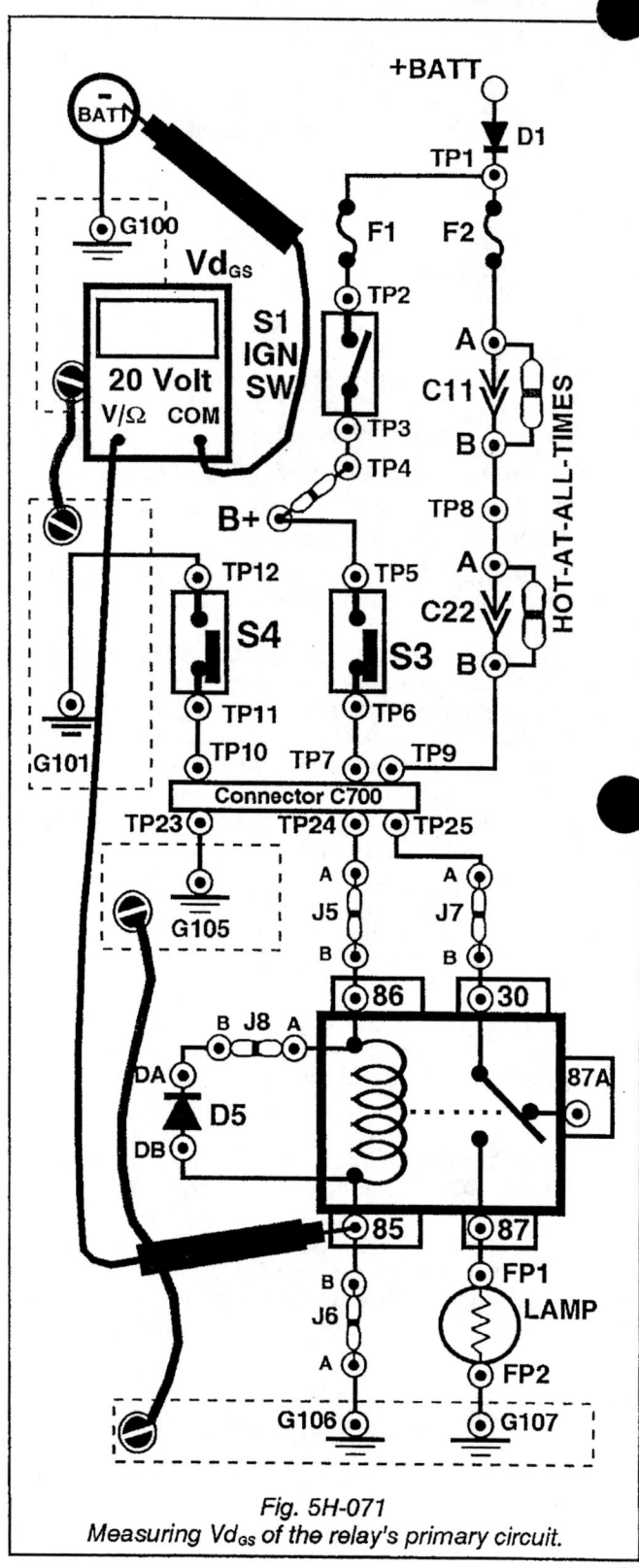

Fig. 5H-071
Measuring Vd_{GS} of the relay's primary circuit.

Vehicle Electronics Hands-On Troubleshooting Training Program

VEEJER ENTERPRISES 3701 Lariat Lane, Garland, Texas 75042-5419
Phone: 972-276-9642   Fax: 972-276-8122   Email: sales@veejer.com   Web Site: www.veejer.com

Measure Vd_{GS} of Ground Side of Relay Secondary Circuit

The Vd of the ground side of the relay secondary circuit is shown in Figure 5H-072. Notice the **redundant ground connections** and how they affect the load of the lamp. All redundant grounds for the relay secondary circuit load are verified to be good if Vd_{GS} is 0.10V or less.

> **Lesson 16** discusses checking the Vd of the ground side of a circuit, Vd_{GS}.
> **Lesson 40** discusses Vd_{GS} in relay circuits.

Current must be flowing when measuring Vd_{GS}. If the lamp is ON current is flowing. If the lamp is OFF current is not flowing and this measurement cannot be done. Scan the top of the PCBs if the relay is not energized.

Follow this carefully.

Place the DMM on the 20-30-40 volt range and connect the test leads as shown in Figure 5H-072.

(1) Record the actual reading obtained. _____ V

(2) Write down the numbers with decimal point in the DMM shown in Figure 5H-072.

A reading of about **0.10** volt is normal for Vd_{GS} if the relay load's ground circuit is in good condition. The *lower* Vd_{GS} is in a relay secondary circuit the better. Normally, on a vehicle, Vd_{GS} of most relay secondary loads connected directly to ground are considered good if the Vd_{GS} is no more 0.10V. The reason that Vd_{GS} is lower than 0.10V in the PCBs is due to the short distance of the ground circuit.

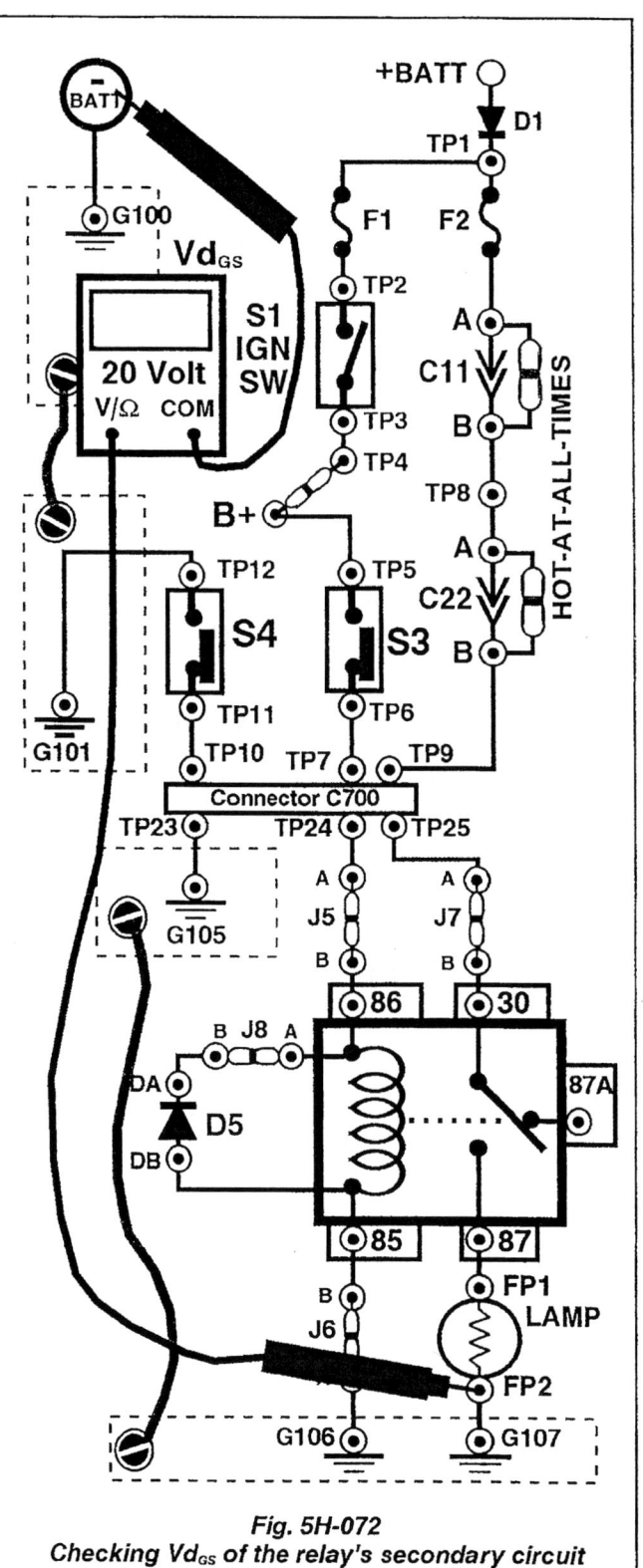

Fig. 5H-072
Checking Vd_{GS} of the relay's secondary circuit

Vehicle Electronics Hands-On Troubleshooting Training Program

VEEJER ENTERPRISES 3701 Lariat Lane, Garland, Texas 75042-5419
Phone: 972-276-9642 Fax: 972-276-8122 Email: sales@veejer.com Web Site: www.veejer.com

Measure Vd$_{LOAD}$ of Relay Primary Circuit

A third Vd check is the Vd of the load as shown in Figure 5H-073. The load in the relay's primary circuit is the relay coil. The term used in *"The"* **Course** for the voltage drop of the load is **Vd$_{LOAD}$**.

> **Lesson 24** covers checking Vd$_{LOAD}$.
> **Lesson 40** covers checking Vd$_{LOAD}$ in relay circuits.

Current must be flowing when measuring **Vd$_{LOAD}$**. If the relay *"CLICKS"* the relay primary circuit (the coil) is energized and current is flowing in the relay primary circuit and Vd$_{LOAD}$ can be performed.

Place the DMM on the 20-30-40 volt range (readout says **0.00**) and connect the test leads as shown in Figure 5H-073.

(1) Record the actual reading obtained. _____ V

(2) Write down the numbers with decimal point in the DMM shown in Figure 5H-073.

Interpreting the Vd$_{LOAD}$ Reading

A reading of close to B+ (13.00 volts present at TP1) is normal for **Vd$_{LOAD}$** of the relay coil. The *higher* the **Vd$_{LOAD}$** reading the better. The closer Vd$_{LOAD}$ is to B+ the more efficient the relay operation and the quicker the relay energizes.

Vd$_{LOAD}$ Low

If **Vd$_{LOAD}$** is too low there are three factors to consider.
(1) B+, the charging voltage produced by the vehicle's generator (alternator) when the engine is running is lower than normal.
(2) **Vd$_{VS}$** is too high due to excess resistance on the voltage side of the circuit.
(3) **Vd$_{GS}$** is too high due to resistance on the ground side of the circuit.

Vd$_{LOAD}$ High

However, if **Vd$_{LOAD}$** is too high there should be concern that the vehicle's charging system voltage is too high. Vd$_{LOAD}$ should never be more than the normal charging voltage produced by the vehicle when considering, ambient temperature, amount of electrical load on the generator and make and model of the vehicle.

For more information on this topic refer to **Lessons 21** and **Lesson 22** from *"The"* Course. They discuss charging system operation, charging system characteristics and correct procedures for testing a vehicle's charging system.

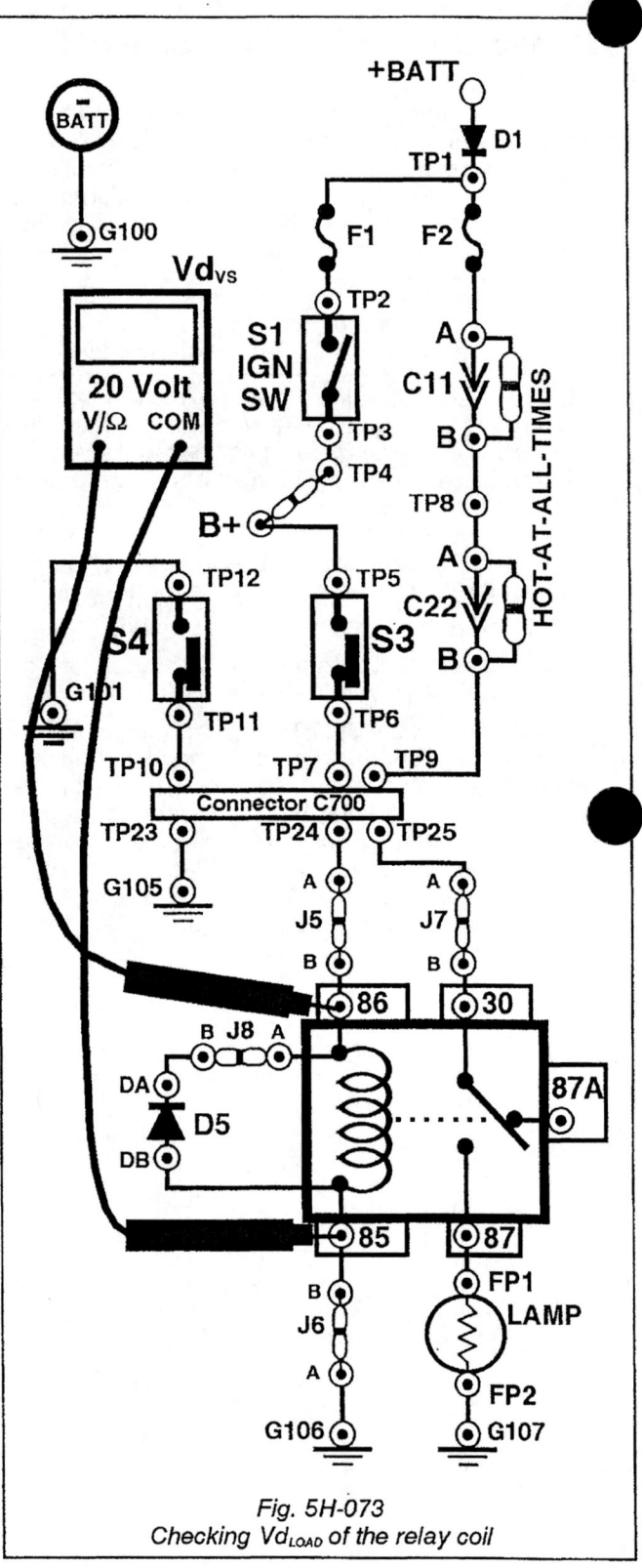

Fig. 5H-073
Checking Vd$_{LOAD}$ of the relay coil

Copyright © 2015 VEEJER ENTERPRISES, Garland, Texas - All Rights Reserved **Student Workbook H-WB115**

Vehicle Electronics Hands-On Troubleshooting Training Program

Measure Vd_{LOAD} of Relay Secondary Circuit

There is also a Vd_{LOAD} on the relay's secondary circuit, the load connected to the relay contacts. This is the device powered up when the relay contacts CLOSE. In the example of the relay circuit board the load is the lamp. Figure 5H-074 illustrates checking the voltage drop of the lamp.

> **Lesson 24** covers checking Vd_{LOAD}.
> **Lesson 40** covers checking Vd_{LOAD} in relay circuits.

Current must be flowing when measuring Vd_{LOAD}. If the lamp is ON current is flowing in the relay secondary circuit and a Vd can be performed.

Place the DMM on the 20-30-40 volt range (readout says **0.00**) and connect the test leads as shown in Figure 5H-074.

(1) Record the actual reading obtained. _____ V

(2) Write down the numbers with decimal point in the DMM shown in Figure 5H-073.

A reading of close to B+ (13.00 volts at TP1) is normal for Vd_{LOAD} of the relay secondary load. The *higher* Vd_{LOAD} the better. The closer Vd_{LOAD} is to B+ the more efficient the load operates.

If the relay is controlling a DC motor through the relay contacts the motor runs at normal rpm provided there is no problem with the motor circuit. If the load is a solenoid the solenoid moves the pintle or armature the proper distance.

A circuit load works best the closer Vd_{LOAD} is to B+.

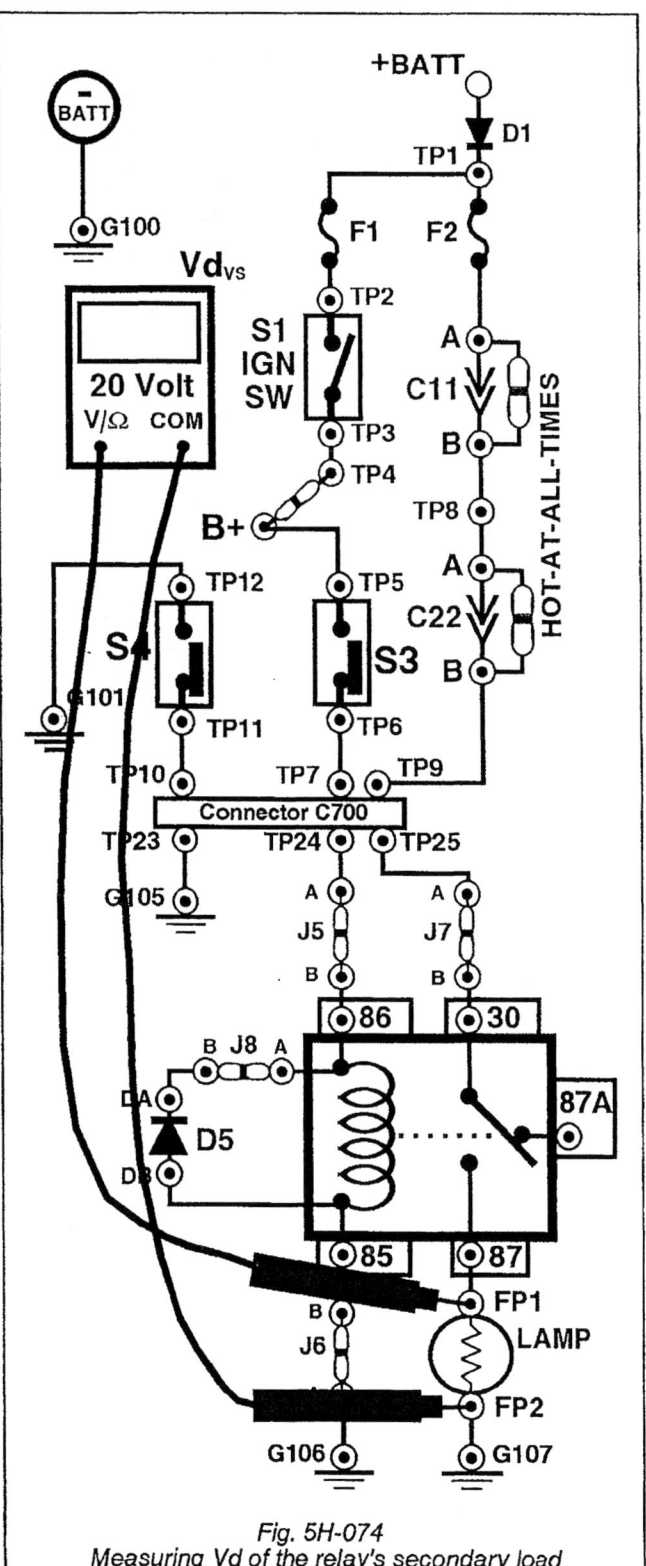

Fig. 5H-074
Measuring Vd of the relay's secondary load

Vehicle Electronics Hands-On Troubleshooting Training Program

VEEJER ENTERPRISES 3701 Lariat Lane, Garland, Texas 75042-5419
Phone: 972-276-9642   Fax: 972-276-8122   Email: sales@veejer.com   Web Site: www.veejer.com

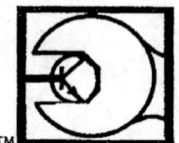

Tracing B+ In Relay Primary Circuit

When measuring a circuit voltage (abbr. "Vc") it *always means* the DMM is understood to be grounded at the battery negative (-BATT). On the vehicle, Vc measurement means the DMM is grounded to the battery negative terminal. On the PCBs the DMM is grounded to the negative or black terminal post. Since the BLACK DMM test lead is understood to be connected to the negative battery terminal and is not shown in Figure 5H-075 to avoid confusion created with the black test lead running across the illustration to the negative terminal.

Figure 5H-075 shows the placement of the RED DMM test lead for each Vc measurement to be made on the voltage side of the relay primary circuit.

> **Lesson 11** covers voltage side of the circuit.
> **Lesson 23** discusses Vc measurements.

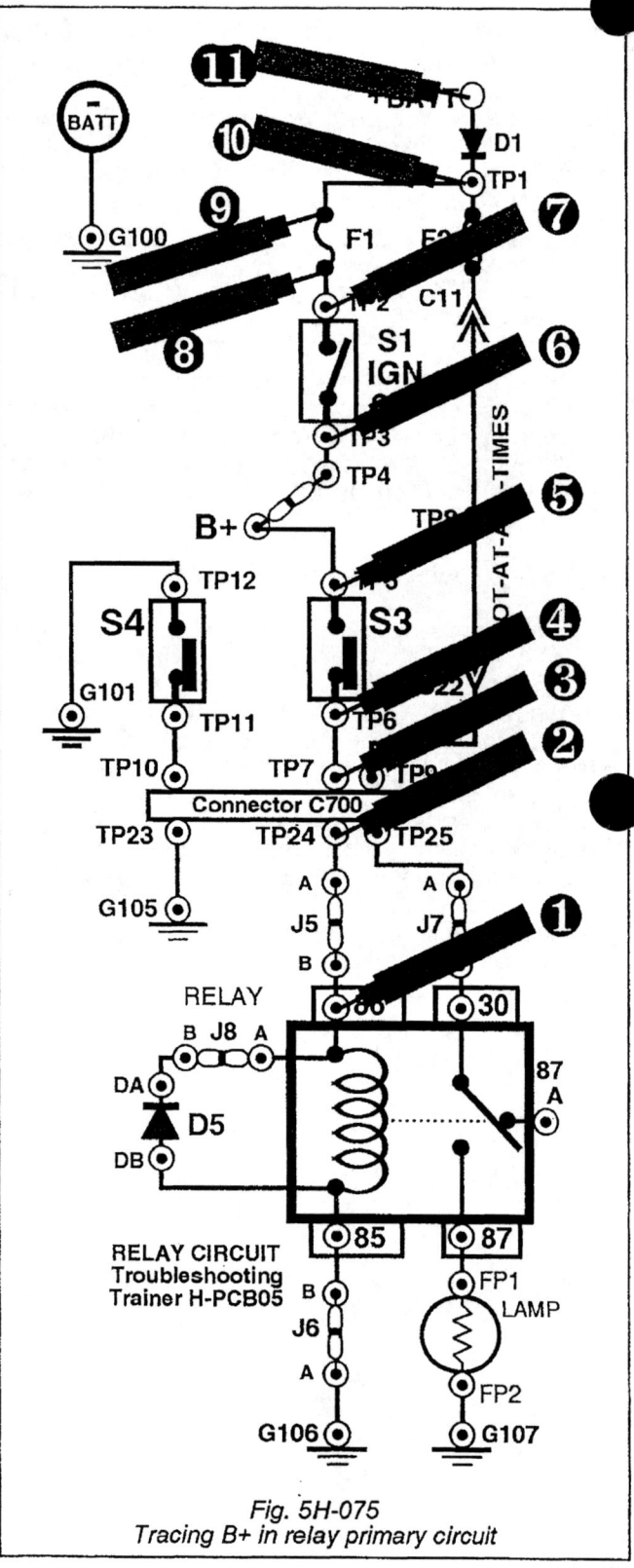

DO THIS:

- Verify a 0ΩR connects the B+ Terminal with TP4.
- Scan the top and bottom of the PCBs to make sure the PCBs have no faults.
- Connect the power supply to the terminals at the top of the Power Board.
- Place S3 and S4 in the ON position (slides-UP).
- Turn S1 ON (toggle UP).
- Ground DMM Black test lead to the black (negative) terminal post, "B-" or 0.00V.
- With the lamp ON, measure the Vc (circuit voltage) at each point in the circuit as shown in Figure 5H-075 beginning at Pin 86 and record readings below.

(1) _____ V (Pin 86)
(2) _____ V (TP24)
(3) _____ V (TP7)
(4) _____ V (TP6)
(5) _____ V (TP5)
(6) _____ V (TP3)
(7) _____ V (TP2)
(8) _____ V (Fuse "cold side")
(9) _____ V (Fuse B+ side)
(10) _____ V (TP1)
(11) _____ V (+BATT Terminal)

Notice the **Vc readings increase** on the voltage side as the measurement point moves up from Pin 86 towards the positive terminal of the voltage source (+BATT). The Test lead at (11) is equal to the B+ of the power supply, H-PS01.

Fig. 5H-075
Tracing B+ in relay primary circuit

Vehicle Electronics Hands-On Troubleshooting Training Program

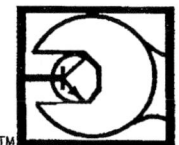

Tracing B+ In Relay Secondary Circuit

The same principles in tracing B+ in a relay's secondary circuit are used: however, the test points follow a different path. The following exercise tracing B+ in the relay's secondary circuit point these out with some notes in italics to highlight points to remember.

DO THIS:

- Verify a 0ΩR connects the B+ Terminal with TP4.
- Scan the top and bottom of the PCBs to make sure the PCBs have no faults.
- Connect the power supply to the terminals at the top of the Power Board.
- Place S3 and S4 in the ON position (slides-UP).
- Turn S1 ON (toggle UP).
- Ground DMM Black test lead to the black (negative) terminal post, "B-" or 0.00V.
- With the lamp ON, measure the Vc (circuit voltage) at each point in the circuit as shown in Figure 5H-076 beginning at Pin 30 and record readings below.

(1) _____ V (FP1- B+ to load)

(2) _____ V (Pin 87)

(3) _____ V (Pin 30)

The difference in voltage between (2) Pin 87 and (3) Pin 30 is the Vd of the relay contacts.

(4) _____ V (TP25)

(5) _____ V (TP9)

(6) _____ V (TP8)

The difference in voltage between (5) TP9 and (6) TP8 is the Vd of Connector C22.

(7) _____ V (F2 "cold-side")

The difference in voltage between (6) TP8 and (7) F2 "cold side" in the Vd of Connector C11.

(8) _____ V (F2 B+ side)

(9) _____ V (TP1)

(10) _____ V (TP1 +BATT Terminal)

The difference between (9) TP1 and (10) the +BATT terminal is the Vd of the polarity diode.

Notice again the **Vc readings increase** on the voltage side as the measurement point moves farther away from load FP1 and closer to the positive terminal of the voltage source (+BATT). Test lead (10) is equal to the B+ of the power supply.

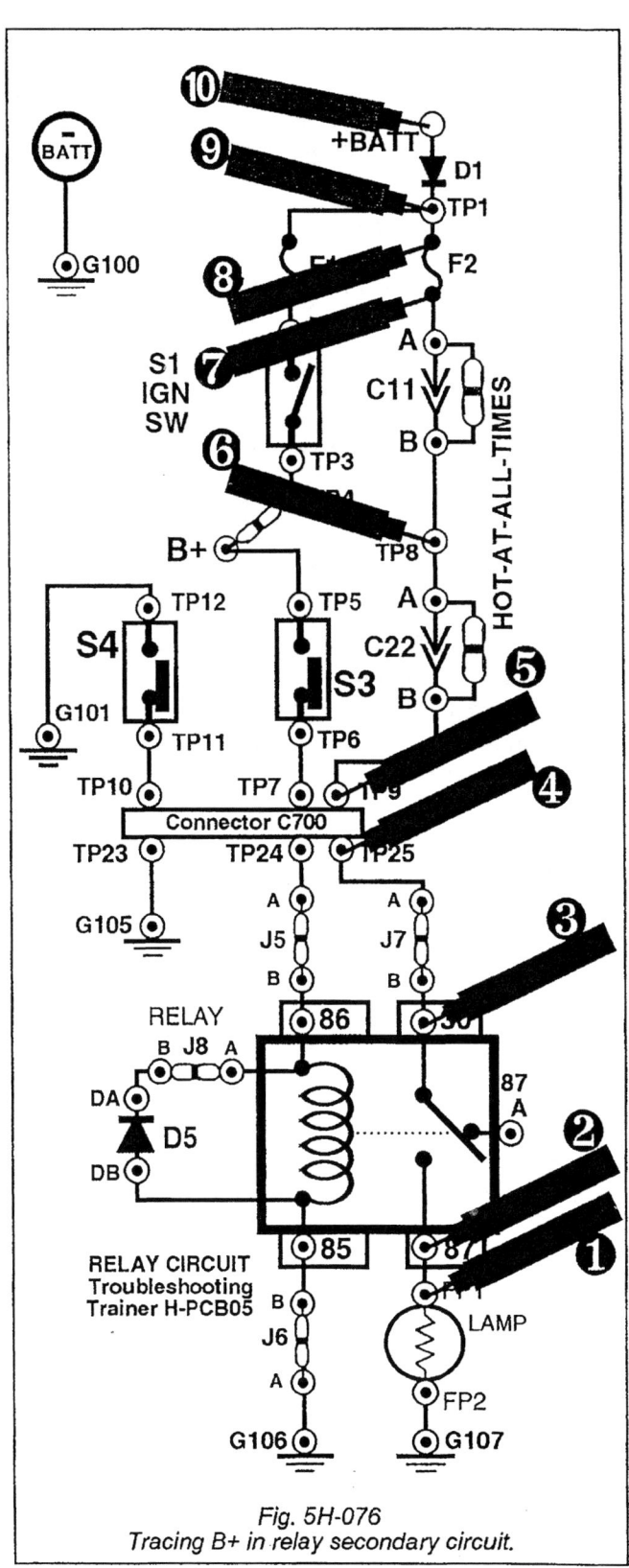

Fig. 5H-076
Tracing B+ in relay secondary circuit.

Vehicle Electronics Hands-On Troubleshooting Training Program

VEEJER ENTERPRISES 3701 Lariat Lane, Garland, Texas 75042-5419
Phone: 972-276-9642   Fax: 972-276-8122   Email: sales@veejer.com   Web Site: www.veejer.com

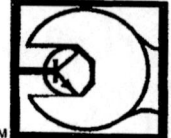

Tracing B- In Relay Primary Circuit

There are two terms, "B+" and especially "B-" that are used in exercise explanations in this hands-on troubleshooting training program.

Most are familiar with the term "B+" which refers to the positive terminal of the battery or the highest positive voltage supply in a circuit. The value of B+ in a vehicle is equivalent to the charging voltage produced by the vehicle's generator when the engine is running or battery voltage if the engine is not running. B+ can also refer to the voltage side of a circuit, or it can be expressed as the B+ side.

The term "B-" (say B minus) resides at the negative terminal of the battery, the -BATT (black) terminal post on the Power Board. **The voltage value of "B-" is 0.00 volt** and is considered the most negative point in a circuit. B- also corresponds to the negative side of a circuit or it can be expressed as the B- side. The next exercise traces the B- side of the circuit, the ground side of the circuit starting at the ground pin of the load.

DO THIS:

- Verify a 0ΩR connects the B+ Terminal with TP4.
- Scan the top and bottom of the PCBs to make sure the PCBs have no faults.
- Connect the power supply to the terminals at the top of the Power Board.
- Place S3 and S4 in the ON position (slides-UP).
- Turn S1 ON (toggle UP).
- Ground DMM Black test lead to the black (negative) terminal post, "B-" or 0.00V.
- With the lamp ON, measure the Vc (circuit voltage) at each point in the circuit as shown in Figure 5H-077 beginning at Pin 85 of the relay and record readings below. Pay particular attention to follow the numerical sequence of the ground test points.

(1) _____V (Pin 85)
(2) _____V (G106)
(3) _____V (G105)
(4) _____V (TP23)
(5) _____V (TP10)
(6) _____V (TP11)
(7) _____V (TP12)
(8) _____V (G101)
(9) _____V (G100)
(10) _____V (-BATT Terminal)

Both test leads are touching B- in Step 10.

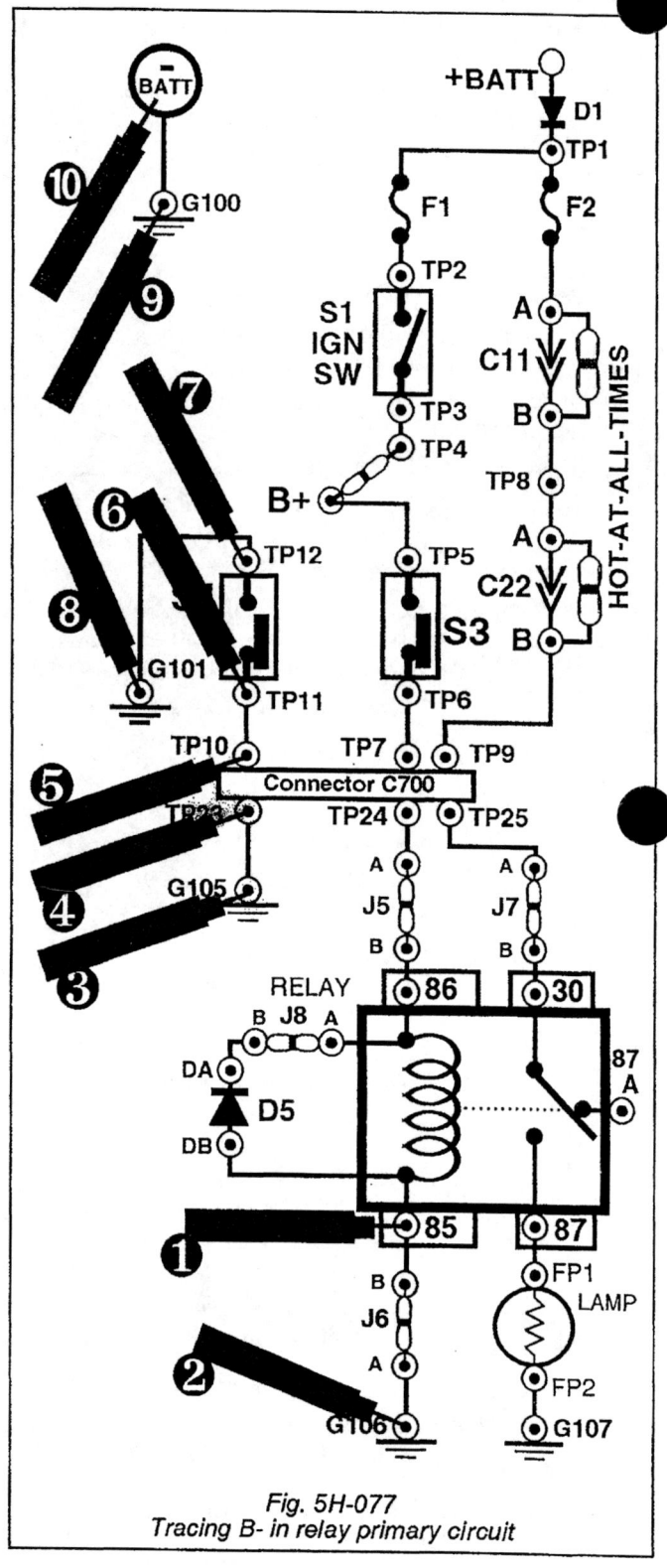

*Fig. 5H-077
Tracing B- in relay primary circuit*

Vehicle Electronics Hands-On Troubleshooting Training Program

VEEJER ENTERPRISES 3701 Lariat Lane, Garland, Texas 75042-5419
Phone: 972-276-9642 Fax: 972-276-8122 Email: sales@veejer.com Web Site: www.veejer.com

Tracing B- In Relay Secondary Circuit

It is also necessary to trace B- through the ground circuit of the relay secondary circuit starting at the load's ground side, pin FP2.

DO THIS:

- Verify a 0ΩR connects the B+ Terminal with TP4.
- Scan the top and bottom of the PCBs to make sure the PCBs have no faults.
- Connect the power supply to the terminals at the top of the Power Board.
- Place S3 and S4 in the ON position (slides-UP).
- Turn S1 ON (toggle UP).
- Ground DMM Black test lead to the black (negative) terminal post, "B-" or 0.00V.
- With the lamp ON, measure the Vc (circuit voltage) at each point in the circuit as shown in Figure 5H-078 beginning at FP2 of the relay and record readings below. Pay particular attention to follow the numerical sequence of the ground test points.

(1) _____ V (FP2)
(2) _____ V (G107)

From this point back to B- at the battery negative terminal, the ground path for the relay secondary circuit is identical to the relay primary (coil) ground path.

(3) _____ V (G106)
(4) _____ V (G105)
(5) _____ V (TP23)
(6) _____ V (TP10)
(7) _____ V (TP11)
(8) _____ V (TP12)
(9) _____ V (G101)
(10) _____ V (G100)
(11) _____ V -BATT Terminal

In the relay circuit of the H-PCB05 Troubleshooting Trainer, the relay's primary and secondary circuits share most of the same ground circuit. This is not always true on an actual vehicle where a relay coil may use one ground circuit path and the load connected to the relay contacts uses a completely different ground path.

Always trace the ground path to determine the ground path for each circuit.

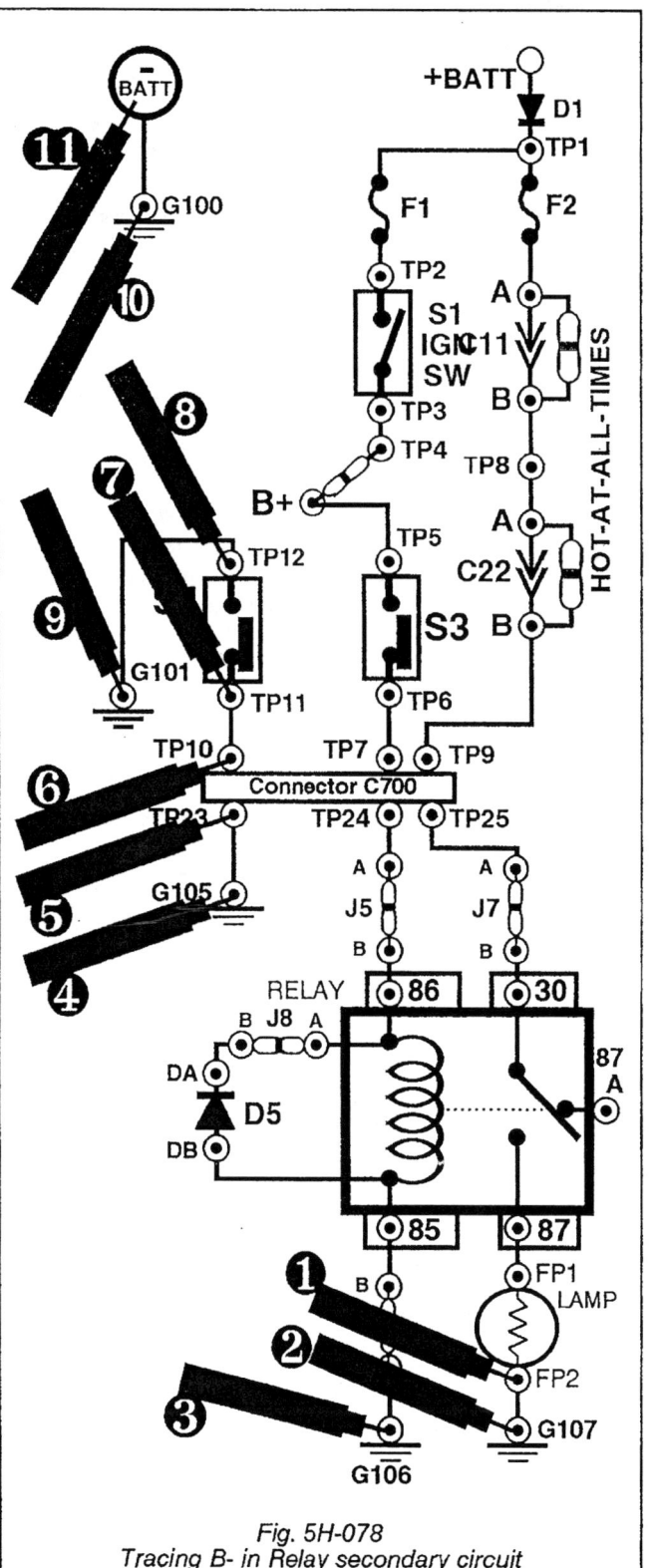

Fig. 5H-078
Tracing B- in Relay secondary circuit

Vehicle Electronics Hands-On Troubleshooting Training Program

VEEJER ENTERPRISES 3701 Lariat Lane, Garland, Texas 75042-5419
Phone: 972-276-9642 Fax: 972-276-8122 Email: sales@veejer.com Web Site: www.veejer.com

Testing Relay Contacts

The contacts in a relay are rated by the amount of current in amps they are designed to handle. If a relay rated with 10 Amp contacts is used in a circuit carrying 25 amps the relay contacts will burn up and the relay will fail. If the relay contacts are burned up the relay will still "CLICK" but the contacts cannot pass secondary load current due to high resistance build up on the burned contact surfaces.

Even if a relay rated with 30 amp contacts is used in a circuit with say 20 amps secondary load current, the relay contacts may eventually fail from arcing every time the contacts CLOSE and especially from the greater arcing that occurs when the relay de-energizes and the contacts OPEN. The greater arcing when the relay de-energizes and contacts OPEN is due to the collapsing electromagnetic field of the secondary load if the load has inductive properties, such as coils, solenoids and DC motors have. The energy released back into the circuit from the inductive load's energy dump jumps across the gap as the contact begins to OPEN causing an electrical arc between the contacts that erodes the contact's surfaces.

> **Lesson 30** covers inductive properties when an electromagnetic field collapses.

Over time a relay can be expected to develop corroded relay contacts that affects the current the contacts can pass to the secondary load. The more resistance build up in relay contacts the less current they can pass to the secondary load.

It therefore becomes necessary, as part of foolproof relay troubleshooting procedures, to evaluate the condition of relay contacts.

The Wrong Way to Check Relay Contacts

The wrong way to test relay contacts is to check the contacts with an ohmmeter to see how much resistance is present between the relay contacts, as shown in Figure 5H-079. This test method would be called a **Static Test** because the relay secondary circuit is not live, or passing secondary load current.

The voltage supply MUST BE removed from the relay secondary circuit because an ohmmeter should NEVER be connected to a live circuit. On the Relay Board, H-PCB05, the 0ΩR in J7 can be removed to disconnect B+ from the relay contacts which is a relatively simple procedure. It would also be acceptable to remove Fuse F2 from the Power Board. On an actual vehicle it probably would be easier to remove the fuse feeding the relay secondary circuit.

DO THIS, as shown in Figure 5H-079:
Remove J7 from the Relay Board.
Connect the Relay Board to the Power Board and energize the relay (CLOSE S1, S3 and S4).
The relay should "CLICK".

Place a digital ohmmeter between relay Pins 30 87. Expect a very small resistance of less than 1 ohm.

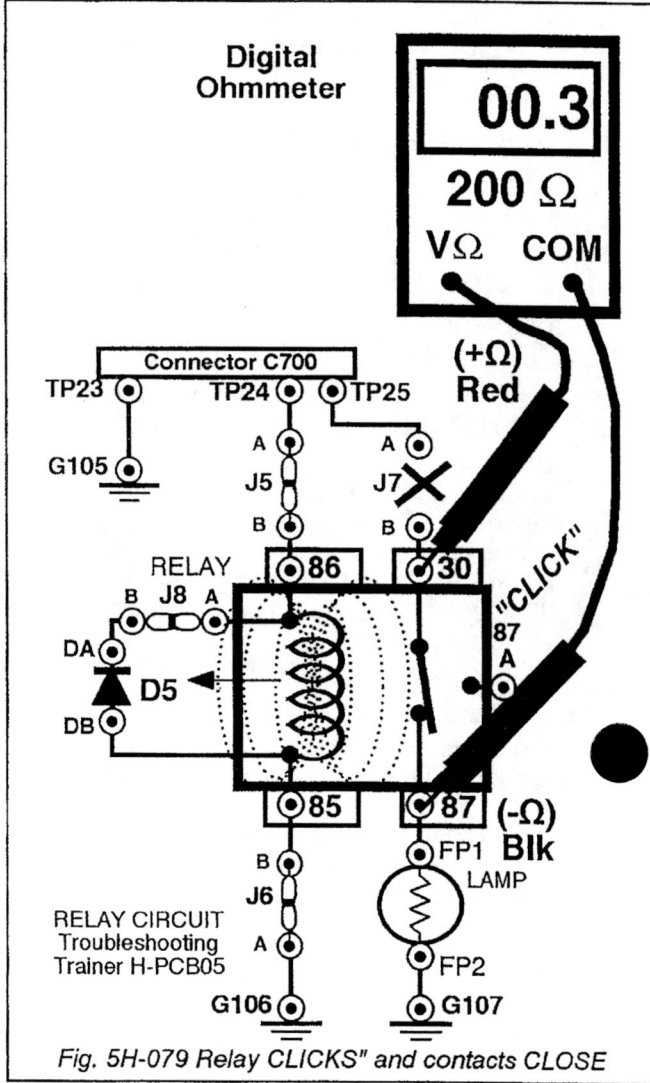

Fig. 5H-079 Relay CLICKS" and contacts CLOSE

The resistance reading on the DMM is the **contact resistance** of the relay contacts as determined by a digital ohmmeter. The problem using an ohmmeter is that there is no load current through the relay contacts to see how load current can pass through the contacts when they are CLOSED. The test current from the digital ohmmeter is not sufficient to put a load current through the relay contacts. The digital ohmmeter only confirms that the contacts have CLOSED but nothing about the quality of the relay contacts and how much current the relay contacts can pass between Pins 30 and 87.

A relay contact **Dynamic Test** is the best method. With load current flowing through the relay contacts, measure the Vd of the CLOSED relay contacts. This is necessary to determine the current handling capability (or condition) of the relay contacts as explained next.

Vehicle Electronics Hands-On Troubleshooting Training Program

VEEJER ENTERPRISES 3701 Lariat Lane, Garland, Texas 75042-5419
Phone: 972-276-9642   Fax: 972-276-8122   Email: sales@veejer.com   Web Site: www.veejer.com

The Correct Way to Check Relay Contacts

In Figure 5H-079A below, a DMM set to the 20-30-40 voltage range is shown measuring the Vd across the CLOSED relay contacts while lamp (load current) is flowing.

DO THIS:
(1) Install the 0ΩR back into J7 on the Relay PCB.
(2) Connect the Relay Board H-PCB05 to the Power Board H-PCB01/02.
(3) Connect Power Supply H-PS01 to the Power Board.
(4) Set the DMM to read DC volts.
(5) Connect DMM test leads as shown, Red to Pin 30 and Black to Pin 87.
(6) Verify the DMM reading is 13.00-14.00 volts while S1, S3 are switched OFF. Leave S4 CLOSED, slide UP.

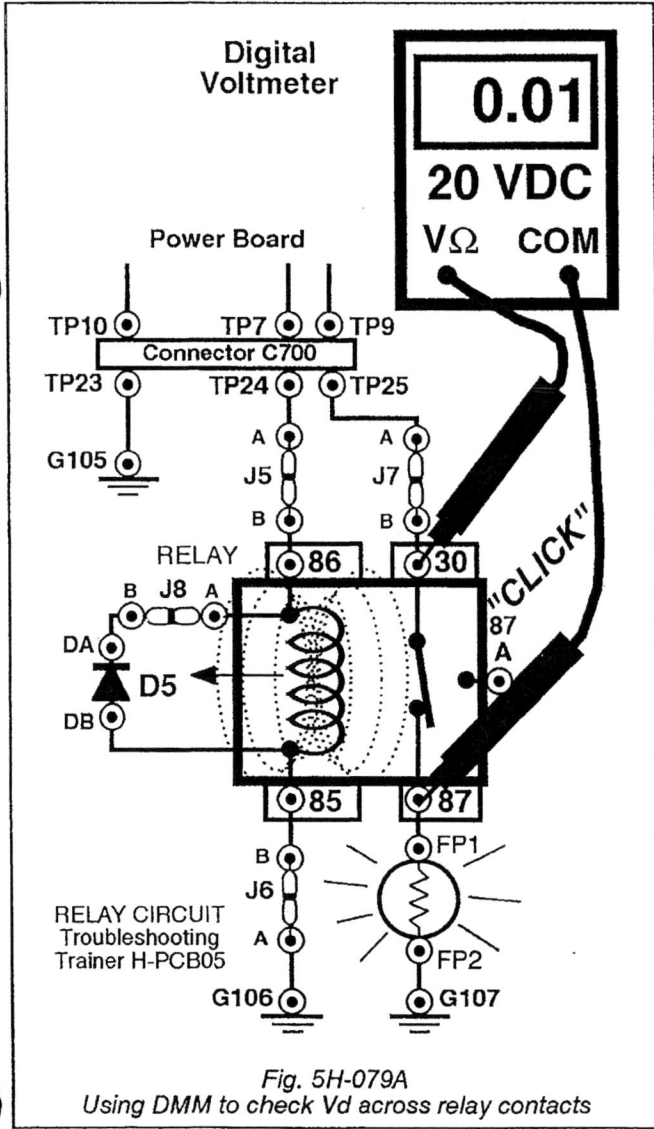

Fig. 5H-079A
Using DMM to check Vd across relay contacts

The reason the DMM reads B+ with all switches OFF and the relay de-energized, is due to the principal of how a DMM measures voltage.

This is a good principle to remember when measuring voltage with a DMM.

> **A DMM reads the difference in voltage between its probe tips.**

The DMM test leads connected to Pins 30 & 87 reads B+ of 13.00 volts with the relay de-energized and the contacts OPEN because the DMM Red test lead "sees" B+ and the Black test lead "sees" B-.

DMMs don't lie. They indicate (read-out) the voltage they "see" between their test lead probe tips. It's up to the technician using the DMM to "see' the circuit the same way the DMM does to understand the meaning of the reading in Step 6. Trace the circuit to "see" this concept as follows.

The Red test lead "sees B+" through J7, C700, Fuse F2, Diode D1 to the +BATT terminal.

The Black test lead "sees B-" through the lamp's filament (which is OFF), through G107, G106, G105, C700, G101, G100 to the black terminal post. The difference in voltage between B+ and B- is in the range of 13.00 volts, the reading on the DMM.

(7) Disconnect the lamp from the relay board and record the reading. _____

(8) Why does the DMM reading drop to zero volt with the lamp disconnected?

_____

(Before you look at the answer at the bottom of this page write your answer above.)

We conclude from this that B+ is the Vd measured across an OPEN connection in a good series circuit. **PUT THE LAMP BACK IN THE CIRCUIT.**

(8) Toggle S1 UP, S3-S4 slides UP to turn ON the relay and verify the lamp is ON.

(9) Record the Vd reading on the DMM.
_____ volt

The Vd reading obtained in Step (9) is the only valid test of the relay contacts because the contacts are passing load current to the load (lamp). We now know the relay contacts are good much more so than a resistance check of the relay contacts using an ohmmeter.

The relay contact Vd on actual vehicle relay circuits according to SAE (Society of Automotive Engineers) specifications is 0.30V (300 mV). The reading obtained in Step (9), 0.01-0.03V, is very much below 0.30V indicating exceptionally good relay contacts while handling load current.

Answer to (8): When the lamp is disconnected the Black test lead no longer can "see" B-. The DMM now "sees" no voltage difference between the test leads with the negative side of the circuit disconnected with the lamp removed.

Vehicle Electronics Hands-On Troubleshooting Training Program

VEEJER ENTERPRISES 3701 Lariat Lane, Garland, Texas 75042-5419
Phone: 972-276-9642 Fax: 972-276-8122 Email: sales@veejer.com Web Site: www.veejer.com

How Electrical Circuits Fail

An electrical circuit will fail in a number of ways. It doesn't matter if the electrical circuit is on an automobile, SUV, truck or piece of heavy equipment, an airplane or a boat, electrical circuits all experience the same type of circuit failures. These failure modes are reviewed with the simple schematic below.

We have presented a troubleshooting plan used in the H-111A Starter Kit and the H-113 DC Motor Circuits. We call it the Texas-Two-Step. Next is a brief review of how circuit fail.

A good circuit.....

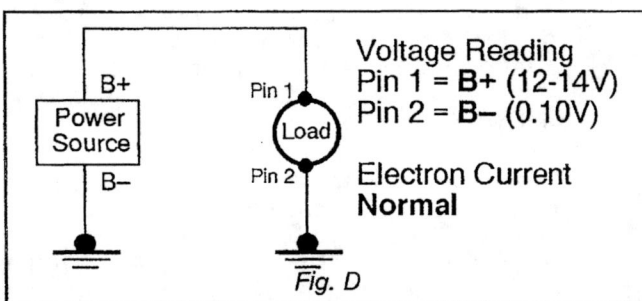
Fig. D

(1) An OPEN circuit on the voltage side.....

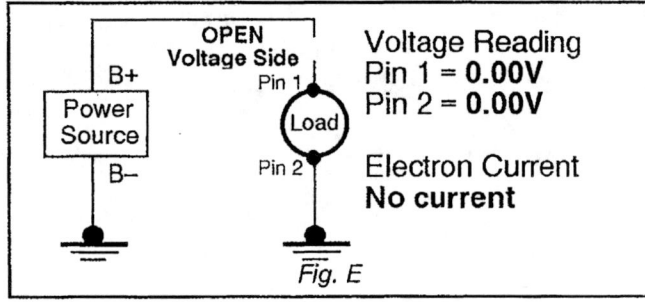
Fig. E

(2) A Vd (voltage drop) on the voltage side.....

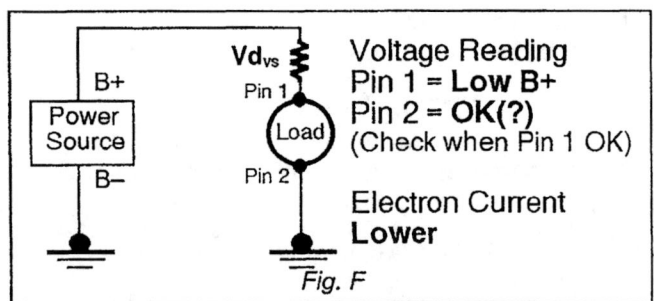
Fig. F

The best way to determine if the circuit has an OPEN or a Vd, the most common circuit failures, is to perform the Texas-Two-Step voltage checks. Measuring electron current is these examples is not as helpful to determine a circuit problem as checking circuit voltages (Vc) tests.

(3) An OPEN circuit on the ground side......

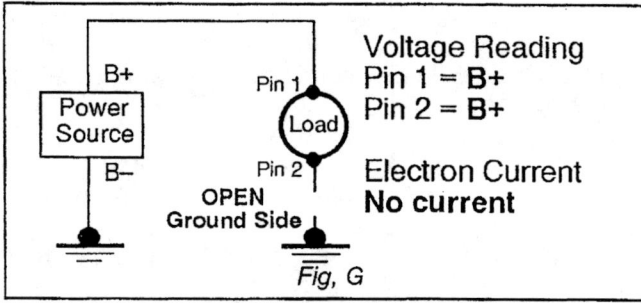
Fig. G

(4) A Vd (voltage drop) on the ground side.....

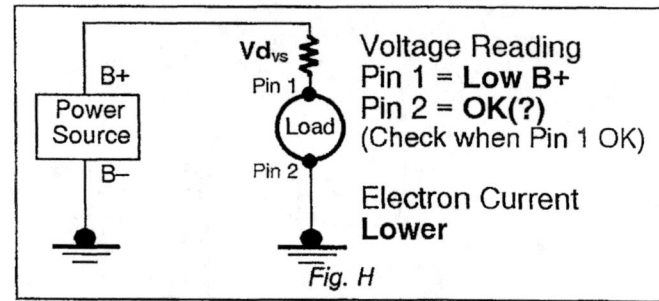
Fig. H

(5) An OPEN circuit load.....

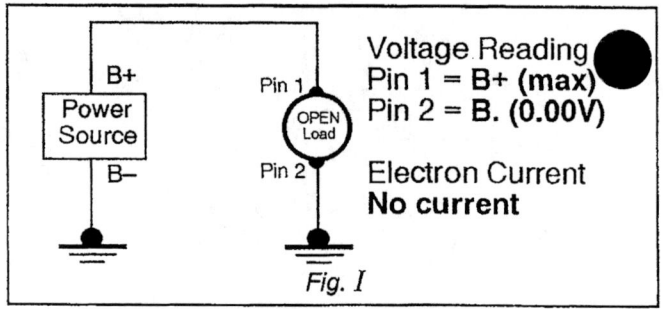
Fig. I

(6) A blown fuse.....

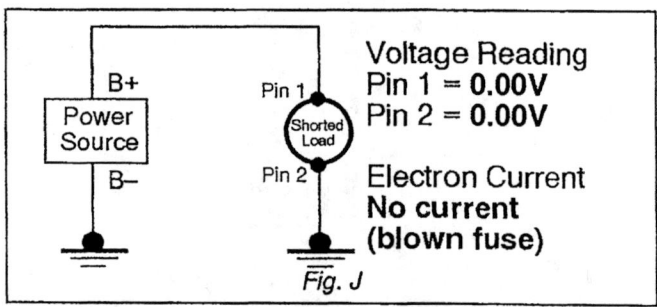
Fig. J

A relay circuit has two circuits that must work together to get the job done, that is operate the load. Either circuit could have a problem or both. As we analyze circuit faults in the relay primary circuit and secondary circuit keep in mind that each is a common circuit fault best determined by measuring the Texas-Two-Step first. We will also test for short-to-ground and short-to-voltage problems later.

Vehicle Electronics Hands-On Troubleshooting Training Program

VEEJER ENTERPRISES 3701 Lariat Lane, Garland, Texas 75042-5419
Phone: 972-276-9642 Fax: 972-276-8122 Email: sales@veejer.com Web Site: www.veejer.com

Introduction - Troubleshooting Relays

We have been covering systematic troubleshooting procedures proven to reveal a circuit problem in the shortest possible time with almost foolproof accuracy. We call this test procedure the "Texas-Two-Step," abbr. "TTS" in "*The*" Hands-On Program.

As we apply the TTS to relay circuit troubleshooting we find there are two circuits involved in a relay circuit.

> **Lesson 23** and **Lesson 24** covers the TTS procedure in detail.
> **Lesson 39** covers the TTS in relay circuits.

The TTS involves two Vc (circuit voltage) measurements at the terminals of a relay circuit's two loads. **The load in the relay primary circuit is the coil. The load in the relay secondary circuit is the lamp** (in this circuit). Remember, the TTS, means the DMM black COM test lead is connected to the battery negative post or **-BATT** terminal.

Figure 5H-080 illustrates the two Vc measurements of the TTS at both primary and secondary relay circuit load terminals.

Turn ON the relay circuit. Verify that the DMM is grounded to the negative terminal post -BATT at the top of the Power Board for each TTS measurement. Perform the TTS and record your readings below.

STEP 1 of the TTS is abbr. as TTS-1 (B+ side):
- Measure the B+ at relay Pin 86 on the relay coil.
- Measure the B+ at FP1 of the lamp.

Expect the reading to be close to B+. The higher the TTS-1 reading the better. **Any electrical problem on the voltage side of the circuit results in a lower TTS-1 reading.**

STEP 2 of the TTS is abbr. as TTS-2 (B- side):
- Measure the B- at relay Pin 85 on the relay coil.
- Measure the B- at FP2 of the lamp.

Expect the reading to be equal to or less than 0.10V for a good ground circuit. The lower the TTS-2 reading the better. **Any electrical problem on the ground side of the load results in a higher TTS-2 reading.**

Record TTS readings below.

Relay Primary	Relay Secondary
TTS-1 _____ volts	TTS-1 _____ volts
TTS-2 _____ volts	TTS-2 _____ volts

Beginning on the next page we investigate the ways a relay circuit fails and how to test and measure relay circuits using the TTS to determine what is wrong with a relay circuit. This is followed by a series of troubleshooting problems to develop live troubleshooting skill.

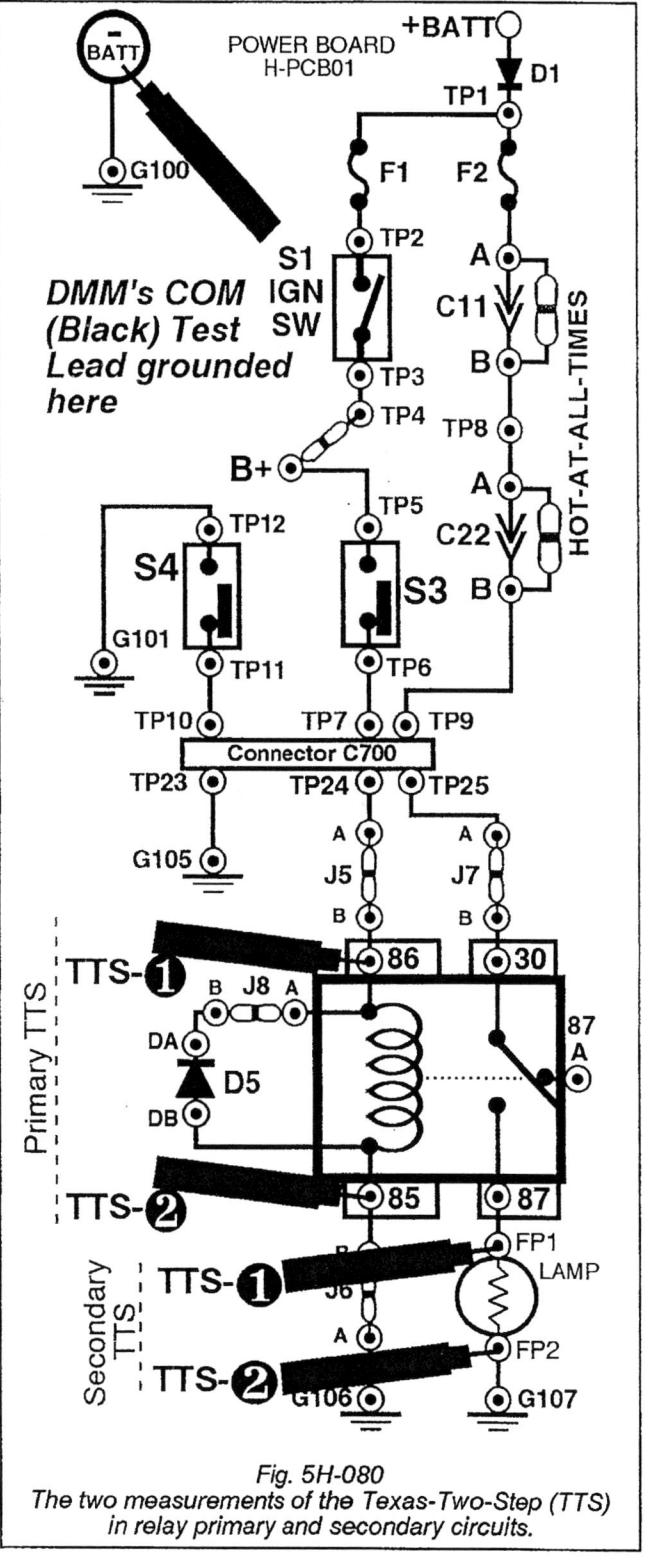

Fig. 5H-080
The two measurements of the Texas-Two-Step (TTS) in relay primary and secondary circuits.

Keep in mind that the following exercises are the same basic problems that happen to all circuits. Study them one at a time and keep the big picture in mind – these are common problems in any circuit.

Vehicle Electronics Hands-On Troubleshooting Training Program

VEEJER ENTERPRISES 3701 Lariat Lane, Garland, Texas 75042-5419
Phone: 972-276-9642   Fax: 972-276-8122   Email: sales@veejer.com   Web Site: www.veejer.com

Relay Circuit Problem Number "1P"
(The "P" in "1P" refers to relay primary circuit)
"OPEN" – Relay Primary Voltage Circuit

Create the Problem:
Create an OPEN circuit on the voltage side of the relay primary circuit by removing the 0ΩR in J5 from the Relay Board H-PCB05 as shown in Figure 5H-081.

> **Lesson 24,** analyzes circuit problem #1.
> **Lesson 41** covers an OPEN on the voltage side problem in relay circuits.

(1) How does an OPEN circuit on the relay primary circuit (relay coil) voltage side affect relay operation?
_____

(2) How does this problem affect the relay secondary circuit?
_____

Do This:
- Turn the circuit ON with S1 (S3 & S4 CLOSED).
- Ground DMM negative test lead to -BATT.
- Since the relay will not "CLICK" perform the TTS on the relay primary load (relay coil) and record the readings below.

(3) TTS-1 reading: _____

   Conclusion: _____

(4) TTS-2 reading: _____

   Conclusion: _____

(5) What is the next troubleshooting step?
_____

(6) What is concluded when B+ is found at J5 Pin A?
_____

DO THIS:
- Slide S3 DOWN to de-energize the relay.
- Install 0ΩR back into J5 on the Relay Board.
- Disconnect Power Supply from wall socket.

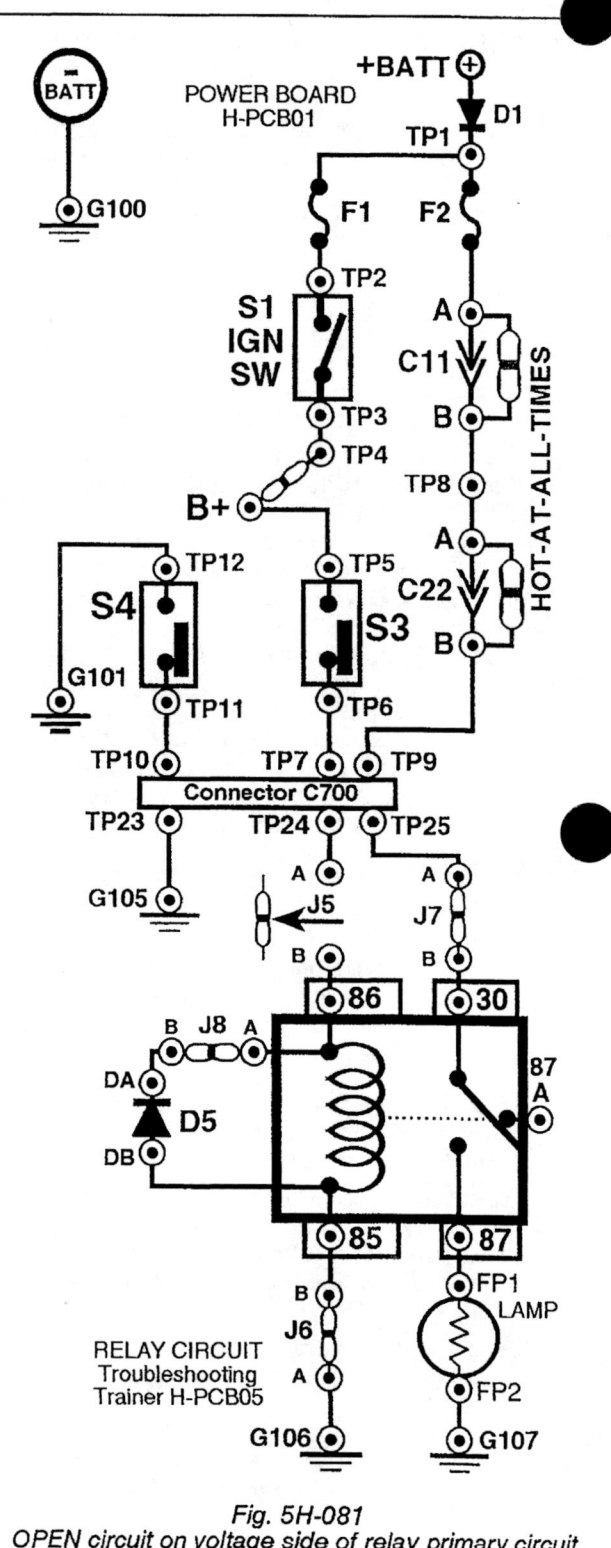

Fig. 5H-081
OPEN circuit on voltage side of relay primary circuit.

Vehicle Electronics Hands-On Troubleshooting Training Program

VEEJER ENTERPRISES 3701 Lariat Lane, Garland, Texas 75042-5419
Phone: 972-276-9642 Fax: 972-276-8122 Email: sales@veejer.com Web Site: www.veejer.com

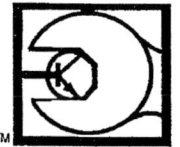

Relay Circuit Problem Number "1S"
(The "S" in "1S" refers to relay secondary circuit)
"OPEN" - Relay Secondary Voltage Circuit

The Problem:
Create an OPEN circuit on the voltage side of the relay secondary circuit by removing the 0ΩR in J7 from the Relay Board H-PCB05 as shown in Figure 5H-081A.

> **Lesson 24**, analyzes circuit problem #1.
> **Lesson 41** covers an OPEN on the voltage side problem in relay circuits.

(1) How does an OPEN circuit on the relay secondary circuit voltage side affect relay operation? _____

(2) How does this problem affect the relay secondary circuit? _____

Do This:
- Turn the circuit ON with S1 (S3 & S4 CLOSED).
- Ground DMM negative test lead to -BATT.
- Since the relay "CLICKS" but the lamp does not turn ON perform the TTS on the relay secondary load (lamp) and record the readings below.

(3) TTS-1 reading at FP1: _____

   Conclusion: _____

(4) TTS-2 reading: _____

   Conclusion: _____

(5) What is the next troubleshooting step? _____

(6) Measure Vc at Pin 87: Reading _____

(7) Measure Vc at Pin 30: Reading _____

(8) Measure Vc at Pin B of J7: Reading _____

(9) What is concluded when B+ is found at J7 Pin A? _____

DO THIS:
- Slide S3 DOWN to de-energize the relay.
- Install 0ΩR back into J7 on the Relay Board.
- Disconnect Power Supply from wall socket.

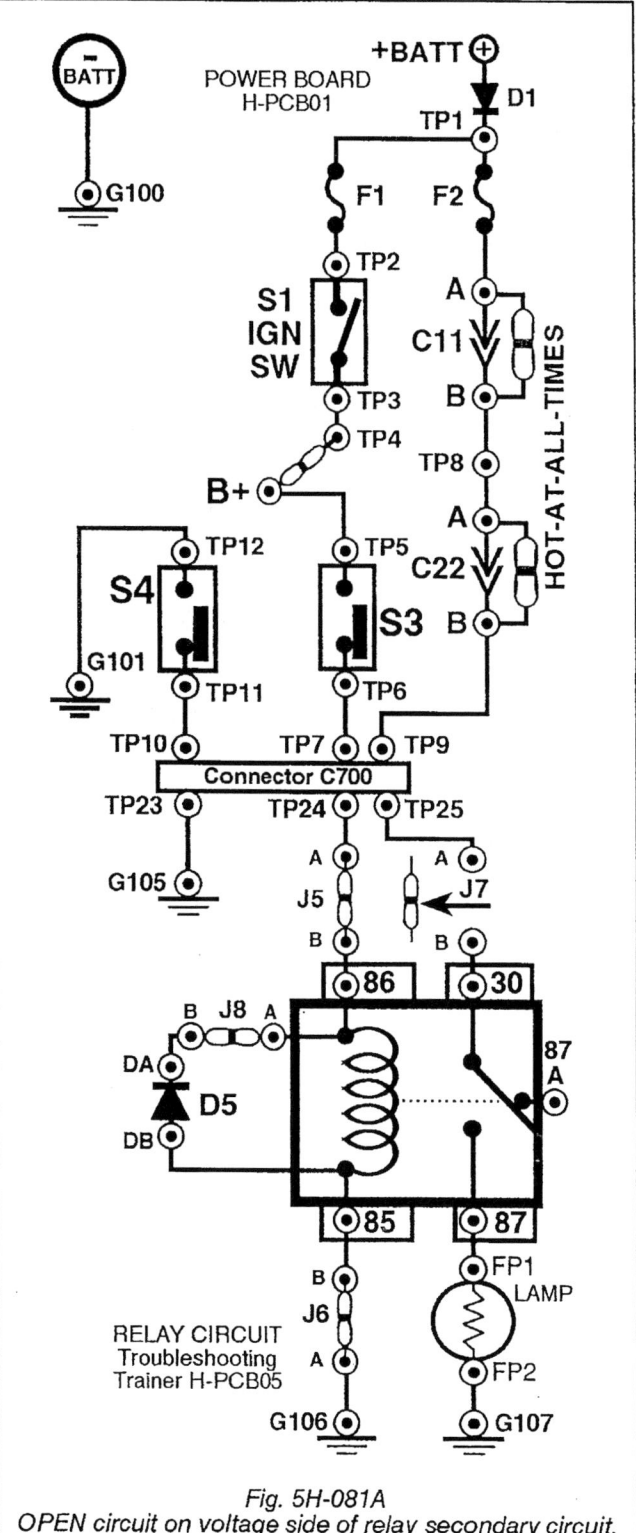

Fig. 5H-081A
OPEN circuit on voltage side of relay secondary circuit.

Vehicle Electronics Hands-On Troubleshooting Training Program

VEEJER ENTERPRISES 3701 Lariat Lane, Garland, Texas 75042-5419
Phone: 972-276-9642 Fax: 972-276-8122 Email: sales@veejer.com Web Site: www.veejer.com

Relay Circuit Problem Number 2P
"Voltage Drop"–Relay Primary Voltage Circuit

The Problem:
Create a Vd (voltage drop) on the voltage side of the relay primary circuit by removing the 0ΩR in J5 from the Relay Board H-PCB05 and replace it with a **560Ω–cc:grn-blu-bro.** A 560Ω resistor creates a large enough Vd to prevent relay operation. If a smaller resistance is used it may not prevent relay operation. The resistor is shown in Figure 5H-082 inserted in J5.

Caution:
Resistor gets hot when relay is energized.

> **Lesson 24,** analyzes circuit problem #2.
> **Lesson 41** covers a Vd on the voltage side problem in relay circuits.

(1) How does a Vd on the relay primary circuit (relay coil) voltage side affect relay operation?
_____

(2) How does this problem affect the relay secondary circuit? _____

(3) TTS-1 reading: _____
    Conclusion: _____

(4) TTS-2 reading: _____
    Conclusion: _____

(5) What is the next troubleshooting step?
_____

(6) What is concluded when you find B+ at J5 Pin A?
_____

DO THIS:
- Slide S3 DOWN to de-energize the relay.
- Leave the 560Ω resistor in J5 and continue working with Problem #2 on the next page for a very important lesson to learn in troubleshooting relay circuits. **It's a troubleshooting principal you should NEVER FORGET.**

Continue with this exercise on next page.

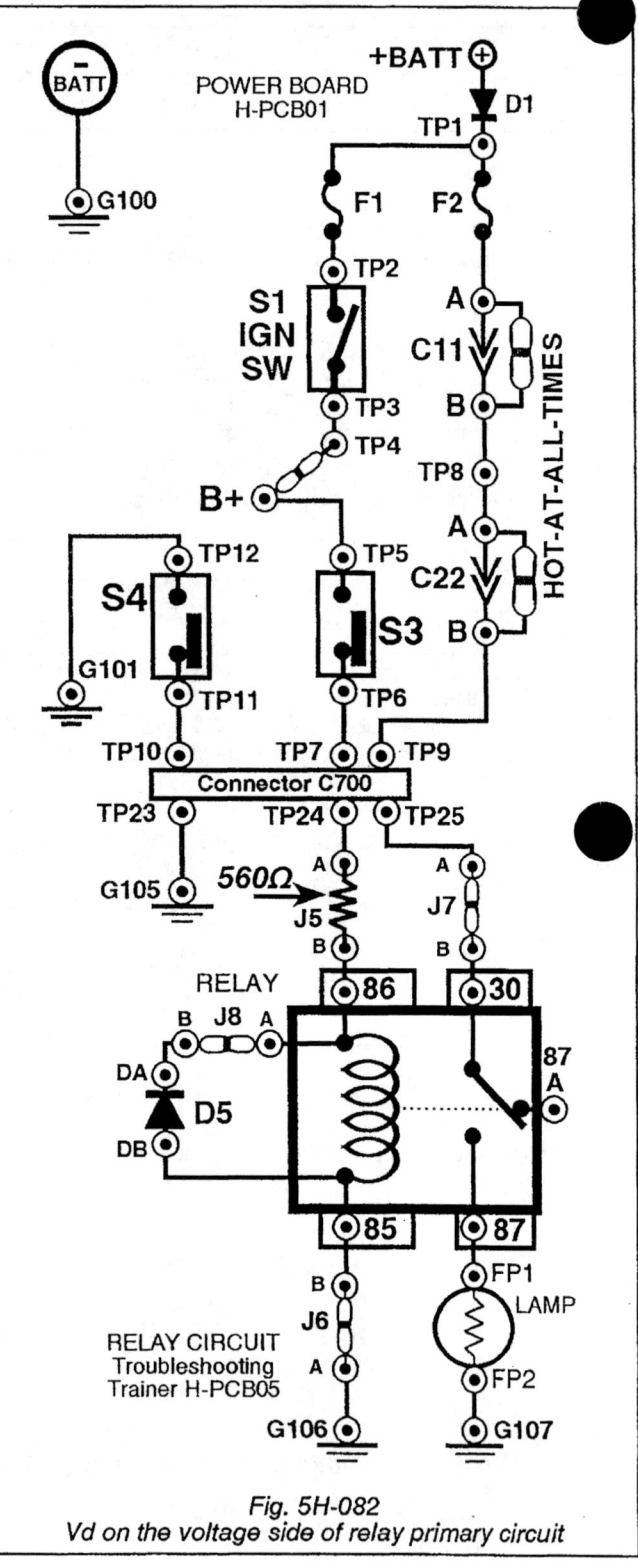

Fig. 5H-082
Vd on the voltage side of relay primary circuit

Copyright © 2015 VEEJER ENTERPRISES, Garland, Texas - All Rights Reserved Student Workbook H-WB115 Page 39

Vehicle Electronics Hands-On Troubleshooting Training Program

VEEJER ENTERPRISES 3701 Lariat Lane, Garland, Texas 75042-5419
Phone: 972-276-9642 Fax: 972-276-8122 Email: sales@veejer.com Web Site: www.veejer.com

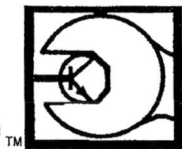

---

2 IMPORTANT LESSONS WHEN A Vd PROBLEM EXISTS ON THE VOLTAGE SIDE OF A RELAY COIL CIRCUIT
These are two voltage side problems peculiar to relay circuits to understand.

Lesson Number 1 – A Vd at Pin 86
Remember? No Current = No Voltage Drop

A common mistake made in vehicle electrical troubleshooting is disconnecting the relay when performing the TTS. This will hide any Vd that is reducing the voltage at Pin 86.

In the Lamp Board (Starter Kit) and DC Motor Board we had the option of disconnecting the load while the resistor Vd was still present in the circuit. We found the TTS reading at Pin 1 of the load was low and became normal with the load was disconnected yet the resistor causing the Vd was still present in the circuit.

The relay cannot be disconnected from the Relay Circuit Board to prove this but the TTS-1 reading at Pin 86 reacts the same way. If the relay is disconnected the TTS-1 reading at Pin 86 appears normal even when the resistor (Vd problem) is present in the circuit.

This troubleshooting principle was discussed in the Lamp Board and DC Motor Board and also applies here in relay primary and secondary circuits, as well.

NEVER DISCONNECT THE LOAD DURING THE TTS READINGS TO VERIFY THERE IS NO Vd AT PIN 86 OR PIN 85.

Any Vd in the relay primary voltage side is concealed when electron current is not flowing because the relay is removed from the relay socket.

LOW B+ READING AT Pin 86 - TRY THIS:
• Turn relay OFF by sliding S3 DOWN (OFF).
• Change the resistor in J5 from 560Ω to 220 ohms **220Ω–cc:red-red-bro.**
• Slide S3 UP (ON) to energize the relay.

(a.) What happens to relay operation?
_____

Since the relay seems to be operating it is not likely the TTS at the relay coil terminals Pin 86 and Pin 85 would be tested. Yet there is a low voltage reading at Pin 86 due to a Vd problem on the voltage side. It's just not big enough yet to cause the relay to fail to energize.

However, if during the troubleshooting steps the TTS on the relay coil was performed the low TTS-1 reading would be recognized and repaired but only if the relay was plugged into the circuit and electron current was flowing.

Check the TTS readings and record the TTS readings with the 220 ohm resistor in J5.

(b.) TTS-1 reading: _____

(c.) TTS-2 reading: _____

(d.) Why does the relay energize with a lower TTS-1 reading on the voltage side?
_____
_____

(e.) What is the lesson to learn from this?
_____

Substitute A Relay In A Vehicle To Test

It may not always be possible to perform the TTS-1 and TTS-2 readings on relays installed in their sockets when you suspect there may be a voltage drop problem with Pin 86 and Pin 85. The bottom of the relay socket may not be accessible or impossible to measure the voltages at Pin 86 and Pin 85.

So Try This! Replace the relay coil with a physical resistor of the proper resistance.

(1) Make sure the relay is turned OFF or de-energized. A relay should never be unplugged while it is operating. This will cause a voltage spike that could damage an transistor driver inside an on-board computer controlling the relay.

(2) Measure relay coil resistance between relay Pins 86 and 85 with a digital ohmmeter to determine what resistor in ohms is needed.
• If the coil measures around 65-75 ohms you can select a resistor that is on the range of 60-100 ohms to be safe. A little higher resistance is better than a little lower.
• The resistor should have a **5 watt rating** so it can safely handle the coil electron current.

(3) Insert the two resistor leads into the relay socket in pin locations for Pin 86 and Pin 85 and turn the relay ON (energize the relay).

(4) Measure the TTS voltage at both sides of the resistor. One side of the resistor is Pin 86, the TTS-1 reading and the opposite side of the resistor is Pin 85, the TTS-2 reading.
• If Pin 86 is low there is a Vd on the voltage side of the relay coil.
• If Pin 85 is more than 0.10V there is a Vd on the ground side of the relay coil.

When finished power down the circuits and then remove the resistor. Install the relay when normal TTS readings are obtained.
Try this on a vehicle for practice.

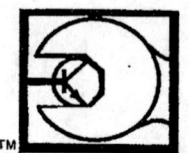

Lesson Number 2
Intermittent Relay Operation

This is the second unusual relay problem that often causes what appears to be **intermittent relay operation.** This happens when the **Vd problem** on the relay Pin 86 side increases to the point it lowers the voltage at Pin 86 enough to prevent the relay contacts from closing.

The relay contacts are trying to CLOSE but just can't quite CLOSE. The Vd problem lowers the electron current through the relay coil which weakens the electromagnetic field.

Yet the relay contacts do CLOSE when the relay is physically bumped or the vehicle hits a hard enough road bump. The kinetic energy of the bump or jarring adds to the weakened electromagnetic field to CLOSE the contacts.

The relay appears to work sometimes and sometimes it doesn't work. It may not be apparent that a physical jarring of the relay is causing what appears to be intermittent relay operation. Let's see how this occurs and how to identify the problem.

DO THIS:
- Turn relay OFF by sliding S3 DOWN (OFF).

- Select a 330 ohm (**330Ω–cc:org-org-bro**) and a 100 ohm resistor (**100Ω–cc:bro-blk-bro**) from the resistor bag. Twist the resistor leads together at one end as shown to create a series network of 430 ohms. Total Resistance = 330 +100 = 430Ω. (SAVE THIS NETWORK FOR LATER USE.)

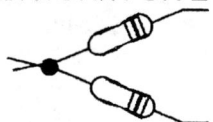

- Insert the 430Ω resistance network into J5 on the relay board. One end plugs into J5-A and the other end plugs into J5-B.

- Slide S3 UP (ON) to energize the relay.

(a.) What happens to the relay?

_____

(b.) Measure the TTS-1 voltage at Pin 86.

_____

(c.) Tap on top of the physical relay until the relay "CLICKS" and describe what happens to the voltage at Pin 86.

_____

_____

Try this several times by sliding S3 OFF and ON. Each time S3 is cycled back ON the relay must be tapped to CLOSE the contacts.

(d.) What happened to the TTS-1 voltage at Pin 86 when the relay energized?

_____

_____

A voltage drop caused by the 430Ω resistor network decreases the B+ to the relay coil just enough so the relay ALMOST, but not quite energizes enough to CLOSE the contacts. The lower B+ at Pin 86 indicates a Vd on the voltage side due to resistance dropping B+ to pin 86.

More resistance in the coil circuit means less coil current and a weaker electromagnetic field that can't quite pull the contacts CLOSED. Tapping lightly on the relay adds kinetic energy to the relay which then helps the weakened electromagnetic field "CLICK" & CLOSE the almost CLOSED contacts. The relay contacts will remain CLOSED at 6.4-6.5V once the relay contacts are CLOSED.

The problem is the relay can't CLOSE the contacts by itself. It needs a bump or a jarring to work. This is what happens when a relay in a vehicle circuit appears to be intermittent.

Perform the TTS on any suspect relay primary circuit (coil) to see if low B+ is getting to the voltage side of the coil. If so, it's an intermittent relay circuit. Trace B+ to find the Vd on the voltage side of the relay coil and repair the problem.

Remove resistor network from J5 and install a 0ΩR.

Both of these two problems are unique to relays and are appropriate to explain along with a Vd problem at the relay coil pin 86.

On the next page we resume studying the basic electrical problems with a Vd on the secondary side of the circuit.

Vehicle Electronics Hands-On Troubleshooting Training Program

VEEJER ENTERPRISES 3701 Lariat Lane, Garland, Texas 75042-5419
Phone: 972-276-9642 Fax: 972-276-8122 Email: sales@veejer.com Web Site: www.veejer.com

Relay Circuit Problem Number 2S
"Voltage Drop" –
Relay Secondary Voltage Circuit

The Problem:
Create a Vd (voltage drop) on the voltage side of the relay secondary circuit by removing the 0ΩR in J7 from the Relay Board H-PCB05 and replace with a **150Ω–cc:bro-grn-bro** resistor, as shown in Figure 5H-083. Any resistance in the relay secondary circuit will affect the operation of the relay secondary load.

Caution: Resistor is hot when relay is energized.

(1) How does a Vd on the relay secondary circuit (relay contacts) affect relay operation?
_____

(2) How does this problem affect the relay secondary circuit?
_____

(3) TTS-1 reading at FP1: _____

   Conclusion: _____

(4) TTS-2 reading at FP2: _____

   Conclusion: _____

(5) What is the next troubleshooting step?
_____

(6) What is concluded when you find B+ at J7 Pin A?
_____

Leave the 150Ω resistor in J7 and continue working with Problem #2S on the next page for a very important lesson to learn in troubleshooting relay circuits. **It's a troubleshooting principal you should NEVER FORGET.**

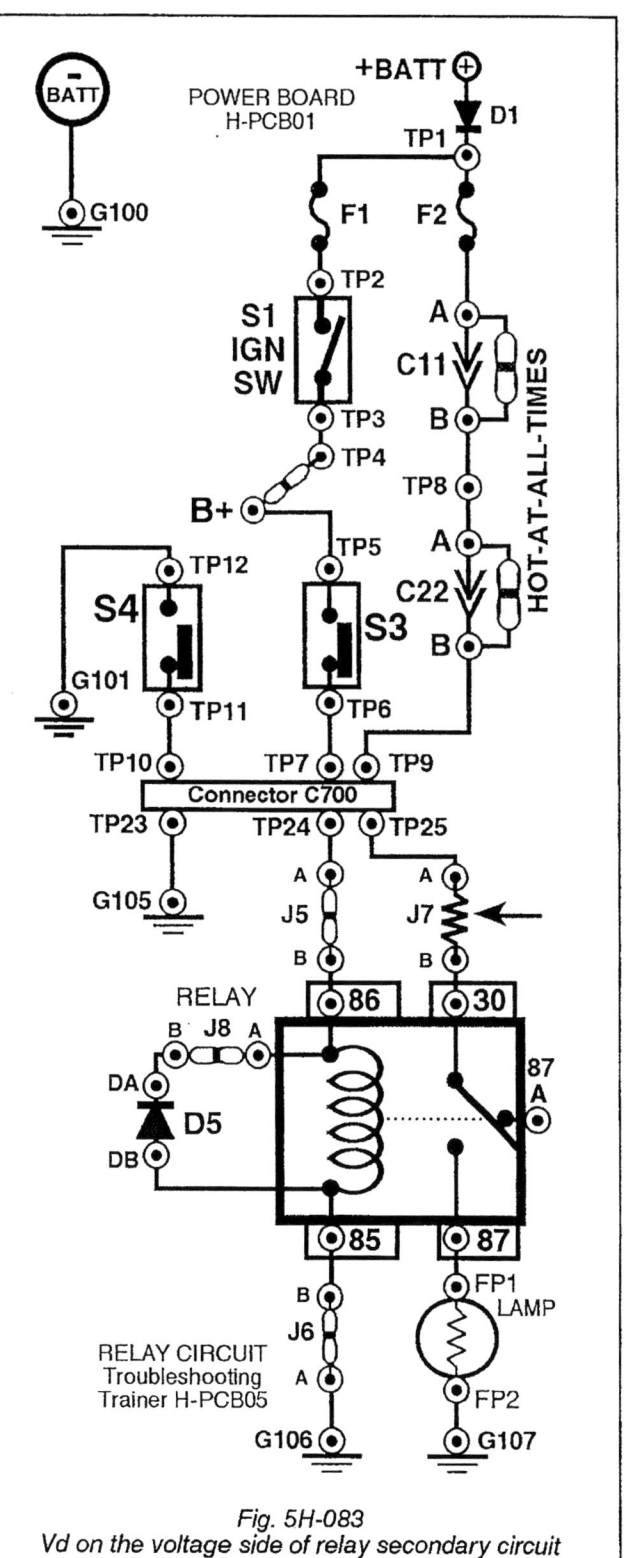

Fig. 5H-083
Vd on the voltage side of relay secondary circuit

Vehicle Electronics Hands-On Troubleshooting Training Program

VEEJER ENTERPRISES 3701 Lariat Lane, Garland, Texas 75042-5419
Phone: 972-276-9642   Fax: 972-276-8122   Email: sales@veejer.com   Web Site: www.veejer.com

IMPORTANT LESSON WHEN A Vd PROBLEM EXISTS ON THE VOLTAGE SIDE OF A RELAY SECONDARY CIRCUIT

We have seen that disconnecting the load hides a voltage drop problem using Figure 5H-084.

If the relay contacts are NOT CLOSED (relay is de-energized) the voltage reading at pin 30 is B+. The relay contacts must be CLOSED to allow electron current to flow in the relay secondary circuit to create a lower voltage at pin 30 indicating a voltage drop is present in the circuit leading to pin 30.

> **Always make sure the relay contacts are CLOSED when measuring the voltage at pin 30.**

DO THIS:
- Slide S3 DOWN to de-energize the relay.
- **Disconnect the lamp from the relay circuit.**
- Slide S3 UP to energize the relay.

(1) Measure the TTS-1 at FP1 and record reading.
_____

(2) Is the resistor still in J7? _____

(3) Explain why B+ is measured at FP1 with the load disconnected.
_____
_____

(4) With the relay energized and the DMM still measuring the voltage at FP1 install the lamp back into the relay board's lamp socket.

(5) Describe the change in the DMM reading as the lamp turns ON.
_____
_____

DO THIS:
- Slide S3 DOWN to de-energize the relay.
- Remove the 150Ω resistor from J7.
  Be careful the resistor is HOT.
- Install a 0ΩR back into J7.

Proceed to the exercise on the next page.

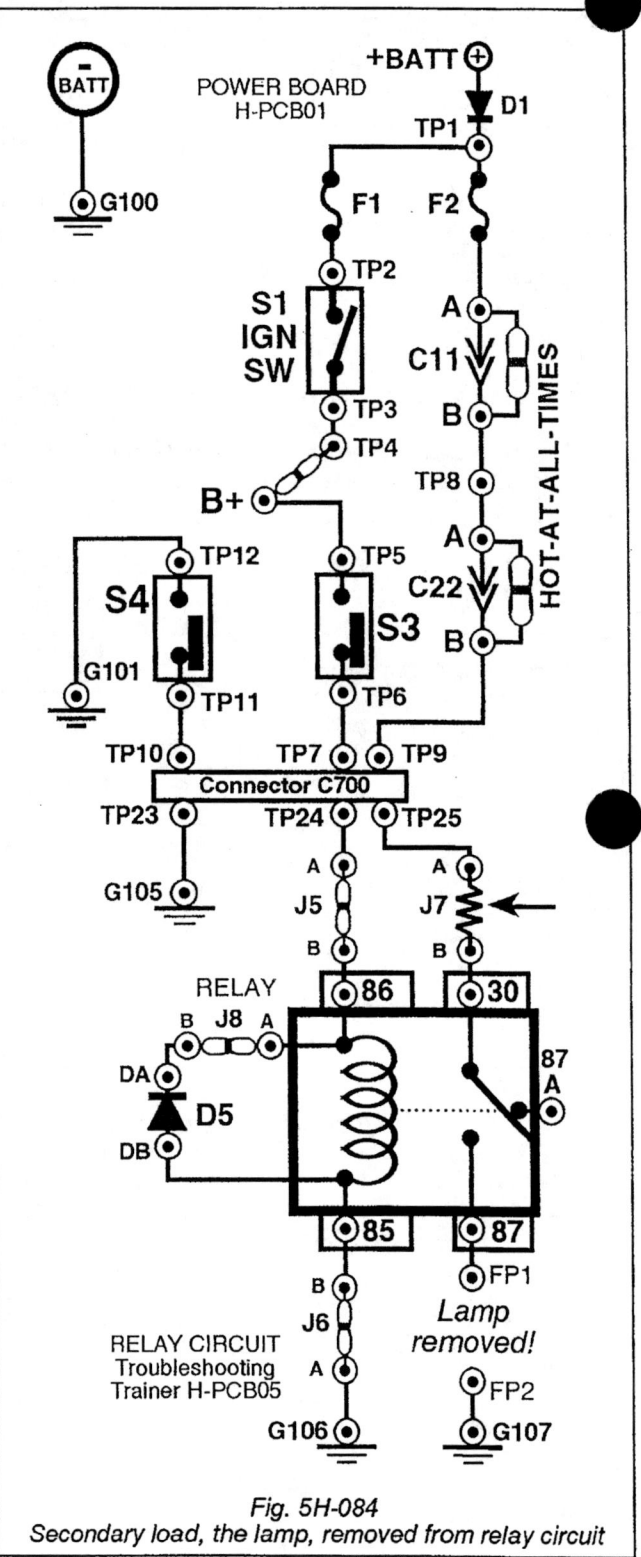

Fig. 5H-084
Secondary load, the lamp, removed from relay circuit

Vehicle Electronics Hands-On Troubleshooting Training Program

VEEJER ENTERPRISES 3701 Lariat Lane, Garland, Texas 75042-5419
Phone: 972-276-9642 Fax: 972-276-8122 Email: sales@veejer.com Web Site: www.veejer.com

Relay Circuit Problem Number 3P
"OPEN" – Relay Primary Ground Circuit

The Problem:
Create an OPEN on the ground side of the relay primary (coil) circuit by removing J6 from the top of the relay board as shown in Figure 5H-085.

Problem Analysis:
How does an OPEN circuit on the relay primary ground side affect relay operation?

_____

Lesson 24 discusses circuit problem #3.
Lesson 41 discusses an OPEN ground on the relay primary circuit.

DO THIS:
- Slide S3 DOWN to de-energize the relay.
- Disconnect the 0ΩR in J6 from the relay circuit.
- Slide S3 UP to energize the relay.

(1) TTS-1 reading: _____

Conclusion: _____

(2) TTS-2 reading: _____

Conclusion: _____

(3) What is the next troubleshooting step?

_____

(4) What is concluded when you find 0V at J6 Pin A?

_____

Remove the fault from the relay board by installing a 0ΩR back into J6 and continue.

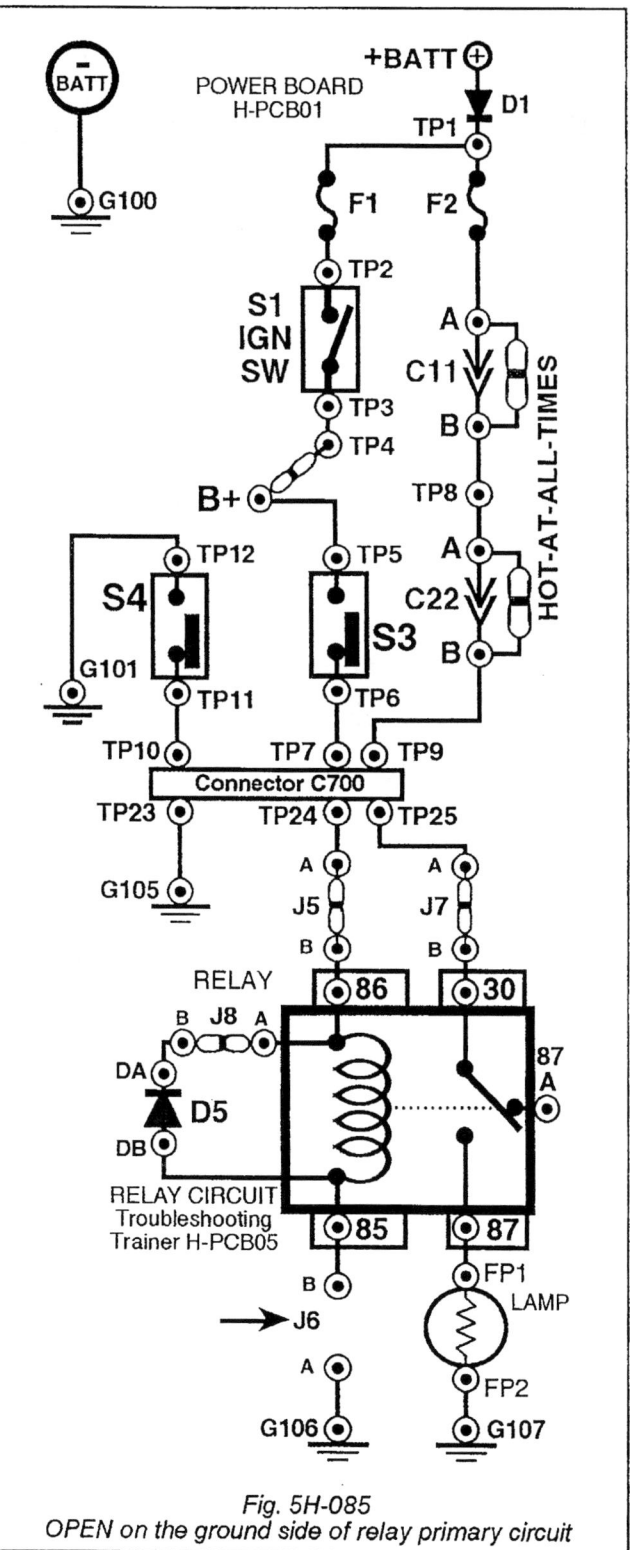

Fig. 5H-085
OPEN on the ground side of relay primary circuit

Vehicle Electronics Hands-On Troubleshooting Training Program

VEEJER ENTERPRISES 3701 Lariat Lane, Garland, Texas 75042-5419
Phone: 972-276-9642 Fax: 972-276-8122 Email: sales@veejer.com Web Site: www.veejer.com

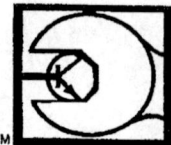

Relay Circuit Problem Number 3S
"OPEN" - Relay Secondary Ground Circuit

The Problem:
An OPEN ground on the relay secondary circuit load, the lamp, is the next circuit problem but it cannot be duplicated on the relay circuit board. There is no provision for opening the ground circuit between FP2 and G107 from the top of the PCB.

Notice in Figure 5H-086 the ground **is drawn OPEN** on the schematic between FP2 and G107 to simulate the problem. No actual measurements are performed in this exercise just answer the following questions.

Problem Analysis:
How does an OPEN circuit on the relay secondary ground side affect relay operation?

_____

_____

> **Lesson 24** discusses circuit problem #3.
> **Lesson 41** discusses an OPEN ground on the relay secondary circuit.

(1) What would the TTS-1 reading be at FP1?

_____

(2) What would the TTS-2 reading be at FP2?

_____

(3) What conclusion is the result of performing the TTS?

_____

(4) What troubleshooting steps are next?

_____

(5) What can be concluded when 0V is found at G107?

_____

Proceed to the next page.

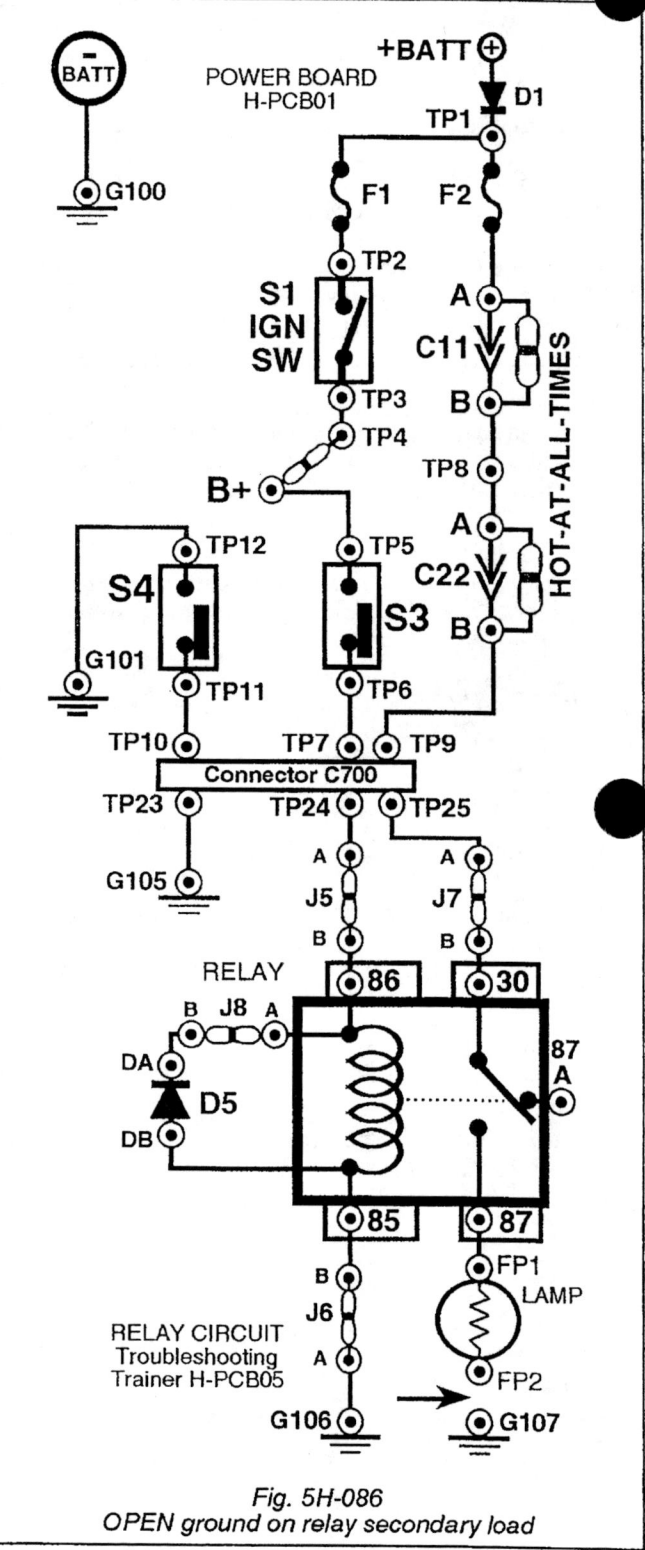

Fig. 5H-086
OPEN ground on relay secondary load

Copyright © 2015 VEEJER ENTERPRISES, Garland, Texas - All Rights Reserved Student Workbook H-WB115 Page 45

Vehicle Electronics Hands-On Troubleshooting Training Program

VEEJER ENTERPRISES 3701 Lariat Lane, Garland, Texas 75042-5419
Phone: 972-276-9642 Fax: 972-276-8122 Email: sales@veejer.com Web Site: www.veejer.com

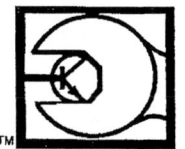

Relay Circuit Problem Number 4P
"Voltage Drop" - Relay Primary Ground Circuit

The Problem:
Insert a Vd on the ground side of the relay primary circuit. Remove J6 from the top of the relay board and insert a 560 ohm resistor **560Ω–cc:grn-blu-bro**. Figure 5H-087 shows the 0ΩR in J6 removed and replaced by a 560Ω resistor which creates a large enough Vd to affect relay operation. If a smaller resistance is used it not affect relay operation.

> **Lesson 24** covers basic circuit problem #4.
> **Lesson 41** cover this problem in relay circuits.

(1) How does a Vd on the relay primary circuit (coil) ground side affect relay operation?
_____
_____

(2) How does this problem affect the relay secondary circuit?
_____

(3) TTS-1 reading: _____
    Conclusion: _____

(4) TTS-2 reading: _____
    Conclusion: _____

(5) What is the next troubleshooting step?
_____
_____

(6) What is concluded finding 0V (B-) at J6 Pin A?
_____

DO THIS:
- Slide S3 DOWN to de-energize the relay.
- Leave the 560Ω resistor in J5 and continue working with Problem #2 on the next page for a very important lesson to learn in troubleshooting relay circuits. **It's a troubleshooting principal you should NEVER FORGET.**

Continue with this exercise on next page.

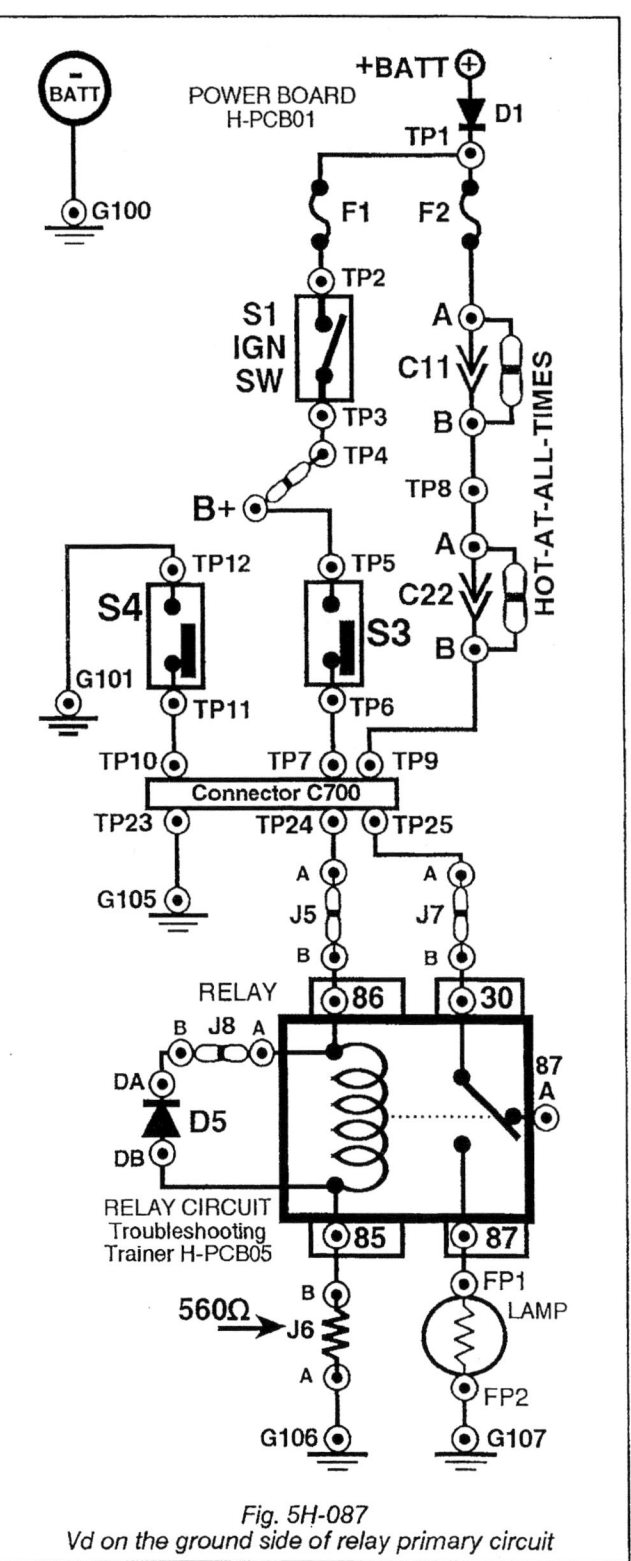

Fig. 5H-087
Vd on the ground side of relay primary circuit

Copyright © 2015 VEEJER ENTERPRISES, Garland, Texas - All Rights Reserved   Student Workbook H-WB115 Page 46

Vehicle Electronics Hands-On Troubleshooting Training Program

VEEJER ENTERPRISES 3701 Lariat Lane, Garland, Texas 75042-5419
Phone: 972-276-9642   Fax: 972-276-8122   Email: sales@veejer.com   Web Site: www.veejer.com

2 IMPORTANT LESSON WHEN A Vd PROBLEM EXISTS ON THE GROUND SIDE OF A RELAY COIL CIRCUIT
These are two ground side problems peculiar to relay circuits to explore here.
(This was discussed in detail on Page 40)

1. Remember? No Current = No Voltage Drop

Do not make the mistake of disconnecting the load when performing the TTS. The relay cannot be disconnected from the Relay Circuit Board to prove this but the TTS-1 result is the same as we found in the Lamp and DC motor circuits. If the relay were disconnected the TTS readings would be normal with the resistor present in the circuit.

The same troubleshooting principle discussed in the Lamp Board and DC Motor Board applies equally in relay primary and secondary circuits. Disconnecting the load in a relay coil circuit stops the electron current and hides any Vd problem.

Relays and Relay Sockets

Most every relay in a vehicle is connected to the vehicle by plugging the relay into a relay socket which is hard wired into the vehicle wiring harness. The relay can be removed from the circuit by unplugging the relay from its relay socket. With the relay removed there is access to the relay pin connections on the relay socket. The TTS cannot be done on the pins of the relay socket with the relay removed because there is no current through the relay primary circuit with the relay disconnected. NEVER DISCONNECT THE LOAD DURING THE TTS ON THE RELAY PRIMARY CIRCUIT BECAUSE ANY Vd PROBLEM PROBLEM IS CONCEALED.

DO THIS:
- Turn relay OFF by sliding S3 DOWN (OFF).
- Change the resistor in J6 from 560Ω to 220 ohms **220Ω–cc:red-red-bro.**
- Slide S3 UP (ON) to energize the relay.

(a.) What happens to relay operation? _____

Note: The voltage drop on the ground side of the relay coil is not big enough yet to prevent the relay from energizing. Perform the TTS.

(b.) TTS-1 reading: _____
(c.) TTS-2 reading: _____
(d.) Why does the relay energize with this TTS-2 reading on the ground side? _____

(e.) What is the lesson to learn from this? _____

2. Intermittent Relay Operation

A second relay problem that often causes **intermittent relay operation** occurs when the Vd on the relay primary ground side finally increases to the point it removes a good ground (B- at 0.10V or less) and prevents the relay from initially energizing.

The relay contacts do finally make contact or CLOSE when the relay is physically bumped or the vehicles hits a road bump. This is identical to the previous problem of intermittent relay operation with a Vd on the voltage side of the relay coil.

DO THIS:
- Turn relay OFF by sliding S3 DOWN (OFF).
- Use the 430Ω resistor network from the previous exercise.

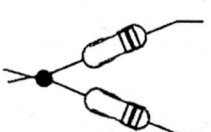

- Insert the 430Ω resistance network in J6 of the relay board and put the 220Ω in the resistor bag.
- Slide S3 UP (ON) to energize the relay.

(a.) What happens to the relay? _____
(b.) Measure the TTS-1 at Pin 86. _____
(c.) Measure the TTS-2 at Pin 85. _____
(d.) What does the voltage at relay Pin 85 represent? _____

(e.) Tap lightly on top of the physical relay until relay "CLICKS" and describe what happens. _____

(f.) What happens to the voltage at Pin 85 when the relay energized? _____

The voltage drop caused by the 430Ω resistor network in J6 provides enough of a poor ground to the relay coil that the relay does not energize The relay coil cannot quite energize with 6-7 volts on the ground circuit. Tapping lightly on the relay adds kinetic energy to the relay which then helps the relay "CLICK" & CLOSE the contacts. The contacts can remain CLOSED at 6.4-6.5V.

This is what happens when a relay in a vehicle circuit appears to be intermittent. Perform the TTS on any suspect relay primary circuit (coil) to see if high B- (more than 0.10V) is getting to the ground side of the relay coil. If so, it's an intermittent relay circuit. Trace B- to find the Vd on the ground side of the relay primary circuit.

Remove resistor from J6 and install a 0ΩR. Go to the next page.

Vehicle Electronics Hands-On Troubleshooting Training Program

VEEJER ENTERPRISES 3701 Lariat Lane, Garland, Texas 75042-5419
Phone: 972-276-9642   Fax: 972-276-8122   Email: sales@veejer.com   Web Site: www.veejer.com

Relay Circuit Problem Number 4S "Voltage Drop" - Relay Secondary Ground Circuit

The Problem:
There is a Vd on the ground side of the relay secondary circuit load. This problem cannot be simulated from the top of the relay circuit board. Notice in Figure 5H-088, the ground of the lamp from Pin FP2, is connected directly to G107. A resistor is drawn in the schematic of Figure 5H-088 to simulate a corroded ground connection.

> Lesson 24 covers basic circuit problem #4.
> Lesson 41 covers this problem in relay circuits.

(1) How does a Vd on the relay secondary circuit (lamp) ground side affect relay operation?
_____
_____

(2) How does this problem affect the relay secondary circuit? _____

(3) What would be the TTS-1 reading at FP1? _____
Conclusion: _____

(4) What would be the TTS-2 reading at FP2? _____
Conclusion: _____

(5) What would be the next troubleshooting step?
_____

(6) What is concluded finding 0V (B-) at G107?
_____

(7) What would the TTS-2 reading be at FP2 if the load (lamp) were disconnected? _____

(8) Explain your answer to Question (7).
_____
_____

DO THIS:
• Slide S3 DOWN to de-energize the relay.

A common mistake made in troubleshooting is to disconnect the load when measuring the TTS.

> **NEVER FORGET!**
> If the load is disconnected the TTS readings will appear normal even if there is resistance on the voltage side or the ground side of the load.
> Remember, "No current = No Vd."

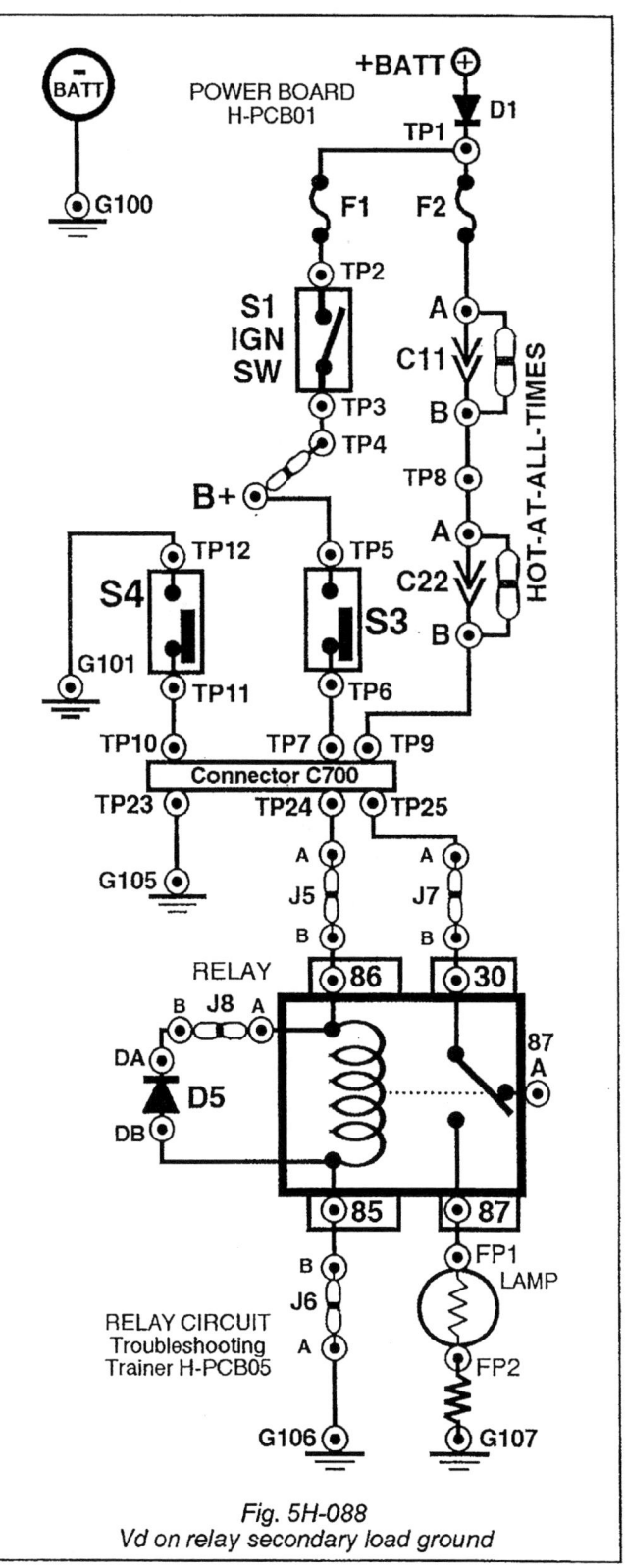

Fig. 5H-088
Vd on relay secondary load ground

Vehicle Electronics Hands-On Troubleshooting Training Program

VEEJER ENTERPRISES 3701 Lariat Lane, Garland, Texas 75042-5419
Phone: 972-276-9642   Fax: 972-276-8122   Email: sales@veejer.com   Web Site: www.veejer.com

Relay Circuit Problem Number 5P
"Open Load" – Relay Primary Circuit"

The problem of an OPEN relay coil (relay primary circuit) cannot be created from the top of the PCBs so we will study this problem through simulation. Figure 5H-089 illustrates an OPEN relay coil winding in the schematic diagram.

> **Lesson 32** covers measuring coil resistance.
> **Lesson 33** covers OPEN coils.
> **Lesson 41** discusses an OPEN relay coil.

Do This:
- Turn the circuit OFF with S1 toggled DOWN (OFF) and S3 slide DOWN.
- Answer the following questions without actually measuring the TTS.

(1) How would an OPEN relay coil affect relay operation? _____

On an actual vehicle, when a relay fails to "CLICK", it would not be wrong to first simply try another relay of the same part number. If the second relay doesn't "CLICK" perform the TTS on the relay coil terminals. The following questions are based on the fact that the relay has an OPEN coil but a new relay is not available so testing is required to prove if the circuit or the relay is defective.

(2) What would be the TTS-1 reading at Pin 86 if the relay coil were actually OPEN? _____

(3) What would be the TTS-2 reading at Pin 85 if the relay coil were actually OPEN? _____

(Since the TTS readings are normal the circuit is providing B+ and B- to the relay coil but the relay doesn't operate. The circuit is doing its job the relay is not.)

(4) What is the next troubleshooting step?
_____

(5) How can relay coil resistance be tested?
_____

(6) How can the correct value of relay coil resistance in ohms be determined?
 (a.) _____
 (b.) _____
 (c.) _____

(7) Since the relay on the relay board is a known good relay, check the coil resistance with a digital ohmmeter connected to Pins 86 and 85, to determine coil resistance, as shown in Figure 5H-089. **Never connect an ohmmeter to a live circuit. Verify that S1 or S3 are OFF to remove voltage from the** relay coil before connecting the ohmmeter.

Coil resistance reading is _____ ohms

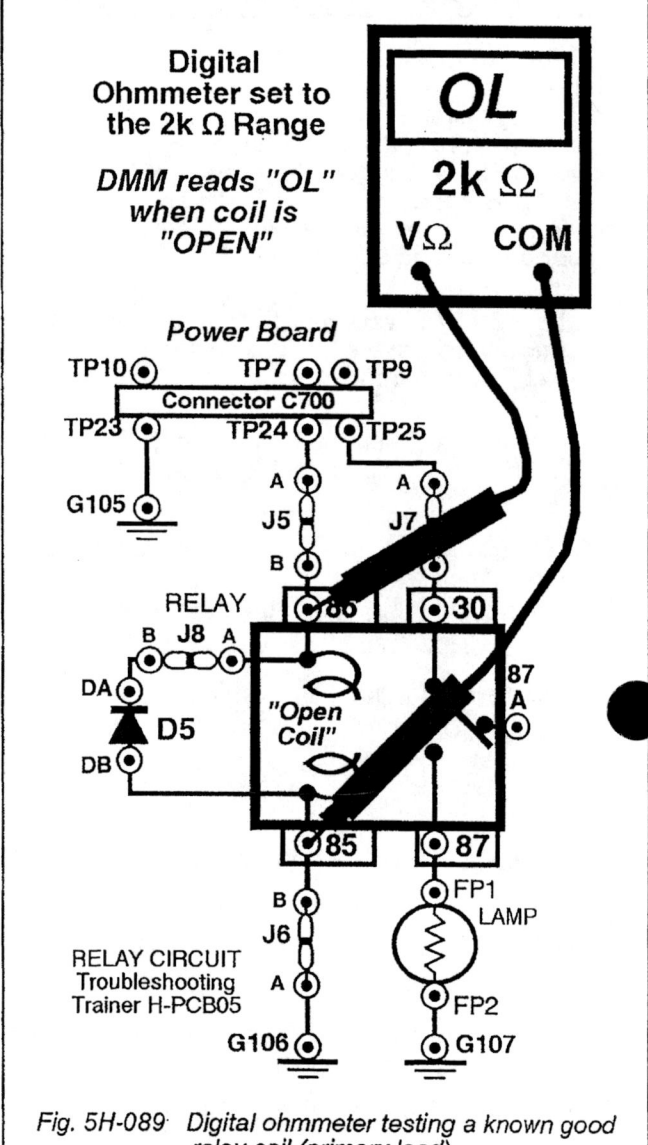

Fig. 5H-089 Digital ohmmeter testing a known good relay coil (primary load)

(8) What would the ohmmeter indicate if the relay coil were really OPEN? _____

Relays with different part numbers can be expected to have different coil resistance values. It is important to know the resistance values of all relays in vehicles you service. Check known good ones with your digital ohmmeter.

Vehicle Electronics Hands-On Troubleshooting Training Program

VEEJER ENTERPRISES 3701 Lariat Lane, Garland, Texas 75042-5419
Phone: 972-276-9642   Fax: 972-276-8122   Email: sales@veejer.com   Web Site: www.veejer.com

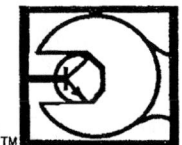

Relay Circuit Problem Number 5S
"Open Load" – Relay Secondary Circuit

The Problem:
Figure 5H-090 illustrates an OPEN load by showing the lamp filament is OPEN but the lamp is still in the circuit.

DO THIS:
- Turn the circuit ON with S1 toggled UP (ON) and S3 slide UP (ON).
- **Simulate an OPEN secondary load by removing the lamp from the lamp socket on the relay board.**
- Do the following exercise.

1. How does an OPEN load in the relay secondary circuit affect relay operation?
   _____

2. What is the TTS-1 reading at FP1? _____

3. What is the TTS-2 reading at FP2? _____

4. What is your conclusion from these TTS readings?
   _____

5. What is the next troubleshooting step?
   _____

6. Check lamp resistance with a digital ohmmeter and record the reading. _____

7. How do you interpret the reading from Step 6?
   _____

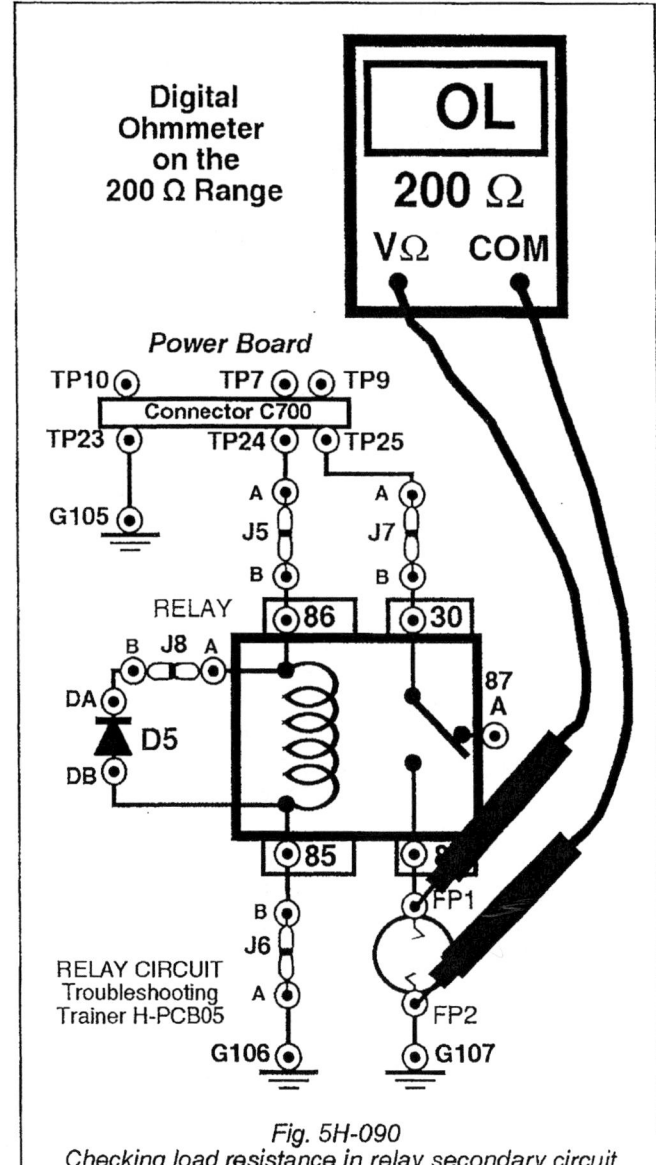

Fig. 5H-090
Checking load resistance in relay secondary circuit

Figure 5H-090 shows a digital ohmmeter checking relay secondary load (lamp) resistance in circuit which means the load is not disconnected from the circuit during the resistance measurement. This is very practical in an actual relay circuit on a vehicle. While the relay is de-energized the contacts are OPEN and no voltage is applied to the load. Since the lamp is drawn as an OPEN lamp in Figure 5H-090, the ohmmeter indicates "OL". When the actual lamp from the relay board is tested a resistance reading is obtained because the lamp is good.

8. With the lamp disconnected from the relay board to simulate an OPEN load, place the ohmmeter test leads at FP1 and FP2 as shown in Figure 5H-090 and record the reading.
   _____

9. How do you interpret the reading from Step 8?

In the real world, if a lamp is OPEN it is often determined by visual inspection of the lamp. If the lamp "looks" good but does not operate then a resistance check would prove if the lamp is OPEN or not.

Checking relay secondary load resistance can be done on any secondary load and sometimes the load may not have to be disconnected during the resistance measurement. If the resistance reading is different when the load is connected to the circuit from when it is not connected to the circuit, always use the resistance reading obtained with the load disconnected for a true load resistance value.

Vehicle Electronics Hands-On Troubleshooting Training Program

VEEJER ENTERPRISES 3701 Lariat Lane, Garland, Texas 75042-5419
Phone: 972-276-9642   Fax: 972-276-8122   Email: sales@veejer.com   Web Site: www.veejer.com

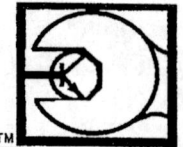

Relay Circuit Problem Number 6P
Relay Primary Circuit—"Shorted Load"

A circuit can develop a shorted load and blow a fuse or the voltage side of the circuit can become shorted to ground and blow a fuse. The latter is where the wire conductor on the voltage side makes physical contact with the chassis. These two possibilities must be considered separately for both the primary and secondary circuits for a total of four exercises troubleshooting shorts-to-ground.

The Problem:
A shorted relay coil (relay primary load) will blow a fuse in an electrical circuit and on the Power Board Fuse F1 would be blown.

If the relay is controlled by a computer, a shorted relay coil could damage the computer. Becoming aware of this potential relay failure and how to detect it can save a major mistake that would smoke a perfectly good computer.

DO THIS:
- **Remove fuse F1 from the Power Board to simulate the fuse is blown or replace F1 with a blown fuse.**
- **Insert A SHORTED Load condition in the relay board by connecting a jumper wire between Pins 86 and 85 to simulate a shorted relay coil winding.**

> **Lesson 8** discusses ohmmeter operation.
> **Lesson 18** discusses resistance testing.
> **Lesson 24** discusses Study Problem #6.
> **Lesson 25** discusses shorts in circuits.
> **Lesson 41** discusses a shorted relay coil.

A review of the essential theory concerning the term "shorts" is helpful in understanding what it means which is often a misunderstood topic resulting in the term "short" being misapplied. The term "short" only involves conditions that result in higher than normal current in a circuit.

(1) What blows a fuse?
_____

(2) What are two reasons for current in a circuit to increase?
   (A) _____
   (B) _____

(3) What is a short in a circuit?
_____

(4) What two ways can a circuit develop a short?
   (A.) _____
   (B.) _____

Figure 5H-091 shows a wire connected across Pins 86 and 85 to introduce a "shorted load" without the relay coil actually being shorted. Connect a wire as shown. The Power Board is not shown but is understood to be connected to the relay board.

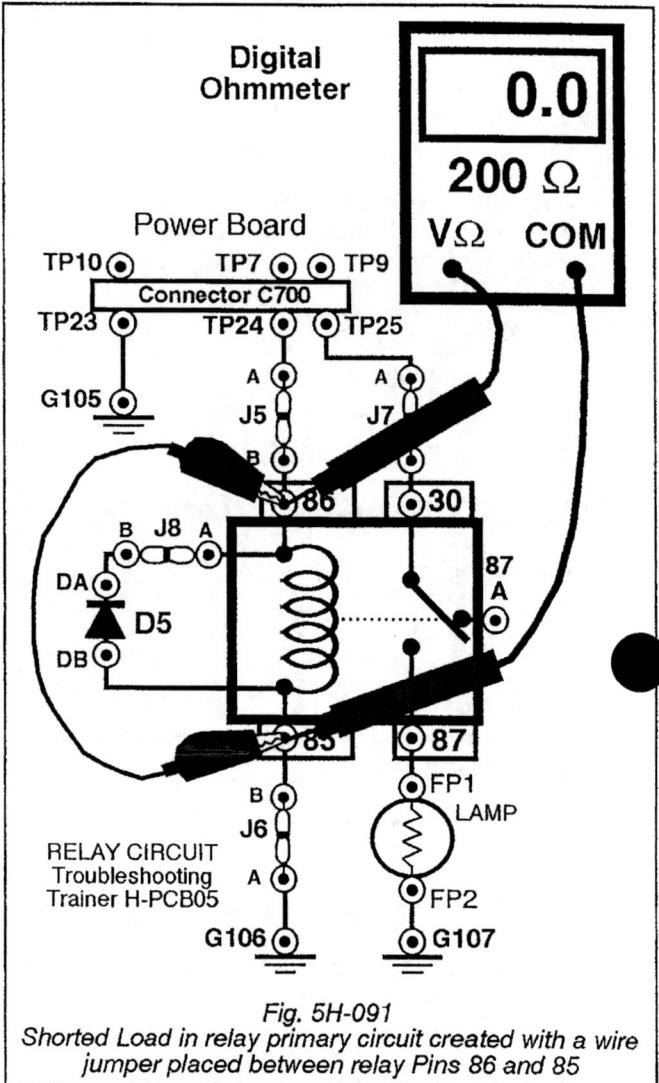

Fig. 5H-091
Shorted Load in relay primary circuit created with a wire jumper placed between relay Pins 86 and 85

(5) What would happen to Fuse F1 if the relay circuit were to be connected to a live Power Board?
_____

(6) If a relay circuit blows the relay primary circuit fuse F1 the first step in troubleshooting the problem is to check relay coil resistance with a digital ohmmeter.

(7) What would the ohmmeter reading be:
   if the relay coil **is not** shorted? _____
   if the relay coil **is** shorted? _____

- **Remove the wire short between Pins 86-85.**
- **Install a good fuse in F1.**

Copyright © 2015 VEEJER ENTERPRISES, Garland, Texas - All Rights Reserved   Student Workbook H-WB115

Vehicle Electronics Hands-On Troubleshooting Training Program

VEEJER ENTERPRISES 3701 Lariat Lane, Garland, Texas 75042-5419
Phone: 972-276-9642 Fax: 972-276-8122 Email: sales@veejer.com Web Site: www.veejer.com

Relay Circuit Problem Number 6S
Relay Secondary Circuit—"Shorted Load"

The Problem:
A shorted LOAD on the relay contacts (relay secondary circuit) will blow a fuse feeding B+ to the relay secondary circuit.

On the Power Board this is Fuse F2. If the relay secondary circuit's fuse does not blow it would damage the wiring harness and possibly burn up the relay contacts. Becoming aware of this possible relay secondary circuit failure and how to detect it will make troubleshooting relay problems more effective.

A shorted load on the relay secondary circuit has no effect on the relay primary circuit.

In Figure 5H-092 the Power Board is not shown but is understood to be connected to the relay board. This was done to have room to show the digital ohmmeter performing a resistance test of the relay secondary load.

DO THIS:
- **Remove fuse F2 from the Power Board to simulate the fuse is blown.**

- Insert a SHORTED Load condition in the relay secondary circuit by connecting a jumper wire across the lamp at Pins FP1 and FP2 to simulate a shorted load on the relay secondary circuit.

(1) What would happen to Fuse F2 if the relay circuit were to be connected to a live Power Board?
_____

(2) If a relay circuit blows the relay secondary circuit fuse F2 the first step in troubleshooting the problem is to check relay secondary _____ _____ with a digital ohmmeter.

(3) What would the ohmmeter reading be if the relay secondary load (lamp):
   is not shorted? _____
   is shorted? _____

- **Remove the wire short across the lamp Pins FP1 and FP2.**

- **Install a good fuse in F2.**

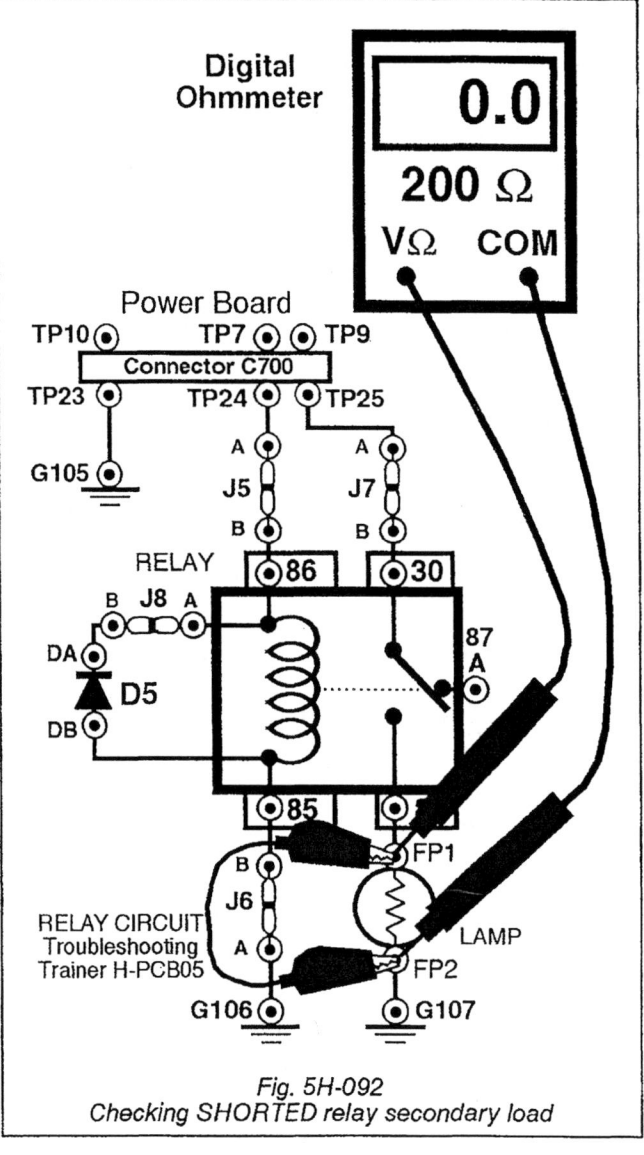

Fig. 5H-092
Checking SHORTED relay secondary load

Troubleshooting a "short" in a circuit, a circuit where a fuse "blows" either immediately or after a few seconds, requires a systematic troubleshooting approach. Whenever a blown fuse is encountered, first check load resistance. It is a simple measurement that doesn't take a lot of time. If the load is shorted the load must be replaced and a new fuse installed. That may take care of the problem and it is fast. Up to this point we have covered troubleshooting the shorted load as a reason a fuse blows.

Another reason for a fuse to blow, besides a SHORTED load condition, occurs when the voltage side of the circuit, the "hot" wire as some call it, touches the chassis or is "grounded". The next two exercises cover a fuse blowing due to a voltage side short to ground.

Vehicle Electronics Hands-On Troubleshooting Training Program

VEEJER ENTERPRISES 3701 Lariat Lane, Garland, Texas 75042-5419
Phone: 972-276-9642 Fax: 972-276-8122 Email: sales@veejer.com Web Site: www.veejer.com

Relay Circuit Problem Number 6P
Relay Primary Circuit—"Short-to-Ground"

The Problem:
The voltage side wiring in a relay's primary or secondary circuit may make contact with the chassis (ground) and blow the fuse. This type of problem is called a **short-to-ground.**

Specifically, the wire conductor on the voltage side is surrounded by wire insulation usually a plastic material. If the insulation is penetrated, the wire conductor touches the chassis. If the wire is "hot" (connected to B+) high current flows and the fuse blows. Some might call this problem a pinched wire problem. Figure 5H-093 is showing the troubleshooting procedure for finding a short to ground.

DO THIS:
- Disconnect H-PS01 Power Supply from wall socket.
- Remove Fuse F1.
- Connect a jumper wire from -BATT to TP7. This inserts a simulated short-to-ground problem in the voltage side of the relay primary circuit at TP7.
- Ground DMM to -BATT and select the Ohms test for a 400 reading. If DMM is manually selectable select the 2k Ohm Range. If DMM Auto ranges allow DMM to Autorange on Ohms and it will automatically select the correct ohmmeter range.
- Connect Red test lead to COLD side of F1. This is the lower fuse terminal that does not have B+ when the fuse is removed.

Note: Carefully follow this exercise.

(1) What does the ohmmeter indicate? _____

   Conclusion: _____

(2) Disconnect the jumper wire from TP7 to remove the short to ground. What does the ohmmeter indicate? _____

   Conclusion: _____

Reconnect the ground jumper wire to TP7 to insert the short to ground again and verify the ohmmeter indicates the short to ground is back.

To determine where in the voltage side of the relay primary circuit the short exists simply disconnect portions of the circuit until the ohmmeter indicates OL (short not seen anymore). In this way the circuit can be narrowed down to the smallest part to identify the location of the short to ground.

(3) Slide S3 Down (OFF) and record DMM reading.

   _____

   Conclusion: _____

(4) Slide S3 UP and DMM "sees" short again. Disconnect the relay board from C700 and record the DMM reading. _____
   Conclusion: _____

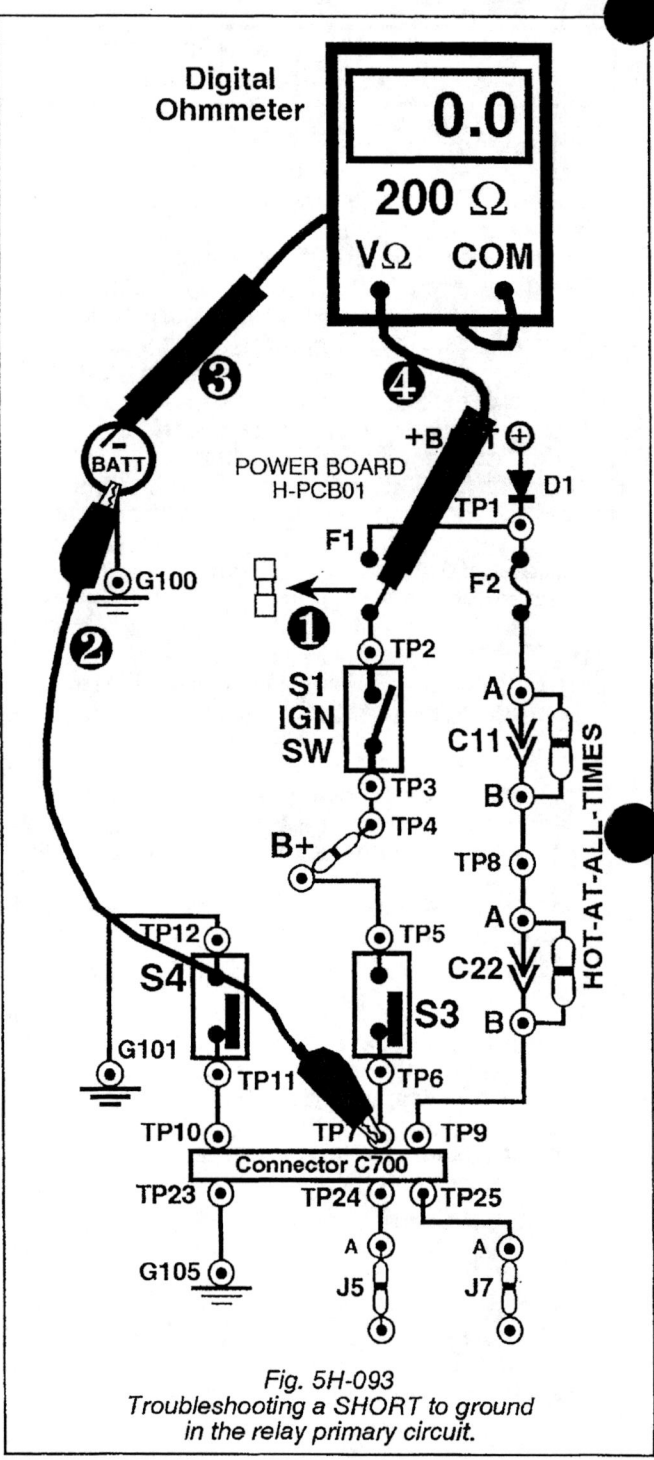

Fig. 5H-093
Troubleshooting a SHORT to ground in the relay primary circuit.

The short to ground in the voltage side of the relay primary circuit has to be in the length of wire between TP6 and TP7. To confirm this is the short location, leave S3 OFF (slide DOWN) and the relay board disconnected. Touch Red test lead to either TP6 or TP7. Ohmmeter reads 0 ohm which indicates the short-to-ground is located there.

Vehicle Electronics Hands-On Troubleshooting Training Program

VEEJER ENTERPRISES 3701 Lariat Lane, Garland, Texas 75042-5419
Phone: 972-276-9642   Fax: 972-276-8122   Email: sales@veejer.com   Web Site: www.veejer.com

Relay Circuit Problem Number 6S
Relay Secondary Circuit—"Short-to-Ground"

The Problem:
A short-to-ground can occur in a relay's secondary circuit. Figure 5H-094 shows the DMM connected into the circuit. Since the illustration is a little complicated with DMM test leads crossing each other and other detail that is hard to see, take a few moments to study the illustration and follow these directions first. It was done this way to fit the illustration in the space available.

DO THIS:
- Disconnect H-PS01 Power Supply from wall socket.
- Install Fuse F1 and Remove Fuse F2.
- Connect a jumper wire from -BATT to J7-B on the relay board. This inserts a simulated short-to-ground problem in the voltage side of the relay secondary circuit at J7-B.
- Ground DMM to -BATT and select the Ohms test for a 400 reading. If DMM is **manually selectable** select the 2k Ohm Range. If DMM **Auto ranges** allow DMM to Autorange on Ohms and it will automatically select the correct ohmmeter range.
- Connect Red test lead to COLD side of F2. This is the lower fuse terminal that does not have B+ when the fuse is removed.

Once all the "**DO THIS:**" is completed and you have studied the schematic of Figure 5H-094, we begin to discuss troubleshooting a short-to-ground on the secondary side of a relay circuit. The same concepts were used with the Starter Kit and The DC Motor Board to troubleshoot shorts-to-ground.

The first symptom noticed on an actual relay circuit on a vehicle with a short-to-ground on a relay's secondary side is a fuse is blown which would be Fuse F2 on the Power Board.

Place the DMM on Ohms and connect as shown in Figure 5H-094 and the reading is 0 ohms since it "sees" the short-to-ground created at J7-B. If the DMM is set to the 200 Ohm range the DMM reads approximately 00.5 (Ω). If the DMM is set to the 2k Ohm range the DMM reads approximately .001 (Ω).

Next disconnect circuitry to isolate what part of the circuit has the short-to-ground. This circuit does not have many points suitable for disconnecting but there are two options to consider first. Disconnect the relay board or the 0ΩR in J7.

If the relay board is disconnected it would break the DMM ground through C700 so the DMM Black test lead and ground jumper would have to be moved from the -BATT terminal to TP23 on the relay board. If we leave the relay board connected to the Power Board and remove just the 0ΩR from J7 on the relay board it's easier to deal with since the DMM Black test lead and wire jumper can stay where they are.

(continue this exercise on next page)

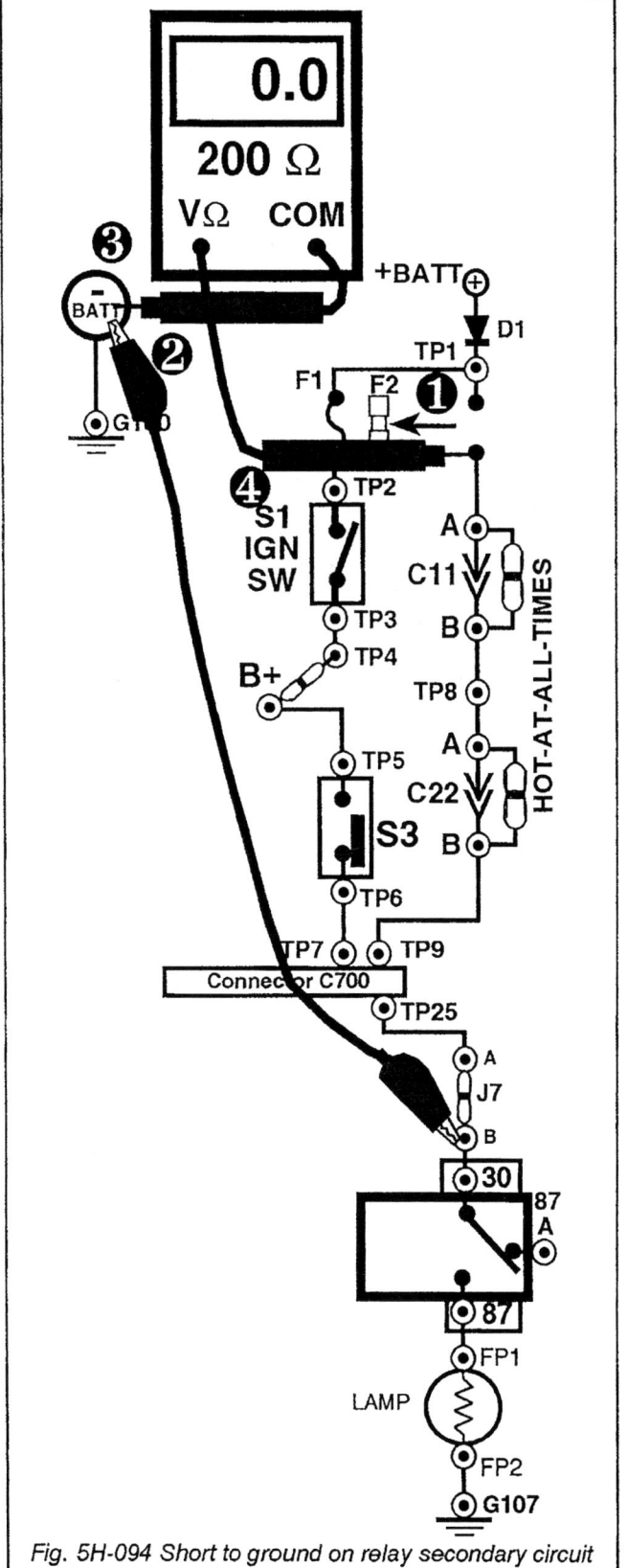

Fig. 5H-094 Short to ground on relay secondary circuit

Vehicle Electronics Hands-On Troubleshooting Training Program

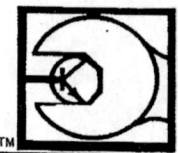

VEEJER ENTERPRISES 3701 Lariat Lane, Garland, Texas 75042-5419
Phone: 972-276-9642 Fax: 972-276-8122 Email: sales@veejer.com Web Site: www.veejer.com

Remove the 0ΩR in J7, as shown in Figure 5H-094A to disconnect the circuit between Pins A and B of J7 which separates all circuitry below J7-B.

Note the reading on the DMM goes to "OL". This means the DMM cannot "see" the short to ground at J7-B from the cold side of Fuse F2.

Leave the 0ΩR out of J7 during the next step. Move the DMM Red test lead from the cold side of F2 to J7-B or Pin 30 of the relay.

The DMM reads 0Ω because it "sees" the short-to-ground again. Pin 30 of the relay is in contact with Pin 87A since the relay is de-energized. Move the Red test lead to relay Pin 87A just to see the short at that point.

Since no wire is connected to Pin 87A the short-to-ground is coming from Pin 30. We can conclude that the wire between J7-B and Pin 30, as long as it might be in a wiring harness, is shorted to ground at some point in the wire. This places a short-to-ground in the wire that can be "seen" by a DMM's ohmmeter at any point in the wire the test lead touches.

Once the wire between J7-B and Pin 30 in a vehicle harness is known to have the short-to-ground, simply follow along the wire in the vehicle looking for the spot where the insulation is penetrated allowing the conductor inside the insulation to make physical and electrical contact with the chassis (ground).

DO THIS:
- Remove the wire jumper acting as the short.
- Install Fuse F2.
- Install a 0ΩR in J7.
- Verify relay board is fully operational by performing the TTS on the relay primary load (coil) and secondary load (lamp).

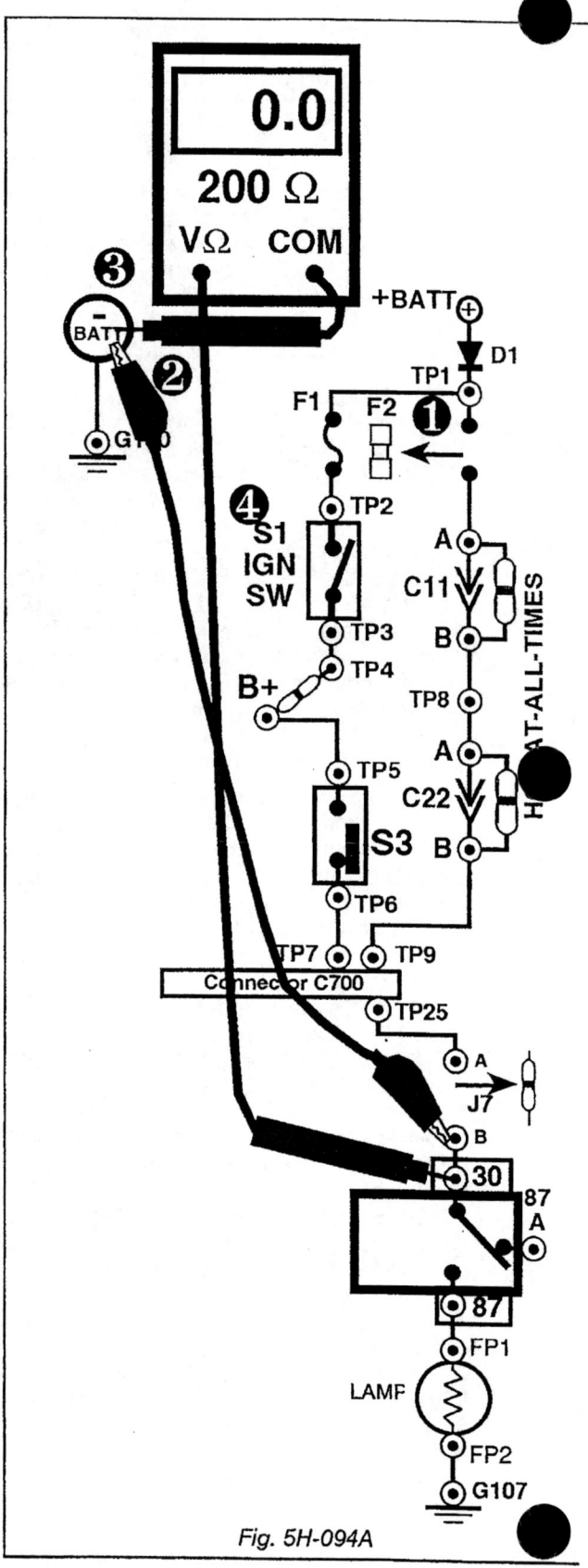

Fig. 5H-094A

Vehicle Electronics Hands-On Troubleshooting Training Program

VEEJER ENTERPRISES 3701 Lariat Lane, Garland, Texas 75042-5419
Phone: 972-276-9642 Fax: 972-276-8122 Email: sales@veejer.com Web Site: www.veejer.com

Relay Circuit Problem Number 7
"Short-to-Voltage" – Relay Circuit

The Problem: A short-to-voltage problem occurs in a wiring harness when a wire carrying B+ runs along the harness and adjacent to a control wire of a second electrical circuit. The control wire is defined as the wire that gets B+ or B- to turn a circuit ON.

If the insulation becomes hot and melts, the two wires may make physical contact and transfer the B+ in one wire to a second control wire as shown in Figure 5H-095. The B+ in the wire to Lamp 1 transfers its B+ to a second circuit, Lamp 2's control wire, when Lamp 1 is supposed to be switched OFF. The result is the second circuit, Lamp 2, operates when its control switch (S1) is OFF and as long as the wire to Lamp 1 has B+. This type of problem is called a **short-to-voltage**.

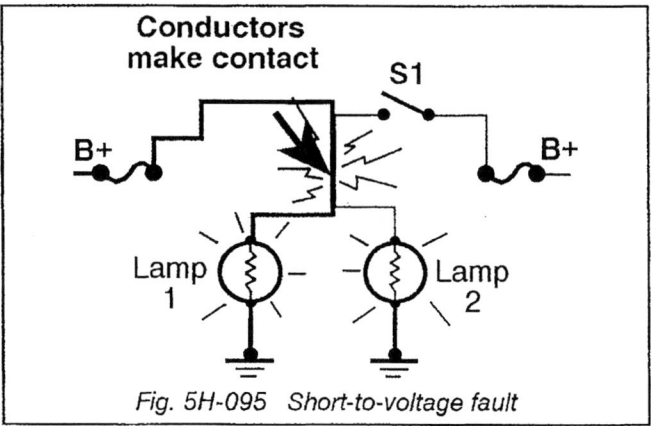

Fig. 5H-095 Short-to-voltage fault

Figure 5H-096, to the right, is a schematic of the relay circuit used for this exercise. Follow these instructions.

DO THIS:
- Set up and energize the relay.
- With the lamp ON, slide S3 DOWN (OFF).
- Verify the relay is de-energized and lamp is OUT.
- Connect a wire jumper from TP8 on the Power Board (hot-at-all-times) to J5-A on the Relay Board (switched B+ with S3).

As soon as the wire jumper makes electrical contact between the two circuit points, a **short-to-voltage** occurs which turns ON (energizes) the relay while the switch S3 is OFF. The B+ from the relay secondary circuit (hot-at-all-times) is providing B+ to Pin 86 of the relay, through the short-to-voltage, causing it to energize and CLOSE the relay contacts which turns ON the secondary load.

In Figure 5H-096, the short-to-voltage occurs in the wire from TP6 (below S3) to Pin 86. Anywhere the short-to-voltage exists in that part of the relay primary circuit will turn ON the relay when S3 is OFF.

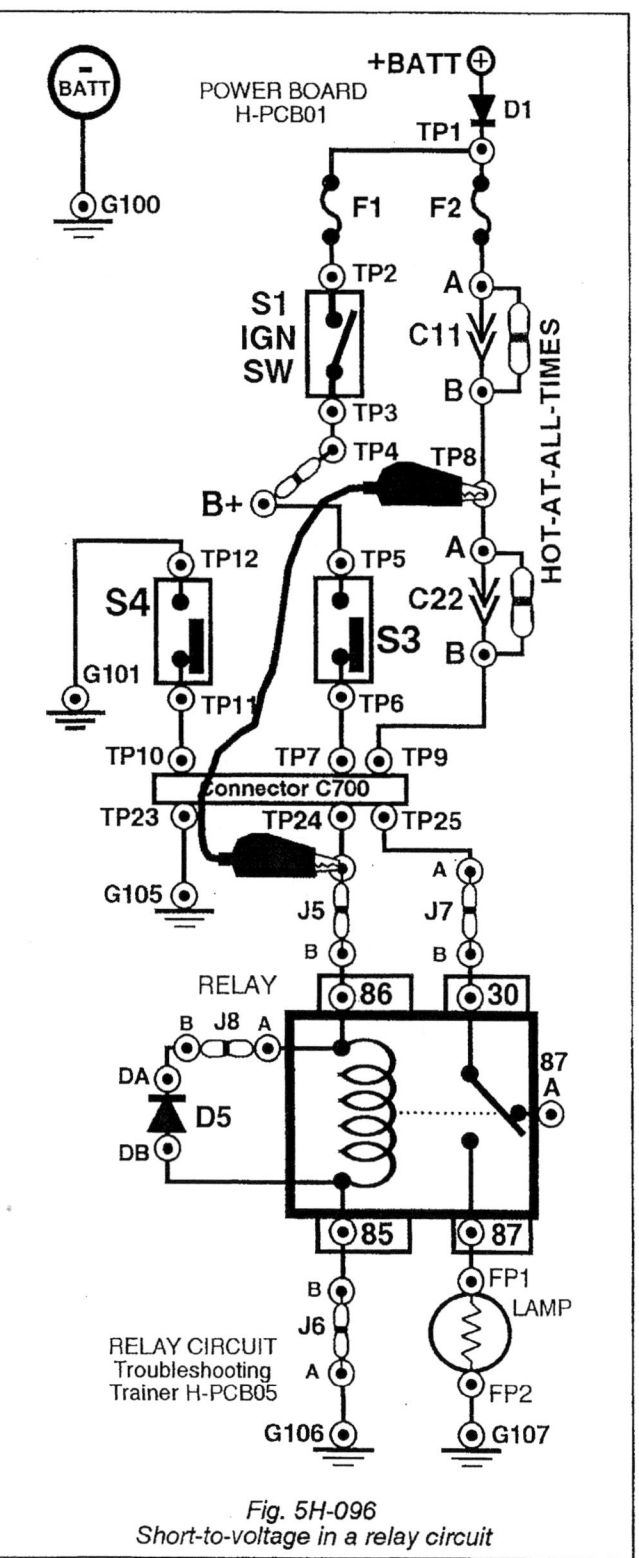

*Fig. 5H-096
Short-to-voltage in a relay circuit*

(continue this exercise on the next page)

Sometimes a short-to-voltage may do no harm although it operates another circuit when that circuit may need to be in the OFF condition which can be a problem in itself. A short-to-voltage can take other forms than discussed this far, such as, when the relay secondary circuit is shorted to the relay primary circuit below the control switch S3.

Yet the underlying principle of a short-to-voltage problem is always the same. B+ makes contact with another circuit turning it ON when that circuit should be OFF. This means the short-to-voltage must make contact with the control side wire of the circuit that should be OFF to be noticed.

If the short-to-voltage occurs above S3 (TP5 side) it wouldn't be noticed. The relay would not turn ON until S3 is switched ON which is normal operation.

DO THIS: (Use only one wire jumper)
(1) Move the jumper wire from J5-A to connect between TP5 and TP8 as shown in Figure 5H-096A. **Wire #1 connects above switch S3.** Control the relay by turning S3 ON/OFF. The relay operates normally with S3 as if nothing is wrong with the short-to-voltage above the switch. The only problem this short-to-voltage problem may present is a fuse blows because it handles more current that it is rated to handle while it is providing power for two circuits instead of one.

(2) Move the jumper wire from TP5 back to J5-A. **Wire #2 connects to control side of switch S3.**

Troubleshooting Shorts-to-Voltage

Identify the voltage source supplying the current to the wrong circuit by disconnecting B+ feeds until the circuit that is not suppose to be ON turns OFF. Then trace that section of wiring to find where the short-to-voltage exists. One of the easiest ways to disconnect B+ is to remove fuses from the fuse box or fuse panel until the circuit that is not suppose to be ON turns OFF.

DO THIS:
- With the jumper wire between TP8 and J5-A the relay is ON, Lamp ON. **Disconnect Fuse F2.**
- Note the relay turns OFF.
- Slide S3 ON/OFF and listen to the relay *"CLICK"*. S3 is now able to control the relay although the short-to-voltage is still present but no B+ is coming through F2 so lamp doesn't turn ON when relay *"CLICKS"*.
- **Remove jumper wire between TP8 and J5-A.**
- **Install fuse in F2.**
- **Verify proper relay circuit operation.**

Any circuit with a short-to-voltage problem that does not have visual indicators it is ON (light turns ON) or audible indicators (CLICKS) when it is ON can be troubleshot by using a DMM to detect voltage in the control wire of the circuit. If you suspect any circuit is ON and you know it should be OFF perform the TTS. Those two readings will indicate if the circuit is indeed ON. Leave the DMM test lead on control side of the load and disconnect fuses till the voltage at that point changes to the OFF reading.

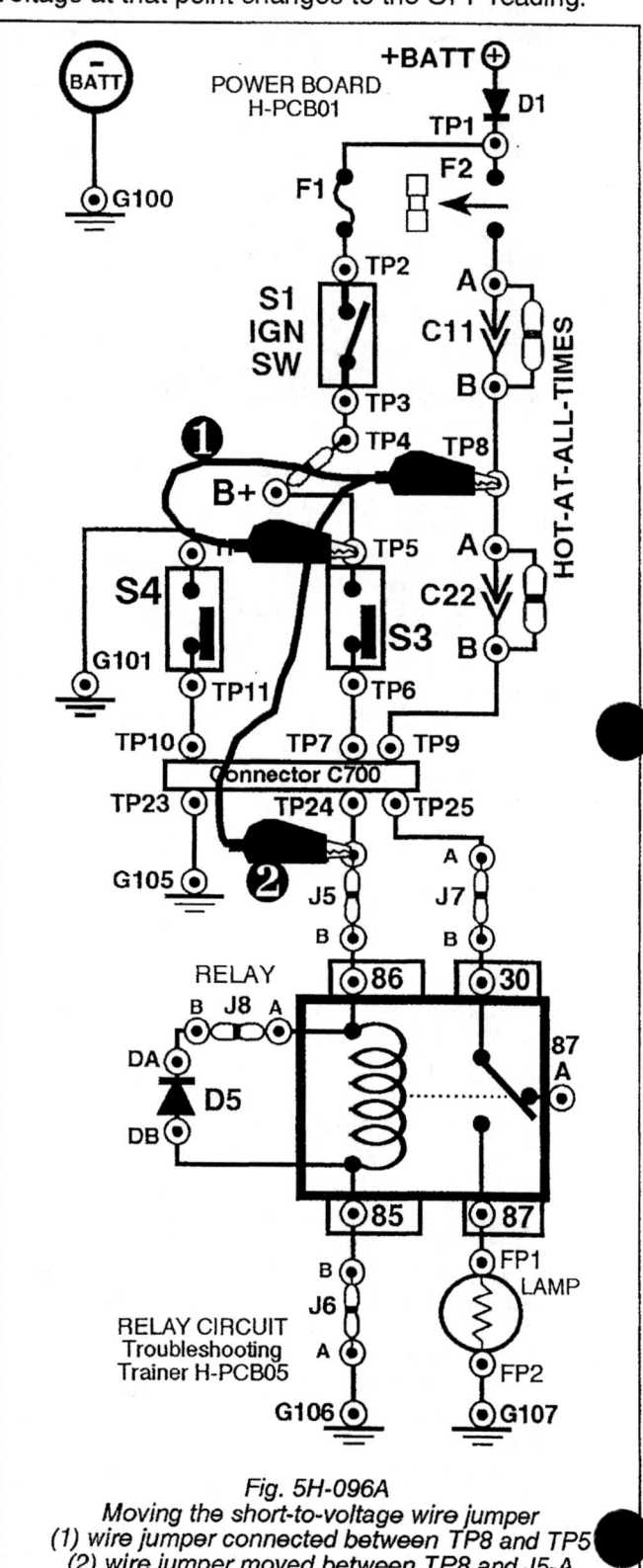

Fig. 5H-096A
Moving the short-to-voltage wire jumper
(1) wire jumper connected between TP8 and TP5
(2) wire jumper moved between TP8 and J5-A

Vehicle Electronics Hands-On Troubleshooting Training Program

VEEJER ENTERPRISES 3701 Lariat Lane, Garland, Texas 75042-5419
Phone: 972-276-9642   Fax: 972-276-8122   Email: sales@veejer.com   Web Site: www.veejer.com

Current in Relay Primary Circuit

Current in an electrical or electronic circuit is the flow of electrons from the negative terminal through the circuit to the positive terminal.

Electrons are shown as ⊖ in Figure 5H-097. Use a highlighter to mark the path of electrons. Tracing current in a circuit is a way to discover unusual things about a circuit crucial to under-standing the circuit but possibly overlooked if the path for current were not traced throughout the circuit. Figure 5H-097 illustrates the path of electron current through the relay primary circuit. Trace the current path through the relay schematic using the following word description.

(1) Electron current ⊖ leaves the -BATT terminal and enters the engine block. G100 is the engine ground in this example. Current channels through the engine block to the redundant ground. "Channeling" is the streaming of electron current through a solid metallic mass such as the engine block or the sheet metal.

(2) Current channels through the Accessory or Sheet Metal Ground Strap and enters the sheet metal designated G101.

(3) Current flows up through G101 and down through the CLOSED contacts of S4.

(4) Current flows through TP11-TP10 through C700 to TP23 and channels through the sheet metal designated G105.

(5) Current flows through the ground strap between G105 and the sheet metal that connects to the sheet metal of G106 and G107.

(6) Current channels through the sheet metal ground up through J6 into relay Pin 85.

(7) Current flows through the relay coil creating an electromagnetic field around the coil that CLOSES the relay contacts.

(8) Current leaves Pin 86, flows up through J5-TP24 through C700 to TP7-TP6 through the CLOSED contacts of S3 to the B+ Terminal.

(9) Current flows up through the 0ΩR between the B+ Terminal and TP4, through the CLOSED contacts of the Ignition Switch S1 and through the Fuse F1.

(10) Current returns to the +BATT terminal.

Relay Secondary Circuit Current

Current through the relay secondary circuit is very similar. Trace the relay secondary current.

Once current reaches G106 it is also available to G107. As soon as the relay contacts CLOSE, current flows up through the Lamp, through the CLOSED relay contacts (Pins 87-30), through J7, through C700 (TP25-TP9), through connector C22, TP8, connector C11, Fuse F2, against the arrow in diode D1 to return to +BATT.

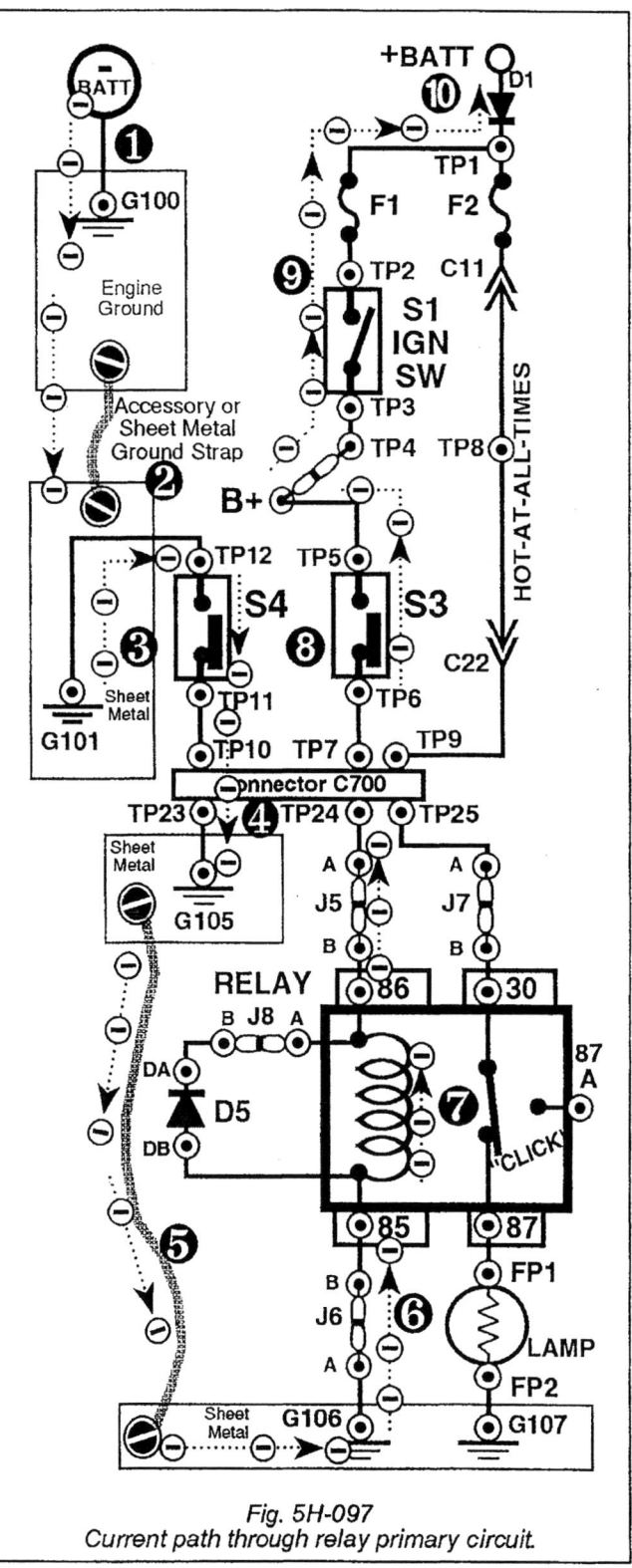

Fig. 5H-097
Current path through relay primary circuit.

Computer Control of Relays

A vehicle computer can control a relay by one of two ways just like S3 and S4 control the relay on the relay board. All it takes is a small current through the relay coil to CLOSE the relay's contacts. Figure 5H-098 reviews both relay coil control options using mechanical switches S3 and S4.

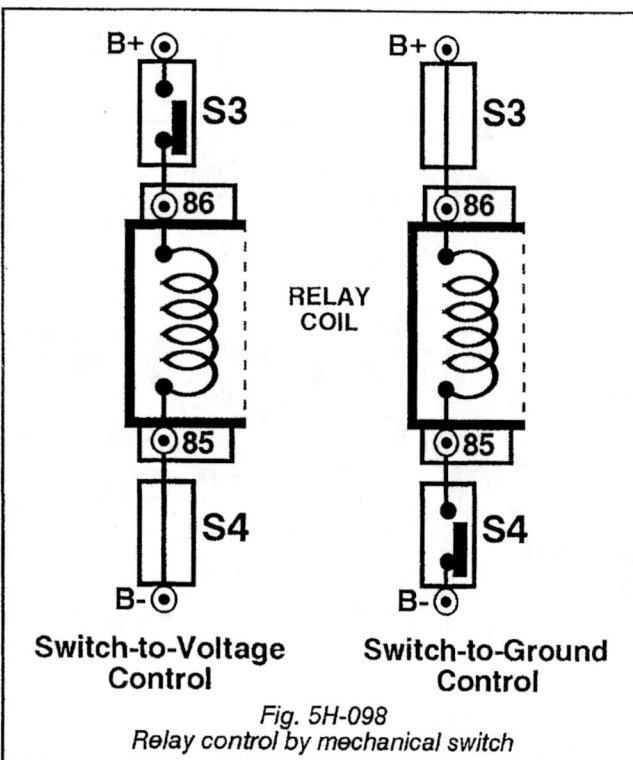

Fig. 5H-098
Relay control by mechanical switch

In **switch-to-voltage control**, S3 switches the voltage (B+) to Pin 86 to energize the relay while Pin 85 is permanently grounded through the CLOSED contacts of S4. In **switch-to-ground control**, S4 switches the ground (B-) to Pin 85 to energize the relay while Pin 86 is permanently connected to voltage (B+) through the CLOSED contacts of S3.

Computer Control of Relays

A vehicle computer controls a relay with a small current using an inexpensive, low power, light weight solid-state transistor switch called a **Driver Transistor** to provide relay coil current. When the relay contacts are CLOSED high current is switched to a high current load such as a fuel pump or blower motor. This allows a computer to control a load needing high current (several amps to hundreds of amps) with a small transistor driver. The driver transistor has to handle only the coil current. The relay contacts switch the high current. The relay contacts can be designed to handle hundreds of amps if necessary to supply high current load requirements. Without relays the computer's driver transistors would be very large and heavy solid-state components generating a lot of heat, waste power and add considerable cost to a vehicle computer just to provide the high current needed by a high current load. A relay solves the problem. Figure 5H-098A shows the two ways a computer using a small transistor driver controls a relay coil. The transistor driver's job is to provide the coil current needed to energize the relay like a mechanical switch does.

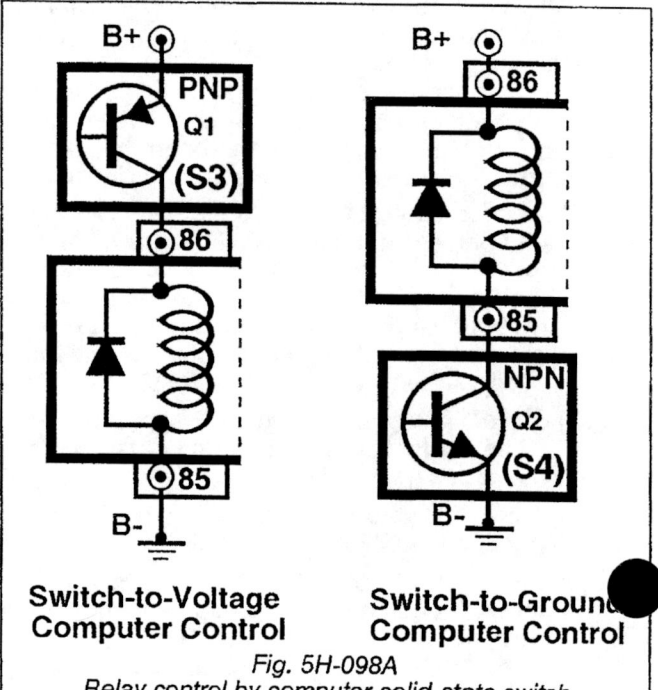

Fig. 5H-098A
Relay control by computer solid-state switch

The relay coil on the left is a switch-to-voltage solid-state control circuit using a PNP type transistor driver, Q1. The "Q" is the recognized method to number transistors in a circuit for purposes of identification. Notice in switch-to-voltage control the computer is on the voltage side of the load like S3. The driver transistor switches B+ to Pin 86 just like S3 would do. Pin 85 is connected directly to ground.

The relay coil on the right is a switch-to-ground solid-state control circuit using a NPN type transistor driver, Q2. Notice with switch-to-ground the computer is on the ground side of the load like S4. The driver transistor switches B- to Pin 85 just like S4 would do. Pin 86 is connected directly to B+ voltage.

The purpose of the diode across the relay coil is to absorb the energy dump and prevent a dangerous voltage spike that occurs every time the relay coil de-energizes.

Lessons to reference from "*The*" Course
Lesson 45 covers the NPN Transistor circuit
Lesson 46 cover the PNP Transistor circuit
Lesson 48 covers spike voltage suppression
Lesson 60 covers computer control of relays

Vehicle Electronics Hands-On Troubleshooting Training Program

VEEJER ENTERPRISES 3701 Lariat Lane, Garland, Texas 75042-5419
Phone: 972-276-9642 Fax: 972-276-8122 Email: sales@veejer.com Web Site: www.veejer.com

How Relays Damage Computers

There are two major ways a relay can knock out the transistor driver in a vehicle computer which means the computer must be replaced. If the defective relay is left in the vehicle circuit and a replacement computer installed, the relay problem will eventually or suddenly knock out the new computer. Not until the defective relay is replaced with a known good relay will the computer survive. It is clear then that a thorough understanding of relay failures is necessary to prevent knocking out replacement vehicle computer. This is the reason we have covered checking relay coil resistance with a digital ohmmeter and spike diodes with an analog ohmmeter in the beginning of this training manual.

Figure 5H-099 shows the relay board connected to the Power Board and a DMM measuring **relay coil load current**. The explanation of this test procedure follows below.

1. Low Relay Coil Resistance

If relay **coil resistance** begins to decrease due to coil windings shorting together when the relay gets warm, driver transistor current increases. Increased driver current will overheat and eventually burn up a computer's transistor driver. But even if a digital ohmmeter indicates the correct resistance is present (a static test) in a cold relay coil it doesn't prove the relay coil has the proper resistance when it gets warmed up from passing current (a dynamic test).

To verify a relay coil is still operating properly when warm, place a digital ammeter in series with the relay coil and measure relay coil current as shown in Figure 5H-099. Make sure the DMM is set to measure mA as explained in Figure 5H-099.

Expect a DMM reading of approximately 30 mA for the relay used in the relay board H-PCB05. Notice that as the relay remains energized and the relay coil warms up that the relay coil current decreases about 1-3 mAmps. **This is what you are looking for in a good relay coil winding.** As the relay coil gets warm, its resistance increases a slight amount causing the slight decrease in coil current. **That's good!** This means as a good relay coil gets warm, its resistance increases, the current decreases slightly then the coil current holds steady at the lower mAmp reading.

If the relay coil were defective, the relay current would INCREASE as the relay coil got warm because the relay coil's resistance is decreasing. **That's bad!** This results in an increase in transistor driver current and a doomed transistor driver. How much can relay coil current increase? A good relay coil will be within 10% of normal current drain that is determined from checking a known good relay. A relay may also be load current tested faster by applying some heat to the relay with a hair dryer for one minute to get it warm.

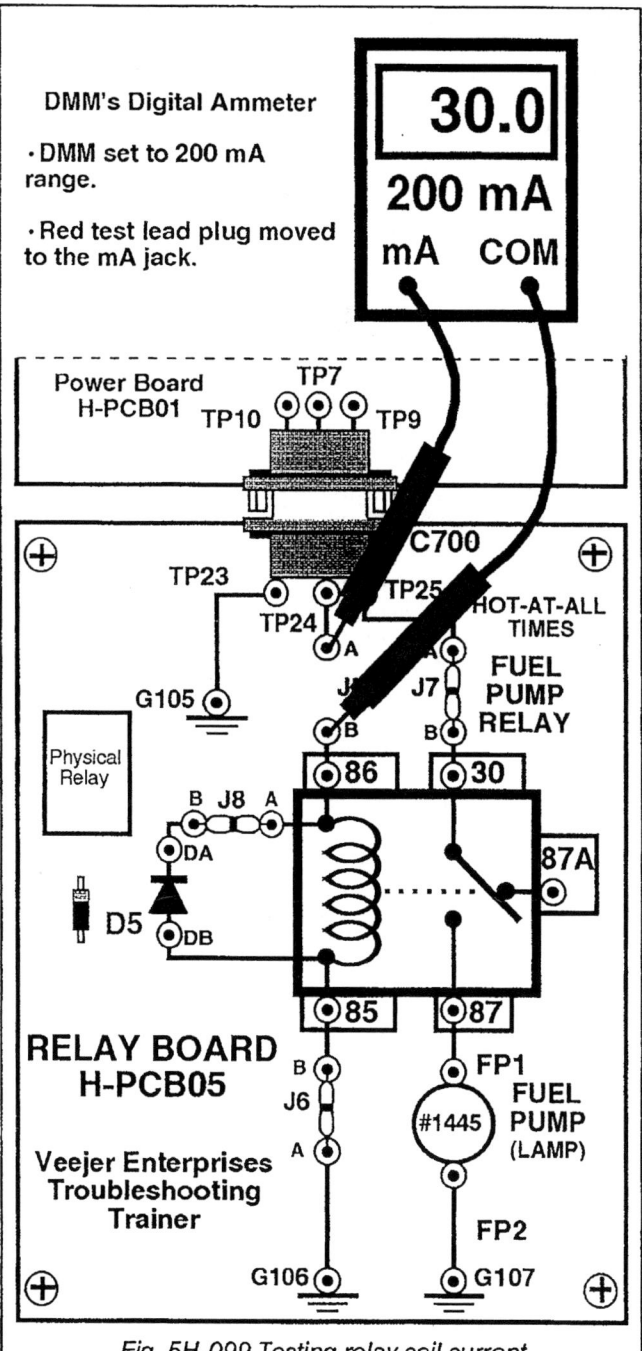

Fig. 5H-099 Testing relay coil current

Calculating Relay Primary (Coil) Current

Ohms Law is used to calculate relay coil current.

$I = E \div R$ *(basic Ohm's Law formula for current)*
"E" is voltage in volts, B+ is 13.0 volts; "R" is coil resistance in ohms measured with a DMM ohmmeter at about 410 ohms. Insert volts and ohms into formula. Divide the voltage by the ohms and the answer is in Amps:

$I = 13.0V \div 410\Omega$

$I = 0.0317$ Amps or 31.7 mA

Copyright © 2015 VEEJER ENTERPRISES, Garland, Texas - All Rights Reserved

Vehicle Electronics Hands-On Troubleshooting Training Program

VEEJER ENTERPRISES 3701 Lariat Lane, Garland, Texas 75042-5419
Phone: 972-276-9642   Fax: 972-276-8122   Email: sales@veejer.com   Web Site: www.veejer.com

2. Spike Suppression Diode Failure

The **diode** across the relay coil protects the driver transistor from a voltage spike when the relay coil powers down as explained earlier in this manual. See Figure 5H-057.

If the diode becomes OPEN, as shown to the right in Figure 5H-099A, a voltage spike, sometimes called an **energy dump,** is generated as the relay coil powers down with enough power to knock out the transistor driver in the PCM. Here's what happens.

The electromagnetic field collapses as soon as the transistor driver in the PCM is commanded to shut OFF current to the relay coil. The electromagnetic field rapidly dumps its stored energy back into the circuit. Pin 86 becomes very negatively charged with excess electrons due to all the electrons coming from the collapsing field while Pin 85 becomes very positively charge due to a deficiency of, and in desperate need of electrons.

The electrical imbalance of electrons between Pin 86 and practically none at Pin 85 produces a current surge of electrons seeking to get to Pin 85 and neutralize the charge difference between Pins 86 and 85. Electrons will get to Pin 85 one way or the other.

We discussed earlier how this normally happens through the spike suppression diode D5. In the example of Figure 5H-99A we are showing the spike suppression diode as OPEN therefore no electrons can pass through the diode to get to Pin 85.

This forces electrons to take a path the long way around the circuit to get to Pin 85. Electrons depart Pin 86, travel up through the voltage side of the relay primary circuit into B+. This pushes electrons out of B- so electrons then travel up through the ground circuit to get to Pin 85.

In the longer path of this current surge is a transistor solid-state driver in the PCM which is switched OFF, as shown in Figure 5H-099A to the right. The current surge has enough energy to punch through the transistor driver resulting in permanent damage to the driver. One current surge through the transistor driver destroys it and the PCM must be replaced.

The current surge is called a "voltage spike" because a lab scope, used to measure the amplitude of the energy dump, displays voltage and not current.

The spike suppression diode or a spike suppression resistor provides a shorter path for electrons to get from Pin 86 to Pin 85 which eliminates the longer path through the circuit saving the transistor driver in the PCM.

We have covered testing methods to check the condition of a spike suppression diode while still connected to a relay coil in Figure 5H-066 through Figure 5H-068C in this manual.

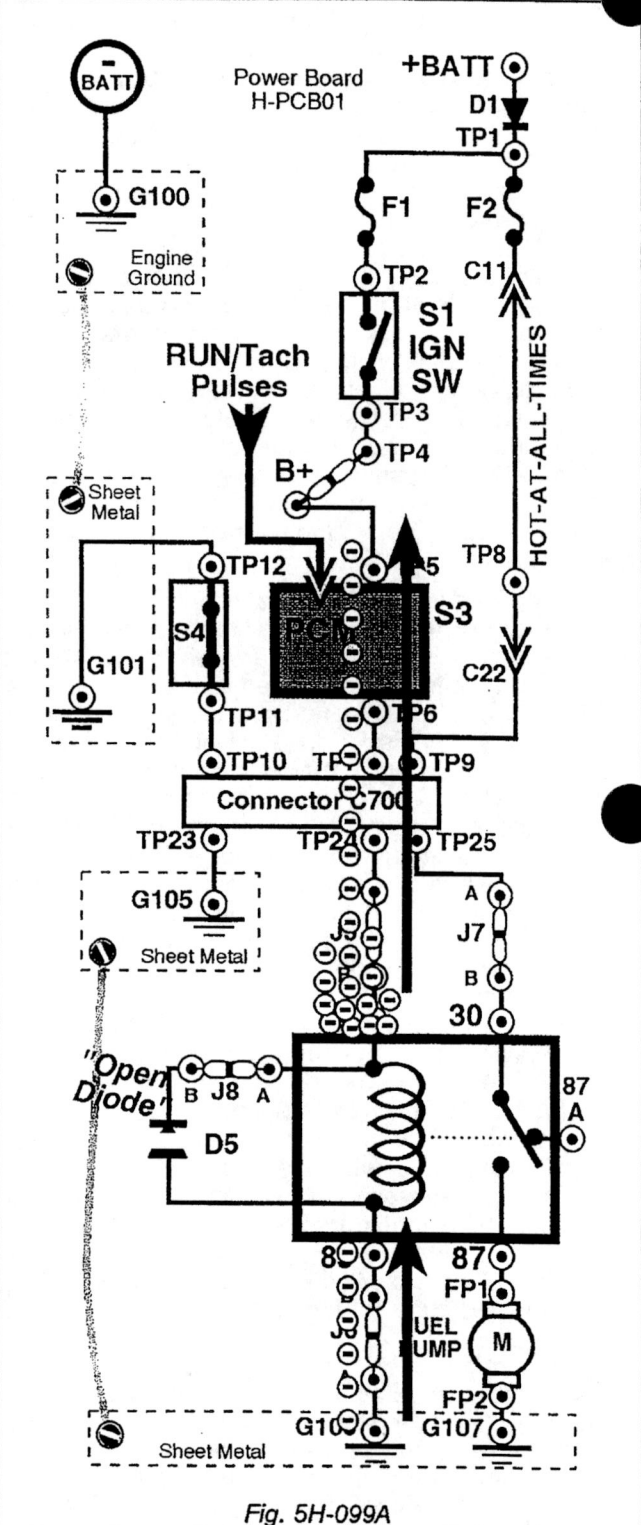

Fig. 5H-099A
Energy from collapsing electromagnetic field destroys computer if spike suppression diode is defective.

Vehicle Electronics Hands-On Troubleshooting Training Program

Relay Circuit Troubleshooting Exercises

For all troubleshooting problems to follow, the relay is designated as the **Fuel Pump Relay** and the lamp is designated as a **Fuel Pump**. The relay circuit board, H-PCB05, is the same circuit board but the troubleshooting schematic has been modified in Figure 5H-6CCFP to the right to represent a fuel pump circuit on an actual vehicle.

In a vehicle the fuel pump is controlled by a **PCM (Powertrain Control Module)** through a fuel pump relay. The circuit example we use in this training program is that a relay CLOSES its contacts to supply B+ to an electrically operated fuel pump that is permanently grounded. This is similar to many vehicles on the road today. To accomplish this scenario with the relay circuit there are two changes to the relay circuit schematic to be discussed involving the operation of switch S3 as the PCM and using the lamp to represent the fuel pump.

Switch S3 and Fuel Pump Control

Fuel pump relay control is provided for by a transistor driver in the PCM which is wired into the vehicle's wiring harness to provide switch-to-voltage control of the fuel pump relay. Figure 5H-100 shows how this is represented in the relay schematic using the Power Board connected to the Relay Board.

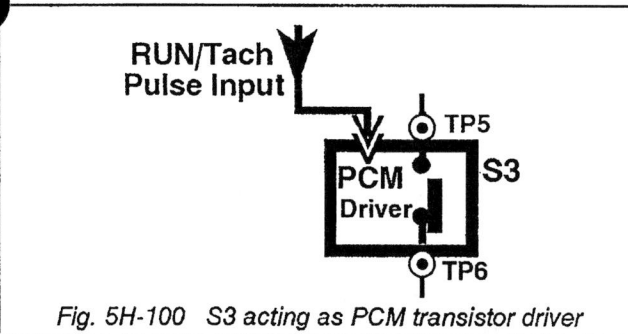

Fig. 5H-100 S3 acting as PCM transistor driver

The PCM must receive **RUN** or **TACH** pulses, to energize the transistor driver to supply current to the fuel pump relay coil. When the engine is cranked, RUN/TACH pulses arrive at the PCM input to alert the PCM to turn ON the fuel pump relay transistor driver to send a current through the relay coil. The relay contacts CLOSE and B+ is supplied to the fuel pump. The fuel pump operates and builds up **fuel pressure in the fuel rail** which provides fuel to the cylinders when the fuel injectors OPEN under command of the PCM.

Pulses to the PCM are provided by a CRANK sensor, a TACH sensor or some other means determined by the manufacturer to be a reliable indicator the engine is requiring fuel such as in cranking and running. Anytime RUN/TACH pulses are not presented at the PCM input the PCM is programmed to turn OFF the fuel pump relay transistor driver and stop current through the relay coil to de-energize the fuel pump relay.

Notice in the schematic below, Figure 5TS-6CCFP, the **new labeling of fuses F1 and F2,** and a DC motor symbol is drawn in place of the lamp which is the actual component on the relay board. The lamp is used to simulate the fuel pump motor.

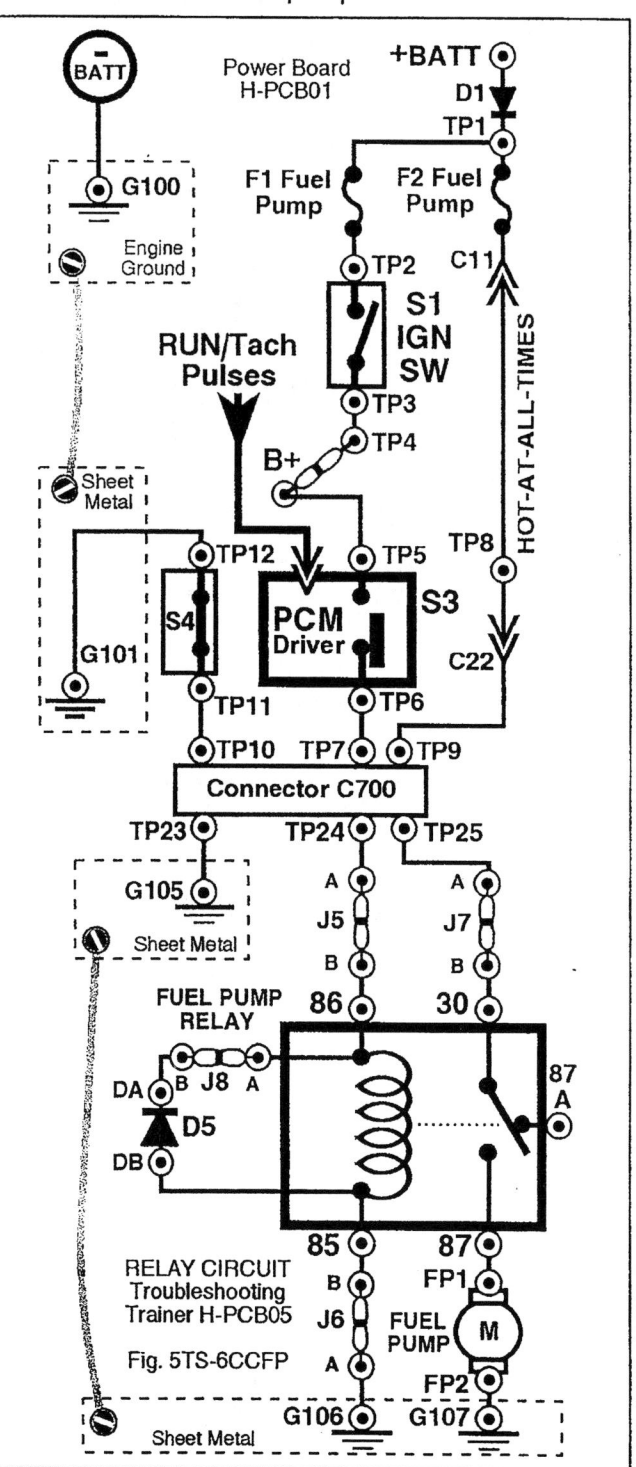

Discussion continues on next page

Vehicle Electronics Hands-On Troubleshooting Training Program

VEEJER ENTERPRISES 3701 Lariat Lane, Garland, Texas 75042-5419
Phone: 972-276-9642 Fax: 972-276-8122 Email: sales@veejer.com Web Site: www.veejer.com

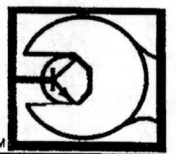

In a car, the PCM initializes the fuel pump relay for 2 seconds when the ignition switch is first turned ON. To keep the relay energized the PCM must receive RUN/TACH pulses. If pulses stop the PCM turns the fuel pump relay OFF after 2 seconds. During the troubleshooting problems the student simulates the PCM is receiving RUN/TACH pulses and turns ON its relay fuel pump transistor driver **by sliding S3 UP** as in Figure 5H-100A.

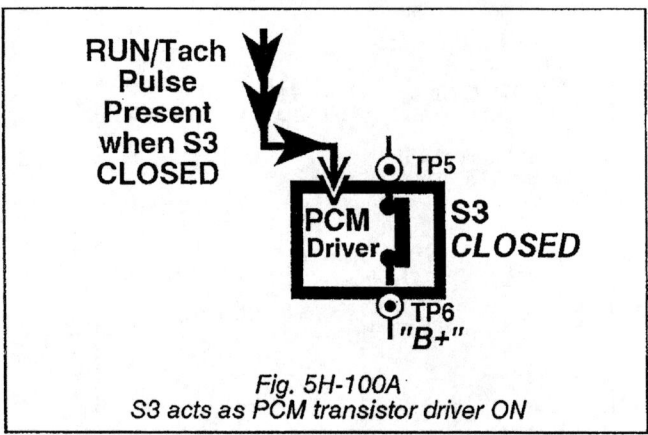

Fig. 5H-100A
S3 acts as PCM transistor driver ON

S3 CLOSED represents the PCM is producing output voltage and current to energize the fuel pump relay. When S3 is CLOSED (PCM driver ON) B+ appears at TP6.

S4 is left in the ON position at all times (slide UP) to permanently ground Pin 85 of the relay as shown in Figure 5H-100B.

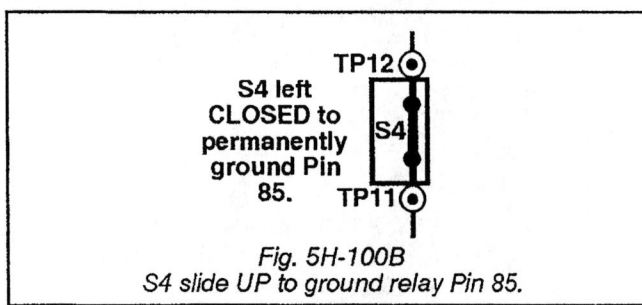

Fig. 5H-100B
S4 slide UP to ground relay Pin 85.

For all troubleshooting problems to follow leave S4 in the CLOSED position (slide UP). Use only S3 to control the relay for all troubleshooting problems.

Lamp Corresponds to Fuel Pump

The lamp is designated as the fuel pump for all troubleshooting problems to follow and the brightness of the lamp corresponds directly to the capacity of fuel pump operation and the amount of fuel pressure in the fuel rail. No specific psi is given for fuel pressure and it is simply expressed as low or high fuel pressure or no fuel pressure.

Normal Bright Lamp = Good fuel pressure

Figure 5H-100C shows the lamp is a normal brightness and represents the fuel pump is running at full capacity and fuel rail pressure is normal.

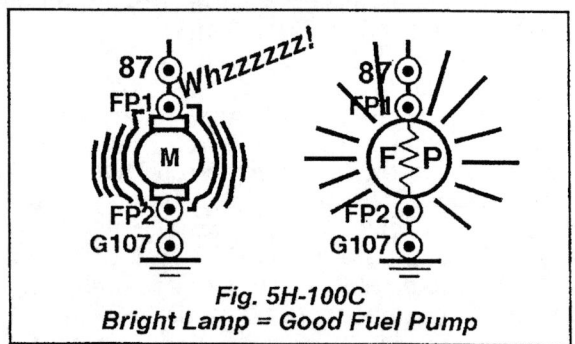

Fig. 5H-100C
Bright Lamp = Good Fuel Pump

Dim Lamp = Low fuel pressure

Figure 5H-100D indicates the lamp is dim which represents weak fuel pump operation resulting in low fuel pressure in the fuel rail with corresponding driveability problems associated with low fuel pressure. This type of problem would be related to a voltage drop in the relay secondary circuit.

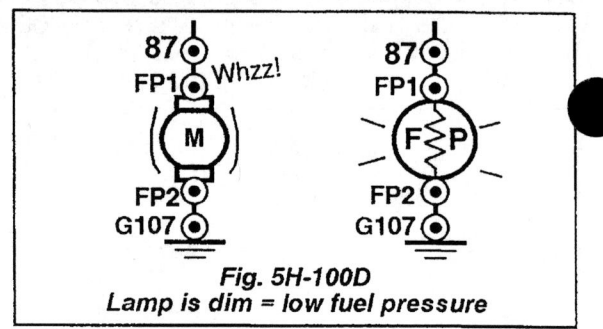

Fig. 5H-100D
Lamp is dim = low fuel pressure

Lamp is OUT = Fuel pump not operating

Figure 5H-100E shows the lamp is out representing the fuel pump is not operating. This could be due to several possibilities in either the relay primary or secondary circuit and what makes troubleshooting so vital to finding the circuit problem.

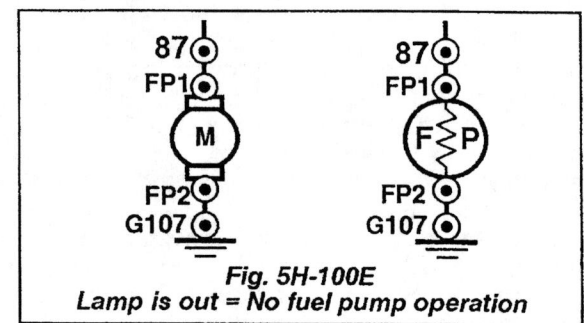

Fig. 5H-100E
Lamp is out = No fuel pump operation

During each troubleshooting problem the func of the lamp is visually determined then related to that condition would affect fuel pump operation.

Vehicle Electronics Hands-On Troubleshooting Training Program

VEEJER ENTERPRISES 3701 Lariat Lane, Garland, Texas 75042-5419
Phone: 972-276-9642   Fax: 972-276-8122   Email: sales@veejer.com   Web Site: www.veejer.com

Troubleshooting Problem Format

You are now ready to begin practice exercises troubleshooting relay circuit problems with the relay circuit corresponding to a vehicle's fuel pump circuit.

To the right is an sample of the format used to write down each troubleshooting problem. The box at the top of each problem contains the problem number and special instructions. Look up this problem number in the Instructor Guide to find out how to insert the fault in the circuit for that problem. **In a tech school the Teacher inserts problems.**

Begin troubleshooting and writing down all troubleshooting steps, the reading obtained and check if the reading is good or bad.

After "Does the Fuel Pump Relay *"CLICK"*? **check Yes or No** as appropriate. The second question is "Performance of the Fuel Pump." Describe how the fuel pump is operating, such as, weak (lamp dim) or dead (lamp OUT).

This is followed by Troubleshooting Step 1. Step 2 etc. Decide what is the first DMM measurement (Hint: TTS-1) and describe the test point from the schematic diagram. Record the DMM reading after "Reading" and then check off if the reading is good or bad. Continue taking readings in Step 2 (Hint: TTS-2) and describe where you are measuring. Record the DMM reading and check good or bad until you know what the problem is in the circuit. Take as many steps as necessary to isolate the problem in the circuit.

If the relay *"CLICKS* the relay primary circuit, Pins 86–85 are OK. Start troubleshooting on the relay secondary circuit at FP1 and FP2.. If the relay DOES NOT *"CLICK* begin troubleshooting the relay primary circuit at Pins 86–85.

Record specifically what the problem is after "The Problem Is." This will be necessary as you go back and review your troubleshooting when finished. A final reminder is given to remove the fault if no one is to use the PCBs after you for this problem. School teachers remove problems. Consult the Instructor Guide for answers after completing troubleshooting problems.

About Schematic Diagrams:

The schematic diagram is on the right hand column of every odd number page for easy reference. This saves time thumbing back and forth through the book looking for a schematic diagram. It cannot be stressed enough how important it is to develop the habit of relying on the printed schematic diagram in deciding troubleshooting steps, such as tracing B+ or B– instead of relying on the white ink (silk screen) on top of the board.

When working on a vehicle, there is no silk screen available on the vehicle to guide you in troubleshooting. You must learn to rely on schematic diagrams then so now is the time to practice!

Problem 00

Consult Instructor Guide IG05 to insert this problem.
Slide S4 UP and leave it CLOSED.
Use switch S3 as the PCM to control the fuel pump relay.
Description of the vehicle driveability problem:
A description of the driveability problem is provided here to correlate the problem with an actual driveability or vehicle electrical problem relating to the fuel pump circuit problem in the PCBs.

Does the Fuel Pump Relay "CLICK"? Yes ___ No ___
Performance of the Fuel Pump: _____

Troubleshooting Step 1: __TTS-1_____
Reading: _____ Good: ___ Bad: ___

Troubleshooting Step 2: __TTS-2_____
Reading: _____ Good: ___ Bad: ___

Troubleshooting Step 3: _____
Reading: _____ Good: ___ Bad: ___

Troubleshooting Step 4: _____
Reading: _____ Good: ___ Bad: ___

Troubleshooting Step 5: _____
Reading: _____ Good: ___ Bad: ___

Troubleshooting Step 6: _____
Reading: _____ Good: ___ Bad: ___

Troubleshooting Step 7: _____
Reading: _____ Good: ___ Bad: ___

Troubleshooting Step 8: _____
Reading: _____ Good: ___ Bad: ___

Troubleshooting Step 9: _____
Reading: _____ Good: ___ Bad: ___

Troubleshooting Step 10: _____
Reading: _____ Good: ___ Bad: ___

Troubleshooting Step 11: _____
Reading: _____ Good: ___ Bad: ___

Troubleshooting Step 12: _____
Reading: _____ Good: ___ Bad: ___

The Problem Is: _____

What did you learn from troubleshooting this problem?

_____

Vehicle Electronics Hands-On Troubleshooting Training Program

VEEJER ENTERPRISES 3701 Lariat Lane, Garland, Texas 75042-5419
Phone: 972-276-9642 Fax: 972-276-8122 Email: sales@veejer.com Web Site: www.veejer.com

More Tips Troubleshooting Relays

When measuring voltage and resistance while troubleshooting these relay problems make use of all the information possible. For example, Pin 86 is the voltage side of the coil. There is a wire from Pin 86 connecting to the top of the coil. This connection point could be accessed from J8 Pin A.4. A resistance measurement between Pin 86 and J8 Pin A would reveal if that wire is OPEN.

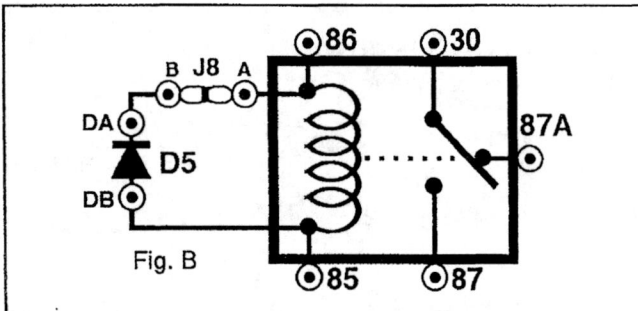

Fig. B

The same principle applies at Pin 85, the ground side of the coil. A wire from Pin 85 connects to the bottom of the coil. This connection point could be accessed from pin "DB" on the diode. A resistance measurement between Pin 85 and "DB" would reveal if that wire is OPEN.

The same principle could apply to the relay contacts. If the wire from Pin 30 connects to the top of the swinging contact, B+ would appear on Pin 87A when the relay is de-energized. If not, then the wire from Pin 30 to the top of the swinging contact is OPEN. If 87A has B+ when the relay is de-energized but no B+ appears at 87 when the relay is energized, then the wire from the bottom contact to Pin 87 is OPEN.

Warning:

- DO NOT LEAVE A GOOD 3A FUSE IN F1 OR F2 WHILE TROUBLESHOOTING ANY PROBLEM WITH A SHORTED LOAD OR A SHORT TO GROUND ON THE VOLTAGE SIDE.
- NEVER SWAP FUSES BETWEEN F1 AND F2 AS THIS MIGHT BLOW THE OTHER FUSE AND CHANGE THE DYNAMICS OF THE PROBLEM.
- THE POWER SUPPLY WILL GET HOT AND POSSIBLY BURN UP AS WELL AS DAMAGE THE CIRCUIT BOARDS IF THE WRONG SIZE FUSE IS USED AND IT DOES NOT BLOW. THIS TYPE OF DAMAGE VOIDS THE WARRANTY. EITHER PUT A BLOWN FUSE IN F1 OR F2 AS REQUIRED FOR A SPECIFIC PROBLEM OR REMOVE F1 OR F2 COMPLETELY IF A BLOWN FUSE IS NOT AVAILABLE TO SUBSTITUTE.
- THE WARRANTY IS VOID IF THE POWER SUPPLY IS BURNED UP OR THE CIRCUIT BOARDS ARE DAMAGED FROM NOT FOLLOWING THESE INSTRUCTIONS OR USING THE WRONG FUSE.

75 Practice Troubleshooting Problems

Read this FIRST before starting . . . .
TROUBLESHOOT PROBLEMS IN NUMERICAL ORDER. You will encounter variations of the basic relay circuit problems reviewed in this Student Manual. Before you begin the troubleshooting problems make sure you understand the basic problems and the DMM readings of the TTS that indicate a good circuit and which side of the relay circuit, primary or secondary has the fault.

Scan the top and bottom of the PCBs to make sure there are no faults in the PCBs before inserting a problem. **Have someone else install the problem for you if possible so you do not have any idea what type of problem is inserted.** Follow directions in the Instructor Guide for inserting the fault in each problem. Be careful to use only the resistors specified to ensure the problem shows up as intended. In and troubleshoot one problem at a time.

ABOUT FUSES F1 AND F2.

If you encounter a blown fuse in either F1 or F2 it means the inserted circuit fault blew the fuse. **DO NOT SWAP THE BLOWN FUSE WITH THE OTHER GOOD FUSE OR YOU WILL BLOW THE GOOD FUSE. WHEN YOU ENCOUNTER A BLOWN FUSE BEGIN TROUBLESHOOTING THAT CIRCUIT FOR A SHORT-TO-GROUND PROBLEM.**

After the fault is inserted begin troubleshooting the problem. Record test readings under the correct Problem Number in the Student Manual. **Write down the actual DMM readings for each step.** The purpose of troubleshooting each problem is to determine what is wrong in the circuit. Once you know what the problem is write a short summary of what is wrong with the circuit at the bottom of each problem in the text.

A schematic diagram of the complete relay circuit is in the right hand column of every odd numbered page for ready reference.

Check the I/G (Instructor Guide) for the correct answers only AFTER completing a troubleshooting problem. DO NOT look at the answers BEFORE troubleshooting a problem.

Problem Number 75 on the next page is the first relay circuit problem. The Instructor Guide H-IG05 explains how to insert the circuit failure for each problem and provides the troubleshooting answers for review later.

Copyright © 2015 VEEJER ENTERPRISES, Garland, Texas - All Rights Reserved Student Workbook H-WB115 Page 65

Vehicle Electronics Hands-On Troubleshooting Training Program

VEEJER ENTERPRISES 3701 Lariat Lane, Garland, Texas 75042-5419
Phone: 972-276-9642 Fax: 972-276-8122 Email: sales@veejer.com Web Site: www.veejer.com

Problem 75
Consult Instructor Guide IG05 to insert this problem.
Slide S4 UP and leave it CLOSED.
Use switch S3 as the PCM to control the fuel pump relay.
    Description of the vehicle driveability problem:
Engine cranks but engine won't run. Checked spark & fuel. There is no fuel pressure in the fuel rail. Fuel Pump not running for initial 2 seconds. A brand new relay did not work.

Does the Fuel Pump Relay "CLICK"? Yes ___ No ___
Performance of the Fuel Pump: _____

Troubleshooting Step 1: ___TTS-1_____
Reading: _____ Good: ___ Bad: ___

Troubleshooting Step 2: ___TTS-2_____
Reading: _____ Good: ___ Bad: ___

Troubleshooting Step 3: _____
Reading: _____ Good: ___ Bad: ___

Troubleshooting Step 4: _____
Reading: _____ Good: ___ Bad: ___

Troubleshooting Step 5: _____
Reading: _____ Good: ___ Bad: ___

Troubleshooting Step 6: _____
Reading: _____ Good: ___ Bad: ___

Troubleshooting Step 7: _____
Reading: _____ Good: ___ Bad: ___

Troubleshooting Step 8: _____
Reading: _____ Good: ___ Bad: ___

Troubleshooting Step 9: _____
Reading: _____ Good: ___ Bad: ___

Troubleshooting Step 10: _____
Reading: _____ Good: ___ Bad: ___

Troubleshooting Step 11: _____
Reading: _____ Good: ___ Bad: ___

Troubleshooting Step 12: _____
Reading: _____ Good: ___ Bad: ___

The Problem Is: _____

What did you learn from troubleshooting this problem?

_____

REMINDER: Remove the circuit fault from the bottom of the PCBs. Verify normal operation of the relay circuit.

Problem 76
Consult Instructor Guide IG05 to insert this problem.
Slide S4 UP and leave it CLOSED.
Use switch S3 as the PCM to control the fuel pump relay.
    Description of the vehicle driveability problem:
Engine cranks but engine won't run. Checked spark & fuel. There is no fuel pressure in the fuel rail. Fuel Pump not running for initial 2 seconds.

Does the Fuel Pump Relay "CLICK"? Yes ___ No ___
Performance of the Fuel Pump: _____

Troubleshooting Step 1: ___TTS-1_____
Reading: _____ Good: ___ Bad: ___

Troubleshooting Step 2: ___TTS-2_____
Reading: _____ Good: ___ Bad: ___

Troubleshooting Step 3: _____
Reading: _____ Good: ___ Bad: ___

Troubleshooting Step 4: _____
Reading: _____ Good: ___ Bad: ___

Troubleshooting Step 5: _____
Reading: _____ Good: ___ Bad: ___

Troubleshooting Step 6: _____
Reading: _____ Good: ___ Bad: ___

Troubleshooting Step 7: _____
Reading: _____ Good: ___ Bad: ___

Troubleshooting Step 8: _____
Reading: _____ Good: ___ Bad: ___

Troubleshooting Step 9: _____
Reading: _____ Good: ___ Bad: ___

Troubleshooting Step 10: _____
Reading: _____ Good: ___ Bad: ___

Troubleshooting Step 11: _____
Reading: _____ Good: ___ Bad: ___

Troubleshooting Step 12: _____
Reading: _____ Good: ___ Bad: ___

The Problem Is: _____

What did you learn from troubleshooting this problem?

_____

REMINDER: Remove the circuit fault from the bottom of the PCBs. Verify normal operation of the relay circuit.

Vehicle Electronics Hands-On Troubleshooting Training Program

VEEJER ENTERPRISES 3701 Lariat Lane, Garland, Texas 75042-5419
Phone: 972-276-9642   Fax: 972-276-8122   Email: sales@veejer.com   Web Site: www.veejer.com

---

Problem 77

Consult Instructor Guide IG05 to insert this problem.
Slide S4 UP and leave it CLOSED.
Use switch S3 as the PCM to control the fuel pump relay.
    Description of the vehicle driveability problem:
Engine cranks but engine won't run. Checked spark & fuel. There is no fuel pressure in the fuel rail. Fuel Pump not running for initial 2 seconds. A brand new relay did not work.

Does the Fuel Pump Relay "CLICK"?   Yes ___   No ___
Performance of the Fuel Pump: _____

Troubleshooting Step 1: __TTS-1_____
Reading: _____ Good: ___ Bad: ___

Troubleshooting Step 2: __TTS-2_____
Reading: _____ Good: ___ Bad: ___

Troubleshooting Step 3: _____
Reading: _____ Good: ___ Bad: ___

Troubleshooting Step 4: _____
Reading: _____ Good: ___ Bad: ___

Troubleshooting Step 5: _____
Reading: _____ Good: ___ Bad: ___

Troubleshooting Step 6: _____
Reading: _____ Good: ___ Bad: ___

Troubleshooting Step 7: _____
Reading: _____ Good: ___ Bad: ___

Troubleshooting Step 8: _____
Reading: _____ Good: ___ Bad: ___

Troubleshooting Step 9: _____
Reading: _____ Good: ___ Bad: ___

Troubleshooting Step 10: _____
Reading: _____ Good: ___ Bad: ___

Troubleshooting Step 11: _____
Reading: _____ Good: ___ Bad: ___

Troubleshooting Step 12: _____
Reading: _____ Good: ___ Bad: ___

The Problem Is: _____

What did you learn from troubleshooting this problem?

REMINDER: Remove the circuit fault from the bottom of the PCBs. Verify normal operation of the relay circuit.

Copyright © 2015 VEEJER ENTERPRISES, Garland, Texas - All Rights Reserved   **Student Workbook H-WB115**

Vehicle Electronics Hands-On Troubleshooting Training Program

VEEJER ENTERPRISES 3701 Lariat Lane, Garland, Texas 75042-5419
Phone: 972-276-9642   Fax: 972-276-8122   Email: sales@veejer.com   Web Site: www.veejer.com

Problem 78
Consult Instructor Guide IG05 to insert this problem.
Slide S4 UP and leave it CLOSED.
Use switch S3 as the PCM to control the fuel pump relay.
Description of the vehicle driveability problem:
Engine cranks but engine won't run. Checked spark & fuel. There is no fuel pressure in the fuel rail. Fuel Pump not running for initial 2 seconds. A brand new fuel pump and fuel pump relay did not fix it.

Does the Fuel Pump Relay "CLICK"? Yes ___ No ___
Performance of the Fuel Pump: _____

Troubleshooting Step 1: __TTS-1_____
Reading: _____ Good: ____ Bad: ____

Troubleshooting Step 2: ___TTS-2_____
Reading: _____ Good: ____ Bad: ____

Troubleshooting Step 3: _____
Reading: _____ Good: ____ Bad: ____

Troubleshooting Step 4: _____
Reading: _____ Good: ____ Bad: ____

Troubleshooting Step 5: _____
Reading: _____ Good: ____ Bad: ____

Troubleshooting Step 6: _____
Reading: _____ Good: ____ Bad: ____

Troubleshooting Step 7: _____
Reading: _____ Good: ____ Bad: ____

Troubleshooting Step 8: _____
Reading: _____ Good: ____ Bad: ____

Troubleshooting Step 9: _____
Reading: _____ Good: ____ Bad: ____

Troubleshooting Step 10: _____
Reading: _____ Good: ____ Bad: ____

Troubleshooting Step 11: _____
Reading: _____ Good: ____ Bad: ____

Troubleshooting Step 12: _____
Reading: _____ Good: ____ Bad: ____

The Problem Is: _____

What did you learn from troubleshooting this problem?

_____

REMINDER: Remove the circuit fault from the bottom of the PCBs. Verify normal operation of the relay circuit.

Problem 79
Consult Instructor Guide IG05 to insert this problem.
Slide S4 UP and leave it CLOSED.
Use switch S3 as the PCM to control the fuel pump relay.
Description of the vehicle driveability problem:
Engine runs but it takes a little longer than normal crank time to start the engine. Battery checks good. Engine seems to run OK once engine is running but fuel pressure is low. A brand new fuel pump and fuel pump relay did not fix it.

Does the Fuel Pump Relay "CLICK"? Yes ___ No ___
Performance of the Fuel Pump: _____

Troubleshooting Step 1: __TTS-1_____
Reading: _____ Good: ____ Bad: ____

Troubleshooting Step 2: ___TTS-2_____
Reading: _____ Good: ____ Bad: ____

Troubleshooting Step 3: _____
Reading: _____ Good: ____ Bad: ____

Troubleshooting Step 4: _____
Reading: _____ Good: ____ Bad: ____

Troubleshooting Step 5: _____
Reading: _____ Good: ____ Bad: ____

Troubleshooting Step 6: _____
Reading: _____ Good: ____ Bad: ____

Troubleshooting Step 7: _____
Reading: _____ Good: ____ Bad: ____

Troubleshooting Step 8: _____
Reading: _____ Good: ____ Bad: ____

Troubleshooting Step 9: _____
Reading: _____ Good: ____ Bad: ____

Troubleshooting Step 10: _____
Reading: _____ Good: ____ Bad: ____

Troubleshooting Step 11: _____
Reading: _____ Good: ____ Bad: ____

Troubleshooting Step 12: _____
Reading: _____ Good: ____ Bad: ____

The Problem Is: _____

What did you learn from troubleshooting this problem?

_____

REMINDER: Remove the circuit fault from the bottom of the PCBs. Verify normal operation of the relay circuit.

Vehicle Electronics Hands-On Troubleshooting Training Program

VEEJER ENTERPRISES 3701 Lariat Lane, Garland, Texas 75042-5419
Phone: 972-276-9642   Fax: 972-276-8122   Email: sales@veejer.com   Web Site: www.veejer.com

Problem 80

Consult Instructor Guide IG05 to insert this problem.
Slide S4 UP and leave it CLOSED.
Use switch S3 as the PCM to control the fuel pump relay.
Description of the vehicle driveability problem:
Engine runs but it seems to crank longer before it starts to run. Battery checks good. Vehicle has less than normal power & sluggish acceleration. A new fuel pump was installed but it made no difference in driveability. All fuel filters have been replaced. A new relay did not fix the problem. Fuel pressure drops at higher rpm.

Does the Fuel Pump Relay "CLICK"?   Yes ___ No ___
Performance of the Fuel Pump: _____

Troubleshooting Step 1: __TTS-1_____
Reading: _____ Good: ___ Bad: ___

Troubleshooting Step 2: __TTS-2_____
Reading: _____ Good: ___ Bad: ___

Troubleshooting Step 3: _____
Reading: _____ Good: ___ Bad: ___

Troubleshooting Step 4: _____
Reading: _____ Good: ___ Bad: ___

Troubleshooting Step 5: _____
Reading: _____ Good: ___ Bad: ___

Troubleshooting Step 6: _____
Reading: _____ Good: ___ Bad: ___

Troubleshooting Step 7: _____
Reading: _____ Good: ___ Bad: ___

Troubleshooting Step 8: _____
Reading: _____ Good: ___ Bad: ___

Troubleshooting Step 9: _____
Reading: _____ Good: ___ Bad: ___

Troubleshooting Step 10: _____
Reading: _____ Good: ___ Bad: ___

Troubleshooting Step 11: _____
Reading: _____ Good: ___ Bad: ___

Troubleshooting Step 12: _____
Reading: _____ Good: ___ Bad: ___

The Problem Is: _____

What did you learn from troubleshooting this problem?
_____

REMINDER: Remove the circuit fault from the bottom of the PCBs. Verify normal operation of the relay circuit.

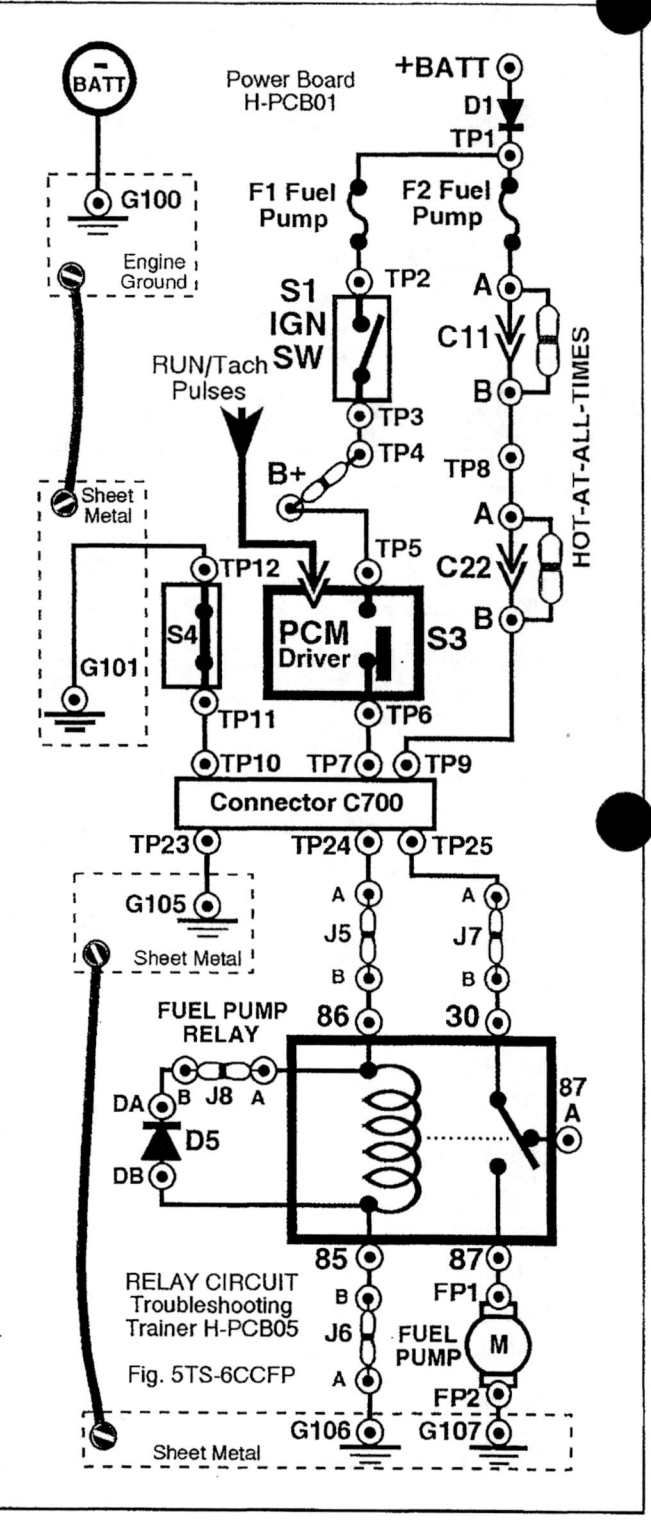

Vehicle Electronics Hands-On Troubleshooting Training Program

VEEJER ENTERPRISES 3701 Lariat Lane, Garland, Texas 75042-5419
Phone: 972-276-9642 Fax: 972-276-8122 Email: sales@veejer.com Web Site: www.veejer.com

Problem 81
Consult Instructor Guide IG05 to insert this problem.
Slide S4 UP and leave it CLOSED.
Use switch S3 as the PCM to control the fuel pump relay.
Description of the vehicle driveability problem:
Engine cranks but will not start. Checked spark & fuel. There is no fuel pressure in the fuel rail. Fuel Pump not running for initial 2 seconds. A new fuel pump and relay did not fix the problem.

Does the Fuel Pump Relay "CLICK"? Yes ___ No ___
Performance of the Fuel Pump: _____

Troubleshooting Step 1: __TTS-1_____
Reading: _____ Good: ___ Bad: ___

Troubleshooting Step 2: ___TTS-2_____
Reading: _____ Good: ___ Bad: ___

Troubleshooting Step 3: _____
Reading: _____ Good: ___ Bad: ___

Troubleshooting Step 4: _____
Reading: _____ Good: ___ Bad: ___

Troubleshooting Step 5: _____
Reading: _____ Good: ___ Bad: ___

Troubleshooting Step 6: _____
Reading: _____ Good: ___ Bad: ___

Troubleshooting Step 7: _____
Reading: _____ Good: ___ Bad: ___

Troubleshooting Step 8: _____
Reading: _____ Good: ___ Bad: ___

Troubleshooting Step 9: _____
Reading: _____ Good: ___ Bad: ___

Troubleshooting Step 10: _____
Reading: _____ Good: ___ Bad: ___

Troubleshooting Step 11: _____
Reading: _____ Good: ___ Bad: ___

Troubleshooting Step 12: _____
Reading: _____ Good: ___ Bad: ___

The Problem Is: _____

What did you learn from troubleshooting this problem?

_____

REMINDER: Remove the circuit fault from the bottom of the PCBs. Verify normal operation of the relay circuit.

Problem 82
Consult Instructor Guide IG05 to insert this problem.
Slide S4 UP and leave it CLOSED.
Use switch S3 as the PCM to control the fuel pump relay.
Description of the vehicle driveability problem:
Engine cranks but engine won't run. Checked spark & fuel. There is no fuel pressure in the fuel rail. Fuel Pump not running for initial 2 seconds. A brand new relay did not work.

Does the Fuel Pump Relay "CLICK"? Yes ___ No ___
Performance of the Fuel Pump: _____

Troubleshooting Step 1: __TTS-1_____
Reading: _____ Good: ___ Bad: ___

Troubleshooting Step 2: ___TTS-2_____
Reading: _____ Good: ___ Bad: ___

Troubleshooting Step 3: _____
Reading: _____ Good: ___ Bad: ___

Troubleshooting Step 4: _____
Reading: _____ Good: ___ Bad: ___

Troubleshooting Step 5: _____
Reading: _____ Good: ___ Bad: ___

Troubleshooting Step 6: _____
Reading: _____ Good: ___ Bad: ___

Troubleshooting Step 7: _____
Reading: _____ Good: ___ Bad: ___

Troubleshooting Step 8: _____
Reading: _____ Good: ___ Bad: ___

Troubleshooting Step 9: _____
Reading: _____ Good: ___ Bad: ___

Troubleshooting Step 10: _____
Reading: _____ Good: ___ Bad: ___

Troubleshooting Step 11: _____
Reading: _____ Good: ___ Bad: ___

Troubleshooting Step 12: _____
Reading: _____ Good: ___ Bad: ___

The Problem Is: _____

What did you learn from troubleshooting this problem?

_____

REMINDER: Remove the circuit fault from the bottom of the PCBs. Verify normal operation of the relay circuit.

Vehicle Electronics Hands-On Troubleshooting Training Program

VEEJER ENTERPRISES 3701 Lariat Lane, Garland, Texas 75042-5419
Phone: 972-276-9642 Fax: 972-276-8122 Email: sales@veejer.com Web Site: www.veejer.com

Problem 83

Consult Instructor Guide IG05 to insert this problem.
Slide S4 UP and leave it CLOSED.
Use switch S3 as the PCM to control the fuel pump relay.

Description of the vehicle driveability problem:
Engine cranks but engine won't run. Checked spark & fuel. There is no fuel pressure in the fuel rail. Fuel Pump not running for initial 2 seconds. A brand new relay did not fix the problem.

Does the Fuel Pump Relay "CLICK"? Yes ___ No ___
Performance of the Fuel Pump: _____

Troubleshooting Step 1: __TTS-1__
Reading: _____ Good: ___ Bad: ___

Troubleshooting Step 2: __TTS-2__
Reading: _____ Good: ___ Bad: ___

Troubleshooting Step 3: _____
Reading: _____ Good: ___ Bad: ___

Troubleshooting Step 4: _____
Reading: _____ Good: ___ Bad: ___

Troubleshooting Step 5: _____
Reading: _____ Good: ___ Bad: ___

Troubleshooting Step 6: _____
Reading: _____ Good: ___ Bad: ___

Troubleshooting Step 7: _____
Reading: _____ Good: ___ Bad: ___

Troubleshooting Step 8: _____
Reading: _____ Good: ___ Bad: ___

Troubleshooting Step 9: _____
Reading: _____ Good: ___ Bad: ___

Troubleshooting Step 10: _____
Reading: _____ Good: ___ Bad: ___

Troubleshooting Step 11: _____
Reading: _____ Good: ___ Bad: ___

Troubleshooting Step 12: _____
Reading: _____ Good: ___ Bad: ___

The Problem Is: _____

What did you learn from troubleshooting this problem?

_____

REMINDER: Remove the circuit fault from the bottom of the PCBs. Verify normal operation of the relay circuit.

Fig. 5TS-6CCFP

Vehicle Electronics Hands-On Troubleshooting Training Program

VEEJER ENTERPRISES 3701 Lariat Lane, Garland, Texas 75042-5419
Phone: 972-276-9642   Fax: 972-276-8122   Email: sales@veejer.com   Web Site: www.veejer.com

Problem 84
Consult Instructor Guide IG05 to insert this problem.
Slide S4 UP and leave it CLOSED.
Use switch S3 as the PCM to control the fuel pump relay.
Description of the vehicle driveability problem:
Engine cranks but engine won't run. Checked spark & fuel. There is no fuel pressure in the fuel rail. Fuel Pump not running for initial 2 seconds. A brand new relay did not work.

Does the Fuel Pump Relay "CLICK"? Yes ___ No ___
Performance of the Fuel Pump: _____

Troubleshooting Step 1: _____
Reading: _____ Good: ___ Bad: ___

Troubleshooting Step 2: _____
Reading: _____ Good: ___ Bad: ___

Troubleshooting Step 3: _____
Reading: _____ Good: ___ Bad: ___

Troubleshooting Step 4: _____
Reading: _____ Good: ___ Bad: ___

Troubleshooting Step 5: _____
Reading: _____ Good: ___ Bad: ___

Troubleshooting Step 6: _____
Reading: _____ Good: ___ Bad: ___

Troubleshooting Step 7: _____
Reading: _____ Good: ___ Bad: ___

Troubleshooting Step 8: _____
Reading: _____ Good: ___ Bad: ___

Troubleshooting Step 9: _____
Reading: _____ Good: ___ Bad: ___

Troubleshooting Step 10: _____
Reading: _____ Good: ___ Bad: ___

Troubleshooting Step 11: _____
Reading: _____ Good: ___ Bad: ___

Troubleshooting Step 12: _____
Reading: _____ Good: ___ Bad: ___

The Problem Is: _____

What did you learn from troubleshooting this problem?

_____

REMINDER: Remove the circuit fault from the bottom of the PCBs. Verify normal operation of the relay circuit.

Problem 85
Consult Instructor Guide IG05 to insert this problem.
Slide S4 UP and leave it CLOSED.
Use switch S3 as the PCM to control the fuel pump relay.
Description of the vehicle driveability problem:
Engine cranks but engine won't run. Checked spark & fuel. There is no fuel pressure in the fuel rail. Fuel Pump not running for initial 2 seconds. A brand new relay did not work.

Does the Fuel Pump Relay "CLICK"? Yes ___ No ___
Performance of the Fuel Pump: _____

Troubleshooting Step 1: _____
Reading: _____ Good: ___ Bad: ___

Troubleshooting Step 2: _____
Reading: _____ Good: ___ Bad: ___

Troubleshooting Step 3: _____
Reading: _____ Good: ___ Bad: ___

Troubleshooting Step 4: _____
Reading: _____ Good: ___ Bad: ___

Troubleshooting Step 5: _____
Reading: _____ Good: ___ Bad: ___

Troubleshooting Step 6: _____
Reading: _____ Good: ___ Bad: ___

Troubleshooting Step 7: _____
Reading: _____ Good: ___ Bad: ___

Troubleshooting Step 8: _____
Reading: _____ Good: ___ Bad: ___

Troubleshooting Step 9: _____
Reading: _____ Good: ___ Bad: ___

Troubleshooting Step 10: _____
Reading: _____ Good: ___ Bad: ___

Troubleshooting Step 11: _____
Reading: _____ Good: ___ Bad: ___

Troubleshooting Step 12: _____
Reading: _____ Good: ___ Bad: ___

The Problem Is: _____

What did you learn from troubleshooting this problem?

_____

REMINDER: Remove the circuit fault from the bottom of the PCBs. Verify normal operation of the relay circuit.

Vehicle Electronics Hands-On Troubleshooting Training Program

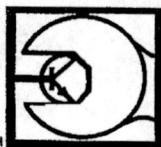

VEEJER ENTERPRISES 3701 Lariat Lane, Garland, Texas 75042-5419
Phone: 972-276-9642   Fax: 972-276-8122   Email: sales@veejer.com   Web Site: www.veejer.com

Problem 86

Consult Instructor Guide IG05 to insert this problem.
Slide S4 UP and leave it CLOSED.
Use switch S3 as the PCM to control the fuel pump relay.

Description of the vehicle driveability problem:
Engine runs but it cranks a long time before it starts to run. Fortunately the battery checks good. Vehicle has very little power & very poor acceleration. All fuel filters have been replaced and a new fuel pump made no difference.

Does the Fuel Pump Relay "CLICK"?   Yes ___   No ___
Performance of the Fuel Pump: _____

Troubleshooting Step 1: _____
Reading: _____   Good: ___   Bad: ___

Troubleshooting Step 2: _____
Reading: _____   Good: ___   Bad: ___

Troubleshooting Step 3: _____
Reading: _____   Good: ___   Bad: ___

Troubleshooting Step 4: _____
Reading: _____   Good: ___   Bad: ___

Troubleshooting Step 5: _____
Reading: _____   Good: ___   Bad: ___

Troubleshooting Step 6: _____
Reading: _____   Good: ___   Bad: ___

Troubleshooting Step 7: _____
Reading: _____   Good: ___   Bad: ___

Troubleshooting Step 8: _____
Reading: _____   Good: ___   Bad: ___

Troubleshooting Step 9: _____
Reading: _____   Good: ___   Bad: ___

Troubleshooting Step 10: _____
Reading: _____   Good: ___   Bad: ___

Troubleshooting Step 11: _____
Reading: _____   Good: ___   Bad: ___

Troubleshooting Step 12: _____
Reading: _____   Good: ___   Bad: ___

The Problem Is: _____

What did you learn from troubleshooting this problem?

_____

REMINDER: Remove the circuit fault from the bottom of the PCBs. Verify normal operation of the relay circuit.

RELAY CIRCUIT Troubleshooting Trainer H-PCB05
Fig. 5TS-6CCFP

Copyright © 2015 VEEJER ENTERPRISES, Garland, Texas - All Rights Reserved   Student Workbook H-WB115   Page 73

Vehicle Electronics Hands-On Troubleshooting Training Program

VEEJER ENTERPRISES 3701 Lariat Lane, Garland, Texas 75042-5419
Phone: 972-276-9642   Fax: 972-276-8122   Email: sales@veejer.com   Web Site: www.veejer.com

Problem 87
Consult Instructor Guide IG05 to insert this problem.
Slide S4 UP and leave it CLOSED.
Use switch S3 as the PCM to control the fuel pump relay.
Description of the vehicle driveability problem:
The car won't run and was towed in to shop. Customer says there is a buzzing noise under the hood. Spark is good but very low fuel pressure. Noticed when the ignition key is ON there is a buzzing noise under the hood coming from the fuel pump relay. Changed the relay and it still buzzes.

Does the Fuel Pump Relay "CLICK"? Yes __ No __
Performance of the Fuel Pump: _____

Troubleshooting Step 1: _____
Reading: _____ Good: ____ Bad: ____

Troubleshooting Step 2: _____
Reading: _____ Good: ____ Bad: ____

Troubleshooting Step 3: _____
Reading: _____ Good: ____ Bad: ____

Troubleshooting Step 4: _____
Reading: _____ Good: ____ Bad: ____

Troubleshooting Step 5: _____
Reading: _____ Good: ____ Bad: ____

Troubleshooting Step 6: _____
Reading: _____ Good: ____ Bad: ____

Troubleshooting Step 7: _____
Reading: _____ Good: ____ Bad: ____

Troubleshooting Step 8: _____
Reading: _____ Good: ____ Bad: ____

Troubleshooting Step 9: _____
Reading: _____ Good: ____ Bad: ____

Troubleshooting Step 10: _____
Reading: _____ Good: ____ Bad: ____

Troubleshooting Step 11: _____
Reading: _____ Good: ____ Bad: ____

Troubleshooting Step 12: _____
Reading: _____ Good: ____ Bad: ____

The Problem Is: _____

What did you learn from troubleshooting this problem?
_____

REMINDER: Remove the circuit fault from the bottom of the PCBs. Verify normal operation of the relay circuit.

Problem 88
Consult Instructor Guide IG05 to insert this problem.
Slide S4 UP and leave it CLOSED.
Use switch S3 as the PCM to control the fuel pump relay.
Description of the vehicle driveability problem:
Engine cranks but won't run. Checked spark & fuel. There is no fuel pressure in the fuel rail. Fuel Pump not running for initial 2 seconds. **A brand new relay solved the problem. Boss says to check the relay and tell him how the relay failed or I will be fired.**

Does the Fuel Pump Relay "CLICK"? Yes __ No __
Performance of the Fuel Pump: _____

Troubleshooting Step 1: _____
Reading: _____ Good: ____ Bad: ____

Troubleshooting Step 2: _____
Reading: _____ Good: ____ Bad: ____

Troubleshooting Step 3: _____
Reading: _____ Good: ____ Bad: ____

Troubleshooting Step 4: _____
Reading: _____ Good: ____ Bad: ____

Troubleshooting Step 5: _____
Reading: _____ Good: ____ Bad: ____

Troubleshooting Step 6: _____
Reading: _____ Good: ____ Bad: ____

Troubleshooting Step 7: _____
Reading: _____ Good: ____ Bad: ____

Troubleshooting Step 8: _____
Reading: _____ Good: ____ Bad: ____

Troubleshooting Step 9: _____
Reading: _____ Good: ____ Bad: ____

Troubleshooting Step 10: _____
Reading: _____ Good: ____ Bad: ____

Troubleshooting Step 11: _____
Reading: _____ Good: ____ Bad: ____

Troubleshooting Step 12: _____
Reading: _____ Good: ____ Bad: ____

The Problem Is: _____

What did you learn from troubleshooting this problem?
_____

REMINDER: Remove the circuit fault from the bottom of the PCBs. Verify normal operation of the relay circuit.

Copyright © 2015 VEEJER ENTERPRISES, Garland, Texas - All Rights Reserved

Vehicle Electronics Hands-On Troubleshooting Training Program

VEEJER ENTERPRISES 3701 Lariat Lane, Garland, Texas 75042-5419
Phone: 972-276-9642 Fax: 972-276-8122 Email: sales@veejer.com Web Site: www.veejer.com

Problem 89

Consult Instructor Guide IG05 to insert this problem.
Slide S4 UP and leave it CLOSED.
Use switch S3 as the PCM to control the fuel pump relay.
  Description of the vehicle driveability problem:
Engine cranks but engine won't run. Checked spark & fuel. There is no fuel pressure in the fuel rail. Fuel Pump not running for initial 2 seconds. A brand new relay did not fix the problem.

Does the Fuel Pump Relay "CLICK"? Yes __ No __
Performance of the Fuel Pump: _____

Troubleshooting Step 1: _____
  Reading: _____ Good: ___ Bad: ___

Troubleshooting Step 2: _____
  Reading: _____ Good: ___ Bad: ___

Troubleshooting Step 3: _____
  Reading: _____ Good: ___ Bad: ___

Troubleshooting Step 4: _____
  Reading: _____ Good: ___ Bad: ___

Troubleshooting Step 5: _____
  Reading: _____ Good: ___ Bad: ___

Troubleshooting Step 6: _____
  Reading: _____ Good: ___ Bad: ___

Troubleshooting Step 7: _____
  Reading: _____ Good: ___ Bad: ___

Troubleshooting Step 8: _____
  Reading: _____ Good: ___ Bad: ___

Troubleshooting Step 9: _____
  Reading: _____ Good: ___ Bad: ___

Troubleshooting Step 10: _____
  Reading: _____ Good: ___ Bad: ___

Troubleshooting Step 11: _____
  Reading: _____ Good: ___ Bad: ___

Troubleshooting Step 12: _____
  Reading: _____ Good: ___ Bad: ___

The Problem Is: _____

What did you learn from troubleshooting this problem?

_____

REMINDER: Remove the circuit fault from the bottom of the PCBs. Verify normal operation of the relay circuit.

Fig. 5TS-6CCFP — RELAY CIRCUIT Troubleshooting Trainer H-PCB05

Copyright © 2015 VEEJER ENTERPRISES, Garland, Texas - All Rights Reserved Student Workbook H-WB115 Page 75

Vehicle Electronics Hands-On Troubleshooting Training Program

VEEJER ENTERPRISES 3701 Lariat Lane, Garland, Texas 75042-5419
Phone: 972-276-9642 Fax: 972-276-8122 Email: sales@veejer.com Web Site: www.veejer.com

Problem 90
Consult Instructor Guide IG05 to insert this problem.
Slide S4 UP and leave it CLOSED.
Use switch S3 as the PCM to control the fuel pump relay.
Description of the vehicle driveability problem:
Engine runs but it cranks a long time before it starts to run. Fortunately the battery checks good. Vehicle has very little power & very poor acceleration. All fuel filters have been replaced. Fuel pressure drops a lot at higher rpm.

Does the Fuel Pump Relay "CLICK"? Yes ___ No ___
Performance of the Fuel Pump: _____

Troubleshooting Step 1: _____
Reading: _____ Good: ___ Bad: ___

Troubleshooting Step 2: _____
Reading: _____ Good: ___ Bad: ___

Troubleshooting Step 3: _____
Reading: _____ Good: ___ Bad: ___

Troubleshooting Step 4: _____
Reading: _____ Good: ___ Bad: ___

Troubleshooting Step 5: _____
Reading: _____ Good: ___ Bad: ___

Troubleshooting Step 6: _____
Reading: _____ Good: ___ Bad: ___

Troubleshooting Step 7: _____
Reading: _____ Good: ___ Bad: ___

Troubleshooting Step 8: _____
Reading: _____ Good: ___ Bad: ___

Troubleshooting Step 9: _____
Reading: _____ Good: ___ Bad: ___

Troubleshooting Step 10: _____
Reading: _____ Good: ___ Bad: ___

Troubleshooting Step 11: _____
Reading: _____ Good: ___ Bad: ___

Troubleshooting Step 12: _____
Reading: _____ Good: ___ Bad: ___

The Problem Is: _____

What did you learn from troubleshooting this problem?
_____

REMINDER: Remove the circuit fault from the bottom of the PCBs. Verify normal operation of the relay circuit.

Problem 91
Consult Instructor Guide IG05 to insert this problem.
Slide S4 UP and leave it CLOSED.
Use switch S3 as the PCM to control the fuel pump relay.
Description of the vehicle driveability problem:
Engine runs but it takes a little longer crank time to start the engine. Battery checks good. Engine seems to run OK once engine is running but fuel pressure is a little low and drops some at higher rpm.

Does the Fuel Pump Relay "CLICK"? Yes ___ No ___
Performance of the Fuel Pump: _____

Troubleshooting Step 1: _____
Reading: _____ Good: ___ Bad: ___

Troubleshooting Step 2: _____
Reading: _____ Good: ___ Bad: ___

Troubleshooting Step 3: _____
Reading: _____ Good: ___ Bad: ___

Troubleshooting Step 4: _____
Reading: _____ Good: ___ Bad: ___

Troubleshooting Step 5: _____
Reading: _____ Good: ___ Bad: ___

Troubleshooting Step 6: _____
Reading: _____ Good: ___ Bad: ___

Troubleshooting Step 7: _____
Reading: _____ Good: ___ Bad: ___

Troubleshooting Step 8: _____
Reading: _____ Good: ___ Bad: ___

Troubleshooting Step 9: _____
Reading: _____ Good: ___ Bad: ___

Troubleshooting Step 10: _____
Reading: _____ Good: ___ Bad: ___

Troubleshooting Step 11: _____
Reading: _____ Good: ___ Bad: ___

Troubleshooting Step 12: _____
Reading: _____ Good: ___ Bad: ___

The Problem Is: _____

What did you learn from troubleshooting this problem?
_____

REMINDER: Remove the circuit fault from the bottom of the PCBs. Verify normal operation of the relay circuit.

Vehicle Electronics Hands-On Troubleshooting Training Program

VEEJER ENTERPRISES 3701 Lariat Lane, Garland, Texas 75042-5419
Phone: 972-276-9642   Fax: 972-276-8122   Email: sales@veejer.com   Web Site: www.veejer.com

---

Problem 92

Consult Instructor Guide IG05 to insert this problem.
Slide S4 UP and leave it CLOSED.
Use switch S3 as the PCM to control the fuel pump relay.
Description of the vehicle driveability problem:
Engine runs but it takes a long crank time to start. Battery checks good. Engine runs poorly with little power. Sometimes engine dies. Fuel pressure very low. New fuel pump and relay didn't fix the problem. Fuel pressure drops dramatically as rpm increases.

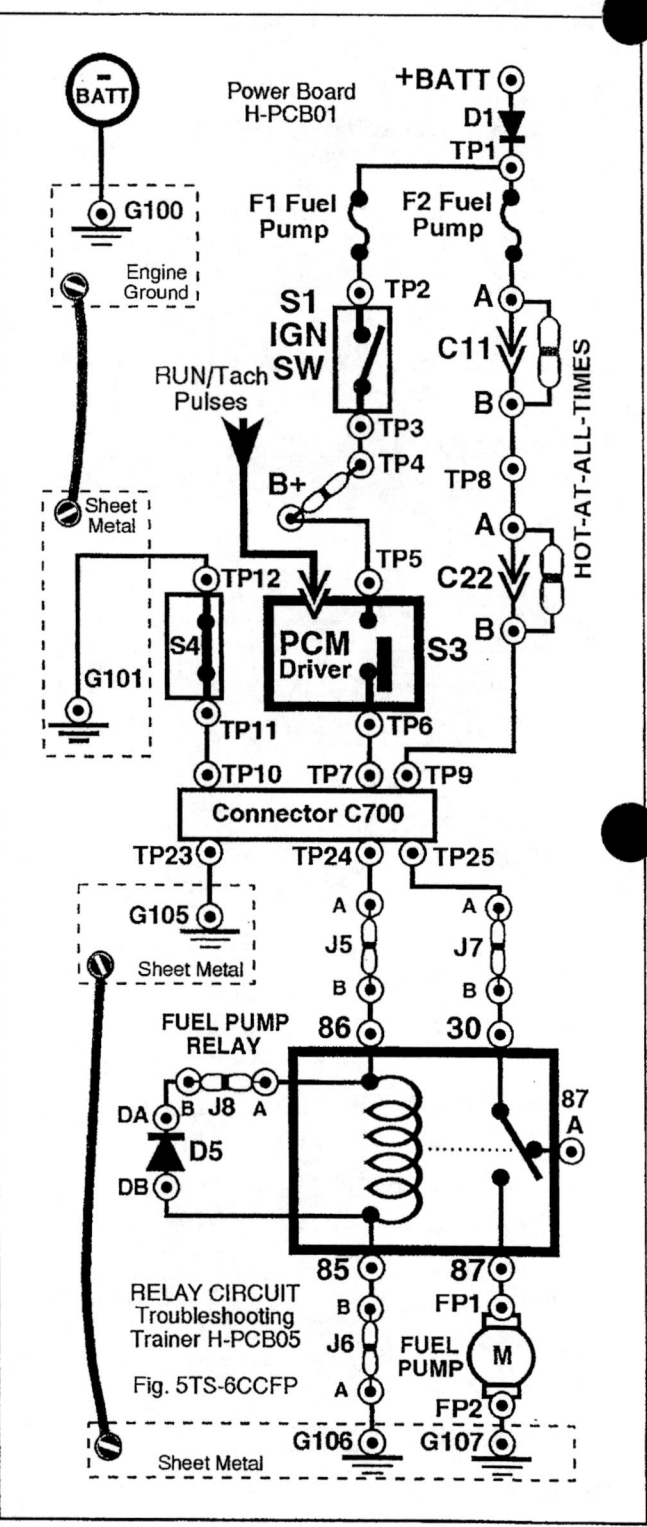

Does the Fuel Pump Relay "CLICK"?   Yes ___   No ___
Performance of the Fuel Pump: _____

Troubleshooting Step 1: _____
Reading: _____   Good: ___   Bad: ___

Troubleshooting Step 2: _____
Reading: _____   Good: ___   Bad: ___

Troubleshooting Step 3: _____
Reading: _____   Good: ___   Bad: ___

Troubleshooting Step 4: _____
Reading: _____   Good: ___   Bad: ___

Troubleshooting Step 5: _____
Reading: _____   Good: ___   Bad: ___

Troubleshooting Step 6: _____
Reading: _____   Good: ___   Bad: ___

Troubleshooting Step 7: _____
Reading: _____   Good: ___   Bad: ___

Troubleshooting Step 8: _____
Reading: _____   Good: ___   Bad: ___

Troubleshooting Step 9: _____
Reading: _____   Good: ___   Bad: ___

Troubleshooting Step 10: _____
Reading: _____   Good: ___   Bad: ___

Troubleshooting Step 11: _____
Reading: _____   Good: ___   Bad: ___

Troubleshooting Step 12: _____
Reading: _____   Good: ___   Bad: ___

The Problem Is: _____

What did you learn from troubleshooting this problem?

_____

REMINDER: Remove the circuit fault from the bottom of the PCBs. Verify normal operation of the relay circuit.

Copyright © 2015 VEEJER ENTERPRISES, Garland, Texas - All Rights Reserved   **Student Workbook H-WB115   Page 77**

Vehicle Electronics Hands-On Troubleshooting Training Program

VEEJER ENTERPRISES 3701 Lariat Lane, Garland, Texas 75042-5419
Phone: 972-276-9642   Fax: 972-276-8122   Email: sales@veejer.com   Web Site: www.veejer.com ™

Problem 93
Consult Instructor Guide IG05 to insert this problem.
Slide S4 UP and leave it CLOSED.
Use switch S3 as the PCM to control the fuel pump relay.
  Description of the vehicle driveability problem:
The customer complains that he has had several PCMs replaced and his car is now out of warranty. He's afraid it will happen again. When the PCM goes bad the engine will crank but will not run. There is good spark but no fuel pressure. After the PCM is replaced the car runs again. What is the problem that causes the PCM failure???

Does the Fuel Pump Relay "CLICK"? Yes ___ No ___
Performance of the Fuel Pump: _____

Troubleshooting Step 1: _____
Reading: _____ Good: ___ Bad: ___

Troubleshooting Step 2: _____
Reading: _____ Good: ___ Bad: ___

Troubleshooting Step 3: _____
Reading: _____ Good: ___ Bad: ___

Troubleshooting Step 4: _____
Reading: _____ Good: ___ Bad: ___

Troubleshooting Step 5: _____
Reading: _____ Good: ___ Bad: ___

Troubleshooting Step 6: _____
Reading: _____ Good: ___ Bad: ___

Troubleshooting Step 7: _____
Reading: _____ Good: ___ Bad: ___

Troubleshooting Step 8: _____
Reading: _____ Good: ___ Bad: ___

Troubleshooting Step 9: _____
Reading: _____ Good: ___ Bad: ___

Troubleshooting Step 10: _____
Reading: _____ Good: ___ Bad: ___

Troubleshooting Step 11: _____
Reading: _____ Good: ___ Bad: ___

Troubleshooting Step 12: _____
Reading: _____ Good: ___ Bad: ___

The Problem Is: _____

What did you learn from troubleshooting this problem?
_____

REMINDER: Remove the circuit fault from the bottom of the PCBs. Verify normal operation of the relay circuit.

Problem 94
Consult Instructor Guide IG05 to insert this problem.
Slide S4 UP and leave it CLOSED.
Use switch S3 as the PCM to control the fuel pump relay.
  Description of the vehicle driveability problem:
Engine cranks but engine won't run. Checked spark & fuel. There is no fuel pressure in the fuel rail. Fuel Pump not running for initial 2 seconds. A new relay and new fuel pump did not fix the problem.

Does the Fuel Pump Relay "CLICK"? Yes ___ No ___
Performance of the Fuel Pump: _____

Troubleshooting Step 1: _____
Reading: _____ Good: ___ Bad: ___

Troubleshooting Step 2: _____
Reading: _____ Good: ___ Bad: ___

Troubleshooting Step 3: _____
Reading: _____ Good: ___ Bad: ___

Troubleshooting Step 4: _____
Reading: _____ Good: ___ Bad: ___

Troubleshooting Step 5: _____
Reading: _____ Good: ___ Bad: ___

Troubleshooting Step 6: _____
Reading: _____ Good: ___ Bad: ___

Troubleshooting Step 7: _____
Reading: _____ Good: ___ Bad: ___

Troubleshooting Step 8: _____
Reading: _____ Good: ___ Bad: ___

Troubleshooting Step 9: _____
Reading: _____ Good: ___ Bad: ___

Troubleshooting Step 10: _____
Reading: _____ Good: ___ Bad: ___

Troubleshooting Step 11: _____
Reading: _____ Good: ___ Bad: ___

Troubleshooting Step 12: _____
Reading: _____ Good: ___ Bad: ___

The Problem Is: _____

What did you learn from troubleshooting this problem?
_____

REMINDER: Remove the circuit fault from the bottom of the PCBs. Verify normal operation of the relay circuit.

Vehicle Electronics Hands-On Troubleshooting Training Program

VEEJER ENTERPRISES 3701 Lariat Lane, Garland, Texas 75042-5419
Phone: 972-276-9642   Fax: 972-276-8122   Email: sales@veejer.com   Web Site: www.veejer.com

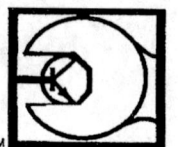

Problem 95

Consult Instructor Guide IG05 to insert this problem.
Slide S4 UP and leave it CLOSED.
Use switch S3 as the PCM to control the fuel pump relay.
Description of the vehicle driveability problem:
Engine cranks but engine won't run. Checked spark & fuel. There is no fuel pressure in the fuel rail. Fuel Pump not running for initial 2 seconds. A new relay and new fuel pump did not fix the problem.

Does the Fuel Pump Relay *"CLICK"*?   Yes ___ No ___
Performance of the Fuel Pump: _____

Troubleshooting Step 1: _____
Reading: _____ Good: ___ Bad: ___

Troubleshooting Step 2: _____
Reading: _____ Good: ___ Bad: ___

Troubleshooting Step 3: _____
Reading: _____ Good: ___ Bad: ___

Troubleshooting Step 4: _____
Reading: _____ Good: ___ Bad: ___

Troubleshooting Step 5: _____
Reading: _____ Good: ___ Bad: ___

Troubleshooting Step 6: _____
Reading: _____ Good: ___ Bad: ___

Troubleshooting Step 7: _____
Reading: _____ Good: ___ Bad: ___

Troubleshooting Step 8: _____
Reading: _____ Good: ___ Bad: ___

Troubleshooting Step 9: _____
Reading: _____ Good: ___ Bad: ___

Troubleshooting Step 10: _____
Reading: _____ Good: ___ Bad: ___

Troubleshooting Step 11: _____
Reading: _____ Good: ___ Bad: ___

Troubleshooting Step 12: _____
Reading: _____ Good: ___ Bad: ___

The Problem Is: _____

What did you learn from troubleshooting this problem?

_____

REMINDER: Remove the circuit fault from the bottom of the PCBs. Verify normal operation of the relay circuit.

Fig. 5TS-6CCFP — RELAY CIRCUIT Troubleshooting Trainer H-PCB05 / Power Board H-PCB01

Copyright © 2015 VEEJER ENTERPRISES, Garland, Texas - All Rights Reserved   **Student Workbook H-WB115**

Vehicle Electronics Hands-On Troubleshooting Training Program

VEEJER ENTERPRISES 3701 Lariat Lane, Garland, Texas 75042-5419
Phone: 972-276-9642   Fax: 972-276-8122   Email: sales@veejer.com   Web Site: www.veejer.com

Problem 96

Consult Instructor Guide IG05 to insert this problem.
Slide S4 UP and leave it CLOSED.
Use switch S3 as the PCM to control the fuel pump relay.
Description of the vehicle driveability problem:
Engine cranks but engine won't run. Checked spark & fuel. There is no fuel pressure in the fuel rail. Fuel Pump not running for initial 2 seconds. A new fuel pump did not fix the problem. Boss asked me to take a look at the problem before anymore time and parts are wasted.

Does the Fuel Pump Relay "CLICK"? Yes ___ No ___
Performance of the Fuel Pump: _____

Troubleshooting Step 1: _____
Reading: _____ Good: ___ Bad: ___

Troubleshooting Step 2: _____
Reading: _____ Good: ___ Bad: ___

Troubleshooting Step 3: _____
Reading: _____ Good: ___ Bad: ___

Troubleshooting Step 4: _____
Reading: _____ Good: ___ Bad: ___

Troubleshooting Step 5: _____
Reading: _____ Good: ___ Bad: ___

Troubleshooting Step 6: _____
Reading: _____ Good: ___ Bad: ___

Troubleshooting Step 7: _____
Reading: _____ Good: ___ Bad: ___

Troubleshooting Step 8: _____
Reading: _____ Good: ___ Bad: ___

Troubleshooting Step 9: _____
Reading: _____ Good: ___ Bad: ___

Troubleshooting Step 10: _____
Reading: _____ Good: ___ Bad: ___

Troubleshooting Step 11: _____
Reading: _____ Good: ___ Bad: ___

Troubleshooting Step 12: _____
Reading: _____ Good: ___ Bad: ___

The Problem Is: _____

What did you learn from troubleshooting this problem?

_____

REMINDER: Remove the circuit fault from the bottom of the PCBs. Verify normal operation of the relay circuit.

Problem 97

Consult Instructor Guide IG05 to insert this problem.
Slide S4 UP and leave it CLOSED.
Use switch S3 as the PCM to control the fuel pump relay.
Description of the vehicle driveability problem:
Engine cranks but engine won't run. Checked spark & fuel. There is no fuel pressure in the fuel rail. Fuel Pump not running for initial 2 seconds. A new relay and new fuel pump did not fix the problem.

Does the Fuel Pump Relay "CLICK"? Yes ___ No ___
Performance of the Fuel Pump: _____

Troubleshooting Step 1: _____
Reading: _____ Good: ___ Bad: ___

Troubleshooting Step 2: _____
Reading: _____ Good: ___ Bad: ___

Troubleshooting Step 3: _____
Reading: _____ Good: ___ Bad: ___

Troubleshooting Step 4: _____
Reading: _____ Good: ___ Bad: ___

Troubleshooting Step 5: _____
Reading: _____ Good: ___ Bad: ___

Troubleshooting Step 6: _____
Reading: _____ Good: ___ Bad: ___

Troubleshooting Step 7: _____
Reading: _____ Good: ___ Bad: ___

Troubleshooting Step 8: _____
Reading: _____ Good: ___ Bad: ___

Troubleshooting Step 9: _____
Reading: _____ Good: ___ Bad: ___

Troubleshooting Step 10: _____
Reading: _____ Good: ___ Bad: ___

Troubleshooting Step 11: _____
Reading: _____ Good: ___ Bad: ___

Troubleshooting Step 12: _____
Reading: _____ Good: ___ Bad: ___

The Problem Is: _____

What did you learn from troubleshooting this problem?

_____

REMINDER: Remove the circuit fault from the bottom of the PCBs. Verify normal operation of the relay circuit.

Vehicle Electronics Hands-On Troubleshooting Training Program

VEEJER ENTERPRISES 3701 Lariat Lane, Garland, Texas 75042-5419
Phone: 972-276-9642 Fax: 972-276-8122 Email: sales@veejer.com Web Site: www.veejer.com

Problem 98
Consult Instructor Guide IG05 to insert this problem.
Slide S4 UP and leave it CLOSED.
Use switch S3 as the PCM to control the fuel pump relay.
Description of the vehicle driveability problem:
Engine cranks but engine won't run. Checked spark & fuel. There is no fuel pressure in the fuel rail. Fuel Pump not running for initial 2 seconds. A new relay and new fuel pump did not fix the problem.

Does the Fuel Pump Relay "CLICK"? Yes ___ No ___
Performance of the Fuel Pump: _____

Troubleshooting Step 1: _____
Reading: _____ Good: ___ Bad: ___

Troubleshooting Step 2: _____
Reading: _____ Good: ___ Bad: ___

Troubleshooting Step 3: _____
Reading: _____ Good: ___ Bad: ___

Troubleshooting Step 4: _____
Reading: _____ Good: ___ Bad: ___

Troubleshooting Step 5: _____
Reading: _____ Good: ___ Bad: ___

Troubleshooting Step 6: _____
Reading: _____ Good: ___ Bad: ___

Troubleshooting Step 7: _____
Reading: _____ Good: ___ Bad: ___

Troubleshooting Step 8: _____
Reading: _____ Good: ___ Bad: ___

Troubleshooting Step 9: _____
Reading: _____ Good: ___ Bad: ___

Troubleshooting Step 10: _____
Reading: _____ Good: ___ Bad: ___

Troubleshooting Step 11: _____
Reading: _____ Good: ___ Bad: ___

Troubleshooting Step 12: _____
Reading: _____ Good: ___ Bad: ___

The Problem Is: _____

What did you learn from troubleshooting this problem?

_____

REMINDER: Remove the circuit fault from the bottom of the PCBs. Verify normal operation of the relay circuit.

Copyright © 2015 VEEJER ENTERPRISES, Garland, Texas - All Rights Reserved Student Workbook H-WB115

Vehicle Electronics Hands-On Troubleshooting Training Program

VEEJER ENTERPRISES 3701 Lariat Lane, Garland, Texas 75042-5419
Phone: 972-276-9642   Fax: 972-276-8122   Email: sales@veejer.com   Web Site: www.veejer.com

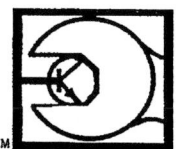

Problem 99

Consult Instructor Guide IG05 to insert this problem.
Slide S4 UP and leave it CLOSED.
Use switch S3 as the PCM to control the fuel pump relay.
Description of the vehicle driveability problem:
Customer complains his car is dead and won't crank in the mornings. Another shop replaced the battery but the problem is the same. Now the other shop wants to replace his generator (alternator) but the customer wants a second opinion. Boss told me to take a look at it before he talks with the customer.

Does the Fuel Pump Relay "CLICK"? Yes ___ No ___
Performance of the Fuel Pump: _____

Troubleshooting Step 1: _____
Reading: _____ Good: ___ Bad: ___

Troubleshooting Step 2: _____
Reading: _____ Good: ___ Bad: ___

Troubleshooting Step 3: _____
Reading: _____ Good: ___ Bad: ___

Troubleshooting Step 4: _____
Reading: _____ Good: ___ Bad: ___

Troubleshooting Step 5: _____
Reading: _____ Good: ___ Bad: ___

Troubleshooting Step 6: _____
Reading: _____ Good: ___ Bad: ___

Troubleshooting Step 7: _____
Reading: _____ Good: ___ Bad: ___

Troubleshooting Step 8: _____
Reading: _____ Good: ___ Bad: ___

Troubleshooting Step 9: _____
Reading: _____ Good: ___ Bad: ___

Troubleshooting Step 10: _____
Reading: _____ Good: ___ Bad: ___

Troubleshooting Step 11: _____
Reading: _____ Good: ___ Bad: ___

Troubleshooting Step 12: _____
Reading: _____ Good: ___ Bad: ___

The Problem Is: _____

What did you learn from troubleshooting this problem?

_____

REMINDER: Remove the circuit fault from the bottom of the PCBs. Verify normal operation of the relay circuit.

Problem 100

Consult Instructor Guide IG05 to insert this problem.
Slide S4 UP and leave it CLOSED.
Use switch S3 as the PCM to control the fuel pump relay.
Description of the vehicle driveability problem:
Engine cranks but it takes a long time to start running. Battery is good. Engine barely runs. Fuel pressure is very low and drops at higher idle rpm.

Does the Fuel Pump Relay "CLICK"? Yes ___ No ___
Performance of the Fuel Pump: _____

Troubleshooting Step 1: _____
Reading: _____ Good: ___ Bad: ___

Troubleshooting Step 2: _____
Reading: _____ Good: ___ Bad: ___

Troubleshooting Step 3: _____
Reading: _____ Good: ___ Bad: ___

Troubleshooting Step 4: _____
Reading: _____ Good: ___ Bad: ___

Troubleshooting Step 5: _____
Reading: _____ Good: ___ Bad: ___

Troubleshooting Step 6: _____
Reading: _____ Good: ___ Bad: ___

Troubleshooting Step 7: _____
Reading: _____ Good: ___ Bad: ___

Troubleshooting Step 8: _____
Reading: _____ Good: ___ Bad: ___

Troubleshooting Step 9: _____
Reading: _____ Good: ___ Bad: ___

Troubleshooting Step 10: _____
Reading: _____ Good: ___ Bad: ___

Troubleshooting Step 11: _____
Reading: _____ Good: ___ Bad: ___

Troubleshooting Step 12: _____
Reading: _____ Good: ___ Bad: ___

The Problem Is: _____

What did you learn from troubleshooting this problem?

_____

REMINDER: Remove the circuit fault from the bottom of the PCBs. Verify normal operation of the relay circuit.

Vehicle Electronics Hands-On Troubleshooting Training Program

VEEJER ENTERPRISES 3701 Lariat Lane, Garland, Texas 75042-5419
Phone: 972-276-9642   Fax: 972-276-8122   Email: sales@veejer.com   Web Site: www.veejer.com

Problem 101
Consult Instructor Guide IG05 to insert this problem.
Slide S4 UP and leave it CLOSED.
Use switch S3 as the PCM to control the fuel pump relay.
Description of the vehicle driveability problem:
Engine cranks but won't run. No fuel pressure. New fuel pump and relay didn't fix the problem.

Does the Fuel Pump Relay *"CLICK"*? Yes ___ No ___
Performance of the Fuel Pump: _____

Troubleshooting Step 1: _____
Reading: _____ Good: ___ Bad: ___

Troubleshooting Step 2: _____
Reading: _____ Good: ___ Bad: ___

Troubleshooting Step 3: _____
Reading: _____ Good: ___ Bad: ___

Troubleshooting Step 4: _____
Reading: _____ Good: ___ Bad: ___

Troubleshooting Step 5: _____
Reading: _____ Good: ___ Bad: ___

Troubleshooting Step 6: _____
Reading: _____ Good: ___ Bad: ___

Troubleshooting Step 7: _____
Reading: _____ Good: ___ Bad: ___

Troubleshooting Step 8: _____
Reading: _____ Good: ___ Bad: ___

Troubleshooting Step 9: _____
Reading: _____ Good: ___ Bad: ___

Troubleshooting Step 10: _____
Reading: _____ Good: ___ Bad: ___

Troubleshooting Step 11: _____
Reading: _____ Good: ___ Bad: ___

Troubleshooting Step 12: _____
Reading: _____ Good: ___ Bad: ___

The Problem Is: _____

What did you learn from troubleshooting this problem?
_____

REMINDER: Remove the circuit fault from the bottom of the PCBs. Verify normal operation of the relay circuit.

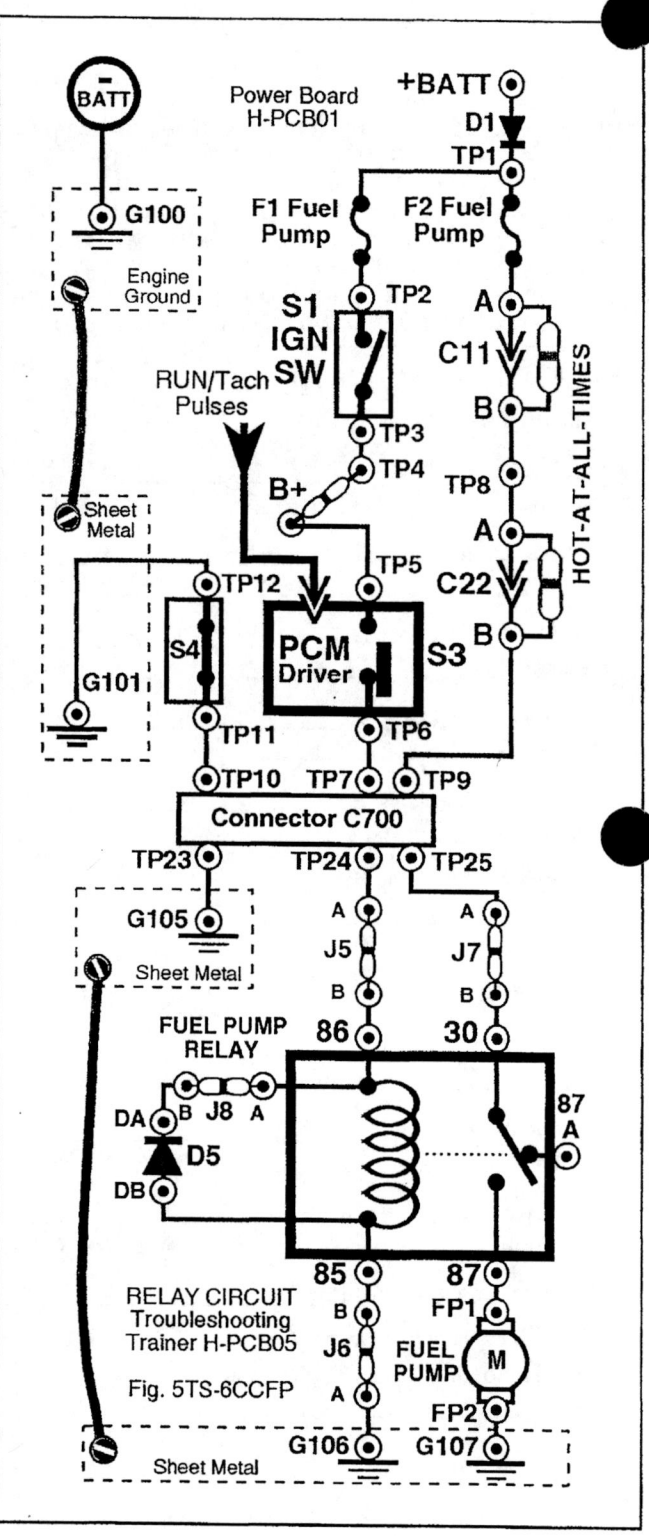

Fig. 5TS-6CCFP — RELAY CIRCUIT Troubleshooting Trainer H-PCB05

Vehicle Electronics Hands-On Troubleshooting Training Program

VEEJER ENTERPRISES 3701 Lariat Lane, Garland, Texas 75042-5419
Phone: 972-276-9642 Fax: 972-276-8122 Email: sales@veejer.com Web Site: www.veejer.com

Problem 102

Consult Instructor Guide IG05 to insert this problem.
Slide S4 UP and leave it CLOSED.
Use switch S3 as the PCM to control the fuel pump relay.
Description of the vehicle driveability problem:
Customer complains of strange electrical problems. Sometimes the car won't crank and sometimes it cranks but won't run. It seems he can get the car to crank and run at times but he has to cycle the ignition key ON/OFF several times.

Does the Fuel Pump Relay "CLICK"? Yes ___ No ___
Performance of the Fuel Pump: _____

Troubleshooting Step 1: _____
Reading: _____ Good: ___ Bad: ___

Troubleshooting Step 2: _____
Reading: _____ Good: ___ Bad: ___

Troubleshooting Step 3: _____
Reading: _____ Good: ___ Bad: ___

Troubleshooting Step 4: _____
Reading: _____ Good: ___ Bad: ___

Troubleshooting Step 5: _____
Reading: _____ Good: ___ Bad: ___

Troubleshooting Step 6: _____
Reading: _____ Good: ___ Bad: ___

Troubleshooting Step 7: _____
Reading: _____ Good: ___ Bad: ___

Troubleshooting Step 8: _____
Reading: _____ Good: ___ Bad: ___

Troubleshooting Step 9: _____
Reading: _____ Good: ___ Bad: ___

Troubleshooting Step 10: _____
Reading: _____ Good: ___ Bad: ___

Troubleshooting Step 11: _____
Reading: _____ Good: ___ Bad: ___

Troubleshooting Step 12: _____
Reading: _____ Good: ___ Bad: ___

The Problem Is: _____

What did you learn from troubleshooting this problem?

_____

REMINDER: Remove the circuit fault from the bottom of the PCBs. Verify normal operation of the relay circuit.

Problem 103

Consult Instructor Guide IG05 to insert this problem.
Slide S4 UP and leave it CLOSED.
Use switch S3 as the PCM to control the fuel pump relay.
Description of the vehicle driveability problem:
Engine cranks but engine won't run. Checked spark & fuel. There is no fuel pressure in the fuel rail. Fuel Pump not running for initial 2 seconds. A new relay and new fuel pump did not fix the problem.

Does the Fuel Pump Relay "CLICK"? Yes ___ No ___
Performance of the Fuel Pump: _____

Troubleshooting Step 1: _____
Reading: _____ Good: ___ Bad: ___

Troubleshooting Step 2: _____
Reading: _____ Good: ___ Bad: ___

Troubleshooting Step 3: _____
Reading: _____ Good: ___ Bad: ___

Troubleshooting Step 4: _____
Reading: _____ Good: ___ Bad: ___

Troubleshooting Step 5: _____
Reading: _____ Good: ___ Bad: ___

Troubleshooting Step 6: _____
Reading: _____ Good: ___ Bad: ___

Troubleshooting Step 7: _____
Reading: _____ Good: ___ Bad: ___

Troubleshooting Step 8: _____
Reading: _____ Good: ___ Bad: ___

Troubleshooting Step 9: _____
Reading: _____ Good: ___ Bad: ___

Troubleshooting Step 10: _____
Reading: _____ Good: ___ Bad: ___

Troubleshooting Step 11: _____
Reading: _____ Good: ___ Bad: ___

Troubleshooting Step 12: _____
Reading: _____ Good: ___ Bad: ___

The Problem Is: _____

What did you learn from troubleshooting this problem?

_____

REMINDER: Remove the circuit fault from the bottom of the PCBs. Verify normal operation of the relay circuit.

Vehicle Electronics Hands-On Troubleshooting Training Program

VEEJER ENTERPRISES 3701 Lariat Lane, Garland, Texas 75042-5419
Phone: 972-276-9642 Fax: 972-276-8122 Email: sales@veejer.com Web Site: www.veejer.com

Problem 104

Consult Instructor Guide IG05 to insert this problem.
Slide S4 UP and leave it CLOSED.
Use switch S3 as the PCM to control the fuel pump relay.
Description of the vehicle driveability problem:
Engine cranks but engine won't run. Checked spark & fuel. There is no fuel pressure in the fuel rail. Fuel Pump not running for initial 2 seconds. A new relay and new fuel pump did not fix the problem. The boss is really ticked at the tech and he asked me to look into it to find out what's wrong.

Does the Fuel Pump Relay "CLICK"? Yes ___ No ___
Performance of the Fuel Pump: _____

Troubleshooting Step 1: _____
Reading: _____ Good: ___ Bad: ___

Troubleshooting Step 2: _____
Reading: _____ Good: ___ Bad: ___

Troubleshooting Step 3: _____
Reading: _____ Good: ___ Bad: ___

Troubleshooting Step 4: _____
Reading: _____ Good: ___ Bad: ___

Troubleshooting Step 5: _____
Reading: _____ Good: ___ Bad: ___

Troubleshooting Step 6: _____
Reading: _____ Good: ___ Bad: ___

Troubleshooting Step 7: _____
Reading: _____ Good: ___ Bad: ___

Troubleshooting Step 8: _____
Reading: _____ Good: ___ Bad: ___

Troubleshooting Step 9: _____
Reading: _____ Good: ___ Bad: ___

Troubleshooting Step 10: _____
Reading: _____ Good: ___ Bad: ___

Troubleshooting Step 11: _____
Reading: _____ Good: ___ Bad: ___

Troubleshooting Step 12: _____
Reading: _____ Good: ___ Bad: ___

The Problem Is: _____

What did you learn from troubleshooting this problem?
_____

REMINDER: Remove the circuit fault from the bottom of the PCBs. Verify normal operation of the relay circuit.

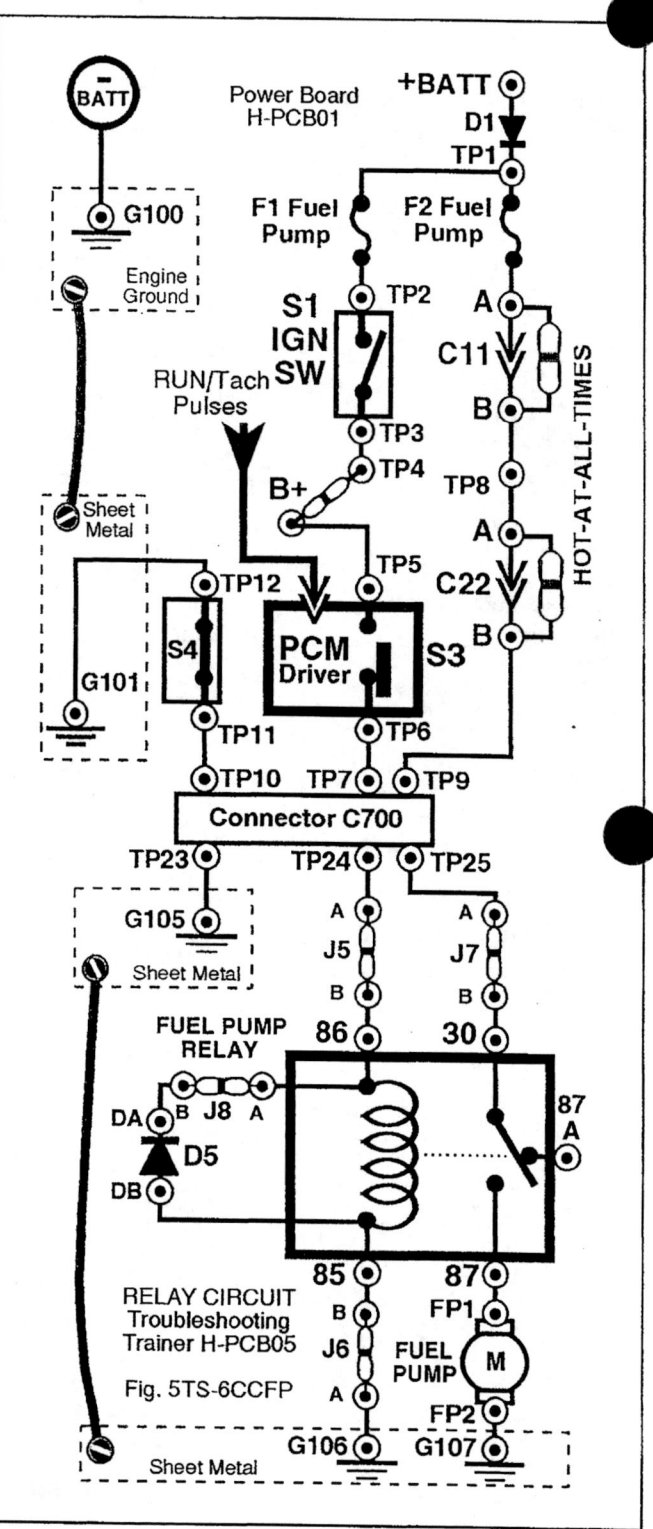

Fig. 5TS-6CCFP

Vehicle Electronics Hands-On Troubleshooting Training Program

VEEJER ENTERPRISES 3701 Lariat Lane, Garland, Texas 75042-5419
Phone: 972-276-9642 Fax: 972-276-8122 Email: sales@veejer.com Web Site: www.veejer.com

Problem 105

Consult Instructor Guide IG05 to insert this problem.
Slide S4 UP and leave it CLOSED.
Use switch S3 as the PCM to control the fuel pump relay.
   Description of the vehicle driveability problem:
Engine runs but it cranks a long time before it starts to run. Vehicle has very little power & very poor acceleration. All fuel filters have been replaced. A new fuel pump and fuel pump relay did not fix the problem. Fuel pressure drops a lot at higher rpm.

Does the Fuel Pump Relay "CLICK"? Yes ___ No ___
Performance of the Fuel Pump: _____

Troubleshooting Step 1: _____
Reading: _____ Good: ___ Bad: ___

Troubleshooting Step 2: _____
Reading: _____ Good: ___ Bad: ___

Troubleshooting Step 3: _____
Reading: _____ Good: ___ Bad: ___

Troubleshooting Step 4: _____
Reading: _____ Good: ___ Bad: ___

Troubleshooting Step 5: _____
Reading: _____ Good: ___ Bad: ___

Troubleshooting Step 6: _____
Reading: _____ Good: ___ Bad: ___

Troubleshooting Step 7: _____
Reading: _____ Good: ___ Bad: ___

Troubleshooting Step 8: _____
Reading: _____ Good: ___ Bad: ___

Troubleshooting Step 9: _____
Reading: _____ Good: ___ Bad: ___

Troubleshooting Step 10: _____
Reading: _____ Good: ___ Bad: ___

Troubleshooting Step 11: _____
Reading: _____ Good: ___ Bad: ___

Troubleshooting Step 12: _____
Reading: _____ Good: ___ Bad: ___

The Problem Is: _____

What did you learn from troubleshooting this problem?

_____

REMINDER: Remove the circuit fault from the bottom of the PCBs. Verify normal operation of the relay circuit.

Problem 106

Consult Instructor Guide IG05 to insert this problem.
Slide S4 UP and leave it CLOSED.
Use switch S3 as the PCM to control the fuel pump relay.
   Description of the vehicle driveability problem:
Engine cranks but engine won't run. Fuel Pump not running for initial 2 seconds. Another relay from the car's relay box fixed the fuel pump problem. The boss doesn't believe the relay is bad and wants to know what's wrong with the original relay before he orders a new one.

Does the Fuel Pump Relay "CLICK"? Yes ___ No ___
Performance of the Fuel Pump: _____

Troubleshooting Step 1: _____
Reading: _____ Good: ___ Bad: ___

Troubleshooting Step 2: _____
Reading: _____ Good: ___ Bad: ___

Troubleshooting Step 3: _____
Reading: _____ Good: ___ Bad: ___

Troubleshooting Step 4: _____
Reading: _____ Good: ___ Bad: ___

Troubleshooting Step 5: _____
Reading: _____ Good: ___ Bad: ___

Troubleshooting Step 6: _____
Reading: _____ Good: ___ Bad: ___

Troubleshooting Step 7: _____
Reading: _____ Good: ___ Bad: ___

Troubleshooting Step 8: _____
Reading: _____ Good: ___ Bad: ___

Troubleshooting Step 9: _____
Reading: _____ Good: ___ Bad: ___

Troubleshooting Step 10: _____
Reading: _____ Good: ___ Bad: ___

Troubleshooting Step 11: _____
Reading: _____ Good: ___ Bad: ___

Troubleshooting Step 12: _____
Reading: _____ Good: ___ Bad: ___

The Problem Is: _____

What did you learn from troubleshooting this problem?

_____

REMINDER: Remove the circuit fault from the bottom of the PCBs. Verify normal operation of the relay circuit.

Vehicle Electronics Hands-On Troubleshooting Training Program

VEEJER ENTERPRISES 3701 Lariat Lane, Garland, Texas 75042-5419
Phone: 972-276-9642 Fax: 972-276-8122 Email: sales@veejer.com Web Site: www.veejer.com

Problem 107

Consult Instructor Guide IG05 to insert this problem.
Slide S4 UP and leave it CLOSED.
Use switch S3 as the PCM to control the fuel pump relay.
  Description of the vehicle driveability problem:
No fuel pressure and fuel pump is not running. Another tech is starting to change the fuel pump but the boss told me to look at the car before the new pump is installed. The other tech has found a blown fuse and replaced it and it blew again so he says the fuel pump is "shorted out."

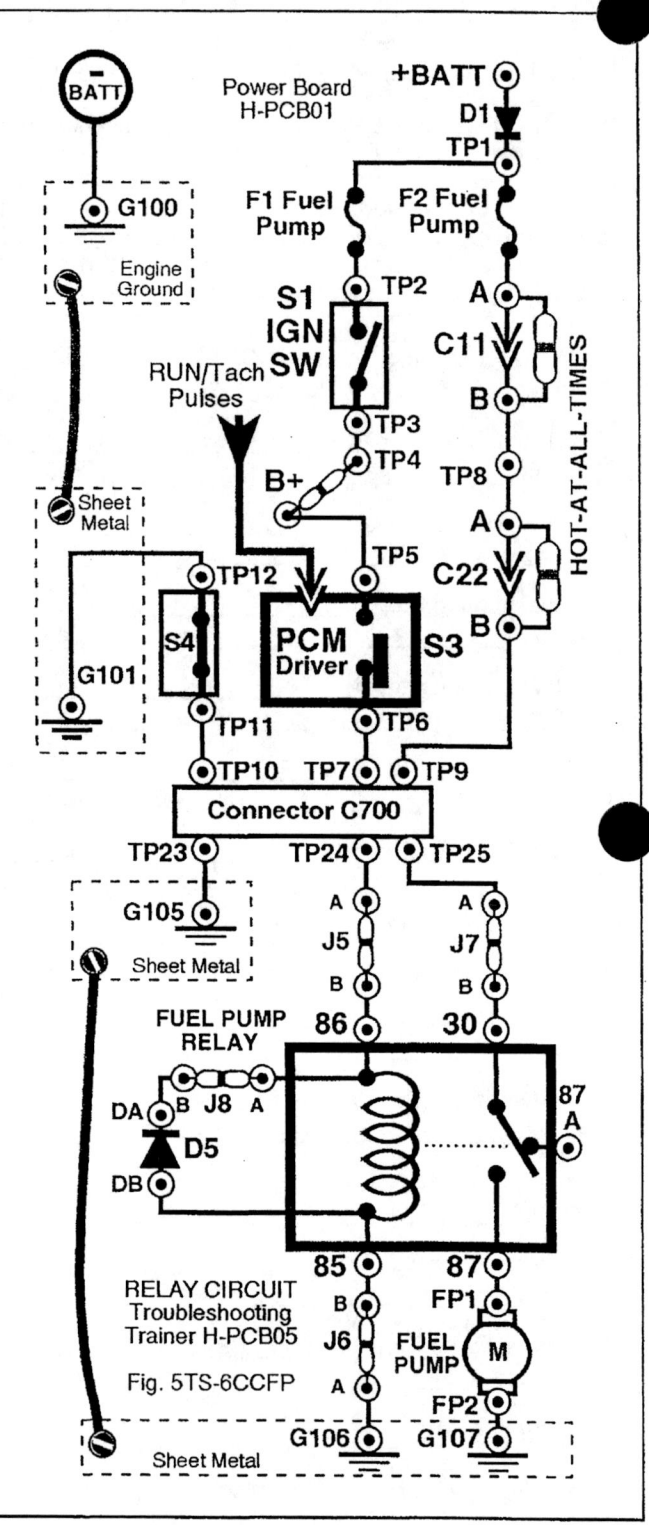

Fig. 5TS-6CCFP

Does the Fuel Pump Relay "CLICK"? Yes __ No __
Performance of the Fuel Pump: _____

Troubleshooting Step 1: _____
Reading: _____ Good: __ Bad: __

Troubleshooting Step 2: _____
Reading: _____ Good: __ Bad: __

Troubleshooting Step 3: _____
Reading: _____ Good: __ Bad: __

Troubleshooting Step 4: _____
Reading: _____ Good: __ Bad: __

Troubleshooting Step 5: _____
Reading: _____ Good: __ Bad: __

Troubleshooting Step 6: _____
Reading: _____ Good: __ Bad: __

Troubleshooting Step 7: _____
Reading: _____ Good: __ Bad: __

Troubleshooting Step 8: _____
Reading: _____ Good: __ Bad: __

Troubleshooting Step 9: _____
Reading: _____ Good: __ Bad: __

Troubleshooting Step 10: _____
Reading: _____ Good: __ Bad: __

Troubleshooting Step 11: _____
Reading: _____ Good: __ Bad: __

Troubleshooting Step 12: _____
Reading: _____ Good: __ Bad: __

The Problem Is: _____

What did you learn from troubleshooting this problem?

_____

REMINDER: Remove the circuit fault from the bottom of the PCBs. Verify normal operation of the relay circuit.

Vehicle Electronics Hands-On Troubleshooting Training Program

VEEJER ENTERPRISES 3701 Lariat Lane, Garland, Texas 75042-5419
Phone: 972-276-9642 Fax: 972-276-8122 Email: sales@veejer.com Web Site: www.veejer.com

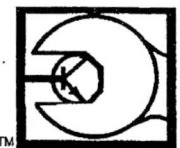

Problem 108

Consult Instructor Guide IG05 to insert this problem.
Slide S4 UP and leave it CLOSED.
Use switch S3 as the PCM to control the fuel pump relay.
Description of the vehicle driveability problem:
Engine will not crank. Battery and starter motor have been replaced. Fuel Pump not running for initial 2 seconds.

Does the Fuel Pump Relay "CLICK"? Yes ___ No ___
Performance of the Fuel Pump: _____

Troubleshooting Step 1: _____
Reading: _____ Good: ___ Bad: ___

Troubleshooting Step 2: _____
Reading: _____ Good: ___ Bad: ___

Troubleshooting Step 3: _____
Reading: _____ Good: ___ Bad: ___

Troubleshooting Step 4: _____
Reading: _____ Good: ___ Bad: ___

Troubleshooting Step 5: _____
Reading: _____ Good: ___ Bad: ___

Troubleshooting Step 6: _____
Reading: _____ Good: ___ Bad: ___

Troubleshooting Step 7: _____
Reading: _____ Good: ___ Bad: ___

Troubleshooting Step 8: _____
Reading: _____ Good: ___ Bad: ___

Troubleshooting Step 9: _____
Reading: _____ Good: ___ Bad: ___

Troubleshooting Step 10: _____
Reading: _____ Good: ___ Bad: ___

Troubleshooting Step 11: _____
Reading: _____ Good: ___ Bad: ___

Troubleshooting Step 12: _____
Reading: _____ Good: ___ Bad: ___

The Problem Is: _____

What did you learn from troubleshooting this problem?

_____

REMINDER: Remove the circuit fault from the bottom of the PCBs. Verify normal operation of the relay circuit.

Problem 109

Consult Instructor Guide IG05 to insert this problem.
Slide S4 UP and leave it CLOSED.
Use switch S3 as the PCM to control the fuel pump relay.
Description of the vehicle driveability problem:
Engine cranks but will not start. Checked spark & fuel. There is no fuel pressure in the fuel rail. Fuel Pump not running for initial 2 seconds and found Fuse F1 is blown.

Does the Fuel Pump Relay "CLICK"? Yes ___ No ___
Performance of the Fuel Pump: _____

Troubleshooting Step 1: _____
Reading: _____ Good: ___ Bad: ___

Troubleshooting Step 2: _____
Reading: _____ Good: ___ Bad: ___

Troubleshooting Step 3: _____
Reading: _____ Good: ___ Bad: ___

Troubleshooting Step 4: _____
Reading: _____ Good: ___ Bad: ___

Troubleshooting Step 5: _____
Reading: _____ Good: ___ Bad: ___

Troubleshooting Step 6: _____
Reading: _____ Good: ___ Bad: ___

Troubleshooting Step 7: _____
Reading: _____ Good: ___ Bad: ___

Troubleshooting Step 8: _____
Reading: _____ Good: ___ Bad: ___

Troubleshooting Step 9: _____
Reading: _____ Good: ___ Bad: ___

Troubleshooting Step 10: _____
Reading: _____ Good: ___ Bad: ___

Troubleshooting Step 11: _____
Reading: _____ Good: ___ Bad: ___

Troubleshooting Step 12: _____
Reading: _____ Good: ___ Bad: ___

The Problem Is: _____

What did you learn from troubleshooting this problem?

_____

REMINDER: Remove the circuit fault from the bottom of the PCBs. Verify normal operation of the relay circuit.

Vehicle Electronics Hands-On Troubleshooting Training Program

VEEJER ENTERPRISES 3701 Lariat Lane, Garland, Texas 75042-5419
Phone: 972-276-9642   Fax: 972-276-8122   Email: sales@veejer.com   Web Site: www.veejer.com

Problem 110

Consult Instructor Guide IG05 to insert this problem.
Slide S4 UP and leave it CLOSED.
Use switch S3 as the PCM to control the fuel pump relay.
Description of the vehicle driveability problem:
Customer complains his second battery has failed. If the car sits over night the engine cranks slowly but does crank. If the car sits over the weekend the battery is dead. He has had the fuel pump relay and fuel pump changed but still has the same problem.

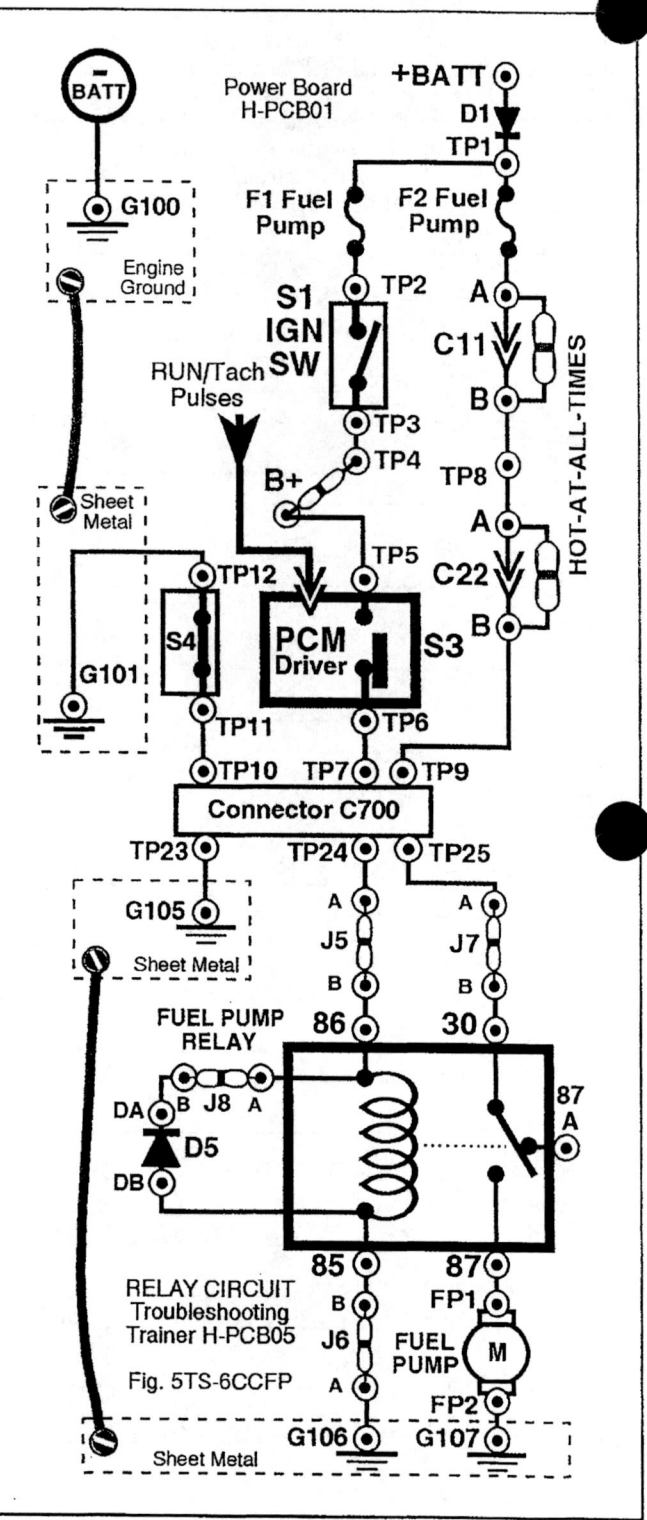

Does the Fuel Pump Relay "CLICK"?   Yes ___   No ___
Performance of the Fuel Pump: _____

Troubleshooting Step 1: _____
Reading: _____   Good: ___   Bad: ___

Troubleshooting Step 2: _____
Reading: _____   Good: ___   Bad: ___

Troubleshooting Step 3: _____
Reading: _____   Good: ___   Bad: ___

Troubleshooting Step 4: _____
Reading: _____   Good: ___   Bad: ___

Troubleshooting Step 5: _____
Reading: _____   Good: ___   Bad: ___

Troubleshooting Step 6: _____
Reading: _____   Good: ___   Bad: ___

Troubleshooting Step 7: _____
Reading: _____   Good: ___   Bad: ___

Troubleshooting Step 8: _____
Reading: _____   Good: ___   Bad: ___

Troubleshooting Step 9: _____
Reading: _____   Good: ___   Bad: ___

Troubleshooting Step 10: _____
Reading: _____   Good: ___   Bad: ___

Troubleshooting Step 11: _____
Reading: _____   Good: ___   Bad: ___

Troubleshooting Step 12: _____
Reading: _____   Good: ___   Bad: ___

The Problem Is: _____

What did you learn from troubleshooting this problem?

_____

REMINDER: Remove the circuit fault from the bottom of the PCBs. Verify normal operation of the relay circuit.

Vehicle Electronics Hands-On Troubleshooting Training Program

VEEJER ENTERPRISES 3701 Lariat Lane, Garland, Texas 75042-5419
Phone: 972-276-9642 Fax: 972-276-8122 Email: sales@veejer.com Web Site: www.veejer.com

Problem 111

Consult Instructor Guide IG05 to insert this problem.
Slide S4 UP and leave it CLOSED.
Use switch S3 as the PCM to control the fuel pump relay.
Description of the vehicle driveability problem:
Engine runs but it seems to crank longer before it starts to run. Vehicle has less power & sluggish acceleration. A new fuel pump was installed but it made no difference in driveability. All fuel filters have been replaced. A new relay did not fix the problem. Fuel pressure still drops at higher rpm.

Does the Fuel Pump Relay "CLICK"? Yes ___ No ___
Performance of the Fuel Pump: _____

Troubleshooting Step 1: _____
Reading: _____ Good: ___ Bad: ___

Troubleshooting Step 2: _____
Reading: _____ Good: ___ Bad: ___

Troubleshooting Step 3: _____
Reading: _____ Good: ___ Bad: ___

Troubleshooting Step 4: _____
Reading: _____ Good: ___ Bad: ___

Troubleshooting Step 5: _____
Reading: _____ Good: ___ Bad: ___

Troubleshooting Step 6: _____
Reading: _____ Good: ___ Bad: ___

Troubleshooting Step 7: _____
Reading: _____ Good: ___ Bad: ___

Troubleshooting Step 8: _____
Reading: _____ Good: ___ Bad: ___

Troubleshooting Step 9: _____
Reading: _____ Good: ___ Bad: ___

Troubleshooting Step 10: _____
Reading: _____ Good: ___ Bad: ___

Troubleshooting Step 11: _____
Reading: _____ Good: ___ Bad: ___

Troubleshooting Step 12: _____
Reading: _____ Good: ___ Bad: ___

The Problem Is: _____

What did you learn from troubleshooting this problem?

_____

REMINDER: Remove the circuit fault from the bottom of the PCBs. Verify normal operation of the relay circuit.

Problem 112

Consult Instructor Guide IG05 to insert this problem.
Slide S4 UP and leave it CLOSED.
Use switch S3 as the PCM to control the fuel pump relay.
Description of the vehicle driveability problem:
Engine cranks but will not start. Checked spark & fuel. There is no fuel pressure in the fuel rail. Fuel Pump not running for initial 2 seconds. A new fuel pump and relay did not fix the problem.

Does the Fuel Pump Relay "CLICK"? Yes ___ No ___
Performance of the Fuel Pump: _____

Troubleshooting Step 1: _____
Reading: _____ Good: ___ Bad: ___

Troubleshooting Step 2: _____
Reading: _____ Good: ___ Bad: ___

Troubleshooting Step 3: _____
Reading: _____ Good: ___ Bad: ___

Troubleshooting Step 4: _____
Reading: _____ Good: ___ Bad: ___

Troubleshooting Step 5: _____
Reading: _____ Good: ___ Bad: ___

Troubleshooting Step 6: _____
Reading: _____ Good: ___ Bad: ___

Troubleshooting Step 7: _____
Reading: _____ Good: ___ Bad: ___

Troubleshooting Step 8: _____
Reading: _____ Good: ___ Bad: ___

Troubleshooting Step 9: _____
Reading: _____ Good: ___ Bad: ___

Troubleshooting Step 10: _____
Reading: _____ Good: ___ Bad: ___

Troubleshooting Step 11: _____
Reading: _____ Good: ___ Bad: ___

Troubleshooting Step 12: _____
Reading: _____ Good: ___ Bad: ___

The Problem Is: _____

What did you learn from troubleshooting this problem?

_____

REMINDER: Remove the circuit fault from the bottom of the PCBs. Verify normal operation of the relay circuit.

Vehicle Electronics Hands-On Troubleshooting Training Program

VEEJER ENTERPRISES 3701 Lariat Lane, Garland, Texas 75042-5419
Phone: 972-276-9642 Fax: 972-276-8122 Email: sales@veejer.com Web Site: www.veejer.com

Problem 113

Consult Instructor Guide IG05 to insert this problem.
Slide S4 UP and leave it CLOSED.
Use switch S3 as the PCM to control the fuel pump relay.
 Description of the vehicle driveability problem:
Engine cranks but engine won't run. Checked spark & fuel. There is no fuel pressure in the fuel rail. Fuel Pump not running for initial 2 seconds. A new relay and new fuel pump did not fix the problem.

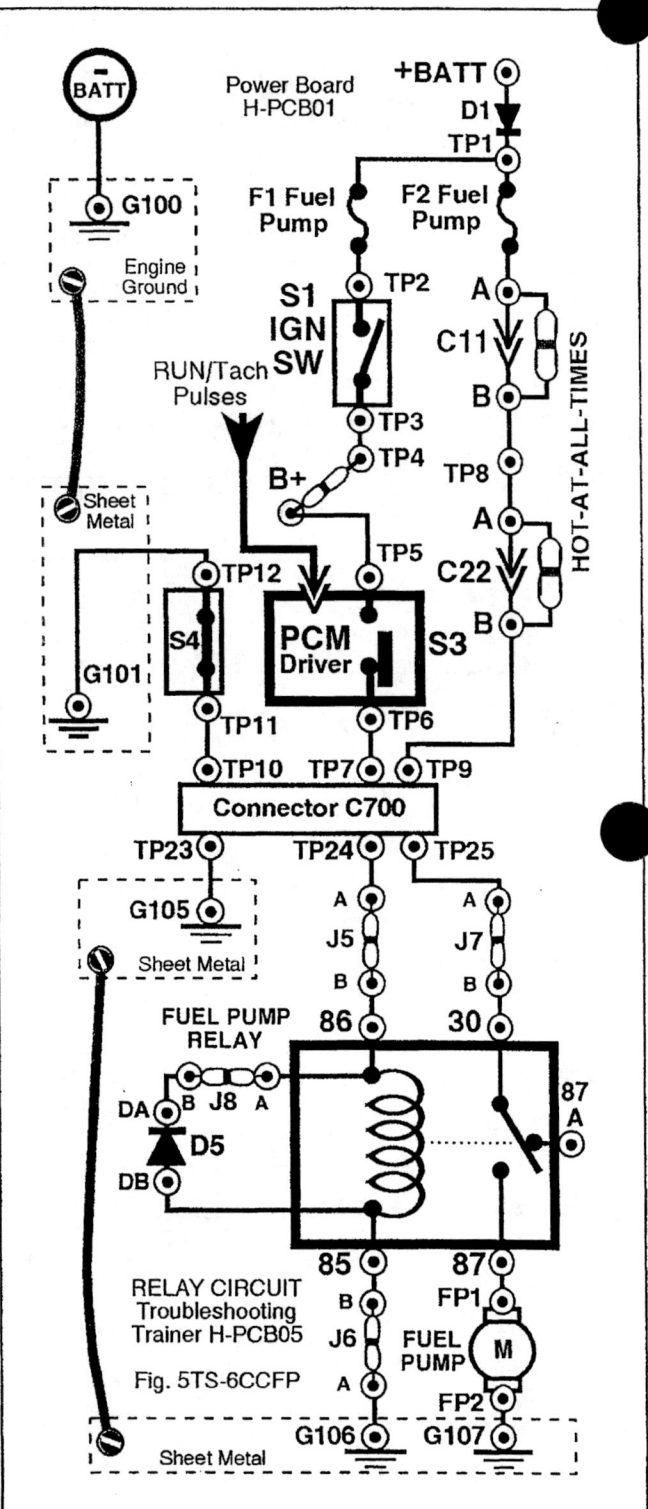

Does the Fuel Pump Relay "CLICK"? Yes ___ No ___
Performance of the Fuel Pump: _____

Troubleshooting Step 1: _____
Reading: _____ Good: ___ Bad: ___

Troubleshooting Step 2: _____
Reading: _____ Good: ___ Bad: ___

Troubleshooting Step 3: _____
Reading: _____ Good: ___ Bad: ___

Troubleshooting Step 4: _____
Reading: _____ Good: ___ Bad: ___

Troubleshooting Step 5: _____
Reading: _____ Good: ___ Bad: ___

Troubleshooting Step 6: _____
Reading: _____ Good: ___ Bad: ___

Troubleshooting Step 7: _____
Reading: _____ Good: ___ Bad: ___

Troubleshooting Step 8: _____
Reading: _____ Good: ___ Bad: ___

Troubleshooting Step 9: _____
Reading: _____ Good: ___ Bad: ___

Troubleshooting Step 10: _____
Reading: _____ Good: ___ Bad: ___

Troubleshooting Step 11: _____
Reading: _____ Good: ___ Bad: ___

Troubleshooting Step 12: _____
Reading: _____ Good: ___ Bad: ___

The Problem Is: _____

What did you learn from troubleshooting this problem?
_____

REMINDER: Remove the circuit fault from the bottom of the PCBs. Verify normal operation of the relay circuit.

Vehicle Electronics Hands-On Troubleshooting Training Program

VEEJER ENTERPRISES 3701 Lariat Lane, Garland, Texas 75042-5419
Phone: 972-276-9642 Fax: 972-276-8122 Email: sales@veejer.com Web Site: www.veejer.com

Problem 114
Consult Instructor Guide IG05 to insert this problem.
Slide S4 UP and leave it CLOSED.
Use switch S3 as the PCM to control the fuel pump relay.
Description of the vehicle driveability problem:
Engine cranks but will not start. Checked spark & fuel. There is no fuel pressure in the fuel rail. Fuel Pump not running for initial 2 seconds and found Fuse F1 is blown.

Does the Fuel Pump Relay "CLICK"? Yes ___ No ___
Performance of the Fuel Pump: _____

Troubleshooting Step 1: _____
Reading: _____ Good: ___ Bad: ___

Troubleshooting Step 2: _____
Reading: _____ Good: ___ Bad: ___

Troubleshooting Step 3: _____
Reading: _____ Good: ___ Bad: ___

Troubleshooting Step 4: _____
Reading: _____ Good: ___ Bad: ___

Troubleshooting Step 5: _____
Reading: _____ Good: ___ Bad: ___

Troubleshooting Step 6: _____
Reading: _____ Good: ___ Bad: ___

Troubleshooting Step 7: _____
Reading: _____ Good: ___ Bad: ___

Troubleshooting Step 8: _____
Reading: _____ Good: ___ Bad: ___

Troubleshooting Step 9: _____
Reading: _____ Good: ___ Bad: ___

Troubleshooting Step 10: _____
Reading: _____ Good: ___ Bad: ___

Troubleshooting Step 11: _____
Reading: _____ Good: ___ Bad: ___

Troubleshooting Step 12: _____
Reading: _____ Good: ___ Bad: ___

The Problem Is: _____

What did you learn from troubleshooting this problem?

_____

REMINDER: Remove the circuit fault from the bottom of the PCBs. Verify normal operation of the relay circuit.

Problem 115
Consult Instructor Guide IG05 to insert this problem.
Slide S4 UP and leave it CLOSED.
Use switch S3 as the PCM to control the fuel pump relay.
Description of the vehicle driveability problem:
Engine cranks but will not start. Checked spark & fuel. There is no fuel pressure in the fuel rail. Fuel Pump not running for initial 2 seconds and found Fuse F2 is blown.

Does the Fuel Pump Relay "CLICK"? Yes ___ No ___
Performance of the Fuel Pump: _____

Troubleshooting Step 1: _____
Reading: _____ Good: ___ Bad: ___

Troubleshooting Step 2: _____
Reading: _____ Good: ___ Bad: ___

Troubleshooting Step 3: _____
Reading: _____ Good: ___ Bad: ___

Troubleshooting Step 4: _____
Reading: _____ Good: ___ Bad: ___

Troubleshooting Step 5: _____
Reading: _____ Good: ___ Bad: ___

Troubleshooting Step 6: _____
Reading: _____ Good: ___ Bad: ___

Troubleshooting Step 7: _____
Reading: _____ Good: ___ Bad: ___

Troubleshooting Step 8: _____
Reading: _____ Good: ___ Bad: ___

Troubleshooting Step 9: _____
Reading: _____ Good: ___ Bad: ___

Troubleshooting Step 10: _____
Reading: _____ Good: ___ Bad: ___

Troubleshooting Step 11: _____
Reading: _____ Good: ___ Bad: ___

Troubleshooting Step 12: _____
Reading: _____ Good: ___ Bad: ___

The Problem Is: _____

What did you learn from troubleshooting this problem?

_____

REMINDER: Remove the circuit fault from the bottom of the PCBs. Verify normal operation of the relay circuit.

Vehicle Electronics Hands-On Troubleshooting Training Program

VEEJER ENTERPRISES 3701 Lariat Lane, Garland, Texas 75042-5419
Phone: 972-276-9642   Fax: 972-276-8122   Email: sales@veejer.com   Web Site: www.veejer.com™

Problem 116
Consult Instructor Guide IG05 to insert this problem.
Slide S4 UP and leave it CLOSED.
Use switch S3 as the PCM to control the fuel pump relay.
   Description of the vehicle driveability problem:
Engine cranks but engine won't run. Checked spark & fuel. There is no fuel pressure in the fuel rail. Fuel Pump not running for initial 2 seconds. A new relay and fuel pump did not fix the problem.

Does the Fuel Pump Relay "CLICK"? Yes ___ No ___
Performance of the Fuel Pump: _____

Troubleshooting Step 1: _____
Reading: _____ Good: ___ Bad: ___

Troubleshooting Step 2: _____
Reading: _____ Good: ___ Bad: ___

Troubleshooting Step 3: _____
Reading: _____ Good: ___ Bad: ___

Troubleshooting Step 4: _____
Reading: _____ Good: ___ Bad: ___

Troubleshooting Step 5: _____
Reading: _____ Good: ___ Bad: ___

Troubleshooting Step 6: _____
Reading: _____ Good: ___ Bad: ___

Troubleshooting Step 7: _____
Reading: _____ Good: ___ Bad: ___

Troubleshooting Step 8: _____
Reading: _____ Good: ___ Bad: ___

Troubleshooting Step 9: _____
Reading: _____ Good: ___ Bad: ___

Troubleshooting Step 10: _____
Reading: _____ Good: ___ Bad: ___

Troubleshooting Step 11: _____
Reading: _____ Good: ___ Bad: ___

Troubleshooting Step 12: _____
Reading: _____ Good: ___ Bad: ___

The Problem Is: _____

What did you learn from troubleshooting this problem?

_____

REMINDER: Remove the circuit fault from the bottom of the PCBs. Verify normal operation of the relay circuit.

Copyright © 2015 VEEJER ENTERPRISES, Garland, Texas - All Rights Reserved **Student Workbook H-WB115 Page 93**

Vehicle Electronics Hands-On Troubleshooting Training Program

VEEJER ENTERPRISES 3701 Lariat Lane, Garland, Texas 75042-5419
Phone: 972-276-9642   Fax: 972-276-8122   Email: sales@veejer.com   Web Site: www.veejer.com

Problem 117
Consult Instructor Guide IG05 to insert this problem.
Slide S4 UP and leave it CLOSED.
Use switch S3 as the PCM to control the fuel pump relay.
Description of the vehicle driveability problem:
Engine cranks but engine won't run. Checked spark & fuel. There is no fuel pressure in the fuel rail. Fuel Pump not running for initial 2 seconds. A new relay and new fuel pump did not fix the problem.

Does the Fuel Pump Relay "CLICK"?   Yes ___ No ___
Performance of the Fuel Pump: _____

Troubleshooting Step 1: _____
Reading: _____ Good: ____ Bad: ____

Troubleshooting Step 2: _____
Reading: _____ Good: ____ Bad: ____

Troubleshooting Step 3: _____
Reading: _____ Good: ____ Bad: ____

Troubleshooting Step 4: _____
Reading: _____ Good: ____ Bad: ____

Troubleshooting Step 5: _____
Reading: _____ Good: ____ Bad: ____

Troubleshooting Step 6: _____
Reading: _____ Good: ____ Bad: ____

Troubleshooting Step 7: _____
Reading: _____ Good: ____ Bad: ____

Troubleshooting Step 8: _____
Reading: _____ Good: ____ Bad: ____

Troubleshooting Step 9: _____
Reading: _____ Good: ____ Bad: ____

Troubleshooting Step 10: _____
Reading: _____ Good: ____ Bad: ____

Troubleshooting Step 11: _____
Reading: _____ Good: ____ Bad: ____

Troubleshooting Step 12: _____
Reading: _____ Good: ____ Bad: ____

The Problem Is: _____

What did you learn from troubleshooting this problem?

_____

REMINDER: Remove the circuit fault from the bottom of the PCBs. Verify normal operation of the relay circuit.

Problem 118
Consult Instructor Guide IG05 to insert this problem.
Slide S4 UP and leave it CLOSED.
Use switch S3 as the PCM to control the fuel pump relay.
Description of the vehicle driveability problem:
Engine cranks but will not start. Checked spark & fuel. There is no fuel pressure in the fuel rail. Fuel Pump not running for initial 2 seconds and found Fuse F1 is blown.

Does the Fuel Pump Relay "CLICK"?   Yes ___ No ___
Performance of the Fuel Pump: _____

Troubleshooting Step 1: _____
Reading: _____ Good: ____ Bad: ____

Troubleshooting Step 2: _____
Reading: _____ Good: ____ Bad: ____

Troubleshooting Step 3: _____
Reading: _____ Good: ____ Bad: ____

Troubleshooting Step 4: _____
Reading: _____ Good: ____ Bad: ____

Troubleshooting Step 5: _____
Reading: _____ Good: ____ Bad: ____

Troubleshooting Step 6: _____
Reading: _____ Good: ____ Bad: ____

Troubleshooting Step 7: _____
Reading: _____ Good: ____ Bad: ____

Troubleshooting Step 8: _____
Reading: _____ Good: ____ Bad: ____

Troubleshooting Step 9: _____
Reading: _____ Good: ____ Bad: ____

Troubleshooting Step 10: _____
Reading: _____ Good: ____ Bad: ____

Troubleshooting Step 11: _____
Reading: _____ Good: ____ Bad: ____

Troubleshooting Step 12: _____
Reading: _____ Good: ____ Bad: ____

The Problem Is: _____

What did you learn from troubleshooting this problem?

_____

REMINDER: Remove the circuit fault from the bottom of the PCBs. Verify normal operation of the relay circuit.

Vehicle Electronics Hands-On Troubleshooting Training Program

VEEJER ENTERPRISES 3701 Lariat Lane, Garland, Texas 75042-5419
Phone: 972-276-9642 Fax: 972-276-8122 Email: sales@veejer.com Web Site: www.veejer.com

Problem 119
Consult Instructor Guide IG05 to insert this problem.
Slide S4 UP and leave it CLOSED.
Use switch S3 as the PCM to control the fuel pump relay.
Description of the vehicle driveability problem:
Engine cranks but engine won't run. Checked spark & fuel. There is no fuel pressure in the fuel rail. Fuel Pump not running for initial 2 seconds. A new relay did not fix the problem.

Does the Fuel Pump Relay "CLICK"? Yes ___ No ___
Performance of the Fuel Pump: _____

Troubleshooting Step 1: _____
Reading: _____ Good: ___ Bad: ___

Troubleshooting Step 2: _____
Reading: _____ Good: ___ Bad: ___

Troubleshooting Step 3: _____
Reading: _____ Good: ___ Bad: ___

Troubleshooting Step 4: _____
Reading: _____ Good: ___ Bad: ___

Troubleshooting Step 5: _____
Reading: _____ Good: ___ Bad: ___

Troubleshooting Step 6: _____
Reading: _____ Good: ___ Bad: ___

Troubleshooting Step 7: _____
Reading: _____ Good: ___ Bad: ___

Troubleshooting Step 8: _____
Reading: _____ Good: ___ Bad: ___

Troubleshooting Step 9: _____
Reading: _____ Good: ___ Bad: ___

Troubleshooting Step 10: _____
Reading: _____ Good: ___ Bad: ___

Troubleshooting Step 11: _____
Reading: _____ Good: ___ Bad: ___

Troubleshooting Step 12: _____
Reading: _____ Good: ___ Bad: ___

The Problem Is: _____

What did you learn from troubleshooting this problem?

_____

REMINDER: Remove the circuit fault from the bottom of the PCBs. Verify normal operation of the relay circuit.

Copyright © 2015 VEEJER ENTERPRISES, Garland, Texas - All Rights Reserved **Student Workbook H-WB115**

Vehicle Electronics Hands-On Troubleshooting Training Program

VEEJER ENTERPRISES 3701 Lariat Lane, Garland, Texas 75042-5419
Phone: 972-276-9642 Fax: 972-276-8122 Email: sales@veejer.com Web Site: www.veejer.com

Problem 120

Consult Instructor Guide IG05 to insert this problem.
Slide S4 UP and leave it CLOSED.
Use switch S3 as the PCM to control the fuel pump relay.
Description of the vehicle driveability problem:
Engine runs but it seems to crank longer before it starts to run. Vehicle has less power & sluggish acceleration. A new fuel pump was installed but it made no difference in driveability. All fuel filters have been replaced. A new relay did not fix the problem. Fuel pressure still drops at higher rpm.

Does the Fuel Pump Relay "CLICK"? Yes ___ No ___
Performance of the Fuel Pump: _____

Troubleshooting Step 1: _____
Reading: _____ Good: ___ Bad: ___

Troubleshooting Step 2: _____
Reading: _____ Good: ___ Bad: ___

Troubleshooting Step 3: _____
Reading: _____ Good: ___ Bad: ___

Troubleshooting Step 4: _____
Reading: _____ Good: ___ Bad: ___

Troubleshooting Step 5: _____
Reading: _____ Good: ___ Bad: ___

Troubleshooting Step 6: _____
Reading: _____ Good: ___ Bad: ___

Troubleshooting Step 7: _____
Reading: _____ Good: ___ Bad: ___

Troubleshooting Step 8: _____
Reading: _____ Good: ___ Bad: ___

Troubleshooting Step 9: _____
Reading: _____ Good: ___ Bad: ___

Troubleshooting Step 10: _____
Reading: _____ Good: ___ Bad: ___

Troubleshooting Step 11: _____
Reading: _____ Good: ___ Bad: ___

Troubleshooting Step 12: _____
Reading: _____ Good: ___ Bad: ___

The Problem Is: _____

What did you learn from troubleshooting this problem?

_____

REMINDER: Remove the circuit fault from the bottom of the PCBs. Verify normal operation of the relay circuit.

Problem 121

Consult Instructor Guide IG05 to insert this problem.
Slide S4 UP and leave it CLOSED.
Use switch S3 as the PCM to control the fuel pump relay.
Description of the vehicle driveability problem:
Engine cranks but engine won't run. There is no fuel pressure in the fuel rail. Fuel Pump not running for initial 2 seconds. Borrowed relay from another circuit and fuel pump runs. Boss wants to know what's wrong with the old relay before he orders a new one.

Does the Fuel Pump Relay "CLICK"? Yes ___ No ___
Performance of the Fuel Pump: _____

Troubleshooting Step 1: _____
Reading: _____ Good: ___ Bad: ___

Troubleshooting Step 2: _____
Reading: _____ Good: ___ Bad: ___

Troubleshooting Step 3: _____
Reading: _____ Good: ___ Bad: ___

Troubleshooting Step 4: _____
Reading: _____ Good: ___ Bad: ___

Troubleshooting Step 5: _____
Reading: _____ Good: ___ Bad: ___

Troubleshooting Step 6: _____
Reading: _____ Good: ___ Bad: ___

Troubleshooting Step 7: _____
Reading: _____ Good: ___ Bad: ___

Troubleshooting Step 8: _____
Reading: _____ Good: ___ Bad: ___

Troubleshooting Step 9: _____
Reading: _____ Good: ___ Bad: ___

Troubleshooting Step 10: _____
Reading: _____ Good: ___ Bad: ___

Troubleshooting Step 11: _____
Reading: _____ Good: ___ Bad: ___

Troubleshooting Step 12: _____
Reading: _____ Good: ___ Bad: ___

The Problem Is: _____

What did you learn from troubleshooting this problem?

_____

REMINDER: Remove the circuit fault from the bottom of the PCBs. Verify normal operation of the relay circuit.

Vehicle Electronics Hands-On Troubleshooting Training Program

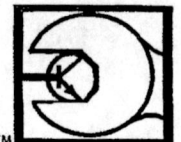

VEEJER ENTERPRISES 3701 Lariat Lane, Garland, Texas 75042-5419
Phone: 972-276-9642   Fax: 972-276-8122   Email: sales@veejer.com   Web Site: www.veejer.com

---

Problem 122
Consult Instructor Guide IG05 to insert this problem.
Slide S4 UP and leave it CLOSED.
Use switch S3 as the PCM to control the fuel pump relay.
Description of the vehicle driveability problem:
Engine cranks but engine won't run. Checked spark & fuel. There is no fuel pressure in the fuel rail. Fuel Pump not running for initial 2 seconds. A new relay did not fix the problem.

Does the Fuel Pump Relay "CLICK"? Yes ___ No ___
Performance of the Fuel Pump: _____

Troubleshooting Step 1: _____
Reading: _____ Good: ___ Bad: ___

Troubleshooting Step 2: _____
Reading: _____ Good: ___ Bad: ___

Troubleshooting Step 3: _____
Reading: _____ Good: ___ Bad: ___

Troubleshooting Step 4: _____
Reading: _____ Good: ___ Bad: ___

Troubleshooting Step 5: _____
Reading: _____ Good: ___ Bad: ___

Troubleshooting Step 6: _____
Reading: _____ Good: ___ Bad: ___

Troubleshooting Step 7: _____
Reading: _____ Good: ___ Bad: ___

Troubleshooting Step 8: _____
Reading: _____ Good: ___ Bad: ___

Troubleshooting Step 9: _____
Reading: _____ Good: ___ Bad: ___

Troubleshooting Step 10: _____
Reading: _____ Good: ___ Bad: ___

Troubleshooting Step 11: _____
Reading: _____ Good: ___ Bad: ___

Troubleshooting Step 12: _____
Reading: _____ Good: ___ Bad: ___

The Problem Is: _____

What did you learn from troubleshooting this problem?

_____

REMINDER: Remove the circuit fault from the bottom of the PCBs. Verify normal operation of the relay circuit.

Copyright © 2015 VEEJER ENTERPRISES, Garland, Texas - All Rights Reserved   Student Workbook H-WB115

Vehicle Electronics Hands-On Troubleshooting Training Program

VEEJER ENTERPRISES 3701 Lariat Lane, Garland, Texas 75042-5419
Phone: 972-276-9642   Fax: 972-276-8122   Email: sales@veejer.com   Web Site: www.veejer.com

Problem 123

Consult Instructor Guide IG05 to insert this problem.
Slide S4 UP and leave it CLOSED.
Use switch S3 as the PCM to control the fuel pump relay.
Description of the vehicle driveability problem:
Engine runs but it seems to crank longer before it starts to run and fuel pressure is low. All fuel filters have been replaced. A new fuel pump was installed but it made no difference.. A new relay finally fixed the problem. Boss again wants to know what's wrong with the old relay before he orders a new one.

Does the Fuel Pump Relay "CLICK"? Yes ___ No ___
Performance of the Fuel Pump: _____

Troubleshooting Step 1: _____
Reading: _____ Good: ___ Bad: ___

Troubleshooting Step 2: _____
Reading: _____ Good: ___ Bad: ___

Troubleshooting Step 3: _____
Reading: _____ Good: ___ Bad: ___

Troubleshooting Step 4: _____
Reading: _____ Good: ___ Bad: ___

Troubleshooting Step 5: _____
Reading: _____ Good: ___ Bad: ___

Troubleshooting Step 6: _____
Reading: _____ Good: ___ Bad: ___

Troubleshooting Step 7: _____
Reading: _____ Good: ___ Bad: ___

Troubleshooting Step 8: _____
Reading: _____ Good: ___ Bad: ___

Troubleshooting Step 9: _____
Reading: _____ Good: ___ Bad: ___

Troubleshooting Step 10: _____
Reading: _____ Good: ___ Bad: ___

Troubleshooting Step 11: _____
Reading: _____ Good: ___ Bad: ___

Troubleshooting Step 12: _____
Reading: _____ Good: ___ Bad: ___

The Problem Is: _____

What did you learn from troubleshooting this problem?

_____

REMINDER: Remove the circuit fault from the bottom of the PCBs. Verify normal operation of the relay circuit.

Problem 124

Consult Instructor Guide IG05 to insert this problem.
Slide S4 UP and leave it CLOSED.
Use switch S3 as the PCM to control the fuel pump relay.
Description of the vehicle driveability problem:
Engine cranks but engine won't run. Checked spark & fuel. There is no fuel pressure in the fuel rail. Fuel Pump not running for initial 2 seconds. A new relay and new fuel pump did not fix the problem.

Does the Fuel Pump Relay "CLICK"? Yes ___ No ___
Performance of the Fuel Pump: _____

Troubleshooting Step 1: _____
Reading: _____ Good: ___ Bad: ___

Troubleshooting Step 2: _____
Reading: _____ Good: ___ Bad: ___

Troubleshooting Step 3: _____
Reading: _____ Good: ___ Bad: ___

Troubleshooting Step 4: _____
Reading: _____ Good: ___ Bad: ___

Troubleshooting Step 5: _____
Reading: _____ Good: ___ Bad: ___

Troubleshooting Step 6: _____
Reading: _____ Good: ___ Bad: ___

Troubleshooting Step 7: _____
Reading: _____ Good: ___ Bad: ___

Troubleshooting Step 8: _____
Reading: _____ Good: ___ Bad: ___

Troubleshooting Step 9: _____
Reading: _____ Good: ___ Bad: ___

Troubleshooting Step 10: _____
Reading: _____ Good: ___ Bad: ___

Troubleshooting Step 11: _____
Reading: _____ Good: ___ Bad: ___

Troubleshooting Step 12: _____
Reading: _____ Good: ___ Bad: ___

The Problem Is: _____

What did you learn from troubleshooting this problem?

_____

REMINDER: Remove the circuit fault from the bottom of the PCBs. Verify normal operation of the relay circuit.

Vehicle Electronics Hands-On Troubleshooting Training Program

VEEJER ENTERPRISES 3701 Lariat Lane, Garland, Texas 75042-5419
Phone: 972-276-9642   Fax: 972-276-8122   Email: sales@veejer.com   Web Site: www.veejer.com

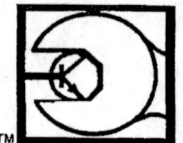

Problem 125
Consult Instructor Guide IG05 to insert this problem.
Slide S4 UP and leave it CLOSED.
Use switch S3 as the PCM to control the fuel pump relay.
Description of the vehicle driveability problem:
Engine cranks but engine won't run. Checked spark & fuel. There is no fuel pressure in the fuel rail. Fuel Pump not running for initial 2 seconds. A new relay and new fuel pump did not fix the problem.

Does the Fuel Pump Relay "CLICK"?   Yes ___   No ___
Performance of the Fuel Pump: _____

Troubleshooting Step 1: _____
Reading: _____ Good: ___ Bad: ___

Troubleshooting Step 2: _____
Reading: _____ Good: ___ Bad: ___

Troubleshooting Step 3: _____
Reading: _____ Good: ___ Bad: ___

Troubleshooting Step 4: _____
Reading: _____ Good: ___ Bad: ___

Troubleshooting Step 5: _____
Reading: _____ Good: ___ Bad: ___

Troubleshooting Step 6: _____
Reading: _____ Good: ___ Bad: ___

Troubleshooting Step 7: _____
Reading: _____ Good: ___ Bad: ___

Troubleshooting Step 8: _____
Reading: _____ Good: ___ Bad: ___

Troubleshooting Step 9: _____
Reading: _____ Good: ___ Bad: ___

Troubleshooting Step 10: _____
Reading: _____ Good: ___ Bad: ___

Troubleshooting Step 11: _____
Reading: _____ Good: ___ Bad: ___

Troubleshooting Step 12: _____
Reading: _____ Good: ___ Bad: ___

The Problem Is: _____

What did you learn from troubleshooting this problem?

_____

REMINDER: Remove the circuit fault from the bottom of the PCBs. Verify normal operation of the relay circuit.

Fig. 5TS-6CCFP — RELAY CIRCUIT Troubleshooting Trainer H-PCB05

Copyright © 2015 VEEJER ENTERPRISES, Garland, Texas - All Rights Reserved   Student Workbook H-WB115   Page 99

Vehicle Electronics Hands-On Troubleshooting Training Program

VEEJER ENTERPRISES 3701 Lariat Lane, Garland, Texas 75042-5419
Phone: 972-276-9642 Fax: 972-276-8122 Email: sales@veejer.com Web Site: www.veejer.com

Problem 126

Consult Instructor Guide IG05 to insert this problem.
Slide S4 UP and leave it CLOSED.
Use switch S3 as the PCM to control the fuel pump relay.
  Description of the vehicle driveability problem:
Engine cranks but engine won't run. Checked spark & fuel. There is no fuel pressure in the fuel rail. Fuel Pump not running for initial 2 seconds. A new relay and new fuel pump did not fix the problem.

Does the Fuel Pump Relay "CLICK"? Yes ___ No ___
Performance of the Fuel Pump: _____

Troubleshooting Step 1: _____
Reading: _____ Good: ____ Bad: ____

Troubleshooting Step 2: _____
Reading: _____ Good: ____ Bad: ____

Troubleshooting Step 3: _____
Reading: _____ Good: ____ Bad: ____

Troubleshooting Step 4: _____
Reading: _____ Good: ____ Bad: ____

Troubleshooting Step 5: _____
Reading: _____ Good: ____ Bad: ____

Troubleshooting Step 6: _____
Reading: _____ Good: ____ Bad: ____

Troubleshooting Step 7: _____
Reading: _____ Good: ____ Bad: ____

Troubleshooting Step 8: _____
Reading: _____ Good: ____ Bad: ____

Troubleshooting Step 9: _____
Reading: _____ Good: ____ Bad: ____

Troubleshooting Step 10: _____
Reading: _____ Good: ____ Bad: ____

Troubleshooting Step 11: _____
Reading: _____ Good: ____ Bad: ____

Troubleshooting Step 12: _____
Reading: _____ Good: ____ Bad: ____

The Problem Is: _____

What did you learn from troubleshooting this problem?

_____

REMINDER: Remove the circuit fault from the bottom of the PCBs. Verify normal operation of the relay circuit.

Problem 127

Consult Instructor Guide IG05 to insert this problem.
Slide S4 UP and leave it CLOSED.
Use switch S3 as the PCM to control the fuel pump relay.
  Description of the vehicle driveability problem:
Engine cranks but engine won't run. There is no fuel pressure in the fuel rail. Fuel Pump not running for initial 2 seconds. A new fuel pump did not fix the problem. Swapped the relay with another and the relay works. The boss doesn't believe the relay is bad so I will show him what's wrong with the relay.

Does the Fuel Pump Relay "CLICK"? Yes ___ No ___
Performance of the Fuel Pump: _____

Troubleshooting Step 1: _____
Reading: _____ Good: ____ Bad: ____

Troubleshooting Step 2: _____
Reading: _____ Good: ____ Bad: ____

Troubleshooting Step 3: _____
Reading: _____ Good: ____ Bad: ____

Troubleshooting Step 4: _____
Reading: _____ Good: ____ Bad: ____

Troubleshooting Step 5: _____
Reading: _____ Good: ____ Bad: ____

Troubleshooting Step 6: _____
Reading: _____ Good: ____ Bad: ____

Troubleshooting Step 7: _____
Reading: _____ Good: ____ Bad: ____

Troubleshooting Step 8: _____
Reading: _____ Good: ____ Bad: ____

Troubleshooting Step 9: _____
Reading: _____ Good: ____ Bad: ____

Troubleshooting Step 10: _____
Reading: _____ Good: ____ Bad: ____

Troubleshooting Step 11: _____
Reading: _____ Good: ____ Bad: ____

Troubleshooting Step 12: _____
Reading: _____ Good: ____ Bad: ____

The Problem Is: _____

What did you learn from troubleshooting this problem?

_____

REMINDER: Remove the circuit fault from the bottom of the PCBs. Verify normal operation of the relay circuit.

Vehicle Electronics Hands-On Troubleshooting Training Program

VEEJER ENTERPRISES 3701 Lariat Lane, Garland, Texas 75042-5419
Phone: 972-276-9642   Fax: 972-276-8122   Email: sales@veejer.com   Web Site: www.veejer.com

Problem 128
Consult Instructor Guide IG05 to insert this problem.
Slide S4 UP and leave it CLOSED.
Use switch S3 as the PCM to control the fuel pump relay.
  Description of the vehicle driveability problem:
Engine cranks but engine won't run. Checked spark & fuel. There is no fuel pressure in the fuel rail. Fuel Pump not running for initial 2 seconds. A new relay and new fuel pump did not fix the problem.

Does the Fuel Pump Relay "CLICK"? Yes ___ No ___
Performance of the Fuel Pump: _____

Troubleshooting Step 1: _____
  Reading: _____ Good: ___ Bad: ___

Troubleshooting Step 2: _____
  Reading: _____ Good: ___ Bad: ___

Troubleshooting Step 3: _____
  Reading: _____ Good: ___ Bad: ___

Troubleshooting Step 4: _____
  Reading: _____ Good: ___ Bad: ___

Troubleshooting Step 5: _____
  Reading: _____ Good: ___ Bad: ___

Troubleshooting Step 6: _____
  Reading: _____ Good: ___ Bad: ___

Troubleshooting Step 7: _____
  Reading: _____ Good: ___ Bad: ___

Troubleshooting Step 8: _____
  Reading: _____ Good: ___ Bad: ___

Troubleshooting Step 9: _____
  Reading: _____ Good: ___ Bad: ___

Troubleshooting Step 10: _____
  Reading: _____ Good: ___ Bad: ___

Troubleshooting Step 11: _____
  Reading: _____ Good: ___ Bad: ___

Troubleshooting Step 12: _____
  Reading: _____ Good: ___ Bad: ___

The Problem Is: _____

What did you learn from troubleshooting this problem?
_____

REMINDER: Remove the circuit fault from the bottom of the PCBs. Verify normal operation of the relay circuit.

RELAY CIRCUIT Troubleshooting Trainer H-PCB05
Fig. 5TS-6CCFP

Copyright © 2015 VEEJER ENTERPRISES, Garland, Texas - All Rights Reserved   **Student Workbook H-WB115   Page 101**

Vehicle Electronics Hands-On Troubleshooting Training Program

VEEJER ENTERPRISES 3701 Lariat Lane, Garland, Texas 75042-5419
Phone: 972-276-9642 Fax: 972-276-8122 Email: sales@veejer.com Web Site: www.veejer.com

Problem 129
Consult Instructor Guide IG05 to insert this problem.
Slide S4 UP and leave it CLOSED.
Use switch S3 as the PCM to control the fuel pump relay.
Description of the vehicle driveability problem:
Engine cranks but engine won't run. Checked spark & fuel. There is no fuel pressure in the fuel rail. Fuel Pump not running for initial 2 seconds. A new relay and new fuel pump did not fix the problem.

Does the Fuel Pump Relay "CLICK"? Yes ___ No ___
Performance of the Fuel Pump: _____

Troubleshooting Step 1: _____
Reading: _____ Good: ___ Bad: ___

Troubleshooting Step 2: _____
Reading: _____ Good: ___ Bad: ___

Troubleshooting Step 3: _____
Reading: _____ Good: ___ Bad: ___

Troubleshooting Step 4: _____
Reading: _____ Good: ___ Bad: ___

Troubleshooting Step 5: _____
Reading: _____ Good: ___ Bad: ___

Troubleshooting Step 6: _____
Reading: _____ Good: ___ Bad: ___

Troubleshooting Step 7: _____
Reading: _____ Good: ___ Bad: ___

Troubleshooting Step 8: _____
Reading: _____ Good: ___ Bad: ___

Troubleshooting Step 9: _____
Reading: _____ Good: ___ Bad: ___

Troubleshooting Step 10: _____
Reading: _____ Good: ___ Bad: ___

Troubleshooting Step 11: _____
Reading: _____ Good: ___ Bad: ___

Troubleshooting Step 12: _____
Reading: _____ Good: ___ Bad: ___

The Problem Is: _____

What did you learn from troubleshooting this problem?

_____

REMINDER: Remove the circuit fault from the bottom of the PCBs. Verify normal operation of the relay circuit.

Problem 130
Consult Instructor Guide IG05 to insert this problem.
Slide S4 UP and leave it CLOSED.
Use switch S3 as the PCM to control the fuel pump relay.
Description of the vehicle driveability problem:
Engine cranks but engine won't run. Checked spark & fuel. There is no fuel pressure in the fuel rail. Fuel Pump not running for initial 2 seconds. A new relay and new fuel pump did not fix the problem.

Does the Fuel Pump Relay "CLICK"? Yes ___ No ___
Performance of the Fuel Pump: _____

Troubleshooting Step 1: _____
Reading: _____ Good: ___ Bad: ___

Troubleshooting Step 2: _____
Reading: _____ Good: ___ Bad: ___

Troubleshooting Step 3: _____
Reading: _____ Good: ___ Bad: ___

Troubleshooting Step 4: _____
Reading: _____ Good: ___ Bad: ___

Troubleshooting Step 5: _____
Reading: _____ Good: ___ Bad: ___

Troubleshooting Step 6: _____
Reading: _____ Good: ___ Bad: ___

Troubleshooting Step 7: _____
Reading: _____ Good: ___ Bad: ___

Troubleshooting Step 8: _____
Reading: _____ Good: ___ Bad: ___

Troubleshooting Step 9: _____
Reading: _____ Good: ___ Bad: ___

Troubleshooting Step 10: _____
Reading: _____ Good: ___ Bad: ___

Troubleshooting Step 11: _____
Reading: _____ Good: ___ Bad: ___

Troubleshooting Step 12: _____
Reading: _____ Good: ___ Bad: ___

The Problem Is: _____

What did you learn from troubleshooting this problem?

_____

REMINDER: Remove the circuit fault from the bottom of the PCBs. Verify normal operation of the relay circuit.

Copyright © 2015 VEEJER ENTERPRISES, Garland, Texas - All Rights Reserved

Vehicle Electronics Hands-On Troubleshooting Training Program

VEEJER ENTERPRISES 3701 Lariat Lane, Garland, Texas 75042-5419
Phone: 972-276-9642 Fax: 972-276-8122 Email: sales@veejer.com Web Site: www.veejer.com

Problem 131

Consult Instructor Guide IG05 to insert this problem.
Slide S4 UP and leave it CLOSED.
Use switch S3 as the PCM to control the fuel pump relay.
Description of the vehicle driveability problem:
Engine cranks but engine won't run. Checked spark & fuel. There is no fuel pressure in the fuel rail. Fuel Pump not running for initial 2 seconds. A new fuel pump did not fix the problem. My boss is something else. He wants to know what's wrong with the relay.

Does the Fuel Pump Relay "CLICK"? Yes ___ No ___
Performance of the Fuel Pump: _____

Troubleshooting Step 1: _____
Reading: _____ Good: ___ Bad: ___

Troubleshooting Step 2: _____
Reading: _____ Good: ___ Bad: ___

Troubleshooting Step 3: _____
Reading: _____ Good: ___ Bad: ___

Troubleshooting Step 4: _____
Reading: _____ Good: ___ Bad: ___

Troubleshooting Step 5: _____
Reading: _____ Good: ___ Bad: ___

Troubleshooting Step 6: _____
Reading: _____ Good: ___ Bad: ___

Troubleshooting Step 7: _____
Reading: _____ Good: ___ Bad: ___

Troubleshooting Step 8: _____
Reading: _____ Good: ___ Bad: ___

Troubleshooting Step 9: _____
Reading: _____ Good: ___ Bad: ___

Troubleshooting Step 10: _____
Reading: _____ Good: ___ Bad: ___

Troubleshooting Step 11: _____
Reading: _____ Good: ___ Bad: ___

Troubleshooting Step 12: _____
Reading: _____ Good: ___ Bad: ___

The Problem Is: _____

What did you learn from troubleshooting this problem?

_____

REMINDER: Remove the circuit fault from the bottom of the PCBs. Verify normal operation of the relay circuit.

Fig. 5TS-6CCFP — RELAY CIRCUIT Troubleshooting Trainer H-PCB05

Vehicle Electronics Hands-On Troubleshooting Training Program

VEEJER ENTERPRISES 3701 Lariat Lane, Garland, Texas 75042-5419
Phone: 972-276-9642 Fax: 972-276-8122 Email: sales@veejer.com Web Site: www.veejer.com™

Problem 132

Consult Instructor Guide IG05 to insert this problem.
Slide S4 UP and leave it CLOSED.
Use switch S3 as the PCM to control the fuel pump relay.
Description of the vehicle driveability problem:
Engine cranks but engine won't run. Checked spark & fuel. There is no fuel pressure in the fuel rail. A new relay and new fuel pump did not fix the problem. While under the hood I accidentally bump the relay box and hear a buzzing noise coming from the fuel pump relay when the ignition key is on.

Does the Fuel Pump Relay "CLICK"? Yes ___ No ___
If no then tap on the relay.
Performance of the Fuel Pump: _____

Troubleshooting Step 1: _____
Reading: _____ Good: ____ Bad: ____

Troubleshooting Step 2: _____
Reading: _____ Good: ____ Bad: ____

Troubleshooting Step 3: _____
Reading: _____ Good: ____ Bad: ____

Troubleshooting Step 4: _____
Reading: _____ Good: ____ Bad: ____

Troubleshooting Step 5: _____
Reading: _____ Good: ____ Bad: ____

Troubleshooting Step 6: _____
Reading: _____ Good: ____ Bad: ____

Troubleshooting Step 7: _____
Reading: _____ Good: ____ Bad: ____

Troubleshooting Step 8: _____
Reading: _____ Good: ____ Bad: ____

Troubleshooting Step 9: _____
Reading: _____ Good: ____ Bad: ____

Troubleshooting Step 10: _____
Reading: _____ Good: ____ Bad: ____

Troubleshooting Step 11: _____
Reading: _____ Good: ____ Bad: ____

Troubleshooting Step 12: _____
Reading: _____ Good: ____ Bad: ____

The Problem Is: _____

What did you learn from troubleshooting this problem?
_____

REMINDER: Remove the circuit fault from the bottom of the PCBs. Verify normal operation of the relay circuit.

Problem 133

Consult Instructor Guide IG05 to insert this problem.
Slide S4 UP and leave it CLOSED.
Use switch S3 as the PCM to control the fuel pump relay.
Description of the vehicle driveability problem:
Engine cranks but engine won't run. Checked spark & fuel. There is practically no fuel pressure in the fuel rail. A new relay and new fuel pump did not fix the problem.

Does the Fuel Pump Relay "CLICK"? Yes ___ No ___
Performance of the Fuel Pump: _____

Troubleshooting Step 1: _____
Reading: _____ Good: ____ Bad: ____

Troubleshooting Step 2: _____
Reading: _____ Good: ____ Bad: ____

Troubleshooting Step 3: _____
Reading: _____ Good: ____ Bad: ____

Troubleshooting Step 4: _____
Reading: _____ Good: ____ Bad: ____

Troubleshooting Step 5: _____
Reading: _____ Good: ____ Bad: ____

Troubleshooting Step 6: _____
Reading: _____ Good: ____ Bad: ____

Troubleshooting Step 7: _____
Reading: _____ Good: ____ Bad: ____

Troubleshooting Step 8: _____
Reading: _____ Good: ____ Bad: ____

Troubleshooting Step 9: _____
Reading: _____ Good: ____ Bad: ____

Troubleshooting Step 10: _____
Reading: _____ Good: ____ Bad: ____

Troubleshooting Step 11: _____
Reading: _____ Good: ____ Bad: ____

Troubleshooting Step 12: _____
Reading: _____ Good: ____ Bad: ____

The Problem Is: _____

What did you learn from troubleshooting this problem?
_____

REMINDER: Remove the circuit fault from the bottom of the PCBs. Verify normal operation of the relay circuit.

Vehicle Electronics Hands-On Troubleshooting Training Program

VEEJER ENTERPRISES 3701 Lariat Lane, Garland, Texas 75042-5419
Phone: 972-276-9642   Fax: 972-276-8122   Email: sales@veejer.com   Web Site: www.veejer.com

Problem 134

Consult Instructor Guide IG05 to insert this problem.
Slide S4 UP and leave it CLOSED.
Use switch S3 as the PCM to control the fuel pump relay.
Description of the vehicle driveability problem:
Engine cranks but will not start. Checked spark & fuel. There is no fuel pressure in the fuel rail. Fuel Pump not running for initial 2 seconds. A new fuel pump and fuel pump relay did not fix the problem.

Does the Fuel Pump Relay "CLICK"? Yes __ No __
Performance of the Fuel Pump: _____

Troubleshooting Step 1: _____
Reading: _____ Good: __ Bad: __

Troubleshooting Step 2: _____
Reading: _____ Good: __ Bad: __

Troubleshooting Step 3: _____
Reading: _____ Good: __ Bad: __

Troubleshooting Step 4: _____
Reading: _____ Good: __ Bad: __

Troubleshooting Step 5: _____
Reading: _____ Good: __ Bad: __

Troubleshooting Step 6: _____
Reading: _____ Good: __ Bad: __

Troubleshooting Step 7: _____
Reading: _____ Good: __ Bad: __

Troubleshooting Step 8: _____
Reading: _____ Good: __ Bad: __

Troubleshooting Step 9: _____
Reading: _____ Good: __ Bad: __

Troubleshooting Step 10: _____
Reading: _____ Good: __ Bad: __

Troubleshooting Step 11: _____
Reading: _____ Good: __ Bad: __

Troubleshooting Step 12: _____
Reading: _____ Good: __ Bad: __

The Problem Is: _____

What did you learn from troubleshooting this problem?

_____

REMINDER: Remove the circuit fault from the bottom of the PCBs. Verify normal operation of the relay circuit.

Copyright © 2015 VEEJER ENTERPRISES, Garland, Texas - All Rights Reserved   Student Workbook H-WB115   Page 105

Vehicle Electronics Hands-On Troubleshooting Training Program

VEEJER ENTERPRISES 3701 Lariat Lane, Garland, Texas 75042-5419
Phone: 972-276-9642   Fax: 972-276-8122   Email: sales@veejer.com   Web Site: www.veejer.com

Problem 135
Consult Instructor Guide IG05 to insert this problem.
Slide S4 UP and leave it CLOSED.
Use switch S3 as the PCM to control the fuel pump relay.
Description of the vehicle driveability problem:
Engine cranks but engine won't run. Checked spark & fuel. There is no fuel pressure in the fuel rail. Fuel Pump not running for initial 2 seconds. A new relay and new fuel pump did not fix the problem.

Does the Fuel Pump Relay "CLICK"? Yes ___ No ___
Performance of the Fuel Pump: _____

Troubleshooting Step 1: _____
Reading: _____ Good: ___ Bad: ___

Troubleshooting Step 2: _____
Reading: _____ Good: ___ Bad: ___

Troubleshooting Step 3: _____
Reading: _____ Good: ___ Bad: ___

Troubleshooting Step 4: _____
Reading: _____ Good: ___ Bad: ___

Troubleshooting Step 5: _____
Reading: _____ Good: ___ Bad: ___

Troubleshooting Step 6: _____
Reading: _____ Good: ___ Bad: ___

Troubleshooting Step 7: _____
Reading: _____ Good: ___ Bad: ___

Troubleshooting Step 8: _____
Reading: _____ Good: ___ Bad: ___

Troubleshooting Step 9: _____
Reading: _____ Good: ___ Bad: ___

Troubleshooting Step 10: _____
Reading: _____ Good: ___ Bad: ___

Troubleshooting Step 11: _____
Reading: _____ Good: ___ Bad: ___

Troubleshooting Step 12: _____
Reading: _____ Good: ___ Bad: ___

The Problem Is: _____

What did you learn from troubleshooting this problem?

_____

REMINDER: Remove the circuit fault from the bottom of the PCBs. Verify normal operation of the relay circuit.

Problem 136
Consult Instructor Guide IG05 to insert this problem.
Slide S4 UP and leave it CLOSED.
Use switch S3 as the PCM to control the fuel pump relay.
Description of the vehicle driveability problem:
Engine cranks but engine won't run. Checked spark & fuel. There is no fuel pressure in the fuel rail. Fuel Pump not running for initial 2 seconds. A new relay and new fuel pump did not fix the problem.

Does the Fuel Pump Relay "CLICK"? Yes ___ No ___
Performance of the Fuel Pump: _____

Troubleshooting Step 1: _____
Reading: _____ Good: ___ Bad: ___

Troubleshooting Step 2: _____
Reading: _____ Good: ___ Bad: ___

Troubleshooting Step 3: _____
Reading: _____ Good: ___ Bad: ___

Troubleshooting Step 4: _____
Reading: _____ Good: ___ Bad: ___

Troubleshooting Step 5: _____
Reading: _____ Good: ___ Bad: ___

Troubleshooting Step 6: _____
Reading: _____ Good: ___ Bad: ___

Troubleshooting Step 7: _____
Reading: _____ Good: ___ Bad: ___

Troubleshooting Step 8: _____
Reading: _____ Good: ___ Bad: ___

Troubleshooting Step 9: _____
Reading: _____ Good: ___ Bad: ___

Troubleshooting Step 10: _____
Reading: _____ Good: ___ Bad: ___

Troubleshooting Step 11: _____
Reading: _____ Good: ___ Bad: ___

Troubleshooting Step 12: _____
Reading: _____ Good: ___ Bad: ___

The Problem Is: _____

What did you learn from troubleshooting this problem?

_____

REMINDER: Remove the circuit fault from the bottom of the PCBs. Verify normal operation of the relay circuit.

Vehicle Electronics Hands-On Troubleshooting Training Program

VEEJER ENTERPRISES 3701 Lariat Lane, Garland, Texas 75042-5419
Phone: 972-276-9642   Fax: 972-276-8122   Email: sales@veejer.com   Web Site: www.veejer.com

Problem 138

Consult Instructor Guide IG05 to insert this problem.
Slide S4 UP and leave it CLOSED.
Use switch S3 as the PCM to control the fuel pump relay.
Description of the vehicle driveability problem:
Engine cranks but engine won't run. Checked spark & fuel. There is no fuel pressure in the fuel rail. Fuel Pump not running for initial 2 seconds. A new relay and new fuel pump did not fix the problem.

Does the Fuel Pump Relay "CLICK"?   Yes ___ No ___
Performance of the Fuel Pump: _____

Troubleshooting Step 1: _____
Reading: _____ Good: ___ Bad: ___

Troubleshooting Step 2: _____
Reading: _____ Good: ___ Bad: ___

Troubleshooting Step 3: _____
Reading: _____ Good: ___ Bad: ___

Troubleshooting Step 4: _____
Reading: _____ Good: ___ Bad: ___

Troubleshooting Step 5: _____
Reading: _____ Good: ___ Bad: ___

Troubleshooting Step 6: _____
Reading: _____ Good: ___ Bad: ___

Troubleshooting Step 7: _____
Reading: _____ Good: ___ Bad: ___

Troubleshooting Step 8: _____
Reading: _____ Good: ___ Bad: ___

Troubleshooting Step 9: _____
Reading: _____ Good: ___ Bad: ___

Troubleshooting Step 10: _____
Reading: _____ Good: ___ Bad: ___

Troubleshooting Step 11: _____
Reading: _____ Good: ___ Bad: ___

Troubleshooting Step 12: _____
Reading: _____ Good: ___ Bad: ___

The Problem Is: _____

What did you learn from troubleshooting this problem?

_____

REMINDER: Remove the circuit fault from the bottom of the PCBs. Verify normal operation of the relay circuit.

Problem 139

Consult Instructor Guide IG05 to insert this problem.
Slide S4 UP and leave it CLOSED.
Use switch S3 as the PCM to control the fuel pump relay.
Description of the vehicle driveability problem:
Engine cranks but will not start. Checked spark & fuel. There is no fuel pressure in the fuel rail. Fuel Pump not running for initial 2 seconds. A new fuel pump and fuel pump relay did not fix the problem.

Does the Fuel Pump Relay "CLICK"?   Yes ___ No ___
Performance of the Fuel Pump: _____

Troubleshooting Step 1: _____
Reading: _____ Good: ___ Bad: ___

Troubleshooting Step 2: _____
Reading: _____ Good: ___ Bad: ___

Troubleshooting Step 3: _____
Reading: _____ Good: ___ Bad: ___

Troubleshooting Step 4: _____
Reading: _____ Good: ___ Bad: ___

Troubleshooting Step 5: _____
Reading: _____ Good: ___ Bad: ___

Troubleshooting Step 6: _____
Reading: _____ Good: ___ Bad: ___

Troubleshooting Step 7: _____
Reading: _____ Good: ___ Bad: ___

Troubleshooting Step 8: _____
Reading: _____ Good: ___ Bad: ___

Troubleshooting Step 9: _____
Reading: _____ Good: ___ Bad: ___

Troubleshooting Step 10: _____
Reading: _____ Good: ___ Bad: ___

Troubleshooting Step 11: _____
Reading: _____ Good: ___ Bad: ___

Troubleshooting Step 12: _____
Reading: _____ Good: ___ Bad: ___

The Problem Is: _____

What did you learn from troubleshooting this problem?

_____

REMINDER: Remove the circuit fault from the bottom of the PCBs. Verify normal operation of the relay circuit.

Vehicle Electronics Hands-On Troubleshooting Training Program

VEEJER ENTERPRISES 3701 Lariat Lane, Garland, Texas 75042-5419
Phone: 972-276-9642   Fax: 972-276-8122   Email: sales@veejer.com   Web Site: www.veejer.com

Problem 140

Consult Instructor Guide IG05 to insert this problem.
Slide S4 UP and leave it CLOSED.
Use switch S3 as the PCM to control the fuel pump relay.
Description of the vehicle driveability problem:
Engine cranks but will not start. Checked spark & fuel. There is no fuel pressure in the fuel rail. Fuel Pump not running for initial 2 seconds. A new fuel pump and relay did not fix the problem.

Does the Fuel Pump Relay "CLICK"?   Yes ___   No ___
Performance of the Fuel Pump: _____

Troubleshooting Step 1: _____
Reading: _____   Good: ___   Bad: ___

Troubleshooting Step 2: _____
Reading: _____   Good: ___   Bad: ___

Troubleshooting Step 3: _____
Reading: _____   Good: ___   Bad: ___

Troubleshooting Step 4: _____
Reading: _____   Good: ___   Bad: ___

Troubleshooting Step 5: _____
Reading: _____   Good: ___   Bad: ___

Troubleshooting Step 6: _____
Reading: _____   Good: ___   Bad: ___

Troubleshooting Step 7: _____
Reading: _____   Good: ___   Bad: ___

Troubleshooting Step 8: _____
Reading: _____   Good: ___   Bad: ___

Troubleshooting Step 9: _____
Reading: _____   Good: ___   Bad: ___

Troubleshooting Step 10: _____
Reading: _____   Good: ___   Bad: ___

Troubleshooting Step 11: _____
Reading: _____   Good: ___   Bad: ___

Troubleshooting Step 12: _____
Reading: _____   Good: ___   Bad: ___

The Problem Is: _____

What did you learn from troubleshooting this problem?

_____

REMINDER: Remove the circuit fault from the bottom of the PCBs. Verify normal operation of the relay circuit.

Fig. 5TS-6CCFP — Relay Circuit Troubleshooting Trainer H-PCB05 / Power Board H-PCB01

Copyright © 2015 VEEJER ENTERPRISES, Garland, Texas - All Rights Reserved   Student Workbook H-WB115   Page 109

Vehicle Electronics Hands-On Troubleshooting Training Program

VEEJER ENTERPRISES 3701 Lariat Lane, Garland, Texas 75042-5419
Phone: 972-276-9642   Fax: 972-276-8122   Email: sales@veejer.com   Web Site: www.veejer.com

Problem 141

Consult Instructor Guide IG05 to insert this problem.
Slide S4 UP and leave it CLOSED.
Use switch S3 as the PCM to control the fuel pump relay.
Description of the vehicle driveability problem:
Engine cranks but will not start. Checked spark & fuel. There is no fuel pressure in the fuel rail. Fuel Pump not running for initial 2 seconds. A new fuel pump and relay did not fix the problem.

Does the Fuel Pump Relay "CLICK"? Yes ___ No ___
Performance of the Fuel Pump: _____

Troubleshooting Step 1: _____
Reading: _____ Good: ___ Bad: ___

Troubleshooting Step 2: _____
Reading: _____ Good: ___ Bad: ___

Troubleshooting Step 3: _____
Reading: _____ Good: ___ Bad: ___

Troubleshooting Step 4: _____
Reading: _____ Good: ___ Bad: ___

Troubleshooting Step 5: _____
Reading: _____ Good: ___ Bad: ___

Troubleshooting Step 6: _____
Reading: _____ Good: ___ Bad: ___

Troubleshooting Step 7: _____
Reading: _____ Good: ___ Bad: ___

Troubleshooting Step 8: _____
Reading: _____ Good: ___ Bad: ___

Troubleshooting Step 9: _____
Reading: _____ Good: ___ Bad: ___

Troubleshooting Step 10: _____
Reading: _____ Good: ___ Bad: ___

Troubleshooting Step 11: _____
Reading: _____ Good: ___ Bad: ___

Troubleshooting Step 12: _____
Reading: _____ Good: ___ Bad: ___

The Problem Is: _____

What did you learn from troubleshooting this problem?

_____

REMINDER: Remove the circuit fault from the bottom of the PCBs. Verify normal operation of the relay circuit.

Problem 142

Consult Instructor Guide IG05 to insert this problem.
Slide S4 UP and leave it CLOSED.
Use switch S3 as the PCM to control the fuel pump relay.
Description of the vehicle driveability problem:
Engine cranks but will not start. Checked spark & fuel. There is no fuel pressure in the fuel rail. Fuel Pump not running for initial 2 seconds. A new fuel pump and relay did not fix the problem.

Does the Fuel Pump Relay "CLICK"? Yes ___ No ___
Performance of the Fuel Pump: _____

Troubleshooting Step 1: _____
Reading: _____ Good: ___ Bad: ___

Troubleshooting Step 2: _____
Reading: _____ Good: ___ Bad: ___

Troubleshooting Step 3: _____
Reading: _____ Good: ___ Bad: ___

Troubleshooting Step 4: _____
Reading: _____ Good: ___ Bad: ___

Troubleshooting Step 5: _____
Reading: _____ Good: ___ Bad: ___

Troubleshooting Step 6: _____
Reading: _____ Good: ___ Bad: ___

Troubleshooting Step 7: _____
Reading: _____ Good: ___ Bad: ___

Troubleshooting Step 8: _____
Reading: _____ Good: ___ Bad: ___

Troubleshooting Step 9: _____
Reading: _____ Good: ___ Bad: ___

Troubleshooting Step 10: _____
Reading: _____ Good: ___ Bad: ___

Troubleshooting Step 11: _____
Reading: _____ Good: ___ Bad: ___

Troubleshooting Step 12: _____
Reading: _____ Good: ___ Bad: ___

The Problem Is: _____

What did you learn from troubleshooting this problem?

_____

REMINDER: Remove the circuit fault from the bottom of the PCBs. Verify normal operation of the relay circuit.

Copyright © 2015 VEEJER ENTERPRISES, Garland, Texas - All Rights Reserved

Vehicle Electronics Hands-On Troubleshooting Training Program

VEEJER ENTERPRISES 3701 Lariat Lane, Garland, Texas 75042-5419
Phone: 972-276-9642 Fax: 972-276-8122 Email: sales@veejer.com Web Site: www.veejer.com

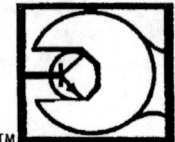

Problem 143

Consult Instructor Guide IG05 to insert this problem.
Slide S4 UP and leave it CLOSED.
Use switch S3 as the PCM to control the fuel pump relay.

Description of the vehicle driveability problem:
Engine cranks but will not start. Checked spark & fuel. There is no fuel pressure in the fuel rail. Fuel Pump not running for initial 2 seconds and found Fuse F2 is blown.

Does the Fuel Pump Relay "CLICK"? Yes ___ No ___
Performance of the Fuel Pump: _____

Troubleshooting Step 1: _____
Reading: _____ Good: ___ Bad: ___

Troubleshooting Step 2: _____
Reading: _____ Good: ___ Bad: ___

Troubleshooting Step 3: _____
Reading: _____ Good: ___ Bad: ___

Troubleshooting Step 4: _____
Reading: _____ Good: ___ Bad: ___

Troubleshooting Step 5: _____
Reading: _____ Good: ___ Bad: ___

Troubleshooting Step 6: _____
Reading: _____ Good: ___ Bad: ___

Troubleshooting Step 7: _____
Reading: _____ Good: ___ Bad: ___

Troubleshooting Step 8: _____
Reading: _____ Good: ___ Bad: ___

Troubleshooting Step 9: _____
Reading: _____ Good: ___ Bad: ___

Troubleshooting Step 10: _____
Reading: _____ Good: ___ Bad: ___

Troubleshooting Step 11: _____
Reading: _____ Good: ___ Bad: ___

Troubleshooting Step 12: _____
Reading: _____ Good: ___ Bad: ___

The Problem Is: _____

What did you learn from troubleshooting this problem?

_____

REMINDER: Remove the circuit fault from the bottom of the PCBs. Verify normal operation of the relay circuit.

Fig. 5TS-6CCFP — RELAY CIRCUIT Troubleshooting Trainer H-PCB05

Vehicle Electronics Hands-On Troubleshooting Training Program

VEEJER ENTERPRISES 3701 Lariat Lane, Garland, Texas 75042-5419
Phone: 972-276-9642 Fax: 972-276-8122 Email: sales@veejer.com Web Site: www.veejer.com

Problem 144
Consult Instructor Guide IG05 to insert this problem.
Slide S4 UP and leave it CLOSED.
Use switch S3 as the PCM to control the fuel pump relay.
Description of the vehicle driveability problem:
Engine cranks but will not start. Checked spark & fuel. There is no fuel pressure in the fuel rail. Fuel Pump not running for initial 2 seconds and found Fuse F1 is blown.

Does the Fuel Pump Relay "CLICK"? Yes ___ No ___
Performance of the Fuel Pump: _____

Troubleshooting Step 1: _____
Reading: _____ Good: ___ Bad: ___

Troubleshooting Step 2: _____
Reading: _____ Good: ___ Bad: ___

Troubleshooting Step 3: _____
Reading: _____ Good: ___ Bad: ___

Troubleshooting Step 4: _____
Reading: _____ Good: ___ Bad: ___

Troubleshooting Step 5: _____
Reading: _____ Good: ___ Bad: ___

Troubleshooting Step 6: _____
Reading: _____ Good: ___ Bad: ___

Troubleshooting Step 7: _____
Reading: _____ Good: ___ Bad: ___

Troubleshooting Step 8: _____
Reading: _____ Good: ___ Bad: ___

Troubleshooting Step 9: _____
Reading: _____ Good: ___ Bad: ___

Troubleshooting Step 10: _____
Reading: _____ Good: ___ Bad: ___

Troubleshooting Step 11: _____
Reading: _____ Good: ___ Bad: ___

Troubleshooting Step 12: _____
Reading: _____ Good: ___ Bad: ___

The Problem Is: _____

What did you learn from troubleshooting this problem?

_____

REMINDER: Remove the circuit fault from the bottom of the PCBs. Verify normal operation of the relay circuit.

Problem 145
Consult Instructor Guide IG05 to insert this problem.
Slide S4 UP and leave it CLOSED.
Use switch S3 as the PCM to control the fuel pump relay.
Description of the vehicle driveability problem:
Engine cranks but will not start. Checked spark & fuel. There is no fuel pressure in the fuel rail. Fuel Pump not running for initial 2 seconds and found Fuse F2 is blown.

Does the Fuel Pump Relay "CLICK"? Yes ___ No ___
Performance of the Fuel Pump: _____

Troubleshooting Step 1: _____
Reading: _____ Good: ___ Bad: ___

Troubleshooting Step 2: _____
Reading: _____ Good: ___ Bad: ___

Troubleshooting Step 3: _____
Reading: _____ Good: ___ Bad: ___

Troubleshooting Step 4: _____
Reading: _____ Good: ___ Bad: ___

Troubleshooting Step 5: _____
Reading: _____ Good: ___ Bad: ___

Troubleshooting Step 6: _____
Reading: _____ Good: ___ Bad: ___

Troubleshooting Step 7: _____
Reading: _____ Good: ___ Bad: ___

Troubleshooting Step 8: _____
Reading: _____ Good: ___ Bad: ___

Troubleshooting Step 9: _____
Reading: _____ Good: ___ Bad: ___

Troubleshooting Step 10: _____
Reading: _____ Good: ___ Bad: ___

Troubleshooting Step 11: _____
Reading: _____ Good: ___ Bad: ___

Troubleshooting Step 12: _____
Reading: _____ Good: ___ Bad: ___

The Problem Is: _____

What did you learn from troubleshooting this problem?

_____

REMINDER: Remove the circuit fault from the bottom of the PCBs. Verify normal operation of the relay circuit.

Copyright © 2015 VEEJER ENTERPRISES, Garland, Texas - All Rights Reserved   Student Workbook H-WB115

Vehicle Electronics Hands-On Troubleshooting Training Program

VEEJER ENTERPRISES 3701 Lariat Lane, Garland, Texas 75042-5419
Phone: 972-276-9642 Fax: 972-276-8122 Email: sales@veejer.com Web Site: www.veejer.com

Problem 146

Consult Instructor Guide IG05 to insert this problem.
Slide S4 UP and leave it CLOSED.
Use switch S3 as the PCM to control the fuel pump relay.
Description of the vehicle driveability problem:
Customer complains of the battery going dead overnight. Another shop couldn't find anything wrong.

Does the Fuel Pump Relay "CLICK"? Yes ___ No ___
Performance of the Fuel Pump: _____

Troubleshooting Step 1: _____
Reading: _____ Good: ___ Bad: ___

Troubleshooting Step 2: _____
Reading: _____ Good: ___ Bad: ___

Troubleshooting Step 3: _____
Reading: _____ Good: ___ Bad: ___

Troubleshooting Step 4: _____
Reading: _____ Good: ___ Bad: ___

Troubleshooting Step 5: _____
Reading: _____ Good: ___ Bad: ___

Troubleshooting Step 6: _____
Reading: _____ Good: ___ Bad: ___

Troubleshooting Step 7: _____
Reading: _____ Good: ___ Bad: ___

Troubleshooting Step 8: _____
Reading: _____ Good: ___ Bad: ___

Troubleshooting Step 9: _____
Reading: _____ Good: ___ Bad: ___

Troubleshooting Step 10: _____
Reading: _____ Good: ___ Bad: ___

Troubleshooting Step 11: _____
Reading: _____ Good: ___ Bad: ___

Troubleshooting Step 12: _____
Reading: _____ Good: ___ Bad: ___

The Problem Is: _____

What did you learn from troubleshooting this problem?

_____

REMINDER: Remove the circuit fault from the bottom of the PCBs. Verify normal operation of the relay circuit.

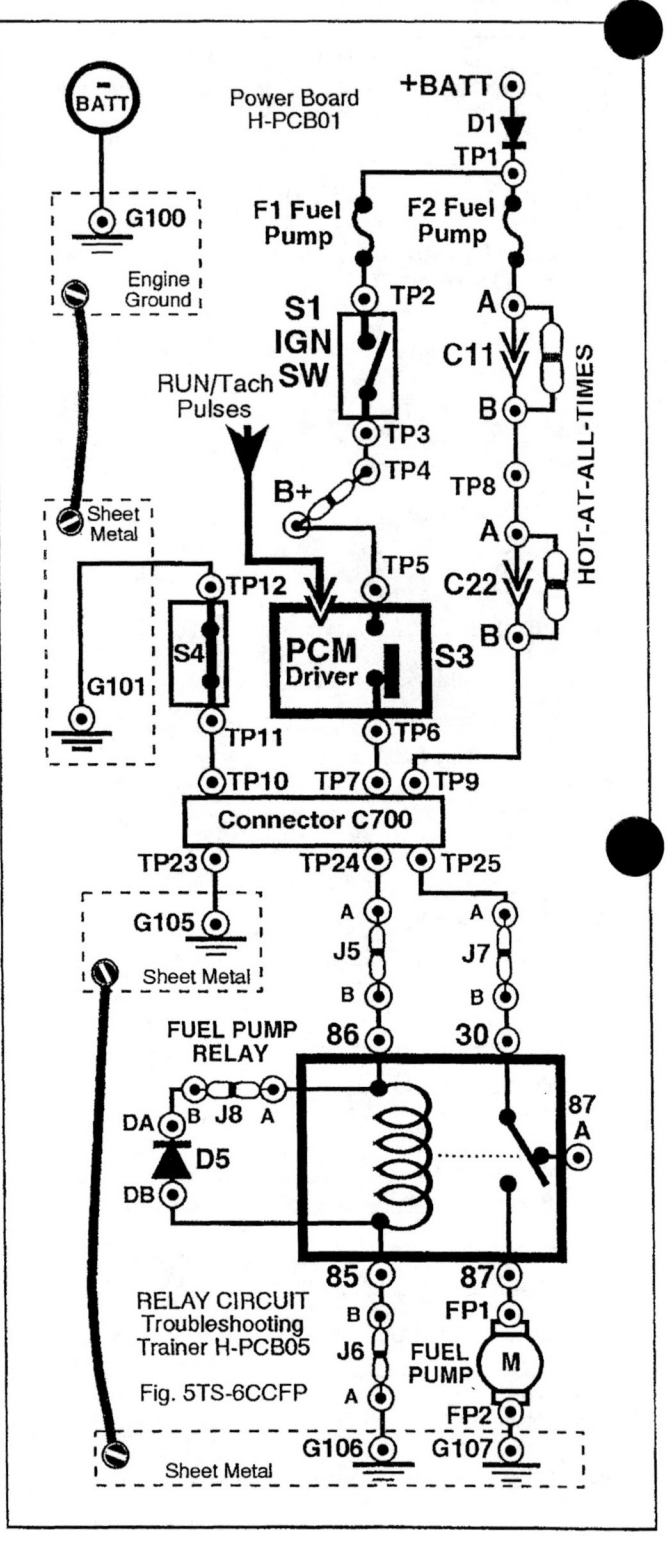

Fig. 5TS-6CCFP RELAY CIRCUIT Troubleshooting Trainer H-PCB05

Vehicle Electronics Hands-On Troubleshooting Training Program

VEEJER ENTERPRISES 3701 Lariat Lane, Garland, Texas 75042-5419
Phone: 972-276-9642 Fax: 972-276-8122 Email: sales@veejer.com Web Site: www.veejer.com

Problem 147
Consult Instructor Guide IG05 to insert this problem.
Slide S4 UP and leave it CLOSED.
Use switch S3 as the PCM to control the fuel pump relay.
Description of the vehicle driveability problem:
Engine cranks but will not start. Checked spark & fuel. There is no fuel pressure in the fuel rail. Fuel Pump not running for initial 2 seconds and found Fuse F2 is blown. Disconnect fuel pump relay and fuse still blows.

Does the Fuel Pump Relay "CLICK"? Yes ___ No ___
Performance of the Fuel Pump: _____

Troubleshooting Step 1: _____
Reading: _____ Good: ___ Bad: ___

Troubleshooting Step 2: _____
Reading: _____ Good: ___ Bad: ___

Troubleshooting Step 3: _____
Reading: _____ Good: ___ Bad: ___

Troubleshooting Step 4: _____
Reading: _____ Good: ___ Bad: ___

Troubleshooting Step 5: _____
Reading: _____ Good: ___ Bad: ___

Troubleshooting Step 6: _____
Reading: _____ Good: ___ Bad: ___

Troubleshooting Step 7: _____
Reading: _____ Good: ___ Bad: ___

Troubleshooting Step 8: _____
Reading: _____ Good: ___ Bad: ___

Troubleshooting Step 9: _____
Reading: _____ Good: ___ Bad: ___

Troubleshooting Step 10: _____
Reading: _____ Good: ___ Bad: ___

Troubleshooting Step 11: _____
Reading: _____ Good: ___ Bad: ___

Troubleshooting Step 12: _____
Reading: _____ Good: ___ Bad: ___

The Problem Is: _____

What did you learn from troubleshooting this problem?

_____

REMINDER: Remove the circuit fault from the bottom of the PCBs. Verify normal operation of the relay circuit.

Problem 148
Consult Instructor Guide IG05 to insert this problem.
Slide S4 UP and leave it CLOSED.
Use switch S3 as the PCM to control the fuel pump relay.
Description of the vehicle driveability problem:
Fuel pump relay "CLICKS" but fuel pump won't run. Replaced the fuel pump and it still won't run. I should have checked the circuit more carefully.

Does the Fuel Pump Relay "CLICK"? Yes ___ No ___
Performance of the Fuel Pump: _____

Troubleshooting Step 1: _____
Reading: _____ Good: ___ Bad: ___

Troubleshooting Step 2: _____
Reading: _____ Good: ___ Bad: ___

Troubleshooting Step 3: _____
Reading: _____ Good: ___ Bad: ___

Troubleshooting Step 4: _____
Reading: _____ Good: ___ Bad: ___

Troubleshooting Step 5: _____
Reading: _____ Good: ___ Bad: ___

Troubleshooting Step 6: _____
Reading: _____ Good: ___ Bad: ___

Troubleshooting Step 7: _____
Reading: _____ Good: ___ Bad: ___

Troubleshooting Step 8: _____
Reading: _____ Good: ___ Bad: ___

Troubleshooting Step 9: _____
Reading: _____ Good: ___ Bad: ___

Troubleshooting Step 10: _____
Reading: _____ Good: ___ Bad: ___

Troubleshooting Step 11: _____
Reading: _____ Good: ___ Bad: ___

Troubleshooting Step 12: _____
Reading: _____ Good: ___ Bad: ___

The Problem Is: _____

What did you learn from troubleshooting this problem?

_____

REMINDER: Remove the circuit fault from the bottom of the PCBs. Verify normal operation of the relay circuit.

Vehicle Electronics Hands-On Troubleshooting Training Program

VEEJER ENTERPRISES 3701 Lariat Lane, Garland, Texas 75042-5419
Phone: 972-276-9642 Fax: 972-276-8122 Email: sales@veejer.com Web Site: www.veejer.com

Problem 149
Consult Instructor Guide IG05 to insert this problem.
Slide S4 UP and leave it CLOSED.
Use switch S3 as the PCM to control the fuel pump relay.
   Description of the vehicle driveability problem:
Fuel pump relay "CLICKS" but fuel pressure is low. Replaced the fuel pump and a new one won't run any better. I should have checked the circuit more carefully before I wasted time changing parts.

Does the Fuel Pump Relay "CLICK"? Yes ___ No ___
Performance of the Fuel Pump: _____

Troubleshooting Step 1: _____
Reading: _____ Good: ___ Bad: ___

Troubleshooting Step 2: _____
Reading: _____ Good: ___ Bad: ___

Troubleshooting Step 3: _____
Reading: _____ Good: ___ Bad: ___

Troubleshooting Step 4: _____
Reading: _____ Good: ___ Bad: ___

Troubleshooting Step 5: _____
Reading: _____ Good: ___ Bad: ___

Troubleshooting Step 6: _____
Reading: _____ Good: ___ Bad: ___

Troubleshooting Step 7: _____
Reading: _____ Good: ___ Bad: ___

Troubleshooting Step 8: _____
Reading: _____ Good: ___ Bad: ___

Troubleshooting Step 9: _____
Reading: _____ Good: ___ Bad: ___

Troubleshooting Step 10: _____
Reading: _____ Good: ___ Bad: ___

Troubleshooting Step 11: _____
Reading: _____ Good: ___ Bad: ___

Troubleshooting Step 12: _____
Reading: _____ Good: ___ Bad: ___

The Problem Is: _____

What did you learn from troubleshooting this problem?

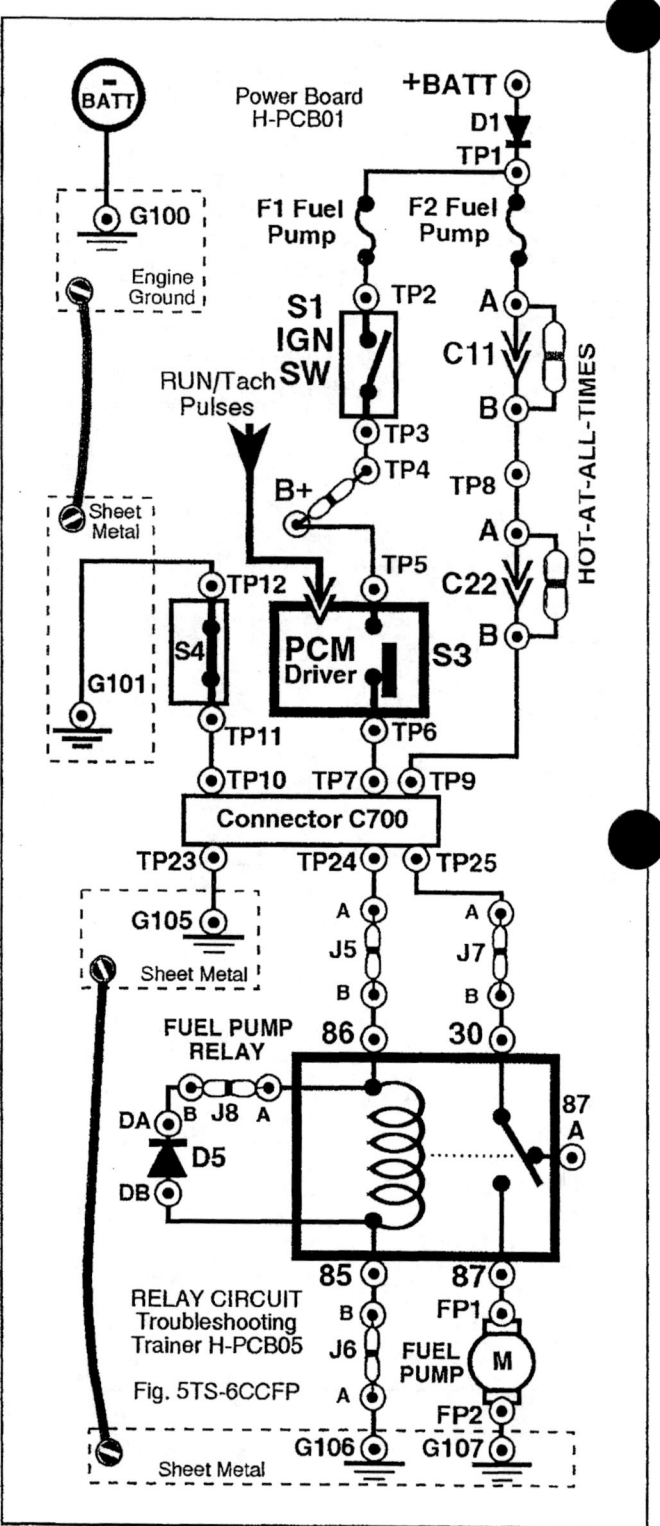

Fig. 5TS-6CCFP

REMINDER: Remove the circuit fault from the bottom of the PCBs. Verify normal operation of the relay circuit.

Copyright © 2015 VEEJER ENTERPRISES, Garland, Texas - All Rights Reserved Student Workbook H-WB115 Page 115

Vehicle Electronics Hands-On Troubleshooting Training Program

VEEJER ENTERPRISES 3701 Lariat Lane, Garland, Texas 75042-5419
Phone: 972-276-9642 Fax: 972-276-8122 Email: sales@veejer.com Web Site: www.veejer.com

Tips On Developing Troubleshooting Skill
Practice – Practice – Practice – Practice

Once all the problems have been completed for the first time you can still use the PCBs to keep your troubleshooting skills sharp and ready to go if you continue practicing by repeating troubleshooting exercises. Just randomly remove a 0ΩR U-jumper from the bottom of the PCBs and begin troubleshooting. After you find the problem replace the 0ΩR U-jumper. You can also select a resistor from the Resistor Bag and insert it in the location of a selected wire U-jumper and begin troubleshooting. After you find the problem remove the resistor and insert the wire U-jumper back in that U-jumper location. Do not insert a resistor into a U-NO-jumper location. This might possibly damage the PCBs.

To practice troubleshooting shorts to ground and shorted loads you can insert a wire jumper into a U-NO-jumper location **AND change fuse F1 or F2 as appropriate to a blown fuse or remove it from the circuit to prevent damaging the power supply and PCBs.** After the problem is found remove the 0ΩR and replaced the fuse with a good 2A fuse.

Conduct A Troubleshooting Contest

Insert a problem in the PCBs and then keep time each student or technician troubleshoots the same problem. Mix up the problems and keep score. The one with the least amount of time spent is the Top Troubleshooter.

Check off each troubleshooting problem when completed.

75 _____
76 _____
77 _____
78 _____
79 _____
80 _____
81 _____
82 _____
83 _____
84 _____
85 _____
86 _____
87 _____
88 _____
89 _____
90 _____
91 _____
92 _____
93 _____
94 _____
95 _____
96 _____
97 _____
98 _____
99 _____
100 _____
101 _____
102 _____
103 _____
104 _____
105 _____
106 _____
107 _____
108 _____
109 _____
110 _____
111 _____
112 _____
113 _____
114 _____
115 _____
116 _____
117 _____
118 _____
119 _____
120 _____
121 _____
122 _____
123 _____
124 _____
125 _____
126 _____
127 _____
128 _____
129 _____
130 _____
131 _____
132 _____
133 _____
134 _____
135 _____
136 _____
137 _____
138 _____
139 _____
140 _____
141 _____
142 _____
143 _____
144 _____
145 _____
146 _____
147 _____
148 _____
149 _____

**"The" Vehicle Electronics *Hands-On*
Troubleshooting Training Program
Written by Vince Fischelli**
Published by Veejer Enterprises Inc
Garland, Texas USA
Copyright © 2004-2015 Veejer Enterprises. No part of this manual or training material may be reproduced, photocopied, entered into a computer data base or copied by any means. All rights reserved.
Phone: **972-276-9642**   Fax: **972-276-8122**
Email: **sales@veejer.com** Web Site: **www.veejer.com**

Vehicle Electronics Hands-On Troubleshooting Training Program

VEEJER ENTERPRISES 3701 Lariat Lane, Garland, Texas 75042-5419
Phone: 972-276-9642 Fax: 972-276-8122 Email: sales@veejer.com Web Site: www.veejer.com

Problem 137
Consult Instructor Guide IG05 to insert this problem.
Slide S4 UP and leave it CLOSED.
Use switch S3 as the PCM to control the fuel pump relay.
Description of the vehicle driveability problem:
Very strange acting car. Fuel pump makes buzzing and squeaking sounds from the relay panel when the ignition key is turned ON. Fuel pressure very low and barely comes up after the key is turned ON.

Does the Fuel Pump Relay "CLICK"? Yes ___ No ___
Performance of the Fuel Pump: _____

Troubleshooting Step 1: _____
Reading: _____ Good: ___ Bad: ___

Troubleshooting Step 2: _____
Reading: _____ Good: ___ Bad: ___

Troubleshooting Step 3: _____
Reading: _____ Good: ___ Bad: ___

Troubleshooting Step 4: _____
Reading: _____ Good: ___ Bad: ___

Troubleshooting Step 5: _____
Reading: _____ Good: ___ Bad: ___

Troubleshooting Step 6: _____
Reading: _____ Good: ___ Bad: ___

Troubleshooting Step 7: _____
Reading: _____ Good: ___ Bad: ___

Troubleshooting Step 8: _____
Reading: _____ Good: ___ Bad: ___

Troubleshooting Step 9: _____
Reading: _____ Good: ___ Bad: ___

Troubleshooting Step 10: _____
Reading: _____ Good: ___ Bad: ___

Troubleshooting Step 11: _____
Reading: _____ Good: ___ Bad: ___

Troubleshooting Step 12: _____
Reading: _____ Good: ___ Bad: ___

The Problem Is: _____

What did you learn from troubleshooting this problem?

REMINDER: Remove the circuit fault from the bottom of the PCBs. Verify normal operation of the relay circuit.

Copyright © 2015 VEEJER ENTERPRISES, Garland, Texas - All Rights Reserved **Student Workbook H-WB115**